The Complete Works of Rather of Verona

medieval & renaissance
texts & studies

VOLUME 76

The Complete Works of Rather of Verona

Translated with an Introduction and Notes

by

PETER L. D. REID

Medieval & Renaissance texts & studies

Binghamton, New York

1991

A generous grant from the Faculty Research
and Awards Committee of Tufts University
has assisted in meeting the publication costs of this volume.

Library of Congress Cataloging-in-Publication Data

Ratherius, of Verona, 890 (ca.)–974.
[Works. English. 1991]
  The complete works of Rather of Verona / translated with an
introduction and notes by Peter L. D. Reid.
    p. cm. — (Medieval & Renaissance texts & studies ;
v. 76)
  Translated from the Latin by Peter L. D. Reid.
  Includes bibliographical references and indexes.
  ISBN 0–86698–087–3
  1. Theology—Middle Ages, 600–1500.   2. Ratherius, of
Verona, 890 (ca.)–974.   I. Reid, Peter L. D.   II. Title.
III. Series.
BX1749.R3713   1991
270.3—dc20   90–43450
                                                                    CIP

This book is made to last.
It is set in Bembo, smythe-sewn,
and printed on acid-free paper
to library specifications.

Printed in the United States of America

Table of Contents

Rather's Works

(As numbered in CCCM 46, pp. xxiv–xxxi.)

Not included in this translation:

Nos. 7, 8, 9, 61 (four legal documents called *commutationes*)
No. 34 (fragmentary)

Preface

Rather is one of the few writers of medieval times, or indeed of classical times, to have included an element of autobiography in his works. He frequently tells us of his experiences and his reactions to them, of his inner thoughts and his assessment of himself. It was this element that led me to put together a few of the more autobiographical writings in translation and submit them to MRTS. Professor Mario Di Cesare then suggested that, since Rather's works had not been translated into any modern language, his full corpus should be attempted rather than some isolated pieces. Our original plan was to print an English translation facing a page of Rather's Latin text in three volumes, but the sheer bulk of such a project and problems with copyrights drew us to the single volume of translations alone.

I am indebted in this to a long line of scholars, starting with the brothers Ballerini in their pioneering work on Rather in Verona in the eighteenth century, up to the most recent work on Rather's sources by François Dolbeau in his *Ratheriana* series. I would like to acknowledge also personal help, direct or indirect, over the last two decades from Bengt Löfstedt, Philip Levine, Louis Lumaghi, Roel Vander Plaetse, Paul Meyvaert, and my colleagues at Tufts University, particularly Jack Zarker, Steven Hirsch, and Steven Marrone. And my particular thanks are due to Mario Di Cesare, Michael Pavese, and their editorial team for their help in the finishing stages of this project. Finally, I am grateful to Dean Mary Ella Feinleib and the Tufts University Faculty Research Fund for an award that made this publication possible.

Tufts University, 1990   Peter L. D. Reid

The Complete Works of Rather of Verona

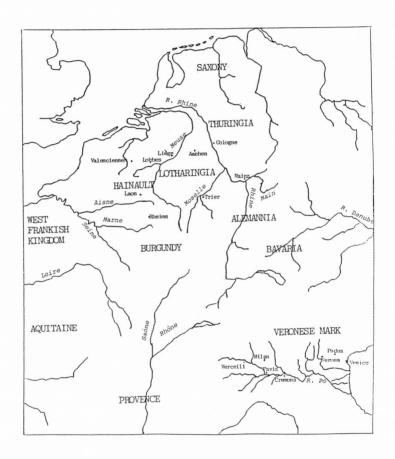

Places mentioned in the text

Introduction

Rather (Ratherius, Ratheri, Raterio, Rathier), "bishop of Verona but monk of Lobbes" as he signs himself, has been called by Erich Auerbach "an outstanding example of literary talent and . . . by far the most interesting and important writer of his time."[1] From the time that he left his monastery in 926 till his death almost fifty years later, his life was one of conflict and turmoil. He lost four bishoprics, Verona thrice and Liège once, he spent two years in prison and two in exile, and even in his eighties he was at odds with his godson, Folcuin, who had given him refuge. He was famous for his erudition, that is, his knowledge of the literary *artes*, but despised it as vainglory. In his zeal to reform corrupt practices in the Church he made enemies wherever he went. But conflict inspired him to write, and his writings reveal an astonishing self-awareness.

Rather[2] was born of noble family in Liège in the late 880s[3] and as a child was offered as an oblate to the monastery of Lobbes in Hainaut, on the west side of Lower Lotharingia (Lorraine). It was a time which witnessed "the final dismemberment of the empire of Charlemagne"[4] after the deposition of the emperor Charles the Fat (887). Europe was being battered by raiders on both east and west flanks. To the east of Lotharingia, the East Frankish kingdom made up of the five great duchies of Saxony, Bavaria, Thuringia, Franconia, and Alemannia or Swabia, under Louis the Child (893–911), son of the emperor Arnulf (896–899), was facing successive waves of Magyars, Hungarian peoples of Finnish origin. To the west was the kingdom of the West Franks, whose king, Odo (d. 898), was hard-pressed by Danish Vikings; the Annals of St. Vaast (an. 884) tell how "the Northmen cease not to slay and carry into captivity the Christian people, to destroy the churches and to burn the towns. Everywhere there is nothing but dead bodies — clergy and laymen, nobles and common people, women and children. There is no road or place where the ground is not covered with corpses. We live in distress and anguish before this spectacle of the destruction of the Christian people."[5] At the same time Odo was facing revolts from powerful

counts and bishops; in opposition to him Fulk, archbishop of Reims, in 893
crowned Charles the Simple (879–929), who became sole king on Odo's death
(898).

When Rather came of age, he took his vows as a monk under abbot Hilduin,
the cousin of Hugo, marquess of Provence. The sorry condition of the Church
at this time can be seen in a conciliar statement put out by the bishops of the
adjacent province of Reims in 909:

> The cities are depopulated, the monasteries ruined and burned, the land
> is reduced to a solitude. As the first men lived without law or constraint,
> abandoned to their passions, so now every man does what pleases him,
> despising the laws of God and man and the ordinances of the Church. The
> powerful oppress the weak, the land is full of violence against the poor
> and the plunder of the goods of the Church. Men devour one another like
> the fishes in the sea. In the case of the monasteries some have been de-
> stroyed by the heathen, others have been deprived of their property and
> reduced to nothing. In those that remain there is no longer any observance
> of the Rule. They no longer have legitimate superiors, owing to the abuse
> of submitting to secular domination. We see in the monasteries lay abbots
> with their wives and their children, their soldiers and their dogs. . . . God's
> flock perishes through our [i.e., the bishops'] charge. It has come about
> through our negligence, our ignorance and that of our brethren, that there
> is in the Church an innumerable multitude of both sexes and every condi-
> tion who reach old age without instruction, so that they are ignorant even
> of the words of the creed and the Lord's Prayer.[6]

The problems of the Church were to affect Rather for the rest of his life.

In the year 911, Charles secured a treaty with Rollo the Viking and extended
his kingship into Lotharingia on the invitation of some Lotharingian nobles, who
felt that their natural allegiance lay to the west rather than to the east, where
the non-Carolingian Conrad had been elected to the kingship on the death of Louis
(911).[7] But Charles' authority in Lotharingia was questioned when the people of
Liège elected Hilduin, Rather's abbot, as bishop in preference to Charles' nominee,
Richer. The dispute over the bishopric was eventually decided by the pope, who
rejected Hilduin's claim. Then in 926 Hilduin's cousin Hugo seized the throne
of Italy; Hilduin joined him and was made bishop of Verona, with the promise
of the archbishopric of Milan when that office became vacant. Rather accompanied him, expecting to become bishop of Verona when Hilduin moved to Milan.
He was now in his thirties, an austere monk known for his piety and erudition.

But when in due course Hilduin was promoted to Milan (931), Hugo was
reluctant to let Rather succeed him as bishop of Verona and was only persuaded

to promote him by a letter from the pope and by the fact that Rather, who was ill at the time, might not live long (no. 10). His first tenure of the see of Verona began in October, 931.[8] Within three years Rather was in prison.

The key texts for Rather's fall are: *Praeloquia* 2.24 (giving the month: February, 934); *Praeloquia* 3.25–28 (the letter to Ursus); *Praeloquia* 4.5–7 (where he claims that he has been sentenced unjustly, without a hearing, and merely on his reputation, without regard to his motives or intentions); *Praeloquia* 5.12 (telling of his betrayal by the faction led by the archdeacon); *Praeloquia* 5.27 (where he regrets that his rebellious action harmed so many sons of the Church); the letter to the pope (no. 10) c. 4 (where he gives a brief history of his claim to the see of Verona); *Dialogus confessionalis*, no. 19, c. 24 (where he admits that since he could have prevented the events which led to mutilations and executions, he is therefore responsible for them), and c. 2 (where he confesses that he broke his oath of loyalty to Hugo); and Liutprand, *Antapadosis* 3.48–52.

These sources leave plenty of room for controversy and speculation.[9] Liutprand sets the historical scene: Arnold, duke of Bavaria, invaded Italy and was gladly received in Verona by Count Milo and Bishop Rather inasmuch as they were the ones who had invited him. After his defeat by King Hugo and retreat to Bavaria, the king recovered Verona and banished Rather to prison in Pavia. We do not know why Rather invited Arnold (if indeed he did). Furthermore, Rather was not immediately imprisoned on the king's retaking of Verona; it was not until the receipt of a mysterious letter some time later, as we learn from Rather himself (*Praeloquia* 3.27), that the king imprisoned him. In the *Praeloquia* Rather does not deny his culpability, but he stresses that his motives were excellent and laments that he was condemned unheard (5.13), so that he could not explain his motives. Behind all this lurks the shadowy figure of Hilduin, Rather's patron and now archbishop of Milan. Though Rather does not mention him by name, it can only be he that is referred to in 1.25 with such bitterness at his ingratitude.

Imprisoned in Pavia for two and a half years (February 934–August 936), Rather spent his time writing the *Praeloquia* (no. 1), "Prefaces," which he seems initially to have conceived only as an introduction to a longer work detailing the duties of Christ's athlete. But the prefaces expanded to include the material of the larger whole — and much more besides — and the name *Praeloquia* was never changed. In book 6 he claims that it is mostly culled from the fertile fields of the Fathers with very little that is his own; he also regrets his lack of books and the fact that so many texts had to be quoted from memory. In fact, far from being merely a *florilegium* of the Fathers, it is a unique kind of a work that covers the duties of human beings in their many capacities, from the humblest servant to the king, from the doorkeeper to the prelate, and includes issues such as the relationship between church and king and between canon law and civil law, criticism of corrupt practices and corrupt individuals in the Church, and his own personal apologia. Citations from the Fathers are used to buttress his case, not to provide the mass of his text. The sheer number of the citations from Scripture, the Fathers, and the classics, for a prisoner deprived of books,[10] testify to a mind of extraordinary capacity.

The premise of the whole work, and indeed the basis of most of his writing, is the requirement of Benedict's Rule (c. 1) to provoke the devil to combat. Rather expands the metaphor into the combat of the arena: one must train like an athlete in order to provoke the devil; one must learn to trip him up (by abstinence, alms, and prayer), one must impress the Judge, one must strive for the (eternal) prize and the applause of the (celestial) spectators. This work of his will be a kind of manual of training for this contest, a contest which lasts one's whole life since the devil is king of this world.

Though the *Praeloquia* was written in prison between February 934 and August 936, there are two indications of later additions: (1) in book 5, c. 12, he draws the attention of Bishops Wido and Sobbo, who had invited him to a synod, to a specific passage of interest to their agenda. We know from another letter, no. 2, that he had to turn down their invitation because he was "in exile," viz. in Como, so that addition can be dated between August 936 and early 939. (2) In the last chapter of book 5, he refers to being at Laon on Christmas Day and being invited by the abbess to the sisters' chapter on St. Stephen's day; the governance of the abbey of St. Amand was on his mind. Since he also mentions that he has already been bishop, this could not have happened prior to his leaving for Italy in 928, so the passage must have been written after 939 and must be a later addition; in the surviving manuscript it is an addition written on another folio and pointed to book 5, line 982.

After two and half years in prison, he was moved to house arrest in Como, with Bishop Azzo (bishop of Como, 937–947). A letter (no. 2) survives from this period, to Archbishops Wido of Lyons and Sobbo of Vienne, refusing their summons and sending them a copy of the *Praeloquia* — or perhaps only a part of it (5.13 ff.?); he also mentions his destitution and asks for resources. Released two and a half years later, in February 939, he seems to have spent the next seven years in Provence and Lobbes, perhaps visiting Reims (no. 5A) and Laon (*Praeloquia* 5.33). This last reference also suggests that he was anticipating being made abbot of the abbey of St. Amand.

Extant letters of this period show him seeking support for his claim to the see of Verona among various bishops and archbishops, in particular Rodbert (no. 5), archbishop of Trier, and Otto's brother Bruno (no. 6), the imperial chancellor, to both of whom he sent copies of his *Praeloquia*. In support of his claim, both now and in later polemics, he frequently cites canon law, relying often on the Pseudo-Isidorian canons, known now as the False Decretals.[11] In 946 he regained his see of Verona, but this second tenure lasted only two years. The details can be found in no. 10, a letter written to the pope in 951 recounting his sad plight. King Hugo had been forced to take his son Lothar as co-ruler, while most of the real power was held by Berengar; it was reported to Rather that the king regretted his action against him and would receive him back. When Rather returned to his seat, he was first arrested by Berengar on the prompting of Manasses, Berengar's appointee as archbishop of Milan, who had held the see of Verona since 934. Then, when after three and a half months he reached Verona, Milo, count of Verona, treacherously worked behind his back to encourage the clergy to revolt, while pretending to be his supporter. Threats of violence eventually persuaded him to go once more into exile (948).

Again, he wandered the north looking for support. Meanwhile, after the deaths of King Hugo and his son Lothar, Berengar seized the throne of Italy, and his rough treatment of Lothar's widow, Adelaide, gave the ambitious Otto I of Germany a pretext for intervening in Italy. Otto's son Liudolf made the first move across the Alps, bringing Rather with him,[12] but quickly returned north without reaching Verona. Then Otto himself came south, reached Pavia in September 951 without opposition, and (supported now by Manasses and other bishops in the north) claimed title to Berengar's throne. But he soon had to return to Germany to face a rebellion fomented by his son Liudolf. In the seat of Verona, for political reasons, he confirmed, not Rather, but Milo's nephew, also called Milo, who had bought it from Berengar. All these events are referred to in no. 10, a letter to the pope written in late 951; at the same time he wrote a letter to the bishops of Italy, Gaul, and Germany (no. 11) and one to all the Faithful (no. 12), begging for their support in his campaign to regain Verona.

A wanderer again, Rather received hospitality from Otto's brother Bruno, the chancellor, and when Bruno became archbishop of Cologne in 953, Rather was appointed by him bishop of Liège. Both positions were important for the security of Lotharingia, Otto's western province, and again Rather found himself a victim of political forces. He was immediately challenged by Rodbert, archbishop of Trier, as part of a plot by Baldric, bishop of Utrecht, to place his nephew Baldric in that see; this in turn was part of a wider manoeuvre of two local counts, Rudolf and Reginar, to break Lotharingia out of German control. Some of the details of events at this time can be seen in the fragmentary letter to Baldric the younger (no. 15). Within a year, after issuing a strongly worded statement (no. 14) of his intentions never to abandon his see, Rather was forced to retire into exile once again.

He found refuge for some months with Archbishop William of Mainz, a natural son of Otto, where he wrote the extraordinary work *Phrenesis* (no. 16); he seems also to have made a collection of his writings at this time, collecting them into twenty books, then reducing them to twelve "out of respect for a certain individual" (perhaps Rodbert, whose death was reported to him while he was writing *Phrenesis*, the last to be written though serving as preface to the rest). Amongst the twelve volumes which he describes only nos. 10, 11, 12, 14, 15 (?), and 16 of his extant works can be identified.

In late 955, with Bruno's support, he was given as abbot to the small monastery of Alna near Lobbes. A life of Bruno records Rather's letter of gratitude (no. 17). While there he wrote his *Confessional Dialogue* (no. 19). Another letter to Bruno (no. 21) indicates that Bruno was still trying to have him restored to Liège, a position that Rather no longer wanted.

In 961, Otto made a second incursion into Italy, to oust a resurgent Berengar and to aid the pope against the Roman aristocracy. He secured Verona and, leaving Count Ernest, and, later, Bucco, in charge, continued on south. Rather, now in his seventies, was restored once more to his bishopric[13] (an appointment confirmed by the bishops in synod at Pavia), replacing Milo, who seems to have yielded on the understanding that he would succede when Rather died. His third tenure was again marked by conflict. He tells us (no. 33) that he was not received with fatherly love, that he was injured and almost destitute, that he was constantly undermined by both Milo, with whom he had patched up a costly reconciliation, and Count Bucco, who was nominally his protector. His own attitude, his obstinate self-righteousness and intolerant outspokenness, cannot have helped. Scorning the material world as the product of the devil and putting all his thought on that future world which his advanced age now made imminent, he further alienated many of the higher clergy by his biting censure of their sloth and greed. But the heart of the conflict was economic. The higher clergy, having grown rich in Church revenues at the expense of the minor orders, justified this state of affairs by telling the minor orders that they too would soon succede to their positions and the wealth and power that went with them, just as they themselves had succeded to their predecessors. Rather saw that it was this wealth which caused so much corruption in the higher orders and that the resultant poverty of the lower orders demoralized them and led them to neglect their duties. He thought that the Church of Verona could only grow and improve spiritually if the pattern of distribution that had become traditional in the Church of Verona was altered to one more in accord with the canons,[14] and he accordingly set about trying to effect this redistribution.[15] He was quite prepared to remove stipends and benefices from clerics who abused them (*ingrati*, "ingrates") and bestow them on juniors more worthy to receive them.[16] In his earlier tenures he had already antagonized some of the higher clergy by his reforming zeal, but he must now have felt more secure with Otto's support behind him.

His first work of this period, *On the Translation of St. Metro* (no. 23), written in 962, hints at the criticism he was already receiving. The letters, sermons, and tracts of the next six years detail the conflict that reached its climax in 968 with his public "trial" and ejection from Verona.

The four sermons of 963 (no. 24–27) give little indication of the conflict, but a letter of November of that year to Bishop Hubert of Parma (no. 28), known since the Ballerini as *On Contempt of the Canons*, relates the issues he had with the higher clergy. He found them avaricious in their handling of the resources of the church, lax in their discipline and neglectful of their spiritual duties, worldly in their gambling, sexual incontinence, gluttony and drinking, and rebellious to their bishop. They have challenged Rather's right to the see (supporting Milo whom Rather had replaced) and have even drawn some of the lower clergy to their side. The year 964 gives us two sermons (nos. 29, 31), a short reply to critics who had misunderstood a point he had made (no. 30), a short work (no. 32) *On his Own Sin* (or "mistake" — *lapsus*), referring enigmatically to something he did or said in church (perhaps an unseemly shouting match with his opponents?), and a fragment of a work attacking Count Bucco (no. 33), in which he cites some hostile actions of the count, who was supposed to be protecting him.

Early in 965 Rather went on the offensive against his enemies, the clerics who supported Milo. Most of them had been ordained or promoted by Milo and so owed him loyalty. In a decree of February 12th (no. 35) he annulled the ordinations performed by Milo on the grounds that Milo had never been the rightful bishop of Verona. But this action hurt not only his enemies but also others who had received promotions during the years before Rather's return. It caused such an outcry that he was forced to moderate it in a decree of the following day (no. 36). But his enemies must have realized how vulnerable they were to such actions; they seem to have become all the more determined to oust Rather and have Milo reinstated.

They could do little while Otto was in Italy, but when Otto returned to Germany later in the year, Rather's position became precarious. Otto's policy in northern Italy had been to increase the power of the bishops at the expense of the feudal barons, and when he left Italy sporadic agitation broke out against his appointees, including Rather. The disaffected clergy of Verona seized their chance. In some general disturbances he was arrested and the episcopal palace was damaged, but he was released on the intervention of Count Bucco. He now moved his household to the Curtis Alta and tried to fortify it, but again was forced to move; a new residence he tried to build was destroyed. Eventually Bucco managed to restore order and brought to trial those involved in the attack on the bishop. They were found guilty of perjuring their oath to the emperor and fined. All these events are covered in a letter to Milo (no. 40) and the extraordinary *Qualitatis coniectura cuiusdam*, "Examination of an Individual's Quality" (no. 41), where he puts into the mouth of a critic the worst things possible that could be said of himself—and thereby gives us a self-portrait and apologia. He also tells us that his enemies were undermining him at court and that he was offered a substantial payment to yield to Milo, which Bishop Hubert of Parma urged him to accept. But he was not without his own supporters at court; Otto's sister-in-law Judith, duchess of Bavaria and mother of Henry of Bavaria, seems to have stood by him (no. 39). He does acknowledge, however, that if he receives clear indication that Otto wants him to yield, he will do so (no. 40).

In Lent the next year (966), he called a synod of his clergy and instructed them in the duties which they were failing to observe (no. 43). Three other works of that year, *De nuptu illicito*, "On an Illicit Marriage" (no. 44), a *Sermon on Mary and Martha* (no. 45), and *De otiose sermone*, "On Otiose Speech" (no. 46), all in their tone reflect the tensions of the conflict. In December, he wrote to the clergy (no. 47) that he was planning to go to Rome to ask of a synod being convened certain questions relating to episcopal authority. "[Since I returned] you have never stopped provoking me," he says, "and denying me every privilege of episcopal rank."

In April of the next year (967), a synod was held at Ravenna by the emperor's command; this synod reaffirmed the stand against priests' uxuriousness (though a year later, in no. 52, he tells Ambrose that his clergy have ignored that stricture). In November Otto passed through Verona on his way to the imperial coronation in Rome; he (and his court) enjoyed Rather's hospitality, conferring on the bishop when he left a privilege (no. 48) by which all the properties and rights of the Church of Verona were restored, including royal protection against any who infringed on those rights.[17] Rather now felt strong enough to correct the imbalance of income between the higher and lower clergy, and he issued a decree, *Judicatum* (no. 49), allocating more of the resources to the lower clergy, on the ground that they did most of the work but labored in destitution. It was met with renewed opposition and even open rebellion by the higher clergy (nos. 51, 52). They started spreading false accusations of Rather. Among other things, they charged him with looting the episcopal palace—though the damage and pilfering there had been done by Otto's couriers passing through Verona or by his enemies in the town. They also attacked him for rebuilding the Church of St. Zeno with funds given by Otto for the relief of the poor. One of them even went to Rome and acquired (Rather says "bought") a papal injunction against implementation of the *Judicatum* (no. 53). They seem to have won over the new count of Verona, Nanno, who now supported them before the emperor.

Rather's quarrel with the clergy dominates ten works between April and July, 968 (nos. 52, 53, 54, 57, 58, 59, 60, 63, 64, 65): five are sermons, stressing the theme of brotherly love and urging his enemies to reconciliation, five are letters — to one of his enemies, to Nanno, to the empress Adelaide, and two to Ambrose, Otto's chancellor. The last letter to Ambrose (no. 65) outlines some of the incidents between April and July; he tells how the feud has come to a head in a public confrontation (it can hardly be called a "trial") presided over by Count Nanno and fears that he is now without support even from the emperor. Shortly after the trial he left Verona for the north.

For the rest of his story we must now go to Folcuin's account in his *Acts of the Abbots of Lobbes* (see *Sources for Rather's Life*). Rather appealed to Folcuin, abbot of Lobbes and one whom Rather "had taken up from the baptismal font," for an escort to help him return to Lobbes. He arrived with "masses and heaps" of gold and silver. With this he bought from King Lothar the abbey of St. Amand, but stayed in it only one night before returning to Alna, the small monastery of which he had been abbot in the years before his third tenure of Verona. Similarly, he bought the monastery of Haumont but left that also. Then he forced Folcuin out of Lobbes and took over his position, supported by Bishop Everaclus. When Everaclus died, his successor Notger investigated the conflict between Folcuin and Rather and reconciled them; Rather returned to Alna, where he lived out the rest of his life. He died in his late eighties on a visit to a friend in Namur in 974 and was buried with honor in the Church of St. Ursmar in Lobbes.

How reliable is Folcuin's account? Can we reconcile his narrative of Rather's simoniacal dealings with the ardent strictures against simony that are a constant refrain in Rather's own works? Can we reconcile Folcuin's account of Rather's wealth when he returned to the north with Rather's own reports of his near-destitution in Verona? The reader who has shared Rather's innermost thoughts in the *Praeloquia* through to the final letter to Ambrose reads Folcuin's account with some surprise. The contentious nature is the same, but the business dealings seem out of character. One might conclude either that his earlier attacks on simony had been hypocritical, or that he felt so depressed by how he had been treated in Verona that he determined to use whatever resources he could carry with him for material security in his late old age. Though Folcuin is recounting events in which he had a personal interest, one should not immediately reject his tale; he seems to write without personal animosity, since, given these facts, he could have used them in a much more damning manner.

Rather's writings are almost the only sources for this tumultuous career, so full of misfortune largely brought on by his reforming zeal and fractious nature.

Hence, as Misch has shown,[18] they are a valuable record of autobiography, a unique document of the thoughts, motives, and meditations of a singularly articulate and well-read individual of the tenth century. The saintly monk of Lobbes, promoted to authority in Italy far from home, was shocked by the mores of the churchmen he was to oversee. His attempts to reform them led first to resentment, then to betrayal, then to violence. He replied with polemical tracts and scathing denunciations of vice. He suffered miserably, but consoled himself with the thought that he was doing God's work and would reach his ultimate reward. He might have remained an erudite monk (in fact, at times of extreme stress, he considers abandoning his see and retiring to Lobbes), but his nature could not be satisfied with an inactive role. He had entered the arena as Christ's athlete to combat the devil and his agents in this world; he could not leave the field, nor could he, as shepherd of the people of Verona, abandon his flock. But he constantly questioned his own motives, afraid that he was acting more for vainglory than for true virtue, more in arrogance than in humility, more out of ambitious lust for power than the desire to lead God's flock. As he said, on no one was he harder than on himself. This inner questioning, the repeated meditation on his own worth, gives us a glimpse of self-analysis rare before modern times.

It is perhaps unfortunate that so much of what has survived of his work is polemical and defensive; the picture that inevitably emerges from such writings is that of a cranky exile who self-righteously attacks the faults of the people he meets, who is constantly at odds with the clergy he supervises, and who is always so dependent on the magnates of the state that he must whine about his troubles to get their support. This negative picture tends to block from our view the other one which can be detected: the scholar with his nose always in a book, the collector and copier of manuscripts, the prelate universally admired for his writings and his eloquence, the teacher of Latin so concerned to make things easier for his pupil that he wrote a text for him (called *Sparadorsum*, "Spare the back"—knowledge of it would save the student many beatings!), the conscientious bishop so anxious for the moral and spiritual health of his flock, the zealous builder of churches, the generous bestower of charity, and, above all, the gentle Christian so ready to forgive his enemies. One can frequently detect his concern for the more humble members of society, the poor in the diocese and the impoverished lower orders in the clergy. He also seems to have had quite a sense of humor, an ability to clown that brought even his enemies to laughter, though he censures this quality in himself (no. 41).

Apart from what Rather reveals of himself, his work is also valuable to us now for its picture of life among the Italian clergy of that time. In *Praeloquia* 4, c. 10 and 5, cc. 8–12, he describes as typical a self-indulgent prelate, given to reading classical literature rather than patristic or biblical, who wears exotic dress and expensive jewels, who neglects his flock, who gambles, sports with horse, dog, and falcon, prefers the company of actors and entertainers to that of clerics, enjoys lavish banquets off priceless furnishings—in short, a man of the world whose goal is wealth not devotion. Most of the works of his last tenure of Verona (nos. 23–65) find similar fault with the clerics he has to oversee; and he implies in *Qualitatis coniectura cuiusdam*, "Examination of an Individual's Quality" (no. 41) that he was criticized by them for not living as extravagantly as was expected of a bishop. He continually complains of his poverty, even to the emperor (as can be seen by the emperor's *privilegium* to him, no. 48), but his motive is not a higher standard of living for himself so much as the desire to relieve the poverty of the lower orders in the Church and to build and restore churches. His enemies seem to have sneered at him as a carpenter; he admits that he took part personally in the rebuilding of churches destroyed by Hungarian invasions and justifies spending money given by the emperor for feeding the poor on this building program (no. 53).

Classical scholars have long acknowledged the debt we owe to Rather for his interest in classical Latin texts. His part in the transmission of Livy, for instance, has been carefully detailed by Guiseppe Billanovich.[19] His works show not only an easy familiarity with many classical authors but also the expectation of a similar familiarity in his readers. *Phrenesis* (no. 16), for example, addressed to Archbishop Rodbert of Trier, is full of veiled allusions to Persius which imply that the archbishop also knows his Persius very well. Citations from Avianus, Boethius, Cicero, *Dicta Catonis*, Fulgentius, Horace, Josephus, Juvenal, Lucan, Martianus Capella,[20] Ovid, Persius, Pliny the Elder, Pliny the Younger, Phaedrus, Publilius Syrus, Sallust, Seneca, Statius, Suetonius, Terence, and Vergil have been identified in his work,[21] and mention is made of Plautus, Catullus, and Prudentius' *Psychomachia*. The reference to Catullus (no. 45, c. 4) is of considerable interest since it establishes the existence of a Catullus manuscript in Verona in 966; since the archetype of all our extant manuscripts was brought back to Verona from France in the thirteenth century, it has been conjectured that Rather himself may have taken it with him when he left Verona in 968.[22]

I have examined elsewhere[23] some aspects of his use of classical authors, but two points may be repeated here. Firstly, his reputation for classical learning was renowned, both attested by other writers (see the *Testimonia*) and implied in his own writings. From a letter to Archbishop Rodbert of Trier (no. 5) we can infer that the archbishop had consulted him on certain literary questions; he also tells us there explicitly that when he first came south he was "pressed by the questions of certain men of Milan." Secondly, in his letter to Rotbert (no. 5) he excuses himself from discussing (classical) literature with him on the ground that he must now (that is, since becoming a bishop in 931) "meditate on God's law day and night" and can find no time for secular learning. Thirty-five years later, in the *Sermon on Mary and Martha* (no. 45), he chides himself for reading pagan authors when he ought to be meditating on God's law. In the *Praeloquia* (4.10) too, he rebukes prelates in the Church for embracing the "foolish wisdom of the world" (i.e., the pagan classics) rather than the eternal wisdom of the Scripture. He justifies study of the pagans only as far as such study can be brought to use for the Church. In three passages (*Praeloquia* 4.10; no. 5, *Letter to Rodbert*; no. 23, *Translatio S. Metronis* 1–2) he cites Exodus 12.35 and the instruction to the Israelites to borrow from the Egyptians gold and silver which they would not repay, interpreting it as a command to plunder the pagan classics to decorate God's Tabernacle.[24] He leaves us in no doubt that the attractions of classical literature were to be borrowed for stylistic embellishment of Christian writings, not enjoyed for their own sake.

But for all his learning Rather's works are not easily assigned to traditional genres. Even his sermons are unusual for the degree to which his personal feuds[25] and his own failings[26] interpose themselves. Some works defy categorization. *Qualitatis coniectura cuiusdam*, "Examination of an Individual's Character" (no. 41), a work of self-criticism that turns into self-justification, has no literary antecedents at all. Similarly *Phrenesis* (no. 16) and the *Dialogus confessionalis* (no. 19), both consciously learned works with much self-analysis, are hard to relate to earlier literary traditions. These can all best be regarded as experiments in autobiography; their originality perhaps results from the fact that he does not have a general audience in mind—in fact at times the audience seems to be himself. His most famous work, the *Praeloquia* (no. 1), does have a general audience in mind, but it equally is hard to place in literary tradition. At first glance one might be reminded of Boethius' *Consolation of Philosophy*, a work he cites or alludes to about fifteen times in all; Rather likewise is in prison, also in Pavia, consoling himself with the thoughts of the great philosophers and theologians who have gone before him; his writing too affords him an outlet for his miseries, a companionship for one to whom even books are denied. Where Boethius' aim is to transmit the philosophy of Plato and Aristotle to his countrymen, Rather's purpose in writing is to arm Christ's athlete for combat with the devil, the king of this world, largely by means of the writings of greater authorities. But Boethius always manages to rise above his own problems and to maintain his discourse in the ethereal realms of philosophy. Rather too often slips from the great thoughts of the Fathers into criticism of contemporary behavior; and he cannot keep his own apologia separate. The result is a fascinating document; but it is not a literary masterpiece. Neither the *Praeloquia* nor any of his other works have later imitators, or even a later readership. Though an attempt has been made to see him as a pre-Gregorian reformer,[27] there is no evidence at all of his influence in either ecclesiastical or literary affairs.

Finally, a word must be said about Rather's style.[28] He is not an easy author to read. He tends to cite an authority to prove a point and that citation prompts another, which in turn prompts another, and so on until the reader has forgotten or missed the original point; then he will suddenly revert back to his argument as though there had been no digression, but the reader has already lost the train of thought. This characteristic tends to make hard work for the reader, but for an editor or translator to prune or cut in the interest of readability would not be in the spirit of Rather's work. He himself demands that reading *be* hard work, on the ground that anything easily understood is soon despised.[29] In many works he is deliberately obscure, using a convoluted word order or complicated syntax, as though he were writing only for the erudite, to exclude the masses.[30] He loves to use unusual words: archaic words that go back to Plautus and Terence (e.g., *silicernius*, "decrepit," from Terence's *silicernium*, "funeral feast"); Greek words (e.g., *metrographia*, "verse-writing"); dialect forms (e.g., *scardus*, "sparing"); new coinages (e.g., *inperaggressibilis*, "inaccessible"). In his autograph glosses of the Martianus Capella manuscript mentioned above, he draws attention to a host of unusual words, often ones with a Greek base. This style of writing, called "hermeneutic" by M. Lapidge and M. Winterbottom,[31] was particularly in evidence in the tenth century; Atto, bishop of Vercelli, for instance, exhibits the same tendencies.

Another device is his frequent invocation of an imaginary listener or critic, in the style of the satirist; but if he already has a real addressee in mind (as for instance King Hugo in *Praeloquia* 4), the introduction of a second "you" can be confusing. The problem becomes particularly acute in *Phrenesis*, where it is aggravated by his addressing himself in the second person, and in the *Dialogus confessionalis*, where it is often unclear who "you" is: a confessor, an abbot, a monk, God, or himself.

To these difficulties we might also add his penchant for using long-winded circumlocutions and extended *topoi* so characteristic of prose writers of the period. Auerbach, in examining the letter to Ursus in *Praeloquia* 3, cc. 25–28, shows how much of it is based on a *topos* identifying sin with death. Ursus seems to have called Rather "a stinking corpse," and Rather's letter, mingling accusation with self-accusation, expands on the notion of the corpse as sinner, infecting others with the stench of sin.[32]

These features of his style combine to make the task of translation particularly formidable. Should the obscurities, the mannerisms, the essential *style* be preserved to do justice to its author and to convey his flavor? If so, much is unintelligible. Should he be rigorously pruned, paraphrased, annotated, revised?

What then is left of Rather? It is not surprising that Rather's work, except for short excerpts, has not been translated into any modern language. In making this attempt, I have chosen to keep closely to the original, however unpalatable the result, rather than to paraphrase or sweeten the style.

This volume translates all the extant works known to have been written by Rather, according to the catalogue in Corpus Christianorum *Continuatio Mediaevalis* 46, with the exception of nos. 7, 8, 9, 61 (four *commutationes*) and 34 (fragmentary). An additional work, a sermon on St. Donatianus, edited by François Dolbeau, is added as no. 5A. They are numbered, and here translated, in chronological order. Glosses and marginalia in Rather's hand have been detected in a number of manuscripts; some are collected and edited by Claudio Leonardi in Corpus Christianorum *Continuatio Mediaevalis* 46A. They are of great interest to philologists but not suitable for translation; likewise two other short fragments edited by Bernard Bischoff in the same volume.

Some of the translations of biblical texts are taken from the revised King James version; the Psalms are numbered according to the Vulgate.

Editions Used

Fritz Weigle, *Die Briefe des Bischofs Rather von Verona* (Weimar, 1949) = MGH *Die Briefe der deutschen Kaiserzeit*, I = Weigle, Epist.

Fritz Weigle, "Urkunden und Akten zur Geschichte Rathers in Verona," *Quellen und Forschungen aus italienischen Archiven und Bibliotheken* 29 (1938–39): 1–40 = Weigle, Urkunden

Corpus Christianorum, *Continuatio Mediaevalis* XLVI, *Ratherii Veronensis Opera Minora*, ed. Peter L. D. Reid (Turnhout, 1976) = CC Opera Minora

Corpus Christianorum, *Continuatio Mediaevalis* XLVIA, *Ratherii Veronensis Opera, Fragmenta, Glossae*, ed. Peter L. D. Reid, François Dolbeau, Bernard Bischoff, Claudio Leonardi (Turnhout, 1984) = CC Opera Maiora

Abbreviations

Ball. = P. and H. Ballerrini, *Ratherii episcopi Veronensis opera nunc primum collecta* (Verona, 1765) = Migne, *Patrologia Latina* vol. 136 (Paris, 1853).

Friedrich = O. Friedrich, *Publilii syri Mimi Sententiae* (Hildesheim, 1964).

Hinschius = P. Hinschius, *Decretales Pseudo-Isidorianae et Capitula angilramni* (Leipzig, 1863).

Bíblíoɡraphy

[Fuller bibliographies can be found in Louis Lumaghi, "Rather of Verona: Pre-Gregorian Reformer" (Ph.D. dissertation, University of Colorado, 1975), 165–98, and A. Stainier, *Index Scriptorum Operumque Latino-Belgicorum Medii Aevi* I (Brussels, 1973), 107–25.]

Amman, Emile, and Dumas, Auguste. *L'Église au Pouvoir des Laiques (888–1057)*. Paris, 1943.

Auerbach, Erich. "Lateinische Prosa des IX. und X. Jahrhunderts (Sermo humilis, 2)." *Romanische Forschungen* 66 (1954): 20–38.

———. *Literary Language and its Public in Late Latin Antiquity and in the Middle Ages*. Trans. Ralph Manheim. Bollingen Series 74. New York and London, 1965.

Avesani, R. "La cultura veronese dal sec. IX al sec. XII." *Storia della cultura veneta* I, 1 (Vicenza, 1976): 263.

Ballerini, P. and H. *Ratherii episcopi Veronensis opera nunc primum collecta, pluribus in locis emendata et ineditis aucta: praefatione generali, vita auctoris, admonitionibus notisque illustrata*. Verona, 1765 = Migne, *PL* 136. Paris, 1853.

Beccaria, A. *I codici di medicina del periodo presalernitano (secoli IX, X, XI)*. Rome, 1956.

Billanovich, G. "Dal Livio di Raterio al Livio del Petrarca." *Italia Medioevale e Umanistica* 2 (1959): 103–78.

Bischoff, B. "Palaographie und fruhmittelalterliche Klassikeruberlieferung." *Mittelalterliche Studien* III (Stuttgart, 1981): 71.

———. *Anecdota Novissima. Texte des vierten bis sechzehnten Jahrhunderts. Quellen und Untersuchungen zur Lateinischen Philologie des Mittelalters*. Stuttgart, 1984.

Bolgar, R. R. *The Classical Heritage and its Beneficiaries*. Cambridge, 1954.

Carusi, E.-Lindsay, W. M. *Monumenti paleografici veronesi* I. Rome, 1928.

Cavallari, Vittorio. *Raterio e Verona: aspetti di vita cittadina nel X sec*. Biblioteca di Studi Storici Veronesi VI. Verona, 1967.

———. *Ricerche sul Conte Cittadino e sulle Origine delle Autonomie*. Biblioteca di Studi Storici Veronesi VIII. Verona, 1971.

Cipolla, C. *Fonti edite della storia della regione Veneta dalla caduta dell' Impero Romano sino alla fine del secolo X*. Venice, 1882–83. (Monumenti storici pubbl. dalla R. Dep. di st. patr., Ser. IV, Miscel. vol. II.)

———. "Lettere inedite di Raterio vescovo di Verona." *Studi e Documenti di storia e diretto* 24 (1903): 50–72.

———. *Compendio della Storia Politica di Verona*. Verona, 1899.

Daniel, N. *Handschriften des zehnten Jahrhunderts aus der Freisinger Dombibliothek. Studien uber Schriftcharakter und Herkunft der nachkarolingischen und ottonischen Handschriften einer bayerischen Bibliothek.* Munich, 1973.

Dawson, Christopher. *Religion and the Rise of Western Culture.* London, 1950; repr. New York, 1958.

Dolbeau, F. "Un sermon inédit de Rathier pour la fête de saint Donatien." *Analecta Bollandiana* 98 (1980): 335–62.

————. "Ratheriana I: Nouvelles recherches sur les manuscrits et l'oeuvre de Rathier." *Sacris Erudiri* 27 (1984): 373–431.

————. "Ratheriana II: Enquête sur les sources des *Praeloquia.*" *Sacris Erudiri* 28 (1985): 509–56.

————. "Ratheriana III: Notes sur la culture patristique de Rathier." *Sacris Erudiri* 29 (1986): 151–221.

Duckett, Eleanor. *Death and Life in the Tenth Century.* Ann Arbor, 1967.

Ebert. A. *Allgemeine Geschichte der Literatur des Mittelalters im Abendlande*, III. Leipzig, 1887.

Fliche, A. *La réforme grégorienne*, I. Louvain-Paris, 1924.

Gessler, J. "Les catalogues des bibliothèques monastiques de Lobbes et de Stavelot." *Revue d'histoire ecclesiastique* 29 (1933): 82–95.

Hauck, Albert. *Kirchengeschichte Deutschlands*, III. Leipzig, 1920.

Hinschius, P. *Decretales Pseudo-Isidorianae et Capitula Angilramni.* Darmstadt-Eberstadt, 1963.

Hirzel, O. *Abt Heriger von Lobbes, 990–1007.* Leipzig-Berlin, 1910.

Klinkenberg, H. M. "Versuche und Untersuchungen zur Autobiographie bei Rather von Verona." *Archiv fur Kulturgeschichte* 38 (1956): 265–314.

Kurth, G. "Rathier." In *Biographie nationale ... de Belgique ...* XVIII. Bruxelles, 1905.

————. *Notger de Liège et la civilization au Xe siècle*, I. Paris-Brussels-Liège, 1905.

————. *La cité de Liège au Moyen-Age*, I. Brussels-Liège, 1909.

Leonardi, Claudio. "Raterio e Marziano Capella." *Italia Medioevale e Umanistica* 2 (1959): 73–102.

————. "Von Pacificus zu Rather. Zur Veroneser Kulturgeschichte im 9. und 10. Jahrhundert." *Deutsches Archiv* 41 (1984): 390–417.

Löfstedt, Bengt. "Bemerkungen zur Sprache des Ratherius von Verona." *Italia medioevale e umanistica* 16 (1973): 309–15.

Lotter, Fr. *Die Vita Brunonis des Ruotger. Ihre historiographische und ideengeschichtliche Stellung.* Bonn, 1958.

Lowis, D. W. "A Saint in the Dark Ages." *London Quarterly and Holborn Review* 156 (1931): 189–96.

Lumaghi, Louis F. "Rather of Verona: Pre-Gregorian Reformer." Ph.D. dissertation, University of Colorado, 1975.

Manitius, M. *Geschichte der lateinischen Literatur des Mittelalters*, II. Munich, 1923.

McKitterick, Rosamond. *The Frankish Kingdoms under the Carolingians, 751–987.* Harlow, 1983.

Misch, Georg. *Geschichte der Autobiographie.* Vol. 2. Frankfurt, 1955.

Monticelli, G. *Raterio, vescovo di Verona (890–974).* Millenari Rappresentativi. Milan, 1938. Soon to be produced in English translation by Buchervertriebsanstalt.

Mor, C. G. *L'età feudale* I. Milan, 1952.

———. "Spigolature storico-giuridiche dall' epistolario rateriano." *Biblioteca di Studi Storici Veronesi* 4 (1953): 45–56.

———. *Verona della Caduta dell'Impero al Commune.* Studi di Verona II. Verona, 1964.

Moreau, E. de. *Histoire de l'Église en Belgique II.* Brussels, 1945.

Muzzioli, G. "Il codice veronese LX (58) (+ Casan. 378) e il vescovo Raterio." *Atti del Congresso internazionale di diritto romano e di storia del diritto, Verona, 1948.* Milan, 1953.

Ongaro, G. *Coltura e scuola calligrafica veronese del secolo X.* Venice, 1925.

Pavani, G. *Un vescovo belga in Italia nel secolo decimo, Studio critico-storico su Raterio di Verona.* Turin, 1920.

Pirenne, H. *Histoire de Belgique*, I. Brussels, 1929.

Pivano, S. *Stato e Chiesa da Berengario I ad Arduino (888–1015).* Turin, 1908.

Raterio da Verona. Centro di Studi sulla spiritualita medieval e, X. (G. Vinay, Ilarino da Milano, G. Miccoli, O. Capitani, C. G. Mor, G. Polara, collabor.) Todi, 1973.

Reece, Benny. *Learning in the Tenth Century.* Greenville, 1968.

Reid, Peter L. D. *Tenth Century Latinity: Rather of Verona.* Malibu, 1981.

Rose, V. *Verzeichnis der lateinischen Handschriften der Koniglichen Bibliothek zu Berlin* I. *Die Meerman-Handschriften des Sir Thomas Phillipps.* Berlin, 1893.

Schneider, F. *Mittelalter bis zur Mitte des dreizehnten Jahrhunderts.* Leipzig-Wien, 1929.

Schwark, Bruno. *Bischof Rather von Verona als Theologe.* Konisberg, 1916.

Sergio, Balossi. "Raterio, vescovo di Verona (sec. X), ed il suo pensiero sui medici." *Scientia Veterum* 87 (1966): 6–13.

Silvestre, H. "Comment on rédigeait une lettre au Xe siècle. L'épître d'Éracle de Liège a Rathier de Vérone." *Le Moyen-Age* 58 (1952): 1–30.

Stainer, A. *Index Scriptorum Operumque Latino-Belgicorum Medii Aevi* I. Brussels, 1973.

Tamassia, Nino. "Raterio e l'età sua: note per la storia giuridica Italiana del secolo X." *Studi giuridici dedicati e offerti a Francesco Schupfer* II (Turin, 1898): 85–94.

Tonolli, Umberto. *Un Precursore della Riforma Ildebrandia: Appunti Storico-critici sulla Synodica di Raterio e sull' Admonitio.* Tortona, 1908.

Vogel, A. *Ratherius von Verona und das Zehnte Jahrhundert.* Jena, 1854; repr. Leipzig, 1977.

Warichez, J. *L'abbaye de Lobbes depuis les origines jusqu'en 1200.* Louvain-Paris, 1909.

Weigle, Fr. "Die Briefe Rathers von Verona" *Deutsches Archiv* 1 (1937): 147–94.

————. "Ratherius von Verona im Kampf um das Kirchengut 961- 968." *Quellen und Forschungen aus italienischen Archiven und Bibliotheken* 28 (1937–38): 1–35.

————. "Urkunden und Akten zur Geschichte Rathers in Verona." *Quellen und Forschungen aus italienischen Archiven und Bibliotheken* 29 (1938–39): 1–40.

————. "Zur Geschichte des Bischofs Rather von Verona. Analekten zur Ausgabe seiner Briefe." *Deutsches Archiv* 5 (1941–42): 347–86.

————. *Die Briefe des Bischofs Rather von Verona.* Weimar, 1949.

————. "Il processo di Raterio di Verona." *Studi Storici Veronesi* 4 (1953): 28–44.

Williams, Schafer. "Pseudo-Isidore from the Manuscripts." *Catholic Historical Review* 43 (1967): 58–66.

————. "The Pseudo-Isidorian Problem Today." *Speculum* 29 (1954): 702–7.

1

Praeloquia

CC, 46a Opera Maiora 3–196   Pavia/Como 935–937

∾

The meditations in exile of a man called Rather, bishop of the Church of Verona but a monk of Lobbes, arranged in six books, which he has decided to call "A Book of Prefaces," since they "preface" a work of his called *Agonistic*[1] [Christ's Athlete].

Preface

Since I have leisure,[2] and since the convenience of the time and the conditions of my present position are equally favorable, I have decided to gather into this little book, in the name of the Lord, a few of the countless salves of God's Word, which may daily be applied to God's athlete as he enters the arena of this world to grapple with the Adversary, summoning his whole strength and bracing his arms; so may he deserve to take the winner's crown in the contest. To make this clearer for someone who is not perhaps so ready to grasp it: I will try, I say, as far as God allows, to gather from any source at all words of pious prayer which our champion may address to our referee, to the spectators on high, and to the supporters of his cause, begging them to support him, so that they may rout the enemy with terrifying shouts and blows alike.

The reader or peruser of this work should know that it most applies to the man who is a recluse somewhere, either of his own accord or by another's command, who strips off all the anxieties of the present world and unloads himself completely of all the distractions of transitory things (which obscure the watchtower of the mind) — whether for the pursuit of true wisdom; or for the defence of justice and truth (which is the proper function of the blessed, as the Lord himself testifies [Mt. 5.10]); or, as often happens, for the correction of some fault. I have written it down for my own sake; but for many others it is indispensable (if they should deign to read it). If anyone finds it beneficial to himself in any particular, I ask him to call it, as I do, "A Book of Training for Christ's Athlete" (or "Health-giving"). And indeed he will be able to find it inspirational for the fight and most beneficial for his health—if he is prepared to take its contents at their true worth. For on the one hand it stirs you to the fight; on the other it soothes and heals the blows inflicted by the Adversary with a miraculously effective fomentation. Here, it goads you strong and sturdy for the battle, there, it rallies you weak and broken, and refreshes you hurt. The humble and timid it rouses to courage; the proud and over-confident it humbles with rebuke and shows on whose strength one ought to rely. For the idle and slothful it removes peace of mind; for those fighting bravely it reveals the rewards. It preaches opposition to temptation; it promises the palm of victory.

So up, approach the track, read on, and find out for yourself whether all this is so. You will find that almost none of it is my own (which would by necessity cause you to despise it), but everything is culled from the sayings of the holy Fathers. First reread this preface, separate from the six books of *Praeloquia*, brief in terms of substance but a little fuller in worth; for in it, perhaps, you will receive some benefit which will fire you with desire to read what follows, and show you clearly what my inspiration was for putting it all down. I further beg you, reader or copier of this work, by him who lives for ever and by his fearful judgement, and by the love with which God "so loved us and gave Himself up for us, a fragrant offering and sacrifice to God" [Eph. 5.2], not to leave out this preface which I put down here by way of forewarning, if ever you take the trouble to read or copy it. Some things are found in these books which not even the author himself fully approves, such as, for instance, what he writes about the doings and sufferings of a certain Origen[3] in books 3 and 4. But because in that part the work is bolstered by great statements of God's Word, give pardon, reader, I pray, to a writer describing events[4] some of which he witnessed but some he only heard about, some reliable but some doubtful. Do not care about the details of the events, whether they be true, false, or questionable, so long as you are the more prepared to accept the truth and healthful doctrine of the arguments, the less you see them veer from the straight path.

Book 1

[Rather outlines the moral duties and quality of a Christian according to his or her position in society, that is, as soldier, craftsman, physician, and the rest.]

Contents of this *Praeloquium* [Rather's own index]:

Here begins the first book of Bishop Rather's *Agonistic* [Christ's Athlete].

1. All the Lord's commands apply to the whole Church in general, yet certain of them are appropriate to particular individuals according to differences in the times, or in their ranks, or conditions, or age, or moral state, or desires, or sex, or motivation. In times of peace you are commanded to give your cloak, while in persecution you are ordered to lay down even life itself for your brother [Mt. 5.40; 1 Jn. 3.16]. The Lord says "Sell everything which you have and give it to the poor, and come, follow me" [Mt. 19.21], but if everyone did this at once, who would till the fields? Again, if everyone were to leave his wife, how would there be any reproduction? When He says "Give alms" [Lk. 12.33], what will the person who has kept nothing for himself give? When He says "To everyone who asks you give yourself" [Lk. 6.30],[5] (as seen in Matthew), He covers

everyone, He commands all, He excuses none. If you have something to give, give it, do not delay; if you do not have anything, give yourself, offer the kindly desire of a generous heart. For "there is glory in the heavens to God and on earth peace, to men of good will" [Lk. 2.14]; and the psalmist says: "In me, O God, are your vows" [Ps. 55.12]. Again, when He says "Love the Lord thy God with all thy heart and with all thy mind and with all thy strength, and thy neighbor as thyself" [Lk. 10.27], and "Thou shalt not steal, thou shalt not kill or commit adultery; thou shalt say no false witness nor desire the property or wife of your neighbor" [Lk. 18.20],[6] He addresses everyone, young and old, male and female, slave and free, rich and poor, cleric and layman. He spares none, He excludes no one, He embraces all. No one who disobeys these commands is guiltless, no one can commit these without sin. In these commandments there are clearly no distinctions among men.

I.2. Do you wish to be a Christian, a good Christian out of many Christians, out of the people, out of the congregation, the assembly, the city, the outskirts, the fields? Then be a righteous, industrious worker, content with your own, deceiving no one, wronging no one, not abusing or slandering anyone. Fear God, pray to the Saints, attend Church, respect the priests, offer to God the tythes and first-offerings of your labor, give to charity as much as you can, love your wife, know none other than her, be continent of her — with her agreement — on certain days (that is, feast days and days of fasting) out of fear of God, bring up your children in the fear of God, visit the sick, bury the dead; render to others what you wish for yourself; do not do to others what you do not want done to yourself [Tob. 4.16].

II. 3. Are you a soldier? Besides the above, hear what John the Baptist says: "Rob no one by violence nor falsely accuse any one, and be content with your wages" [Lk. 3.14]. But if you cannot receive wages by campaigning, earn your living by working with your hands; turn your back on brigandage, beware of murder, and avoid sacrilege.

"What sacrilege?" you ask.

That, of course, which the psalmist mentions so alarmingly; listen: "Those who said, Let us take possession for ourselves of God's sanctuary, make them like a wheel, O my God, and like chaff before the face of the wind: as fire consumes the forest, as the flame sets the mountain ablaze, so wilt thou pursue them with thy tempest and terrify them with thy wrath" [Ps. 82.13–16], and the rest. "God's sanctuary" is whatever has been offered to the Lord and belongs to his house;[7] this is made clear by Moses' words: "Everything which is offered as sacred to the Lord belongs to the holy men of the Lord and comes under the jurisdiction of the priests" [Lev. 7.9, 27.21]. Hear how much God is displeased by brigandage: "For the misery of the destitute and the cries of the poor, I shall now arise, says the Lord" [Ps. 11.6]. Rising—that is, preparing himself for vengeance—he makes clear what He himself will do when he says: "But the Lord will not have vengeance on any of his elect that cry to him but will have patience in them; Amen, I say unto you that he will have vengeance on them speedily" [Lk. 18.7–8]. Hear what this vengeance is: "The vengeance of the flesh of the impious," he says, "is fire and worms" [Eccli. 7.19].

You say: "But then fire will be extinguishable, and worms mortal."

In answer the prophet says: "Their worm will not die and their fire will not be put out" [Is. 66.24]. By *flesh* understand that the whole man is expressed through the lesser part, just as often in the Scriptures he is understood by *soul* alone through the greater part. Again: "The Lord has no favorites at the poor man's expense and will listen to the prayer of the wronged; he will not despise the orphan's prayer nor the widow, if she pour her complaint of grief. How the tears run down the widow's cheeks and her cries accuse the man who caused them. From her cheeks they climb to heaven and the Lord hearing them will not take delight in them" [Eccli. 35.16–18]. And again: "The bread of the needy is the life of the poor man; he who takes it away from him is a man of blood; he who takes away bread in sweat is like one who kills his neighbor" [Eccli. 34.25–26]. The Apostle John says: "You know that every murderer has no part in the kingdom of Christ and of God" [1 Jn. 3.15].

4. But since the Lord says "Make friends for yourselves of the mammon of unrighteousness" [Lk. 16.9], perhaps you think you can buy salvation with your loot? Listen to the same preacher as above: "A sacrifice derived from ill-gotten gains is contaminated, a lawless mockery that cannot win approval" [Eccli. 34.21]. And again: "The most High is not pleased with the offering of the godless, nor do endless sacrifices win his forgiveness for sins. For whoever offers sacrifice from the possessions of the poor is as one who sacrifices a son before his father's eyes" [Eccli. 34.23–24]. Wherefore Maximus also, talking about fasting, says: "What does it profit not to eat one's own bread and snatch the bread of the wretched?" And again: "You will give a coin to a poor man justly, if you did not take it from another."[8] Again, the same preacher as above: "Do not offer tainted gifts, for God will not accept it; for the Lord is a judge and with him there is no consideration of a person's standing" [Eccli. 35.14–15]. The prophet also says: "Woe to you who plunder; will you not also be plundered?" [Is. 33.1]. Job also says: "The soul of the injured will cry and the Lord does not let him go unavenged" [Job 24.12]. And truly: "For to thee," says the psalmist, "the poor man commits himself, and thou wilt be the helper of the fatherless" [Ps. 9.34].

Therefore, adding these few to the infinite testimonies of God's law, so practice your soldiery in this temporal world that you do not damn your living soul in the world to come.

III.**5**. Are you a craftsman? Listen: "The prayer of a craftsman is in the working of his craft, adapting his soul and seeking the law of the Highest" [Eccli. 38.39]; so you can understand that through your very products you can offer to God an acceptable praise (of prayers, that is), if you earnestly try to adapt your soul to God and to seek the law of the Highest by keeping the words of his commandment. This happens if the craft which serves for the livelihood of your body you endeavor to practice in such a way that it also serves some livelihood of your soul. From it make your alms, give a tythe of it to the Lord. Remember that from everything which He has conferred, He always demands what is his own. Be afraid that if you take his part from him, you will rather deprive yourself of your own, that is, the present and future part.

IV.**6**. To move now in my admonition from craftsmen as a class to particular kinds of craftsmen:

Are you a physician? Obey to the letter the Lord's command to you: "Physician, heal thyself" [Lk. 4.23]; that is, when you cure sickness of the body in others, be sure to attend to the health of your habits in yourself. This comes about if in the very act of healing you strive to serve your creator. Toward the poor abide by that command which the Lord gives in the gospel: "You received without pay, give without pay" [Mt. 10.8]; and toward the rich by that of the Apostle: "Let no man circumvent his brother in business, because the Lord is an avenger in all things" [1 Th. 4.6]—that is, you should charitably help the poor without charge for the love of God, but in good faith give treatment to the rich for the payment you receive, lest deceiving them you experience God as avenger.

"But," you say, "I did not receive without payment as you maintain, because I paid my teachers a fee and I bought the various medicines at a price, and I often have to be up all night working hard for the sake of the sick and their treatment."

But the Lord says: "Without me you can do nothing" [Jn. 15.5]. The Apostle also: "What do you have that you did not receive?" [1 Cor. 4.7]. And again, "Who first gave it to him and it will be repaid?" [Rom. 11.35]. James also: "Every good endowment and every perfect gift is from above" [Jas. 1.17]. Imagine that God addresses you in this manner:

Who gave you the merchandise which you have offered? Was it not I? Did I not give your teacher his skill in teaching and you the wit to receive it? Or has it escaped you that all wisdom is from the Lord God? Who could have given him the will with which he taught you even for a fee, if I had utterly taken it away from him? Who allowed you to pay the price for the medicines? By whose aid do you enjoy the skill, desire and satisfaction in your labors? Lastly, when you work, who supplies the outcome to your work? Have you not learned by much experience that your labor achieves nothing unless I decide to bestow health? When in two cases of similar sickness treatment restores one to life but lays out the other for burial, what is your part in all this? By what merits of yours, what privilege, what reward, what prayers? Understand, then, that I am the bestower of gifts, the examiner of actions, and pursue your craft so humbly, charitably, carefully, and cautiously, that you realize I am present everywhere, so that you may merit to receive in this world a favorable outcome to your work and in the next a reward in proportion to your own labor.

7. Observe also that there is no small difference between light and dark, between truth and falsehood, between the works of the devil and the generosity of God, and consider what concerns *medicine*, what the quackery of magicians. To use drugs, herbs, and different parts of God's creation to achieve in his name what the diligence of experts has discovered under his inspiration is proper to physicians. To use auguries, chantings, and other superstitious and sacrilegious practices is the work of sorcerers or magicians. There is a type of sorcerer in Africa who is not harmed by snakes; and when they want to test their children, to see if they are really theirs or not, they put them among snakes; and if they are someone else's children, the snakes devour them.[9] The Marsi in Italy, like the Psylli in Africa, were snake charmers who either killed snakes or did not allow them to hurt.

There is a cure for a carbuncle or sore commonly called *malampnum*; you make it, so they say, as follows: finely grind the herb called *radix* [radish] by the Franks, squeeze out the juices and apply the mixture to the sore, keeping it there until the same hour as that at which it had been applied, at the same time making sure that the sick man is given the juice of the radish to drink, to prevent the poison from turning inward to the heart; and let him be given it to eat, as much as he can, but in small quantities to prevent it becoming distasteful, continuously up to the hour at which it was applied.

But some quite unmentionable token applied to the wound like a stamp on a document does no good even if it may *seem* to give some relief, because it is an evil thing; in fact, it causes deadly danger to the soul.

You ask: "But why is it that such superstitions often seem to bring real bodily health?"

I, or rather, Reason itself answers: "Why is it that the devil, though he never stands in truth (as the Lord attests), often seems to speak true? Surely for this the word of Truth will not be invalidated which says: 'He was a murderer from the beginning and has nothing to do with the truth because there is no truth in him'?" [Jn. 8.44].

8. But I am afraid that in saying this I may abandon you in total ignorance to error and that you will either tell those abominable lies to some Christian to deceive him or be deceived yourself, so I will set down a few thoughts, not of my own, but of someone whom you cannot doubt at all, so that you can be quite satisfied on this point. Aurelius Augustine of august memory says in the fourth book of *De Trinitate* [c. 17.23]:

> Even though we find that the proud and treacherous powers of the air have spoken through their own agents certain things about the city and fellowship of the saints and about the true Mediator, which they have heard from the holy prophets or angels, they have done so in order to seduce God's faithful to their own falsity by means of these truths which are alien to themselves. But God acts through unconscious agents so that his Truth may resound on all sides, in the faithful for their salvation and in the wicked for their incrimination.

Augustine says this in order to show why the devil often speaks true.

But why does the devil sometimes seem to provide a cure for the body? Listen to the words of the martyr Mark, as told in the passion of St. Sebastian: "The devil's whole strategy of war, his whole plan of deceit, is to snatch the body from its pains of punishment and to make the soul subservient to vices. Let us in opposition strive not to yield to the enemy but to despise the body and succour the soul." That this is so is clear also from the admission of that same great liar when wracked by God's power through Bartholomew the Apostle, as we read in that saint's passion.

So much for the devil's wicked will to seduce with words and deceive with seeming benefits, by which means he often drags men through false goods to true evils, though God in his justice permits him.

Now something should be said (as Augustine does in the second book of the same work) about the devil's power for good, whereby through God's mercy he often, though against his will, leads the faithful to good and the wicked to their due perdition, the former when they are scourged by this power and so corrected, the latter when they are subjected to it and punished; for those that are deceived by this power ascribe it to the deceiver himself. If you look for more persuasive argument than this, you want to exceed human ability — and you know it is written: "Do not seek things higher than yourself" [Eccli. 3.22].

> I see (Augustine says [*De Trinitate* 3.7–8; 12–13], after further discussion of this matter) what can occur to the weak mind (as to why such miracles also come about through the arts of magic); for the magicians of Pharaoh likewise made snakes and other such things [Ex. 7.11]. But it is much

more remarkable that the power of the magicians which could make snakes entirely failed when it came to very tiny flies; for the gnats, the third plague to strike the proud people of Egypt [Ex. 8.16–19], were tiny flies. The magicians surely failed there, when they said: 'This is the finger of God' [Ex. 8.19]. From this it can be understood that not even the fallen angels themselves and the powers of the air, who have been thrust down out of their dwelling in that sublime ethereal purity into that deepest darkness as though into a prison of their own kind, through whose agency the magicians' arts have whatever power they have, can do anything unless the power is given them from on high. Now that power is given them either for deceiving the deceivers—just as it was given against the Egyptians and against the magicians themselves, so that they might seem admirable for seducing those spirits by whom the things were done (but in fact were going to be damned by God's truth)—or to warn the faithful not to desire to do anything of the kind as though it were some great deed (and that is why this information has been handed on to us by the authority of Scripture); or, finally, for training, testing, and manifesting the patience of the righteous. For it was not by any small power of visible miracles that Job lost everything which he had, both his sons and the very health of his body [Job 1]. Nor for that reason should you think that this stuff of visible matter is controlled by these fallen angels at their command, but rather by God, by whom this power is given as far as He who is unchangeable in his sublime spiritual seat decides. For condemned criminals in a mine control water and fire and earth to make of it what they wish—but only as far as they are permitted. And those wicked angels should not be called creators just because through their agency the magicians resisting God's servant created frogs and snakes; it was not the wicked angels who created these frogs and snakes. For of all things which are corporeally and visibly born certain hidden seeds lie hidden in these corporeal elements of this world. Some are the seeds visible to our eyes, such as those of fruits and living things; others are the hidden seeds of those seeds, out of which, on the creator's command [Gen. 1.20–25], water produced the first swimming and flying creatures, and earth produced the first seedlings and the first animals after its own kind. Nor were the seeds at that time brought forth into offspring of this sort in such a way that that power was all used up in those things that were produced; often the right circumstances for them to break out and make up their species are missing.

For consider: the tiniest shoot is a seed; properly planted in the earth it makes a tree. Of this shoot there is an even tinier seed, a grain of the same kind, and this is visible to us still. Of this grain too there is a seed.

Although we cannot see it with our eyes, we can infer its existence from reason, since if there were no such force in these elements, there would not be produced from the earth so many things which had not been sown there; nor would there be so many animals, the result of no previous mating of males and females, either on land or in water, which still grow and produce others by coitus, although they themselves arose with no mating of parents. Bees certainly do not conceive the seeds of their young by coition but they gather them with their mouths as though they were sprinkled over the ground. The creator of these invisible seeds is the creator of all things himself, since all things that are born and come forth to our eyes receive from hidden seeds the first beginnings of their growth and the increments of their due size, and they take their distinctive shapes, as it were, from these original patterns. We do not say that parents are the "creators" of men nor farmers the "creators" of fruit, though when their outward motions are applied God's power works within to create them. In the same way neither wicked angels nor even good angels should be considered as creators, if in the subtlety of their bodily senses they have known of the seeds of these things hidden beneath what we can see and then scatter them secretly with the proper moderating of the elements and thus provide opportunities for things to be produced and for their growth to be accelerated. But neither the good angels do this, except as far as God orders, nor do the wicked ones unrighteously, except as far as he righteously permits. For the malice of the wicked has its own wicked will, but the power to act he receives only in justice, whether for his own punishment or for that of others or for the punishment of the wicked or for the glory of the good.

9. Again, further on Augustine says [*De Trinitate* 9.16–19]:

It is one thing to create and then control the creature from the innermost and highest fulcrum of causes, which only God the Creator does; but it is quite another thing to make external adjustments from without, according to the powers and faculties allotted by him, so that whatever is created comes out at this time or at that, in this manner or in that. All these things have already been created in their original and primordial nature in a combination of the elements but they come forth when the opportunity is given. For just as mothers are pregnant with offspring, so the world itself is pregnant with the causes of things that are born, and these are not created in it except from that highest essence where nothing either dies, or is born, or begins, or ceases to be. But the external application of outside influences, which although not natural still follow natural laws, so that the things which are held hidden in the secret womb of nature burst forth in some way and are produced without, unfolding the proper measures, numbers, and weights which they have received in secret from him, who has disposed everything in due measure, number, and weight, is something that not only wicked angels but even wicked men can do, as I have shown in the example of agriculture above.

Don't be put off by the fact that the world of animals is a seemingly different system, in that they have the breath of life with instinctive appetites and self-defences. Even in this one can see how many men have knowledge of what animals are usually produced from what herbs, or flesh, or what juices of anything, so placed, or so buried, or so crushed, or so mixed; who is so mad as to dare call himself creator of them? Is it then any wonder that, just as any wicked man can know whence these or those worms or flies are born, so wicked angels by their more subtle sensitivity for the more hidden seeds of elements know whence frogs and snakes are born, and by applying to the elements surely known moderations of their environments, cause frogs and snakes to be created but do not create them? Men do not wonder at those things which are usually done by men. But if anyone perchance wonders at the speed of the elements,[10] in that those animals were made so quickly, he should note how this also is achieved by men according to the degree of human capability. How does it happen that the same bodies breed worms faster in summer than in winter, faster in warmer spots than in cooler ones? These things are achieved by men with the greater difficulty, in proportion as their earthly sluggish limbs are lacking in subtlety of the senses and physical mobility. Hence the easier it is for any kind of angels to draw attendant causes out of the elements, the more amazing is their speed in actions of this kind.

But there is no creator but He who originally shaped these elements, nor can anyone be a creator but He who originally has control over the measures, numbers, and weights of all that exists. And God alone is the single Creator from whose ineffable power it comes about that what these angels could do if they were permitted they cannot do because they are not permitted. For the only reason why the magicians who made frogs and snakes could not make the tiniest flies was that the greater power of God forbidding it was present through his spirit. Even the magicians themselves admitted this when they said, "This is the finger of God" [Ex. 8.19]. But what they can do by nature but cannot do when prohibited, and what they are not allowed to do by the condition of their very nature, is very hard for man to search out, in fact impossible, except through the gift of God, which the apostle mentions, saying, "To another the ability to distinguish between spirits" [1 Cor. 12.10]. For we know that a man can walk, but even that he cannot do unless he is permitted, but that he cannot fly even if he is permitted. So too those angels can do certain things if they are permitted by more powerful angels under God's ultimate command; but some things they cannot do, even if those others were to permit them, because He, from whom they have received such a measure of natural powers, does not permit it; even through his own angels He does not often permit those things to be done which He has conceded that they are able to do. Excepting then those things which happen in the normal course of seasons in the general scheme of nature, such as the rising and setting of the stars, the reproduction and death of animals, the countless varieties of seeds and buds, the mists and clouds, the snow and the rain, lightning and thunder, thunderbolts and hail, winds and fire, cold and heat, and all such; and excepting also those things which are rare in the same scheme, such as eclipses and unusual appearances of stars, and weird phenomena and earthquakes and the like—excepting all these, then, whose first and highest cause is none other than the will of God (hence also in the Psalm [148.8], when some things of this sort had been mentioned—"fire and hail, snow and vapor, stormy wind"—so that no one should believe that those are brought about either fortuitously or only from physical causes or even from causes that are spiritual but existing apart from the will of God, it adds immediately, "fulfilling his word"); excepting these, then, as I had begun to say, there is also another kind, which, though from the same corporeal substance, are nevertheless advanced to our senses in order to announce something from God, and these are properly called miracles and signs.

10. You have here, on the authority of so great a teacher, that devils can also do many things through their angelic nature which they cannot do if God forbids it; but they can do nothing unless given the power from on high either for deceiving the faithless (such as the Egyptians, who are imitated by those who either venerate the devil's deceptions as divine or desire them as efficacious—and they are much more to be hated than those who practice them, or rather than those through whom these quasi-virtues are practiced) or for warning or proving the faithful: for warning them lest, desiring to do similar things, they become like them; for proving them so that, instructed by these, practiced and made manifest, they may show how much they have been removed from the devil and made subject to God.

For who of those persons who today are so deceived in such matters to the point of perdition of their souls that over those whom they call witches[11] they set up Herodias, the killer of Christ's Baptist, as a queen, or rather as a goddess, declaring that a third part of the whole world was given her, as though this was the payment for killing the prophet, when rather they are devils who with such illusions deceive unhappy women and—more execrable than women because most damned—men, who, I say, of people deceived like this, seeing a man being whipped, like the admirable Job, by miraculous power—this too through devils—would urge him to say, and would believe it justly said, "The Lord gives, the Lord takes away, as the Lord pleases, so it is done" [Job 1.21]? No, he would ascribe it to wicked angels or to certain pitiable men and would urge that some controller—or "rainmaker" as he is called—be summoned and begged with gifts to deign to cure it, as once Mercury healed the companions of Ulysses by the touch of his wand. For not to mention the loss of such glory as was Job's, they would not do this about a mere trifle, a penknife or shoelace. We have often seen this done by people in whose hearts the words of our oft-mentioned Augustine has not sounded: "You rejoice that you have found your stuff; are you not sorry that you have perished? It were much better for your tunic to perish than your soul."[12] And the words of the psalmist: "Let all who do vain things be confounded" [Ps. 24.4]. The Apostle's words also concerning a much less serious sin: "You observe days and months and years; I am afraid I have labored over you in vain" [Gal. 4.10–11]. And from the fourth book of Kings: "Is there not a God in Israel that you go to consult Beelbezub god of Ekron? Therefore, the Lord says this to King Ahaziah, you shall not come down from the bed to which you have gone, but you shall surely die" [2 Kg. 1.3–4].

11. Consider from this last example: though some may often seem to be "cured" by such means (in fact, either by God's mercy they desire penitence or by God's justice they are abandoned to themselves), see what they merit when God's judgment finally catches them; for if the just judge avenged everything in this world, there would be no need for that Final Judgment; but if he punished none, almost no one would believe that he cared for human affairs. Therefore, you should know that—according to the opinion of a very wise man[13]—it is not proper for you to seek the help of vile spirits, you whom Wisdom wishes to raise to such an excellence, so that he can make you like to a god, as far as concerns the blessings he concedes, at any rate. Understand that this is the nature of men's minds (as the same teaches you), that whenever they throw out true opinions they take on false ones; and practice—as I suggested at the beginning of this section— what the true (because proven) skill of doctors inspired by God has discovered, rather than what wretched witches' craziness inspired by the devil has proposed. In this way it comes about that no darkness of unbelief will cloud that true vision which directs the proper course of action; and because of the good of your knowledge and the help of the cure conceded by God you will receive your gift

from kings, in fact—as it is said—from the king of all kings, as much the temporal gift as the eternal. "Teaching also shall exalt your head" and "You will
be praised in the sight of the great"; "Your skill will be known among men
and the Highest will also give your knowledge to be honored among his things
of wonder; practicing these, you will mitigate pain and make sweet medicines
and healthful salves, and your works will not be consumed, but the peace of
God will ever be over the face of your earth" [Eccli. 38.2–8].

V.**12.** Are you a businessman? Listen: "Many have sinned out of want, and
he who seeks to be rich will turn away his eyes. As a peg is fixed in the joint
between stones, so dishonesty squeezes in between buying and selling. Sin will
be cursed along with the sinner. If you have not held resolutely to the fear of
the Lord, your house will soon be in ruins" [Eccli. 27.1–4]. And again: "Nothing is more wicked than the greedy man. There is nothing more unrighteous
than the love of money; for such a man has his soul for sale" [Eccli. 10.9–10].
The Lord also in the Gospel says: "Take heed and beware of all greed; for a
man's life on earth does not consist in the abundance of his possessions" [Lk.
12.15]. And the same as above says: "Gold and silver has been the ruin of many"
[Eccli. 8.3]. And: "The man who is greedy and grasping has his property without
reason; he who acrues unjustly gathers for others; others will live in luxury on
his riches" [Eccli. 14.3–4]. And again: "How hard it is for a merchant to keep
clear of wrong or for a shopkeeper to be ignorant of dishonesty" [Eccli. 26.28].

This being the case, consider, I beg you, how dangerous to your soul is the
office you are allotted, and know that you, as well as the brigand, are called—
though a little more pardonably—a publican. For the very name which you hear
yourself called by the crowd—*cupidenarius*, "cash-coveter"[14]—shows that you
serve a vice and not a little one. For cupidity, as the Apostle says, is the root
of all evils [1 Tim. 6.10].

13. Yet do not despair. For it is written: "The blessing of the Lord is on
the head of those that sell" [Pr. 11.26]—but consider what sellers. Do then,
while there is yet time, what I tell you: "Lend to your neighbor in his time
of need; for he who lends to his neighbor shows mercy, and by supporting him
he keeps the commandments" [Eccli. 29. 1–2]. So call Christ to your house,
prepare a banquet and dinner for him, wash his feet, wet him with your tears,
dry him with your hair, feed him, clothe him, warm him, give him drink and
hospitality. He will not scorn to step aside to your house, in fact he boldly comes
in; he daily asks to be received, though you ought to press him; he thinks not
of his own need but of your greed. Then hurry to his house, address his disciples, reward them, beg them to offer you pardon, counsel, and indulgence and
to ask the same of God. Consider, while you amass wealth at home, how much
damage you are amassing for your soul. "For what," says the Lord, "does it

profit a man, if he gains the whole world and suffers damage to his soul?" [Mt. 16.26]. And the Apostle: "The world and its desires are transitory" [1 Jn. 2.17]. Be afraid, therefore, that while you yearn insatiably for things transitory, you will be deprived of things eternal. So be a good doctor to yourself; from the instrument of your avarice bear aid to your soul. "Make friends for yourself," says the Lord, "out of the mammon of iniquity" [Lk. 16.9]. Saying this, he does not urge you to fraud, but he invites you to correction after you have committed fraud. For example, you ought not indeed to take anything by force nor collect anything with evil intention, nor cheat anyone in any dealing; you may be sure, since the Apostle declares and testifies it, that the Omnipotent is an avenger of this [1 Th. 4.6]. Be content with your daily bread; hope for everything from God, who also daily feeds the flying creatures. What he gives you, accept with grateful thanks and share with others; what he denies you, do not yearn for but praise his justice.

14. But you have transgressed his commands and seized goods by force, you have amassed wealth by fraud, loved usury and extravagance, yielded to your desires, been ungrateful to God who gives you, though unworthy, everything, and have not shared it with others as the Lord commands. You have often longed for what he did not choose to give and not obtaining it have murmured against him. After all these things which ought not to have happened, he still does not want to damn you. He shows you the wealth of his goodness, and for that poison of avarice he supplies you the antidote of kindness, saying, "So that when you fail, they may take you into the eternal tabernacles" [Lk. 16.9]. What you have badly sought, wickedly discovered and foully amassed, pay out to those who, when life fails you, may be able to return you payment in heaven, match your loan, join your scattered investments into one portfolio, or rather multiply it a hundredfold. Be sure though, if it can be done — that is, if those from whom you have borrowed anything are present, and if there is a sufficient supply to do so — that first, following Zacchaeus [Lk. 19.8], you pay back at least the capital, even if you cannot, or will not, pay back the fourfold interest.

Remember also how many perjuries you have committed in that aggrandizement, how many lies in that accumulation, and in addition consult your own good, knowing that most truly the devil is father of the lie [Jn. 8.44], as the Lord himself declares, who (we also know) in the law cried "Thou shalt not commit perjury in the name of the Lord thy God" [Lev. 19.12]; and in his own person: "I say to you, do not swear at all" [Mt. 5.34]. Hence also the same wise man as above says: "Better a thief than a habitual liar; yet both shall come to a bad end" [Eccli. 20.27]. And again: "Do not inure your mouth to oaths; for there is great ruin therein; let the naming of God not be habit with you, and do not swear by the names of the blessed, for you will not be free from them" [Eccli. 23.9–11]. Elsewhere also: "Speech full of swearing will make the hair stand on end" [Eccli. 27.15]. Bristling of the hair usually occurs from sudden fear or excessive shame; if you want to know where it happens, listen to the Apostle in particular: "It is a fearful thing to fall into the hands of the living God" [Heb. 10.31]. And to Job speaking about the places of punishment: "Where no order but everlasting horror dwells" [Job 10.22].

But in case, perhaps, you are not led by my authority, which is negligible, and refuse to take advice from me, hear certain words of the Holy Spirit which are pertinent to your salvation, as contained also in the hagiographers: "Fear the Lord with all your soul and honor his priests." "Love your Maker with all your might" and "Do not leave his ministers without support. Honor God with your whole heart and honor his priests and be open-handed; give him the first-fruits as you have been commanded and cleanse yourself of negligence with a few gifts. Be open-handed to the poor, so that your well-being may be complete. Do not go to law with a great man, for fear of falling into his power. Do not quarrel with a rich man, lest he happen to take up suit against you. Do not withhold your kindness even when a man is dead, nor turn your back on those who weep, but mourn with those who mourn. Do not be slow to visit the sick; for by such visits you will win their affection." What more? "Whatever you are doing, remember the end that awaits you; then all your life you will never go wrong" [Eccli. 7.31–40; 8.1–2].

VI.**15**. Are you an advocate or pleader? Consider whose name you have taken and show yourself a faithful minister of so good a cause. For it is said of the Lord that we have him as "an advocate with the Father" [1 Jn. 2.1]. Neglect your pleading at times to preserve your love.

VII.**16**. Have you been appointed a *locothete*,[15] whom we call *comes palatii* or judge? Consider whom you too will have as examiner or judge; weigh how heavy a yoke you bear and believe that there is none heavier. For the only man who can uninhibitedly judge the fault of another is he who has no cause to be judged for his own. Listen: "Judge not," he says, "and you will not be judged; condemn not and you will not be condemned" [Mt. 7.1]. Hear also another, yet one taught by his spirit: "Do not aspire to be a judge, unless perchance you have the strength to end injustice; for you may be intimidated by a man of rank and place a stumbling block in the way of your nimbleness" [Eccli. 7.6].

But you say: "These words of yours seem to sound as if God does not want there to be judges at all. Then where is the law? Where right? Where the very distinction between good and bad? Everyone will be allowed to do everything with impunity; theft will be praised equally with giving; vices will share the same glad crown with virtues. Who will divide an inheritance between brothers?

Who will defend the widow from her abuser? Or the virgin from the rapist? Who will protect the poor?"

God does not say "I forbid that there be any judgment among men in this present world," but "I tell you of danger, so that you may avoid sin. For what is dangerous to a person ought not everywhere to be desired by many."

17. Then as I consider, I have hardly ever been able to see a judge without greed; and greed certainly does not make just decisions, in fact, it blinds the hearts of judges. Therefore, I want there to be judges not robbers, embezzlers, or abusers; I want judges, but true judges, not men thirsting after wealth. For a certain person counselling his friend about sharing the burden of power said: "Choose judges who hate avarice" [Ex. 18.21]. Also the Book of Wisdom begins thus: "Love justice, ye who judge the earth" [Wisd. 1.1]. Also, Jesus the son of Sirach, says: "In giving judgment be a father to orphans and like a husband to their mother; then the Most High will call you his son and his love for you will be greater than a mother's" [Eccli. 4.10–11]. The Lord also in Deuteronomy: "Cursed be he who perverts the justice due to the sojourner, the fatherless, and the widow" [Dt. 27.19]. And again the same as above: "Do not leave behind you one who will curse you; for when a man curses you in bitterness of soul his prayer is heard; God who made him will hear him" [Eccli. 4.5–6]. And again: "Do not love a lie against your brother, nor pile sin upon sin, for even one is enough to make you guilty" [Eccli. 7.13]. The psalmist also: "How long will you judge unjustly and show partiality to the wicked? Give justice to the weak and fatherless, maintain the right of the afflicted and the destitute; rescue the weak and the needy; deliver them from the hand of the wicked" [Ps. 81.2–4]. And another says: "Do not take account of poverty when making your judgment" [Eccli. 35.16, Lev. 19.15]. You should know that this must be observed when, as often happens, the rich man has the just cause, the poor man the unjust cause. And the same: "Hear and judge righteously, whether he be citizen or foreigner; let there be no distinction of persons. You will hear the small just as the great, nor will you take anyone's person in judgment, for the judgment is God's" [Dt. 1.16–17]. A judge is named as though from "saying right" (*iudex, ius-dicere*); to say the right is to judge justly.

Finally, hear one of whose authority you can have no doubts: "The good judge ought to decide nothing of his own will nor judge anything in accordance with his own wishes nor deliver an opinion prepared and pondered at home, but should announce everything according to the law and right, obeying what is decreed and indulging his own will in nothing."[16] In saying this, how well he harmonizes with the words of the highest judge and only one without falsity, who says: "Just as I hear, so do I judge" [Jn. 5.30]. So you should judge just as you hear, and so you should decide according to the facts of the case. Avoid catching anyone in his words, detest the example of the pharisees who watched in ambush how they might catch the Lord in his words [Mt. 22.15]. Remember that you offend not only in words but in many things every day, while the justest Judge looks on. Even when you judge justly, see that you do not demand a fee or any service, so that it will seem to be of you that the Lord complains: "Oppressors have despoiled my people" [Is. 3.12]. Hear rather his advice: "Justly pursue what is just" [Dt. 16.20]. He unjustly pursues what is just who seeks profit instead of justice and does not scruple to sell justice itself. But let this little suffice; for if you wish to be instructed further, read the book of Isidore which applies to you.

VIII.**18**. Are you a witness? Take heed of what he says: "The false witness will not be unpunished" [Pr. 19.5]. And according to the verses of a certain poet:

This one hides the truth, that one bears false witness; each sins equally:
the one because he is no use, the other because he tries to obstruct.[17]

I think that there is no greater wrong than giving false witness, because he is held guilty both to the Lord whom he takes in vain and to the judge whom he deceives—and thus he brings all the judge's fault onto himself—and to the neighbor whom he hurts—and thus he brings that one's whole calamity onto his own soul. Also, it is easier, as someone says, to avoid a bully than to turn aside a liar.[18]

IX.**19**. Are you a procurator or steward (called *gastaldus* in general currency but *major* in the Frankish speech) or *thelonearius* or minister of any other public office? Consider what it is that you are steward of, knowing that it was most truly said, "To whom more is given, more is demanded of him" [Lk. 12.48], even with the interest of punishment. This was why I advised at the beginning that you should consider what ministry it is, since I know that there are different kinds of ministries, and some are lighter, some more burdensome; among them I know that there is none more burdensome than that which the Italians call *curatura*. Since its very name urges that earthly property be constantly attended to, this office compels the wretched soul to be abysmally neglected. For all types of vices flow into it as if into some kind of asylum, and though it is the duty of that office to punish every vice, no vice is found of which the officeholder in general is not held guilty. For it is the procurator's duty to deliver thieves to the prison, though he himself seems to do almost nothing else every day but rape and loot, and in the scale of evil it is less an offence, I think, to steal things without violence than to demand of anyone under the rack that it be given; it is less to practice brigandage under pressure of poverty than in ardour of greed defraud anyone for one's lord or someone else or even for oneself, a fraud which seems to avoid neither perjury nor robbery. This is proved by Wisdom which says: "It is better to be a thief than a habitual liar, yet both will come to the same bad end" [Eccli. 20.27]. And again, about the sin of perjury: "The man given to swearing is lawless to the core; the scourge will never be far from his house; if he goes back on his word, his sin will be upon him; if his oath was insincere he will not be acquitted; his house will be filled with trouble; if he hides his perjury he will sin twice over" [Eccli. 23.12–14]. To hide a perjury is to swear cunningly. He is doubly delinquent who does this, because he is held guilty to God, whose watching eye he does not fear, and to his neighbor, whom he does not fear to cheat. He is doubly delinquent because he incurs the brand of both deceit and perjury.

20. The procurator lays down penalties for adulterers and whores, though his whole life, foully devoted to debauchery and drunkenness (which often are stimulants to fornication and adultery), quite clearly shows that he does the very things which he damns in others. To the sum of his perdition: if an adulterer or whore perchance finds something to offer him, he immediately wins over the procurator, who should be the avenger of his crime, as his protector; and thus in him is fulfilled what we read in the psalm: "If you saw a thief you ran with him, and you took your part with adulterers" [Ps. 49.18]. What more? To be brief: let us say that this is the sort of case where one man seems to be picked, as it were from thousands of men, who ought to be delivered to eternal perdition for the correction or good of the others. But what do I do, who see this very kind of office being sought by some for a price? What of it, I say? Have you never seen cords being purchased by someone from which should be made the rope to hang him? Then ascribe also the cunning of this wretch to madness of this sort.

21. But I fear that while fiercely reprehending a crime like a Pharisee, I may seem to remove all hope of correction; let me show, then, the riches of God's goodness and reveal how even you can be saved. Above all, I give you this advice: disentangle yourself, if in any way you can, from that deadly net, and so at last taking refuge in the salvation of penitence, seek the cure of satisfaction which your sin warrants. If you cannot do this in full, following with great fear what has been commanded, avoid above all cruelty, then deceit, then greed and rapacity and drunkenness no less; and finally attend to that verse of the psalm which we noted [Ps. 49.18]. In other words, do not, won over by a fee or deceived by some kind of "pity," cover up any theft or defend any crime which you ought to chastise. In avenging crimes, so pursue what your office demands that you never forget what the Lord in a parable addressed to all in general, but particularly to you, with the ending as follows: "Wicked servant, should you not have had mercy on your fellow-servant, just as I had mercy on you?

And in anger his lord delivered him to the jailers" [Mt. 18.32]. But also, I beg you, remember this often: "Whoever of you is without sin be the first to cast a stone at her" [Jn. 8.7]; and in your actions never fail to prop yourself up with charitable gifts. If with these you assail the holy ears of the Omnipotent in humility of heart, you will one day merit that he will deign himself to come to you and in his own person to visit you, as once he visited Zacchaeus [Lk. 19.10] and Matthew, and care for you and reply to those who once despaired that you could be saved: "I have come not to call the righteous but sinners to repentance" [Mt. 9.13].

X.22. Are you a *patronus*[19] or, in the common parlance of the many, a *senior*? Listen: "What you wish men to do to you, do you also to them" [Mt. 7.12]. And likewise Moses says: "The work of a hireling shall not stay with you till morning" [Lev. 19.13]. Understand that "work" is used for "reward for work," just as you often read that by "efficient" is meant that which is effected and by "continent" that which is contained. Another says: "He who sheds innocent blood and he who cheats a hireling of his wages are brothers, the one destroying, the other building; what have they gained except toil? When one prays and the other curses, whose voice will God hear?" [Eccli. 34.27–29]. And in Malachi: "I will be a swift witness against sorcerers, against adulterers, against those who swear falsely, against those who oppress the hireling in his wages" [Mal. 3.5]. Note what Jerome said in explanation of this passage: "Let us in no way think them light sins, perjury and depriving a worker of his wages," and the others here attached, which are compared to sorcery, poisoning, and adultery.[20] The Apostle also says: "He who does not take care for his own and particularly for his household, denies his faith and is worse than the infidel" [1 Tim. 5.8]. Remember that God said in the beginning of the creation of man: "Increase and multiply and fill the earth and subdue; and have dominion over the fish of the sea and over the birds of the air and the beasts of the earth" [Gen. 1.28]. Understand that men have been given dominion not over men but over fish, birds, and beasts, and God has made all men equal in nature; but owing to the inequality of their ways, some have been made subject to others to such an extent that some often dominate even men better than they. Hence our ancestors preferred to call those who had dominion over the others fathers of their country, dictators, and consuls, rather than kings, thinking it would be hateful if men were said to be ruled, like cattle, by anyone.

You must remember, as Gregory tells you, that our holy Fathers were not kings of men but shepherds of flocks.[21] Augustine also says about natural equality and the social bond of friendship: "For each man is part of the human race, and the nature of man is a social thing and has great natural good, and it also has the power of friendship; for this reason God created all men from one, that they might be bound in their society not only by their likeness in race, but also by the bond of kinship."[22] Blessed Pope Leo also, clarifying the same topic most enlighteningly, says [*Tract.* 41]: "We share even with slaves the fact that we were created in the likeness of God, and they are separate from us neither in their carnal nor in their spiritual origin. We are sanctified by the same spirit, we live in the same faith, we join in the same sacraments." Severinus Boethius, treating many aspects of the same topic so that they could be quite clear even to the blind, concludes as follows: "If you look at your origins and Creator, God, no one is degenerate, except a person who in vice espouses the worse cause and abandons his own origin."[23] This opinion is confirmed also by another, blessed in name [Benedictus] and action and words, who says in a certain place: "Whether slave or free we are all one with Christ, as we do equal service under one Lord, because there is no distinction of persons before God; before him we are distinguished only if we are found better in good works than others and humble."[24]

23. But note this, whoever you are who arrogantly boast in the pride of high blood: since the whole race of man on earth comes from like origin, and you have been created from the same material, not different, from the same single father and the same mother as any slave, that if we are all also one in Christ [Rom. 12.5]—that is, redeemed at one price, reborn in the same baptism—everyone who puts himself before the rest is doing his best to split that unity of brotherhood and to deny His paternity—and without doubt His regeneration and redemption also—by which we are made His sons, and it is apparent, if I may say so, that he denies Him. But if we are only distinguished before God by being found humble and better than others in good works, he who serves you humbly is proved to be better than you who arrogantly despise him; he who faithfully delivers you the service he promised is nobler than you who deceive him with lies; he who guarding the laws of nature does not abandon his own origin[25] is better born than you, who, feeding vice with vice, violate the force of friendship and its great natural good.

And so, most rightly accepting all this, inasmuch as it is supported by the truest authority of the most truthful and stands sure with no inconsistency, we arrive at this certain conclusion: men are distinguished from each other not by nature but by will. To enlighten the ignorance of fools and to restrain the impudence of the haughty: He who in the Gospel says, "My Father is ever working and I work with him" [Jn. 5.17], daily while we watch humbles this man and exalts that one, "because he raises the needy man from the dust and lifts the poor man from the dunghill, to place him with the chieftains" [Ps. 112.7–8]; so that, you see, when someone boasts of his noble birth and scorns those who rise to the highest honors from poor and humble positions, he should note that

that could have happened to his ancestors too, and he should try to check his pride. "For every good gift and every perfect endowment is from above" [Jas. 1.17]; and: "There is no power but from God" [Rom. 13.1]; this is most clearly shown by the sons of nobles who have been reduced to infamous poverty and the offspring of slaves who have obtained the illustrious inheritances of the highest offices, in whatever sphere they have won them. For let us examine any commander's son you like, whose grandfather is known to have been a judge, great-grandfather a tribune or *sculdascio*[26] and *his* father before him a knight: who knows what *his* father was? a seer or painter? coach or birder?[27] fishmonger or potter? tailor or sausage-maker? muleteer or groom? knight or farmer? slave or free? Who remembers after all? For

the fates will give thrones to slaves, triumphs to captives,[28]

as a certain satirist once put it, though one ought rightly to ascribe it not to the fates but to the will of the Omnipotent. What if one of those ancestors had once been promoted from some mean position to the highest office, as Varro[29] tells us happened to a certain piper, who so delighted the people with his talent that he won election to the throne? Is there something which could make that piper a noble when the pipe brought it out, which was unable to when his own nature brought it forth?

24. But let us leave this doubtful and perhaps even incredible tale, and bring to the fore something which we can clearly show not with the cunning tales of the pagans but with definite statements of the Holy Scriptures. When his brothers were rejected, David was elected king by God, because by God's gift he preceded them in kingship; was he any the nobler in birth? Or was his progeny different because of his kingship from those which he produced naturally without kingship? Was he noble because he was king and his brothers ignoble because they were mere soldiers? Or rather (which is true) did he win this nobility for himself by God's grace by his own virtue, so that he who was unknown in family became illustrious by his actions? Hence Cicero in his case against Sallust finely says:

I would like him to tell me whether these Scipios and Metelli whom he cites had any reputation and glory before their own achievements and blameless lives commended them? But if this was the beginning of their name and dignity, why will the same not equally be thought of us?

And again:

Therefore do not keep throwing men of old at me. For it is better for me to be distinguished by my own achievements than to lean on the reputation of my ancestors, and to live in such a way that I am for my posterity the beginning of their nobility and an example of virtue.[30]

The opposite is done today. For a man would rather have his ancestor praised than himself. Boethius says: "Another man's distinction will not make you shine unless you have your own."[31]

But to return to what we see happening every day: do you not see that today many people, whether by compliancy or some talent, not only win their freedom but even become their masters' heirs; and that sometimes after a noble (though unequal) marriage a slave's offspring are even given preference over those of the master?

Whether it actually happened or not, this story has been reported. A certain rich man's son had epilepsy. All the skill of the most experienced doctors could do nothing for him; his mother and father had given up all hope of his recovery. When, lo, one of the slaves suggested that on the first full moon of the month of April they collect in a glass vase the flowers of the persic tree, well cleaned; this was to be buried under the roots of the same tree by someone they chose, everyone else being kept in ignorance; the same man who planted it was to return on the same day a year later, at the same hour if possible, and digging up the vase he would find the flowers turned to oil and the weed dried; this was to be placed under the altar, with the priest not knowing anything about it, and nine masses were to be celebrated over it; it was to be sanctified and immediately after the onset of the sickness was to be given to the sick boy to drink nine times a day, together with the Lord's prayer—but with this change, that after "deliver us from evil" [Mt. 6.13] the giver should say: "O God, deliver this man named X from epilepsy"—and on the nine days on which he heard the mass each day, he should take after his fast some unleavened bread and lenten fare, and thus with God's mercy he would get well again. It was done (if it really did happen); he got well, the slave was given his freedom, was even made an heir, his medicine was tried by many, to many it also brought healthful remedy.

I have chosen to tell this tale for two reasons, firstly so that those reading it may try it for themselves and with my help a cure for this sickness may become available to some; secondly, so that I may by this example warn you to whom my words are addressed "not to seek beyond yourself"[32] and not to be foolish enough to want to put yourself before anyone especially beholden to you, as if you were nobler than they; be assured that you are of the same condition, mortality, and dust as they are. The world's honor, if it be carefully analyzed, stands not in nobility of birth but in possessions, to such an extent that we seem to value not men themselves but the trappings which surround them, and his offspring will be more glorious if fortune, passing (so to speak) from you to him, makes his rich and yours poor; or rather—to tell the truth without hesitation—the will of the Omnipotent has wanted to elevate his offspring and humble yours. All of this let the words of the wise man, if not the evidence of your own eyes, persuade you: "I have seen the slave sitting in the seat of the lords" [Eccles. 10.7], and another, though far inferior: "The son of well-born parents makes way for the rich man's slave."[33]

25. I have known in some people a certain foul vice, which I cannot leave untouched since I have experienced it myself, as if I can read it in a book. You will find a man of the nobility[34] destitute of almost everything, stripped of power and rank (if indeed he ever had any) and utterly cast down in all that ambition dictates and nobility demands, struggling to defend himself against that harsh calamity of fortune. Not able to do anything on his own account (for that is the nature of this kind of effort), he does not hesitate to seduce—with sweet-sounding enticements—someone else[35] into following him, someone who could quietly, with comfortable resources, stand firm on his own or in another's service with great profit. So he [Hilduin] tries to reduce him [Rather] from great success to monstrous failure. But though the glory of the former rose at the expense of the latter and his gains increased with the latter's losses,[36] you'll see him either giving no thanks of worthy repayment at all, or, if any compensation small or large was made and even the slightest division or discord crept in, forgetful of the past friendship, forgetful of the latter's goodwill, which was such that persuaded not by any gift (which usually deceives and entices the eyes) but by that "love which is strong as death" [Cant. 8.6], he [Rather] neglected himself entirely and chose, even at great peril to his life, to help the former [Hilduin] recover his lost glory, or even greater glory, rather than to look after his own interests and to satisfy his own needs, though they could have easily been satisfied. Forgetful of the things which each had then and which could have increased from day to day and in which he [Rather] was strong when he was tripped up, you'll see him [Hilduin] taunt the latter with the situation into which the latter (the duped teller of this tale) fell for his sake. Forgetful of those things which he [Hilduin] saw him have, you'll see him remind the latter of those which (thanks to him) he does not now have. Remembering only what he conferred,[37] he forgets what he took away.[38] He tells of the honors to which he raised him, is silent about those of which he deprived him; he is silent about the glory of the latter's nobility,[39] while mentioning the mark of poverty which he himself imposed. This great wrong demands another place, its own volume,[40] for its true description. Let what has been briefly mentioned here suffice to stir your mind in warning, if you wish to have God propitious.

XI.**26.** Are you someone's hireling, or client, or retainer? Hear what the Lord commands: "What you do not wish done to you do not do to another" [Tob.

4.16]. To show how this applies to you: just as you do not wish to be cheated of your due pay for service by your patron, so you should take care that he never be cheated of his due service by you, lest he seem to have a complaint against you. Wisdom says: "Many treat a loan as a windfall and bring trouble on those who helped them. Until he gets a loan, a man kisses his neighbor's hand and humbles his voice in his promises, but when it is time to repay, he postpones it, he pays back only perfunctory promises and alleges that time is too short" [Eccli. 29.4–6]. Take the time of repayment which you have promised as the time of your service when you shook hands with your *senior*. Take care then not to be slow, haughty or disloyal in fulfilling what you promised, or you will seem to be applying the blessed Job's words to yourself: "The stupid man is elevated in his pride and like the ass's colt thinks that he has been born free" [Job 11.12]. You can see by Job's statement that you are in no way born free, since he very clearly says that "man is born for toil" [Job 5.7]; and toil seems rather to apply to service than to freedom. Hence a certain wise man says on this subject: "Fodder and burden for the ass, bread and discipline and work for the servant" [Eccli. 33.25]. So Seneca says: "To receive a benefit is to sell one's freedom."[41] Do not, therefore, claim as your own this liberty which you have sold for a price; do rather what Solomon says, when noting that no person ought to be more friendly to yourself than you: "My son, if you become surety for your neighbor, you have given your pledge for a stranger; then do this, my son, and save yourself, for you have come into your neighbor's power; go, hasten and importune your neighbor; give your eyes no sleep and your eyelids no slumber" [Prov. 6.1, 3–4]. Since you ought to do all this for any friend, as I have said, even to the letter (saving the mystical interpretation which is the privilege of the leaders of the Church), it befits you much more to do it for yourself for two reasons: to prevent your patron rightly saying of you that you have not repaid his favors with due service, and so that the Lord who sees everything from heaven may not come as an avenger (as the Apostle says [1 Th. 4.6]) when he sees you deceive your brother in the give and take of commerce. And so remember most often the words: "Understand your neighbor from yourself" [Eccli. 31.18], and again: "Many have refused to lend money, not because of malice but because they feared to be needlessly defrauded" [Eccli. 29.10]. So you can understand from your own experience that it is not always the fault of the patron if he sometimes holds back the pay of a hireling or retainer, but it is the wickedness, idleness, or pride of the latter that causes this. Hence the writer mentioned above says: "Ingrates in particular teach people to become mean."[42] And so, pondering this carefully and with concern, as faithfully and earnestly as you can, prepare your heart manfully for service, being sure that the Father, whose servants you both are, will watch your toil and trouble from the heavens, and if he sees you deceived by your patron, he will charge him with it on that fearful day of his righteous judgment, accusing him of fraud to his face. But if you do not justify that same pay with worthy work, you will be required to earn it with punishment, when there will be no help or bail given by your guarantor.

XII.27. Are you an adviser [*consiliarius*]? Beware the words of the Prophet: "Woe to you who say bad is good and good bad" [Is. 5.20]. For as the old proverb has it: "If you come into the service of a powerful and prosperous man, either honesty or friendship must be destroyed."[43] Remember that we say that the Jews crucified Christ, though it was not they but Roman soldiers who crucified him; so you should realize that the whole burden of responsibility falls on the one who unscrupulously gave this advice. Hence we revile Caiphas, who said: "It is fitting that one man die for the people" [Jn. 18.14], more than Pilate, who said: "Take him and judge him according to your laws" [Jn. 18.31]. Hence also the Apostle said: "Not only those who do but also those who consent to the doer are worthy of death" [Rom. 1.32]. And note that he does not say those who "order" or "counsel" but "those who consent," which is far less; so you should realize how deadly is wicked counsel, when even consent to the act is that noxious. For, as Seneca says, "He who can help a dying man, if he does not help him, kills him."[44] Today the opposite is done; for a man would rather find a compliant person than a friend.

A friend, as Gregory says, means "guardian of the soul."[45] But today a greater number are found of those who "say to the seers, See not, and to the prophets, Prophesy not to us what is right; speak to us smooth things, prophesy illusions" [Is. 30.10]. But such is not, is not, I repeat, friendship, but the greatest enmity. For whoever kills a man in that part in which he is to live for ever is the greatest murderer. The law of friendship, as Laelius says, is that we should demand honesty of our friends and act honestly for our friends.[46] Every advice ought to be three things: honest, good, feasible. If one of these attributes is lacking, the advice is not acceptable. "A friend," we read in the Book of Wisdom, "is all smiles when you are fortunate but will turn against you when trouble comes" [Eccli. 37.4]. Recognizing this, the aforesaid Pope Gregory of happy memory writes to someone: "Choose as your advisors those who love *you*, not your property."[47] You, therefore, who are chosen one out of a thousand to be someone's advisor, remember in whose place you stand; and loving your friend not for his property but for himself, give him honest advice, work honestly in his cause; for we read that the Lord was called "Angel of great counsel" [Is. 9.6], and if we wish to be his imitators, we should give no one advice except that which is sound, just, and honest, lest doing otherwise we be judged not counsellors but betrayers of our friend, and called not fellow-workers of goodness but inventors of wickedness and therefore supporters of the devil.

XIII.**28**. Are you a lord? Do not exalt yourself; remember that you and your servant have one Lord and that therefore you are a fellow-servant. For though a certain wise man, pondering the arrogance of wicked servants, most wisely says: "Bread and discipline and work for the servant" [Eccli. 33.25], yet see that you do not impose on him anything that he cannot handle or that demands harsh service. Know that discretion is the mother of all virtues,[48] since, according to the admonishment of blessed Pope Leo [*Tract.* 41], one thing that ought to make you more gentle in everything is the fact that you use the service of someone with whom you share the same service to one God. Hence someone says most finely: "He who is cruel to his servants shows that in his dealings with others he does not lack will but power."[49] Therefore, the punishment of Pharaoh should frighten you; remember that God watches the miseries of the wretched from heaven; give your servant each day a period of time in which he can — not be idle in rest but — serve his creator. If, or rather because, discipline is necessary, let it be moderate. But if perchance he wrongs you, if he steals something, if he cheats you, if he runs off, whatever he has done wrong, take care to correct it all in such a way that you seem not to satisfy your anger but to rebuke a delinquent, not to exact vengeance but to chasten a fault and so to save the soul of a wrongdoer. And in all these things do not forget that terrible sentence which says, "Wicked servant, I released you from all your debt when you asked me; ought you not therefore to have had pity on your fellow-servant, just as I had pity on you? Then in anger his lord handed him over to the jailers" [Mt. 18.32–34]. But if he is faithful and obedient, hear this: "If you have a faithful servant, let him be as your own soul to you. Do not cheat him of his liberty nor leave him destitute" [Eccli. 33.31, 7.23].

XIV.**29**. Are you a servant? Do not fret; if you serve your lord faithfully, you will be the freedman of the Lord of all; for we are all brothers in Christ. And so listen to the Apostle saying: "Servants, be submissive to your masters with all fear" [1 Pet. 2.18]. What *fear*? and what does he mean by *all* ? First, the fear of God, then that of his earthly lord; then that servile *fear* which perfect love casts out [1 Jn. 4.18], that is, fear that you will be beaten or whipped, or that you will be imprisoned, and ultimately that you will be put into eternal fire for your contempt. For "whoever resists power, resists God's ordinance; for there is no power but from God" [Rom. 13.1–2]. Also the psalmist says: "You have placed men over our heads" [Ps. 65.12]; and according to the opinion of someone: "He who tries to resist God must necessarily lack great good and incur great evil, because he has gone against the highest Good and become an adherent to the worst evil."[50] And finally that chaste *fear* which remains for ever and ever, namely that if you are lazy or indolent, you will lose the glory promised in the future for those who do strong work. Therefore, any hours you steal from your lord, give to your creator. And lest you think that it is fortuitous, that is, without God's providence, that you have been subjected to service in whatever rank it happens, listen to Isidore:

> Because of the sin of the first man, God's punishment of servitude has been imposed on the human race, in such a way that those whom he sees as not suitable for freedom, of these in his mercy he demands servitude; and though this happened through the original sin, yet the just God differentiated the life of men, making some slaves and some lords, in such a way that the licence of slaves to do ill should be controlled by the power of their lords. For if all were without fear, who would there be to restrain anyone from evil? For that reason also kings and princes were chosen over the nations, that they might restrain their peoples from evil by their terror and coerce them with laws to live aright. For as far as rationality is concerned, God "has no partiality [Rom. 2.11]; God chose what is low and despised in the world, and even things that are not, to bring to nothing things that are, so that no flesh"—that is, fleshly power—"might boast in the presence of God" [1 Cor. 1.28–29]. For the one Lord gives counsel to lords and servants alike: subjection and servitude are better than pride and liberty; for there are found many who freely serve God, appointed under shameful lords, who, although subject to them in body, are yet superior to them in mind.[51]

Comforted then by this testimony of so great a man, as true as it is eloquent, be a faithful and good servant, ever keeping in your heart the counsel which the angel Agar gave to the handmaiden Sarah: "Return to your mistress and be humble under her hand" [Gen. 16.9].

XV.30. Are you a teacher? Remember that you owe your students both discipline and love, by the example of him above who is teacher of all, who chastises and reproves him whom he loves [Pr. 3.12] and who used to call his disciples not servants but friends [Jn. 15.15]. And discipline them both verbally and corporally and correct the error of their ways, in such a way that you also nourish the delinquent with love.

XVI.31. Are you a student? Know that you owe obedience to your teachers and that morality holds that a man demand of those under him the behavior which he remembers that he once showed to his superiors. To compose a mixed harangue (addressed to both teachers and students at once) in a parliamentary kind of way: Are you a student? Then hear, you too, the Lord commanding, "What you want others to do to you, do you to them also" [Mt. 7.12]. Likewise, are you a teacher? Listen: "Do not want to be called Rabbi" [Mt. 23.8]. Are you a student? Listen: "Do what they say but do not do what they do"

[Mt. 23.3]. Are you a teacher? Hear: "Whoever causes one of these little ones who believe in me to sin, it would be better for him to have a great millstone fastened around his neck and to be drowned in the depth of the sea" [Mt. 18.6]. Are you a student? Beware: "There will come a time," says the Apostle, "when people will not endure sound teaching, but they will accumulate for themselves teachers to suit their own likings" [2 Tim. 4.3]. Are you a teacher? Note: "Desiring to be teachers of the law, without understanding either what they are saying or the things about which they make assertions" [1 Tim. 1.7]. Are you a student: "Outdo one another in showing honor" [Rom. 12.10]. A teacher? "Not domineering over those in your charge but being examples to your flock" [1 Pet. 5.3].[52]

Lastly, are you a teacher or called one or do you want to be called one? The responsibility of the teacher is to keep the laws, lest you be called one wrongly. Desire rather to give benefit than to give commands. Are you a student? Study to be humble and obedient so that some time you may be of benefit both to yourself and to many others. Are you a teacher? Teach humbly what you know. A student? Be full of desire to learn what you do not yet know. A teacher? Desire rather to be loved than feared; for, as Augustine [Ambrose] says, downcast and overharsh cruelty turns many away.[53] Hence also Gregory says: "If anyone has bestial habits, he should live alone like a beast."[54] A student? Strive by your compliance to win the love of your teacher; for the poet sings for you thus:

Wisdom is the conqueror of Fortune; but we say that those are happy also, who have learned by life's experience to bear life's ills and not throw off the yoke.[55]

Are you a teacher? Take care to temper your teaching with this art, so that you seem to be set over your students to fashion them rather than blunt them. For some of them have such slow and forgetful minds that it is difficult for them to grasp those first elements of letters, still less are they able to understand any of those deeper branches of learning. And some, to use Augustine's words, are so stupid that they little differ from cattle.[56] But some are so sharp of mind and industry that often from their own intelligence and learning they understand more than their masters teach them. There are also those who grasp what is difficult and miss what is easy. There are those who find it difficult to understand but firmly retain something once they have understood it. There are those who grasp it easily but lose it more easily. There are those who grasp it easily and lose it with great difficulty. You should tell the latter nothing else than that they should nourish the keen sharpness of their intellect with the practice of study; otherwise, by not learning what they can, they may offend their creator with their ingratitude and, empty of knowledge, they may some time receive punishment for their contempt. For the rest, know also that you must temper your instruction and discipline according to the capacities of individuals and their differing intellects; otherwise, if you try to instruct them in doctrines beyond their capability, they may fall into a deeper hovel of ignorance. Read St. Augustine's Book of Soliloquies and there you will find clear instruction on this, yet not discordant with mine here.[57]

But perhaps it is not available and cannot be found when you look for it? I tell you, as I read there, that it is the duty of good teaching to arrive at wisdom in a certain order, and success is scarcely credible without order. Therefore, I urge you to handle the students mentioned above with such talent of teaching that, like doctors who try to make the sun visible to the bleary-eyed, teaching of easiest understanding be offered them first, then something more difficult, though not much more difficult; then something which is removed from this in some small part, which can, by certain parallel lines of thought, widen the vision a little; then something close to that light, then some easier part of wisdom itself, then more difficult, then—but only if it can somehow be grasped—the splendor of the truth should be shown them. But if you do otherwise, it is preferable for the student to go with bleary eyes around the tavern in the morning and to take some advantage home, than, utterly obscuring the full glory of the midday sun, to grasp at the very darkness with some desire but without any fruit.

32. Just as different levels of understanding are found in listeners, so also there are different aspirations in teachers. For some are of such obdurate will that, though they desire to be called "masters," they do not desire to imbue others with any art of doctrine. They desire to be called "doctors" but driven by envy absolutely decline to be taught. These, of course, are those who bury the treasure of their wisdom in the cavern of their heart and are spitted on the shaft of execration in the judgment, according to the proverb: "He who hides the grain will be cursed among the people" [Pr. 11.26].

There are others, on the other hand, who seem so generous that they rather appear to *pour out* their doctrine than to bestow it; of these it is said in the law (as Gregory points out) that the man who allows the flow of his seed should be excluded from the priesthood [Lev. 15.2].[58] For he who "allows the flow of his seed," that is, who pours out to no purpose those things which in the hearts of his hearers ought to have generated offspring of good virtues, is seen to render them sterile listeners by the superabundance of his own words. Though there is a fivefold division of this kind of teacher, only one seems to militate for virtue: that is, if someone is of such burning charity that he would pour himself totally, if it were possible, into the heart of the listener, as the Apostle says, "I wish you all to be like me myself" [1 Cor. 7.7]. And again: "Our mouth is open to you, O Corinthians, our heart is wide; you are not restricted by us, but you are restricted in your own affections" [2 Cor. 6.11–12]; as though he had said: though the vessel of your heart which holds it is narrow, the hand of charity which pours it is not narrow. The second division seems to serve flattery, when anyone under the pretext of teaching wants to please some magnate and introduces satire and violates doctrine. The third is criticized for militating for avarice; for many in greed of gain make money by saying what ought to be kept unsaid. The fourth particularly serves pride, when someone, in order to appear to know much, often reveals what he ought to have kept hidden, contrary to the psalmist's words: "I have hidden your word in my heart, that I might not sin against thee" [Ps. 118.11]. Hence Augustine, explaining this verse, says: "He who reveals the mysteries lessens Christ's glory." With this the words of the poet fit very finely:

Is your knowledge to be totally worthless unless other people know that you have it?[59]

Impetuous speech on its own makes up the fifth division; for many people, immoderately relaxing their tongue when speaking somewhat loosely, say without thinking something that they would like to recall but cannot.

Of these five divisions, the first is to be praised and kept to, the second and fifth to be pitied and corrected, the third and fourth to be completely avoided. After these, there are those who brazenly presume to teach others what they have not learned themselves; of these the Apostle says: "They wish to become teachers of law, not understanding either what they are saying nor the things which they assert" [1 Tim. 1.7]. These often disdain to become disciples of truth and become masters of error. There are also some who, according to the Apostle, are always learning but never come to knowledge of the truth [2 Tim. 3.7]. There are also those who say at great length what they do not understand. On the other hand, there are those who have great understanding but lack eloquence. But he is to be praised whom both eloquence and understanding make illustrious, while that first one I mentioned is to be faulted for his presumption, and the second not reviled but rather embraced, unless perchance he be full of envy or greed, or empty of kindness or charity, as often is the case; this last I pray you earnestly to beware.

XVII.33. Are you rich? Do not be like the proud rich man who scorned Lazarus [Lk. 16]. Be afraid that if you deny a poor man a crumb, you may want a drop of water and not receive it. Do you seem to have many possessions? Dispose of them so that you may truly possess.

"How," you say, "will I truly possess? Do I not truly possess things now when I enjoy them?"

You need not ask me this question; ask yourself, commune with yourself, debate with yourself. Tell me, I say, in what things do your riches lie?

"In my possession of property," you say, "of servants, of maids, of horses, oxen and other animals; in the homage of my followers, in my delight in dogs and hawks, in abundance of clothes, utensils, food, wine and oil, of arms, silver, gold, jewels."

Fine. Now I want to cross-examine you. Tell me, if you please, has the weather never touched these possessions of yours?

"How could it be otherwise?" you say.

But, I ask, how can you claim that you have ever truly possessed what the weather could take away? For what can become not yours at the whim of someone or something else is not logically yours. Hence also the words of the wise man: "Do not call yours what can be changed."[60] But let us look at the rest. Perhaps you possess those more securely. Can servants, maids, horses, or oxen be seized by bandits or stricken with disaster? Do not these also in the end share with you the lot of death? Cannot clothes be destroyed by moths?

"I know a remedy for that," you say.

Good. But do you know a remedy against their destruction by fire?

"No," you say, "but I put them in the same vault that keeps my gold as well; it is an arched cellar and fire cannot get at it."

I grant you that; but will they always be there? Will they never come out?

"Yes, they will, obviously."

What then?

"If they are all right, fine; if they are destroyed, they are destroyed."

Where then is all your careful safekeeping? What was the use of guarding them so long, if you have lost them so quickly? And even if no disaster happens, who takes his wealth with him when he goes from here? Do I not see you being put almost naked into your sepulchre with your thumbs tied? And if this is your fate, I can almost call you fortunate, because I have often heard of rich men being devoured by wolves.

34. "What then must be done?" you say. "Should everyone waste in idleness, do no work, beg? Who is to give if everyone begs?"

"No," says the Lord, "I do not command that, in fact I utterly forbid it. For I have said to you that 'you will eat your bread in the sweat of your brow' [Gen. 3.19]. When I said that, I called for work, but you on the contrary want not to work but to take from those who do work, and while idle yourself in sin and sensuality, you impose work on others, despite the fact that you have heard me say in the psalms: 'You will eat of the work of your hands; you are happy and it shall be well with you' [Ps. 127.2]. And through the Apostle: 'He who does not want to work let him not eat either' [2 Th. 3.10]. Work therefore, enjoy the fruit, pay out, dispose, I say. Just as I do not cease to give, or rather to entrust, just so you too cease not to pay out; and ever keep to your work because I have ordered it, so that you may have something to spend and there should be no need to hoard. For leisure—except on certain days for my sake—is inimical to the soul;[61] at no time do I want you to be at leisure; for though I have said through the Prophet, 'Have leisure,' I added: 'and see that I am the Lord' [Ps. 45.11], so that you can understand that you must take care to serve me. What need do you have of hoarding, when you receive enough every day as a gift from me? What is the point of saving when you do not know who you are saving for?"

"I save for my sons," you say.

"Perhaps they will die before you."

"I will give it for their souls," you say.

"When? After hell has swallowed them down? Have you not heard the psalm saying: 'In hell who will remember you?' [Ps. 6.6]. Have you not read: 'His brother will not redeem him, will a man redeem him?' [Ps. 48.8]. Finally, have you not heard me say: 'These will go into eternal punishment, but the just will go into eternal life?' [Mt. 25.46]."

"But," you say, "how can anything be eternal which, when once obtained, can be nullified by someone's gift?"

"Have you not heard, 'Wherever the wood falls, there will it be?' [Eccle. 11.3]."

35. Therefore, if you wish to give for your soul or for anybody's soul, give it while you have it, while it is still in your control, in your power, in your disposition, while you can still be redeemed, while you can be set free. For your riches can travel before you, they cannot follow you. Begin to give while you are here with a sound constitution, and if you should fall sick, pay out the more earnestly. Then if death comes, you need not fear; what you have spent here will profit you there. Only let not God judge that you have begun too late, let Him not mark the compulsion, let Him approve the will, let Him not condemn your intent; let Him consider that *here* in health you wanted to give, let Him see that you began to do so, that you wanted *here* to complete your giving. For He judges you on your wish and intent.

But perhaps you say, "My parents left for me, can I not leave for my sons or nephews or other heirs?"

Woe to those who left everything to you and took nothing for themselves—or rather took much; for what they took will never fail; for they took for themselves perpetual damnation and everlasting fire. As though God cannot feed you without their generosity, God who feeds the whole world every day!

"My father left it to me," you say.

And who left it to your father?

"Grandfather," you say.

Who left it to your grandfather?

"My great grandfather."

To your great-grandfather who?

"So and so."

To him who?

"Why do you tire me with your questions?" you say; "Adam, if not some-one else."

To Adam who?

"God."

Then it was God's, nay, whether you like it or not, it still is all God's; even if He does not receive it from you, He has it of himself. "The earth is the Lord's and its fulness" [Ps. 23.1]. But woe to those who left so many heirs behind them that the Lord never won the place of heir. Break the chain, break it, I beg you, my son, or to your damnation you will be bound by it as well as they. Take the Lord as your heir, so that He may take you as consort of His kingdom. Share your sons' inheritance with Him and make Him their brother. If you are not willing to do this, neither will you share His inheritance. But whether you will or nay, I will prove with your own words that you do not own your riches.

"Do so," you say.

Pay out, I say.

"I will not," you say.

Why not?

"I am afraid."

Of what?

"Poverty."

So your riches belong to poverty not to you; for an owner forbids, a subject is forbidden. There, I have caught you by your own admission: not only do you not own your riches, but you are even possessed by poverty, which your very riches serve.

But I see why you have strayed; for though you are a slave to avarice, you have not even dared to name it and have chosen to take refuge under the cover of poverty, though it is clear that you do not *fear* poverty but abhor it. It would be better for you to revile avarice, for love of which you abhor poverty. For why should you fear poverty? Do you not see that the poor, whom God feeds every day, have greater merit than the rich? Do you not know that the poor are raised to such a pinnacle that the Lord himself calls them brothers in that judgment where your only single comfort will be if you merit to be placed on the right side for the service rendered to *them*? So do you scorn them? Or perhaps the brotherhood of God himself is vile to you?

36. "I am ashamed of poverty," you say.

Why?

"Those who honor me now will look down on me when I am poor; 'it is a fine thing to be pointed at and have people say, this is he.'"[62]

But Reason says the opposite: "The cares of man! What great vanity there is in things!"[63] Is this what I see you yearning for so avidly? How futile it is the psalm can tell you: "I have seen a wicked man overbearing and towering like a cedar of Lebanon; again, I passed by, and lo, he was no more; I sought him and he could not be found" [Ps. 36.35–36]. Look, there is another mistress.

"What?"

Pride. For what will anybody's scorn do to you if you are humble and self-possessed? Throw a shaft at a marble column and you will see what happens.

"Now I am happy," you say, "I am delighted, I am at peace."

Look, a third mistress, luxury; but root that third one out, for you are not at peace; not without good reason does God in the Gospel couple anxiety with riches [Lk. 8.14], because He penetrates the hearts of all men and well knows what worry torments wretched rich men. Wisdom also says: "Everything pre-eminent is more troubled with pains than has delight in honors."[64] This he would not say if he did not well know what troubles the rich carry in their hearts. Finally, considering yourself and examining yourself in the censure of proper judgment, ask your heart what it is that straitens it so stringently, what keeps you awake and denies you sleep; what makes you restless and steals your peace, what is that confusion between love and fear, what the worry and what the frequent sighing—and you will see clearer than light how you toil under the savage sickness of anxiety, with what confusion of mind you are torn, by what tempests of pain you are blown, you who claim that you are at peace, content and happy. Though it may delight you for a while, you well know how much earthly wealth often pricks the heart. For you are happy while you win it, but distraught when you lose it. You pant for it when you demand it, you are in terror when demands are made on you. Like the ant-lion[65] indeed, you seem like an ant to some and a lion to others.

To add to your misery also, you must often fear those whose power you appear to exceed beyond measure. Hence someone says most eloquently: "How is the rich man at rest, when his very possessions make him ever anxious with their pricks, for fear that they be lost."[66] Also Seneca[67] says that it is much worse for a king than a slave; for a slave fears one individual, but a king fears many. So placed under such mental stress and quite self-deluded, so to speak, what can you say is yours, since you are yourself subject to another's power? The Lord puts it well: "You cannot serve both God and mammon" [Mt. 6.24], after first saying that no one can serve two masters.

37. But do not think that I am saying this about all rich men; you should know that there are two types of rich man, one good, the other bad, one proud, the other humble. For who does not know that King David was very rich? Who said that Abraham and Job were paupers? And yet David says: "I am needy and poor" [Ps. 69.6]. Abraham also: "I will speak to my Lord since I am dust and ashes" [Gen. 18.27]. And Job says: "if I have rejected the cause of my manservant or my maidservant when they brought a complaint against me" [Job 31.13]. See how much humility there is in this type of rich man. To this type belongs the man of whom it is said: "Blessed is he who considers the poor" [Ps. 40.2]. And elsewhere: "The cedars of Lebanon which the Lord has planted, there the sparrows will build their nests" [Ps. 103.16–17]—that is, certain powerful magnates in this world, in whose possessions nests, that is monks' cells, are built (so Augustine interprets)[68] and shrines are constructed by monks, virgins, and widows, and in them gather visitors and pilgrims, wanderers, prisoners, and beggars. To this type of rich man belongs also he whose praise is sung by the psalmist: "Glory and riches are in his house and his justice remains for ever" [Ps. 111.3]. To this type also belong those who demand nothing else of their wealth than the ransoming of souls and the necessary food for themselves and their families and the means to be generous. The richest, though not the most monied, are those who, according to the opinion of a certain wise man, do not seek after riches but if they have some, spend most wisely and carefully [Wisd. 8.5]. Of these Isidore says: "Certain humble men are rich, who are not swollen with pride of property, such as most of the saints of the Old Testament, who were both affluent in wealth and yet strong in humility." And again about both kinds he says: "Some are damned for the human property which they have loved too greedily; others are saved when they praise and admire the most beautiful providence of the creator in the beauty of their property, or when through charitable action they purchase heavenly goods with it."[69]

38. But now let us look at, and beware, that other kind of rich man. "Woe to you rich," says the Lord, "who have your comfort" [Lk. 6.24]. And in the psalm he says: "They will leave their wealth and their sepulchres will be their homes for ever" [Ps. 48.11, 12, 17, 20]. And again: "Be not afraid when one becomes rich and when the glory of his house increases." And further on: "He will go to the generation of his fathers, and will never more see the light." Job also says something expressive: "They lead their days in prosperity and on the point they will go down to hell" [Job 21.13]. And another says: "Come now, you rich, weep and howl for the miseries that are coming upon you. Your riches are rotten and your garments moth-eaten; your silver and gold have rusted and their rust will be evidence against you and will eat your flesh like fire. You have laid up treasure on earth and have fattened your hearts in delights in a day of slaughter; you have brought anger on yourselves in the last days. Behold, the wages of the laborers who mowed your fields, which you fraudulently withheld, cry out and their cries have reached the ears of the Lord of Hosts; you have killed the righteous man and he did not resist you" [Jas. 5.2–6].

But just as there is no greater means of salvation for the good rich man than true humility, so there is no more certain cause of ruin for him than his pride. For by it he not only destroys himself, but he oppresses, burns, and tortures others and despises those better than himself. Hence also the psalmist says: "When the wicked man is proud, the poor man is burned" [Ps. 9.23]; and again: "Have mercy upon us, O Lord, for we have had more than enough of contempt; too long our soul has been sated with the scorn of those who are at ease" [Ps. 122.3–4].

Also the Apostle giving them medicine says: "As for the rich in this world, charge them not to be haughty nor to set their hopes on uncertain riches" [1 Tim. 6.17–19]; and to all in general: "They are to do good, to be rich in good deeds, liberal and generous, thus laying up for themselves a good foundation, so as to grasp the true life." Look how the camel taking off the load of its hump can pass through the needle's eye [Mt. 19.24], how the twisting snake taking off its load can assume the wings of a dove [Ps. 54.7] and rest on the branches of the tree raised from a grain of mustard seed [Lk. 13.19] and be enriched not only with this but with so great a privilege that on his back Madian and Epha and Sheba bring gold and frankincense to the Lord's temple [Is. 60.6].[70] The Ishmaelite traders also bring gum, balm, and myrrh grown in Gilead [Gen. 37.25]—that is, the holy preachers bring the word of the Scriptures like a cargo of spices and a valuable treasure of wisdom with which to enrich others and fire them with the vapor of good thought to love of the Lord and offer to their infirm minds the medicine of good example, so that all can assuredly see that what is impossible for men is quite possible for God [Mk. 10.27]. Truth itself told us how this can happen when he said in the Gospel: "He who receives a prophet in the name of the prophet will receive a prophet's reward" [Mt. 10.41]. And the Apostle: "One carry another's burden and thus you will fulfill Christ's law" [Gal. 6.2].

Therefore, rich man, receive for Christ's name anyone prophesying in His name and you will receive the reward of prophecy itself along with him; help the righteous man with your wealth and you will receive the merit of his righteousness. For this is to carry on your back the riches of the traders—that is, those doing good deeds—to give them help in their good deeds. The help bestowed on them wins for you their fellowship and their fellowship acquires the eternal Kingdom as the gift of Him who lives and rules for ever.

XVIII.39. Are you of moderate wealth? Listen to the Apostle: "Not that others should be eased and you be burdened, but that as a matter of equality at the present time your abundance should supply their want" [2 Cor. 8.13–14]. And that of Tobias: "If you have much, give abundantly; if little, that too try to impart freely" [Tob. 4.9]. But if you are absolutely poor, consider the widow's two mites [Lk. 21.2]. Perhaps you do not even have these? You have a cup of cold water [Mt. 10.42].

"I have no well," you say, "no spring or stream; there is no river and no cup at all."

But even here the Lord's advice is available; listen to the angels' song in the Gospel: "Glory to God in the highest, and on earth peace to men of good will" [Lk. 2.14]. But the miser, according to Jerome, lacks what he has as much as what he does not have.[71]

But alas for my folly, what have I achieved? For while I speed along faster than I should, I have left out completely the greatest vice of certain rich people as well as the moderately wealthy. To take a step back in my address: I will say again, I will repeat, I will cry out, I will declare it, I will not leave it out; yet I will not say it in my own voice, but I will shout it out in the words of another; for it is of such importance and quality that I dare not keep it back, even if I am unable to express it in my own words—I could, I suppose, somehow, but reason tells me not to; it has already been most eloquently expressed by another [Chrysostom]. But it is possible that this work of mine will come into the hands of someone who is quite unfamiliar with his words; for I know that there will certainly be many people who will be so knowledgeable both about these things and about much else also which is remote from my experience that they will disdain even for a moment to look at my work, still less to want to take it up and read it. Therefore, I here use the words both of this one and of many others like him more willingly than my own, so that those who cannot read it elsewhere may be able to find their sayings here and my own thoughts may be able to find some added weight by being paired with theirs.

40. Speak then, I beg you, sir, most admired for your power of expression, knowledge and brilliance, most deservedly called Golden Mouth,[72] speak out, powerful performer of God's grace, which you seem to carry with you in your name. He says:

> That man cannot show pity, who, when his own possessions are spread far and wide does not suffer another to have property close by. When he joins up properties, enlarges his boundaries, reviles the poor, harries the not-so-poor, shuts out his neighbor, and subjects all those dwelling round him to assaults and persecution, who alone benefits from a public calamity when by either hoarding supplies or buying up the crops or inflating the price or pushing up interest rates he seeks out means for making profits

and working evil. Can such a man carry out the offices of pity, who takes pleasure in the wailing of children and the weeping of widows? When he is delighted by plunder of this sort and feeds on its spoils? Who is rich in treasure but not merit? In possessions not quality? In name not worth? Can he be touched by pity or moved by humanity if his greed is not satisfied by his own property nor bounded by another's? Even if he gave to a poor man, he would still be worse if he takes from one what he gives to another and he feeds the hungry with the bread of the hungry and clothes the naked with clothes stripped from another, since it is written: "He who offers sacrifice from the substance of a poor man is like one who sacrifices a son before his father's eyes" [Eccli. 34.24].

Behold, careful reader, you can see if you will three distinctions of the rich in one type: those who grab and do not give, those who grab much and give little, and in the middle those who are said neither to seize nor to give but are intent on piling up their profits, who lay up a double treasure, that is, one here for another (though they know not who) and one in the future, the anger of God, for themselves. Now let us learn from his honeyed voice how another type, that of good men, faces off against these. He says:

That man is truly rich, who, rich in mercy as much as in riches, divides his resources amongst the poor, who shows himself rich as much by giving as by having, who remembers that he has riches for one purpose, to lend out at interest to God, to feed Christ, to clothe the Lord; who does not seek to leave his patrimony to an ungrateful heir, but desires to commend it to Christ for the poor; who entrusts his wealth to heaven rather than the world; who desires to be more able in action than in the power of his substance; who transfers his treasures to heaven; who lives in order to do good deeds, who does good deeds in order to merit eternal life; who is moved by the misfortunes of widows, touched by the pain of children, takes up the cause of the suffering and condemns the arrogance of the proud.

41. Now that you have explained so eloquently and clearly—more clearly than anyone else by the span of ten fingers and the two hands of action—how the humility of the good rich tears open the threefold heart of the proud and lays bare to those wanting to know and be forewarned its inner recesses which are so contrary to humility, now I ask you to show what torments these same rich people bear also in this world and so loosen the reins for us to push on to other matters. He says:

To have wealth and not to do these things is to have the ability to show mercy and to refuse to do so. The wretch counts as entrusted to himself what he may transfer to an heir through his own torments and is not permitted to touch of his own because he is compelled to save it for future generations after him; he hoards more anxiously than he acquires; he guards with more trouble than he grabbed; awake he is troubled about acquiring a fortune, asleep he is troubled about keeping it; neither his waking hours are happy nor his sleep secure nor his day joyful nor his night safe; he chases around, he is in torment, he groans, and—as though what he acquires does him some good—desires to increase that which he must leave to another, even an ingrate, with much torment, so that he has a pile of anxiety in proportion to the weight of his patrimony.

42. This being succinctly and eloquently proven, let the moderately wealthy man hear, I beg (whatever mists of self-excuse he hides behind), what befits him from your words, O most clear-sighted one.

There is no wretched person except the man who refuses to show pity, because no one desiring to pity will be able *not* to have something to give. No one will be able to leave empty-handed the man who asks him except him who *refuses* to favor him; for the means of pity are not limited: either unless one gives much, what is given cannot be acceptable, or the poor demand from someone so much that those who are asked are unable to give; someone is compelled either to give much out of a moderate amount or to give a large proportion out of a little—though God's pity is grateful when a moderate amount is willingly given out of a moderate means.

Behold, rich man, with your greed exceeding even your pride and cruelty; behold, moderately rich, most tenacious; if I have seemed in my haste to spare you, this learned speaker has not spared you, every word of the Holy Scripture does not spare you. Therefore, I beg and advise you too not to flatter yourselves in anything, lest sometime you be suddenly seized away and be saved by none [Ps. 49.22].

XIX.**43**. Are you a beggar? Hear the Apostle: "He who does not want to work, let him not eat" [2 Th. 3.10]. Hear also the proverb of wisdom: "Every lazy man is ever in need" [Pr. 21.5]. And again: "The lazy man has refused to plough because of the cold; therefore he will beg in summer and none will give to him" [Pr. 20.4]. And again: "Need and shame on him who abandons discipline" [Pr. 13.18]. And again: "The lazy hand has brought about want" [Pr. 10.4]. "One man pretends to be rich, yet has nothing; another pretends to be poor yet has great wealth" [Pr. 13.7]. Again: "He who tills his land will have plenty of bread, but he who follows worthless pursuits has no sense" [Pr. 12.11]. And: "Go to the ant, thou sluggard; consider her ways and be wise. Without having any chief or officer or ruler, she prepares her food in summer and gathers her sustenance in harvest. How long will you lie there, O sluggard? When will you arise from your sleep? A little sleep, a little slumber, a little folding of the hands to rest, and poverty will come upon you like a vagabond and want like an armed man" [Pr. 6.6–11].

I have extended these quotations in a line in this way, to warn you to consider what causes you to be a beggar, in case perchance, like many, you wish to amass wealth under this excuse or to give in to laziness. There are many poor, as you have heard above [c. 37], whose pride exceeds the arrogance of the rich; though on the other hand there are rich men whose humility is greater than the pliancy of many paupers. Thus Truth says truly, "Blessed are the poor in spirit, since theirs is the kingdom of heaven" [Mt. 5.3], so that you may know that some people in the most wretched condition of poverty cheated both here of the world's joys because of their destitution and in the future of the kingdom of God because of the wickedness of their merits, are totally banished and excluded from this beatitude. "Wealth is a good if sin has not tainted it," says Wisdom, "and poverty is wicked in the mouth of the ungodly" [Eccli. 13.30].

Hence also Jerome says most acutely: "Wealth does not hinder the rich man if he use it well; nor does his need make a poor man more commendable, if amid his want and rags he does not beware of sinning."[73] Both Abraham and daily examples are available to prove both these points: one of them was a friend of God in the most abundant wealth, and others caught in crime every day pay the penalty before the laws. Hence also Isidore says: "There is an arrogance in some paupers who have no wealth to elevate them, but their only motivation is pride."[74] Even though they lack wealth, yet for the arrogance of their heart they are condemned more than the proud rich. Augustine also, talking about weak people, says: "O what great evils the blind do! evils from which the evil mind abstains."[75]

44. Since this is so, you too be earnest in serving God in humility as far as you are able, I pray, so that you may merit to be placed with the sheep on the right hand in that Final Judgment, and to be called "brother" and "blessed" by that highest righteous judge, not to be put with the goats on the left because of your pride and branded for avarice and cursed from the face of God and sequestered from the blessed. For you should surely know that you must not cease from works of mercy, since the Lord testifies that to offer a cup of cold water to your neighbor does not lack its reward [Mt. 10.41–42]. You find also the song of the angels in the Gospel: "Glory to God in the highest, and on earth peace to men of good will" [Lk. 2.14]. Thus also John Chrysostom most eloquently, as always, says:

So that no one can be excused on the grounds of not having anything, gratuitous duties of mercy are laid down, so that the Lord is shown to have given even the poor themselves their duties for behavior. Providing a cup of cold water to a prophet is promised a prophet's reward. Visiting the sick or one in prison is to visit God, so that he who cannot show mercy out of his own property can be rewarded for his good will. So it is now quite clear that men ought not to cease from the offices of mercy in proportion to their resources, so that their labors can be rewarded with heavenly rewards. So when the merciful begin to be examined and the unfruitful condemned, then the man of mercy may rejoice because he has been merciful, and the unfruitful find the punishments which he least expected.[76]

So thinking this over carefully, and putting aside all excuse, even if you are mutilated or utterly deprived of all use of your limbs, if only your mind within is whole and functioning, earnestly offer whatever you can to God, knowing that you are in debt to all at whose expense you are fed. But woe to you if you cannot live by your own work, and idling in sloth live off the work of another.

"But my infirmity makes me," you say.

Then give thanks to God and see that you do not complain, and pray for those whose wealth keeps you.

"I am healthy at least," you say, "but I am hard-pressed by a large family."

If you can, I say, refrain from sex with your wife's consent and work with your hands, so that thereby you will be able to sustain both yourself and others.

"I cannot," you say.

Then bewail your vice, for it is serious and crippling; beg what is enough, avoid overextravagance, see that you do not feed mice and worms with it. You who are healthy, help others, visit the sick, bury the dead, share with all the blessing of the Lord that is given to you; be an eye to the blind, an ear to the deaf, a tongue to the mute, a foot to the lame; and do not ever be anxious about the morrow for your own sake. If your way is by the church, do not step off it until you beg therein both pardon for yourself for your sins and eternal life for your benefactors.

Book II

[Rather outlines the moral duties of a Christian in his or her human capacity, that is, as man, woman, husband, wife, celibate, and the rest.]

Contents of this *Praeloquium*:

1. Under your guidance, O God, I have now in brief completed my first book; now still presumptuously counting on your support, I straightway begin this second little book, a modest one since I am as nothing, a wordy one though I am dejected.[1] I will say things that I have read, for the most part, and some things that I have discovered for myself. For though I have been brought from the dawn of infancy almost to the high noon of my life,[2] I still suffer the dark night of various calamities, shut up and secluded in this triple-gated prison—I who once seemed to the crowd one destined to free them from the darkness and lead them to the wondrous light of your sight; now denied access to my flock because I refused to entrust them to the treacherous wolf—as it is said and would that it were truly said—I have been exposed to punishment merely because I feared exposing them to danger, and subjected to the power of this world because I believed that I ought to be subject to you alone, Lord. But knowing that nothing is done in this world created by you that is quite contrary to your will, supported by your comfort I sustain this storm in peace, believing that

this stormy sea can very easily be stilled by you if and when you wish it; for you in the beginning made the sand the sea's boundary, saying: "Thus far will you come and no further, but your waves will be broken upon you" [Job 38.11].

Then thunder forth still, Christ, I beg you, with your commandment from heaven; and what you have decreed with frequent threats through many prophets and even in your own person, forbid also now; mercifully pitying your wretched suppliant, speak mercifully from the deep to him who cries out shut in by fearful darkness; say, "Come out, be released from the bondage of prison"; say it, do not prevent it. I know that what seems long and even difficult to the one who desires it is quick and very easy for the one who disposes. If in the meantime here you put some thoughts in my mind, I will try with your help to collect them as matter for this little work, leaving the rest to your mercy, at whose nod I know that all things prosper.

I.2. Are you a man [*vir*], taking the word from "manliness" [*virtus*] or "vigour" [*vireo*] or "strength" [*vires*] or "force" [*vis*] and the verb "rule" [*rego*]—as I heard someone claim, quite appropriately it seems to me.[3] Avoiding feminine softness, keep your heart steadfast in virtue. For the Apostle says: "The soft will not possess the kingdom of God" [1 Cor. 6.10]. This you can then achieve if you trust in your strength and raise the power of your mind to heaven, subjecting your flesh to your soul and your soul to God, ever firm and unyielding with God's help against the pleasures of the world, ever keeping the words of the psalmist in sight: "Act *manfully* and let your heart take courage, all ye who hope in the Lord" [Ps. 30.25]; and those of the Lord to Job: "Gird up your loins like a *man*" [Job 38.3]. Consider that you have been commissioned to fight the Lord's battles against the spirits of the air also, who are signified by the kings of the Canaanites, so that you may merit entrance to the land of promise (since you have already been brought from Egypt through the Red Sea, that is, the baptism consecrated by Christ's blood, and are going through the desert of this world) and think that the words, "Comfort ye and be strong" [Deut. 31.23; Jos. 1.6], have been said to you. How much soft and dissolute willpower harms the efforts even of perfect men is shown by the falls of Lot, the most righteous, and Samson, the strongest, and Solomon, the wisest. The death of Isboseth [2 Sam. 4.5–8] also indicates whether the security of the heart ought to be entrusted to womanly or manly charge.

II.3. Are you a woman? Try to apply the softness, which you bear in name, to the virtue of obedience, not to the vice of sensuality. For in the beginning you were called "virago" [Gen. 2.23], that is, "strong woman," so you should always remember that you must be strong against vices and compliant and obedient to the Lord's commands. Opposing the devil—a man with his mind, a woman with her flesh—try, you too, to overcome the mad passions of vice and pleasure with steadfast strength of mind, noting that in the Holy Scriptures there are many examples available to you; in the Old Testament, though all men are consumed with fear (as though with the sleep of death) of the enemy who terrorizes the whole world, you may read that many women won a wondrous victory by God's grace, and in the New, many forgetting their feminine weakness fought a manly struggle and, overcoming the enemy, merited with their triumph the palm of glory and the eminent crown of victory.

III.4. Are you a husband or a wife? Consider what faithfulness you owe to your spouse and to whose faith one is held witness and champion. For you can learn by the testimonies of Holy Scripture that marriage is a good, according to that condition of life and death in which we have been created, and that to violate this good is great sin, especially since the Lord in the beginning wished to make the binding of this pact so insoluble that He fashioned husband and wife not each individually but one from the other, showing by his subsequent commandments why He did this, when He said: "For this reason a man will leave his father and mother and remain with his wife, and they will be two with one flesh" [Gen. 2.24]. They will be two, He said, with one flesh. Therefore, if—or rather because—the strength of this union is so great, those who, by sinful abuse, either by committing adultery or utterly abandoning their wives or husbands, rend this bond of such faith and indissoluble love, should consider how serious and noxious a charge they bring on themselves, particularly since they have clear commandments about this both in the Gospel and in the Lord's Apostle; and if the violation of love, by the introduction of hatred, in two people who are brothers by spiritual regeneration, is branded with the charge of homicide, what will it be when not only the spirit but one flesh also is torn apart by an abominable separation?

5. You should know that there are two kinds of marriage, one without blemish, the other with fault but venial; to these is added something that is adultery, even though the committer of it violates no one's bed, because in himself he violates the temple of God, in which he ought to have lain. The first of these the creator himself graciously honored to such an extent that he deigned not only to command it but even to take part in the nuptials [Jn. 2.1–11], and, by performing his first miracle, to enhance it with his gift. This kind is strong in the love of children, so that a multitude of people may be propagated to fill the world and to hold lawful dominion over the creatures subjected to them [Gen. 1.28] and to pay due reverence to the creator, so that the City of God also may be filled with the number of those predestined. The second kind is venial and allowable, conceded by the Apostle only for reasons of fornication, that is, to prevent a man who cannot control his lust from sinning through adultery or any forbidden desires or—what is incomparably worse—from being driven

to unnatural acts in any way; for it is on account of these that "it is better to marry than to burn" [1 Cor. 7.9]—that is, to be consumed up to the point of release or unlawful or unclean ejaculation and not to be restrained by any love of God or fear of hell. See how much marriage can do, even with fault, when it is allowed in cases of need on account of something worse.

Augustine, in his book against Jovinianus the heretic, *On the Good of Marriage* [11–12], says it well:

> Intercourse that is necessary for procreation is without fault and is the only true marriage. He who goes beyond this need is subject to lust, not reason; however, even this one may supply to a spouse, though not demand of one, to avoid damnable sin in fornication.
>
> But if both partners are subject to such concupiscence, they clearly do not observe the object of marriage; yet if in their union they love what is honorable more than what is dishonorable—that is, what belongs to marriage more than what does not belong to marriage—this, on the Apostle's authority, is conceded them with pardon, though marriage does not encourage this sin, but it does mitigate it, provided that they do not turn God's mercy away from themselves either by not abstaining on certain days (to leave time for prayer and through this abstinence to make their prayers commendable in the same way as through fasting) or by changing natural practice into that which is against nature—which is more damnable in a spouse. If that natural practice slides beyond the marital right, that is, beyond the need for procreation, it may be venial in a wife; however, it is damnable in a whore. That which is beyond nature is execrable in a whore but it is even more execrable in a wife.

6. Again, in the book addressed to Valerius[4] against new heretics, about the words of the Apostle, "I want you to be without worry" [1 Cor. 7.32], he says:

> This I tell you, brothers: the time is short, that is, the people of God will not now be propagated by [temporal] generation in the flesh, but will now be gathered by generation in the spirit. Therefore, "those who have wives" should not be subject to carnal concupiscence; "those who weep" with sadness at the present ill should rejoice in hope of the future good; "those who rejoice" for temporal good should fear the eternal judgment; "those who buy" should in their having so possess it that they do not in loving it cling to what they possess; and "those who take advantage of this world" should ponder that they pass on and do not remain. For the form of this world passes away. But "I want you to be free from worry," that is, I want you to raise your heart to him in whom past times do not pass away.

Then he adds:

"The man without a wife ponders those things which are the Lord's how he may please God; the married man ponders the things which are of this world" [1 Cor. 7.32-34]; and in this way the Apostle clarifies in a manner what he had said above: "Let those who have wives live as though they had none." For those who have wives in such a way that they ponder "those things which are the Lord's how they may please God," and not, in "the things which are of this world," ponder how to please their wives, live as though they had none. This felicitously happens when their wives are such that their husbands do not please them just because they are rich or exalted or noble-born or good lovers, but because they are faithful, religious, chaste, and upright men. Just as these qualities are to be embraced and praised amongst married people, so others are to be tolerated lest they slip into damnable sins—fornication or adultery; to avoid this evil, even those conjugal acts of intercourse which are not motivated by desire for procreation but serve overmastering concupiscence (in which they are bade not to refuse one another [1 Cor. 7.5] lest Satan tempt them through their lack of self-control) are not indeed required by commandment but are conceded with pardon. For thus it is written: "Let a man render his due to his wife, likewise also a wife to her husband. A woman does not have rule over her own body but the husband does; likewise a man does not rule over his own body but the wife does. Do not refuse one another except perhaps by agreement over a season that you may devote yourselves to prayer; but then come together again lest Satan tempt you through lack of self control. I tell you this by way of concession not of command" [1 Cor. 7.3-5].

Where pardon is given, that some fault exists will not be denied. Since, therefore, intercourse without the intent to produce children is culpable (for that is the proper purpose of marriage), why does the Apostle concede it with pardon? Because when spouses are not continent they demand the duty of the flesh from each other not in desire of procreation but to satisfy their lust. Yet this desire does not become a fault because of the marriage but it receives pardon because of the marriage. For which reason even in this case marriage is commendable because marriage causes that which does not pertain to it to be pardoned because of itself; for the intercourse by which lust is satisfied is not done in such a way that the offspring which marriage demands is prevented.

But it is one thing to have intercourse only with the desire for procreation (that has no fault); it is quite another to seek carnal pleasure through intercourse, not excluding with one's spouse—which has venial fault; for although intercourse does not take place for the sake of procreation, yet for the sake of this lust procreation is not obstructed whether by wicked spell or wicked act. Those who do this [that is, those who prevent conception by some spell or act], although they may be called "spouses" are not, nor do they retain any reality of marriage, but they use an honorable name to veil a wickedness. They are betrayed when they reach the point of exposing children that are born to them unwanted; for they hate to nurse or keep those they were afraid to conceive. When dark wickedness is so savage to its own whom it has conceived, it comes to light clearly in its iniquity and the secret shame is revealed in its cruelty. Sometimes this lustful cruelty or cruel lustfulness reaches the point that it even procures the poisons of sterility: and if these avail not, it snuffs out and destroys the conceived fetus in the vitals, wanting its offspring to die rather than live; or, if it was already alive in the womb, to be killed before being born. If both partners are like this they are not spouses; and if they have been like this from the beginning, they made a pact not for marriage but for wantonness. If both are not like this, I dare say, either she is in some way a whore of her husband or he is an adulterer of his wife.

Again, further on [1.17.19], Augustine says:

In marriage these marital blessings are loved: offspring, faith, vows—(1) offspring not just for birth alone but for rebirth; for it is born for punishment unless reborn for life; (2) faith, not such as the unfaithful enthusiasts of the flesh have between themselves; for who, however wicked, wishes for an adulterous wife? or what woman, however wicked, wishes an adulterous husband? This good in a marriage is natural, but of the flesh. But the member of Christ the Consort ought to fear adultery for his consort not for himself, and to hope for, from Christ, the reward of the faith which he shows to his spouse; (3) the vows, which not even separated or adulterous spouses lose, let them keep chastely and in harmony. For it is they alone which keep even a childless marriage in upright standing, when the hope of offspring, the object of their union, is now gone. So whoever wants to praise marriage should praise these marital blessings in marriage; but carnal concupiscence is not to be thought a part of marriage but only something to be tolerated; for it is not a good that comes from natural marriage but an evil that arises from primordial sin.

Lo, by the testimony of so holy and learned a teacher, I have shown why I said in the beginning that marriage was a good and why the adulterer or utter deserter of marriage incurs so noxious a charge—because, that is, it is both beneficial and blameless if it takes place only for the sake of procreation according to the Lord's command; and it is both beneficial and venial if it is held for the purpose of avoiding the sin of fornication, following what is conceded by the Apostle.

7. As to the fact that some men because of poverty marry rich wives, so that their brides may solve the many problems of need, whether this belongs to that conceded marriage or not, I leave to others to decide. This alone, following Augustine, I declare: marriage is further to be praised also by the fact that in itself it can make pardonable even what does not pertain to it.[5] But I know that some people think such marrying for wealth belongs to the third kind of marriage, pointing out that in the beginning the creator of everything said, "It is not good that the man should be alone; let us make him a helper like to himself" [Gen. 2.18]. But whatever the motivation for marriage—procreation of children or avoidance of fornication or escape from poverty— so strong is the faith and sacrament belonging to marriage that a wife once divorced cannot be the wife of any other than the divorcer: and if married again, however holy, pure, noble, and chaste she may be, she is held to be a whore by Truth; and the man she marries is himself an adulterer, since the Lord testifies and says: "Whoever dismisses his wife except by reason of fornication is an adulterer and whoever marries a divorced woman is an adulterer" [Mt. 19.19].

Note that, though it is otherwise quite forbidden, divorce is allowed in the case of fornication, because, that is, when she fornicated, she broke the bond and ceased to be one flesh. So adulterers of both sexes should know and understand what a detestable sin they commit, if, against the creator's express command, what God has joined together they separate either by adultery or divorce, since they cannot be one flesh except by keeping faith to each other and guarding the sacrament. But whatever is forbidden to women is clearly forbidden to men also, as reason shows, as far as relates to their contract: and it is quite abhorrent if what the stronger sex demands of the weaker, it does not, when overcome and enslaved by lust, allow to the weaker. This contract and sacrament I mean to be the marriage vows or records, by which man and wife are insolubly bound to each other while God the just judge attends, watches, and witnesses.

Then let this whole topic which I have set forth convince you, I beg, so that, because you have now with wiser counsel left burning Sodom, that is, the forbidden hot lusts of the flesh, but have not yet decided to climb into the mountains, that is, the heights of celibacy, you can at least in Segor [Gen. 19.23], that is, the middle ground between these two, which is understood to be carnal marriage, live as chastely and continently as possible, loving your wife according to the Apostle's command [Eph. 5.25], as Christ loved the Church, and knowing none other but her, being continent of her with her consent on those days on which the Church by law calls for continence, and keeping perpetual faith with her, knowing that if you deceive or circumvent her in any business, the swift avenger and just judge and true witness who sees everything from heaven and whose commandment you have transgressed will speedily be present.

8. One thing I dare not pass by: childish is the opinion of those who take the words "They will be two in one flesh" [Gen. 2.24; 1 Cor. 6.16] to refer to a *child*; that is, that because of the seed of the male and the flower of the woman, out of which, according to physicians, offspring is produced in the womb, *two*, i.e., the father and mother, *in one flesh*, i.e., the child, *are made one*. For if it were so, a whorish union would have as much worth as a marriage, provided that children resulted from it; though the Apostle clearly said that such people also were one body, this was not because of the generation of children but because of the act of coitus. For he says: "Do you not know that he who joins himself to a whore becomes one body with her? But he who becomes united with the Lord becomes one spirit with him" [1 Cor. 6.16–17].

If it were as they say, that child would be able to say what only the single-born Son of God, coessentially and coeternally God remaining with God, could truly say: "My Father is in me and I in Him" [Jn. 10.38]. And: "My Father remaining in me does these works" [Jn. 14.10]. And "I and my Father are one" [Jn. 10.30] — using *one* in the singular and *are* in the plural so that you may understand that they are two in one substance, godhead, eternity, majesty, operation, will, and power; and, as I said, the child would be able to say: "I and my father and mother are one, and my father and mother are in me and I am in them"; and madder still, "I am the father and mother of myself, because in me they are both one who had before been two, which could not happen unless they had ceased to exist in themselves but were turned into me."

But what when not just one, but two or twenty-two or more children are born? Of them it ought to be said — they ought not to be left out — it ought to be said, I repeat: "they are two in twenty fleshes!" Rather we should understand that they will be two in one flesh, in one law, in one love and faith of the flesh, in one bond of the flesh, in one contract of the flesh, so that two bodies should be bound to each other in so strong a union that nothing is allowed to one which is not allowed to the other; for example, he should not go to the body of another woman nor she to that of another man, deserting the body that is proper for them; and just as body cannot be separated from body without great pain, so a wife cannot be separated from her husband without great sin; otherwise, those who have remained in perpetual virginity, as we read many of the saints have done even joined in marriage, or those who are childless, and old men too whose bodies are nearly used up, would seem deprived of this right of charity, or rather of this blessing of marriage, which is only a blessing because of that insoluble bond by which God wanted to make two from one so that those who have been separate from each other in body might be one in love and faith in each other: so that a third might be made from these two, a third who now would be not one with them but would leave them and join with another, with whom, following their example, he would become two in one flesh; and so the generations of men would be propagated, different from beasts and other living creatures in this blessing, in that the latter, having no reason and not knowing how to be one in love and affection, lapse into promiscuous matings, while the former, having reason, are strengthened by a solid pact, joined even in the flesh by a single love and emotion.

9. But if you make the objection that Jacob had two wives, and David also, and Solomon had even more, I invite you to probe the mystery of it because "all this happened as a warning" [1 Cor. 10.11]; and I boldly state that even here the city of our God and His holy mountain have been prophesied, in which a man is allowed to have but one wife—and a wife but one husband—with whom he may chastely live, whether for procreation or to avoid fornication, and forever keep the faith which he swore to her and the sacrament, particularly since that too looks to a greater authority, namely, the Church and Christ; for the Apostle says of it: "This is a great sacrament"—that is, mystery—"I say in Christ and in the Church" [Eph. 5.32]; that is, if I may dare add to this a little, that just as husband and wife are two in one flesh, so Christ, since he is truly God, and also truly man in his body which is the Church [Col. 1.24], remains one from two natures and cannot ever be separated from the Church, for which he shed his own blood in the wedding; just so is it not allowed for a man to leave his true wife nor for a wife to leave her true husband. Just as legitimate divorce from each other can occur in the case of fornication, so also any soul seeking after other lovers in fornication, that is, diverse sins or suggestions of wicked spirits, is repudiated by him, unless perchance it is reconciled again to him through repentance, just as also the Apostle teaches us a wife can be reconciled to her husband [1 Cor. 7.11].

10. Where also the Apostle declares that the two in flesh are one flesh [Eph. 5.31], this too is not to be taken lightly, but we must state that they were two at the beginning, because the one was formed out of the other, and they were one flesh, because they were, as it were, one body: he in that rib which was taken from him, she because she had her whole body in him, from whom the rib was taken, and was created for him. Likewise Christ also is one with the Church, inasmuch as He is the head of the Church, as He witnesses in the Gospel, saying: "Nobody ascends into heaven except he who descended out of heaven, the Son of man, who is in heaven" [Jn. 3.13]. As if He had said more openly: "No one will enter into the kingdom of heaven unless united and as it were

co-embodied with Him who thus made man descended from heaven, so that he may be in heaven through the power of His divinity, filling heaven and earth." Christ and the Church are two, inasmuch as it is made up of men, and pure men, and He is true man and true God. So much for this; let me now hurry on to the rest.

IV.**11.** Are you a wife? Remember that everything I have noted above applies to you, with the addition of the special commandments given by God the Creator to you, both through Christ and through his servants by word and example, and most of all through the Apostle. To you in particular God the Creator said: "You will be in the power of your husband and he will be lord over you" [Gen. 3.16]. Thus Peter used Sarah as an example when he wanted to tell you how you ought to behave, saying: "As Sarah obeyed Abraham calling him lord, whose daughters you are if you do right" [1 Pet. 3.6]. In order, therefore, that you may merit becoming a daughter of the patriarchs in doing right, make sure you obey your husband also using words of humility, preferring submission and solemnity, so that the words of Wisdom may apply to you: "Blessed is the husband of a good woman, the number of his years is doubled" [Eccli. 26.1], that is, he is blest with joy both of this present world and of the future. And again: "The upright woman delights her husband; he will live out his days in peace; a good wife means a good life; she is the Lord's gift to him for his good deeds" [Eccli. 26.2]. And truly. "For," says the Apostle, "the unbelieving husband will be saved through his believing wife" [1 Cor. 7.14].

On the other hand, according to the same as above, "It is heartache and grief when a wife is jealous of a rival and her tongue is like a lash" [Eccli. 26.8–9]. A jealous woman is a quarrelsome one or one who makes her husband jealous. A jealous man is one who watches over his wife's chastity with heartache and anxiety. Thus also the Lord is called jealous by Moses [Ex. 34.14], because, just as a husband carefully guards his wife's chastity, so He, both with the fear of punishment and the promise of his kingdom, guards and restrains us from committing adultery away from Him. Again: "A quarrelsome woman is a great anger; both her abuse and wickedness will not be covered; but grace on top of grace is the woman who is holy and modest" [Eccli. 26.11, 19]. The Apostle also, instructing Titus on matters of the Church, tells him how he should instruct you, saying among other things: "Teach what befits sound doctrine, bidding the older men be sober, serious and sensible, sound in faith, in love and in steadfastness. Bid the older women likewise to be reverent in behavior, not slanderers, or slaves to drink; they are to teach what is good and so train the young women to love their husbands, to be sensible, chaste, sober, domestic, kind, and submissive to their husbands, that the word of God may not be discredited" [Tit. 2.1–5]. To the Ephesians also he says: "Wives, be subject to your husbands as to the Lord; for the man is the head of the wife, just as Christ is head of the Church and himself is savior of its body. As the Church is subject to Christ, so let wives also be subject in everything to their husbands" [Eph. 5.22–32].

He instructs men also: "Husbands, love your wives, as Christ loved the Church and gave himself up for her, that He might sanctify her. Even so husbands should love their wives as their own bodies. For no man ever hates his own flesh but nourishes it and cherishes it, as Christ does the Church, because we are members of his body from his flesh and from his bones. For this reason a man shall leave his father and mother and be joined to his wife and the two shall become one. This is a great mystery and I take it to mean Christ and his Church." In other words: though it happens in the human and carnal union that the two embracing one another become one flesh, yet the mystery refers to Christ and the Church; because, just as Eve was fashioned from the rib of a man, so from Christ's side the Church was redeemed and grew, and just as the head of the wife is her husband, so the head of the Church is Christ. Hence he adds: "However, let each one of you love his wife as himself" [Eph. 5.33], because, that is, Christ did likewise by giving Himself up for the Church; and he adds: "Let the wife fear her husband."

12. There, you have heard from the Apostle's commands what you ought to be towards your husband; now, what you ought to be towards yourself hear from the words of St. Cyprian, bishop and martyr:

Bodily modesty lies in not coveting other people's property, avoiding all uncleanliness, not wanting to eat before the appointed hour, not raising a laugh, not speaking empty and false words, having your habit proper in every detail and in accordance with what is appointed, both of your hair and of your dress, as is fitting; not to enter taverns with the worthless, to look at no one with arrogance, not to let the eyes wander, not to walk with showy or lascivious gait, to appear second to none in beginning good work, to bring no abuse or embarrassment on anyone, to slander no one, not to mock old men, not to argue with a better, not to meddle in things which you do not know, and even the things which you do know not to reveal them all. These things make a person loved by his neighbors and acceptable to God.[6]

To return to our subject: if then you have a good husband, imitate Sarah, Rebecca, Rachel, and Elisabeth; but if he is wicked and cruel, you have also models to imitate—in the New Testament, Anastasia and Theodora, in the Old, Abigail, the wife of Nabal of Carmel, and Esther, wife of Assuerus. Finally, hear the words of the Apostle: "The unbelieving husband will be saved by his believing wife" [1 Cor. 7.14]; and again: "He will be saved through the generation of his sons" [1 Tim. 2.15] — where you should take them not as sons of the flesh but sons of the mind, whom you are told to "take and dash against the rock" [Ps. 136.9]; that is, to raise all your works and thoughts to Christ, so that, whatever good you do, you may try to attribute not to yourself but to him without whom you can do nothing good.

V.**13**. Are you celibate? Consider how you have climbed the highest peak of sanctity and the higher you stand the more carefully you should beware headlong fall. And remembering the Lord's words, "Because you can do nothing without me" [Jn. 15.5], know that especially in this matter you need his mercy and grace, because, as Jerome the man of truth says, "To live in the flesh but beyond the flesh is God's gift, not human merit."[7] Hence also, as Gregory says, the celibate is not commanded but commended; for it is stupid, or rather very arrogant, for dust or ash to presume that it can do by its own virtue what nature gave not to it but to angels along with God's gift. For thus Truth himself says: "The sons of this age marry and are given in marriage, but in the resurrection they will neither marry nor take wives, but will be as angels in heaven" [Lk. 20.34–35]. And elsewhere he says, on the same subject, "Whoever wishes to take, let him take" [Mt. 19.12], showing that not everyone who wishes climbs the citadel of such high eminence but only he to whom God has granted the ability.

Therefore, trust not at all in yourself but in him without whom you can do nothing. "Whom do you surpass in beauty? go down" (as the Prophet says) "and dwell with the uncircumcised" [Ezek. 32.19] — that is, humbly go down with those who are not only joined in marriage but also have care of the flesh in concupiscence, not preferring yourself to anyone, in your own estimation, as though the rest were sinners; since you have been given chastity, be singularly holy; for you know that certain vices at times dominate people, and God permits it, so that when converted they may afterwards learn by whose pity they have been redeemed from captivity and by whose virtue they have been snatched from the power of the cruel tyrant, and they may thank their Savior the more, the greater the danger from which they have been freed. But on the other hand, you know that sometimes to some reprobates come certain gifts of sublime virtues, in which they grow proud and fall even more severely; this happens so that the elect may be cowed by their fall and not presume about themselves, but may fix more firmly the footstep of their heart in God's mercy. For this reason the Apostle finely says: "He who stands, let him see that he does not fall" [1 Cor. 10.12].

14. The psalmist shows the particular cause of such a fall when he prays: "Let not the foot of arrogance come over me nor the hand of the wicked move me; there the evil-doers have fallen" [Ps. 35.12]. And rightly so; for since the Scriptures say that "before a fall the heart is exalted" [Pr. 16.18], you should know that no one falls from virtue to any vice unless he first happen to jump from the rock of humility into the quicksand of pride with a leap of vanity and inconstancy; for if no secret pride came first, the visible fall of lust would not follow.[8] Hence also Prosper says:

> The man given to concupiscence of the flesh seems indeed to have no pride, especially since his very passion seems to bow him down before sensuality; and yet, unless he were first a rebel to God, whose wholesome commandment about preserving chastity he despised in the presumption of his proud spirit, no desire would propel him into wantonness. In his heart contempt and fear of God have long been at odds; but either contempt of God predominates and his proud heart accepts desire and loses its chastity, or fear holds fast, and his soul, subject to God, shouts down desire and pride at the same time.

So much for the particular cause of a fall. Now, about the general cause of such an event, listen to Prosper again:

> Many revert to sensuality from a base self-indulgence in food and wine; others are inflamed by unclean thoughts to lose their chastity; some are turned from their goal of chastity by the offerings of opportunity; some are brought under the yoke of debauchery by the examples of those who live lives of damnation. There are others whose lives are inflamed by a foul tongue which shows their guilty conscience—those who first either utter shameless talk or willingly listen to it and then as the sickness worsens gradually slide from integrity. But just as dirty thoughts sully the mind, so, if the thoughts are pure, they purify it. Hence it is that that corporal emission, which happens to a man asleep without any sin, is sinful when it occurs while he is awake. What happens to the man asleep is quite different from what the man awake does; in the former, the excess of moisture is expelled by nature, in the latter his base concupiscence is brought to light.

Therefore, so that you do not underestimate the gift of chastity and lose it, remember the prophet's command: "How have you fallen from heaven, Lucifer, you who arose in the morning?" [Is. 14.12]—that is, you appeared glorious and admirable to all in the splendor of your virginity; for this kind of glory is not innocence but trickery; for, as I said, it is from the sin of pride that a disastrous fall of this sort happens; for with these two vices—lust and pride—in particular, or rather in total, the devil trips up the whole class of lost souls; yet one depends on the other. For just as through pride one passes into the profanity of lust, so from lust one slides into obdurateness and, alas, continues on downwards to the point of despising the creator; and in this way at last his heart, which ought through its humility and purity to have been God's temple, becomes by its pride and foulness a haunt of demons and (to parallel the metaphor) the devil's shrine. For this is what the Lord himself says to blessed Job (and we cannot disagree): "Under the lotus plants he lies, in the covert of the reeds and in the marsh" [Job 40.16]. Beware, then, all you who still enjoy the great privilege of chastity, that you do not attribute it to your own merits when you reject lust, and so fall into pride; and while you avoid pride, take care not to slide slothfully into lust. To enable you to do this, keep the fear of hell in your mind's eye, and as a nail drives out a nail, so let the fear of this fire drive out the fire of that vice.[9] Let consideration of our earthly fragility also check your fearful pride. Thus it comes about that, defended both from the poison of pride and from the fire of lust by Christ's aid, you may eternally rejoice in the company of the angels, since you have imitated the angelic life while on earth.

VI.15. Are you a father or a mother? Remember that you owe your children discipline, and obey the Apostle's admonitions [Eph. 6.4] so that at the same time you avoid the fate of Eli the priest [1 Sam. 2.12–25]. "Fathers," says the Apostle, "do not provoke your sons to anger, lest they become puny-hearted" [Col. 3.21].

VII.16. Are you a son or daughter? Remember that you owe respect to your parents; for the sole-begotten, who was conceived not from sin as you were, but from the Holy Spirit, was born of the Virgin; and after He had been found in the Temple, and had taught his parents (that is, his Virgin Mother and his most chaste provider,[10] called for that reason father) about the power of his divinity and they had not understood, "He went down," says the Evangelist, "with them and came to Nazareth and was obedient to them" [Lk. 2.51]. Why then should you disdain to be obedient to your parents, when the Lord, who creates and nourishes everything, did not disdain to obey his provider also? It often happens that a father is poor while his son is rich. What, I ask you, is there worse in the whole of nature? While others are usually arrogant from pride in their father's nobility, you to your own disgrace dismiss your father branded with the mark of poverty to wander the streets as a beggar. As he begs, what does his beggar's cry show if not that you are newly rich, raised out of poverty and elevated, a "made" man[11] (as was lately invented by those who boast that they "make" men), a spurious foundling and a bastard? If one were even falsely to charge you with this, would that not have been good cause for a fight?

All this is as far as relates to the world. But in relation to God: since He says through the psalmist, "Blessed is he who considers the poor and needy" [Ps. 40.2], whom do you consider, I ask, who do not even look with pity on your beggar-father? To whom do you provide alms, you who do not even acknowledge nature itself in your own father? Though pity should be shown to all, even to those outside the faith, but especially, as the Apostle says, "to the household of the faith" [Gal. 6.10], what do you show to these who are not only of the household of the faith but also the household of your blood, even the source of your birth? Or, as someone commenting on the Decalogue says so well: "He who does not show honor to his parents, whom will he be able to spare?"[12] Therefore, you should give something to everyone, but to your father you should entrust everything; put your whole estate under his control. And so, whether you are a father or a son or any blood-relative, hear the words of the Apostle: "He who has no thought for his own, and particularly for his household, has denied his faith and is worse than the infidel" [1 Tim. 5.8].

VIII.17. Are you a widow? You have Anna [Lk. 2.37] for your model, so to speak. But if you wish to live differently, listen to the Apostle: "A widow who is self-indulgent is dead even while she lives" [1 Tim. 5.6].

IX.18. Are you a virgin? Rejoice humbly in the Lord and beware of ceasing to be that which you are. You have Mary, the mirror of modesty, the title of chastity, the mark of humility, the glory of purity. Study her song; it is pattern enough for your behavior. See on what virtue she most relied, so that she merited enrichment with the privilege of such a sublime and excellent gift, granted to none other before or since, and study how you too can imitate her. To make it easy for you: if you humbly ask her how, she herself would wisely reply: "He has regarded the humility of his handmaiden" [Lk. 1.48]. There is the reason; for this very thing He had long ago promised through the prophet: "To whom will I look but to him who is humble and contrite in spirit and trembles at my word?" [Is. 66.2]. And so the single cause of our perdition is pride, the single cause of our recovery is humility. Humility is the mother of all virtues, the ornament of all behavior; without it there is no virtue; without it all virtue is not virtue but vice.

To close, I offer you three authorities in succession whose word you cannot doubt, all brilliant teachers, all chief pontiffs, all admired by the whole world, one prelate of Rome [Gregory], one of Milan [Ambrose], one of Hippo [Augustine]. "There is," says the first, "no virginity of the flesh which sweetness of the mind does not improve."[13] "It befits," says the second, "a virgin to be the more humble the more she is chaste."[14] "A humble marriage," says the third, "is better than a proud virginity."[15]

X.19. Are you a child? Let him nourish you in this world who nourished Samuel in the temple [1 Sam. 2.11]. Listen then, as you are able—and be earnest as you are able, and try and strive and follow as you are able—to Wisdom, who says: "How long, little ones, will you love your infancy?" [Pr. 1.22]. Know that your Father is present and that He daily summons you in the morning of your life. For when you grow older, when you want to read or learn, or at any rate to ask, you will find that some children five years old, and (a still greater miracle) even three years old [Cirycus], have of their own will gone forth to martyrdom, have resisted the powers of the world with wisdom and strength, have performed miracles in the name of the Lord, have bravely borne torments, have steadfastly derided their torturers, have willingly undergone for the Lord a death as precious as it is immature, and have clearly shown, by the signs and miracles attending their dead bodies, that they have won the crown of victory together with the palm of glory; and—an even more incredible wonder—you will find many brave virgins of that age, who in conflict with the devil have come through victorious for the love of Christ's name. You will also find other wretches of the same age who, after remission of the original sin, have won hell by their own deserts and have brought this to the notice of men by certain clear indications, with the merciful permission of Him who wished this to be written for your forewarning.

XI.20. Are you a boy? Listen to the Apostle: "Do not be boys in your thinking; be babes in evil but in your thinking be mature" [1 Cor. 14.20]. Imitate Him of whom it is said that "He increased in wisdom and stature and in favor with God and men" [Lk. 2.52]. For following His divinity, He remained perfectly complete, having nothing in which He could grow because He existed thus without a beginning; so that He cannot have any end by diminishing either. But according to His humanity, which He took on for your sake, He wished to grow in order to show you how you ought to grow, in fact He offered himself in order that you should grow. Therefore, be aware also that your Father is present and calls you to cultivate the vineyard [Mt. 20.1–16] the more earnestly, as your bodily limbs seem to grow for working and your mental abilities seem to grow for understanding. For with the addition of a conjunction, he invites you and those behind you saying: "Go ye *also* into my vineyard"; elsewhere it will be clear why He does this. Remember also that death, though untimely, comes unexpectedly on babes, boys, and young men, just as it comes of necessity to old men.

XII.21. Are you a young man? Listen to the Lord: "I say to you, Arise" [Lk. 7.14]. Hear also the Apostle: "Rise, ye who sleep, and arise from the dead and Christ will give you light" [Eph. 5.14]. And do not be angry that I seem to rouse you so fearfully right at the beginning; know that I do this as much for your age, which is liable to every kind of slip, as for the forked road at the very entrance of life; the letter [Y] of Pythagoras of Samos[16] can remind you of this, in case you should ever want to forget it. But let the word of one who has already on many occasions helped, increased, adorned, and strengthened this work on which I labor—St. Augustine—be present at once, I pray, in case I seem to fail at all in my explanation: "Youth," he says, "is freer toward love, less cautious for a fall, more fragile toward weakness, less amenable to reproof."[17] What lessons also Ecclesiastes and the Books of Proverbs and Wisdom, inspired by the prophecies of the authors both of the Old and the New Testament, both of the shadow of the Truth and of Truth itself, use to strengthen and defend you against youth's dangers, it would take too long to tell; it would obstruct my theme which moves on to other things.

But in case I seem to cheat you of some lessons at a time when you need many, I urge you, if you will, to turn the ear of your heart to the psalmist's words when he asked a question and at once received advice that is applicable to you also: "How can a young man keep his way pure? By keeping your commandments" [Ps. 118.9]. To use St. Augustine's words here too: note that he straightway offers you the curing cup not found by human presumption but received from God's inspiration. For your mind, which is degenerate in its stock, will begin to give better fruit if it is sprinkled with the seeds of the words of heaven—but these the heavenly Father is wont to sow only in a furrow.[18] Hear finally the minister of this most fertile sowing: "All things should be done decently and in order" [1 Cor. 14.40]. So direct the gaze of your heart to his nod and do not follow the crooked way of the twisting serpent [Is. 27.1]. Prepare the way of the Lord coming to you; make straight the paths of your God [Lk. 3.4]; for He deigns to proceed only by a straight path, as the Scripture says: "The ways of the Lord are straight, but the paths of the reprobate are crooked" [Dan. 3.27, Pr. 2.15]. If, therefore, you wish to follow Christ, walk on the road by which He goes, lest it be said of you: "Alas, those who have left the straight paths!" [2 Pet. 2.15].

22. Observe the better advice which the prophet in Lamentations urges: "It is good for a man that he bear the yoke in his youth" [Lam. 3.27–28]; and as though you ask, "Why?" he adds: "He will sit alone in silence."

"Nothing else worthwhile?" you ask; "for men think that these are the worthwhile things: to go hemmed in by great crowds of people attaching to your side, to be surrounded by a thronging crowd of flatterers—that is what is said to be great happiness. You urge me to take up my yoke, that I may sit *alone*, when I see many take it up so as to be thronged by vast crowds."

He continues and adds what that one sitting alone merits: "for he will raise him aloft."

"Where will I be raised?" you say; "why will I be raised? So it may be said of me, 'He who raises himself will be humbled' [Lk. 14.11]? Or so that I can say: 'Raising me up thou hast crushed me' [Ps. 101.11]?"

No, but so that it may be said of you: "He who dwells in the shelter of the most high will stay under the protection of the God of heaven" [Ps. 90.1]; and so that you may be able to sing in gladness: "You have held my right hand and you have led me in your will and have raised me with glory" [Ps. 72.24]; and so that many will be able to say in praise of you, or rather of God: "Blessed is he whom you have chosen and raised, for he will live in your halls" [Ps. 64.5].

As to where He will raise you, ask Paul: "Who raised us up with him and made us sit with him in heaven" [Eph. 2.6]. And the Lord himself: "Where I am there also will be my minister" [Jn. 12.26]. Minister, therefore, for Christ and you will be with Christ.

"Where?"

"In their sight," Scripture says, "He was raised up and a cloud received Him out of their sight; while the angels said, 'Here is Jesus who was taken up from you into heaven'" [Acts 1.9–11]. If therefore you wish to belong to Him, study to cleanse the earth from your heart, so that lightened and free, on the wings of your virtues, that is, on wings not weighed down with any of the things which you have shown above that you yearn for, you may be able to climb to heaven where He is.

23. "I don't want to object," you say, "but the psalmist says: 'Raising me, you have crushed me' [Ps. 101.11]."

In case you happen to think that I have understood it superficially, I tell you (as well as I can if not as well as I ought) that the sentence should be taken in its good meaning rather than in its bad: that is, that raised on the summit of virtues, you are crushed in humility gratuitously, or rather he crushes you, yet not "in the whirlwind and hailstorm" [Is. 30.30], but "in the spirit of gentleness" [1 Cor. 4.21] which can "unbend the crushed" [Ps. 145.8], which "touches the mountains and they smoke" [Ps. 103.32], and "mortifying brings to life again, taking away the breath" [1 Sam. 2.6] of those who aim high so that they fail and "return to their dust" [Ps. 103.29] — that is, recognize that they are dust — commanding them, "The greater you are, humble yourself in everything" [Eccli. 3.20]. For thus you will be able to recognize Him, who alone puts the humble on high and raises the sorrowing to safety, and to know that you ought to attribute nothing to your own merits but solely to Him, whom we know to be author, giver and rewarder of good. As has been observed before me, by the one evil of vainglory you can be cast from the highest to the lowest, but by the one good of humility you can be drawn from the lowest to the highest.

But if you still ask — and think that you have not been answered to your satisfaction — how you can be raised aloft, know from the teaching of the Apostle that "the body which is corrupted weighs down the soul" [Wisd. 9.15]; nor can anyone raise himself to the highest by his own efforts, unless he is raised by the grace of Him who came down to the lowest for our sake. But because in this quotation [Lam. 3.28], which I have included for your sake, not only "will raise him aloft" is said, but also—which you seemed for a while to deny—"he will sit alone and in silence," I do not think we should pass it by, but we should zealously ask what this *sitting* is and what this *silence* is and what they mean. Perhaps it will then be clear that the virtue of contemplation of God is born out of gravity and cleanliness of the heart and silence of the mouth; that enthronement, which also imitates the enthronement of the heavenly kingdom, is acquired by contemplation, that is, when the mind's thought has been restrained and cleared of all the greed and dirt of mortal things.

24. So lest I begin to wander over many topics: there is still present, fresh in your ears, she who was mentioned just now in the Gospel, Mary; for on the sixth day of the seventh month from the turn of the year—but the eighth from the time of this calamity which oppresses me, or rather disciplines me—this reading is duly assigned,[19] which will help me much, I believe, with God's support, to investigate what I have undertaken. Let us see therefore, so that we may believe; let us believe so that we may see. What is it that I say? Let us see that it is God alone who uncovers the hidden from the darkness, let us believe that he is present to us always, but particularly when we speak about him. Let us believe those things which we do not yet know about him, so that we may be able to see and understand while believing. For thus he said: "If you believe, you will see" [Jn. 11.40]. Let us find out how that most holy sinner, that most chaste courtesan, bore the yoke, how she sat alone, how in silence she was raised aloft [Lk. 7.36–47]; and if today's reading does not help, we have to help us all the clearest and most fitting lessons about the Mary of the other reading [Lk. 10.39–42]—but only if she is believed to be the same person.

Come now: "A certain Pharisee asked Jesus to dine with him, which He did, and while doing so there was present a certain woman who had been a sinner in the city." Wait here a moment; note that it says "had been"; why does it not say "was"? Surely she had not already heard, "I say to you, her many sins are pardoned because she loved much"? But the evangelist knew that the cause of the woman's coming was from the mercy of the Lord, who drew her in; for He himself drew her inside in his mercy, who outside was about to take her up in his gentleness. And therefore, when He saw her and chose to draw her in, converted she ceased to be what she had been and began to be what she would be in the future through the pity of Him who took her up. For thus He promises through the prophet: "At whatever hour a sinner is converted and mourns, he will be saved" [Ezek. 33.12].

Now let us try what follows: "She brought an alabaster flask of ointment and standing behind him at his feet weeping, she began to wet his feet with her tears, and wiped them with the hair of her head, and kissed his feet and anointed them with the ointment."

There is the yoke which she bore. For she offered from herself as many sacrifices as she had previously had pleasures; she won over to herself every kind
of delight, when, leaving herself nothing of herself, she broke into so many tears
of heavenly desires; she burned with the fire of divine love, who had previously
burned with the fire of passion; she washed with her tears the stains of her sins,
which she had caused by the thrill of her unwholesome pleasures; her hair, her
eyes, her whole body in addition, she subjected to this yoke, all of which she
had once armed in contempt of the creator; she converted a multitude of vices
into virtues, so that whatever in sin had served the world, or rather the devil,
might wholly serve God in penitence. Lo, from the present reading you know
the yoke which this Mary bore.

25. Now, to move onto something else as I promised: let another woman
show how she sat alone in silence, and sitting raised herself aloft; and with God's
help let her round off my whole argument: "Jesus entered a village and a woman named Martha received him into her house; and she had a sister called Mary
who sat at the Lord's feet and listened to his teaching" [Lk. 10.38–41]. There
you have one sitting and listening in silence.

"But surely not *alone?*"

Listen: "Martha stood and said: 'Lord, do you not care that my sister has
left me to serve *alone?*'" You have here also *alone* if you please; for two had
already been mentioned, Martha and her sister Mary; Martha served alone; Mary
sat in silence and listened alone; and rightly was she silent when she has such
an advocate speaking for her. There, as I believe, is nothing left in doubt about
the *sitting* nor about the *being in silence.*

Now let us see the *raising aloft* as well, and seeing it let us embrace it, and
embracing it let us desire it for ourselves. "Martha, Martha, you are anxious
and troubled about many things"—she is addressed twice, I believe, either because of his love or because she did not now minister to one as Mary did, but
served two, seeking the things of heaven while ministering the things of earth.
This that other Mary had once done also, as the reading discussed above shows;
but lightened of these, her yoke now thrown off, and free, of her own accord
she submitted all her limbs to the feet of the Lord. And so Martha alone was
not alone; Mary was alone; Mary was alone because she served many: Martha
was alone because she served one. "For one thing is needful"; for those many
things receive no fruit if they do not arrive at the one, and for that reason the
many lack the one, but the one does not lack the many. "Mary has chosen the
good portion which shall not be taken away from her." Look how she is *raised
aloft*, who, after carrying the yoke, desired to sit alone in silence. For clinging alone to Him alone, she merited Him alone, God himself alone, as her
portion.

26. "But," you say, "why are you so quick to say that this *portion* is God? As yet you have given no evidence for this belief."

I have given no evidence because it is quite clearly stated there above: "He who serves me," He says, "follows me; and where I am there will my servant be also" [Jn. 12.26].

"And so," you say, "Martha who served will be there, not Mary who sat."

You would be right if she sat in laziness; you would be right if she had not already been serving. For many things are served, though one would be enough; but one thing is arrived at by the service of many.

"What is that one thing then?"

God, to be sure.

"And what are the many?"

The works of mercy. By works of mercy God is arrived at. When that goal is reached, all action ceases, because there is no necessity for action. The fruit remains for which the action was done; the Love alone remains for which it was done; Love alone, individually, singularly, clings to Him alone, individually, singularly, forever. There is nothing more industrious than that very sitting of which you try to accuse Mary, though it seems more than anything else like inactivity, so that by a like definition even rest in this world can be called industrious.

But in case perhaps you should think that from want of quotations I have not given any example to help us, you have the blessed young person, the holy adolescent—in fact Mary herself who bore the yoke—saying in the same Lamentations [3.24]: "God is my portion, said my soul, therefore will I await him." And the psalmist: "My portion is in the land of the living" [Ps. 141.6]. But hear what will never be taken from her: "But thou art the same and thy years have no end; the children of thy servants shall dwell secure there and their seed shall be established forever" [Ps. 101.28–29]; and: "My part is the Lord for everlasting" [Ps. 72.26]. Thanks be to God that in our reasoning we have been brought to this point, that, by that very hesitation of yours, I may urge you to raise the yoke with Mary and minister with Martha, so that afterward you may be able to sit well with the same Mary, with whom also sitting well—that is, taking time out from worldly matters for contemplation, and hearing the soundless word of God—you may happily be able to choose the best part and win it and possess it.

27. And so this sweet yoke, this light burden, which can so lighten and raise you that you merit having God himself as your portion, which does not press down and twist the neck but adorns and honors it; do not delay; do not hesitate to raise it in your youth, I beg; otherwise you may perchance wish to raise it later, and there will be no opportunity, and it will be said to you: "If you have not found this in your youth, how will you find it when you are old?" [Eccli. 25.5]. Anticipate, therefore, the years of age with due action and due correction, knowing that it is more desirable for you to be able to say truly, "O God who feedeth me from my youth" [Gen. 48.15], and "O God, you have taught me from my youth" [Ps. 70.17], than, remembering your lapses, to pray in apprehension and in tears, saying, "Do not remember, Lord, the sins of my youth and my indiscretions" [Ps. 24.7]. For the former is the bulwark of salvation, the latter is the medicine of a sick man; a remedy is sought for a wound, but grace is bestowed on the healthy.

For since the life of man on earth is a service [Job 7.1], is it not better bravely to undergo the campaigns of that service in your youth, so that in old age you may attain the place of higher rank among the emeriti, than to waste your youth in idleness and then strive to give your hand to service, when age both impedes the service and weakens the limbs, as strength fails and the less resolute shoulders are denied hope of winning the contest? Particularly since age itself does not promise such a span of life in which, your work complete, you will be able to change your service so as to be dignified with the honors of a higher rank; but rather you will have to be content, with weary limbs and no announcement of your praises preceding you, at least to be numbered among those who ask for a donative for their first assignment, or with the provincials who offer the knights their tithe of tribute; and for that reason the preacher above says that it is a good thing to raise the yoke in youth [Lam. 3.17].

For he who takes it up after the time of youth is past meets with many opposing forces; unaccustomed vices provoke him, his evil habits press him down; his very conscience goads him; the sins he has practiced make him unstable; he strives against himself, and falls; he wishes to wipe out the old, but his actions do not follow his will, and, like a bird caught in the nets, where he wants to free the foot of his action, he is held back by the toils of his habitual practice. And so, for this one, his whole being is in danger, while for the other it is in good. Finally, the other will sit alone, finding few people, or even none at all, worthy of his company, and serenely and in holiness he will have time for the divine offices; enriched by the revelations and rewards of the angels, harried by no pleasures of wantonness neither past nor present, nor touched by the titillations of itching flesh, he will rejoice alone, at peace, free, and sure of his salvation.

28. Therefore, whoever you are who strive for this singular height, practice first communally in the field of the living; give your careful presence and attention to serious men; learn to give honor to your elders, love to your peers, an example to your juniors; follow the authority and instruction of wise men, and believe that in it God himself speaks to you. When you sit in the council of elders, keep your hand on your mouth, listen attentively, keep learning intent-

ly, so that by taking in the views of your elders, you may earnestly gather something to keep in your older age.

Also I ask you to refrain at times from talking with your contemporaries, so that you do not by the very practice of it grow used to small-talk and, being yet green in years, easily slip into speaking forbidden words; and so that aloof you may be able to listen to the precepts of the elders, to the words of the ancients, to the oracles of the prophets and the teachings of the apostles. For he is worthy of praise who would rather learn in silence what he ought to say than utter his thoughts before he has learned to speak. If the grace of God concedes that your genius be enriched with these, we must add the counsel that was shrewdly given by the above [Augustine] to a certain insolent but articulate young man: "You should neither become vain by attributing to yourself more than is necessary, nor again become cold by casting yourself out and despairing."[20] Meanwhile, note that you at your leisure are summoned by the Father to cultivate his vineyard [Mt.20.7], not in simple terms like those in the morning at first, but with the addition of the conjunction "also," which you should understand to be a criticism: "Go ye *also* to the vineyard"; that is, those of you also who ought to have been present in the morning, and at the third hour, or at least at the sixth, hurry up and work your hire for that half of the day that remains.

XIII.29. Are you an old man? Rejoice in the Lord, you who have been brought this far, not only because you have already avoided many reefs and sandbanks, many chances of shipwreck, but also because the harbor to which you seem to be heading is close by, if only you are grave, honest, serious, graced with good habits, decorated with virtues, venerable in the eld of your mind, honey-toned in the beauty of your words, and if you can say with the psalmist, "My old age is fruitful in mercy" [Ps. 91.11]. But if otherwise—heaven forbid!—be not angry, I beg, if I, a younger man, dare to advise you, as far as I see affects you; I do so, you see, by virtue of my office. No age should appear too late for learning that which is necessary; and though (as someone before me seemed to say very effectively) it is more fitting for old men to teach than to learn, yet it is far more appropriate for them to learn than not to know what they teach, or rather what they do, so that we cannot overstate it.

Hear then, you too, what Ecclesiastes says: "If a man has lived many years, he ought to remember the dark time and the many days; when they come the past is shown as vanity" [Eccli. 11.8]. And: "The child of a hundred years will be accursed" [Is. 65.20]. And again: "A venerable old age is not long lasting nor computed by the number of years" [Wisd. 4.8]. Hear also the watchman saying to all in general but to you in particular: "Morning comes and also the night; if you enquire, enquire; turn and come back again" [Is. 21.12]. Hear also the Apostle: "Everything that grows old and ages is near death" [Heb. 8.13].

But as I look at those white hairs of snow upon your head, I confess that I am in considerable doubt where to start my address; I would like, if I could, to confer reverence on age and learning on foolishness. But let the propitious one be here, I beg, who once turned the meaningless braying of an ass into human speech [Num. 22.28]. I will reread the passages of Gospel reading read today; and if perchance you find anything of your own, do not, I beg, impute it to me who only recites it, but take what is applicable to you as yours and convert it for use to yourself, even if you think it offered in disparagement.

30. "A certain man had a fig tree planted in his vineyard" [Lk. 13.6], and the rest. If this reading still does not convince you that trees signify men, read a clearer passage in Daniel, which tells of a dream of a great and lofty tree; when its many attributes and honors had been described, and it was finally ordered hewn down, it was interpreted as the king in his loftiness, and its loss indicated him whom eminence highlighted. For he was exalted like a tree almost up to heaven by countless honors and dignities, as though by some blessed combination of the elements; but lopped from his eminence he fell from honor, was abandoned by his supporters, like a tree abandoned by birds in flight; "seven times passed over him" and then he again returned to his former sublime state [Dan. 4.10–30].

There are also many things in the Scriptures which signify one thing literally and another thing allegorically, but they demand careful study by the reader. Let us see, then, what happened to this tree, whether it be you or me or both of us or anyone to whom what is said of it applies. "He came seeking fruit in it and found none" [Lk. 13.6–9]. Who came? He whose vineyard, whose fig tree it was. If you are the fig tree, then he who planted you is the Lord. For He himself says: "The vineyard, my elect, I planted you" [Jer. 2.21]. If you do not believe this, there is a parable in another reading [Mt. 21.33–43] to prove it. The vineyard in which He planted you is the Church. He comes seeking fruit in you and does not find any. How many times? Let Him tell you himself; for I do not want to make anything up or distort the truth for my own purposes, or you will think me a foolish babbler instead of a sure champion of doctrine. He said to the husbandman of the vineyard: "Lo, it is now three years since I came looking for fruit on this fig tree and I do not find any." *Three years*, remember. Let us look at another. I said that you were the tree, the vineyard was the Church, that certain person—the lord of the vineyard—was God; whom am I to call the husbandman of the vineyard? For if He had said "the husbandman of the *fig tree*," you might perhaps have understood it as the heart, or perhaps some angel to whom you have been entrusted, as some people think—and quite rightly. But since He does not say *the husbandman of the tree* but *the husbandman of the vineyard*, He requires someone else, someone who has undertaken to care not only for you but for the other fig trees as well, in fact to guard the complete vineyard.

What then? Are we in difficulties? No; but if a little, fine. For what is found with greater difficulty is held more sweetly, as Ambrose testifies,[21] and the slower the understanding, the more pleasing the achievement. For I could show you right now the husbandman of the vineyard, as far as he who is master of all deigns to "bedew the valley" of my puny powers by means of those "mountains" who have already sufficiently dealt with this question;[22] but I wish to draw you on with the example of more eminent authority, so that you may be rendered more ready to search and, perceiving that I have not found these ideas out of my own head but have gathered them out of the Scriptures, may become more capable as you get more eager.

31. "A certain man," says another reading (but likewise this too from the Gospel), "was rich, who planted a vineyard and put round it a fence and rented it to other farmers" [Mt. 21.33–41]. This parable, because it is complete and has been clarified by the interpretations of many, can help to show more clearly the interpretation of the one now under investigation. For now those wicked husbandmen of the vineyard, who not only refused to surrender the fruit but abused and even killed the servants, and in addition did not keep their hands off the heir himself, were put to a miserable death.

Now the vineyard is rented to the apostles and to their successors, the bishops and priests and other holy orders, each of whom, individually, according to his capacity or ministry, works hard at the vineyard and awaits the coming of the Lord of the vineyard, who comes not to put to death the wicked but to receive fruit that pleases Him and to reward the good husbandmen with generous largesse. Whether the one who has undertaken to cultivate you is a bishop or a priest makes no difference to me. The Lord addresses him about you and complains that you have given forth no fruit. Pointing out your ways to him, He says in his own words (that is, the words of the Scriptures) that you are not converted and have long been fruitless in your actions. "Lo," He says, "it is now three years since I came looking for fruit on this fig tree and I have not found any." This is said when the husbandman of your soul sees in you those things which he knows from the Lord's teaching to be reprehensible; then he hears the Lord complaining about you, that you do not provide Him with the fruit of your labors. By *years* the seasons of age are meant, just as another Gospel passage uses *hours* [Mt. 20.3–12]; if you deny this, there are many testimonies to refute you.

But let us not take too long to arrive at the goal for which we are heading, by laboring to establish proofs for material over which there is no need to split hairs. You should be aware that the Lord has already come to you at three ages.

For he came to you in your infancy and childhood (to take them as one for their proximity), by giving baptism and endowing you with understanding, by providing teachers and demanding the collected fruit. What fruit you offered, you yourself know best. He came a second time in your adolescence and youth, increasing your intelligence, enlarging his gifts and demanding your merits; and I think you remember what you repaid Him at that time. He is present now at this time of your life; look to your actions. For He wants to cut you down.

And do not flatter yourself that if you are cut down, you will grow again as that tree above [Dan. 4.22] did after seven years — that tree was one thing, you are another; that was not a fig tree but a cedar, and not one of "the cedars of Lebanon which the Lord planted" [Ps. 103.16], but one of those of which it is said: "The Lord will break the cedars of Lebanon" [Ps. 28.5]. For although Lebanon is translated *whiteness*,[23] yet there are some like whitened tombs, to whom truth himself says "Woe!" [Mt. 23.27]. This cedar did not stand in the vineyard but in the field. Believe me, if you are cut down uncorrected, you will be sent at once into the fire. For the Father has already threatened: "Every tree which does not bring forth good fruit will be cut down and sent into the fire"[Mt. 3.10]. At the time of that other tree, grace was looked for; now judgment is expected. That one [Nebuchadnezzar], a pagan yet having some good, was rewarded for the present so that he could be corrected for ever; of you, a Christian though a negligent one, it is demanded that you correct your ways here willingly so that you may live for ever.

This explanation has been overlong, since that cutting-down [Dan. 4.22] was nothing else than the loss of kingdom and humanity; but this cutting-down of yours, which is discussed here, is the end of life and the approach of death, which, if it is good, is not death but birth; but if it is bad, it will be endless death, an unfailing failure, a permanent loss, an immutable corruption, a comfortless grief, a ceaseless mourning, an infinite disaster.

32. Remember then — to continue on with the Gospel reading — what this husbandman of yours, be he bishop or any patron praying to God on your behalf, says: "Lord, leave it this year also, until I dig around it and put down manure, to see if it produces fruit; but if it does not, cut it down in the future." How short a time! Yet how sufficient if you are converted! But O how sudden if you turn away, or rather persist in this hardness of heart in which He finds you. Do not say that it is outrageous for me here to take *year* for a single year when I said above that *year* was for *age*. Consider here your age, I beg, think how much you have lived, and see if your age still promises as many periods of time, especially since even in infants the onset of death cannot be ruled out because it often comes before its time. Consider that there is a particular reason why you at your age are called *silicernius* ["funeral feast"]: it is to remind you to pay closer attention to the due end the closer it is. Keep before your eyes the tomb which will receive you as you depart this life, let your sepulcher not escape your view, let the memory of your sins not slip from your thoughts nor the monstrousness of the punishments, the fearful pains, the stern gaze of the judge and that final sentence of eternal damnation. For this is the *manure* by which you can be brought back to a state of production; this is the *digging* of humility which will make you bear the *fruit* of pious action; in other words, let the conscience of your wickedness touch the memory of your thoughts, and, bewailing what you remember that you have done, let the *root* of your heart return to the production of *fruit* through the *digging-round* of confession and the contemplation of your *stinking* deeds.

33. And do not despair at the thought that the time past is too long and that what is left is too short for penitence; consider David, I beg you; look at Zacchaeus [Lk. 19.8], and if you have anything with which to redeem yourself, do as he did. But if you are so poor that you have nothing with which to redeem yourself, and the arrival of death is so imminent, imitate that blessed robber [Lk. 23.40], long a robber, then suddenly confessor and martyr; long a murderer, then a dweller in paradise. Imitate the Ninevehites deleting their long guilts with a penitence of three days [Jon. 3.4–10]. For the goodness of the heavenly doctor is ineffable, unfathomable, incomprehensible, saving some after long satisfaction, others after a moderate one, and yet others after a very brief one, but all with the kindness of his grace alone, none by his own action, as you have heard in the psalm: "For thy mercy is better than life" [Ps. 62.4]. For He supplies the time; He wishes you to chastise your long ways of error with a long period of penance, just as He says to Ananias: "For I will show him how much he must suffer for my name" [Acts 9.16], which is just as if He were to say: I want him who has fought against me for a long time to strive for an even longer time *for* me. David had already absolved his sin and yet God still made him suffer for his sin by killing his son against David's desire, by allowing another to rebel against him, and by sending a plague on the people [2 Sam. 18.5–15, 20.2, 24.15].

But if the time of life be moderate, God does not refuse a moderate penance, provided that the desire be not moderate but great. Hence the holy Fathers very properly established that in the case of penitents the measure of time should not be considered so much as that of pain.[24] But if your very last hour suddenly arrives, while yet you breathe and tremble, let forth your voice in confession to the best of your ability; be penitent that you have reached that point unprepared. But do not despair, do not doubt, cry confidently, pray with your whole heart. He looks into your heart, He considers with what desire you cry. Believe me, I truly promise you that, if He sees that you are penitent with a simple and guileless heart, and that you confess on the very edge of death, He will confer the medicine of salvation. Therefore, let the great clemency of the creator stir you with fear and anxiety; let the sentence of the Apostle James frighten the hardness of your obstinate heart, a sentence that, though fitting all in general, applies to you in particular: "Lo, the Judge stands before the door" [Jas. 5.9]. For the door is each man's unforeseen exit, where irrevocable fate lies in ambush like a thief, watching for the hour in which to seize your soul unexpectedly and take it to the place where it will receive what its merits warrant. You ought to have been watching for this thief since the day of your birth, lest he assail you too early, as often happens. How much more you ought to now, when he is duly at hand by a kind of judicial authority!

34. Therefore, do not act sluggishly, do not slumber, or he will catch you sleeping, that is, relaxing from good deeds. Listen to the salvation-giving words of the Apostle rousing you from this lethargy and sloth: "Now is the hour for us to rise from sleep" [Rom. 13.11]. Henceforth take no holidays, be content with those you have had; with the Jews, you have already sabbathed enough. Put an end now to your relaxation; buckle down to pious work. See that "your flight does not take place in winter or on the sabbath" [Mt. 24.20], that is, that it does not find you cold in charity or relaxing from good work. Know that for you the final hour is already at hand, that already the messenger sent to summon you is here; seize whatever you can to take with you, but know that you will take with you what you have tried here to send ahead. "The axe is already at the root of the tree" [Lk. 3.9], a tree that is dried up from age, withered and fruitless from lethargy; nothing is left for it but to be cut down. You will be cut down, I tell you, you will be cut down; but see that you are not sent into the fire. It is impossible for you not to be cut down, because the Lord of the vineyard complains that you use up space to no purpose. Many trees are being cut down, but they are not being put straight into the fire; but the fruitless ones *are* being put into the fire. Of the others, some become various products, useful tools and vessels, some, the best — but in very few instances — more precious than gold. I tell you this because I know most truly that in this hour, at this time, at this very age which you have reached, you must be cut down; and I do not want you to become fuel for the fire, but a most precious cup in the hand of the heavenly king. May Solomon, the true peacemaker, who has made peace between us and God, and who has allied the earth to those in heaven, deign to drink out of it and offer his fellows the cup of gladness, that is, joy at your conversion and salvation; for his "overflowing cup is very bright" [Ps. 22.5]. Let these words — though few in terms of your benefit, yet ample in terms of my leisure — suffice.

35. Here now (since you have presented me with the opportunity) I think

it worthwhile and very beneficial to add certain passages appropriate both for
you and for me from the same Gospel; may God allow that they be profitable
to us both. But because they have been clearly interpreted with incomparable
eloquence by one whose authority far exceeds mine, I am afraid to sully them
with any additional comments of my own; but I will set them down quoted
just as he wrote them at the end of his homily. After dealing most enlighteningly with certain other points—and some of these have been touched on here (not
indeed as well as befits the subject, but as well as my unimaginative talent could)
to be of benefit to you, old man, in particular, but to myself and many in general, differing in phrasing rather than tenor—Gregory says:[25]

> There are many who hear the rebukes yet still scorn to return to peni-
> tence, and fruitless before God still stand green in this world. Then let
> us hear what the husbandman of the vineyard says: "to see if it produces
> fruit; but if not, cut it down in the future," because, clearly, he who is
> here unwilling to fatten up to fruitfulness by means of rebuke falls to a
> place from which he will no longer be able to rise by means of penitence
> and will be cut down in the future, though here he may seem to stand
> green without fruit. "Now he was teaching in one of the synagogues on
> the sabbath; and a certain woman had a spirit of infirmity for eighteen
> years" [Lk. 13.10]. We have already said a little above that the third visit
> of the Lord to the fruitless tree was what the number of eighteen years
> signifies in relation to the bowed woman. For on the sixth day man was
> made and on the same sixth day all the works of the Lord were completed
> [Gen.1.27]; but when the number six is triangled it makes eighteen. There-
> fore, because man who was made on the sixth day was unwilling to
> make his works complete but was weak before the law, under the law
> and in the beginning of early grace, the woman was bowed for eighteen
> years.

A little later [*Hom. in evang.* 2.31.7–8]:

> We often see what must be done but we do not fulfill it in action; we
> strive and are weakened; the mind sees the course of rectitude but the force
> of action succumbs, assuredly because from the punishment of sin it hap-
> pens that by his gift the good can be seen but through his own deserts
> the sinner is repelled from what is seen. For the habit of sin so blinds the
> mind that it cannot rise to rectitude. It tries and falls back, because, where
> it stands firm for a long time on its own volition, there under pressure
> it falls when the volition is absent.

Again:

If the soul itself does not descend to seek the depths, the wickedness of devils cannot be strong against it and they cannot pass through that which they fear is adamant against them. And as it is we, brothers, we, who give a path to wicked spirits, when we desire worldly things, when we are bowed in our search for temporal things, therefore, be ashamed to yearn for worldly things and to offer the backs of our minds for adversaries to step on. He who is bowed is ever looking at the earth; and he who seeks the depths does not remember at what price he has been redeemed.

Again:

He who carries a hump [Lev. 21.20] is ever looking at the lowest things. Therefore, he is rejected from the priesthood, because whoever is intent upon earthly things alone himself is witness that he is not a member of God, the highest priest.

Again:

If we cannot achieve the highest of the virtues, God himself rejoices that we lament it. From that beginning of justice towards Him, we will be pleasing to Him, since we are punishing the wrongs we have done.

Let it suffice that I have gone this far only off the path of my topic, in delight at so pleasant a meadow of flowers and greenery.[26]

36. Returning now to you (old man), in case I seem to have interrupted my work at all, I urge and advise you, since I know that you are due respect for your age, to compare this with what I said above, and put out every effort on your behalf to acquire salvation; and so that you will not rightly be called "ancient of evil days" [Dan. 13.52], I ask you now to try to "live out half your days" [Ps. 54.24] while you can, and strive to be renewed in mental spirit. And since up till now you have given yourself up to the carnal senses more than you ought, gather yourself together and, becoming a new man by throwing off the old [Eph. 2.24], be young again in God; look at the eighty years now close or past or imminent, do not despise the oncoming gentleness of God; otherwise, being too hard in receiving correction, you will notice the "white flower" [Eccle. 12.5] of your head. But if "the locust" — that is, the erstwhile sprightliness of your steps — has already "grown fat" with the swelling of your feet or of your calves, or (according to the poet)

the knotty gout now makes the joints like the boughs of an old beechtree,[27] await, trembling and fearful, that hour in which you must go to your "eternal home" of good or evil; because afterwards, whatever "mourning occurs in the streets" for you, it will not help you in your torments a bit, you who, while you were here above, scorned to look to your interests and to take counsel for yourself against the straits of coming calamity, though you well knew that calamity was inevitable.

So now, therefore, while there is yet time for fruitful weeping, while the hour is acceptable, while there is time for salvation [2 Cor. 6.2], while you yet live, while you yet are sustained by the judge, I urge you to make every effort toward amelioration. While He puts off the blow of the axe, take counsel about yourself; while He suspends the punishment, correct your life. With God, conversion is neither difficult nor too late; He is pleased by the very beginning of a righteous life. But woe to him who is not allowed to make his conversion before he dies; for, as the one above says, a greater wrath of punishment usually follows great obdurateness and contempt of His gentleness and grace, and the longer he waits, the harder is the unconverted struck;[28] and the more generously His mercy is bestowed in the present, the more severely His justice is imposed on ingrates in the future.

Book III

[Rather examines the position of the king, or chief civil authority, in a Christian community. He focuses particularly on the relationship between the king and the Church. The king must be subject to God, that is, to the Church and its bishops. The king has no authority to judge and punish a bishop. He alludes to his own imprisonment without trial by King Hugo and blames his fellow bishops for not rallying round one of their own in a conflict that pits the civil authority against that of the Church.]

Contents of this *Praeloquium*:

I Are you a king? Let the prerogatives of kingship be your instruction.
II Discern the motives with which anyone does anything.
III Do not sully virtues under the pretext of motives which are at odds with virtues.
IV In fear of God govern what is entrusted to you.

V That the Church is Catholic and its Grace Catholic.

VI That the king should not disdain to be subjected to God's judges.

VII That we have become subjects of abuse and mockery.

VIII That just as bishops are partners of the saints in the ministry of the order, just so also are they in the privilege of honor.

IX That the Holy Spirit is often to be found even in a negligent bishop.

X That a bishop can be judged by no one but by God alone.

XI Prayer of God's devout who are persecuted.

XII The threefold division of the sons of the Church.

1. In the previous two books, by God's gift, I dealt with the prefaces [*praeloquia*] of secular duties, persons, crafts, sexes, and ages, with all the brevity I could, though not with the grace befitting such a topic. Now I struggle to find my way through the vast seas, fraught with ruin because they are filled with many jagged reefs,[1] of dignities, high ranks, or ambitions; facing adverse squalls, I oppose them with Christ himself as bulwark, trying to plough ahead with the three-headed boat of my volumes—but only if His rowing does not fail. His help in this I beg as essential, for he knows that I assume this task with as much hesitation as there is danger in it. For on the one side I fear the storm of the supernal spectator, on the other, this seething sea of politics, and I fear the total loss of my ship, whose skipper, with his oars broken and his tiller lost, tired and pounded by all sorts of rocks, his strength paralysed, not so much carried by his skiff as tossed on the waves, biting his very tongue with trembling teeth, lies on one of the reefs;[2] I fear its loss, I say, since I know that this pitiable misfortune has happened to him because of his headlong course when he could not avoid the double onslaught.[3]

For although we know from the words of Scripture, "The tongues of the wise are like goads and like nails deeply fixed" [Eccle. 12.11], that the constancy of God's authority is so very constant that he spares no one but touches everyone, yet I know that men of sophistication today take great pains to find ways to say what is expedient rather than what is true. They find more advantageous what the comic poet encourages than what the Lord threatens. They value more highly the saying "Flattery begets friends, the truth hatred"[4] than "Whoever is ashamed of me and my words, of him will the Son of Man be ashamed when he comes" [Lk. 9.26]; perhaps the former, as it is more rhetorical (as it were) is thought finer; because it is stylish, it is judged wholesome; whereas the latter, stripped as it is of charming style—or rather, stripped of the dark obscurities of vanity—is for that reason thought by the worldly-wise to be rather simple or rustic and worthy of little regard; they think that the esteem of "Those who say to the seers, See not, and to the prophets, Prophesy not to us what is right, speak to us smooth things, prophesy illusions" [Is. 30.10]⁵ brings profit of no less security.

But let me strive that my words be controlled by the same master, Truth, which is also the Way [Jn. 14.6], who says about himself through the mouth of a prophet: "This is the way, walk by it and do not incline either to the left or to the right" [Is. 30.21], so that I may incline neither to the right by presumptuously attempting things too deep for me [Eccli. 3.22], nor to the left by timidly yielding to falsehood; so that (if I may speak so, though absurdly) neither Terence may rebuke me for having thoughtlessly provoked anyone's hatred against me nor Christ for having preferred anyone's friendship to the truth. To prevent this happening, let me go with cautious steps between these two and so touch the chord of dignity that I keep silent about the person of the citharist.⁶ Let me address the rank in such a way that I leave out the name of the person in that rank; let me address the ambition, in such a way that I do not suffer a lack of charity, of which I should desire an abundance; especially since I believe that there will be no lack of envy from those who hate me, who will not hesitate to criticize me in this part also, since, besides, they know that no wisdom, no authority (save for the reverence of my office) flourishes in me—a fact which here too they can surmise.

I.2. Are you a king? Let the dignity of your position instruct you while you take delight in it. There are certain features of the rank without which the dignity of the position cannot hold up in reality even though the title is there in some form. Practice these therefore, be trained in them, be glorified by them. Be prudent, just, brave, and temperate. Use these virtues as a four-horse chariot, as it were, in which to course the limits of your realm. Let it be your car on this road so that you may merit to be called with holy Elija, the charioteer of Israel [2 Kg. 2.12]. Protected by this four-fold breastplate, do not hesitate to meet the enemy unflinching; for you cannot be conquered by any adversaries if only you merit to be defended by such protection.

II.3. In the first place—before, that is, I address the other qualities befitting your serenity—I wish to instruct you, along with all who are established in high positions, in these individual points, adding that one should earnestly strive to find out the intentions behind people's actions.⁷ For I know, both from personal experience and from reading the works of the ancients, that vices usually masquerade as virtues. Hence Seneca finely says in his prefaces: "The timid man calls himself cautious, the miser calls himself thrifty."⁸ And as one of our number says: "Cunning often wants to appear prudence," that is, that when we trick someone successfully, we congratulate ourselves on having acted prudently. To the contrary the psalmist says (as Peter in his Epistle also says of Christ [1 Pet. 2.22]): "He speaks truth in his heart who has no treachery in his tongue" [Ps.

14.3]. And one of our number says: "The more cunning a scheme is in men's eyes, the greater folly it is in God's eyes."[9] And the psalmist: "His enemies will lick the dust" [Ps. 71.9]. To lick the dust is to take something earthly from someone by means of honeyed words. Though this vice is thought of as sophistication by certain worldly people, it should all the more carefully be avoided by righteous minds, since by this testimony we learn that that person especially is called an enemy of God who, by the flattery of his recommendations, deceives his neighbor with lies, either robbing him of his possessions by duplicity of this kind or, what is worse, abusing him in the manner of the treacherous traitor, as in the words: "In his mouth he speaks peace with his friend and in secret he lays plots against him" [Jer. 9.8]; and: "Saying, Peace, peace, when there is no peace" [Jer. 6.14]: and: "Under his tongue are mischief and iniquity; he sits in ambush with the rich, in hiding-places to murder the innocent" [Ps. 10.7–9]. And a little further on the psalmist says: "He lurks that he may seize the poor, he seizes the poor when he draws him in." Again elsewhere: "His words are smoother than oil and they are his shafts" [Ps. 54.22, 24]. Then in his usual manner, changing from the individual to the type and stating their due reward he says: "But thou, O God, wilt cast them down into the pit of death." Job says, as frighteningly as it is succinct: "Cheaters and feigners provoke the wrath of God" [Job 36.13]; here we should note that He does not say *deserve* but *provoke*, so that you may feel that there is something more fearful involved. We should fear that He will be provoked to such an extent that no one can stand before Him and it will be said: "As I live, the Lord says, this iniquity will not be expiated by sacrifice or by offering for ever" [Is. 49.19; 1 Sam. 3.14].

4. How foul this vice is for any Christian to pursue is shown even by the example of the pagans, who laid it down that any victory won by treachery was shameful; they did this not from any love of God but from their native love of honor.

Again, the vice of impatience often tries to pass for fortitude. For everyone wants to appear brave, when he is insulted and strikes out with his fist. But it is foolish, as one of the most learned says, for a man who has been overcome to say that he is brave. Also, we should observe that madmen are often braver than those in their right minds. The more things virtue despises, according to Augustine, the more it should be esteemed.[10] Wicked cruelty and the desires of burning greed often try to invade the righteous throne, as when a man satisfies his anger and thinks that he serves justice, or, even if what he does is just, he does it for the sake of gain, against the command of him who instructs us: "Do justly what is just" [Dt. 16.20]. Sloth sometimes wants to appear as temperance, as when we avoid doing something impetuously but cannot temper our actions with discernment; and also when without forethought we put off through sloth doing those things which have to be done; thus while we fear a vice, we incur a vice. Often when a man tries to control his anger, he incurs negligence; though not to restrain one's vices is usually a greater sin than to take revenge, and to neglect the delinquent is not less than to hate him. Sometimes, when avoiding the Scylla of trickery we run into the Syrtes of stupidity; often when earnestly avoiding what must be done, in our lethargy we serve the vice of sloth.

5. But what good does it do if you happen to recognize their imitators but do not know by sure signs what the virtues themselves are? Then let us define what they are and it will appear clearer than light what they are not. *Justice*, as already defined by our ancestors, is a state of mind attuned to the common advantage, attributing to each his dignity; hence justice is properly named as though "*iuris status*."[11] *Ius* is the law proper and the just man is he who keeps *ius*, that is, the law proper, or he who pays each man his due,[12] as in the Lord's words: "Render to Caesar what is Caesar's and to God what is God's" [Mt. 22.21]. *Wisdom* is the true knowledge of good and bad things. *Temperance* is firm, tempered self-control over lusts and other improper onslaughts on the mind. This is also called moderation, because it does everything with "mode" or measure. *Fortitude* is the deliberate facing of dangers and resolute endurance of toil. We properly know these four virtues as "royal," so that even some peasant who has them can fittingly be called king, whereas without them even he who holds almost total sovereignty of the world (though abusing it) cannot rightly be called king; for by bad government, as the thinker above says, the greatest empire is lost.[13] How much it benefits not only kings but all men to be clothed in these virtues, he testifies who says in the praises of Wisdom: "For he teaches temperance and wisdom and justice and virtue, than which nothing on earth is more useful to men" [Wisd. 8.7]. Let the careful reader note that these four are the four virtues I have been discussing. Happy is he to whom it is said: "You wear all these like a garment."

III.6. After considering this introduction, I beg your majesty not to disdain to receive what must now be said in such a way that points which have perhaps long been unknown or overlooked may be made clear and corrected. First, I ask you not to want to dilute these virtues somehow and use them as a cloak for other qualities which perhaps are not in harmony with them. Be prudent, I say, not cunning (though prudence is often understood under the name of cunning, as: "It is a cunning man's part to discern his way" [Pr. 14.8]); be brave, not proud; be temperate, not slothful or remiss; be just, not cruel. Honor God; govern yourself first, or rather, commend yourself to the Ruler. Note what trees are thrashed by the greater blasts of wind; consider what buildings fall with the most ruin, and, so that you do not incur the words of Wisdom, namely, that "The hardest judgment will fall on those who command," and "The powerful will suffer torments powerfully," and "The greater punishment awaits the mighty" [Wisd. 6.6–9], hold earnestly in your heart that "Blessed are the merciful, for they shall receive mercy" [Mt. 5.7]; so that you can at the same time avoid the "judgment without mercy" which awaits those "who have no mercy" and understand that "no one is pitiable except him who has refused to pity" [Jas. 2.13].

And do not think yourself brave when you are insulted and strike with the sword, nor be glad when you lord it over a wide domain; listen to what was said long before us: "He is first subject who wishes to have others subject to him."[14] To what he is subject, I leave to you to discover; for the Lord can very pertinently teach you on this point when He says, "No man can serve two masters," and, "You cannot serve both God and Mammon" [Mt. 6.24]. And the Apostle who says: "Let not sin reign in your mortal body" [Rom. 6.12], and, "He who sins is a slave of sin" [Jn. 8.34]; and, "By whom a man is overcome, to him is he also enslaved" [2 Pet. 2.19]. And in Daniel it says: "The chief of the kingdom of the Persians resisted me" [Dan. 10.13]. *Demons* of fornication and pride, or spirits of other vices, are called that for no other reason than that they have as their subjects those whom they *dominate*, those, that is, who are enslaved to those vices.

7. Now that you have clearly understood this, consider what the Lord says through the prophet: "Woe to those of you who join house to house, who add field to field until there is no more room. Do you not live alone in the land? All these things are in my ears, says the Lord of Hosts." And after a few verses: "Therefore hell has enlarged its mouth and opened it beyond measure and the nobility and people of Jerusalem shall go down into it, those in high places and the glorious." And again: "Woe to those of you who acquit the guilty for a bribe and deprive the innocent of his justice. Therefore, as fire devours stubble and wood and the heat of flame burns it up, so their root will be like ashes and their seed will rise as dust" [Is. 5.8, 9, 14, 23–24].

Consider, I beg, how serious is the sin of greed, which can consume you and your people and your whole seed. But if everything goes to your liking, if the necks of all your enemies suddenly bow to you, do not, because of it, become excited in expressing useless joy. Remember what was promised by the psalmist to the man despised by God's justice: "Thy judgments are taken from his sight; he will dominate all his foes" [Ps. 10.5]. Remember also that to *hopeless* cases doctors deny nothing that they want to eat.

IV.8. You, on the other hand, should fear God, govern — or rather nourish — the people committed to you, respect the pious, honor bishops; know that they have been set over you, not you over them, and — to amplify it — that they have been given to you as gods by the one supreme and only God and as angels by the Angel of great Counsel [Is. 9.6] himself. If you think I lie, ask your predecessor

Constantine, ask the psalmist, ask the Lord. "You," says the former, "have been given to us as gods by God and it is not fitting that man should judge gods."[15] "God stands in the middle of gods," says the psalmist, and a little further on: "I have said, You are gods"; and: "The God of gods, the Lord, speaks" [Ps. 81.1,6; 49.1]. And the Lord himself says to Moses: "See, I have made you as god to Pharaoh" [Ex. 7.1]; and: "Do not revile the gods" [Ex. 22.28]; and again: "Bring him near to the gods" [Ex. 22.8]; and again in the psalm: "He who makes his angels spirits and his ministers flame of fire" [Ps. 103.4], that is, he makes his preachers both spiritual and fervent in love. And through the Prophet: "The lips of the priest will keep justice, and they will seek the law from his mouth because he is an angel of the Lord of Hosts" [Mal. 2.7].

In the Revelation of St. John, when you hear "the angels of the seven churches," understand that they are none other than the bishops of the churches. Notice what He says also in the Gospel, what power He gives them: "Whatever you bind or earth shall be bound also in heaven and whatever you absolve on earth shall be absolved also in heaven" [Mt. 16.9]. The prophet also had said the same thing, though obliquely, in the psalm: "Thy friends, O God, are greatly honored, their leadership is greatly strengthened" [Ps. 138.17]. Whose? The apostles', the evangelists', bishops', clergy's, monks' — who, renouncing the world and refusing to have anything in this world, rightly are leaders with God and judge the world, preferring to rule those who have gold than to have gold themselves.[16] "The princes of the people are gathered with the God of Abraham, since the mighty gods of the earth are highly exalted" [Ps. 49.10].

There you have clear evidence that the princes of the people themselves are the gods of the earth. But what is this principate? What is the purpose of this principate? "To bind their kings in shackles and their nobles in iron chains, to execute on them the judgment written" [Ps. 149.8–9]. See what principate they have received, for what purpose they have received it, how the principate itself is bolstered. When? Here and in the future. Where? Through all the world. Wherever Christ is worshipped, his priest is honored second to him, in fact in the priest Christ himself is honored.

V.9. Let no one therefore single out Jerusalem or Rome or Alexandria or any other church for the prerogative of this principate, excluding the rest; the Church is catholic, its grace is catholic. There are no more; the rock on which it stands is one; the Church also is single. For of it the Scripture says: "She is the only child of her mother" [S. of S. 6.8], that is, of regenerative grace. The whole Church has only one law. Though nations may differ in their customs as regards rites and practice, all are hallowed by a single spirit, just as all people are washed by a single baptism. And though there are different levels of grace [1 Cor. 12.4], in that some people are higher than others in the Church (as also there are ranks in heaven), yet the givers of grace are not divided; for there is one giver, one creator, and it is He who alone is God in essence, nay, something that cannot be understood and which we define better by worshipping and believing than by rationalizing, philosophizing, or discussing, namely, that He is of substance, lives, is powerful, knows and understands; ever remaining the same He splits up into single parts as He wishes, however He wishes, through whom He wishes, and therefore it is said: "There is no power but from God; what powers there are are ordained by God" [Rom. 13.1], that is: it has been established by his ordinance, what is to be given to any power as its privilege, what power is to be placed above or below another power; that is, the highest power should be that which apportions, controls, and governs everything (inasmuch as everything has been created by it) and contains the universe; this power is followed by that which He appointed over the others (so far as — to pass over those above the heavens — applies to those in heaven, which are called by us "ecclesiastical") when He said: "Whatsoever you bind on earth will be bound also in heaven" [Mt. 16.19].

For He did not say "something you bind will be bound," so that you could have the option of understanding that something else could remain untouched by this law, but "Whatsoever" — that is, *everything* — "you bind on earth will be bound also in heaven." I have not been able to find, either by meditation or by reasoning or by reading, any power which can supercede this one, since there seems to be nothing excluded in its definition, and only through it can anything which is to control subordinates seem to be duly and Christianly appointed.

10. If perchance we find someone who disagrees with this, let him prove it from the holy Scriptures, and I believe it, provided that I do not hear that the Holy Spirit proceeding from the Father and the Son and inspiring where he wishes, can be given by a man; even if an angel says it, I do not agree, but on the contrary with the Apostle call whoever says it anathema [Gal. 1.8].

Another argument which is put forward as though it were invincible is the Apostle's saying, "Beloved, be subject to every human institution, whether it be to the king as supreme" [1 Pet. 2.13]; this would have some weight to support it if it said "supreme over a god" or "supreme over bishops." But as it is silent on this, we should understand that he is supreme only over worldly men and that in order for justice to be kept he should be paid the honor due him, that is, one greater than all worldly creatures but not greater than heavenly beings (but even this not on his own account but on account of God), keeping the reverence due to the sublime powers to whom both that human power and every soul is instructed to be subject [Rom. 13.1]; and these are none other than those who have received, through the Holy Spirit in the apostles and their successors, the power of binding, judging, and absolving all men from the Supreme Power himself.

VI.11. Do not disdain, then, O king, to be subject to such as these, because, whether you will or no, you will have them as gods and angels and chiefs and judges. They can bind you, they can absolve you. For you are set over some men; they are set over you and all men. So venerate them with whatever respect you can, so that they too may venerate you with worthy return. See that you do not happen to do them any injury; in fact, do your best to avenge any injury done them, as far as you have the power and reason dictates. Do not grieve the Holy Spirit [Eph. 4.30] which is in them in any business; beware lest it not work out for you. Remember, if you have read it — if not, read it — what threats the Lord made for them in the book of Genesis, in the persons of Abraham and Sarah [Gen. 20.3], and again of Isaac and Rebecca [Gen 26.11], and again of Jacob in flight from Laban [Gen. 31.29], and take it as a warning for your action. Look at the the Ark of the Covenant also, which signifies them mystically, taken by the Philistines and put in the temple of Dagon [1 Sam. 5.2], and think ahead for yourself, remembering what happened to them. Consider what Uzzah, which is translated "Strong of the Lord," merited because he wanted to set the Ark on a cart drawn by stumbling oxen [2 Sam. 6]; and if perchance you see in them any indications of a negligent life, beware of trying to correct and punish them on your own account; otherwise, while you strive to appear the "strong of the Lord," you may become the victim of the striking angel. Consider also the prophet sent to Bethel and devoured by the lion for his disobedience [1 Kg. 13.24]; and besides the king's hand which was dried up [1 Kg. 13.4], consider in that beast which lacked reason in what veneration you as a creature endowed with reason ought to hold the living, since the lion did not dare to seize even the dead prophet's ass for his fault.

Consider the two groups of fifty who slandered Elija [2 Kg. 1.20, 12], and be afraid of the fire of heavenly wrath. Again, think of the forty boys who mocked Elisha in Bethel [2 Kg. 2.24], and restrain your tongue, hand, and might from the abuse and hurt of prophets, which indeed is what the clergy are. But if — to let these examples I have offered suffice — you have perchance desired, if you have presumed, if you have taken it upon yourself, either perhaps led by them or puffed up in your own might, to believe that you have been set over them — though you have not been, since man ought not and cannot be set over God, nor terrestrial being over heavenly one, nor worm be prince over angel, nor king rule over a King who is more substantial — then you can be satisfied that you have been brought by your own wicked sin to the condition of those boys. Take care not to be driven into a worse state by the wicked charioteer and do not try to put any of them — even if they be universally disgraced, provided they be firm in the Catholic faith—to any punishment in the manner of slaves, since they should rather perform the function of masters. You should know that this was the practice not indeed of Catholics but of tyrants whose portion is far from yours.

But if priests' delinquency in some fault or sin require that they be brought forward for a whipping, so that they be the "malleable trumpet" [Num. 10.2] in the Church of the Lord, do not be the hammer yourself, because the hammer is blunted when the trumpet is forged. For though the propitious Lord punishes all their desires and visits their transgressions with the rod and their iniquity with scourges [Ps. 88.33], do not you be that rod. Hear what has been said: "Who spares the rod hates the child" [Pr. 13.24]. Be afraid, then, that while any one of them chastised by you is spared because he is loved, you as the broken rod will not be spared because you are despised; and while he, because he is loved, benefits through correction to eternal life, you, because you are despised, fail through your wickedness to the point of damnation. Palaces are swept by brooms, but when the brooms are worn out they provide fuel for the fire. Gold is purged by fire, not consumed, but wood on which flames feed is reduced to ashes.[17]

12. "But," you say, "the sons who please the best are whipped [Heb. 12.6]; what is surprising if negligent servants are whipped?" I say: But though they are negligent, they still do not belong to the category of slaves that should be whipped by anyone. I am boldly, and even insolently, telling you what they are so that you will not offend through ignorance; yet I tell you the more freely as the words are not my own but from divine Scripture. It would be miraculous if such great and ineffable attributes—incomprehensible even to those who enjoy them—could be conferred by a man. How would God differ from man or what need would there be for God to be prayed to, if dust[18] could bestow such great virtues? To think this is nothing less that to want to ascend to heaven. To say this is nothing else than to raise your throne above the stars of heaven— that is, the bishops, if only they are what they are said to be. To try this is nothing else than to try to climb above the height of the clouds—which God is witness that the bishops are, since He says through the prophet: "I will order my clouds not to pour rain upon them" [Is. 14.13–14]—and to think that you are like a god. Bishops are gods, lords, christs, heavens, angels, patriarchs, prophets, apostles, evangelists, martyrs, anointed, kings, princes, judges (not only of men but of angels), rams of the Lord's flock, shepherds of his sheep (not any sheep but those washed with Christ's blood), teachers, heralds of the coming judge, spies, the pupil of the Lord's eye [Zech. 2.8], friends of the living God, sons of God, lights of the world [Phil. 2.15], stars of heaven, pillars of the Church, doctors of souls, doorkeepers of paradise; they carry the keys of heaven [Acts 1.9], they can bolt and bar heaven, they are the clouds which the Lord put as

his ascent, the foundations on which the whole building of God's temple stands. Whoever moves any one of these foundation-stones with a single push (omitting the rest for brevity's sake and reasoning about this alone) what, I ask, does he do in regard to the building placed upon it?

13. The Lord shouts for them, He threatens for them, He fights for them, even though you are unaware of it. He shouts, I say, He shouts and does not hide it, He is not silent, so that you cannot by any chance say, "I did not know." He shouts and says: "Do not touch my anointed" [Ps. 104.15]. He tells you this that you may know, may beware, may come to your senses; in fact, He tells you this so that you will not try nor presume nor dare to do so: do not touch them nor even revile them. He shouts and cries and thunders this, saying: "You shall not revile your gods" [Ex. 22.28]. Do not, therefore, make excuses that you did not know. Strengthening them and goading them and encouraging them not to be afraid, He says: "Do not fear but believe, because I have conquered the world" [Jn. 16.33].

"*I*" He says, "*I* your God, your father, your brother, your head, *I* by nature what you are by duty, *I* the sharer in you, *I* the Christ, the anointed, *I* the shepherd, the priest, bishop, highest pontiff, *I* the King of Kings, *I* have overcome the world. Whom do you fear? He has been overcome. Whom are you afraid of? He lies under your feet. To prove it, whoever you are that is afraid, even perhaps one groaning in chains in prison, raise your hand, raise the standard, hoist the trophy, show the flag, unfurl the ensign. You will see what that pride, that haughtiness, that arrogance, that stiffness, that straight neck of the daughters of Babylon [Is. 47.1], that tower of Senaar [Jos. 6], those walls of Jericho, those mighty walls of Cariath-Sepher [Jos. 15.16], will do, will try, how they will yield, will beg, will totter, collapse in ruin, and prone and humble will worship the despised, injured, vilified, imprisoned, bound, naked, servile, thirsty, and totally wretched individual man of God. For you are my witnesses [Lk. 24.48], and he who spurns you spurns me [Lk. 10.16] and he who grieves you has grieved me and he who does wrong receives the wrong that he has done [Col. 3.25] and he who touches you is as one who touches the pupil of my eye" [Zech. 2.8].

VII.14. But we bishops *have* been touched, crushed, scorned, driven, routed; the structure which seemed to stand on our foundation has fallen. "Other lords have possessed us without you" [Is. 26.13]; "we have become a taunt to our neighbors, mocked and derided by those round about us" [Ps. 78.4], an example, a spectacle, a fable, "their song the whole day through" [Lam. 3.14].

"Understand, O dullest of the people," He says, "fools, when will you be wise? He who planted the ear, does he not hear? He who formed the eye, does he not see [Ps. 93.8]? But why do you wonder if the world hates you, which hated me before you? For if you had been of the world, it would love what was its own [Jn. 15.18–19]. Why do you look for the friendship of the enemy, when I would not cast you from the friendship of my company, nor would the world itself judge you worthy of its friendship? See that you do not seem to refuse to be in the body of Christ, if you are not willing to face the hate of the world along with Christ the head.[19] For what do they do to you which they have not already done to me and my ancestors? If they persecuted me, they will persecute you also [Jn. 15.20]. Just as I am with you till the end of time [Mt. 28.20], so there will be people who will hate me in you, who will persecute you and scorn your words, not because it is yours but because it is mine; for if it were yours, that is, of the world, carnal, and supporting vices, it would be loved. Why do you want to collect the tares before the harvest, not caring if you tear up the good ears with them at the same time, when you see that often in such action the good have perished with the wicked? Rather mine, says the Lord, is the vengeance, I will repay" [Heb. 10.30].

VIII.15. But if you charge that I ought not to apply what was written about the saints to us who are far below their feet, I answer that in this world, just as we are partners to them in the ministry of the order, so also are we their partners both in the dignity of the name and in the privilege of honor. If we study to conform our life to theirs, we will be sharers also in their eternal glory. But if not—which heaven forbid—we who seem here to perform the office of honor and ministry in common with them will there be separated from them. For if it were not so, what would that Christianity which we have undertaken to uphold be worth? And if our episcopate were not sanctified by the same spirit as theirs, what benefit would there be in the people being baptized by chrism sanctified by our ministry? And what would be the benefit of the celebration of the Mass, the benediction and the consecration of diverse objects or even the show of any worship of the divine? Therefore, either pronounce that Christianity has failed, and deny the truth of what Truth himself who knows no lie says, "Lo, I am with you always to the close of the age" [Mt. 28.10], and declare that He did not receive what He prayed for to the Father when He said: "I do not pray for these alone, but also for those who will believe in me through the words of these" [Jn. 17.20]. It then follows that what the angel who foretold his birth said, "He will reign in the house of Jacob for ever" [Lk. 1.33], will also be absurd. Or—if you cannot accept this—whether you will or no, you will allow our priesthood to have the same honor and dignity as theirs, because it is one and the same thing, whether before the law, under the law or under grace, first presaged in figures and mysteries, afterwards shown by Truth himself, and the kinds of words also are the same and signify the same.

For as long as the people are the flock, so long is the bishop shepherd; as long as the word of God will be heralded, so long will the herald be called angel and will *be* one; so long as the chrism will be prepared, so long will the preparer be called the Christ; so long as prophecy will be read, so long will the reader be called prophet—unless perhaps you choose to consider false the words of the proverb, "When prophecy shall fail, the people will be scattered" [Pr. 29.18], and you want to take in the past sense and not in the present or future the words, "Whoever receives the prophet in the name of the prophet will receive the reward of the prophet" [Mt. 10.41]. Also, as long as these insignia will last, so long will their scorners, deriders, and persecutors have the same charges as for the ancients; nor will their punishment be dissimilar, except that their insolence is struck harder than their ignorance, their contempt harder than their excess, since the Lord says: "If I had not come and spoken to them, they would not have sin" [Jn. 15.22]; and: "The last state of that man becomes worse than the first" [Mt. 12.45]. Again: "Lo, you have become healthy, go and sin no longer, lest something worse happen to you" [Jn. 5.14]; and: "It will be better for the lands of the Sodomites and Gomorrahites in the Day of Judgment than for that city" [Mt. 10.15], which has heard the word of God but scorned to believe; and: "Woe to you, Corozain, woe to you, Bethsaida"; and concluding: "For Tyre and Sidon on that day it will be better than for you" [Mt. 11.21–22]. And the Apostle: "It had been better for them not to know the way of truth than after knowing it to turn back again" [2 Pet. 2.21]. Through Moses, the Lord himself also says: "And the priest shall make atonement for the person who in ignorance has sinned, because he has sinned unwittingly, and he shall ask pardon for him and he shall be forgiven. But the person who does anything with a high hand will be cut off from his people because he has been a rebel against the Lord; and therefore he will be cut off and his iniquity shall be upon him" [Num. 15.27–31]. Countless other testimonies affirm that judgment is more severe on those who sin knowingly than on the unknowing; hence in the psalm it says: "Living let them descend into hell" [Ps. 54.16]; for the living denote those who know what they should do, the dead are those who have no knowledge.

16. How much reverence should be paid even to a negligent priest is shown also by Moses; when Aaron had made the calf for the children of Israel to worship, though Moses killed twenty-three thousand of the people, he rebuked the man who was the author of the crime with only the lightest charge, saying: "What did this people do to you that you have brought a great sin upon them?" [Ex. 32.21]. Notice, therefore, how improper it is for any lay person even to criticize a priest for any wrong, if such a mighty prophet in an unspeakable crime like this did not dare even to rebuke rather harshly the author of the crime, though he put the rest to death, thinking that in view of the dignity of the office that was God's prerogative alone; for when someone persecutes a bishop, he does not persecute that bishop but the blameless highest priest, Christ himself, in him; nor is it the culpable bishop that is hurt, but the Holy Spirit itself dwelling in that bishop by the blessing of grace. When the person of the priest is touched, the very pupil of the eye of the Lord is touched [Zech. 2.8], because it is through him that the Church is nourished and administered by God. Therefore, persecutor of priests, whoever you may be, since by this action you also sin against the Holy Spirit, be afraid that there will be found no one to absolve you of this; for, apart from that leading sentence which says this, it is declared elsewhere that "if a man has sinned against a man, God can mediate for him; but if a man sins against the Lord, who can intercede for him?" [1 Sam. 2.25] — in which you should understand not every sin but a particular one. And rightly so; for in the same history [1 Sam. 11.12] we read that David sinned against one of his most loyal soldiers and yet won pardon; and the sons of Eli who abused the Lord's sacrifice were destroyed by the avenging sword [1 Sam. 2.4]. Consider then, I pray, how wrathful God's justice must be if this true sacrifice is abused[20] — and this on a daily basis — by the removal of a bishop, since He showed his wrath in such severe punishment in what was for Him the *foreshadowing* sacrifice; or do you perhaps not know that there is a great difference between the shadow and the reality, the flesh of the beast and the flesh of the Redeemer, the ash of the calf and the consecration of the Eucharist?

IX.17. But that the Holy Spirit is often present even in a sinful bishop is shown also by the example of Caiphas, who, according to the Gospel, was able to prophesy so truthfully about the Lord because he was chief priest of that year [Jn. 11.49–51]. That this is not unbelievable we can establish by certain similar, though very different, considerations. For example, when the sun enters a sewer, it lights up the sewer as clearly as the finest chamber; let there be any ordure inside the sewer, in the sun's rays it has no dark spots, and no filth even, but only as much increase or diminution of light as it would have if a wall of the purest gold lay there. If you were then to throw some object into the sewer, you would not be able to reach the ordure with it before striking the sun's rays. The same, of course, happens in the wrong or honor done to any bishop, even the most depraved. For it is the light of grace, the benediction, the Holy Spirit, Christ the very Light of justice [Mal. 4.2] dwelling in them that is honored or wronged; and before the striker's blow can reach the victim, He himself who illuminates the noxious one is struck. For it was not without point that He to whom nothing is impossible said that tasteless salt should not be put on the manure heap [Lk. 14.34–35], but so that you should know, in addition to anything else, that the bishop (who is here understood by the word "salt" because he ought to season the minds of the faithful with the spice of the heavenly word, so that they can be the food of God) can and must be chastened by some penance when he goes wrong by no one at all but the Omnipotent himself. For who would dare to judge a judge, to chasten an angel (still less to bind one) except He who is above the angels?

In one and the same person there is often found both good blood and bad health; and when one ignorant of curing tries to bring back good health, he often upsets the good blood. Take the spirit of benediction as the good blood, the negligent action—or as you like to call it, the criminal action—of the bishop as the bad health; beware while you try to correct the sickness of the victim in your incompetence—for you do not perform a doctor's function—that you do not seem to damage rather the Holy Spirit. Take a well also: it shows very clear water both for drinking and washing, yet some foreign matter often lies close to its mouth, but not so as to prevent drinking or to dirty the washing; but when a bucket is put into it, and we try to take it out, the water is muddied. This third analogy is appropriate warning, since you have a priest referred to as a *well* in a certain person's work and in the Gospel the Holy Spirit referred to as *water* [Jn. 7.38].

X.18. That they can be judged or rebuked by none but God himself, the Apostle testifies when, answering some critics, he says: "Here now stewards are examined so that each faithful one may be found"; and assuming the priest's person while he defends his own, he says: "My judge is the Lord" [1 Cor. 4.2–4]. The Lord himself says of the Pharisees: "Do what they say but do not do what they do" [Mt. 23.3]. He did not say "Punish them"—as recently the world knows was done by a certain person,[21] very absurdly and therefore unworthy of telling. But to tell some of it, though but a fraction, and to make my claim that I neither cover it up through fear nor approve it to gain favor: would that He had shouted to him [King Hugo] from heaven as He did to Saul [Acts 9.4], or would that he himself had known that God had already shouted, as is contained in the writings of Truth: "Men have taken my judgments for themselves"; he would not then so rashly have raised his throne or tribunal against Him.

But to allude to his action briefly (it rather deserves the general lament of all): I say that he has given priests or doctors of souls the greatest example by this action, if they wish to follow it; for they now know with how much censure they themselves ought to hold and bind those who should be bound, if those who should be bound make such an effort to hold and bind those binding them, and with what diligence the shepherds ought to recall the straying sheep from their errors, if the delinquent sheep themselves try with such vigilance to bring back the shepherds from their excesses even by blows or, more accurately, bites in a manner not so much savage as preposterous.

19. But perhaps against this you say: "I have heard that many [bishops] were sent into exile by my predecessors." To this I reply: And were they not also put in prison?[22] Of course, if you want to have as predecessors those who we hear or read did this, you will find that many bishops were mutilated by them, blinded, excoriated, burned at the stake, nailed to the cross, beheaded. But ask who those predecessors were and see if it is in your interest to be their successor. Assuredly, I have heard that the Lord himself, the high priest himself, the Consort himself, the head of all with no exception (as far as the office of bishops is concerned), God himself says in the Gospel: "Lo, I send you prophets, sages, and scribes; some of them you will kill and crucify; others you will flog in your synagogues and hound from city to city, so that on you will fall the guilt of all the innocent blood spilt on the ground, from innocent Abel to Zachariah, son of Barachiah, whom you murdered between the sanctuary and the altar; Amen, I say to you, all this will come on this *generation*" [Mt. 23.32–36]. And again: "Fulfill then the measure of your fathers." And again: "Just so did their fathers treat the prophets" [Lk. 6.26]. And: "Gather first the weeds and tie them in bundles" [Mt.13.30], that is, join like to like.

In these examples you have one *generation*. Give me a second.

"The generation of the just will be blessed" [Ps. 111.2].

Give me if you can a third.

"I cannot," you say.

Then if you cannot, see in which of these two groups you find those who we read did the things you mentioned above, and measure your action from theirs and your reward from theirs, and choose which you want: either with that most wicked generation pay the penalty not only for your own actions, but also for those which they have done from Abel to the last "rememberer of the Lord" and "son of benediction" (for that is what those two names signify);[23] or restrain your tongue, might and hand from persecuting any cleric even of the lowest rank (for they are called prophets, sages and scribes), so that you may be blest with the generation of the just and be able to reign with them for ever. For if you think little of punishing a delinquent bishop or even a priest, do not, I beg, think light of the many whom the Gospel reading has just shown you, killed from the beginning to the end of time. For if you do not fear to injure one, consider whether you are able to stand torments for the injuries done to all. If I tried to tell you this on my own account, you could indeed say that I had made it up for my own sake. But since you hear it in the words of Truth, who threatens nothing rashly, who promises nothing idly, what refuge, I ask, do you find?

XI.20. Consider also the continual prayer under God's altar of the souls of those killed for the Lord's testament; and with no less fear for the altar itself— since you are aware that it is the same as he who is both priest and victim— observe, I beg, whose punishment they demand: "How long, Lord, holy and true," they say, "will you not vindicate us and avenge our blood on the inhabitants of the earth?" [Rev. 6.10]. O what terrible thunder! It shows that he who is not awakened to it is not sleeping but utterly dead. They are not speaking about those who have killed us clergy, for they know that those are already being tortured in hell for ever; even if they were speaking about them, they would not dilute at all that sentence of the Lord's stated above; but they are speaking about those who are on the earth now who still persecute others, even though not such as ourselves, yet of our body, of our members (though weak yet, as I was), of our brotherhood, of our ministry, of our rank and office — they persecute them, thrust them into prison, torture them with hunger, torment them with cold, send them into exile, drive them from their rightful seats, and injure them with divers kinds of affliction. This also is the daily cry of the universal Church throughout the world; this she cries here, where contemplating the form of her own head in a mirror and glass darkly [1 Cor. 13.12], mixed with evil weeds, she often suffers worse from her own members than from outsiders; this she cries also there, where now exalted in certain of her members, she sees the head himself, the author, face-to-face, and she cries the more earnestly since she is free: "Let the groaning of the captives reach thy presence, turn it back on our neighbors sevenfold" [Ps. 78.11–12].

Then be afraid, O neighbor hearing this, that is, anyone of the same house, the same family, faith, and redemption, any Catholic; be afraid, good Christian king; and though you are glad when you hear the Church say each day, "Lord, save our king," be afraid of what follows: "And hear us on the day that we call upon you" [Ps. 19.10]. For quite clearly you get little benefit from prayers that are said for you, when those who say the prayers for you are not even allowed to live in peace. The Apostle commands: "Pray for kings, leaders, and all set up in authority"; but see what follows: "So that we may live a quiet and peaceful life" [1 Tim. 2.2]. Beware, then, lest God be invoked *against* you when what you have just heard is sung; that is, when the imprisoned cry out, their fellows cry for them too, being of one will in voice as in love.

21. "But," you say, "they are not heard if they curse, since by God's command they ought to pray *for* those who persecute them" [Mt. 5.44].

Fine. What of the fact that the prayer is often turned back onto the head of the one praying [Ps. 34.13]? Therefore, lest you childishly flatter yourself, hear the Lord's words: "Will not God vindicate his chosen who cry to him day and night and will he not have patience in them? I tell you, he will vindicate them soon enough" [Lk. 18.7–8]. And Job: "The soul of the wronged will cry, and God will not let him go away unavenged" [Job 24.12]. Another says: "Do not let someone curse you behind you; for if he curses you in bitterness of soul his prayer shall be heard; God who made him will hear him" [Eccli. 4.5]; and:

"Whoever turns his ear from the cry of a poor man himself will cry and will not be heard" [Pr. 21.13]; and: "Seeing, I saw the affliction of my people and heard their cry" [Ex. 3.7]; and: "The blood of Abel cries to me from the earth" [Gen. 4.10]; and: "The Lord has heard the poor man's desire; the just have cried and the Lord has heard them" [Ps. 10.17]; and: "The Lord is close to those who are of troubled heart and he will save the humble in spirit" [Ps. 33.18–19].

But how do you know whether it is with you converted—that is, by their intercession for you—or damned that they enjoy salvation, since the holy prayer turns not onto you but on the breast of those who said it? In this ought you not to fear the prayers of the afflicted one more than the prayers of the whole Church, your prayers among them, shouting against you for the afflicted one, "Help us, Lord, our Savior" [Ps. 78.9], and "God, look to my help" [Ps. 69.2], and "Lord, free my soul from the lips of wickedness and from the treacherous tongue" [Ps. 119.2], and "Let all who do evil unto your servants be confounded" [Dan. 3.44], and "Free us, God, in your wonderful ways and give glory to thy name" [Dan. 3.43]? When those who have been freed pray for this and countless things like this, they cry without doubt for those who will be freed, a fact proven true by experience.

Do you not hear it said every day that it is customary in the world for a king to speak up for a king, though they may be the worst enemies, since each looks to his own interest, and a bishop for a bishop, a cleric for a cleric, a monk for a monk, a lay person for a lay person, a judge for a judge, a butler for a butler, and—to come to the lowest stations—a baker for a baker, a cook for a cook? If then *we* help each other, in whom there is such imperfection of love, out of fellowship in the same rank, what do you think *they* [the saints] do for their colleagues, who, striving not only to climb that citadel of love than which there is none higher [1 Cor. 13.13], but even—if it were possible—to transcend it, lay down their life for their friends and even pray for their very enemies? Surely you do not think that those who were afraid to neglect even their enemies would abandon us who defer them their due of honor (though much more remissly than is proper) and daily summon their aid and protection?

But perhaps you say: "*They* are willing to help, yes, but they cannot because of our sins."

What kind of beatitude, I ask, is one which some unsatisfied longing torments? What kind of felicity is one which is troubled by some unattainable want? What could be more childish than to think this? What could be found more perverse than to say it?

But while I say all this without interruption, perhaps you are pondering in your mind: "What should be done if one of the clergy rebel against my rule?"[24]

How that could happen I cannot think. For how would he who holds a higher honor want yours? For who is thought greater even in your opinion: he who is instituted or he through whom someone is instituted? You have read that the Lord instructed Samuel, saying: "Take the horn of oil and go, annoint this one" [1 Sam. 16.1] or that one as king; and you have also read that Nathan and Zadoch annointed Solomon [1 Kg. 1.45]. See if you can find anywhere that any king *annointed* — though we may read that they *appointed* — any of the priests or prophets, and you will see which of them holds the higher place after God.

XII.22. All the sons of the Church, among whom you also are numbered — but only if you do not disdain it, if like Absalom punished by the avenging tree [2 Sam. 18.9] you do not attack your father[25] with the sword, if you do not gnaw your mother's vitals[26] with your viperous mouth, and yet you do, you do; you are numbered among them, but see that you do not cheat yourself of their heredity and co-heredity — all the sons of the Church, I say, are *either* of the Lord's lot and are called clerics and monks, or they are servants of the Church and fellow-servants of the bishop, *or* they are workers, serf and free, or nobles of the realm. The earth is the Lord's [Ps. 23.1] and is committed to your protection; its produce *either* is sacred to the Lord and belongs to the priests' right [Lev. 27.21] and cannot be taken away by anyone except one who is not afraid of committing public sacrilege; *or* it belongs to your imperial right, and I think (but I do not judge) that no one can take any away without danger of losing his head; *or* it belongs to the local community and anyone who tries to infringe upon this right is restrained by legal sanction.

But that the priesthood is conferred by God alone just as kingship is — in fact, much more eminently than kingship — a thousand testimonies prove, yet I will note here only those which now come to mind. Moses was told: "Lo, I have set you up as god to Pharaoh" [Ex. 7.1]. And indeed that was no earthly king, it was not any earthly power, but the voice of the Lord himself speaking out of the bush, the voice which "gives strength to his king and raises the horn of the Christ" [1 Sam. 2.10], in fact, *His* Christ (His annointed); which said in the psalm, "I have spoken, you are gods" [Ps. 81.6]. *I*, it says, not any man, *I* have spoken, I have established, I who also created you men; I have spoken; not to any man have I conceded that he should speak, that he should have power, that he should dare; by me men were created; by me you have been called "gods," which no one could do except God, which none could concede except the Lord of all, and that very force — no other — that very power, that command, that majesty said: "I have given you as watcher over the house of Israel" [Ezek. 3.17]; and to another: "To everything to which I shall send you, you will go" [Jer. 1.7]; and: "Lo, I have establised you today over nations and over kingdoms, that you should tear out and destroy and scatter and plunder and build and plant" [Jer. 1.10].

Finely put, and in full agreement from the New Testament: "Whatsoever you bind on earth will be bound also in heaven" [Mt. 18.18]; and one of these addressed says: "To some we are the fume of death in death, to others the breath of life to eternal life" [2 Cor. 2.16]. Wisdom itself also says: "Through me kings reign and establishers of law decide the right" [Pr. 8.15]. What "establishers of law" does he mean if not the revealers of the Scriptures, who then seem to establish the laws of God when they studiously unravel the mysteries; for these are as nothing to the ignorant, just as "nothing is clean to the polluted" [Tit. 1.15]. If perchance this displeases you, another version puts it more clearly: "Through me kings reign and the powerful write up justice," with which that very same Wisdom, now clothed in flesh, agrees, saying: "Every teacher taught in the kingdom of heaven is like a father of the household who offers from his store both the new and the old" [Mt. 13.52].

He said this also in another place—but still in the Gospel—to one man, and in him to all of the same rank, but to him in particular: "I will give you the keys of the kingdom of heaven" [Mt. 16.19]; and again, with greater authority (if it is right to say this), as He had by now defeated mortality, triumphed over death, been clothed in immortality, fulfilled his resurrection with his Ascension imminent, He says: "Feed my sheep" [Jn. 21.17]. Mine, He says, mine; mine by creation, by redemption, by right, mine not yours, mine not Tiberius', mine not Claudius', mine not Constantine's, mine not Theodosius', mine not Mauritius', mine not Charles'. To all the disciples in general He says: "Receive the Holy Spirit. Whosoever's sins you forgive or pronounce unforgiven, forgiven or unforgiven they remain" [Jn. 20.22–23]; and: "Going into the whole world preach the Gospel to every creature" [Mk. 16.15]. Remembering this, he who was first commanded and in whom the whole catalogue of preachers was commanded said: "The Lord instructed us to preach to the people" [Acts 10.42]; and placed before the princes and magistrates he said: "One must obey God before men" [Acts 5.29]. And in his passion his colleague Paul in an Epistle says: "We come as Christ's ambassadors" [2 Cor. 5.20]; and elsewhere: "How will they preach if they are not sent out?" [Rom. 10.15]. By whom are they sent, I ask, if not by Him who had said: "I sent you to reap what you have not sown" [Jn. 4.38]?

23. There you have briefly, but sufficiently, the rights of the priesthood conferred by God himself through the Holy Spirit. Let no one continue to call what is uniquely the gift of God the gift of man. Mastered by this authority, the person who, though in ignorance yet blaspheming God, says to God: "I made him[27] and him," must cease. Otherwise, wishing to make himself equal to God in some aspect, he will be cast down with him [Satan] who wanted to erect his throne in heaven against him [Is. 14.13]. For so universally do we hold it as certain that no created substance is a creator, that, if anyone thinks at all otherwise, no one can be found more insane than he. But if a bishop in particular has been made by man, when the whole world in general has been created by God, it is ridiculous that idols should seem, if not to be worshipped, at least to be respected; for it was said in the psalm: "The idols of the nations are the works of men's hands" [Ps. 113.4].

Even more perversely he says, "God gave him bones and flesh; I conferred the rest." Here you have the unthinkable—God placed below man. For how much those marks of grace by which a man is called an angel, or rather a god, are different from that condition by which he is called dust and ashes, I believe no rational person is ignorant. So see how much this person, who could make an angel out of dust and a god out of ashes (but only if they are two separate substances in this sense, or rather non-sense), which he claims he has done, is preferred to him who could only create the dust and ashes—which is all that he seems to concede to God! Even to listen to this is unbearably obscene and utterly abhorrent (though it has never been heard or said except, alas, in this age of ours, yet I think the prophet said to a certain person: "O shepherd and idol abandoning the sheep" [Zech. 11.17], calling him "shepherd"—in a manner of speaking— for his usual office and "idol" because he thinks this gift was conferred on him by a man; and he "abandons the flock" in its need because he does not know what reward, or from whom, he will receive for defending it, overcome in the judgment of his conscience). It is especially abhorrent since by this hypothesis he can also believe that something can be thought to exist without God. Alas, what unbearable wretchedness of soul, to be utterly lacking in knowledge of one's Creator!

24. But to return to what I had begun: there is no shortage of critics, even in the bishop's household, who follow the example of those who in the year before last put together a Thyestean banquet against a certain bishop, and now too chime in certain slanders against him.[28] And it is not outsiders that are doing this but intimates, who should have been produced as witnesses of his good. It is not enemies who do this, I say, but treacherous friends, men who were once close to his heart, once sweet acquaintances, who "received sweet food with him in the house of God, walking with him as if in agreement" [Ps. 54.15], praising him to the heavens and pronouncing him blessed, righteous and holy, with support as deceptive as it was flattering; may God spare them and "not let death come over them so that they descend *living* into hell" [Ps. 54.16], that is, knowingly contriving hellish deeds and not bewaring the sudden onset of death. This is what the rest of the traitors are doing, not terrified by any divine punishment, which this one has already paid, or so some think at any rate, in return for such action. To one of them he wrote from exile in this manner:[29]

25. "Alas, my son, what will I do? Whom first shall I lament—myself dead[30] or you abusing the dead (as though you were not subject to the same condition of dying!), or rather, what's much more lamentable, inhaling the stench of the dead through your nose, breathing it in through your mouth, absorbing it into your lungs to die a far worse death, and, even worse, infecting others so that they can die along with you? Or do you not know, my son, that there is a fortress called Comacchio overlooking the sea near you in which the dead are said to kill the living?[31]

"Talking with you, my son, in affection—as always—I would tell you (if I had the chance of such conversation) how I think I am rightly open to criticism in the particular matters which you charge me with (and would that you charged me falsely!), not to mention the countless other things which are known to you and to me and to everyone (as well as those known only to God), which are equally lamentable. But since any chance of conversation is quite impossible, I will briefly address you for the moment on paper.

"First, I lament that I could be found the kind of person that could be called 'dead' by you. Secondly, that I have turned you into a critic by my own example (just as you now are leading others), in that in your presence I too—alas—have often forgotten myself and criticized others, even people better than me. Thirdly, I am afraid of causing the death of those who listen to me, who are in danger from the stench of your infection[32] as well as from my own. Cease, my son, from accusing me in this action, and cease no less from imitating me; in it, if it is as you assert, I have been very damaging to myself and even more so to you. You have counsel of salvation to heed on this matter; God's pity, foreseeing that there would be no lack of such stinking tombs of corpses, offered counsel to the living to prevent their being killed by the stench of these, saying: 'Do what they say, but do not do what they do' [Mt. 23.3]. For though I as the putrid matter have been the cause of your death, yet you should know that, no matter who is the author of the sin by which you die, no matter the rank, you will be written down as dead among the dead.[33] For God says: 'He shall die in his iniquity, but his blood I will require at your hand' [Ezek. 3.18]. And in truth, what benefit did Eve get from saying, 'The serpent deceived me' [Gen. 3.13]? I write this to you so that you will restrain yourself, as I am concerned for you, and I do it so earnestly because I not only wish you to be freed from death,[34] but I also do not want to be held guilty of your blood.[35] You can be freed; I do not despair that He to whom wishing is the same as being able can make it happen, nor should you despair of its happening, since you read that He raised one dead for four days[36] (and I remember that I taught you this in that talk on parricide[37] which you wrote down with your own hands); so that I now may be summoned forth to life by the call of God's pity, though you still say that I stink like one four days dead (which he knows better than you). For I have sisters[38] weeping over me (and I pray that you be numbered among them—that is, that there be in you the love of a sister and not that of a parricide). If with such love in you you declare that I stink—as you can truly do—I am not angry, indeed I demand that you do, as long as I merit to hear the Lord's sweet voice promising resurrection to me and a miracle to you. I only ask that you look to the danger of those listening and not downplay your own danger also. For you are not unaware, I think, even if you do not remember it, of God's declaration: 'Whoever speaks evil of his father or mother, let him surely *die* in *death*' [Lev. 20.9; Mt. 15.4].

26. "When you recall these words to mind or reread them here, you will notice the double death[39] and recognize the two conditions attaching to them individually (that is, the condition proper to each), the one [*die*] being mortally mortal alone, the other [*death*] immortally mortal and mortally immortal; so do not forget, I beg, what foul spots you put on your mother (who is of course—I tell you again lest you give it only perfunctory attention—the Church, if you are indeed her son, if your father or any proper parent does not say of you, 'They went out from us but they are not of us' [1 Jn. 2.19]—but be so, I pray, be so, I beg), do not forget, I say, what foul spots you put on your mother when you brand your father with so foul a charge of sin. For the love of husband and wife, just as it is an unbreakable bond, so does it share sufferings, since they have share in the same honor also.[40]

"All this, my son, you would not have dared to do if you had been willing to remember the words, 'Honor thy father and mother' [Ex. 20.12]; you would value regeneration more highly than generation,[41] if you remembered the command, 'Do not touch my anointed' [Ps. 104.15]; and: 'Whoever touches you is like one who touches the pupil of my eye' [Zech. 2.8]; and: 'he who spurns you, spurns me' [Lk. 10.16]; and: 'Do not abuse your gods' [Ex. 22.28]; and: 'He who speaks evil against the king, speaks evil against the law' [Jas. 4.11]. That the priesthood of the Church is *kingly*, one statement of Peter by itself, besides countless others, should be able to persuade you: 'You are a chosen race, he says, a royal priesthood' [1 Pet. 2.9]. You would have kept in mind also the words of a certain most holy Pope in the Decretals: 'I think that there is no worse crime than for Christians to speak evil against their priests.'[42] You would have noted also the power of Cham's curse and have feared to lay bare your father's shame as he did.[43] You would not have taken lightly also the canons and councils of the Holy Fathers, in which you could have seen that many have been damned for this reason, if you had read them. You would have been afraid of being handed over to the Curia and of serving it in shame all the days of your life without hope of restitution.[44] You would have remembered the vengeance done for Blessed Narcissus[45] and would not have thought that our arch-deacon[46] must have been struck down by accident just because *you* do not yet suffer anything—since the longer an unconverted man waits the harder he is struck down (which may the Almighty avert from you and your fellows).

27. "And[47] perhaps, my son, those critics of mine, while wanting to appear hostile to me and amenable to you, have deceived you, just as once those others tried to deceive the assembly of saints, by showing in the Council someone's amputated arm, pretending it was Arsenius';[48] just as you also deceived a certain person [Hugo]—may God forgive you—in your hatred of me; when he produced a letter full of insults originally sent him by that aforesaid teacher of yours [the archdeacon] and trying to find out the author had made you willingly admit that you were the writer of it, you left out the others, who were not as closely related to you as I was, and presented me as the author of the letter and the originator of the whole scheme; and of course when you said this of your own accord, you could, if you had wanted, have told the truth and still have excused yourself and only slightly accused me. This you no doubt would have done, if you had looked to my interests with as much love as I looked to yours and all my flock's, and especially to that of your aforementioned father-in-law [the archdeacon] when I agreed to that letter (my motive is known to God).

"For when another letter came from the other side, as you well know, the fierce clan[49] hostile to us saw it and was rightly suspicious (since it was on behalf of a life which had often foundered on many occasions in similar business) and twisted all the blame, such as it was, onto the same archdeacon and onto certain nobles of our side, and onto the whole clergy in particular, saving me (though shipping me away) because of the relationship which I had with their leaders and with their chief himself [Arnold] (as he said). Then they tried to loot all the house of God and to mutilate and imprison all the elders of the city and to string up the aforementioned [the archdeacon] and those who afterwards with him were the leaders of my betrayal. What a night I spent then, God knows.

"You too, who declare that you know nothing good of me, with what prayers, supplications, bribes, and promises I won life and freedom both for you and for him [the archdeacon] by the intervention of my friends, you, as I said, know best, yet you have kept silent about all this and chosen rather to volunteer only that information which would kill me. For when day dawned it was decided—not by me alone, as you claimed, but by everyone of both parties, ours [the Veronese] and the outsiders [the Bavarians] (who was the leader of the scheme I do not really know other than the devil)—that such a letter should be written as was written, and if the archdeacon should venture to send it, he should be cleared of the charge as though through ignorance; but if not, he would be subject to execution for it. This was done as much on my part as on theirs, as I said; but thanks be to God that when I looked to your good, I neglected myself, so it seems; and when I spared you, though aware of your scheme to some degree, I betrayed myself.

28. "There is a story in the *Tripartite History*,[50] my son, about a man whose occupation was tending the herds; he killed a man and fled in fear into the desert; there, following the example of the holy Fathers, he practiced good deeds and became a hermit, and always blessed the crime which had been the cause of so much good for himself. I tell you this so that you may learn from it how much your action was to my benefit, when you accused me so viciously in order to destroy me utterly. If you were here now and allowed me, I would cover with sweet kisses the hand that wrote that letter, because it was the cause, the occasion and the high-point of my whole salvation, I think. By it I think I have been snatched from eternal death and returned to life; because of it I think it has come about that I seem to be clear of the sins whose stench still endangers you,[51] by which you are corrupting almost the whole Church committed to my care with deadly, pestilential infection—though everything may not be entirely as you say it is—as well as countless other sins far remote from your ken; but I take no security from this; for that would not be appropriate seeing that I lack certainty. I think that I have benefited from this incident so much that I see that I should embrace no one more than you, since you were the cause of so much good to me.

"How fortunate I am in my very misfortune, even if nothing else had happened to me because of it[52] than to get to know you and your like. So I not only pardon you for it but even thank you heartily; and, my son, because you have now undeniably done me good, I advise you to be careful not to let your hatred of me damage you at all. To be brief, since the messenger is in haste away and paper is in short supply: may the righteous pity of the Almighty spare you as you repent, I pray; nay, may He kindly concede that you do repent, I beg; for He knows that I am suffering this from you without due cause, as far as wrong done to you is concerned—if one can be said to 'suffer' a benefit in this manner of speaking—so that through you your fellows may be corrected also and not be called a name derived from yours, Ursians or Ursines, but may rightly merit to be called a name derived from Him who said, 'Learn from me that I am gentle and humble in heart' [Mt. 11.29], and who said through one of his own, 'Obey those put in authority over you and be subject to them' [Heb. 13.17], that is, Christians or Lambs, that is, gentle not fierce, lovers of their shepherds, not deriders of them.

"If this prayer of mine succeeds, I cannot hide my joy, still less stifle it; if not, I impute its failure to my sins. But may God's pity concede this at least, I beg: that while you recount my sins against me, or rather against yourself,

He may remit them; while you write them down, He may delete them, and make you realize in this present world that you inestimably damage yourself while striving to do me irreparable hurt, thereby benefiting me beyond words. May you be strong in the Lord corrected, I pray, my son. Amen."

29. Among these (if I may dare to say so) stand the idols[53] set up on every side, who give no sound, even for their own cause; they seem to shout, as it were, by their very silence that they are totally devoid of reason. But I ask them to be angry rather with themselves, not with me. I do not know or say that they are in fact "idols," but I greatly fear that they are rightly called so, when I hear them patiently bear being called "man-made";[54] in fact they give bountiful thanks to whoever says it. For they will not be man-made if I say so, nor will they not be if I keep silent; but they will be if *they* say so or consent at all. O, how much better to be called "fulfilled" than "makeling." "Every man will be fulfilled provided he be like his teacher" [Lk. 6.40]. But woe to him who does not have as his teacher the Lord himself who says this; we cannot be like Him by comparison, but we ought to be like Him by imitation, and not in every way but the way in which He commanded us; who, though He rendered tribute to the world, paying to Caesar what was Caesar's and to God what was God's [Mt. 22.21], yet showed how much He trod down that world by his very humility, and showed how, subjected to Him, it should be put down by you also, after He had said: "All power in heaven and earth has been given me" [Mt. 28.18]; He warns you in the words of one, a disciple to him but a teacher to you, He warns you which you should rather fear: the lord or the servant, the master or the subject, the giver or the possessor, when he says: "You must obey God rather than men" [Acts 5.29]. And this he cried out to you not in the pulpit or lectern, but before the princes of the world, amid threats and abuse, among his very murderers; this you do not even dare to say, still less to do, though now the very emperors are subject to you.[55]

30. But to return now to my purpose: the priest and the levite pass by [Lk. 10.30–36], not understanding that they go down by the same road, nor do they bring any first-aid to their wounded brother;[56] and (to make the sentence, "Where iniquity abounds, most men's love will grow cold" [Mt. 24.12], apply to this time also — may God avert it!) no one is found who, even out of respect, fear or love of God, dares, or rather is willing, to feed him hungry, refresh him thirsty, clothe him naked, visit him sick or imprisoned, comfort him in mourning, cherish him troubled, and such visitation is forbidden to no one; we can read that this was not forbidden to anyone by that generation of the ancients either, as the Epistles of Paul written in prison clearly show [Philem. 10–11; Acts 24.23], in which he seems to mention those ministering to him and does not fear that they will be apprehended, since he knows that both he and they fear God more than Nero.

31. I will now state that I have the same belief in the Catholic faith as St. Augustine, though the liveliness of his acumen for inquiry, the capacity of his intellect for remembering, the skill of his eloquence for uttering it and the quality of his life for meriting this with God's grace were all far superior to mine; and casting from my mouth or spitting from my heart every heresy against God, even if perchance I cannot detect it, I confess that I believe in the equal, co-essential, or (to put it thus) eternally consubstantial Unity of the Trinity, the Trinity of the Unity, that is Father and Son and Holy Spirit, creator and governor of all things that exist, whether in heaven or on earth, and (if we needs must add it) in the sea and in all the abysses, with one and the same substance of Godhead so remaining, with the persons keeping their own distinction, that He is Father who created all things, Son through whom all things were created, Holy Spirit in which all things were created. I pronounce the Father as the authority for the Son, the Son as the Wisdom of the Father, the Holy Spirit as the community of the Father and the Son. Believing that in these three there is one and the same equality of the Godhead, understanding that there is nothing prior or posterior in these, nothing greater or less, I believe that the Father takes existence from himself and not from any other, that the Son exists from the Father alone, and that the Holy Spirit exists from the Father and the Son, and that the Father begot the Son in an eternal and ineffable way; that the Son was begotten of the Father alone ineffably and eternally, not made, just as light is begotten of light or word in the heart or, to make myself clearer, anything that can be said; that the Holy Spirit, that is, the consubstantial love of both, has never been absent from there, and that it proceeds from the one to the other and from the other to the one without localization, movement, or finiteness, and therefore also ineffably, that it is sent by the Father and the Son to inspire the hearts of the elect, and that it comes from itself temporally; that the Son was born of the Father without a mother eternally and of the Mother without a father temporally. When I hear that He was conceived of the Holy Spirit, I do not understand that the Holy Spirit was another father, but believe that the Word, remaining eternally in the heart of the Father, when He wished, left his Father by his own and his Father's will and came into the world in such a way that he neither left his Father nor heaven itself; the Word was made visible to men through the body, which the whole Trinity together fashioned in the womb of the Virgin Mother from the substance of the same Mother who remained ever a Virgin.

When I hear, "The Word was made flesh" [Jn. 1.14], I profess that God was not turned into man, but with the substance of unchangeable Godhead remaining the Word united man to himself so that, just as man is a single entity from body and rational soul, so Jesus Christ is one from man and God, not a composite but co-existing ineffably. When I hear that He suffered, died and was buried, and on the third day rose and ascended the heavens, I ascribe neither the separation to Christ nor the capacity to suffer to God; but just as man, who of course is flesh and soul, is said to be killed by someone though the rational soul is not touched by death, so God, I believe, suffered, without suffering, all those things in the man which He assumed.

When I say, "I believe in the Holy Spirit," and immediately add, "The holy Church," I do not think of a quaternity thereby, but confess that I believe that the holy Church is Catholic alone, through one baptism, that is, the Catholic baptism, and by God's grace and by the faith which works through love [Gal. 5.6]; through these also I believe that we will receive the communion of saints and remission of sins, if we are willing. As to the resurrection of the flesh, just as I know and confess that in our Lord Jesus Christ's case it was real and not fantastical, so I confess that it will happen for all, as much for the reprobate as for the elect; but it will happen for the elect that they will go with body and soul into eternal life, for the reprobate that they will go, likewise with body and soul, into eternal punishment; but as the former go without fear of being expelled through justice, so the latter go without any hope of recovery through mercy.

32. Pardon me, reader, I pray, pardon me as, impudently and simplistically, I essay all this about the ineffability of such great incomprehensibility, pondering it rather than explaining it; for wretched and blind, not seeing with the eyes with which such things ought to be considered, that is, the blessed eyes of a pure heart, not seeing but groping, I have assembled these thoughts. And just as when we want to tell a blind man of things he cannot see, we are unable to unless we supply an analogy of things he has seen; so I, lacking the proper attributes of God, because they do not occur to us in this contagion of mortality, have suggested them through images easy for my grasp but not entirely foreign to the authority of Holy Scripture, and in my reasoning have asked my heart what it feels about God and his creation, trying, that is, to find out whether, being indeed censurable on other points in the opinion of many and damnable in my own, I could be found culpable in my assertion of the Catholic faith, and therefore could rightly be expelled from the presulate committed to me, that is, that of the Church of Verona (but only if the authority of the Universal Council decreed it); my heart, though moved by the ineffability of the matter and the novelty of the attempt, yet did not put off answering that God's power has created all things in his wisdom. When my puny mind's barrenness, hazy with the dust of my vices, compared this answer with the creed which we call Athanasian or Nicene, and perceived that it did not differ at all from it, I ventured—not with the tenacity of a defender but with the security of one believing that I had found what I had been looking for—"to believe in my heart and so be justified and to confess with my lips and so be saved" [Rom. 10.10], that the governor and creator of all things is the Unity of the Trinity and the Trinity of the Unity. I therefore rejoice, if I am not in error; but if I am, then I long and yearn to be corrected in all love.

Book IV

[Rather continues to examine the position of the bishop in conflict with the king, with particular reference to his own case (c. 5 f.). He concludes with the duties of a king in respect to charity and material support for Christian institutions.]

1. A weary traveller, though able to complete his journey within the day, usually postpones it till the next, so that his late arrival may not deny his tired body the chance of rest. The busy sailor too, if ever the wind blows contrary and keeps him from his proper coast, usually seeks the shore of some island nearby, where he can obtain small boats and use their help, as Paul once did [Acts 27.17], lest the ship strike a reef. This example (not inappropriate if examined) has led me too to put off my address of one day to the next, in case my very prolixity weary the reader and my importunate eloquence bring some danger (as often happens) to certain persons who may contradict it; for even the apostles themselves filled with the Holy Spirit were reported as "being filled with new wine" [Acts 2.13] at the third hour; still less would I be thought at sundown to be sober in my speaking.

2. After straying in somewhat leisurely fashion, it seems, in pursuing the matter which presented itself in the case of idols,[1] or shepherd and image (since I discussed points not entirely relevant and fear that I may have hurt someone), let me now hurry on to enquire, as I set out to do, what a bishop is able or required to do or think against you, the king. But because I have expatiated somewhat, let me repeat the points in order as they were made. I said, unless I am mistaken, that bishops are instituted by God alone, just as kings are but much more eminently than kings, because kings are also instituted by bishops, but bishops,

though they can be chosen or appointed by kings, cannot be ordained by kings. Nor do I regret saying this. For the Lord himself, who alone can bear witness for himself, provides the testimony when he says: "I have sent you to reap" [Jn. 4.38]; and there are many other testimonies to this, countless I say. But woe to those usurping the position—not commanded, permitted, not sent; woe to those about whom it is said: "Kings have reigned and not from me, princes there have been and I have not known it" [Hos. 8.4]. Woe to those climbing in by another route and not entering by the door [Jn. 10.1]; from which woe may the good Shepherd free them, who, alone Omnipotent, can turn "woe" into "well done," not punishing severely in the future life those whom he kindly concedes to be converted in this one. I said that the sons of the Church were either clerics and monks, or servants or workers, serf and free, or nobles of the realm; that the Lord's earth is entrusted to your protection, O king; that the produce of it is either sacred to the Lord and belongs to the right of the priests, or belongs to your right or to that of the local communities.

3. This I stated before[2] and have repeated now, so that I may try to understand, if I can, what difference, what disagreement, there can be between you and a bishop, since you should be his protector and he should be your shepherd; he should provide you with spiritual sustenance, you should provide him with carnal sustenance, from your own substance, not from his. For one of them says quite pointedly: "If we have sown a spiritual crop for you, is it too much for us to reap from you a carnal harvest?" [1 Cor. 9.11]. He should bless you, you should honor him. Finally, your temporal benefits have been allotted by the Lord with such balance that you ought not to encroach on his, because they are not his but the Lord's, nor should he desire yours except only for the salvation of your soul. For he is told: "Not seeking the gift but the fruit" [Phil. 4.17]. But you are addressed in a prayer to God (and would that it were not in vain): "Those who have said, Let us seize the sanctuary of God, put them down, O my God, like a wheel" [Ps. 82.13], etc.; and: "You shall not muzzle a threshing ox" [1 Cor. 9.9].

4. The words of the good bishop should usually be these: "Let every soul be subject to the governing authorities" [Rom. 13.1]; and: "Render to Caesar the things that are Caesar's and to God the things that are God's" [Mt. 22.21]; and: "Pay all of them their dues, taxes to whom taxes are due, revenue to whom revenue is due" [Rom. 13.7]; and: "There is no authority but from God" [Rom. 13.1]; and: "Obey your leaders and submit to them" [Heb. 13.17]; and what someone most finely says: "Obedience which is shown to one's elders is shown to God";[3] and the sayings of others of this sort. If the bishop thinks, preaches, and admonishes nothing else against you, he should not only not offend you with this, but should much rather please you, since he is supporting your in-

terest. But if he does otherwise (heaven forbid), and you cannot keep your patience but decide to punish him, there is a way in which you may do him harm and not bring so heavy a sin onto your own head. Bishops have their general conventions, their universal synods, ancient canons, written councils, decretals of the holy Fathers, sanctions of various popes. There is nothing that can happen among them for which they cannot find the appropriate court among themselves. Finally, there is the universal seat, the capital and chiefest because it is foremost among the very heads of the Church, the nourisher, mother, judge, and instructor of everyone. If anything improper is done by any or in any bishop, before that seat it can be judged, examined, or punished with legal sanction. Therefore, consult the Church authorities, refer the matter to them, hand over the case to them. If any crime is found to have been committed against you, it will be punished strictly, believe me, in the court of the canons. There is no other who can raise his hand against a bishop with immunity and without offence to God; you cannot find him even if you could fly with wings.

5. Perhaps you say to the contrary (and indeed I heard this said yesterday with no less madness than stupidity):

"What need of a judge when we already have his guilt[4] as self-evident? For his reputation is such that everyone knows that he must rightly be condemned."

You could have said all this quite correctly if you had taken it from his own confession made in the council according to the canons. But what a seat of pestilence [Ps. 1.1], on which the holy one, the gentle king of Sion, who was made man for us, refused to sit! O wicked court that should be suppressed at its very root! Wicked sentence, belonging only to this world, where thousands of our saints have been arrested merely at the shouts of a seditious mob and the prisons crammed with innocents! Worthy sentence! The very opposite of the Lord's command, "Do not judge according to appearance, but according to right judgment" [Jn. 7.24]; and "I judge as I hear" [Jn. 5.30], referring to himself.

"As I hear," He said, not "as I have heard." For when the charges of the prosecutors have been made and the defence of the accused follows, the judge who is just and not violent can discern the just man, so that he can truthfully say: "I judge as I hear," that is, as the law itself requires, not as the talk of madmen babbles, as the defendant who is present states, not as his enemies who are absent plot. Thus someone has said very cleverly: "he hurries to punish who judges swiftly"[5] — to punish, not to decide. "For by your words you will be justified," he said, "and by your words you will be condemned" [Mt. 12.37], that is, both in man's court and in God's, mercifully and justly; mercifully, for God said: "You first should tell your wickedness that you may be judged" [Is. 43.26]; justly, since "Out of your own mouth do I judge you, wicked servant" [Lk. 19.22].

Here you should see that a certain warning, as it were, has been put between you and God; for each man is judged justly out of his own mouth, and he is judged mercifully if he first tells his wickedness.

Hence it is that boys being educated in school who confess their faults spontaneously sooner deserve pardon, but the obstinate ones are whipped for a long time. Truth himself, who makes this warning, says: "The measure you give will be the measure you get" [Mt. 7.2], that is, just if just, merciful if merciful. This sentence too should be carefully weighed: "Let him who is without sin among you be the first to throw a stone at her" [Jn. 8.7]. Beware also imitating the Pharisees, who looked to catch the Lord in his words [Mk. 12.13]; for this reason also, man's laws tried very carefully to provide for ignorant defendants. If, then, a lay person cannot be condemned unless convicted by his own mouth, how much less ought he, whose judgment is in God's hand alone, to be subjected to imprisonment on the complaints of the envious. For you know with what object that disreputable rumour was started; and if you know from what cause or incident it *arose*, in what spirit was it *spread*—the spirit of charity or the spirit of envy?

6. So that our reasoning may come to the point, stay a little, I beg, and let us see. This too the ancient law forbids, for a priest to take a widow or one divorced [Lev. 21.14]; and virgins consecrated to God should be so far removed from the sight, contact or speech of any man, the more they strive to keep chaste for that bridegroom "most pure and lovely above all the sons of men" [Ps. 44.3], and stay devoted to him not only in deed, word, and hearing, but even in thought (as far as it is possible for any human being earnestly striving with God's help). The holy canons also forbid bishops any kind of cohabitation with women, excepting those specified there. You may see a woman sometimes talk with a bishop, that is, have a private audience, and it is noised abroad among the people. Do you wish or think that he should at once be deposed as one defamed, as though by this alone he is "self-evident" (as you said)?[6] How do you know that he is not compelled to hold this audience for some reason of piety that is hidden from you, but clear to God and him, that is, for winning a soul—just as we read that a certain anchorite of no small fame converted a certain infamous harlot? Again, another of the same rank, no less valiant, in a certain city brought into a hospice harlots that had been hired for a price, as the custom is; and when he was so defamed for it that people shouted that he should be burnt at the stake, such a crowd of converted women shone forth renouncing the world, that in that densely populated Alexandria, which had counted three thousand of them when he entered, scarcely one harlot could be found when he departed.

7. You say: "What if his sons also approve the crime?"[7]

I answer; who knows this except himself and God? Have you not read, "But while men were sleeping, his enemy came and sowed weeds among the wheat and went away" [Mt. 13.25]? by which you may understand that when one man sows the words of doctrine, another can creep in to sow the seed of wantonness. Let me mention another thing: "A drunken bishop," the canons say, "should either desist or be deposed."[8] And we often see many of this rank who seem to be enslaved to this kind of vice, when we are quite ignorant of their intention in what they do. For it can happen that a man pretends to be a drunkard and feasts with drunkards, according to the apostle [1 Cor. 5.11], in order to win them over for Christ, or does it with some other secret — but good — motive. Do you then think it right that he be deposed at the crowd's insistence because of a scandal of this kind, without any confession from his own mouth?

"But riots, piracy and wars, serious crimes, justify even execution, besides other punishments."

But the Lord says: "It is necessary that stumbling blocks come" [Mt. 18.7]; and: "Nation will rise against nation and kingdom against kingdom" [Lk. 21.10]; and Job: "Nothing happens in the world without cause" [Job. 5.6]; so, some cause or occasion arising, a revolution may occur in a city, as often happens, or a break with the monarchy, and deaths may result, and everyone might say that the bishop had plotted the whole business. Do you think that he should be deposed with no prior examination in the court of the canons or any confession on his part? Or (what is much more inappropriate) that he should be harmed because of the people's clamor, himself alone denying it? What if he will be innocent of such offence? How do you surmise that he is not?

"Because," you say, "he associated with wrong-doers while the action was going on, he was arrested with them."

So you decide that one should consider not what he was planning but where he was, though we know that the Lord to the contrary judges not on the action but on the intention. For what if he did this with a good or just intention? For example, just as Jeremiah the prophet did, who, as St. Gregory says,[9] when he could not restrain the people from entering Egypt, out of love strove to go there with them himself [Jer. 43.6–7]. Again, when Italy was invaded by the Lombards, which of the bishops do we read abandoned his flock and crossed over to Mauritius? Again, did not this saint [St. Gregory] I have just mentioned do the same? This same Mauritius was suspicious of him, though the saint had baptized Mauritius' son in the baptismal font, and daily rebuked Gregory because he had obtained the primacy of the Apostolic seat by his own support, action, and decree, though he had at first shunned it unwilling, and, after refusing it, had afterwards obtained it with Mauritius' consent (and later regret however); Gregory decided that he had to act in this way because of the citizens' wickedness and the enemy's invasion, so that he abandoned the flock entrusted to him and crossed over to Constantinople.

Did not also Father Augustine of most excellent memory, pressed by a similar situation, decide that this was the action to be taken or demonstrate it by his example? Asked for his name by the enemy, he is said to have replied that he was a servant of Christ, and the enemy in like manner responded that he was a whip of Christ; ought he to be justly condemned because for that reason he opened the city to the enemy? Do you then judge that all bishops should be deposed who, knowing that citizens, their sons, are rebels to kings have not handed them over to be punished, but on the contrary have sung masses for them, have baptized their children, have counselled them, confirmed them, forgiven them their sins and reconciled them to God?

8. But[10] perhaps you think that what you say is right because you remember that the Lord said, "If you offer your gift at the altar," and the rest [Mt. 5.23]; and because, just as medication does not help the wound if the steel is still in it, so penitence does not help the man whose heart is still at discord with his neighbor,[11] still less with the Lord, since the Lord's most important words were: "If you do not forgive men their sins, neither will your Father forgive you your sins" [Mt. 6.15]. But who is the one to know this if not God himself who knows everything? How do you know whether a man's heart is positively inclined, though his actions are negative? Have you not read: "If possible, live peaceably with all men" [Rom. 12.18]? Have you not heard, "Whoever wishes to be a friend of this world is set up as an enemy of God" [Jas. 4.4]? Do you not know the words, "Whoever has said to his father or his mother, 'I regard you not,' has kept thy covenant" [Dt. 33.9]? Do you not remember the words spoken to Josaphat, when he offered help to Ahab, "Do you offer help to the wicked and join in friendship with those that hate the Lord?" [2 Chr. 19.2]. Does not the psalm come to your mind, "Have I not hated them that hate thee, O Lord, and have I not loathed your enemies?" [Ps. 138.21] and "I hate those who do perverseness" [Ps. 100.3] and that whole psalm? And "The just man will rejoice when he sees their punishment" [Ps. 57.11] and "Have I not hated the unjust?" [Ps. 118.113]. Finally, remember the Lord's words, "I have not come to bring peace but the sword" [Mt. 10.34], and Job on friendship with the impious: "The folds of his flesh cleave together . . . one sticks to another and not even a breath can come between them" [Job 41.14, 7].

With so many possible motives, who but God alone can know, except either by a person's own words or by certain interpretations of his actions, with what intention he does anything, since even though we know his intention to be wholly bad, yet it is our duty to attend vigilantly to make him better? For is Job to be condemned when he says, "I have been a brother of snakes and a companion of ostriches" [Job 30.29]? Is Lot to be condemned in the crime of the men of Sodom [Gen. 19]? Those too, to whom the apostle says, "In the midst of a crooked

and perverse generation, among whom you shine as lights in heaven, holding
fast the words of life" [Phil. 2.15-16]? Is that angel, or rather bishop, to be
condemned to whom it is said in the Apocalypse, "I know where you dwell,
where Satan's seat is, and you hold fast my name and you have not denied my
faith" [Rev. 2.13]? Are Noah and his sons to be condemned, because they were
with the serpents in the ark [Gen. 7]? Is the Church as a whole to be condemned,
to which are addressed the words, "like a lily among brambles, so is my love
among maidens" [S. of S. 2.2]?

9. If the ship of the Church ought not to be neglected in a calm, how much
less should it be in a storm! And if the flock should not be deserted when the
wolf feigns away, how much less should it be when he prowls the fold! If the
healthy are to be saved, should the sick be completely neglected? Where will
be "Those who are well have no need of a physician but those who are sick"
[Mt. 9.12]? Who has ever cast out a dear son, even one driven mad—since even
though he could not be tied, he could at least be guarded in some way? Since
we see that that is often done for the meanest of servants in good health, when
consideration is taken for their safety, how much more ought it to be done for
beloved sons, if there be need? Assuredly, the pious Lord considering the safety
of his pastors, foreknowing that they would be particular targets of the wolf's
attack, conceded this to them: "If you are persecuted in one city, flee to another"
[Mt. 10.23]. But what was to be done in a general emergency, he shows both
by his own example and that of the hired hand, saying: "The good shepherd
gives his life for his sheep, but the hired hand runs away" [Jn. 10.11-12]. And
elsewhere: "Now when these things begin to take place, look up and raise your
heads, because your redemption is drawing near" [Lk. 21.28]; and again: "And
so watch at all times, praying that you may be found worthy to escape all these
things that will take place and to stand before the Son of Man" [Lk. 21.36].
Therefore, we are commanded to give our life for our sheep, to lift up our hearts,
to watch and pray, not to flee in a communal crisis, since this we are specifically
prohibited from doing.

10. Therefore,[12] stop increasing your crime [negligent bishop] by defending
it (though you have already spoken to excess), or you will rather seem fit to
be deposed from both temporal and eternal honor, because, though you share
the honor, you do not understand it; and so you should be compared to a beast
of burden [Ps. 48.13] rather than a bishop, to a sheep rather than a shepherd,
when you cheapen yourself so and try so impiously to oppose the laws which
have been made by God especially for you—if you would only be what you are
called. For up to now you have opposed me in this matter with that Gigantomachia and Theomachia of yours—or rather Idolomachia—and you have not
allowed this fault to be kept hidden, since, though you wear the habit, you fol-

low the way of vainglory rather than true monasticism; by not only rereading the *Gigantomachia* more often than the *Psychomachia*, and even admiring it, you show that you are more a worshipper of idols than a bishop of Christ. In fact, you hint that you are an idol, when, chased by giants—or rather, by Him who exulted like a giant to run his course [Ps. 18.6]—to avoid being caught, arrested, and cast down, you try to protect yourself with frivolous evasions and conceits, as though you were found hiding (though you could not be hidden) behind a tree from his heat [Ps.18.7], that is, on the point of being punished by him, covered with the leaves of the wild fig [Gen. 3.7], not clothed with the innocence of the true Lamb, colored with the dyes of India [Job 28.16], not whitened with the snow on Selmon [Ps. 67.14–15]. Nor do you want to take on the wings of the dove, that is, the virtue of simplicity, with which you might fly to your rest, but the wings of the stork with which you might be lifted aloft to your passing away; nor are they covered with silver, so that your nether parts may have the likeness of gold, but in silver turned to dross [Is. 1.22]; the gold rather of Ethiopia [Job 28.19], which is not equal to Wisdom, is what you desire rather than that best gold of Ophir [1 Kg. 10.11], which our true Peace "who made us both one" [Eph. 2.14] ordered to be brought to Him on ships, with which to adorn the ceilings or vessels of his temple, that is, the hearts of those in whom He deigns to dwell and to hide his longed-for treasure.

You prefer to embrace the foolish wisdom of the world [1 Cor. 1.27], which is confounded by the weak and despised—our "fairest of the sons of men" [Ps. 44.3]—rather than that eternal and true wisdom; you seek the empty wisdom esteemed by those teachers of yours whom you commend and extol and glorify. The vessels borrowed from the Egyptians [Ex. 12.35][13] you pile up not among the utensils of the Lord's tabernacle, but among the ornaments of that same Egypt, making the Lord's cloth with them serve the queen of heaven [Jer. 44.17], that is, worldly pomp. You bring in Jugurtha defeated by Marius[14] by a trick rather than worldly pomp subjected by Christ with the cross; or Siphax[15] captured rather than the dragon cut down by Michael [Rev. 12.7] and now triumphant in our battle, whom you ought to have crushed rather than emulated. You recall to mind Scipio, Pompey, Deiotarus, and eloquent Cato, rather than Peter, Paul, and John, beloved of the Lord. You read Lucan[16] more often than the canons celebrated by Christian teachers, or rather described by triumphant heroes in the loveliest passages of holy Scripture. You prefer the law relating to crime, rather than the Rule established for living righteously, the valor

> that strove greater in a tiny frame[17]

of Statius, rather than the power which "is made perfect in weakness" [2 Cor. 12.9] of the apostle.

Therefore, you should fear that you will be struck down from the mountains without hands, since you are not afraid to offend against Him, suspecting—or rather, teaching—that the "many-peaked mountain" [Ps. 67.17] is the fertile mountain of God, enriching whom He wishes and as He wishes with parcels of his grace [1 Cor. 12.4]—which you dare to say is done by a man (though sometimes it can partly be done *through* a man); and therefore, because you are of the earth when you utterly renounce the heavens and speak only of the earth, you should be afraid that you will be devoured by the ancient Serpent, since you yearn to be his food. For this is what He who cannot lie promised that serpent: "Earth"—that is, earthly men—"you shall eat all the days of your life" [Gen. 3.14]. But since you uttered this so cleverly (or so you thought), you ought to have remembered that Cariath-Sepher [Jos. 15.15] (that is, "the city of letters") has already been destroyed by Joshua, who "gives life in spirit to those whom the letter kills" [2 Cor. 3.6], and that now the kingdom of God does not consist in talk but in power [1 Cor. 4.20]; that now our strong man, a second David, "to whom the Lord swore and will not change his mind" [Ps. 109.4], saying, "You are priest for ever," has struck the Valley of Salt[18]—that is, the rhetoric of the proudly wise—noted by the word "valley" because "everyone who exalts himself will be humbled" [Lk. 14.11], not because "the valleys will deck themselves with grain" [Ps. 64.14], but because "he who humbles himself will be exalted" [Lk. 14.11], by Him, that is, who "makes springs rush forth in the valleys" [Ps. 103.10] so that "the waters pass between the hills"—not those waters which once "stood above the mountains" [Ps. 103.6] of the churches, that is, covered them for a while with the tide of persecutions.

Now, thanks be to God, though to your own hurt you try to recall them, they have fled from God's rebuke, they have risen and sunk down to the place which God has appointed for them [Ps. 103.8], that is, the Lord has for ever established them so that they may not be gathered together again, even though they wish to cover the earth; for although the kingdom of God still labors in some parts and "its adversaries are many" [1 Cor. 16.9], yet already in the greatest part of the world a "wide and clear door is opened" [2 Cor. 2.12] for the apostle's teaching—not, to be sure (that I may say this too), among those mountains of cataclysm (those by whom the Church is watered, washed, and cleansed, as you in your lofty wisdom try to teach) does the Lord make "His springs gush forth," but among those whom He "waters from his lofty abode" [Ps. 103.10,13], those, that is, on whose summit He is established [Is. 2.2], which also is "the stone cut from the mountain without hands" [Dan. 2.34], that is, Christ born in the flesh from the seed of David [Rom. 1.3] without man's participation. The Church, I say, is not washed in the waters of Egypt, which cascade in waterfalls, but in "the waters of Siloe, which move in silence" [Is. 8.6]. For though

"Abanar and Pharphar, the rivers of Damascus" [2 Kg. 5.12–14], were thought better than all the waters of Israel in the judgment of Naaman the Syrian, yet he could not be cleansed of his leprosy unless he was washed in our Jordan seven times (a number not without mystical significance). Also, the Church, when handed over to physicians, that is, lying magicians (to whom you too still adhere when you introduce Cicero's concepts and rhetoric in the Church's cause), could be cured by none of them, though it has been able to endure much.[19] For in this my cause I so laugh at both your "affirmation" and your "negation" that in the case of the former I say it is more wholesome and wise to answer as the apostle does, "If we say that we have no sin, we deceive ourselves and the truth is not in us" [1 Jn. 1.8]; in the latter I staunchly avoid running in the number of those who "hold fast to their purpose" [Ps. 63.6] (that is, their evil purpose), and even prefer, while the Catholic faith is still safe and the pit (that is, the loss of our office) avoided, humbly to yield to the words of others than obstinately to pursue contention.

11. This whole argument has been to establish this: if any bishop be found to be such as you claim—heaven forbid!—he cannot be judged by any man, unless by himself, excepting the authority of the canons. He is judged by himself by making a pure confession between himself and God or any trusted person he chooses, so that he will not be harshly judged by God, but may be justified by first confessing his wickednesses against himself and forestalling the words of the accuser [Pr. 18.17]. He is judged by canon authority if under proper examination in the council he announces his guilt out of his own mouth. He is judged by the Lord in many ways, when either infirmity or loss or attacks of enemies or any other kinds of catastrophe punish him with God's affliction, not, indeed, on God's commands, but with His permittence (according to the psalmist); so that either he is afflicted in this present world, so as not to be damned in the future one, or so that the steel of his mind may become as sharp as a needle, honed by the file of other people's perversity, and with it he too may be able to prune the vicious outgrowths of the heart in others.

12. That all this is so, let me prove by the Lord's sayings, not by Cato's. That bishops must be judged by no man, the apostle shows, referring to them when he says of himself, "It is the Lord who judges me" [1 Cor. 4.4], and "The spiritual man judges all things but is himself judged by no one" [1 Cor. 2.15]; and the Lord also, when he declares that salt that has lost its taste should not even be put on the dunghill [Lk. 14.35]. A bishop must be judged by himself; the same apostle says, "If we judge ourselves, we would not be judged" [1 Cor. 11.31]; and consider too the words about Moses: "He placed also the bronze laver, in which Aaron and his sons were to wash when they entered the shrine, which he had made from the mirrors of women who ministered at the door

of the tabernacle" [Ex. 38.8]. He is judged by the Lord as the Lord's words show: "I will punish their transgressions with the rod and their iniquity with scourges" [Ps. 88.33], though this is not said by Him whom we read in the Gospel washed the feet of his disciples [Jn. 13.5].

How a bishop is to be judged by canon authority he shows very clearly when He says, "I judge as I hear" [Jn. 5.30], and "Out of your own mouth do I judge you" [Lk. 19.21]. This too, you should realize, must be taken into account in the present instance: the extent to which you think the Lord is present, when by some clearer indication of His presence and agency the defendant is revealed and exposed, either forced against his will but nevertheless stating palpable truth and freely confessing, or found guilty by some just and legal process. "Do not pronounce judgement before the time," says the apostle, "before the Lord comes, who will bring to light the things now hidden in darkness" [1 Cor. 4.5].

There is a certain kind of royal protection called popularly *mundeburdis*, a special privilege which so protects the holder of it with the king's authority that he cannot be harmed by anyone, either by force or by court decision, even if caught in the act, until he gets a hearing in the presence of his royal majesty. If the authority of a human being is so respected, if one can be protected by mere words written on a bit of paper today, which if destroyed tomorrow by fire or water or mold carry no weight, with what respect and fear ought one to observe the edicts of him whose words do not pass on when the earth and heavens pass on [Mk. 13.31]? What clearer protection can you find for defending in particular the leaders or ministers, whom the most powerful King of Kings placed in his Church, than His words, "Do not touch mine annointed" [Ps. 104.15]?

There is also a token called a *wiffa*, which protects with avenging sword anyone who has received it as a gift from the king and suffers any loss from another's encroachment. What more terrible token could be found than the bishop's crosier? What clearer *wiffa* do you want than the crown which they wear on their heads? The stole, chasuble, belt, hose, and sandals—even if you could understand no other symbolic meaning in them, what do they mean if not the clearest marks of God's protection and veneration, when you see bishops wear them in distinctive fashion? Not a little do I fear that these symbols will face you at your judgment, when I see them so despised by you, that you would rather have bishops robbed and killed than protected by them.

13. Now that you have read these brief remarks against this iniquitous judgment—and one inappropriate even for a lay person—I ask you whom I addressed above to consider this: since bishops have also their own courts for themselves if they have done wrong, have you ever seen a knight or commoner dare even to criticize, still less to judge, a palatine judge? Are you now satisfied that

bishops are judges of all, not only men but even angels [1 Cor. 6.3]—fallen ones that is? But to stress the point, in case it should escape a mind loaded with diverse and complex problems: I think it should be repeated, and also something added which you still perhaps do not know, or pretend that you do not know. You should be aware that there will be four orders in the judgment: one which will judge with God, another which will be freed in judgment by God, a third which will be damned in judgment, and a fourth which has already been judged and will have no other fate, believe me, than to be tormented by the very felicity of those who are more righteous, as we read in the psalm, "The sinner will see and be irked" [Ps. 111.10], and to groan in anguish of heart [Wisd. 5.3].

To explain this by the clearest examples: Listen to the Lord's promise: "You will sit above the twelve thrones" [Mt. 19.28], that is, on the thrones of the apostles, not only those of the twelve apostles, in fact, but also those of all the righteous of the same office. And in case you think this is something new I have fabricated, listen to one of these apostles, who was already the thirteenth as he was divinely summoned after Matthias [Acts 1.23–26]: "Do you not know," he said, "that we will judge angels?" [1 Cor. 6.31]. Your doubts about where this order sit are vain, since, insofar as they do this [judge angels], they are apostles, as you know—if only the literal meaning of the word does not escape you, as it is Greek. And the psalmist agrees, saying, "The princes of the people gathered with the God of Abraham" [Ps. 46.10]. What they do when "gathered" (that is, exulting in glory and rejoicing in their stations) he says in another psalm: ". . . the two-edged swords in their hands, to wreak vengeance on the nations and chastisement on the peoples, to bind their kings with chains and their nobles with fetters of iron, to execute on them the judgment written" [Ps. 149.6–9].

If you do not understand what the *sword* is, when their hands produced the works for which the saved would be freed in the judgment from vengeance and rebuke, while the damned would be condemned, you should be able to perceive it, as one of them already holding the sword, though not yet openly brandishing it, says: "To some we are a fragrance from death to death, to others a fragrance from life to life" [2 Cor. 2.16]. And Simeon says of the Lord: "Lo, this one has been put here for the fall and resurrection of many" [Lk. 2.34]. And the Lord himself: "It is Moses who accuses you" [Jn. 5.45]; and about the apostles He said: "They will be your judges" [Mt. 12.27], and "The men of Nineveh will arise at the judgment with this generation and condemn it, for they repented at the preaching of Jonah" [Mt. 12.41], and "If I had not come and spoken to them, they would not have sin" [Jn. 15.22]. If, as I said, you do not understand what this sword is, ask Paul and let him answer, "The sword of the spirit which is the word of God" [Eph. 6.17], and—of the final and foremost pride—"Whom the Lord Jesus will kill with the breath of his mouth" [2 Th. 2.8], and "The word of God is living and active piercing to the division of soul and spirit" [Heb. 4.12].

The swords are *two-edged*, that is twice-sharpened; why? Besides what I have just said, consider this: the "written judgment" [Ps. 149.9] is also called "gehenna," that is, double-punishment; the "chains and iron fetters" [Ps. 149.8] readied with harsh severity are sufficiently explained in the Gospel, "Bind their hands and feet" [Mt. 22.13]. So the unrighteous are judged, while the righteous rebuke and punish them with two-edged swords in their hands, because in this world they made no effort to attend to them by imitating their works, but tried not only to scorn their words but even to hound their persons with persecution and death. And because here they have of their own accord kept their hands and feet bound from good works, they will there deservedly have them bound against their will in eternal damnation.

If you say, "They are few who will come to this at some future time," He says, "I will number them" [Ps. 138.18]; and if you say: "Because of Matthias there will be twelve," or "Because of Judas, there will be eleven," or "Because of Paul thirteen," He says, "They are more than the sand" [Ps. 138.18]. Consider how many judges there are, and see if it is a small thing even to rebuke one among so many.

14. You have the order of *judges*. Let me also offer the order of those who will be saved through judgment: "Blessed is he who considers the poor and needy; the Lord will free him in the day of trouble" [Ps. 40.2]. Also the order of those who will be damned: "When it gets hot," says blessed Job, "they will vanish from their place" [Job 6.17], that is, that place on the left, destined for eternal punishment. These two orders the Lord in the Gospel has distinguished, after stating the merits of each: "These will go into eternal punishment, but the righteous will go into eternal life" [Mt. 25.46]. The psalmist identifies a fourth order: "Therefore the wicked do not rise in the judgment" [Ps. 1.5]; to these the Lord refers in the Gospel: "He who does not believe has been judged already, because he has not believed in the name of the only Son of God" [Jn. 3.18].

15. It seems worthwhile here to invalidate the leprous view of a certain person, who in the presence of some well-informed bishops (for shame) dared to reject what is sung in Church, namely that "all the saints will reign with Christ for ever,"[20] declaring that one should neither say nor believe that anyone but God can *reign* for ever, but admit only that the saints *rejoice* with Him. As though "to rejoice with God" were not the same thing as to *reign with him* [Rev. 20.4], to reign the same as to live, to live the same as to exist *for ever*! Unfortunately, he so prevailed in this view that in the presence of Him for whom he labors in this present life he removed the whole hymn, so sweet-sounding and felicitous, from the singing of the Church. This it would be all right to do, if he so piously venerated and understood God's unique deity, sovereignty, and power, by which He rules and governs with his own unique command and control all things that have been created by his own unique nod, that he feared to oppose in impious envy God's gratuitous mercy and merciful grace, which turns the vessels of wrath into vessels of mercy [Rom. 9.22–23], and enriches them with such a gift that with ineffable kindness he allows them not only to be (and to be called) *kings*, but in addition to be and be called *gods*. What blindness, for him to say it and for them to acquiesce in it! What stupidity, if it is supported! For in trying to measure God by themselves, they think that He too, like themselves, envies the success of another; as if God's possessions and power were so straitened and his greed and ambition so vast, that what another gains He should consider as his own loss! When sole possessor of everything he controls his treasury with such just restraint that it cannot be lessened or increased; nor can his power count any gain or loss, though He himself increases and dimishes everything at his own behest and in harmony with characters and causes, giving gains to whom he wishes and losses to whom he wishes, himself unchanging, containing in himself the things subject to change, so illuminating out of himself what must be illuminated under him (though He takes no light away from himself), that He generously allows it to be called light itself. That bishop could also understand the same principle in regard to kings; he should know and declare that He is in reality King of Kings—of those that have been appointed—just as he is Light of Lights—of those that have been lit.

16. To address my words now to the author of the fallacy himself: tell me please, when you say this or silently approve of it or, what is much worse, affirm it in agreement, do you contest the evidence of the apostle?

"In no way," you say.

What hidden meaning, then, is there in his clear statement that "If we endure, we shall also reign with him" [2 Tim. 2.12]? What, when you read in St. John's Revelation, "They shall reign with him for a thousand years" [Rev. 20.6] (taking the finite number to be infinite)? What kingdom do you think He will give to those to whom He will say in the judgment, "Come, ye blessed of my Father, receive your kingdom" [Mt. 25.34], if not this, that *they will reign together*? What earthly king do you hear say that, as they give out prefectures and estates and other such attributes of the kingdom to their own partisans, except when they say it to a son who will reign in partnership or succede to the throne? Or in regard to the judgment in the twelve thrones [Mt. 19.28]: can you not understand that number as the number of those reigning also? When you hear in the psalm, "God, your God, has anointed you with the oil of gladness above your fellows" [Ps. 44.8], what do you understand by "fellows" if not "those reigning together?" In what you read that the angel said to Mary,

"He will reign over the house of Jacob for ever" [Lk. 1.33], what, I ask, do you think it means? Do you think that some kingdom which he did not have before, and which besides could exist everywhere, has been promised somewhere else to his divinity, in which co-eternal and consubstantial with the Father He rules everywhere without beginning and without end, and not rather attributed to his humanity, which He put on for us temporally, by the divinity which He has in One with the Father—the kingdom by which "He will reign over the house of Jacob," that is, over the kingdom of the Church, which He began to do from that time that He was born or from that time that He deigned to ascend the tribunal of the cross for our sake, as the psalmist testifies to all believing Christians when he cries, "Say among the nations, that the Lord reigns from the wood" [Ps. 95.10], that is, from the ascent of the cross, a kingdom which will be without end, with the same Jacob for ever, that is, the head with the body? Or do you think otherwise, and believe that, since no head can live without its members, it cannot reign even temporarily? Or perhaps you do not recall what was said of Him: "With his body which is the Church" [Col. 1.24]? and again: "If also heirs, then heirs of God and fellow-heirs with Christ" [Rom. 8.17]? And of what thing are they heirs of God if not of the kingdom? If—or rather, *because*—he is the Son of the King and we are his brothers—by adoption, not by nature—what are we heir to with him if not to the kingdom?

Finally, when you say in the prayer handed down to you by the Lord himself, "Thy *kingdom* come" [Mt. 6.10], what are you praying for? That He should now hurry to reign whom we never believe not to have reigned? or—and this is the truer—are you praying that you may deserve to reign with him, by adoption, not lineage, by gift, not right, by favor, not due, by concession, not equality, by grace, not nature, by the beneficence of the Giver, not by the sharing of equals? For by noting the differences between Christ's words about the mansions [Jn. 14.2] and the Apostle's about the stars [1 Cor. 15.41], we can rightly understand not only that Christ himself (to whom reigning for ever is essentially the same as living for ever) far excels appointed kings, but also that there is no small difference between them in the nature of their reigning. So stop defending this opinion of yours, my son, or rather this great ignorance, or you will sometime be counted among the number of those who, while trying to defend God, only offend him. Rather, justify your position by your way of life, so that you do not lose so great a privilege. Your prayer is useless, if you have no desire—and even no hopes—of attaining it; for when you say that he is your Father, you do not mean it.

17. Leaving this bishop, I turn now to you, the lengthier subject of my address. Consider this, O king: since a bishop should not even be rebuked by any man, how much less should one be whipped, imprisoned, and tormented with

hunger and thirst, with cold and lack of clothing, and other kinds of afflictions.[21] One other point I ask you to consider, and apply the analogy to yourself. If you had a servant, a careless one but one you loved with such affection that you would put him in the second seat after yourself in any of your functions, in authority and power next to yourself, so much that whatever was proper for you alone to do or decree you would hand over to him to do or decree, whatever he decided you would confirm, whatever he denied you would deny, whomever he blessed you would bless, whomever he cursed you would curse; one to whom you would concede your rights, your insignia, your throne, sceptre, purple, and even your very crown, you would have him addressed by your title, so finally there would be nothing left to you except the very essence, command, and governance by which you controlled and governed him along with your flock, and the fact that whatever he did, decided, decreed, or defined, he did not with his own power but with yours: then, amidst all these honors, imagine him being arrested by one of his fellow-servants who surpassed him in some area, without consulting you (though you were present); imagine him being hurt by him, plagued with hunger, thirst and cold, mocked, insulted, and taunted in contempt of your name which he bore; what, I ask, good king, just prince, would you decide to do in a case like that?

You say: "I know what *I* would do; but this fellow is not as beloved of God as you claim."

How do you know? Don't you see him manifestly honored with the throne, the sceptre, the crown, the purple, and even the very title?

"I was the one who honored him."

You? how? Could you give what you do not even dare to touch? Could you concede what you are even forced to worship? Was what is now so much higher than you ever in your power? Then it is astonishing that what you had for yourself you have given to another! But do not even think this. For if you had been able to give it, you also had the power to take it away. But as it is, though you can rob him of his possessions, drive him from his country, exile him, put him in prison, take out his eyes, flay him, mutilate him, and finally kill him (at your own peril), yet that title, that sceptre, that office, that crown with the purple, that benediction, that power of binding even you yourself (by whom he is held bound in prison) and of absolving, that power of judgment, that primacy, that apostolate, angelicate, pontificate, regnate, pastorate, and finally—what excels all these—that consecration and divinity, you cannot by your might, decision, authority or power take away. Acknowledge, then, that something which, as you see, is so close to God that it cannot be conferred or taken away except by him, is far above you; so inseparably does it merit to be attached to God's company that no one can touch it without touching God. Though all these things can be inflicted on them by a man—against God's wishes, since he forbids it so awesomely, but with his permittence; with the greatest wrong done to God and the greatest distress to the perpetrator—yet the glory of this rank is beyond reckoning; this is also testified by those "who left the presence of the council rejoicing that they were counted worthy to suffer dishonor for the name of Jesus" [Acts 5.41].

18. "I yield," you say, "to such obvious truth; but he [Rather] made a grave rebellion against the Giver when he attacked him [King Hugo] so monstrously."

What is that to you?

"Because he caused a disturbance in my kingdom, he instigated riots, carried out countless robberies."

I do not think so, I say; but let us say that he did, let us say it to humor you. But after you had arrested him and held him prisoner, since God allowed it though against His wishes (for it is not right to say or think that he supports actions which He has forbidden), would that you had remembered that He said to everyone, but particularly to you: "Those who honor me I will honor, and those who despise me shall be lightly esteemed" [1 Sam. 2.30], and: "God gave him a place, but he abused it in pride" [Job 24.23]; and: "They have averted their eyes so that they did not see the heaven nor did they remember the judgments of the just" [Dan. 13.9]. Would that that proverb of the wise man had buzzed in your ear: "He is double victor who controls himself in his victory."[22] And: "He who overcomes his anger overcomes his greatest enemy."[23] And again: "In taking revenge, speed is criminal."[24] And the words of another in this wise: "To conquer the will, restrain one's anger, moderate the triumph, not only raise one's fallen enemy but even enhance his former stature—the man who does this I do not compare to the greatest of men but judge him most like a god."[25]

On the other hand, it is ridiculous, as the person quoted above says, to lose one's innocence by hating one's injurer.[26] Would that you had remembered the story of David, how he found Saul, who was pursuing him, delivered into his hands by God but refused to kill him when urged to do so by his company; instead he said: "May God be propitious to me, that I should not put forth my hand against the Lord's annointed" [1 Sam. 26.11]. Would that you had observed in this story that he first asked for God to be propitious to him, so that he should not do what he could do with justice since God gave him the chance. Woe to him who, according to the psalmist, is given over to his own will [Ps. 80.13], since the Scripture, branding elsewhere some who have become corrupt and abominable to God [Ps. 13.1] in their ways, says, "Do not go after your lusts; turn from thy desire" [Eccli. 18.30], and, "There is a way which seems right to a man but its end is the way to death" [Pr. 16.25]; and some desire what, if their prayer is granted, they receive to their own detriment.

Hence one of the pagans neatly observes: "Nothing is so insane as to long for that which can cause your destruction."[27] Likewise, another says wittily (since Wisdom itself teaches him): "If it is wretched to have wanted perversity, it is more wretched to have had the power for perversity."[28] But Job says: "The tents of robbers are full; but brazenly they provoke God, though he has given everything into their hands" [Job 12.6]. Why are they *robbers* when God has *given*? Surely because, though God justly permits it, they have unjustly burned for booty. Why do they *brazenly provoke*, if not because God has given them the opportunity, for the purpose of chastizing or punishing the delinquent, or to their own detriment, namely so that left to themselves and not prevented by the physician they eat the food from which they are killed, and drink the chalice of the Lord's fury and inebriated by it fall the more deeply into eternal perdition, piling up crimes for which a greater gehenna is set blazing for them, with iniquity ever heaped on iniquity [Ps. 68.28–31] (when, that is, their perverse will reaches its wicked outcome, so that they do not enter into God's justice but are deleted from the book of life and not enrolled with the righteous, while the poor and afflicted are set on high by God's salvation, to magnify him with thanksgiving and praise his name with a song)?

Why then do they provoke God's anger, as I said, if not because, receiving the power with God's permittence (though the disposition of his intent is very secret) they do everything which their temper, greed, or pride dictates, neither fearing the justice of the Permitter, nor weighing his pity, nor fearing God's two-edged sword, nor thinking of his concern for the affliction of the wretched, nor sympathizing with the wretchedness of others when thinking of themselves, nor remembering the prophet's rebuke, where in the mask of impious Babylon the Lord reviles such people, saying, "I was angry with my people, I profaned my heritage; I gave them into your hand; you showed them no mercy . . . nor remembered your end," and concluding after a while in terrifying words: "Evil shall come upon you and you will not know its origin; and disaster shall fall upon you for which you cannot atone, and ruin will come upon you of which you know nothing" [Is. 47.6–11], and the other things than which nothing more terrible can be found?

19. To return to David: if you should point out, in the usual manner of men of this world, that David's action was, yes, an example of great self-control, but that today this is irrelevant, I reply that it is more relevant today than it was then; for then it was quite lawful to take revenge, while now one must not even get angry [Mt. 5.22].

"David's action was correct," you say, "because Saul had been his lord."

You would have acted even more correctly [had you shown mercy], because he [the delinquent bishop] is your shepherd, your prophet, your angel, your judge, your god. But if you want to find some deeper meaning in this action, you should know that David stands symbolically for you and your injury in this "disturbed" (as you call it) kingdom and Saul stands for the rank that has been anointed but persecutes the righteous, the rank of those who have been placed in charge in the Church but are negligent. And so Saul relieves himself [1 Sam. 24.4], when one of that rank breaks the wind of bad opinion about himself. David regretted that he had cut off the skirt of his cloak [1 Sam. 24.6], because it is very fearful for any of the men of this world, even one also anointed like David was, to rebuke one of the bishops even in extreme cases. That our priesthood is a royal one is established both by Peter's testimony [1 Pet. 2.9] and countless others.

I had not intended to put down this testimony in my haste to move on, but because it came spontaneously it could not be rejected; perhaps in its spontaneity it will be no less cogent than the others.

20. It may be that, if we examine it more closely, we will find that the case is not entirely as you say. For I think I understand fully what you want. Since you are yourself the wolf, you would like to find the shepherd timid and the dog barkless. And since you are an open robber of the Church, you would like no one to be found to oppose you.[29] Unbearable burden! Where will be "Not only those who do but also those approving them are worthy of death" [Rom. 1.32]? Where will be what the same apostle says elsewhere: "Whoever wants to be a friend of this world is set up as an enemy of God" [Jas. 4.4]? Where the psalmist's words, "If you saw a thief you ran with him" [Ps. 49.18], that is, made a pact with him? This, as I see it, was the cause of the split, these are the grounds of the charge you [Hugo] make: you wanted to hold all the Church's property and to have the bishop as your hired hand, not the shepherd of Christ's flock.[30] He[31] objected to this and showed it by some kind of resistance, considering you a king, according to the etymology of the word,[32] when you *acted rightly*, but a thief, when you committed sacrilege. But whatever was done, whatever happened amiss (for the argument must be stated as if it *had* been done or *did* happen—and my whole purpose in this work is to prevent it being done or happening), ought not the perpetrator of the deed first to have been lawfully examined in the court of the canons? Then, if lawfully convicted, by being himself the witness, judge, and censor of his own damnation, he would not now be condemned as a bishop, but he would be deposed, if this is what the law required, and another given to the Church in his place, and he could then justly pay the penalty for his crime, if you wished, and so the consecrate ministry would not be violated at all, and the Mother Church would not suffer such infamy for so long a time through the loss of her sons. For where will those sons, whom she ought to produce at least at the time of Easter, be when the Mother Church is, so to speak, a widow without a consort, though her husband is still alive? "What God has joined together, let no man separate" [Mt. 19.6] has been forgotten; for the apostle says, when explaining the prophecy [Gen. 2.24] in praise of the original union of man and wife: "This is a great mystery; I take it to mean Christ and the Church" [Eph. 5.32].

21. To whose fault will it be charged that such a number,[33] who ought to have entered the kingdom of heaven, mercifully delivered by the grace of Christ, have stored up punishment from being wickedly abandoned? For, having digressed a little from the topic, let us return to the point which I earlier discussed at some length: I have learned from the report of certain people, alas!, that during that same Paschal period that he was absent, when there had been no baptism celebrated in that Church, as there was no one to give the chrism, more cases of infant mortality—and only of infants that had not been baptized—occurred in the city than anyone could ever remember before; so that everywhere throughout their homes they could raise a single lament—not in fact willingly stifled by their mothers—for the whole city (if only there were any fear of God in that place), some weeping for the punishment of God's vengeance, others bemoaning the death, both temporal and eternal, of children and mothers.

What, moreover, will the Judge say, when He comes in his awesomeness, who first comes in gentleness to seek and to save what had perished [Lk. 19.10], if not that, as far as they are concerned, He has come in vain, He has sought in vain, since someone—let him beware!—has *hidden*[34] them (if it is not un-catholic to put it this way, metaphorically speaking) so that they cannot be found and saved? He will cry in complaint that in vain has He appointed agents to gather them from all quarters, that in vain has He given his blood for them. Allowed that the bishop erred, what sin did any of *them* commit? What harm did Christ do anyone that He should suffer this? What sin did the Church commit? You think that the fault lies with the delinquent in exile? Let us agree; but you (I mean the author of the deed) still will not evade God's judgment. On the contrary, your punishment has become more severe, the more you have striven to avenge your own injury by injuring him; when He has warned you by his example (inasmuch as for the many like sins which you daily commit—if only one could be found like this one!—he still patiently waits for you to repent in this one also) not only that you should not prosecute him, but that you should not repay your brother evil for evil, but rather good for evil [Rom. 12.17], so that you may merit to be the son of so great a Father; since you have refused to do this, see which father you deserve to be called a son of (for there must be two fathers, just as also there are two generations [the blessed and the wicked]).[35]

Another point: the prophet Elisha, if asked about this, could perhaps have answered you: "You shall not strike him, for you have not taken him with the sword or bow so that you may strike him" [2 Kg. 6.22]. What if God forgives him in that punishment which you have sentenced him to, justly according to you, but unjustly and quite abominably to God and all Christians in respect of his rank, just as we read happened to the robber on the cross [Lk. 23.43] and to some others who were punished for their crimes but merited to receive Christ's grace during the actual torments? Surely you do not think that God leaves unpunished such a loss to his kingdom? For if this one did something wrong, have you corrected it by injuring him? On whose judgment do you do what you are doing? Assuredly, "God suffers nothing to go unavenged" [Job 24.12], as it says in Job. God also, as the Apostle says, "will not be mocked" [Gal. 6.7], though you want to be mistaken, and to be deceived as it were by pretending. A proverb of the wise man also testifies that a crime is never to be avenged with a second crime.[36] For it is quite wrong for the crime charged to be recognized in the one charging it and for a criminal to be condemned by a criminal.

Be awakened, therefore, or rather be terrified, by the terrible thunder of his words which precede that storm of his judgment which will come in the whirlwind [Is. 29.6], and restrain your strength, tongue and hand from the affliction of any cleric, however low in rank, however at fault he may be; for it may be that while God corrects them through you (as He is now correcting others through others), under His training they too with others will "stand in great constancy against you who have straitened them" [Wisd. 5.1], and you and your men, weeping in grief of heart and too late repentant while they judge you harshly, will begin to say: "These are men whom once I held in derision and rebuke" [Wisd. 5.3]. This briefly is what I wanted to show you on this point, though I could continue indefinitely; otherwise, if in ignorance of this you blindly charged into this abominable crime of rebellion against God, I might myself pay the penalty for your perdition. For if I kept silent and refused to prevent this sin when I point out others of much less peril, I would appear to have condoned it.

22. To apply all this to any one of those kings who now energetically govern the kingdom of the north in four divisions:[37] I think that what I have said so far has not been pertinent to you, since I see that you are a Christian ruler and have not corrupted your administration with tyranny nor your power with madness—though I know that there are so many fine teachers in the Church that if, heaven forbid!, you were to be motivated by this kind of madness, they would sufficiently restrain you. Woe to them if they either fear you much, putting God second (though you are of the same condition, the same dust, as they, and can do nothing unless permitted, but have long been far below them in authority of power), or hate you much, though you are their sheep, son, defender, advocate, and patron, and perhaps (which, though coming from evil, is yet closer and more burdensome)[38] bound to them by some kind of oath, since that statement of Pope Clement, "to neglect a friend is no less than to hate him," is quite true. And quite rightly; for as one of the wise says: "Whoever can save a dying man, if he does not help him, is his killer."[39]

A worse woe yet threatens them [bishops] if, though they are watchdogs put over the Lord's flock to defend them with their bark from the constant attacks of wolves [Is. 56.10], they have been so mute that they have not only failed to save them, but have permitted one of their own number — though weak and useless and, being consumed with every kind of sickness, quite unfit for any service, yet one of their own company, also called "watchdog" and "shepherd" — to be strangled by anyone in their presence with their mouths damnably hardened by one of the same rank[40] into an unprecedented silence of the worst kind; for it has been truly said in a case of the same kind: "he has brought death upon a failing man, whoever did not save him when he could." For if there raged today such a persecution as there then was, ought they not to have gladly bowed their necks before the sword for a brother, or rather for Christ? But now, when everyone of you kings is so gentle and giving, so obedient to God, so friendly and kind to men, that he does not hesitate to offer firm and generous support to the prayers of any suppliant, and falls into any error more from ignorance than malice: what excuse can they offer, I ask, except that they entirely neglect themselves when they do not look to you and kill themselves when they desire perhaps that you be betrayed, since they allow it. In fact, I dare to say without hesitation (and I do not think I am wrong in this), that any bishop who is able, wants or dares to give you counsel, support and help as you slide into error of this kind, is one who either does not know God or denies him or wants to be, or is, a traitor to your life, kingdom, and honor both present and future, even though you do not know it, or he does not understand or remember the oath he made to you, when he so wickedly ignores the sentence, "Mark this, you who forget God, lest sometime he may seize you and there be none to deliver you" [Ps. 49.22].

23. But you, good king, most Christian prince, wisely protect yourself from the likes of these in respect of him, by whom each day you are raised to happy issue in your prayers, and make war hereafter on enemies, but preserve your citizens. Take, if you take, from outsiders; give to your own, and so that you may recognize who your own are, remember what kingdom you are called king of and what men's service you often use. Carefully consider the name of your office in Greek[41] and noting the difference between the Greek and Latin meanings acknowledge that you ought to support the people, not press down upon them. Be heavyhanded to the proud, gentle to the lowly, to all be kindly, friendly, discrete, generous, self-controlled, weighing your power in order to benefit people, concealing it so that they will not be afraid. Hear the words of Wisdom, "Mercy and truth protect a king" [Pr. 20.28], and, "Remove wickedness from a king's heart and his throne will be strengthened by clemency" [Pr. 25.5]. To this the common saying too seems concordant, that "he ought not to have power who does not have pity."

Therefore, love the good, as one of the wise rightly says, and pity the wicked. For, as another proverb says, it is best not to eradicate criminals but crimes.[42] Give alms both assiduously, as others do, and continuously. I would tell you also—but I am afraid of your anger; but whether you are angry or not, I do not dare to be quiet; for I fear what I heard in the Gospel yesterday: "Whoever is ashamed of me and of my words, of him will the Son of Man be ashamed when he comes in his glory and the glory of the Father and of the holy angels" [Lk. 9.26].

"What is it that you are trying to say?" you ask.

I say: examine from what source you dispense charity, to whom, for what reason, and how. From what source? That is, do not take away from another; for "whoever offers sacrifice from a poor man's substance, it is as if he sacrificed a son in the sight of his father" [Eccli. 34.24]. For though you are told to make friends for yourself by means of unrighteous mammon [Lk. 16.9], you are not told this so that you may unjustly take from one man what you may generously give to another, but so that you may know that riches, whatever their source, come from wickedness. For, as Jerome says, every rich man is either wicked or the heir of a wicked man.[43] For it is wicked that what God has conferred on all in common, some individuals should amass for themselves; therefore, either he is wicked if he amasses them, or he is the heir of a wicked man if he inherits from the amasser. That profit cannot come about without another's loss is proved both by the old proverb[44] and by daily experience. And so riches are called unrighteous mammon for this reason, because the man who, motivated by the spirit of greed (which is called *mammon* in Phoenician), collects riches, unjustly appropriates for himself what belongs to all in common;[45] just as, on the other hand, it is said of the man who distributes it and gives it to the poor, that "his righteousness endures for ever" [Ps. 110.3].

To whom should you make alms? First to your own, then to all in general. For what good is it to send your own ploughman away naked but clothe another's? Why should you make alms? First as duty; for you are the dispenser of the things which God conferred on you, or rather entrusted to you, and he entrusted much so that you might pay out much; then for the peace and stability of your kingdom; and finally for the past and continuing sins of you and yours; for many untoward things are done by your people with your authority, power, and protection which you are not even aware of. For, as someone says, the burden of a house is perilous and very onerous to the master himself, if the household is vicious in its ways.[46] And so that king, most powerful, strong, just, temperate, wise, and holy, whom you too ought to imitate, cried: "Who can discern his errors? Cleanse thou me from hidden faults, O Lord, and spare thy servant from others'; if they have not dominion over me, I shall be blameless and I shall be cleansed of great transgression" [Ps. 18.13–14]. Look how much he feared this transgression, which he called "great." For as was said before me, whatever proceeds from you comes back to you; also whatever pupils do wrong reflects on the master.

Finally, do not desire in the security of your charity to commit future everyday sins, but erase past ones and beware repeating past ones and future ones. By future sins, I do not mean those which I expect to see happen, but those which can happen in the future if they are not carefully avoided. I prefer to make this point with someone else's authority than my own, which is none beyond my office; for even if I could set it down worthily, I know it would not be received by you with willing heart. For it is difficult, as Gregory says, for one who is not loved to be heard with willing ear, even though he preaches right.[47] So let Aurelius of august memory come to my aid, soothing the ears of your heart with his ten-stringed playing:

> Train yourselves in mercy, in alms, in fasting and prayer; by these, daily sins are purged, which can only creep into our souls through human frailty; don't despise them because they are of less consequence, but fear them because they are more in number. Listen, my brothers; they are small, they are not great. They are not great beasts like the lion, so that one's neck is broken at one bite; but often even little beasts in large numbers kill. If someone is thrown into a place full of fleas, does he not die there? They are not indeed large, but human nature is weak and it can be destroyed by even the tiniest beasts. So also small sins; you consider that they are small, but avoid them all the same because they are many. How tiny are grains of sand. But if too much sand is put on a ship, it sinks it to destruction. How tiny are drops of rain; but do they not fill rivers and sweep away houses? So do not despise these small sins.

> But you are going to say: "Can anyone be without these?" You should not say this, because it is true that no one can. But merciful God seeing our frailty has given us remedies against them. What are these remedies? The remedies of alms, fasting, and prayer. They are three. But to speak true in your prayer, your alms must be perfectly fulfilled. What are perfect alms? To give from your abundant supply to him who has none, and when someone hurts you to forgive him. But do not think, brothers, that you should commit adultery daily and wash it away with daily alms. For greater sins like these, daily alms are not enough to wash them away. It

is one thing to change your life, another to maintain it. Those sins must be changed, so that if you were an adulterer, you are no longer; if you were a fornicator, do not fornicate; if a murderer, do not be a murderer; if you consulted an astrologer or other sacrilegious pests, now cease. Will you think that these can be cleansed by daily alms, if they do not cease to happen? I am talking of those daily sins which one commits easily with the tongue, such as a hard word or when one slips into excessive laughter or everyday trifles of this sort. There are sins even in things which are allowed. If you exceed the mean of lying with your wife beyond what is needed for procreating children, it is sin. For one marries a wife for this purpose—as also the tables where it is written down show—for procreating children. When you want to enjoy your wife more often than the need for procreating children requires, it is now sin; and sins like this are cleansed by daily alms. Again, if perhaps you exceed the mean in food, even those foodstuffs which are allowed, and take more than is necessary, you sin. What I am talking about are everyday sins, but they are sins nonetheless and not unimportant; but because they occur daily and are many, one should be afraid of ruin through their very number. Such sins, I say, brothers, are cleansed by daily alms.[48]

And again after a little:

Whatever you give to actors, to hunters, to base persons, you give to people who kill you. For they kill your souls just by their exhibition of pleasure. So the more you give, the more you are mad. But if you hoarded insanely, you would not be bearable. To hoard insanely is the mark of greed; to give insanely is the mark of extravagance. God wants you to be neither greedy nor extravagant; he wishes you to invest what you have, not to throw it away. You are competing to see who wins out in perversity, you do not attend to who is better. [And would that you did not give your money to such people and say, "We are Christians!"] You waste your money on the favor of the people, and you hang onto your money against the commandments. Look, Christ does not command you; he asks, he is in need. "I was hungry," says Christ, "and you did not give me to eat" [Mt. 25.42]. He wished to be in need for your sake, so that you might have a place to sow the earthly seed he gave and hence might reap eternal life.

You see, my brothers, the mercy of Christ. Thanks be to God that you have heard these mortal perils while still alive. Let none deceive you: God hates these sins and punishes them.

24. Well, best of princes, who would dare to say this to you today? Certainly if I had said it, you would either call me base or subordinate or say that I was mad. I would not be able to endure those jeering friends of yours; their insults against me would have no end. But the ancients had this kind of determined austerity, as well as a wonderful sanctity, so long as purest truth inspired them and the most fervent love fired them. Then too the issue was debated with men whose sudden anger need not be feared, but who rather were glad to be consulted on these matters, as the emperor Theodosius of merciful memory did in those times.[49] But now, alas, to fulfill the prophecy, "The Lord will cut off in one day the head and the tail that bends and bridles" [Is. 9.14], no one is found either among those flattering courtiers or in the Council of Elders who dares to point out to you your danger, at least with any skill, as Nathan did to David [2 Sam. 12.15]; though you are not—God forbid!—some son of Belial so that none can speak with you, nor—thanks be to God—do you wish, I know, to run in the number of those who are addressed (as though individually): "Consider the works of God, that no one can correct him whom God has disdained" [Eccle. 7.14].

And so one must fear that in the Judgment almost no one of this age can speak of his actions to the Lord with a view to receiving that eternal *euge* ["well done"], saying: "I spoke of thy testimonies before kings and was not put to shame" [Ps. 118.46]—when the sin of those (may God separate you from their company!) who said to the Lord God, "Recede from us" [Gen. 26.16], is made clear—when, that is, they did not listen to God's preachers, when he wanted to approach and walk among them and live and cohabit with them, that he might be their God and they might be his chosen people. So that you may avoid the latter kind of counsellor and obtain the former, let me continue in detail what I began about alms, so that thus I may inform you fully on the other points relating to the topic.

25. Take care how you give your alms, that is, humbly, not proudly, in case you chance to hear with Pharissees, "Amen, I say to you, you have received your reward" [Mt. 6.2]. For why should a man be proud about alms, when, even if it could happen—John and James testifying that it cannot, of whom one said, "We all offend in many things" [Jas. 3.2], the other, "If we say that we have no sin, we deceive ourselves and the truth is not in us" [1 Jn. 1.8]—that someone could be without sin, yet the money which he bestows is not his own. For it is called "justice" and not "charity" because the money which is given belongs to him that commands that alms be given; if you pay it out faithfully, you are crowned for justice; if you hoard it greedily you are condemned for injustice; if you give it away arrogantly, you are condemned for fraud—for it is fraud to hand out and distribute the goods credited to you not to the creditor's

will and account but to your own. But if one gives alms to atone for sins and
one takes pride in the fact, it is just as if some sick man poured out his resources
on doctors and, driven frantic, rejoices that in his sickness he has reached this
point of necessity, and counts as a mark of distinction what is a necessity, or
rather a madness, though it would be better for him to possess his wealth in
health than to waste it in sickness.

26. Don't object that I am only saying this because I want to downgrade
your good works in some name, as if I were asserting that there is no merit
in giving alms for one's sins. I do not assert that; in fact, I oppose it with all
my power. For what greater merit is there for a sinner than the blessedness which
is won by remission of sins? For "blessed is he whose transgression is forgiven,
whose sin is covered" [Ps. 31.1]. And so the man who dispenses charity for his
sins does not lose of his substance, since (as can rightly be seen) he has received
his substance for that purpose—if only he has acquired it not wickedly but with
work and skill. And if he has dispensed charity, the mercy of Him who has
come to seek and to save what had perished [Lk. 19.10] is not lacking for him.
As an example of blessed ones we have Zacchaeus, small in size but large in grace;
here he is, crying in inspiration, "Lord, a half of my goods I give to the poor;
and if I have cheated any man of anything, I return him fourfold" [Lk. 19.8].

"But who knows," you say, "whether he pleased Him by doing this?"

The evangelist adds: "But Jesus said to him, Today salvation has come to
this house, since he also is a son of Abraham"—a son, that is, in imitation, not
lineage. For just as Abraham left Chaldea by God's command [Gen. 12], so this
one beloved of God renounced greed. I repeat: he does not lose his substance
if he makes alms for his sins; rather, he wins pardon from it and through God's
grace puts out the flames of wrath and secures eternal life for himself. But he
loses his substance if he gives alms out of vanity; in fact, he wins punishment
and God's anger—punishment because of his deceit, anger because of his pride.
What deceit? That which we have already mentioned, of using resources entrusted to him as his own and distributing it to the fancy of his pride, though
by doing so he is going to receive nothing else from it (to count up the sum
total) than empty wind, that is, the favor of flatterers; and perhaps he does not
even find Him, whom he has sought with his every effort. But he does find
God's anger, which he provokes, and wins him as an enemy, whom he ought
to have won as a friend for that action. For "God resists the proud," though
on the other hand "He gives grace to the humble" [Jas. 4.6].

27. There is beside these a fifth kind of alms, and a sixth far excelling the
rest, forgiveness of a brother's transgression, and a seventh, when by pious preaching we provide the alms of the Word to the ignorant; this fifth one, after a
brief mention of the two following, I prefer to discuss not in my own words

but in the words of him whom I introduced earlier, so that you may not wish to say that I have made them up in my own interest.[50] This is what he says, in this sense and in the same words: "Mercy is rightly due to all the needy, but a greater feeling of charity is due, when affliction has cast people down from wealth and honor into the most abject state of destitution." There you have the lessons of alms-giving, in brief but sufficient for the wise. Let us pass on to the rest.

28. There comes to my mind a remark I heard from a child—but it is not childish, I think, since it is not only very shrewd but true. A boy in my hearing was jokingly asked by another, "Of whom is a man king?" Without a moment's hesitation he replied, "Of him who does his works." This caused me a good deal of surprise at the time, but someone told me later that it was a saying frequently used in assemblies. Applying it to God, I wanted you to hear it just as I chanced to hear it, so that, comparing it with the Lord's words, "No man can serve two masters" [Mt. 6.24], and remembering also the words, "He who sins is a servant of sin" [Jn. 8.34], and "Whatever overcomes a man, to that is he enslaved" [2 Pet. 2.19], you might not only escape the worst master, but, proving your nobility by your ways, resist him with head held high, and scorn to be subject to him, and strive to belong wholly to the best Lord, and by doing his works try to belong to no one else than Him who created you to be a man, or rather, to excel other men. For we know that you must be more careful than the rest to beware lest (as I fear) sometime *the king of Babylon* should *kill your sons*[51]—that is, waste the offspring (if you have produced any for God) of your good thoughts and deeds, or lose by your fault or example what is entrusted to you—*in Reblatha*, which is translated "this much," which is also called by the Lord the broad and spacious path of this life which leads to perdition [Mt. 7.13]—and when you do not raise your hand against him for your slain sons—by repenting, that is, for your transgressions, by changing your ways for the better and seizing the arms of justice—you be *bereft of your very eyes* by the course of overmastering wickedness, and you be thrust into prison by him, to grind like the mighty Samson weakened by woman's charms [Jg. 16.19], at the mill (in whose circle the wicked walk [Ps. 11.9]) of insatiable worldly care—in other words, take care that you be not bereft of the sight of reason, by which you ought to have looked after yourself and those entrusted to you and in your lack of forethought suffer the prison of eternal perdition. For this often happens to a wretched soul; while his virtues gradually fail day by day and he does not flex the biceps of his mind to recover to his former better state, his wretchedness grows and he reaches the point where sin reigns in his mortal body and he is so subjected in obedience to his lusts that, lacking the very light of reason, he neither remembers what he has done nor sees what he ought to do [Rom. 6.12].

Lest this happen to you, fight back at those lusts courageously and expel lust's dominion from your heart; take up the sweet yoke of Christ [Mt. 11.30] and his light burden; make your subjects fight for him under your provident rule, not so much by your commands as by your example, so that you may merit to reign with them for ever. And though it was suggested by a child, do not despise the wholesome lesson above, modest though it be, since you know that God was pleased even with the testimony of those not speaking, as today's solemn feast [the Feast of the Innocents?] shows us.

29. To continue now the course I have set myself: do not think that you are allowed to do everything that your heart's desire suggests. When you hear that "the heart of a king is in the hand of God" [Pr. 21.1], you should know that this can be taken in three ways (as far as I have been able to ascertain), of which the first applies to you, the second to your subjects, and the third (which is to be more firmly held and more carefully preserved) to all in general.

To speak on the first meaning, applied to you personally: you should know that your heart is in God's hand and that he directs it when you try to take to heart what he commands and to fulfill it in action. By "heart" we mean not that piece of flesh under the ribs called "heart," which we know as the source of the rivers of veins, but that power which produces our thoughts; this power, as the Fathers knew, and as great Father Augustine also said, is called "heart" because, just as the heart never stops moving as the pulse of the veins spreads around the body, so we never cease making mental movements.[52] And so we are commanded to love God with all our "heart" [Mt. 22.37], that is, this power of mind; from this "heart" come the terms "heartless," "mutual-hearted," "heart-in-heart," "empty-hearted," and "lazy-hearted." Sinners are told, "Recall it to heart, O transgressors" [Is. 46.8], so that they may understand that they are driven by madness, not ruled by the heart, when, wishing to establish their own will, they scorn to be subject to the will of God who loves only the good and the just, and that God does not turn their heart to good but that the adversary drives madness upon them.

Secondly, you should recognize that this is said so that no one may fear your anger more than is right or seek your favor; "For it is better to hope in the Lord than in princes" [Ps. 117.9]; also another prophet calls that man "accursed" "who puts his hope in man" [Jer. 17.5]. And again: "I the Lord form light and create darkness, I make peace and create woe" [Is. 45.7]. For when he says: "The heart of a king is in the hand of God, he will turn it wherever He wishes" [Pr. 21.1], he wants to tell everyone that you can achieve nothing in your anger except what He has permitted, can bestow nothing by your favor except what He has wished. Wherefore He desires that He alone be feared, He alone be loved, that to him nothing at all should be compared, still less preferred. This idea is beautifully expressed by the apostle in one succinct sentence: "Fear God, honor the king" [1 Pet. 2.17], as if to say: "Fear the Lord, honor his minister."

But why do I weaken the thought by changing a word? He said "Fear God, honor the king" quite deliberately I think. For you become "honored" by the attentions of others, being in yourself subject to the same human condition as they are. For as you well know, the capacity for power rests not in yourself but in the hands of your servants; thus those whom you frighten you fear the more yourself. But as Avianus says, a man ought to measure himself and be pleased by his own merits and not carry (that is, count) as his own the merits of another.[53] See, then, that He too is honored by your service, since you are honored by his commands. Do not use the goods of others and be ungrateful to your Bestower. For when the apostle in another passage said: "Be subject to every human institution," he immediately added "for the Lord's sake" [1 Pet. 2.13], that is, honor the created thing because of the Creator; be subject to whoever is appointed, not in love of the appointed but in love of the Appointer; "whether it be to the emperor as supreme," he goes on—understand "for the Lord's sake"; that is, so that he may recognize with how much reverence he himself ought to be subject to the Creator, since so much is paid by a creature similar in condition. What does the Lord of all rightly demand in his honor, when a servant seems to demand so much from his fellow-servants of a common nature? Fear God, honor the king. Fear the Lord who is whipping you; honor the king as the whip through which you are corrected by Him. Fear your patron, honor the staff by which you are sustained. Venerate your father and do not despise the master who trains you. Tremble at the voice of your father nor scorn the person of your protector.

30. For this is what it says: "The heart of a king is in the hand of God; he will turn it wherever he wishes" [Pr. 21.1]—just as "Everything which he wanted the Lord made in heaven and on earth, in the sea and in all the deeps" [Ps. 134.6], and "In his hands are all the ends of the earth" [Ps. 94.4]. Of this argument, this is the sum, this is the goal, if I am not mistaken: whatever is done, whatever had been done, whatever will be done, be it matter, be it body, be it action, be it passion, is done because God either disposes, wishes, orders, helps, accomplishes it, or approves, concedes, and permits it; it is his disposition and accomplishment; nothing can be done to anyone, either by man or angel or any beast or any breeze or any element or snake or worm or even fly, which can happen without his nod, wish, and power.

By this means also is accomplished what wise men have long held firmly defined, but which only souls that have been thoroughly cleansed can see (as the writer above finely says), namely that everything is so controlled by God's providence and justice that to no one can even death itself happen unjustly, even though perhaps an unjust person may seem to cause it; that in our natures too there is no nature that is not from him, and in our wills there is no good will which he does not support, no bad which he cannot make good use of. For (as the same blessed Augustine, most articulate teacher, very clearly remarks) we believe for certain that He commands all creatures by a double supervision, controling our natures so that they are what they are, and our wills so that they can do nothing without his command or permission.[54] Both of these aspects are clearly seen in the sufferings of Job, who is said both by the Lord's declaration and his own statement to have undergone his blows both in vain and not in vain. For the devil had taken everything from him and yet he said: "The Lord gave and the Lord has taken away; as it pleased the Lord, so it was done" [Job 2.3]. But it is certain that nothing pleases the Lord unless it is just. Even the adversary, who uniquely vaunts himself against God, attributes his strength not to his own malice but to the Lord's power, when he says: "Put out your hand and touch all that he possesses" [Job 1.11]. What the Lord himself says about tiny animals we have heard; for He says: "Are not two sparrows sold for a penny? And not one of them will fall to the ground without your father's will" [Mt. 10.29]. What wonder then if a king's heart is in the hand of God, or any other man's, when even the wing of the smallest bird is in His hand? What is not held in the hand of Him who measures the heaven in his palm and holds the earth in his fist [Is. 40.12]?

And so do not arrogantly wish to assign to yourself alone what is acknowledged to have been given to all creatures in general, that your heart alone is in the hand of God, since, if there is anything outside his hand, it is surely in perdition; in fact, I venture to say that it does not exist. "For you have hated none of the things which you have made" [Wisd. 11.25], was said to God; and the apostle said: "From whom are all things and through whom are all things" [1 Cor. 8.6]. To believe that His hand, that is, His power, is something else than Himself is not only foolishness but madness beyond compare. For to Him knowledge, ability, will, life, and understanding are the same as existence.

31. But in case you say that when you make a wicked plan, God turns your heart to it: know for certain that He wishes no evil nor does He impel anyone's heart to any crime, but it is the devil and one's own will that do so; this the same author as a little above says prettily—and none more prettily than he—in a letter to St. Jerome: "I am sure that the soul has fallen into sin by no fault of God, by no necessity of God's, but by one's own will."[55] But, as I have said many times, I do not deny, in fact I even affirm, that by His own secret—but never unjust—decision He sometimes permits even what He does not want. The reason why this sometimes happens, besides what I said about it above, the apostle gives in his letter to the Romans, saying, "Although they knew God, they did not honor him as God," and, "Therefore God gave them up to a base mind and to improper conduct" [Rom. 1.21,26–28]. In this quote I am careful to admonish you not to take it that God *gives* anyone up to evil. But it says "gave up," that is *permitted* to be given up, just as he says, "I have hardened the heart of Pharaoh" [Ex. 4.21], that is, have *permitted* his heart to be hardened. And David said: "If God arouses you" [1 Sam. 26.19], that is, *allows* you to be aroused; and it says of Shimei, "Let him curse; for the Lord has commanded that he should curse David" [2 Sam. 16.10], saying "commanded" for "allowed." We too in our daily prayer say "lead us not into temptation" [Mt. 6.13], that is, do not allow us to be led into temptation, and other similar things.

Therefore, when you do something good, ascribe it to God; but when some evil, attribute it to yourself. For he has been wont (as the earlier meaning also shows) — though with no merit of ours, yet out of his kindliness — to do many good things not only through our agency but even out of our malice, just as we on the other hand do many evils out of his benefits. This being so, no one should seek anyone's favor or fear anyone's power (even if there be some power claimed by a king) if he abandons God to do so. That power only is to be embraced, that solely to be feared, which compels one to be of service for whatever purpose He wishes, even those He does not love; in whose governance all things have not been left in their own power. In His praise a wise speaker most wisely declaims: "For you know, Lord, how to do good through the wicked, when you turn to succour what has been readied to injury, judging it better to turn injurious blows to good use than to cut out at the roots the causes of evils."[56] But if I were to clearly explain all the things which result from this, or if I wanted to gather all the things that can result, I admit that the week would run out, still less would a day suffice.

32. Coming to the third way of understanding this sentence, let me quote the author above to expedite this, so explaining in two ways that verse of the psalm where it is said by some people: "My soul is ever in *my* hands" [Ps. 118.109], and by some "in *your* hands"; without rejecting the former sense but taking the latter for himself (because the former seems to be said by people speaking as though with security, the latter by people presuming for God's pity alone), Ambrose says in these words: "The prophet knows where to place the protection of his soul and whence to look for help. He wants to set his soul in God's hands, because 'a king's heart is in the hand of God.' Whoever has controlled his own body and is master of himself, fit for future salvation, and has not permitted his soul to be distraught with the body's passions, who controls himself with royal power, is called 'king,' because he knows how to govern himself, so as not to be dragged captive into sin or carried headlong into vice."[57] And another says, as elegantly as succinctly: "If you are ruled by your heart, you are a king;

if by your body, a slave."[58] Likewise another says: "Do you wish to have honor? I will give you great command: command yourself."[59] This is why we commonly call a road which is ancient and straight "royal" and a door by which one enters a hall "royal"; which suggests that anything which proceeding straight shows others by its own example the way of a straight journey and the entrance of the blessed mansion is "royal." For as the etymology of the name itself also implies, taking the word "king" [rex] as derived from "straight" [rectum], it shows that the king must do nothing but what is straight, lest he be at odds with his title. What wonder is it, then, that any good soul ordering his body aright is justly called "royal," when even a road going straight is called "royal" and a door which does not lead astray but provides a proper entrance is called "royal"? The sentence from Proverbs, which regularly provides a source for great boasting for those weak in understanding, "Inspired decisions are in the heart of a king, his mouth does not err in judgment" [Pr. 16.10], is rather to be understood about the King of Kings, as another translation shows: "Nothing false will be said to the King and nothing false will come from his mouth," because, of course, as Bede also explains, he can neither be deceived by any lie nor ever tell a lie.[60]

In the joyfulness of that King is life, because all those who will merit in the final judgment to see His joyful face will be granted eternal life with Him; about these also the same [Bede] says, in explanation of the above:

> Why does it say that the heart of a king, and not rather of all men, is in the hand of God (since it is written that "In his hand are all the corners of the earth" [Ps. 94.4]), unless because he means that any holy person who has learned to win the wars of the vices in himself and gird himself with the armour of virtue is *king*? For just as the Lord fills the ends of the earth and of the air with manifold divisions of waters, and "covers the heights of the sky with water" [Ps. 103.3], so He inclines the heart of a king wherever He wishes; for just as He has bestowed shares of grace on both angels and men according to his will [1 Cor. 12.4], so He makes the hearts of whatever saints He wishes worthy of his gifts, and the Pelagianist has no place, because no one can be saved without God's grace.

33. So that this may now suffice, small though it is yet supported by the great authority of those who say it, I suggest to you some few teachings of one still living. And so leaving you I move on to other topics, pointing out first and foremost that it is essential for you to obey the laws. For you should recognize that your laws will be kept by men only if you too respect them. For, as Isidore says, you are bound by your own laws and should not yourself invalidate the laws which you pass on your subjects by acting against them.[61] The authori-

ty of your voice is just, if you do not let something be allowed to you which you forbid the people. As the proverb truly says: "He ought to fear many whom many fear."[62] To address you in Isidore's words: I urge you to know that "the chiefs of this world sometimes hold the pinnacles of power they have won within the Church so that they may strengthen ecclesiastical discipline through that power. But within the Church, powers would not be necessary, except the power to enforce through fear of discipline that which the priest cannot effect through the word of doctrine."[63] There, that is the power, and the rationale for it, that has been granted to you in the affairs of the Church.

34. Do not, therefore, slip from your duty; following the example of your predecessors restore God's churches, succour the monasteries, enrich them with your wealth; for there will be a time perhaps, when what you spend will be for your salvation. Ask which of the previous kings proceeded justly and wisely. Who sought the will of God, that he might further it? Who ruled the people justly? Who built churches, founded monasteries, set up hospices? Then embrace him, follow him, imitate him. Take care that there never be anyone who can urge you to take something from these institutions for your own use or that of your friends. Know for certain that if they will have reward for what is given, you will have punishment for what is taken away, that if they have won eternal life by giving, you merit hellfire by taking away. For the Church's property holds fire: you cannot make alms out of it nor eat nor drink of it; if you do, it is either by the Church's gift or your own sacrilege. What sacrilege deserves to receive from the laws, you do not need to be told, since you have been appointed avenger over crimes of this sort both by God and by the people. You should know that you have been appointed advocate of God's Church not master (for it would be senseless to be master of one's mother), her protector not steward (which is the bishop, as the Lord's teaching shows [Lk. 12.42]), her patron not minister (which the Lord said was the bishop also, as you can find in the Gospel if you read it [Jn. 12.26]). If you want to usurp more than has been commanded, you should fear that you will be compelled in the Judgment to pay the penalty for your invasion. Listen, the Lord said in the Gospel (to quote it verbatim): "Do not give to the dogs what is holy" [Mt. 7.6]. The same also cried in the law: "Whatever is offered to the Lord is sacred and belongs to the priests' right" [Lev. 27.21; Num. 18.9]. See then that neither you nor any one of them give to the dogs what has been offered either for feeding the poor or for the priests' livelihood.

35. Besides, love your wife, avoid consorting with concubines. That was the practice of former times because of the scanty population. But when the necessity recedes, so also what is done because of the necessity ought to cease, particularly since we know that a New Man has given new commandments [Jn. 13.34].

Choose such ministers and advisers as are proven to love *you*, not your property;[64] nor flatterers so much as friends, that is, guardians of your soul,[65] those,
that is, who will rebuke you in mercy and chide you and not soothe your head,
that is your mind, with the oil of deadly poisonous flattery. Beware also the
deceitfulness of informers; remember that many innocents have already been
betrayed by their lies, among whom, to mention but one because of the danger,
you know that Joseph was imprisoned though innocent [Gen. 39.20]. Realize
that if you are willing to believe them, they will never be lacking, as Hegesippus testifies.[66] See that you do not appear in your actions to be unjust, though
you strive in your edicts, letters, and decrees to be called just. And—if I may
venture to touch on something from the pagans ("Blush, Sidon, for the sea has
spoken!" [Is. 23.4])—note also what the poet says to you in his satire:

> Since the province after a long wait has received you its ruler, put a bridle
> on your anger and a limit on your greed and pity your poor comrades.[67]

Comrades, he says, not servants, not subjects. For, as the apostle says, "We are
all one in Christ" [Rom. 12.5]. But I will try to leave you [kings] now, lest
I seem to wish to criticize the ways of a certain person [King Hugo]; and at
the same time I ought to remember, even too late, that I should not try to swim
against the current.

36. Are you a queen? Much of the advice given above applies to you too; you
have many models to imitate, after Mary the Mother of Christ, Helen, the mother
of Constantine, and Radegund both queen and virgin, and Clotild, mother of
Clodoveus, and Placilla, mother of Theodosius, besides many others. If you are
willing to imitate these, you will both blessedly be able to win here the sceptre of
the present kingdom and very blessedly gain there, where they have already gone
before, the rewards of the heavenly kingdom, if only you do not disdain to follow.

Book V

[Rather examines the general moral duties of a bishop, soon turning
(c. 5 f.) to the faults of the bishops of his age. He attacks them for
their sumptuous living, their sporting and gaming, their lack of sexual restraint, their admiration of pagan literature, and their spiritual
shortcomings. He briefly addresses the clergy in general and, individually, each rank of the clergy, then the monk and abbot.]

I The Bishop
II The Cleric
III The Monk

1. Since I have undertaken to brave the nearby storms with a three-headed boat of volumes,[1] it may perhaps chance that someone will wonder why I have floated my bark on this flood of such unusual size (which by God's gift I have now swum through and so head my very unequal vessel for other territories). He should know that my action has been necessitated mostly by the inclemency of the weather as well as the unsuitability of the season; for the subject has called for not one or two ship's masters only but several, who may cautiously between the fractured reefs guide the ship straight through the seas. For though the vessel of my treatise might rejoice that it has now been delivered from the flood, yet the closeness of Charybdis advised putting arms once more to the sea-breaking oars. The whole work has been so storm-filled with these disasters, that it seems surprising, not that the master suffered shipwreck, but rather that he has come through alive — if indeed he has come through. But now with Christ's auspices from this point also let me approach a gulf of the sea, challenging though it be, for it is no small one. Perhaps this too has brought me some danger — may the helmsman who is Lord of all deliver my bark from it. Hence, summoning many companions while the sea stands moderately calm, let us pray that they take up stalwart oars and speed them through the waters, so that the ship may more swiftly reach the desired shore, returning the sailor snatched from death to our watching friends. Well then, give me now help, O God, and come into my heart, assuring that the route of my address may not turn aside from you in any way.

I.2. Are you a bishop? Let the name itself admonish you, let the office teach you, let its great dignity befit you; weigh the past, settle the present. Consider how lofty is the name which you bear, how sacred, how old it is. Pay heed to your sacrifice received in Abel [Gen. 4.4], your purity transferred in Enoch [Gen. 5.21–24]; remember that your office has been preserved in Noah through his justice [Gen. 6.8]. Realize that the ark is the Church, that the animals are the types of men in their various tempers, that the Flood is the world [Gen. 7.6], and guard against shipwreck. If ever you are given calm, see that drunkenness does not creep in. Ponder that Melchisedech offered bread and wine [Gen. 14.18] and so prefigured your royal priesthood. Abraham pleased God with his faith [Gen. 15.6], the faith in which you live — if only you live righteously — and he was a priest, as you are too — if only you are what you are called. What are Isaac and Rebecca [Gen. 24.67], if not the Lord and the Church? After being offered as God wished, he often offered victims, fed his flock, dug wells —

and if Philistines filled them in he did not wait to dig still more [Gen. 26.15–18]; toiling for himself, but instructing you daily to offer yourself to the Lord God with frequent victims — that is, with mortification of the flesh and contrition of the heart — on the altar of the mind, to commend your priesthood to him from whom you received it; to dig wells — that is, to draw out the Scriptures' inner meaning from their deepest mysteries and offer it to your rational flock, to prevent the thirst of ignorance slaying them. Jacob laying his head on a stone and then pouring oil on it and setting it up for a pillar [Gen. 28.18] — does he not very clearly show that, when you are slumbering at leisure from secular worries or actions, you ought to place the head of your mind on Christ in contemplation, so that you merit to watch the ascent and descent of the angels, that is, where God's words rise above the heavens, and where descending upon us they adapt to our humble level, so that they can somehow be understood. And finally you must understand that you must pour over the stone itself the oil of mercy and brotherly compassion, which is to ever exalt mercy above judgment [Jas. 2.13], so that you too may merit to receive it from the Lord; and that Christ himself should be the head of your actions, the beginning and end and hope of your whole glory, the crown, the pillar, and the blazon of a kind of unstormable citadel — that is, that remaining sober to your brothers but mentally withdrawing to God, you may glory in the Lord, if you glory in anything [1 Cor. 1.31].

Finally, Jacob supplanted his brother, fed his flocks, married two wives, of whom the elder was near-blind but fertile, the younger lovely but infertile [Gen. 29.17]: whom in this did he instruct more than you, who ought to mock the devil's wiles with wise forethought and to bear rich offspring of your works by the practice of an active life of pastoral concern, but through your intention of ethereal contemplation ever cling to God in seeking, knowing, and loving the things which belong to contemplation? For no rank or order do these two types of life alike suit more than the bishop's majesty.

What does Joseph's long damask coat [Gen.37.3, 23] signify if not the mark of your priesthood? When Job offered sacrifice for his sons on the eighth day and sanctified them with blessing in word and act [Job 1.5], whom especially did he instruct but you? And Moses himself is acknowledged as almost totally yours; for you will be able to find nothing in his words and actions which, if you understand it properly, you are not bound to imitate either in the letter or the spirit. What of Aaron and his sons, Joshua, Samson, and all the judges of Israel, and Samuel [1 Sam. 1.20] also, the one granted to his mother's prayers, brought up in the temple too and decked with all the symbols of ecclesiastical office? For the actions of the person, and the very names of the offices also, declare, define, and clarify your standards, as well as your rights and the symbols of your priesthood.

Let us come to David, that most holy prophet, powerful king, brave warrior, aggressive soldier, priest acceptable to God. What did he do, in all that we read of him, but teach you what to do, either spiritually or morally, even in the acts which interpreted literally seem reprehensible? He fed his flock, killed a lion and a bear, felled the giant with his slingshot, quelled the evil spirit with his singing of his psalms, spared his enemy, ran from his son, and danced before the Lord's ark [1 Sam. 17.49, 16.23, 24.7; 2 Sam. 15.14, 6.14]; what in all these actions, taking them spiritually and morally, do you understand but the courage and fortitude of a pastor of the Church, his application to prayer, his endurance, his practice of God's worship, and finally the doctrines of evangelism and priestly life? Solomon and all the kings of Judah and Israel, with all their good actions and with their unction too, whom have they especially taught but you? What need to run through the prophets when you ought to imitate the prophets, expound the prophets, even be a prophet, yourself? For, as the Lord testifies [Mt. 13.52], you ought to bring out of the treasure of your heart what is new and what is old. What does that brave band of Maccabees in all their victorious battles and successes do but advocate your daily battle of prayer, preaching, and pious action against visible and invisible enemies and promise you the palm and crown after your victory? All this from the Old Testament; recognize the antiquity of your ministry and embrace it.

3. In the New Testament, what tongue can list, what intellect can grasp, all the patterns of living that are available to you? Here I have a better homily for you, I think; I want you to study it in its entirety. Ponder the Scriptures, reread the books of God's words, look at the apostles, study the martyrs, attend to the confessors, contemplate, too, the virgins who have overcome even their sex along with the world. Ponder all those witnesses of God who, following Job [Job 10.17], "have been renewed against you"; make peace with these, while they walk with you in this path of the present journey, and win them over to you by giving in to them, and endeavor to teach others to do likewise; for not otherwise will you merit to be called what you are called.

4. Finally, look at the weight which crushes you, consider the burden which you seem to bear; and if you are already good, holy, righteous, and beyond criticism in everything, yet consider your flock, think of those committed to you; weigh carefully whether these too are also righteous. For you have to be presented to the Lord not alone, as others are, but with your whole flock,[2] and you will receive what is fitting not for your own person alone, according as you have acted [2 Cor. 5.10], but also for the actions of the whole congregation committed to you. But if (to pass over the graver faults and mention only the lighter) you should happen to be presented alone, where would be your "well done" [Lk. 19.23]? so that you will not be denied it, listen anxiously to the Book of Wisdom which cries to you and counsels you: "My son, if you have become surety for your neighbor, you have given your pledge for a stranger; then do what is useful for you, and save yourself; for you have come into your neighbor's power; go, hasten and importune your neighbor, give your eyes no sleep and your eyelids no slumber" [Pr. 6.1–4]. Hear also the Lord crying to you through Ezekiel: "I have given you as a spy to the house of Israel" [Ezek. 3.17, 33.7]; and the rest about you in the same book (than which nothing is more threatening). Hear also Jeremiah complaining in Lamentations: "The boys asked for bread and there was none to break it for them" [Lam. 4.4]. If at these words you still slumber and suffer from sluggish lethargy, then let that thunder of his judgment at least awaken you, when He says: "Wicked — and lazy — servant, why did you not give my money to a bank and at my coming I should have collected it with interest?" [Lk. 19.23]. This is what He said to the lazy and slothful.

5. What sort of a charge do we imagine awaits those who, though they have received no "money" in the form of learning, yet boast with shameless impudence of a talent not given them as though it had been given them? Who everywhere claim to be called pastors, though they know no pastures of life, and who want to appear as ministers of the Lord's substance, when they manifestly toil under the scourge of destitution? What does he pay out who takes in nothing? What does he give who has nothing? What does he dispense who lacks everything? Since the Father says, "Feed my sheep" [Jn. 21.17], on what, I ask, does he feed them, when he has himself not even found the very pastures yet? Though the steward ought to be faithful and wise, whom the Lord has set over his household, to give them the measure of barley at the proper time [Lk. 12.42], what does he dispense who in hunger and stupidity toils in lack of what ought to be dispensed? What barley does he hand out who does not even know what barley is? I greatly fear that this one, along with me, may happen to hear:

"Friend, what have you come for?" [Mt. 26.50] or "How have you entered here?" [Mt. 22.12]. By what gate? By what door? On what merits? On what passport? By virtue? Or wisdom? Or learning? Or perhaps the blamelessness of your life commended you, even if you had no skill at preaching? Did I not warn you (what you could have seen even with your eyes of the flesh), when I said: "Can the blind lead the blind? Don't both fall into the pit?" [Lk. 6.39]. How did you come to try what you were not able to do? How did you, who could not even carry yourself, come to take up so burdensome a yoke? How did you, who did not know how to take control over your own life, desire to become a judge of someone else's? How could the wise one not have persuaded you, saying, "About the thing which does not concern you, be not anxious"? Where did you have your ears when the words "Don't seek things higher than yourself" [Eccli. 3.22] were said? Where, when one indescribably superior to you, in wisdom, eloquence, and virtue, as one accustomed to talk with God, and superior not only to you but also to all who are under the heavens, was told: "The business is beyond *your* powers" [Ex. 18.18]? What effect on you did that Gospel sentence, "Cut it down since it still uses up space" [Lk. 13.7], have, since it did not move you, did not terrify you, did not make you leave off what you had begun? What did you think about yourself when you heard me complaining: "Holding the law they knew not me" [Jer. 2.8]? What did you hear when the Psalm said, "They knew not, nor did they understand, they walk in darkness, all the foundations of the earth will be moved" [Ps. 81.5]? When you in your ignorance did not know how to even keep yourself on a sure moral footing, let alone carry others, being so bound up in divers vices and passions of an earthly body, and with the burden of the whole house of God placed on you in addition, what did you think would happen but that the foundation would collapse and the whole structure above it surely fall?

6. These faults, though grave in themselves, are light in comparison with your more serious ones. To touch on those more serious ones, though not entirely dealing with them as they really are (for they beggar both description — not only mine but even that of the most eloquent — and assessment): what torments do we think await those who not only neglect to feed (even if they seem fit to do so) the flock entrusted to them, but to the infamy of the great name they bear, never stop driving themselves into the pit of vices? Who are continually active in secular games, wanton hunting and birding? who

in Teuton fashion are wont to hurl their darts[3]

and make the holy Scriptures quite out of fashion? who take off the clothing of God, put on that of the world, and do not even shrink from dressing in lay garments?

But why do I complain of lay garments, when I often see certain priests dressed (or, what is more accurate, *debased*) in girdles of foreign fashion — and even barbarian fashion, if I may say so — to the shame of the priesthood, so perverting its great dignity that they value more highly being

arrayed in Quirinal robe and Gabine cincture[4]

than in ecclesiastical habit. They would rather be called hunters than teachers, bold than meek, cunning than guileless, Maccabees than bishops! Would that they were real Maccabees in that battle in which Christ appointed them to triumph over the world and its princes! They play ball and do not shun the dice. They are more practiced in the gaming table than in Scripture, in the discus than in the Book. They know better

how much the ruinous ace takes away[5]

than what Truth that leads to salvation commands, prohibits and promises, and

what the lucky sixes bring[6]

than what they themselves should render to God. They would rather embrace actors than priests, players than clerics, drunken spouters than theologians, scoundrels than men of true worth, men of shame than men of modesty, mimics than monks. They yearn for Greek glories, Babylonian show, exotic decoration. They commission golden goblets, silver salvers, cups of even greater value, bowls, or rather conches, of greater weight and of a size unseen in any age. Their

broad-based decanter[7]

is tinged with gold, while the church next door is observed to be grimy with soot.

7. With its stuffed dishes their feast is remarkable both for its very variety and for its many courses. And among all the feasters he who is greedier is thought the more "sumptuous," he who is wittier the more "righteous," he who is richer the more "knowledgeable," he who is more propertied the more "famous"; he is the hero whose name is on everyone's tongue, whose praise is on everyone's lips. To be called *frugal* today is so despised in a bishop that it is reviled even among monks—though generosity (charitably done) by those most liberal in their munificence not only do I not criticise but rightly acclaim it with the highest praise. A bishop also seems to live without purpose if he has no money.

Then, besides, there is ribaldry, then intemperate laughter, often at the expense of those who in their naivety give up those delights in fear of God. Then "the cithern in feasts and the lyre" [Is. 5.12], as the prophet also says; but none remembers the Lord's work nor the woe promised to those acting like this. Then there are the symphony and all kinds of music, the bawdry of singers, the plague of tumblers and dancers, all the talk which belongs to the matter of men and not of God, of the created and not of the creator, of the present world and not of the future, of the worldly master and not of the heavenly Lord. Then the former is celebrated, the latter forgotten; the former's name is sworn to, the latter's not even remembered; the former's health is drunk, the latter in thirst is not even given a drink; the former's stomach is gorged with overeating, the latter, perhaps even in prison, a pauper, lacking a crumb, is not refreshed; the former is advanced in power, the latter is demoted; the former's memory is toasted in the first place, the latter's not even in the second. Besides all this dogs run around the very table, horses gallop, or rather fly on their swift feet, the falcon wings his headlong way, the hawk snatches the raucous crane.

In all this there is no prophet, no apostle, nor any teacher near, the canons are nowhere, the teachings of the Fathers faroff, the decrees of pontiffs distant, the suffering, frugality, humility, poverty, and deeds of the saints remote from the memory of all. Proud Dives is not presented for viewing, nor Lazarus licked, or rather nibbled, by the tongues of dogs [Lk. 16.21]. Balthazar's death for such luxury [Dan. 5.1–4] is not even remembered. No thought comes to mind of the ephah with the cover of lead in the prophet [Zech. 5. 8–9], which for such vices was borne aloft on the wings of a kite[8] in the land of Sennaar, nor does anyone take note of the camel's hump and the eye of the needle [Mt. 19.24]. None remembers the arrival of the Lord's Day. With mouth stuffed in feasting and tongue loosened in bawdry, no one cares to mark someone's recent death with tearful eyes, or to remember that for that reason God commanded us at all times to watch and pray [Lk. 21.36]. It escapes everyone's notice that it was on the day of the feast of the elder brother that the sons of Job were destroyed [Job 1.13–15]. None remembers Lot leaving Sodom [Gen. 19.17] nor Noah entering the ark [Gen. 7.7].

Finally, those canons are consigned to oblivion which require that all the revenues of the Church, which are "the Lord's sacred offerings" [Lev. 27.21; Num. 18.9], be divided into four parts; if this is done properly, there will be no wherewithal for the cup even, let alone the mixing-bowl, punchbowl or conch, or — to mention something even more remarkable (and would that I were exaggerating!) — *cauldron*; and even the daily bread, not to speak of the banquet prepared with regal luxury, will often have to be awaited from God, however late it may be, as did Daniel shut in the den [Dan. 14.30]. I would be lying, did I not have the evidence of so many churches destroyed around the world, of widows, orphans, refugees, countless paupers, prisoners, people in chains, imprisoned, blind, lame, feeble, sick, monks and nuns, people oppressed and imprisoned for their debts. Finally, if anyone can give support or help to any of all these in their time of need and refuses to do so, he will be seen to incur the damnation of the fraudulent steward [Lk. 19.23]. It has been truthfully said by one of no mean authority that any Christian who does not help others to the best of his ability will be *judged*, but a bishop, if he has neglected anyone, will be *condemned*.[9]

8. Yet even if these expenses were all fully and equitably met, they would still not stand in the way of luxury.[10] Ought the teacher to long for what he

teaches others absolutely to avoid? What if the sentence of the apostle were cast at him which says: "While you preach against stealing, do you steal?" [Rom. 2.21]. What if he were struck with the Lord's words when He said, "Cast out first the beam from your own eye" [Mt. 7.5], and "Doctor, heal yourself first" [Lk. 4.23]? Where will be the words of the same Apostle, "I beat my body and subdue it, lest after preaching to others I myself become reprobate" [1 Cor. 9.27]? For, as has already been said by a most skilled and saintly teacher before me, "He whose life is despised, it follows that his teaching also is despised."[11] What does such a preacher say to himself privately when he says to others publicly: "Not in feasting and drunkenness" [Rom. 13.13]; and: "You are humbled under the mighty hand of God" [1 Pet. 5.6]; and: "Touch not the world nor the things of this world" [1 Jn. 2.15]; and: "Whoever wishes to be friend of this world is made enemy of God" [Jas. 4.4]? Granted that he does not want even to teach this, still less do it, what when he is required to cry, "Lift up your hearts"?

9. But leaving the form, let us with a stride move on to the type for a while: drunk with potions of wine, so that in every point (except in the worship of idols—though idolatry is not lacking in their other vice, avarice itself [Eph. 5.5]) they seem like those of whom it was said: "The people sat down to eat and drink and rose up to play" [Ex. 32.6]; abandoning the high and lofty pulpit,[12] they climb into carriages, so to speak, and gigs, and mount their foaming horses decorated with golden bits and silver neckbands, with German trappings and Saxon saddles, and hurry to whatever sport their drunkenness suggests. Then none thinks of the Lord sitting on his ass, mighty and strong in battle [Jn. 12.15; Ps. 23.8]. Then they yearn to outshine even kings in worldly glory, rather than to imitate the poverty of the apostles, to exceed the pleasures of the rich rather than to follow the saintliness of the fishermen.

10. Next, their couch is wonderfully decorated and inlaid with golden pieces, the supports are colored with woven silk, the very mattress is covered with the best cloth, even the stool is dressed with Gothic tapestry. In all this they forget the cradle of our infant Lord, the very swaddling clothes and the manger itself; far from their memory is He who had nowhere to lay his head [Lk. 2.7, 9.58]. Then, when their sleep is broken by anxious cares, rolling around in that delightful bed and quite unable to rest, for their morning hymns they offer up a kind of murmur, fit rather for insult than grace, for scorn rather than acceptance, for execration rather than sympathetic hearing.

11. When it comes to clothing, they are dressed in foreign rather than native garb, as I have said, with their legs smoothly rounded, as though rather fashioned on a lathe than by hand, as it were, so that either one could better be called a column than a calf. The whole body is groomed with such care that the very overcoat, which ought to be made only for warding off cold, the thicker the better, though itself made of the finest cloth, has a border of another material which would be better than the best that could be found; its breadth is not limited to that of others but exceeds it to the measure of a cubit. If any kind of garment is worn on top of this, it is fitted to it with such care and conceit, that the very thing which it was supposed to cover beneath enchants the eye either by its delicate finery or by some trimming, even with loss of material. The skirt, reaching as far as the feet of the person sitting, and fitted with a golden pin, reveals also a golden belt at its top, providing all eyes with a mighty pang of ambition, so that in this alone the saying can seem fulfilled that "when the wicked man is arrogant, the poor man is set afire" [Ps. 9.2]. Then you may see some wear a fur cap instead of a hat and a Hungarian bonnet instead of the priest's cap, or use the sceptre for a cane and think not of the apostle's words, "Not in costly attire" [1 Tim. 2.9], nor remember those of the Lord, "For the rest give alms" [Lk. 11.41], and "What is exalted among men is an abomination in the sight of God" [Lk. 16.15], and of Him who will say, "I was naked and you did not clothe me" [Mt. 25.36], although He himself through his precursor commanded that one cloak, not only out of a thousand, but even out of two, be given to a man in need [Lk. 3.11].

12. Then, after delivering the Mass rather than singing it — or, what's worse, sometimes totally neglecting it — and receiving the bread and wine (which to be sure would be sufficient for a royal feast) — there being none who wants to remember, either literally or metaphorically, the words, "Woe to the earth whose princes feast in the morning and whose king is a slave" [Eccle. 10.16]), they mount their Falerian horses[13] once more (not of course the same ones as yesterday, lest by chance they be cheapened by overexposure!), decorated with golden collars and with silver bits of such weight that only the strongest horses are capable of carrying them, whose (to describe it more ornately in the words of the poet)

golden chains hang dropping from their breast; in gold caparisoned they champ yellow gold with their teeth,[14] and they even flex their limbs on the grassy wrestling-place, vie in sports and grapple on the yellow sand[15]

or

train on their horses, handle their chariots in the dust, or bend eager bows or hurl supple darts with their arms[16]

or, to return to our subjects, practice similar sports; or abandoning the affairs of heaven, they deal with and care for those of the world alone; they who ought to decide ecclesiastical questions settle how the state should be run.

And would that they handled nothing else there, would that this were all that offended God—it would perhaps be pardonable though not commendable. Then what happened lately would not have happened: that is, at this very same time, almost a year ago, they sought to be compliant so that they should not also happen to fall into that state which they had been wont to sing of in the same verse: "He will incline and fall, when he has mastered the poor; for he has said in his heart, God has forgotten, he has turned away his face so he may never see it" [Ps. 10.10–11].

For as calamity came upon him [Rather] and his misfortune grew, they not only thought that he had been abandoned by the Lord, but even kept repeating it, to such an extent that on the very feast of the Mother of God some souls were most severely rebuked because they had given him the kiss of peace in Church (which is usual in the ritual of the Mass); for, blessed and wise themselves!, they thought that he had been damned by God not because he was a sinner but because he had been caught—although guilt is not established by the penalty but by the case, and, according to Aurelius of august memory, the pain of the guilty is a kind of absolution of their sins.[17] And so on the next day[18] none of their promises was made good in fact, yet that chief one [the archdeacon], in whom lay all the hope of a good outcome, sent word through messengers, frequently, that he [Rather] was not to deviate from his plan in any point, promising that he would see everything through to a good end, if he only stood firm in the promised agreement. This he [Rather] did, to his own disadvantage, so it seems and so it can be thought (but in true and clear fact to his own good,[19] as should be believed). He also asked him to send to him at once some leaders of the city. When the other did this, he put a noose, as it were, around his own neck. For with them a deed was done which could in no way escape that Eye which is present everywhere; may the Almighty mercifully either punish it or remit it in this world, lest He chasten it severely in the next.

What more? I can indeed tell a very long story of this, but here I think it should be swallowed because of that danger, which I remember mentioning in the preface of the above book, namely, that the truth itself will generate some hatred for me.[20] So let the nefarious deeds of these men be suppressed; or else, if perchance they are revealed in indiscrete report, the names of the men also may have to be produced, which would lead to great friction and turmoil. Such is the present state of affairs; yet none is found who, in respect of God at least, will stand up for the poor, pray for the damned, who will make the cause of orphans and widows or any of the afflicted his own; this is proved also by this man's affliction, which is relieved by no one.

[Letter of the Same]
Rather in exile to Wido and Sobbo, archbishops, and other fellow-
bishops sitting on the Council.

My Lords, pray take up and deign to read this, instead of hearing me in person. For perhaps it will not be irrelevant to your present business.

13. Nowhere are there councils of the Church, nowhere synods and conventions; ecclesiastical law neither approves nor reproves, accuses or excuses, defends or opposes anything, but everything is commanded, executed, and allowed
by secular might, power, and decision, justly or unjustly; I too am evidence
of this condition, in that I was not condemned by my fellow-bishops but was
sent into exile by lay authorities with no prior hearing, with no advocate to
"build up the wall of my defense and stand in the breach for me, putting himself
as a battlement for the house of Israel and standing in battle in the day of the
Lord" [Ezek. 22.30, 13.5], that is, when the world rejoices and the Lord is dishonored, as far as they are concerned, since this happens not on one occasion
only and not on the testimony of one man only, but often and on the testimony
of very many.

For it was not without purpose that Lazarus lay before Dives' door, but so
that Dives might be damned for not providing what Lazarus lacked in his torments. For since the Lord says in the psalm: "I tested you in the waters of Contradiction" [Ps. 80.8], where, I ask, can or should you show your resolution
for strong devotion and pastoral fortitude, if not where there is — not just any
but — the greatest "contradiction"? And since none is crowned but he who competes rightly [2 Tim. 2.5], from where, I ask you, can he expect or seek a crown,
who runs away when the battle is near and does not anywhere make his fight?
Well? Even though victory cannot be won, is that good reason for always offering the enemy one's back? Have we not often seen, when a soldier has been
pierced through and through, the children rewarded for the father's bravery,
constancy, and devotion? Our battle is far different, but its dangers are greater;
for he who flees dies eternal death, but the fallen soldier, provided he does not
fail in devotion, is not only raised again, but also is eternally crowned for his
wounds. But to him who wins through to victory there is the same crown as
shield, as arms, as victory, namely, God himself, who is all of these things, who
protects those whom He rouses, crowns those whom He protects, raises those
whom He allows to fall, rewards those whom He lets be victors.

For this battle is between no others than God and the adversary; He fights,
He is shut in and besieged, He stands to, He defends the walls; and the victory
comes to us, it is written up and credited to us. Why should anyone show such
listless courage, when his battle is not his own but God's, to such an extent

that he need not even be anxious what or how he is to speak—provided, as I said, that he lack not the devotion for wanting to speak? Why should anyone be afraid, when the very same who is rewarder is also protector and finally also warrior? For He is so much present when you fight, so with you when you battle, that when you are thought to be struck, it is He not you who is struck. For this is what you heard today, as you also read yesterday: "Whoever touches you, it is as though he touches the pupil of my eye" [Zech. 2.8], and "Whoever spurns you, spurns me" [Lk. 10.16].

14. Do not, therefore, pander to the enemy, if you wish to please the General, for you will not be able to win over the latter, if you refuse to dissociate the former from yourself. For the apostle says, excepting no one: "All who wish to live righteously in Jesus Christ suffer persecution" [2 Tim. 3.12]. So a person seems unwilling to live righteously in Jesus Christ who does not suffer persecution for Jesus Christ; he even refuses to be in the body of Christ, as has been said before me, who is not willing to bear the world's hatred with his head.[21]

You say: "I do not dare—the world[22] is dangerous today."

The Lord says: "Out of your own mouth do I judge you, wicked servant" [Lk. 19.22]. For you have forsworn your service if you have lost your courage. Why then did you take up arms? Why then did you enlist? Why did you want to be called shepherd and then decide to run when the wolf came? Why did you take up the staff if you were afraid to face danger? Why did you accept the wage if you did not dare defend the flock? With what conscience do you eat of the milk of the flock if in face of the thief you are afraid either to raise your voice or alert the master or rouse up the dogs? Why do you put on the sheep's wool, if you are so afraid of the goat among the lambs, let alone scorn the roaring lion or bear? Why have you taken my money, if you were afraid to give it out, though able to do so? And why do you defy me so bravely, by so timidly holding yourself subject to him whom I hold under my feet?

"The world is dangerous," you say.

Is there then a storm at sea, if the ship is in danger [Lk. 8.22–25]?

"What do you want me to do?"

Show why you have taken up the oar; surely not to sink your head in bilge-water, doomed man? Rather exert your strength, fight bravely, sail with courage; the harbor is at hand, there lies in the ship, though sleeping for you, One whom the sea and winds obey [Mt. 8.27].

15. "I am afraid," you say, "of offending my lord."

Against this the apostle says: "If I were still pleasing men, I should not be servant of Christ" [Gal. 1.10]. For what will offence to your lord do to you?

"He will reproach me, perhaps, take away what he has given me perhaps."

You would rightly fear all that if you did not have His promise: "Rejoice and be glad; for lo, you have great reward in heaven" [Mt. 5.12]; and if you did not know the words of the apostle: "Who is there to harm you if you are zealous for what is right? But even if you do suffer for righteousness' sake, you will be blessed; but have no fear of them" [1 Pet. 3.13–14].

"I fear something more," you say.

What?

"To die."

That is to say, "There is a lion in the way, I shall be slain in the streets!" [Pr. 22.13]. But hear the Lord: "Not a hair of your head shall perish" [Lk. 21.18]. Hear also a servant of that same order you belong to, that is, Augustine, oft cited here: "Be afraid of death," he says, "if you are able not to die." Hear another: "Whoever is born of man is also going to die." Hear also the Apostle: "For I am ready not only to be imprisoned but even to die for Jesus Christ" [Acts 21.13]. Hear also another—a pagan, to your shame: "More tolerable is the man who orders you to die than he who orders you to live wickedly."[23] A king's anger can kill you; can his favor make you deathless?

But do not be mistaken, I beg you. It is not a king who kills a person, but he who says, "I will kill and I will make live" [Dt. 32.39]. For if, but for him, anyone could kill anyone, the fiery furnace would not have saved the three young men, nor would the starving lions have spared Daniel; Susanna too, condemned by the laws (or so it was thought) would not have been set free so speedily. Jonah too, swallowed by the whale, would not have been vomited up by God's command. For what is there quicker to kill than fire? What more ready to snuff one out than the fury of lions? What harder to release than one condemned by a law which knows no mercy? What more voracious in swallowing than the seadepths, or, rather, the gluttony of a seamonster? Yet none of these, though having the might conceded by God's will, could avail aught against God's protection. Hence we regularly chant to God in church these fine words about one of them: "The fire forgot its strength, for your servants to be freed unharmed."

16. Whether the case is such as I have said or not, you can also consider, if you wish, from the words of Cassiodorus:

Besides, it seems remarkable that incorporeal substance has been bound into very solid limbs, and that two substances so different have been gathered into one conformity, so that the soul can neither dissociate itself when it wants nor hold itself in the body when it recognizes its creator's order. All things are closed to it when it is commanded to stay put; all things are rendered open when it is ordered to depart. For even though a bitterly painful wound is inflicted, life is not lost without the creator's command, just as it is not saved without his gift.[24]

Though led by reason itself, we can understand from our very selves that this is unshakably so, yet we utterly cast out our manly resolution and assume a womanly cowardice. We are disdainful of God and subservient to the world, slothful and effeminate, insatiably eager for vainglory too, we provoke each other, envy each other, we are negligent and unblessed, we swell with pride, we are empty of goodness, we are given up to the pleasures of the flesh, haughty to our brothers, fired with the torches of greed for material possessions, but slow and ineffective in amassing the wealth of the virtues. While we strive for vainglory we lose— wretches alas!—the glory which comes from God; and while regrettably we are earnest to rise arrogantly over our brothers, we become subject to the world over which we ought to have control. And despising the Lord we endure a slave lording it over us; and we who ought to trample on the serpents, scorpions, and all the power of the enemy and have been granted strength to do so [Lk. 10.19], are ourselves daily trampled on in reverse order. So that we can fear that sometime what we read was said in Job will be fulfilled in us too: "He will flee from an iron weapon and will fall on a bronze bow" [Job 20.24], and "Who fear the frost, on them will fall the snow" [Job 6.16]. This happens when temporal anger is feared, and eternal wrath is incurred; when earthly peril is feared, and there rushes down that from above, the inescapable judgment of God's anger.

17. But if, rather, that honor of ours, by which we have not only been made in God's likeness, but also been given the duty of commanding all creatures under heaven, we had been willing to justify by our ways—that is, by being subject to Christ, like those who have gone before us, and disdainful of the world, carrying one another's burdens, as the apostle instructs [Gal. 6.2], helping each other in turn, yielding honor to each other, all of like mind in the Lord, fervent in spirit, zealous in charity for the house of Israel like Elija [1 Kg. 19.10], instructing in doctrine, encouraging each other with mutual support, guilelessly supplying each other according to their necessities, fulfilling our office conscientiously, comforting each other with gladness, having genuine love of God and of our brothers, hating evil, clinging to good, reciprocating our brother's love in turn, not being haughty but associating with the lowly [Rom. 12.7–17]—I confess, not only would we not fear anyone, but we would even be feared by all.

But as it is, for shame, the prophet's words are fulfilled in us: "Each will devour the flesh of his arm, Manasses Ephraim and Ephraim Manasses, and together they are against Judah!" [Is. 9.20]—that is, the glorious Church, as God says— biting each other we are consumed in turn; we are divided and forsaken, each by each. For ever-truthful Truth does not lie saying: "Every kingdom divided against itself is laid waste" [Mt. 12.25].

Irrefutable also is the remark of one who did not know God, who said that in concord small estates increase while in discord even the greatest are dissipated.[25] The apostle's warning should also be kept in mind: "Let us then pursue what makes for peace and let us in turn preserve what makes for upbuilding. He who thus serves Christ is acceptable to God and approved by men" [Rom. 14.18–19]. Again: "Would you have no fear of him who is in authority? Then do what is good and you will receive his approval" [Rom. 13.3]. And: "For it is God's will that by doing right you should put to silence the ignorance of foolish men" [1 Pet. 2.15]. And another's warning: "When the ways of a man please the Lord, he will turn his enemies also to peace" [Pr. 16.7]. And the Lord's words through the psalmist: "If my people had heard me, if Israel had walked in my ways, I would perhaps subdue their enemies with no trouble" [Ps. 80.14–15]. Again in Jeremiah: "If you had walked in God's ways, you would have lived in eternal peace" [Bar. 3.13]. Through Moses also: "Lo, I will send my angel to go before you and ever guard you; only observe and hear my voice and I will be your enemies' enemy and will strike those who strike you" [Ex. 23.20–22].

18. But such vengeance should not be sought at all by perfect men, but whatever is good should be done for the glory of God; adversities should be borne for love of Him rather than vengeance desired. But we, on the contrary, want to avenge ourselves rather than be avenged, to defend ourselves rather than be defended by God; and—since we are unable to effect this—we rush to enter into a pact with the enemy themselves and collaborate with them in evil, rather than to raise our hearts and hands to God and invoke Him as our protector and seize arms against the internal snatcher [Satan], who is never better defeated than when the External Snatcher [God] is loved; and not unlike those who for health, which can only be given by God, make prayers sacrilegiously to springs or trees for worldly goods, we earnestly pray to the earth itself rather than to Him who made earth and heaven.

And so that we be not cheated at all in the desired outcome of our prayers, we abandon utterly Him who put us in control of the world, and abandoning all our office but the name, we ourselves serve the world so much more than others, that whereas others try to render to God what is God's and to the world what is the world's, we render to the world what is God's—that is, all kinds of love and worship—and to God what ought to be the world's—that is, every kind of scorn and contempt; and, to bind ourselves more tightly to the world (in case, that is, we should ever be despised and go unrecognized by it), abandoning our worship, discipline, and habit, we adopt the world's practices and desires and even its dress, to such an extent that we seem to differ from men of the world only in our tonsure and in the fact that we do not take wives as they do, and in the fact that there are certain lauds which we appear to render to the Lord (but only with the mouth, and that rarely), and in nothing else. So that it could be believed that it was about us living in this present age, alas, that the prophet said: "And it shall be, as with the people, so with the priest" [Is. 24.2], and what another deplores in Lamentations: "How the gold has grown dim, how the finest color is changed! The stones of the sanctuary lie scattered at the head of every street" [Lam. 4.1]; and we can also grieve that a large group of stars have fallen from heaven to earth [Rev. 6.13], that is, a large number of priests, whose works ought to have shone among men so that God may be glorified, follow only those who were expelled from heaven to the abyss [Mt. 5.16].

19. Nor does it seem superfluous in their case to add at this point a short but wholesome sentence of a certain priest close to our time: when he saw his bishop (horrible to tell) gaming at the tables, he shook his head and twittered in derision; seeing this, the bishop was angry — and quite rightly, if he was angry at the one he ought to have been angry at — and immediately threatened him with prison, if he did not at once say where canon law forbad him to gamble. The other, pretending fright, since the bishop had ready the rope with which to tie the runaway, threw himself at his feet and said: "Pardon me, lord; for I am struck by such fear that I cannot even remember the first verse of the first psalm, still less cite any of the canon decrees. But I beseech you, pious lord, remind me of it, since in my fright I have forgotten it." Then the bishop, with all the bystanders, dissolved in laughter and on the priest's insistence quoted the first and second verse, saying: "Blessed is the man. . ., but his delight is in the law of the Lord, and on his law he will meditate day and night" [Ps. 1.1–2]. Catching him by the words of his own mouth, the priest in reply instructed the bishop as follows: "Then for the rest of the time, holy father, it is fine to play at the tables."

I decided to tell this story here, so that you can clearly understand in this brief sentence both what you ought to do and what you ought to avoid. But I will try to leave you now, so that I will not seem to be stupidly watering the river when the garden is dry; for I am also afraid that one of these who, according to the poet,[26] turn black to white when they say good is bad and bad good, thinking darkness is light and light darkness, and believing truth falsehood and falsehood truth, may say to me: "You will die because you have spoken lies in the name of the Lord" [Zech. 13.3]. I will rather proceed to other things closer to my calling and therefore more fearsome.

20. Perhaps you have been promoted from a monk? Look from what and to what you have come, that is, from the greatest to the great, from the greatest quiet of the monastery to the great toil of the world, from the calm of a safe bay to the squalls of frequent storms. And so sail circumspectly, you who refused to stay in happy safety in the harbor; try, strive, be earnest to achieve something more sublime than the rest, or rather, more humble and more perfect, knowing that you are pressed by two burdens. For you are required to render to the monk what is a monk's and to the bishop what is a bishop's. See that no one can ever persuade you to change your habit, even if he wants to approve this from precedents of the ancient Fathers, excepting when you come to that divine ministry which requires its own proper vestment; and at the time too when it is not worn on the body, let it not vanish from the heart. Hear the apostle's words: "Incurring damnation for having violated their first pledge" [1 Tim. 5.12]. So temper your eating with fasting, your bodily delights with prayers, and your worldly joy with tears.

But if perhaps you have been promoted from abbot, or, as often happens, have already been in charge of two or even more monasteries, ponder on the cause of this change; and do not spare yourself, I beg you, do not deceive yourself, do not flatter yourself, do not try to hide from yourself what you know best of all. For, as Augustine says, there is no hidingplace from God, even though the one trying to hide is very deceitful;[27] He is not unaware, just because you pretend that you are unaware; so, acknowledge it in humility rather, if you wish Him to pardon you.

The first reparation, as one of the pagans says, is that no guilty person is absolved when judge himself.[28] Think, therefore, whether you have supervised these properly; if you find that you have, regret that you did not persevere in it; if not, for that too let the tears not cease each day in all your life. Remember that you are pressed by as many burdens as the appointments you have been honored with and handled unworthily, being ungrateful to the Bestower; and though you ought to have benefited many people, you have been the cause of some progress to very few, or perhaps even to none at all; in fact, abandoning this monastery, you have migrated from here to another, and have brought no harvest to the pile of the Lord's threshingfloor, either from this brotherhood or from that one, or even in fact from yourself. All the sheaves you ought to have carried you will be required to pay for in the judgment.

21. Do then what I suggest, while there is yet time. While there is still time left for sowing, while still the steward waits, while the keeper of the threshingfloor threshes, does not throw out the chaff, does not pick up the winnowingfan, while he does not yet blow away the chaff: work, sow, gather, give yourself no holidays, grant yourself no entertainment, no rest, no time for leisure, but press on in every way with the sowing, so that you be not short of harvest to bring to the threshing; think of it, too, with your mind's eye all the time, attend to it; ponder daily on it in case the chaff overcome you or there be too many weeds; remember that the wheat must be stored in the granary, but the chaff must be burned in inextinguishable fire [Mt. 13.30]. So fire anew those near you to God's worship with frequent exhortations, and those far away with frequent letters. *Accuse* and *rebuke* [2 Tim. 4.2] their former sloth (and your own too) and invite and charge them, with yourself, to rise up, come alive again, raise their spirits, repair their industry, summon their strength, recharge their constancy, be rekindled in faith, hope, and love for God; and know that you should not accomplish this in words alone but much more in your actions. For the sentence of Pope Leo is true, that examples are stronger than words and it is better to teach by action than by voice.[29] Assist them carefully also in their temporal afflictions. If as abbot you embezzled anything, as bishop restore it. If you remember that you failed in anything when you were abbot, do not be afraid as bishop to make it good.

22. In doing this, do not be afraid that anyone will say that you have once been a sinner or an embezzler. See only that you do not appear abusive to Christ, rebellious to God, or abominable to the Holy Spirit. This happens if you neither wipe out your past sins nor atone for your present by emendation; rather, when this is said about you, rejoice humbly in God, if it is truly said of you with the others: "You were once in darkness, but are now light in the Lord; and such were some of you; but you have been washed, you have been sanctified" [Eph. 5.8; 1 Cor. 6.11]. And so, if someone maligns, criticizes, curses or abuses your action, take firm hope and solid refuge in the help of Him to whom the prophet said: "They will curse but thou shalt bless" [Ps. 108.28]; and raising the eye of your mind, cry without cease, "Remove from me abuse and contempt" [Ps. 118.22]—not the abuse of men which passes, but rather yours which, if it does not cease on earth, finds no end in heaven. For I am afraid that while you judge the past as worthy of reproach (as it is), you will think the present worthy of contempt also. This comes about if the past is corrected sluggishly and the present is practiced negligently. Make use also to your benefit of that prayer of Sarah's: "I beg you, Lord, to clear me of the bonds of this charge or to seize me under the earth" [Tob. 3.15]—not indeed by taking me away in substance before my predestined time, but by totally raising my heart to you.

"This man," they will say, "has become a new prophet, a fresh apostle, a sudden angel; this one is St. Martin, St. Zeno, newly sent down from heaven! These are the signs of vanity," they will say, "hypocrisy, pretence, or inconstancy; this is only a change of attitude, not true religion." What bitter words! But see that it is not true!

23. Watch out also for the hunters' noose hidden close by. For many, frightened, hurt, and shamed by this bitter rebuke, leave the good they have begun and are caught in the hunters' snare. Reply to them in your heart, not with your voice. Watch out for yourself also, as you ponder this. There are within you certain inner caverns where the bandit adversary sets his traps. Say therefore in your heart, but ponder in fear and apprehension, say what was said by someone far superior to you, far dissimilar, and you will not lie: "To change your attitude for the better is not inconstancy but virtue, not fault but grace."[30] There will also be some who, when they see no good deeds of their own (or rather are unwilling to do any), if they see any of yours, begin at once to praise the good deeds and admire them as though they are the greatest. If you believe them, abandoning the evidence of your conscience, I tell you for certain, you will be destroyed thereby. On the contrary, while you maintain the present, you must ever try to remember the past and to ponder the severe and incomprehensible judgments of God; for often fault is incurred when one thinks one is earning grace, and grace is acquired when one is afraid of incurring fault. Keep your tongue not only from vicious words but from otiose ones too, knowing that James said: "If anyone thinks he is religious and does not bridle his tongue but deceives his heart, this man's religion is vain" [Jas. 1.26].

24. But to address you still in a few words, now that I have begun: I urge you, if you have done something in your youth and also if you have done something when placed in the monastery, before, that is, you were promoted to any authority, then carefully review it; perhaps there too you will find something which you ought to fear not a little. You will also understand on what conditions you were promoted, by what necessity chosen. For the pride of human ambition is ever inclined to the worse; it has already consumed all the secular spheres and today is not even absent from the monasteries, in that those to be chosen are appraised not by the merits of their virtues, but by the fame of this putrid worldly "nobility"—so-called, but really *corruptibility*. No one asks who excels the others in obedience, is superior in humility, outshines in wisdom, but whose chest is fuller, whose closet more packed, whose house more opulent, whose stable fuller, and whose properties and benefices more widely extended, whose father is richer, brother more affluent, family nobler, offspring more powerful.

Amidst these considerations not even the white hair of age is honored, but youth takes over the place of the elder, and the office which is all God's is given away as a reward; worldly profit is sought for in the place from which the rewards only of souls ought to be collected. If perchance you find that you have been caught by these traps of human ambition and others which usually accompany this kind, then give no place in your heart to joy, I beg you. For perhaps starting from these beginnings, you have come to the point that your accession to the height of honor which you now hold was due to the support and assistance of the world. If this is the case, how grievous you are I cannot sufficiently say, even if all the limbs of my body were to sound in every kind of voice. But do not think that I say this because I want you to be depressed or in despair; I do not neglect to give you counsel if I can give any; the rest I leave to your own industry.

25. I have quoted many sayings from the various works of the saintly Fathers; reread these and from them gain for yourself the means of salvation. Yet it seems to me that, while you are catching at these, perhaps you are prevented by your dilatoriness from finding and following through the counsel which they have given, namely, that you should in no way despair but place your trust firmly in Him who made everything from nothing, and give yourself wholly to tears, and practice righteous works, not as one who began doing so in infancy itself, but as one who, having given and wasted the whole time of his life to base delights, remembers that you ought for the rest of it, if any time is given, to put yourself into the hands of God alone. And though I know that you have not entered into this rank by the door, but have rather climbed in by another way [Jn. 10.1], yet I do not go as far as to despair of you utterly, because I know that this Father's power is so great that He could make a shepherd out of the very thief, if He wanted, and has often made a sheep out of a wolf, as we read. For what is there that the Omnipotent cannot do? What power does He not have other than what He refuses to have? If He could raise the sons of Abraham out of stones [Mt. 3.9], can He not make a righteous bishop out of a wicked usurper? Could He not restore a dead man, if He could create him when he did not exist?

"These things are very difficult," you say.

For whom? For God? What is difficult for Him who could make everything from nothing? Have you not heard today the words He spoke: "If you can believe, all things are possible for the believer" [Mk. 9.22]? Do you not know that in human affairs also this practice prevails, that the more the sick man is despaired of, the more the doctor is praised, and the more desperate the chance of the soul's death, the more people are corrected by that example? Hence one of our colleagues says after making this point: "Look at David, consider Peter; the higher their position, the heavier their fall; but the heavier their fall, the more welcome the mercy of the Raiser." So the same was wont to pray very beautifully: "O God, who show your omnipotence most in sparing and being merciful, multiply your mercy upon us."[31]

What if He deliberately permitted all these things to befall you so that you should have grounds for praising Him more, by allowing you, that is, to be in more dangers so that you should cry to Him without fail? What if He wanted you to be made an example for those who (for grief!) are appointed today in countless numbers through the whole world, so that they may take some counsel for themselves too, when they see you whom they knew dead revived, so that they may, if possible, escape the fate of anathema decreed by the canons and drive off from themselves the curse of the first of the apostles [Acts 8.20], by the clemency of God and of the Lord's apostles? For He deigned to become a curse for us, to redeem us from the curse not only of the law but also of original and personal sins [Gal. 3.13]. Only do not despair, do not act slothfully, do not bend to the right in pride nor to the left in desperation, do not be deceived by quality of good or quantity, as usually happens, of evil, do not look at others' habits and either arrogantly vaunt yourself or depairingly humble yourself, nor further give place to the adversary within you, nor ever concede to anybody (as far as you can prevail against it, that is) what you regret happened to you, nor allow yourself to slip in these or even similar faults, pondering how difficult it is to rise again after falling.

26. A certain person gives you, and those like you, fine salutary warning, though less harsh than the authority of the canons provides, when he says: "Those who are such, if they are unwilling at the Lord's coming to be removed from the Church, should themselves remove this business—that is, what the Lord saw done in the temple and punished with the whip of cords [Jn. 2.15]—from their hearts and not make the house of God a house of business." But mindful of all this and abjuring[32] that example wherein one says, "I am indeed lustful, but it is my part to conquer lust itself," commit nothing to your own virtue, your own position, or your own strength, but strive to be wholly His, and commit yourself wholly to His protection with every effort of heart and hand, who deigned to create you, redeem you, and summon you. He can keep you a little upright, who was willing to raise you when utterly cast down; He can keep you healthy who was able to heal you when you were contrite; He can speedily make you sensible, who against nature and beyond all hope was willing to correct you when you were infatuated. But although without Him you cannot even will anything good, let alone do it, yet you should not at all believe that you will be saved without any effort on your part, since you can take it for certain that it is for this purpose that you have been created a rational being by God, being conceded freedom of the will.

Endeavor to embrace Him, therefore, not hurriedly and as though in passing, but ceaselessly; with Him you cannot exist but in felicity, without Him you cannot exist but in infelicity. But if meanwhile by the kindly disposition of the just, or rather merciful, Judge, there comes upon you some adversity—sickness, say, or loss of family property, or some other kind of requittal—do not be sad as if you had been despised, but humbly rejoice as if you had been mercifully recognized, knowing and confessing that this has happened to you for your sins, and acknowledge that it is much less than your wickedness deserves. For the rust of such sins cannot be consumed except by the fire of many pains.

And so exult and rejoice in the Lord humbly, because you have chanced to receive requittal for some of your sins in this world; for there was great danger that in the next you would have to atone for them all at the same time, since all know that God leaves nothing unpunished [Job 24.12], while in this way the damned are usually set free from their sin by His mercy. And so in His sight continually accuse yourself and cry thus along with the prophet: "You are righteous, Lord, and right are thy judgments" [Ps. 118.137]; and with another: "You are righteous, Lord, in all that you have returned to us" [Dan. 3.27]; and: "All that you have done to us, Lord, you have done in true justice" [Dan. 3.31]; and: "I will suffer the Lord's anger, since I have sinned before Him, until He himself shall justify my cause" [Mic. 7.9].

27. Do not be slothful in the act of tribulation — as though you were certain that all your sins have been remitted you for your penance or at any rate a part of the graver sins forgiven (though you should not entirely give up hope of this) — but more urgently and attentively engage in vigils, prayers, and fasting beyond what is required; for you do not know what kind of whip you are subject to, whether that by which sons are corrected or that by which servants are whipped or the wicked punished. For since (as Scripture testifies) "every son who is received is chastized" [Heb. 12.6] and "many are the pangs of the sinner" [Ps. 31.10], and: "He rains on sinners traps, fire, brimstone, and the gusting winds" [Ps. 10.7]; and though these seem quite unbearable, yet this is not all but only a "portion of their cup." "I have struck you with an incurable blow, a cruel punishment"; and again: "Why do you cry out over your hurt? Your pain is incurable" [Jer. 30.14–15]; and describing the pain of the eternally damned, he says: "May they be wrapped in their own shame as with a mantle" [Ps. 108.29]; hence twice he prays for the same thing in the psalm: "Lord, rebuke me not in thy anger" [Ps. 6.2]. But another says: "Correct me, Lord, but in mercy and not in thy anger, lest thou bring me to nothing" [Jer. 10.24].

You realize that all of these passages refer to the kind of punishment by which the wicked, like Herod and Pharaoh, are punished both in the present and in the future; and so you should know that, as Gregory says, only those are released by temporal pains from eternal ones who happen here to change from their iniquities.[33] You should also know that you stand in the arena with an adversary who rages the more fiercely, the more he regrets his lost power over you; and furthermore his anger is aggravated by the fact that he is challenged to the contest by you who used once to be his subject.

Those[34] too, whose deceit betrayed you, whose negligence ruined you, whose treachery captured you, whose revolt brought you to this plight, do not hesitate to forgive, being certain that if you let their acts rankle in your heart, then for your own too you will fail to be pardoned (as the voice of Truth tells us [Mt. 5.45]); for if you forgive them, you will sometime rejoice for the forgiveness of your own and will eternally bask in God's blessing. Everything which you suffer, impute to yourself; ascribe everything to your own fault, your own sins. For perhaps this rebellion [against Hugo] of yours was to some purpose, since it was the cause of the penalty you are paying. If not, you have more cause for joy; but if it was, you have more cause to weep, but not in desperation, because none can conceive the richness of God's goodness, still less put a value on it. If this is the case, you should grieve for those who betrayed you, just as much as for yourself and for your supporters, since they were the sons of your own Church, or perhaps (may it not be so) even of the same rank as yourself; for you realize that since you provided the occasion, you were the cause of the death of these sons, and you can repent that so many lights of heaven were obscured by your darkness and extinguished by your fall. But because the mercifully righteous one is wont to punish harshly certain sins in this world, so that He will not find things which He must punish eternally in the next, let the remembrance of His mercy, in this act, that is, refresh you amidst these trials, so that you can sing with the psalmist: "I will rejoice in the Lord, I will exult and be glad in your mercy, because you have seen my humility, you have saved my soul from its distress and have not delivered me into the hand of my enemy; thou hast set my feet in a broad place" [Ps. 30.7-9].

All this you will truly be able to say, if you do not neglect the time given to penance, if you patiently bear the imposed penance, knowing that from the cause of past sin there has arisen this penalty of your present sin, in which, caught in wickedness, you have not even been able to see when sinning that you were sinning, so that you might avoid sin. Earnestly pray, therefore, that God's pity may mercifully both spare you this and also remove and delete the former in this furnace of tribulation, as a result of which you were involved in this one — or rather, in these (I say "these" to recall both the sin and the penance of the sin, applying the sum total to you) — and pray that He may so cleanse you in this world that He find nothing for that devouring but inextinguishable future fire to consume, but rather what his grace may reward and his justice crown.

28. Though you ought greatly to bewail the abandonment of your flock, you should not however do so without consolation; for you know that the chief Shepherd has said through the prophet: "Lo, I will seek out my sheep and visit them, just as a shepherd seeks out his flock on the day when he shall be in the midst of his sheep that have been scattered" [Ezek. 34.12]. Know also that a certain wise man has said that it is necessary for God's help to be present when man's help is lacking.[35] But if the great length of the sentence torments you, and the perdition of those dying without benefit of baptism desolates you, and the fact that your torturers do not care so long as they satisfy their desire for your pain, consider: giving yourself wholly to God's will and disposition, prepared to give your life itself — let alone every kind of loss of honor — for your flock, make use of the words of him who said, "If I am the cause of this storm, pick me up and cast me into the sea" [Jon. 1.12] — only let not the ship of the

Church be in danger any longer because of me, giving up so many sons, alas, to eternal death. May God concede that these words benefit you.

II.29. Are you a cleric? Let the very name fit you, I beg; that is, consider that you ought to be of the Lord's lot,[36] and, longing only for Him, you should greatly fear to lose the fellowship of so great a Good, but rather show yourself worthy of such company. If you are called a canon, see that you do not deviate from the sacred canons. If you happen to reject them, think in which of the orders of judgment you will have to appear, having renounced the lay order and not kept the ecclesiastical order.

Are you a priest? Preserve in your actions the gravity which you seem to bear in the name.

Are you a deacon? Recognizing that you are a minister of the heavenly sacraments, keep yourself chaste in every way, as the apostle commands [1 Tim. 3.8], and worthy of such duties, and celibate in heart and body to God, knowing that so sacred a sacrament, one that has been instituted for cleansing the sins of all, should not be handled with unclean hands.

Are you a sub-deacon? Know that you should be subject not only to God but to all the prelates of the Church, so that you may merit to be raised by the Lord in this world and rewarded in the next.

Are you an exorcist? Do not permit him whom you expel by exorcism from the bodies of others to dominate your own thoughts.

Are you a candle-acolyte? While you minister light to others, do not let yourself a sinner be obscured by the darkness of ignorance, but rather try yourself to be enlightened within and to show others the light of good example.

Are you a reader? Try to do the task that gives you your name industriously, lest you fail in your office.

Are you a doorkeeper? Open your heart to God's coming, close it to the devil's machinations.

III.30. Are you a monk? My only exhortation is that you should carry through to an excellent end what you have begun well—if only you are what you are called, what you are considered, and what you claim in your habit. If otherwise (heaven forbid!), woe to you who hide a wolf in sheep's clothing. But see that you do not despair; rather, drive the wolf from your heart and return the sheep to its own skin. Remember that the Lord, as I have already said elsewhere, has turned a wolf into a sheep, and even into a shepherd.[37] But to accuse you more by excusing him: it is one thing in ignorance of the good to rage like a wolf in the open, another under the pretext of religion to lead others astray by deceiving them, and to provoke God's anger by pretending what is not true. But perhaps you do not do so in pretense, but are slothful and aslumber from negligence? Then repair your strength, resume your constancy, clothe yourself in fortitude like a giant, fight bravely against the demons of wickedness; for not otherwise will you be able to overcome them, and in no other way will you be able to climb to the arduous summit. Ponder the Rule, reread the lives of the holy Fathers frequently, see yourself in these as in a kind of mirror and compare your life to theirs. First, require obedience of yourself, avoid public gatherings, shun associations with worldly men; know that it has been truly said (as I too, alas, have also proved by experience)[38] that the sheep which leaves the fold is an open prey for wolves. If ever obedience or any just necessity requires that you appear in public, let your habit, conversation—or rather very silence—gait, expression, and complexion be an object of admiration, respect, and example to all. Avoid "mine" and "yours" as if they were some kind of sacrilege; without them the condition of all could be one of great peace. After you have fulfilled all the requirements of a true monk, remember that you still sail in that dangerous sea where almost everything is uncertain or doubtful, as much contrary as favorable, as much ruinous as tranquil. So until you come to the harbor, don't think yourself secure, but listen to Ambrose: "The helmsman cannot be praised till he has brought the ship into harbor."[39]

31. Are you an abbot? Remember what you are called and what a difficult and arduous office you have undertaken; and so that I may bring my address to an end with you, note, pray, the dignity of such a name and with the eyes of your mind consider whose place you are taking. A monk[40] is one who, seeing himself aground on the shoals, is almost brought to the point of despair but is held by the anchor of God's almighty mercy, so as not to be cast utterly on the Charybdis of himself; thinking that that fear comes from God's mercy, he returns to himself and abandons putting on the noose with which to strangle himself like Judas; and leaving everything which he possessed in the world, that is, ambition with its property, he seeks a monastery and gives himself wholly to God, saving nothing out of the whole for himself, since he knows and decides that not even his very body should be retained in his own control.[41] He believes that he has been forbidden to consider, let alone say, what to eat or drink or wear, and is confident that all his needs will be provided by the father of the monastery. I think this enough about the monk.

32. What now shall I say about the abbot? In fact, I have already said a little, but let me add a little more. The abbot is of all the monks (if I may be allowed to say so) the most monk, in that he can fast more, pray more, read more, sing more psalms, and more patiently bear fasting, lack of clothing, poverty, insults, scorn, hunger, thirst, cold, wind, rain, snow, hail, abuse, mockery, derision, and finally every misfortune; more than other monks, he can show goodwill to all, even those attacking him with hatred, where he does not help them with good deeds; he is more teachable and quicker to learn than the others; he is wiser

than the others, if that can be, that is, with the other virtues in like proportion; he is fuller of love, stronger in the austerity of his discipline, gentler in his store of kindness, quicker in generosity, more ready to comfort the wretched, more humble and submissive than all. I think this is enough, as about the monk, so about the abbot.

33. But there are some whom I have discovered everywhere who, alas, desire only to command monks but not to *be* monks, I am sure; and so I say that these should be shunned rather than followed, still less is it wise to live by their example: they have clearly pronounced so many monstrous, terrible things about themselves. In fact, I think it opportune to tell of an incident this year which caused me much anxiety. For when I was at Laon on Christmas day,[42] the abbess asked me to come to the sisters' chapter on the Feast of St. Stephen and say, to quote her words, "something good" to them. I consented; and after the usual reading, when the blessing had been asked for and given, I said:

Being asked to say something good to you, beloved, I find nothing else than to relate something which happened to me tonight. Being overly concerned yesterday about the government of the abbey of St. Amand, when at the nocturnal office I stood at vigil (dozing, alas, as often) the reader came to the place in St. Jerome's commentary[43] where the Lord in the Gospel, after some preliminary remarks, continues: "All this will come upon this generation" [Mt. 23.36]; and from the explanation of the same aforesaid doctor I understood it in this way: that he who today unjustly kills his brother, that is, any Christian, incurs greater hurt for himself from all those who from the blood of innocent Abel to the blood of Zachariah the son of Barachiah have committed murder [Mt. 23.36]; for he has their guilt, which he has inherited, as well as his own for what he committed in imitation of them. I was greatly worried by this (as often happens) inferring other concerns from different facts, for reason clearly demanded that what was said of murder could be applied to other crimes as well. I began to say to myself: "Ought you then to be made an abbot with a conscience like that? Be first a monk." For at that time my only thoughts about the presulate were that it too I had held unworthily.

Therefore, because I have far digressed from the point where the ending of this book ought to have been, let us drop our anchor in this spot, so that the pilot may rest a while, and get his strength back more quickly. So let the text of this my address end in praise of the Holy Trinity. To you all praise, glory and thanks, blessed Trinity. Pity, pity, pity me whose name you know, unworthy as I am, yet speaking about you, with my hair unsuitably long.[44]

Book VI

[Rather admonishes the righteous to be humble and the sinner to repent, then similarly addresses other human conditions: health and sickness, wisdom and ignorance, joy and depression. He concludes with a statement of his own motives and methods in writing this.]

[I The Righteous and the Sinner
II The Penitent
III The Healthy and the Sick
IV The Wise and the Ignorant
V The Glad and the Sad
VI The Duties of All Christians
VII Conclusion: God's Athlete
VIII Rather's Aim and Method
IX His Apologia]

1. It is usual for sailors to fear pirates as much as storms; and sometimes they fear the closeness of the harbor itself more than the open sea, when the merchantman laden beyond its size unexpectedly grounds on the shoals and all the hope of their toil is lost together with the toilers, while friends look on from close by. To prevent this happening to me too, I rise and pray, "Save us lest we perish" [Mt. 8.25], (for without you the mind begins nothing of any depth, still less completes it), while in my presumption, highest divine Pilot, I strive to furrow this my sixth bay, with the harbor our goal already in sight. Having thus touched briefly on the holy orders, let me come to various dispositions of men, addressing them too as succinctly as I can.

I. Are you righteous? Pretend, or rather believe, that you are not, so that you can truly be so. Are you a sinner? Strive to your utmost not to be one, while acknowledging that you truly are. For in this way, with God's help, you will some day be able not to be one. Are you righteous? See that you do not fall. Are you a sinner? Try to rise. Are you righteous? Let the fall of the angel terrify you to your caution. Are you a sinner? Let the ascent of Man arouse you to your repentance. You, the righteous one, should not trust in your own action, nor should you, the sinner, despair of God's mercy, because if your condition today is known, what the condition of either of you will be tomorrow is quite unknown. For that both the darkness and the light of the heart can be changed is shown daily by the fall of the upright and the raising of the fallen. Hence the apostle says to certain people, "You were once darkness but now you are light in the Lord" [Eph. 5.8], as elsewhere he also said, "Let anyone who stands see that he does not fall" [1 Cor. 10.12]. Are you a sinner? Hear where you may take heart: "There is more joy in heaven over one sinner that repents than in ninety and nine just men who do not need repentance" [Lk. 15.7]. Are you righteous? Hear what to beware: "I saw Satan like a lightning-bolt falling from heaven" [Lk. 10.18].

2. But perhaps you are neither fully righteous nor fully sinful, but a middle position between the two is your delight? Then you should greatly fear that very tepidity; don't slip back again to the cold! For just as one can progress from tepidity to heat, so often, as Gregory says, one regresses from tepidity to cold.[1] Listen to what is said to the angel of the Church in Laodicea: "Would that you were hot or cold; but as it is, because you are lukewarm, I will spew you out of my mouth" [Rev. 3.16]. Woe to him who is spewed from God's mouth beyond recovery! On the other hand, the psalmist says of the righteous: "They will go from virtue to virtue" [Ps. 83.8]—because, that is, as St. Leo says,[2] knowing that they are trees planted for the Lord in the Church's garden, they not only take care not to fail for the worse, but earnestly endeavor to succeed for the better. Though one of our number has expressed the most beautiful— because gentle—thought, that whoever has achieved even a part of good deeds will not be beyond mercy, yet no less acceptable—because true—is the maxim, one we need to remember, of another, that "whoever does not succeed fails, and whoever acquires nothing loses something."[3] A third, no less an authority, agrees, saying that "every loss proceeds to nothing."[4]

Putting all these together in this way, you must fear that while you do not yearn for amelioration, you will succumb to deterioration, and, being subject to deterioration, you will arrive at nothing. There are some, as Gregory witnesses,[5] from whose company you should try to be set free, who serve God administratively so that they may enjoy the world; on the other hand there are those, in whose number you should try to be found, who serve the world ephemerally so that they may enjoy God. This I consider to be the middle ground of righteousness. But if you are not willing, or are quite unable, to raise yourself to that highest order of pleasing God, at least humbly and firmly hold yourself to this middle position, I beg, so that sometime you do not fall into that lowest one; for you should not be damned just because you cannot be perfect nor should you be worst just because you cannot be best. Finally, that humility in which you think little of yourself, if it is true humility and not rather slothfulness, will sometime be able to raise you to the sublime, as the Lord's words testify [Mt. 23.12].

3. Do not think, as I go through this with you rather gently, that I am urging you, or even perhaps allowing you, to pander to some other vice, as though with pardon, while you abstain from some; for I know from the apostle's teaching that a little leaven leavens the whole lump [1 Cor. 5.6]. Hear what James said: "Whoever keeps the whole law but fails in one point will be guilty of all of it" [Jas. 2.10]. Whether he means this law to be that of the Gospel or of the Old Testament or both at once, I leave to the scholars to uncover; though the Lord himself, when asked, said that on two commandments hang all the law and the prophets [Mt. 22.40], and the apostle said that love is the fulfilling of the law [Rom. 13.10]. We know that Augustine said: "If anyone keeps one commandment and breaks another, it is no benefit to him. If someone avoids avarice but does not avoid adultery, being convicted in the one, he is damned even by the world's laws; and abstinence from one sin does him no good if he is caught in another" [Jas. 2.10].[6]

Though what Augustine says here is very terrifying, yet on this same sentence of the apostle he had already consulted Jerome — and we know this because we read the reply he received.[7] It seems to me that in this place "the whole law" means those ten general commandments, from which is drawn as from a kind of spring every single law defined by the strings of the decachord; that is, since these ten are drawn indissolubly from those first and greatest two and make ten streams, seven pertaining to love of one's neighbor and three to love of God, they so keep the essence of that from which they derive, that you cannot truly embrace or reject one without the other, any more than you can the limbs without the head. For just as he who does not love his neighbor is proved not to love God, since John says: "If anyone says, I love God, and hates his brother, he is a liar" [1 Jn. 4.20] — and not only his brother but even his enemy, since the Lord says: "Love your enemies and pray for those who persecute you, so that you may be sons of your Father in heaven" [Mt. 5.44–45] (but there is no clearer love than that of a father for his son nor clearer rejection than that of a son who does not obey his father's command, whom he is shown not to love) — so those three which derive from the first no one can break who truly keeps that one.

For no one who loves God worships any other than him, nor takes His name in vain, nor does any good other than for the true Sabbath [Dt. 5.14], that is, eternal rest. And just as he who does not love God is proved not to love his neighbor — for he does not even love himself, since the psalmist says: "He who loves wickedness hates his own soul" [Ps. 10.6] — so he who truly loves that first commandment does not neglect the rest which derive from it. For he honors his parents and does not commit adultery and does not kill and does not steal and does not bear false witness or desire his neighbor's wife or any of his possessions. He who has broken any of these is held guilty of all, because he is seen to have transgressed the very source from which all derive, since truly loving God and his neighbor, he can do none of these things which are forbidden; for "love of one's neighbor works no evil" [Rom. 13.10]. I have said all this so that if you wish to maintain even that middle ground of goodness, you should earnestly try to be free from every capital fault.

4. The capital faults, you should know, are those which are forbidden by the Decalogue written on the tablets of stone. To cover under the same meaning those which have already been arranged by St. Augustine: you must know that the first of these is betrayal of your faith, which He forbids you when He says: "The Lord your God, God is one" [Mk. 12.29]. The error of heresy and various superstitions follows this, namely, incantations and what are popularly called *facturae* [magic] and what are called by the psalmist "pride and false gods" [Ps. 39.5], and also those which the Apostle lists, saying: "You observe days and months and years; I am afraid I have labored over you in vain!" [Gal. 4.10–11], and the like, from all of which you are constrained when you hear, "Thou shalt not take the name of thy God in vain" [Ex. 20.7]. Perjury also seems to me to be forbidden in this. From this also pride, vanity, and vainglory or love of the world, for which particularly those who love not God toil in all their business; from these you are restrained when you are commanded to keep the Sabbath, that is, to decline from evil and do good [Ps. 36.27] and cease from sin and serve God; but all of this in humility, not in pride, for the eternal reward, not for the empty glory of the world. You cannot break these three classifications of commandments and prohibitions of evils pertaining to the love of God without contempt of Him.

To the love of one's neighbor the following [Ex. 20.12–17] pertain: "Honor thy father and mother," whereby you are required to honor more especially God the Father and the mother Church and the leaders of the Church, beside your parent in the flesh; "Do not commit adultery," whereby you are checked from all lust; "Thou shalt not kill," whereby you are prohibited from any kind of cruelty; "Thou shalt not steal," whereby you are restrained from greed and avarice; "Thou shalt not bear false witness," whereby you are forbidden lying, perjury, and malicious gossip; "Thou shalt not covet thy neighbor's wife" [Ex. 20.13–17], whereby you are also forbidden adulterous thought.

If you keep these in their entirety, then following the Lord's words to the young man saying that he had kept these [Mk. 10.20], I can urge you to ride up to greater things; but if I catch you failing in any of these, I do not rouse you up to the better, but urge you to correct your injustices, not so that you may climb from virtue to virtue, but so that you may be converted from evil to goodness. For this is not the middle ground of goodness, as you thought;

in fact, it is no ground of goodness at all. For by trespassing against these ten commandments in a single detail, even though you seem to have fulfilled some of them, you are proved to love neither God nor your neighbor; what goodness do you think you have, until you correct those points where you acknowledged that you have failed? When I see you cleansed, either by the practice of good, or by penance and amendment, of those faults which these ten forbid, and adorned with the virtues which they demand, that is, love of God and one's neighbor, faith, and hope, then I think that you have reached the middle ground and urge you either to ride on to the higher, by selling everything and giving to the poor and following Christ, or at least to hold yourself firmly in these virtues, because I know that by these alone you will be not only saved but rewarded, since the psalmist says: "Thine eyes have seen my faults and all will be written in your book" [Ps. 138.16], that is, both the imperfections and the perfections. The "perfections" are what, as I said above, the Lord suggested to the young man, saying: "If you wish to be perfect, go, sell all that you have and give to the poor, and you will have treasure in Heaven, and come, follow me" [Mt. 19.21]. The "imperfections" are what I mentioned above when describing the middle ground of righteousness, by which even worldly men please God, I believe, and by which we hope to merit the grace of the most merciful judge through the worthy fruits of penitence [Lk. 3.8], even after much contempt of Him, and by which we believe that we will receive the wedding garment, which we lost by hurting our brother, together with pardon at least, if not with the crown. I have put down all this not to make you despair but to curtail your presumption and arouse your devotion.

5. You should also know that every tiny sin can often do much harm, though for those converted even the greatest are forgiven by largesse of alms alone—but it is clear that this happens only through the freely-given grace of God, which mercifully helps what it mercifully inspires to come to perfection, and mercifully receives and crowns the perfect. This also happens through love, which extinguishes all sins [1 Pet. 4.8] (for no one truly pities another except in love of God and of him whom he pities); so great is the privilege of this virtue that even the failings of him who has it are accepted, and virtue that is without love is nothing, though it seems to be something, as the apostle says [1 Cor. 13.2–3]. To speak of the faith by which we believe in God: if we believe in Him and worship Him for any other reason than for love of Him and of our own soul, we gain no benefit. What else are we particularly told to expect of Him than that we will enjoy forever His love (or return of love), vision, and recognition? What good do you think it does us not to commit adultery, not to kill, not to steal, not to bear false witness, not to lust after one's neighbor's wife or possessions, for any other reason than for love of God and of our brother? So rest

assured, any good, however small, if you do it out of love, you do it to your own benefit, but if you do it for any other reason, make no mistake, your effort is wasted. If you are restrained from some wickedness out of love of charity, you will not lack reward; if you do it for any other reason, you are not even thought worthy of pardon, let alone grace.

If, therefore, you want to hold that middle ground of righteousness, observe these ten commandments, and do so because of those two, love of God and love of your neighbor. If perchance you slip from these, as quickly as you can run to the pity of the physician whom you love, and confessing that your love is little less than contempt and weeping for it, endeavor to be restored to your place. For He loves even those by whom He is not loved; He would not despise you by whom He is loved, however negligent in some detail you are. Take care, then, to be quickly reconciled to such a friend and to be restored to the place from which you fell; for some who have been restored you see even advanced to better. There is true restitution where there is true confession; and true confession where there is true conversion; and where there is true conversion, there is true healing. For what point is there in showing your wound to the doctor, if you do not wish to be without it? The wounds which are too often shown and not healed become more swollen, to such an extent that they even infect with their stench those by whom they are seen, and are aggravated by frequent touching.

II.6. So are you penitent or do you wish to be so? Consider the rule of penitence laid down in the words of John the Baptist: "Bear fruit that befits repentance" [Mt. 3.8], and a little later: "Let him that has two tunics give one to him that has none" [Lk. 3.11]; and laying down the other works of mercy, he states very clearly that the person who desires to show fruit that befits repentance in harrowing his faults, in order to win mercy from the Lord, ought mercifully to attend to the needs of others. And so he must clothe the naked, if he wishes to receive the lost finery of innocence; he must feed the hungry, if he desires to avoid the deadly hunger of the soul; he must give drink to the thirsty, if he desires to sip the sweetness of God's pity; he must visit the sick, if he wants to escape the sickness of his ways; he must comfort the man confined in prison, if he does not want to face the prison below; he must console those in pain, if he does not want to see eternal pain; he must give hospitality to the pilgrim, if he wants to be received by the Lord in that eternal hostel of paradise; he must ransom the captive, if he longs to be freed through Christ from the devil's noose; he must give solace to the needy, if he wants to be freed from the needs of various troubles; he must bury the dead, if he wishes to avoid the death of eternal damnation; he must free the man arrested for his debts, if he desires to be freed from his own sins. He must save those being led to execution, if he wishes to escape the prison of below; he must overcome the impatience of his heart, if he wants to overcome the raging devil; he must mercifully punish the negligent, if he wishes to placate God the Father punishing him.

7. Besides these means of showing mercy, there is another, even more important, as it was defined by the Lord himself in his own words and attached to them, or rather put before them in rank, quality, and benefit, as follows: "Forgive and you will be forgiven, give and it will be given unto you" [Lk. 6.37]; and: "If you do not forgive men their sins, neither will your Father who is in heaven forgive you your sins" [Mt. 6.15; Mk. 11.26]; and repeating the same a third time in the same sense: "When you stand to pray," He says, "forgive, if you have anything against anyone, so that your Father also who is in Heaven may forgive you your trespasses" [Mk. 11.25]. And fourthly, after a parable to show the same point: "So also my heavenly Father will do to every one of you, if you do not forgive your brother from your heart" [Mt. 18.25], (so that no one should think that he can deceive God by forgiving his brother only with his mouth, since God sees into his very heart). And fifth: "If you offer your gift at the altar, and there remember that your brother has something against you, leave there your gift before the altar and go, first be reconciled with your brother, and then come and offer your gift" [Mt. 5.23].

But perhaps you say: "He whom I have hurt is far away and I cannot reach him."

The angel tells you: "Glory to God in the highest, and on earth peace to men of goodwill" [Lk. 2.14]. And the psalm says: "My vows to thee I must perform, O God, I will render offerings of thanks to thee" [Ps. 65.12]. And the apostle says: "If possible, as far as depends on you, be at peace with all men" [Rom. 12.18], that is, if it can be that he with whom you wish to be at peace also wishes himself to be at peace, then good; but if otherwise, you should keep peace in your goodwill. For the Lord also says: "And if a son of peace is there, your peace shall rest upon him; but if not, it shall return to you" [Lk. 10.6], that is, it will not be missing from your goodwill and reward, even if it has not been accepted by him. And Gregory also says: "So we ought to reach out for our neighbor, however far away and far remote, in our mind and give our heart to him and win him over in humility and goodwill."[8]

Sixth, the Lord says: "The measure you give will be the measure you get" [Mt. 7.2]. Seventh, speaking about the adulterous woman, He says: "Whoever of you is without sin, let him be the first to cast a stone at her" [Jn. 8.7], that is, let him who has in himself no sin whereby he can be struck strike without mercy at the sin of another. Hence Seneca says: "See if you are still wicked and spare those like you."[9] But if you have ceased to be wicked, why should you deny another the place of emendation, so long as this person's character is not at odds with it? Eighth: "Cast out first the beam from thine own eye and then you will see to take the mote from thy brother's eye" [Mt. 7.5], by "mote" meaning sudden, fickle anger, and by "beam" pride, hatred, and grudges. Ninth: "Physician, heal thyself" [Lk. 4.23], that is, correct first the anger or hatred in yourself and then heal the sin of another by rebuking him; like a certain wise man, who was driven into a rage (as I have already related in another volume), and is said to have told the person provoking him: "I would strike you now if I was not angry."[10] If he had happened to say that to one of the faithful, what else would he do but keep his own mind safe and sound and cure the other's madness by the draught of patience. What would this same *pagan* (for shame!) say to us in this kind of situation, carrying a beam in our own eye and trying to remove the mote from another's, if not what the prophet had already said: "Blush, Sidon, says the sea" [Is. 23.4] — as if by that example he were saying: "With what presumption would any Christian with the beam of pride try to remove from another's eye the mote of some vice, when the philosopher sees that I am unwilling to bear even the mote of anger in the eye of my heart, while I try to remove the beam of pride from another's?"

Tenth, the Lord says: "Love your enemies, bless those who hate you, so as to be sons of your heavenly Father, who makes the sun rise over the just and the wicked and rains over the righteous and unrighteous" [Mt. 5.44–45]. Away, then, with all the deceit of those unworthily repenting, or rather provoking God to anger with this pretense, if they think that they in any way merit pardon for their faults, while they keep any hatred of their brother in their hearts; their deceit has been censured by these and many other thunderings of God's voice.

8. For worthy fruit of repentance, this also is particularly important: anyone who thinks he has committed unlawful acts should restrain himself prudently even from lawful ones; he should beware further accustoming his body to the delights of those things which he recognizes as the cause of some sin of his, knowing that it has been most truly said by someone (and would that I too had not recently proved it most clearly by experience, alas!) that it is one thing for a blight to be destroyed, another for it to slumber. For the raging adversary, learning that he has been driven out of someone's heart and striving to avenge the hurt of his expulsion, has a thousand devices for harm, and especially this: he looks for the entrance by which he used to be let in and, unless a strong guard with God's help has been put on it (like the murder of Isboseth whose death occurred unexpectedly while the doorkeeper slept, when he was struck in the groin by assassins, who also picked up grain being cleansed [2 Sam. 4.5]), he is wont frequently to charge in at that point the more fiercely, the more his assault is unexpected; as the Lord says: "When the unclean spirit has gone out of a man, he passes through waterless places seeking rest; and finding none he says, I will return to my house from which I came; and coming home, etc.;

then he goes and brings seven other spirits more evil than himself and they enter and dwell there, and the last state of that man becomes worse than the first" [Lk. 11.24–26].

Behold, what evil arises from negligence, sloth, or torpor! Hence the psalmist, describing the people's troubles physically, showed our situation symbolically, when he said: "Their soul loathed any kind of food and they drew near to the gates of death" [Ps. 106.18]. The food of the soul is prayer, singing psalms, fasting, alms, and continual reading, and the man who loathes them, unless what follows happens — that is, that he cry to the Lord in his trouble to deliver him in his distress — incurs without doubt the risk of eternal death, as Gregory testifies; for temporally also if a man rejects material food, we despair of his life.[11]

9. To take myself as an example in this my undertaking: when the other day I was acting with rather more relaxation than was proper, I felt (for shame) for a very short time (so it seemed to me, but in reality not so short) that bitter sweetness of pleasure titillating and pricking me, even when held in prison and sorely in pain, far more gently indeed than it used to, but again far otherwise than I had thought; so that even in this I could recognize that I ought to have put a guard on the door of my heart, not a weak one but one in every way sturdy, not a womanly one but a manly one. It is proper for me to mention this at this point, O good Jesus, pious, heavenly, wise physician, not in order to reveal it to you (who know everything before it happens [Dan. 13.42]), but (in addition to what is most to be prayed for, namely that when I write it down, you may wipe it out, and when I confess against myself, you may delete it together with countless other graver ones) in order to provide a warning for my readers also in this; that is, so that they may ponder the cause of your just punishment which I suffer and so glorify your justice, considering how guilty I appeared in your sight when I, in my total blindness, thought I was not so. (And now too though struck, prostrate and thirsting after you with my eyes opened for a while, as it seems to me — though you know whether I do so truly — and wanting with your help not so much to emend as correct myself so that I may merit to see you, and considering turning my back on those cruelest of masters, who took me in when I fled from you, and fleeing back to you, I am still held back by the embrace of my inveterate ways and by the tarnish of evil company; wretchedly transfixed by the devil's thrust and smitten by the shafts of sin, I am pierced again.) Let them consider how wretched I was when quite turned away from you, who now appear so useless when turned (in a manner) towards you; how wicked when I cruelly killed myself, who now appear so unrighteous when I beg you mercifully to take me up; what my proud flesh did in favorable times when it is still proud in such calamity; what my impetuous courage yearned for when fortune smiled on its prayers, since it now vanishes when everything

is against it. Also let them gain from my loss some advantage of forewarning (for happy is he whose torments are the instruments of another's learning); and let them earnestly beseech your mercy for wretched me, as they see my numerous faults and realize my urgent need of intercession.

10. But to return to you with whom I was having this talk: I urge that when you do penance, you control your tongue also, not only from wicked words, but even from good ones, as the psalmist teaches you when he says of himself: "When the sinner stood against me, I was silent and humbled and held my peace from good words" [Ps. 38.2–3]; he had previously said: "I put a guard on my mouth." For it is one thing to guard one's mouth so that when justice demands it one speaks with reason, and quite another to hold it tightly so that nothing is spoken. Hence also in another psalm he prays in these words: "Put a guard on my mouth, O Lord, and watch over the door of my lips" [Ps. 140.3]. A door is both opened and closed. By *the sinner* [Ps. 38.2–3] know that the devil is here meant, who, as has already been said, is shown to stand against us most at the time of trial or penitence. The Apostle commanded him who had violated his father's wife to be delivered to Satan for the destruction of his flesh, that his spirit may be saved in the day of the Lord [1 Cor. 5.5]; to be *delivered to Satan* means to Satan's hostility, not to Satan's control, to contest, not to subjection, to death of the flesh, not to loss of the soul, that is, that while the flesh perishes as one fights with the adversary with fasting, vigils, and other bodily torments, the spirit may overcome the enemy and be saved in the day of the Lord.

Hence elsewhere too, when mentioning the secular to exemplify the spiritual, he says: "Every man who strives in the contest abstains from everything" [1 Cor. 9.25]. And truly. For abstinence from some things is recommended for those about to wrestle in the ring too, so that they are given special training food, that is, light food which strengthens and repairs the body and does not slow one down by its weight; and because wantonness also weakens the body, they put metal guards on their loins to avoid nocturnal pollution; all this which they do to win in the flesh a corruptible crown, we ought to do in the spirit in this very different conflict, and so both subject the flesh to the spirit and lay low the devil and take the eternal crown for our victory. "To deliver such a man to Satan" [1 Cor. 5.5] can also be understood in another way more appropriately: Satan is translated as "adversary" or "contrary"; by the name of *contrariety* it means that the sinner is handed over to ways *contrary* to his former life; for example, he who formerly indulged in pleasures now engages in austerity and on days of penance practises whatever is opposed or *contrary* to pleasure, so that as his flesh perishes through affliction by *contrariety* of this kind, his spirit may merit to be saved on the day of the Lord.

11. You should know that there are two kinds of penitence, one where, by the decision of the whole Church, each repents at a fixed time, the other where we repent of our own accord at any time. The latter is fixed by no law other than what each wants to impose upon himself, provided that he knows how to take the medicine of salvation to match his sickness. The former is subject to this condition, that he cannot do anything less exacting than what is commanded, unless it is lightened by the authority of him who imposed it or unless the imposer perhaps deliberately bound him under this condition, that if he himself should be absent, he could ask absolution from another. Neither the former nor the latter penitent is shown to do worthy penance, if he attacks some one vice in self-flagellation but does not fear to commit another like it, or perhaps a worse one, or even several others. For there are some people who, while repenting for a murder they have committed, are planning another murder. There are also some who, while repenting for a murder, do not fear to commit adultery. What happens to these, if not "Woe to the sinner walking the earth by two paths" [Eccli. 2.14]? He tries to *walk the earth by two paths* who seems to seek the path of salvation by harrying one vice, but is proven to follow the path of death by adopting other vices, since the Apostle James quite clearly says that he who offends in one is guilty of all [Jas. 2.10]. What I have said about murder and adultery as examples to prove my point must be understood about the rest.

12. Meanwhile, note what wicked people the Lord takes to Himself when they are converted. For He says: "If the wicked man has turned from his wickedness and has done penance for all the crimes which he has done and has kept all my commandments and has done just deeds, he will live and not die" [Ezek. 18.21–28]. *If*, He says, *he has done penance for all his sins and has kept all my commandments*: do not think that you can delete any sin by penitence if you break the Lord's commandments. He who wants to win indulgence must abandon all his sins and keep all of God's commandments. Do not, therefore, whoever you are who desire to do penance, want to enter that contest with a deceitful heart, lest perchance, while you think that you can deceive God, you seem not indeed to deceive Him but rather to provoke Him, whom you ought to win over by genuine and humble satisfaction.

13. But who is up to this, when no one can accomplish anything by his own strength? Hence, cry daily, or rather continually, even when silent and doing something else, pray and demand: "Create a clean heart in me, O God" [Ps. 50.12]. But if in your efforts you find it hard to cast off that habit of wickedness, do not, I beg, for that reason give up. For that is natural experience of all attempts. For a great stone is with difficulty brought to the top, but it quickly rushes to the bottom; and no one can be perfect from his first origins; for, as St. Augustine says,[12] it is hard for a man to be so changed that he has nothing for which he may be censured. Hold, hold yourself to Christ, cry, "Draw

me behind" [S. of S. 1.3] and "Take my soul out of prison" [Ps. 141.8]. And so that you do not strive with your own strength alone, listen to the same Augustine: "Fight against base lusts without God's help if you can; you can toil but you cannot win."[13] Hence also the psalmist: "If I take the wings of the morning and dwell in the uttermost parts of the sea, even there your hand shall lead me and your right hand shall hold me" [Ps. 138.9], as if he were saying: "However much I try, however I toil, wherever with flight of mind I fly, wherever I climb in moral progress, even with wings, I know that I will fall unless your right hand give me its usual help." How confident he is of that help, he shows elsewhere: "I promise you, my sons, and I am certain, that if anyone is heartfully penitent and does not return to the vomit of sin, he will be safe, only let him not doubt in his faith or seek delights again."[14]

14. In the meanwhile then, should it happen that temptation suddenly attacks and you slip unexpectedly either in thought or word or deed, do not despair, do not abandon your undertaking, do not interrupt the course of doing good in anything, but renew and revive the contest, resume the conflict, fire up your courage again, avenge the hurt. A commander usually loves the soldier who, pierced with many wounds, again attacks the enemy with renewed fight, more than him who never either turned his back or did any stalwart deed, or him who, after once turning his back, showed no courage in attacking the enemy. Hear too the advice of the Holy Scripture on this: "If the anger of one having power rises against you, do not leave your place, for deference will make amends for great offenses" [Eccle. 10.4].

III.15. Are you healthy? Praise God's mercy which watches over you. Are you sick? Praise the pious Father's justice which chastises you. "It is good," says the psalmist, "to confess to the Lord and to sing your name, O highest One" [Ps. 91.2]. How? "Announcing your mercy in the morning and your truth in the night" — *morning* signifying prosperity and *night* adversity, as if he had said: It is good to announce with praise your mercy in prosperity and your justice in adversity. Are you well? Hear by whom you are kept: "The Lord keeps all their bones" [Ps. 33.21]. Sick? Hear your consolation: "Many are the afflictions of the righteous," and the rest [Ps. 33.20]; and: "The sufferings of this present time are not worth comparing with the glory that is to be revealed to us" [Rom. 8.18]. Are you sick? Listen, lest you fret without patience: "He whom the Lord loves He seizes" [Pr. 3.12]. Are you well? Listen, so that you do not presumptuously exult: "If you are left without discipline, in which all have participated, then you are illegitimate children and not sons" [Heb. 12.8]. Are you well? Be afraid that you will be told: "Son, remember the good things you received in your lifetime" [Lk. 16.25]. Are you sick? Yearn to have it said of you: "and Lazarus in like manner evil things." Cling to "now he is comforted here" and fear "and you are in anguish" [Lk. 16.25].

Do not let your very sickness make you lax or your health make you ungrateful; you should know that for some people any sickness or scourge is for growth or trial or for the glory of God alone, but for others it is either for correction or the beginning of woes, that is, that while they are scourged here and not corrected, they begin here to be stricken so as to be tormented forever. For "many are the blows of the sinner" [Ps. 31.10]. Look at Pharaoh, consider Herod. To some people health or other temporal goods are given for trial, or for the benefit of others or as a sentence, and sometimes they are given so that a man, enjoying an abundance of provisions in this world, may strive more willingly for the lasting goods, or so that while he is a good steward of another's property he may sometime come to his own, and while he manages the ephemeral with God's glory, he may come with the fruit of his good work in glory to the eternal. For it is written: "He gave them the lands of the nations" [Ps. 104.44]. So one ought that much the less to be troubled by sickness or conceited over health, the less easily one can understand in this world for what purpose it was bestowed.

IV.16. Are you wise, or want to be, or perhaps are called wise? "Become ignorant[15] in this age," as the apostle says, "so that you may become wise" [1 Cor. 3.18]. Are you ignorant? "Incline your ear to the wise" [Pr. 5.1], as Solomon says, so that you may not be ignorant. Are you wise? Listen: "Do not think more highly than you ought to think" [Rom. 12.3]. Are you ignorant? Listen: "Whoever does not recognize this will not be recognized" [1 Cor. 14.38]. Are you wise? Listen: "Put a measure on your wisdom" [Pr. 23.4]. Are you ignorant? Listen: "How long, children, will you love simplicity and the fools desire what hurts them and the unwise hate knowledge?" [Pr. 1.22]. Are you wise? Listen: "A good understanding have all those who practise it" [Ps. 110.10]. Are you ignorant? Know this: "He who turns his ear from hearing the law, his prayer will be an abomination" [Pr. 28.9]. Are you wise? Beware what the apostle says: "It had been better for them not to know the way of truth than after knowing it to turn back from it" [2 Pet.2.21]. Are you ignorant? See what the Lord says: "Whoever is of God hears God's words; you do not hear because you are not of God" [Jn. 8.47]. Are you wise? Avoid the wisdom of the flesh. Ignorant? Pursue the wisdom of the spirit. Wise? Listen: "Do not be wise in your own esteem" [Pr. 3.7]. Ignorant? "Fear God and shun evil." Wise? Acknowledge your own ignorance. Ignorant? Be bold for wisdom, so that temptation does not subdue you before fear. Wise? Listen: "You will be wise if you do not believe that you are." Ignorant? You are denied wisdom not by your nature but by your negligence. Are you wise? Listen: "Do not seek things too high for you" [Eccli. 3.22]. Ignorant? "Think ever on what God has commanded."[16]

Listen to the same on both sides at once: "Neither is excused, neither he who has read nor he who refused to read, but he who denied what he read has sinned the more." But he who, when he could have learned, refused to learn what to do will not escape; for it is said in Job in the description of a curse of a certain person, whether of the Jews who crucified or of Judas who betrayed the Lord, or spoken to that first pride or the classes of the wicked in general (for the sense applies to both): "The heavens will reveal his iniquity and the earth will rise up against him and his sin will be manifest in the day of God's wrath . . . together with those who said, to the Lord God, 'Depart from us, we do not desire the knowledge of thy ways.'" Again: "They spend their days in prosperity and on the instant they go down to hell" [Job 20.27; 21.14; 21.13]. And Wisdom says the same thing very terribly: "I called and you did not come, and so on; I will also laugh at your death" [Pr. 1.24]. Also the prophet in Lamentations laments: "Therefore my people go into exile for want of knowledge" [Is. 5.13]. And another says: "All wickedness comes from ignorance."[17] And: "He refused to understand so as to do good" [Ps. 35.4]. And again: "They knew not, nor did they understand, they walk in darkness; and the foundations of the earth are shaken" [Ps. 81.5]. The Lord in the Gospel says: "Whoever is of God hears God's words" [Jn. 8.47]. Do not think, either you or that other, that I am calling you to any kind of wisdom other than that which is from God and forbidding you some kind of wisdom by urging another prohibition, for there is none. I shall try as rapidly as I can to establish that there are three kinds of growth of the soul as there are of the body, equating them word for word just as Augustine does, who has offered much good advice in this work already. Augustine says:[18]

> For there is one *growth* in the body which is necessary, whereby it naturally reaches its appropriate size in its limbs; another which is superfluous, as when sometimes people are born with six fingers; and a third which is harmful, which is called a tumor when it occurs; for the limbs are said to *grow* in this way—they do in fact fill a greater space but at the cost of good health. So also in the soul there are certain quasi-natural growths, as when it is said to grow with disciplines which are worthy and proper for living well and blessedly. When we learn things which are more remarkable than beneficial, though they are often pertinent yet they are superfluous and should be counted in that second kind of growth. The harmful kind, whereby the soul is damaged, is that of the liberal arts.

To show how these three are to be taken: this third worst kind of knowledge is to be utterly rejected, the second should be guarded against, and the first should be embraced. For the first is true wisdom, in fact there is no other kind; it counsels nothing but what is worthy, teaches nothing but what is beneficial, and commands nothing but what is acceptable to God.

17. Are you wise? Be also simple. Are you simple? Be also wise. For neither one without the other has any worth to produce virtue. For wisdom without simplicity is cunning, and simplicity without wisdom is silliness. Hear the Lord's words: "Be ye wise as serpents and innocent as doves" [Mt. 10.16]. I want you then to be, as Gregory very finely puts it,[19] knowingly ignorant and wisely unlearned.

V. Are you glad? I would you were so in God. Are you sad? I would you were so for your neglect of God. Are you glad? Hear in what you ought to be glad: "Be glad in the Lord always" [Phil. 4.4]. Are you sad? Hear how you ought to be sad: "Godly grief," says the Apostle, "produces a repentance that leads to salvation, but worldly grief produces death" [2 Cor. 7.10]. The psalm tells you: "Rejoice in the Lord" [Ps. 31.11]. The Apostle also says to you: "Count it all joy my brethren, when you meet various trials" [Jas. 1.2]. He who is glad should hear this in case he grow insolent: "Woe to you who laugh now, for you will weep" [Lk. 6.25]. He who is sad should hear this in case he grow bitter: "Blessed are you who weep now, for you will laugh" [Lk. 6.21]. The glad: "Rejoice because your names are written in heaven" [Lk. 10.20]. The sad: "Again I will see and your heart will rejoice and no one will take away your joy from you" [Jn. 16.22]. The glad: "Rejoicing in hope" [Rom. 12.12]. The sad: "As though sad but ever rejoicing" [2 Cor. 6.10]. Let the sad hear: "Rejoice in the Lord, O ye righteous" [Ps. 32.1]. The glad: "Weep like a maiden [Jl. 1.8]. The sad: "Rejoice and be glad, daughter of Sion" [Lam. 4.21]. The glad: "As she glorified herself and was wanton and glad, so give her a like measure of torment and mourning" [Rev. 18.7]. Let the sad hear: "Is one of you sad? Let him pray in constancy and sing psalms" [Jas. 5.15]. Let the glad hear: "God loves a glad giver" [2 Cor. 9.7].

I have joined these last two together in this way so that the sad person may strive to lessen his grief with constancy, prayer and (if he is fit for this) frequent singing of psalms, so as not to fall into bitterness; and so that the glad may humbly try to show God gladness in no other way than in good works with God's grace, so as not to offend in his gladness, and so as to win merit for his good deeds. For it has been said by someone, most truly I think (for by the saintliness of his words he won for himself the privilege that no one should doubt his testimony): "Whoever gives bread to a poor man and is sad, loses both the bread and the merit."[20] On this point also Augustine, whom I have cited frequently already, says: "If you do good with joy, then you do good; but if with sadness, then it comes from you but you do not do it."[21] When, therefore, temporal joy creeps into your heart too readily, let the strength of your mind within control it, and in grief for the blindness of the present world answer: "What joy will I have who sit in darkness and see not the light of heaven?" [Tob. 5.12].

Again, when intolerable sadness overtakes it, let constancy prevail in the citadel of your mind and say: "Who will separate us from Christ's love? Will tribulation or distress?" [Rom. 8.35].

18. Therefore, since it is in some way natural for everyone to weep rather than to laugh, as we all seem to start off weeping at birth, that person clearly transgresses the law of nature who is too prone to laughter and rarely, or perhaps never, can show heartfelt grief or bring tears to his eyes, either in desire for heavenly things, or for the loss of worldly things or in contemplation of his mortality (which, because of that inevitable fall, is daily subject to as many chances as it meets necessities). That sadness is sometimes more beneficial than gladness, he witnesses who says: "The heart of fools is in the house of mirth, but the heart of the wise is in the house of mourning" [Eccle. 7.5], and the person cited above neatly agrees, saying: "Often the melancholy which usually accompanies gravity is more beneficial."[22] And another says: "God rejoices in our very grief" [Pr. 16.18]. Hence it is said that "The heart is raised up before a fall" [Pr. 16.18], and "Laughter will be mixed with grief and the end of joy will be sadness" [Pr. 14.13] — which, though it can best be understood about future perdition, yet can also be understood about the changes and chances of the present. How then you should regulate your state of mind between these two, he wisely shows you who says: "In the day of ill be not forgetful of good, and in the day of good be not forgetful of ill" [Eccli. 9.27]. Doing this, neither gladness will make you reckless, nor sadness make you desperate, as he of incomparable eloquence quoted a little above finely remarks from his golden mouth, saying: "If there is any joy of the present time, it is so to be handled that the bitterness of the subsequent punishment is never forgotten."[23]

Putting all this together so, each of us should weigh what he ought to rejoice for in the present so as not to be sorry in the future, or what he ought to be sorry for, so as not to be censured for rancor; for men both laugh and weep in the present world, and what they laugh for they should often weep for and what they weep for they should often laugh for. Someone laughs for what should be bewailed as is said of some: "They rejoice when they have done wrong and exult in wickedness" [Pr. 2.14]. Likewise someone weeps when some calamity happens to him, though he should rather rejoice, because "Him whom the Lord loves He snatches" [Pr. 3.12] and "He whips every son whom He receives" [Heb. 12.6]. What then should one rejoice for if not the success of the righteous? What should one be sad for other than their failure? What rejoice for other than their promised felicity? What be sad for other than this long pilgrimage? For there is no desire of the fatherland if there are no tears at all on the pilgrimage; and love lies cold and sluggish in the heart if one cannot at all be glad for one's brother's success and grieve for his failure. Hence also Augustine says: "He hates and abuses his fatherland who thinks that it is well with him when he journeys abroad."[24]

19. There is yet another cause for rejoicing, one not indeed familiar to many but nevertheless demanded by the Lord's commands. After enumerating certain signs preceeding His advent, He said to His disciples: "When these start to come about, look up and raise your heads, for your redemption is approaching" [Lk. 21.28]; as though he had said: When you see those things which you do not love pass on, know that what you have longed and yearned for is near. By this example every Christian ought to be very afraid of grieving at the destruction of the world; otherwise, when caught loving the world by his sympathy for it, he may seem to incur God's enmity, since the apostle terrifyingly thunders: "Whoever wishes to be a friend of this world is established as enemy of God" [Jas. 4.4].

Nor should you grieve in your prayers for earthly matter, because, according to Gregory's words, grief which tries with tears to win ephemeral things bears no fruit[25] (this is proved also by Esau's vain sorrow [Gen. 27.34]), though you ought to pray to God, in moderation however, for even the smallest things, or implore God's help, as Plato says in the *Timaeus*.[26] What should be done in such a case is shown by the prophecy of the prophet Habakkuk, who, after enumerating various disasters of the world, adds in conclusion: "But I will rejoice in the Lord" [Hab. 3.18]. And the psalmist says: "The righteous will rejoice when he sees their punishment" [Ps. 57.11] — knowing, when he sees the punishment of the wicked growing, that the reward of the righteous is close at hand. And again: "My soul refuses to be comforted" [Ps. 76.3]. And so this joy is peculiar to the good; none of the wicked shares in it. For in this world the wicked seem to rejoice and to sorrow equally with the righteous. For they rejoice when they acquire, are sad when they lose. Likewise, the blessed — and yet not likewise, because their motives are different; for the wicked are sad for worldly losses, the blessed for their celestial desires; and yet the blessed rejoice, when, that is, they attain the fruit of their labors and they are sad when they lose, that is, when they see someone leave their company. The blessed are laughing while piously weeping. The wicked are weeping while vainly laughing — and also weeping vainly; for they move from laughter to weeping, from weeping again to weeping, from weeping with laughter to weeping without laughter; one grieves at his neighbor going to the kingdom, when he ought rather to grieve over himself rushing into perdition.

Do not, therefore, presumptuously rejoice, do not vainly weep; rejoice in the Lord, be glad in God your salvation; weep in the world, groan for your heavenly desire; mourn for your sin and for your neighbor's sin, sigh and be sad for this long neglect of God. He will give you joy for your grief, exultation for your mourning, jubilation for your wailing. He is the comfort of the sad, the hope of those who labor, the help of those perishing, who speaks through the Gospel: "Again I shall see you, and your heart will rejoice and none shall take your joy from you" [Jn. 16.22]. For the prophet also had long ago promised this: "The Lord will give you a garland instead of ashes, a mantle of praise instead of a spirit of grief" [Is. 61.3]. Therefore, carry your ashes without worry, you who are promised a garland, wear your spirit of grief ephemerally, you for whom there waits an eternal mantle of praise. Be eager to obey His commands, or rather, gratefully embrace Him as He nurtures you. "Those who mourn," it says, "as though they were not mourning, and those who rejoice, as though they were not rejoicing" [1 Cor. 7.30]; that is, if you weep with sadness at the present ill, rejoice in hope of the future good, and if you rejoice for a temporal gain, fear for eternal judgment. For, as Gregory says, he is well counselled who grieves for the present and hastens towards the eternal.[27]

VI.20. But since I see that I am nearing, with God's approval, the goal of my discourse, I must be careful not to move faster than I should and, having once begun to admonish everybody, not leave someone out or neglect someone; to avoid this, I urge and advise all Christians, all the baptized, every rank, condition, sex, age, and profession, rich, moderate, and poor, healthy and sick, young and old, and even infants, sinners and righteous, clergy and lay, all, I say, without exception, omitting none, all, who wish to have part in Christ's kingdom to stir themselves, to take to heart the parable which the Lord himself told about the king and his good and bad servants; one servant took five talents, one servant took two, and the other one, to be demanded later. For what He there said that the king did, He himself does every day; what He tells happened to the servants, happens on the Day of Judgment to everyone according to their various works; "Let him who has ears to hear" [Mt. 11.15] hear it, understand it, and unhesitatingly acknowledge it. No one can make the excuse that he has not received a talent, even if he seems to be totally crippled, since even infirmity is often given as a gift. Does a man have wisdom? This is the greatest talent, for there is none greater. Does he have riches? That is a lesser talent, but one most fitted for paying out. Does he have some skill? With it he can multiply his talent beneficially. Has he a place with prince or friend? What he cannot do with his own talent, he can do with his lord's. Is he totally deficient? But he still has life; let him only have goodwill as well, he amasses no less profit.

VII.21. Going through all this point by point and under separate headings (profusely it seems, though I had not planned it this way, but nevertheless not without benefit, I think), I have now shown in a few words how God's medicines apply in sum to all and to individuals in particular. It remains now for me to address him for whom I have supplied this "manual for Christ's athlete,"[28] and then to add a few words from St. Augustine about the benefit of vigils. Let us begin it thus in God's name; give me all your attention, then, and listen to what is said with the open ears of the heart.

First, I want to ask you if it is entirely of your own will that you want to enter this singular contest.

"It is," you say.

If it is, then at the very beginning—that is, before you begin this journey that is so arduous and entered upon by few, begun lazily by some and more lazily left off, started courageously by some and finished far otherwise, but by some well begun and finely finished—I urge you first to carefully consider and wisely weigh whether, after starting well, you can carry it through to the goal of finest perfection. The highest good is begun in vain, if it is abandoned before the end; nor is the victim acceptable in the Lord's sacrifice if it lacks a tail [Lev. 3.9]. The brothers' clothes were not mentioned, but Joseph's long coat of many colors was [Gen. 37.23]—of many colors for his many talents and long for his completing of projects. The prophet abuses these sinners, saying, "Let them be like grass on the rooftops" [Ps. 128.6], and He who was wont to give the laborers their coin in the evening says, "He who endures to the end will be saved" [Mt. 20.8–9]. There are thousands of testimonies to show that beginnings of good work have no value if they are not brought to blessed completion. So let the soul striving for the highest be warned by the Lord's parable which we read in the Gospel: "For which of you desiring to build a tower does not first sit down and count the expenses which are necessary, whether he has enough to complete it, lest perchance when he has laid a foundation and is not able to finish it, all who see it begin to mock him and say, 'this man began to build and was not able to finish'?" [Lk. 14.28–30]. It is clear that He said all this so that you should know that it is better for a man to hold himself humbly at the bottom than imprudently to reach for the top and, not gaining it, fail shamefully and give the spectators occasion to mock. Indeed, one should be very careful that, when one strives imprudently to rise from the common goods to those which defy the strength of many and does not persevere to complete that which he attempted at the beginning, that what we read in Job does not happen to him, that "all who see him say, 'where is he?'" [Job 20.7]. That is, that he is found neither here, where he seemed to live well in common with the rest, nor there, where he seemed to have hastened on his own, transcending the rest. You should consider also the many clever traps of the devil and the great envy which he has, specifically, it seems, for those he sees hastening for the sublime. For Satan sees himself fallen to the bottom and grieves beyond words when he sees someone raised to the heights. He does not stop every day walling in each one of these with three kinds of blockade, at the beginning of their intention, in the course of their action, and at the end of their consummation.

22. If you want to learn more fully about these three individually, you have them abundantly described in Gregory's *Moralia* [1.36.52–56]. But if firm in your heart, as I hope, and remembering that "he who watches the winds does not sow and he who considers the clouds does not reap" [Eccle. 11.4], you desire undismayed[29] to enter such a struggle, be careful above all that nothing earthly, worldly, or beastly reside in your heart: "For if a beast touches the mountain it will be stoned" [Heb. 12.20; cf. Ex. 19. 12–13]. Considering then that your bark is still on this great wide sea in which are creatures beyond number, be very wary of the devil-dragon, I advise. Sport with him before he sports with you [Ps. 103.25–26]. Watch for the *snake* in your mind's eye.[30] Know that his nature is such that though he kills a man if he sees him first, he is himself killed if a man sees him first. Watch carefully also for the tongue of viperous suggestion, and, rising up, you will be able to slay the wicked act of aspish beginning; and when you have shown the first face of a *man* at the beginning of the work, be sure not to tail off into the *beast* of unreasoning execution and be marked with the monstrous appearance of the onocentaur.[31] "Avoid the barren company of the hypocrite" [Job 15.34]; beware the bullrush that is damp before the rising of the sun but dry at its rising.[32] Observe that beasts and birds prefer to tread on the prolific but neglected vine rather than the sterile ones. Do not desire to walk the earth by two paths" [Eccli. 3.28], when you both do good out of love of God and want to please men thereby. Do not carry your treasure openly on the road or you will be robbed of it by bandits ambushing the road. Do not snatch at the empty wind of vanity for the source of your eternal reward.

For among all the kinds of craftiness of the multiform serpent with his countless coils and twists, there is no vice which you must more carefully guard against than the foul vice of vainglory. He uses this trick so cleverly in his attack on the blessed that, unless they are very vigilant and on their guard, and take care to avoid his treacherous ambushes not only in their thoughts but in the whole body of their actions, he is wont to strike them unexpectedly and to cast them down more heavily by their very virtue than when he trips them up with vices. Finally, be careful to restrain that tongue of yours. For, as Augustine says, this tongue is so glib and unstable and has the tendency and power to cast down the mind from its citadel, that it often happens that by its very promptness in speaking it incurs an offense which the mind does not intend.[33] And in case you aver that it is a light offense to slip with the tongue, hear what the Apostle James tells you particularly: "If anyone thinks that he is religious and does not bridle his tongue, but deceives his heart, this man's religion is vain" [Jas. 1.26].

And elsewhere: "The tongue is a restless evil, full of deadly poison" [Jas. 3.8]. And again: "Death and life are in the tongue's hands" [Pr. 18.21]. And: "In garrulity sin will not be lacking" [Pr. 10.19]. One of our number has finely added two points saying: "One should not be thought to be saved as long as one does not fear to embrace irregular ways, to take delight in superfluous words, and to be wracked with unruly thoughts."[34]

But thanks be to God. For lo, suddenly, and it seems unexpectedly, while I endeavored to use him to witness the dangers of loquacity, I brought to an end almost the whole business which I had thought could hardly be managed in many volumes of words. Do you wish to be saved, rewarded, and crowned? While you steer clear of irregular actions, avoid also superfluous words, restrain yourself from unclean thoughts, with innocent steps of action follow the voice of the Lord: "Whoever wishes to come after me," He says, "let him deny himself, raise up his cross and follow me" [Lk. 9.23]. To follow, that is, imitate, Christ is to go behind Him by the road He takes, which is: not to strive for worldly things, not to work for ephemeral gains, to decline even the lowest honors, and to willingly embrace adversity and the world's scorn for love of Him, to be willing to benefit everyone, even beyond one's strength, to do hurt to no one but to bear patiently hurt done by someone else, and also for those who do you wrong to repay it with good, if possible, but if not, to ask for pardon for them with constant prayers; and to stir up whomever one can to love of the heavenly kingdom.

23. If with these endeavors of pious will you have first trained yourself in the field of action, you show yourself as a champion athlete, I admit, to the Director of the palaestra, the leaders, and all the spectators, so long as you do not wear yourself out in them (as, alas, happens to some), and always strive for better things; until, after fighting well the good fight, finishing the course in felicity, constantly keeping the faith [2 Tim. 4.7], you are gloriously enriched with the lasting crown of reward.

Since God so disposes (in whose hand we are, my words and myself), I have extended my pious work this far for this reason: that after showing the characteristics of lesser actions and qualities, I may finally come to the very summit which you are trying to reach, whereby, carefully and gradually climbing from the lowest of the Lord's commandments, as though by a ladder, and reaching the higher, nothing further remains for you to seek among the lowest; through an order of living which many cannot reach, you will now merit to cling to those summits.

I have also extended my work this far so that, from whatever order, condition, honor, temper, sex, or age you want to put your hand to that very glorious work of contest, you may find here how you ought first to train yourself in your own sphere, so that in this way you may finally climb in blessed progress to those things which are beyond you, in case sometime, having once put your hand to the plough, you be compelled by the pressure of some domestic duty to turn the eyes of your intention back from your undertaking, and either to make a crooked and useless furrow or to damage the hooves of the ploughing oxen. But if (as I have shown in another work already)[35] someone is found who is compelled, not by his own choice but by another's action, to follow this manner of living either at a definite time or at every time of life, I believe that I have already satisfied him in the latter books.

Here now I think there is nothing further left except to add this, that should he perchance by God's grace be freed from this necessity, at no time ever should he abandon his usual practice of penitence, but for all the rest of his days he should be seen doing His works, because the merciful Lord has now reined him in from the perversities of presumptuous vanity. Doing this, he will appear both to win merit for himself and to give thanks to his teacher and to render satisfaction to the Lord and praise to God, who has whipped him in the present lest He lose him for eternity, disciplining him temporally so as to make him a worthy heir of His eternal kingdom. But if, on the contrary, he decides to turn from this path of our advice, let him look to what he does; I greatly fear that Christ's rebuke, "Was no one found to return and give praise to God?" [Lk. 17.18] may apply to him, and, what is more serious still, that he may be subject to the sentence which the same Lord indicated about the unclean spirit going out and returning with eight [Lk. 11.24–26].

For this reason He also said to the man healed: "Go and sin no more lest worse should happen to you" [Jn. 8.11; 5.14]. And what the prophet bewailed, saying: "You have smitten them and they have felt no anguish; you have consumed them and they have not changed" [Jer. 5.3]. He must also consider, I see, that long sickness often restores people back to life, but afterwards the slightest event utterly extinguishes them from life, while, relaxed in a kind of security, as it were, they let down their guard. So let such a man fear that this will happen to him and take counsel for his salvation while there is time, in case he be unable to when he wants to again.

VIII.24. If perhaps someone is upset that in this preface I have used the modern sayings of teachers in equal measure with the ancient,[36] and wants to call me a "harmonizer" or, more currently, a "compiler" for that reason, as though I wanted to build my own work at other people's expense, I hasten to give the reason. The psalmist says: "Lord, watering His mountains from His higher places" [Ps. 103.13]; as far as I was able to have any understanding since He watered my parched intellect through modern teachers (He also watered their predecessors in His own person, and through those predecessors the moderns, and through the moderns He watered me, who still am too dry—not because of a lack of rain, but because I prefer to be parched in the dust of vices than to be sprinkled with the "copious rain which He has sent down on His heritage" [Ps. 67.10], and I have sheltered myself under an umbrella of wickedness, as it were), it seemed proper to use the sayings of the Fathers, as also those of the Scriptures, without distinction, inasmuch as what they received from their predecessors they have also rained on us their successors. And so the proper interpretation of a passage is clearer through their discernment and there is no need for anyone to err in ignorance and put things in the wrong places, since you find copiously treated in their expositions the special meaning which a scriptural saying has and the proper place it holds; and so, when occasion demands that one mention some of the Scriptures' sayings, there is no need to take on a useless and perhaps perilous task, but one can interpret them just as they have been interpreted by the Fathers.

I have been persuaded to rely more on the Fathers' examples than on those of the Scriptures for two reasons: first because the maze of the Scriptures was still unintelligible to me, and secondly because of the example of the two[37] who in the *Ecclesiastical History* are called the "sons of fat" and "the lamps attending the lampstand of the Law on the left and on the right" [Ex. 35.14], whom Cappadocia—at that time the more fertile than neighboring regions the more it was watered by those very clouds—bore, nourished, and taught, or rather, through whom Cappadocia itself was moistened, nourished, and taught, and so shone more brightly than the rest; who, after studying for thirteen years all the books of the secular Greeks, excepting alone the volumes of divine Scripture, took their understanding of them not from their own presumptuous ideas, but from the writings and authority of their predecessors, who, so it was accepted, themselves received the rule of understanding from the apostolic succession. And because no one knows anything but what he learns (though some speak even what they do not know), when some reason compels me to speak, I have not been able to tell anything but what I know, though I seem to have added some obscure details (albeit few and pertinent to my grievous position).

25. There is also another reason for this hesitation, already mentioned above and not any less important: if someone, not persuaded by my authority (which is none, even if it has something to advance of its own), refused to put any belief in what was said or ought to be said, at least he would not refuse to believe those agreeing with me, who could pluck them from the Scriptures and pass them on to us intelligibly. I, who can find in myself nothing whereby to please another, know how displeasing I am to all, and I verify the truth of the statement that the teaching of a man whose life is despised is also scorned,[38] and for that reason I am afraid of saying anything on my own authority (even if I had any) without their company, in case I myself receive a note of censure from the

Lord, and my readers take from my own words an opportunity of criticizing what I say.

IX. Though I had decided to put at the end of the work my reasons for venturing to write this book, yet because a suitable occasion now presents itself, I think they should more fittingly be given now. While, alas, my sinfulness is doing and meriting much worse, while, wrapped up in my sufferings, I want to inspect what I have lately been, what I am now, what I have not been, what I am not now, what I ought to be or what I ought to have been, and am unable to see, I ponder whence, where, and how I contracted this blindness; but I do not find cause to be angry with or complain about either the Bestower of light or the leaders themselves, but see that it is to be imputed to my own negligence, laziness, and procrastination.

So much for what I have not perceived. But when I come to what I did indeed perceive but having perceived have again forgotten, I attribute that to my own great cruelty and savagery to myself (up to the point of self-destruction), to my own great crime against myself: in that by my own action I have so wounded myself, oppressed myself, and blinded myself, that, if ever I want to raise my eyes to the light which I have lost, I am unfocussed by such a film of my own noxious habits that not only can I not see what I desire and what I summon to my mind like a fleeting dream, but dazzled by the very light I speedily look again with some delight for the darkness itself. Now much exhausted by this long blindness, I keep thinking of the Author of the light that was given but has been lost for a while, to ask Him now, late though it be, to annoint the eyes of my mind with the salve of His mercy, who gave them to me healthy and capable of seeing the light in the beginning, and Himself, who can do everything He wants, make bright the understanding of my heart. And because, as I said, a little of His love has now taken root in my heart, I realize that by that very love, since He who gave it has bestowed it, I have merited Him too; so that I know that I ought not to thrust myself suddenly and presumptuously with my presently fogged vision into that brightness, or my eyes will be dashed by its very brilliance and return with shame to worse darkness than now. And so I think that I should aim for some glimmerings of that light, to which I might become gradually accustomed, so that when my eyes have to some extent been cleared of obstructions by practice on these, I may be able in due course to turn my stricken gaze on the full radiance of the light and to yearn in desire for Him; and to see Him with free vision as often as He will deign to shine on me, and having seen Him to love Him eternally.

To merit to obtain this in full, it seemed best to me to accustom myself to the discipline of those physicians who, discussing this in more modern times (yet with more clarity), have written the books of their art in such a way that in every point they both imitated their masters and instructed their followers—how, that is, the light itself is to be sought, found, held, perceived, loved, with what salve the eyes are to be anointed, with what good they are to be cleared of noxious dust, with what diet they are to be nourished, with what regimen they are to be preserved. Seeing myself most unlearned in all of this, yet long a lover of this same light, I wanted to write this book from their sayings for my own sake, a book in which I might put together nothing contributed by me in my own originality, but mostly found in their healing medicines; and I would not venture on my own to traverse any maze of the Old Testament[39] (in which there is easy access to anything but often more difficult egress), but I would follow them in everything and would tread the avenue worn by the steps of those who, after subjecting the same to thorough inquiry in long familiarity, are now able to proceed freely on their course without the counsel of any guide, preceeded, accompanied, and followed only by the light of the fount which flows around, within, and alongside them.

26. I have done this not so that I might presume to instill learning into anyone with this art, but so that what I had once pondered should not again escape me, as it has done now. Nor is it surprising if few works could be gathered and few remembered (and if remembered, not very eloquently or ornately expressed), though they are quite enough for so modest a work, and books to bring solace are lacking, and I am also without the conversation of friends, while the toil of my misfortune is ever there to cloud the sharpness of my intellect, and pain has blunted my memory; for if the conscience is sick, even eloquence itself is wont to turn dumb, and the badly struck chord does not sound well on the lyre.

Note, then, reader, the torment which drove me to this, the calamity, the crisis, which showed me these paths of writing. The first cause of my forgetfulness (to make it clearer in summary) was fear. To vomit out the whole of the virulent poison: I was afraid that, oppressed as now by slagheaps of vices of every kind, and walled in by the darkness of my wickedness, and bombarded by many noxious cries of worldly care, I would forget them altogether, often rejoicing that I remembered and recalled one of these rather than Him. The second reason was that, because (as I said) I am lacking books and friends to talk with, but that agonizing depression is ever present as well as the grief that constantly gnaws my heart, I should have in this work some comfort and use it like a friend to talk to and be refreshed by it as by a companion. Nor did I complain like the comic poet, saying to myself, "Who will read this?,"[40] seeing that I am the only reader, I am the only lover of this work (even if there is no one else), since lacking other books, I saw that the love of reading within me could be satisfied at least by this. And so let him who wishes read and him who wishes not read; for none can say that I am forcing him to read.

And because for this purpose I have found more spare time than I wanted, I have painted a nearly complete picture of myself in the prefaces,[41] my condition, family, name, entrusted office, my very fortune (if it dare be mentioned) and punishments, mentioning my very torturer [King Hugo] by certain indications and the punishment which awaits him unless he repents—from which I pray that God may free him; and then again, what I have done that ought not to be done, and what I have not done that ought to be done. All of this, though it seems to have been put down as though applying to other people, so that the facts cannot easily be discovered, yet is so relevant to me that it will quickly be clear when offered for inspection. If anyone cares to investigate all these hints thoroughly, he will be able to find that they have been fashioned so carefully, that my shrewd intention can be thought to have labored in divulging them in so lengthy a course of preface. But I have so fashioned the whole body of the work, that moving from prayer to reading and from reading to prayer, I have given no rest or leisure either to our athlete or to the adversary, since by prayer the former fights while the latter is thrown, and by reading the former is aroused while the latter is harassed; in one the powers of the former increase, while the latter's strength fails; in the other the former is coached, while the latter is affrighted. This being so, the prologue seems to be almost entirely mine; in it I ventured to put much of my own, though first explored by others; and the *agonistic* itself is the common property of all those who give their hand to the struggle. Hence you will find nothing of my own invention except the connecting links and, so to speak, the sinews of the limbs. The prayers have been composed by many—though some few at the beginning, which I thought relevant to the present business, have been slipped in by me—and the readings have been taken from the books of the saints. How the preface itself, which I wanted to be very succinct, has become so long a treatise still remains in part a mystery even to me, but as far as I have understood it, it awaits another place for explanation, since it is still not clear what ending God wills for my case.

But, kindly Jesus, I ask for pardon in all this while I do not cease to build up guilt—and you know it well. The reason for making this preface I think I know in part, but whether I have done so properly, in many places I can scarcely understand, and in some I admit that I am quite ignorant. Properly done is everything which is humbly expressed and is not discordant with absolute truth, which you are, O Lord. If anything, then, is properly said, I pray, Lord, that it may benefit me; if anything is discordant, may your mercy pardon it and your majesty concede that someone who understands these things better than I up till now correct it, but no one distort or destroy it. Your majesty, to whose command all things are obedient, can arrange (since for you to wish is the same as to do, to be able the same as to be) that these same thoughts benefit anyone who wishes to pray to you on behalf of poor me; and may you, Merciful One, deign to hear him and repay him in turn for his goodwill. Amen.

Here should be inserted what I promised of St. Augustine about the benefits of vigils: . . . .[42]

Therefore, since we are shown both by these writers and many testimonies of other learned men, and by many testimonies of the Holy Scripture as well, how great are the benefits of vigils, I counsel our champion thus: since he has decided to enter the prize ring against a very vigilant enemy, he should realize that he has to use prizewinning throws in order most vigilantly to keep the strength of his virtues safe against the other's constant trickery. So he should surpass the vigils of others in enthusiasm for addressing the contest, to prevent the enemy, while he sleep, rushing in unexpectedly, made that much the fiercer, the more he is shamed by his previous defeat. When he has opened his eyes, therefore, mindful of His command, "Begin in confession to the Lord" [Ps. 146.1], and remembering also His countless benefits, let him hurl his shaft at the enemy, so that it may prove for him a defence surer than any shield.

End of the sixth book of the *Praeloquia* of Rather, bishop of the Church of Verona but monk of Lobbes.

[Rather, in exile at Como, refuses an invitation from Archbishops Wido and Sobbo to attend a synod. He begs for material and spiritual support, enclosing his *Praeloquia* or excerpts from it.]

～

Rather, exile and sinner, to the saintliest and sweetest fathers, Archbishops Wido [of Lyons] and Sobbo [of Vienne], Bishops Godescalus [of Le Puy en Velay] and Aurelius.[1]

Were I not lacking paper—a fact which particularly shows how straitened my circumstances are—I would put down, fully and at length, a worthy excuse for my—not obstinacy indeed but—inability to obey your summons, an excuse that would be appropriate for worthy lords, blessed pontiffs like yourselves to receive from the most unworthy and unblessed individual of all, though also by God's mercy a fellow-bishop.

But what am I to do? What I cannot declare in adequate terms, I shall endeavor in a few: the particular reason, my lords, that I have not obeyed your lordships' summons is that I am not subject to my own will,[2] and, also, that "no one tries to delve into his own heart."[3] To feel, still less to say, anything negative about one's patron [i.e., King Hugo] (I speak to you who know) is, I judge, an execrable crime. There is no need for me to present myself to anyone's eyes for the purpose of examining my condition. As far as the worse aspects are concerned, "the whole people care for that,"[4] as Terence says; as far as the better, "if I am anything, I am so by the Grace of God" [1 Cor. 15.10]; but I am a thousand times less in every respect than what I am reported to be in the words of my friends. In the middle of these two poles the misery of my misfortune lies open to all eyes. Pity me then, I ask for God's sake, in two ways: by supporting me with your prayers and by helping me with resources. For I am greatly in need of both and I am not unaware that it is your duty to provide them and that you are rich in God's pity for fulfilling that duty.

This little work [i.e., the *Praeloquia*], the product of my sweat, selected from the rest, I direct to your attention; may you read it over with charity, for love of God. Be strong in the Lord, ever mindful of me.

3

Weigle, Epist. 21–27   Como 936–939

[To Peter of Venice, who is planning to become a monk; he outlines the duties of a monk.][5]

✍

1. Since I hear by report that you wish to abandon the world and put your hand to monastic service, I earnestly suggest that in the very beginning you remember the words of the prophet: "If you turn, Israel, says the Lord, turn to me" [Jer. 4.1]. For there are some people who, though they could have attained eternal life as laymen by the demonstration of alms, fasting, and other good works, leave their lay life and turn to monastic life not in truth but only superficially; in some things they keep their faith in the world[6] while observing the monastic routine. By a conversion of this kind they are shown to be false to God, so that they are later proved to be neither monks nor laymen.

This, then, is not conversion to God, my lord, but—and it cannot be said without tears—the worst aversion from God; such a man as this has abandoned not the world but God. For he has abandoned Truth and embraced falsehood. This can be proved by the fact that, when we consider his clothes, his beard, and the other indications of secular life, we do not even need to ask the layman what he is, clearly seeing to what order he belongs; but if this great rascal, who tries to hide the most rapacious wolf under a sheep's skin [Mt. 7.15], is examined according to the Rule, he will in no way be able to say what he is.

2. For he who has ceased to be what he was, and is not at all that which he has set himself to be, has passed with the outward image into not-being. It had been better for him to be a layman in dress and a monk at heart (which happens to many) than to be a monk in dress and lay at heart—an infinite number of whom, alas, are found in today's world. But "woe to the sinner crossing the land by two paths" [Eccli. 2.14]! And woe to wretched me, who know this and say this, and even write it as well, and take no notice of it, to whom it can most rightly be said, "Out of thine own mouth do I judge you, wicked servant" [Lk. 19.22]. Woe to all hypocrites, who, wanting to have both God and the world at the same time, lose the world and find not God but the devil himself, not eternal life, but hell. Woe to the Sarabaites,[7] those who live for themselves in a monk's dress or in a hermitage, that is, follow their own will and refuse to accept the discipline of the Rule. Woe to those seeking God with a double heart and keeping only the practice of the monastery according to the Pharisees [cf. Lk. 18.11] and not caring to have as a monk one who should be in heart the only kind that God requires, whose praise is not from men but from God.[8] Woe to those who serve greed under the name of sanctity, and serve Mammon under the name of Christ [Mt. 6.24] — though we have seen and heard very many monks practice this banditry in the Church under the pretence of receiving alms. Them without a doubt the Lord in His coming will drive out of His temple with a whip made of cords [Jn. 2.15]; for they have made the house of prayer into a den of thieves [Mt. 21.13].

3. What has a monk or hermit[9] to do with the care of the poor? This has been enjoined upon *laymen* so that they should have something whereby they can redeem their sins. But he who has left everything, who has buried himself in a prison, to whom the world has been crucified and he himself with it to the world [Gal. 6.14], who owns nothing any more even down to a single atom [*athomum*], so to speak, and cannot even put his own body in his own power (excepting only in the matter of goodwill, in which he is sufficient), and who ought not even to be anxious about what he is going to eat — ought he to be concerned that he should possess something to give to another? Does he doubt that what Jerome says is true, that "neither the wealth of Darius nor the riches of Croesus can fill up the poor of the world"?[10] And if those whom your solicitude feeds cannot live without your aid, who will sustain them when you are dead? Assuredly He who feeds the world every day while you are alive! For if we read that the raven fed Elijah, it was not thanks to the raven but to God [1 Kg. 17.6]. But don't you be a raven too; it is a rapacious bird. Those campaigning for God often enjoy the solace of creatures like this, but the assistance does not come from them but from God acting through them as agents.

But, good sir, I have not set out to treat of this topic with you now, especially since there are some who do such things with good and simple hearts. We will all stand before the tribunal of Christ [Rom. 14.10]; there it will be apparent with what intent each person has done anything.

Returning then to what I undertook to say: I suggest that if you desire to become a monk, you not do anything else for another person.

[From the same letter.]

4. "Every[11] man," He said, "who leaves his home" [Mt. 19.29], and the rest. What a happy declaration to be requited with such reward! O, what ineffable clemency of the Redeemer! When He says *every man*, none is excepted—no denier of God, no blasphemer, no parricide, no committer of incest, no inveterate adulterer, no arsonist of churches, no habitual perjurer, no individual befouled by any crime, even unheard-of and unspeakable ones, not even, I think, that "accursed salt unfit even for the dunghill" [Lk. 14.34–35]—but *every man* who leaves his father and mother and wife and children and lands for the name of Christ will receive a hundredfold and will possess eternal life.

O happy haven where every shipwrecked sailor is set free; and not only set free but enriched as well in many ways. But every man is set free only if he renounces the desire of possessing along with the thing posessed [1 Tim. 6.10]. For if that worm remains in the root, a tree like this can blossom but cannot at all bear fruit. Also, if he has neither father nor mother nor wife nor children nor property nor anything else left, if he denies this single thing, the *desire* of possessing, he will receive that perfect reward which Peter received [Mt. 19.27]. But woe to the person who hears under the names of Ananias and Saphiras the Apostle saying: "You have not lied to men but to God" [Acts 5.4]. For they sold their possessions but wanted to keep something of worth for themselves and were punished with temporal death; but he, wanting to do the same, is punished with eternal death, unless swift penitence intervenes.

5. Woe, likewise, to him who wears the monastic habit from greed or from the vainglory of this world. He also hears along with Simon Magus: "There is no lot or part in this talk for you" [Acts 8.21].

He who piously begins something but abandons it out of negligence or pride, woe to him too nonetheless. For to him those looking on say: "How have you fallen from Heaven, Lucifer, who used to arise in the morning? You shone in the morning, but you could not carry your splendor through to evening. You began to run well, but you could not happily arrive at the goal. In the morning you entered the vineyard like a prudent man, but like a madman you have not waited for your shilling. You began to run the good race, but you did not endure to the prize" [Is. 14.12; cf. 1 Cor. 9.24].

Nor should it be thought that this apostasy—that is, recession from God—occurs only in those who abandon the habit or monastic way of life and return to the world. You should know that often those persisting in the monastery or hermitage incur a fall that is worse because it is irrecuperable, when they are secretly proud about their life and their conversion, and hate (as the Pharisee hated the publican [Lk. 18]) and criticize those who are fallen in sin or are worldly or perhaps are living somewhat negligently in the monastery, not tolerating them in sympathy but scorning them in self-admiration. Too forgetful of their own former ways and the weakness they share, they do not think what God in His mercy can do about those others also, and look with a haughty and arrogant heart at themselves as though in Heaven and at them as though in hell, not understanding in what fallen devil's sty they themselves are rolling. And so their fall is irrecuperable, as I said, because it is unseen; for if it could have been seen, they could also have been warned of it.

6. The Lord says, "Where thy treasure is, there also is thy heart" [Mt. 6.21]. Where do they have their gaze if not on a secular, earthly—or rather, infernal—treasure? Those in the monastery who waste away in envy or hatred, who stir up quarrels and rivalries, and revile their brother [Gal. 5.20], how do they differ, I ask, from laymen who dispute for property? Those who serve and flatter the princes of this world [1 Cor. 2.6], and take pleasure in being visited by them, and willingly accept their gifts, and even sometimes ask for them, and do not warn them about their sins in such a way that the princes either are converted or dismiss them to live quiet lives in their cells—for whom do these monks campaign? Does not the psalmist pray for the just man to seize him out of pity and rebuke him, but for the oil of the wicked not to anoint his head [Ps. 140.5], that is, the flattery of any hypocrite not to fatten his heart? For adulation acts on the heart of a fool in the same way that a film acts on the eye [cf. Lev. 21.20]. And since one should seek the friendship of laymen for no other reason than to convert and save them, where, I ask, is the sentence: "If anyone wants to be friend of this world, he sets himself up as an enemy of God" [Jas. 4.4]?

In saying this, I do not want to contradict what I said above, nor will I seem to do so if you look carefully at my object. For there are some who, preferring themselves, despise sinners in their hearts; of them the Lord says: "Those who say, Away from me because you are unclean, are the smoke of my fury" [Is. 65.5]. And there are some who, in order to be loved in return, sweetly embrace secular people, and these are rebuked in the person of Josaphat: "You offer help to the wicked and join in friendship with those who hate the Lord" [2 Chr. 19.2]. But since the Lord says, "If they have persecuted me, they will also persecute you" [Jn. 15.20], and since there is no lack—in fact an overabundance—of the wickedness of the impious, even though their author Satan may seem to cease from open hostilities, we wretched, weak, and effeminate are not going to be crowned, but, alas, damned, because we refuse to enter the contest as we ought, but instead give our hand to the adversary, flattering his servants so that we may merit to enjoy the fruits of this world; we ought to have shunned their worldly desires and followed justice [2 Tim. 2.22]. And so we are shown by sure reasoning in no way to be living piously in Christ Jesus, since we obviously do not suffer persecution from anyone for Christ Jesus [2 Tim. 3.12].

I say this in order to advise you, most illustrious, that if you take up the fight for God, you should no longer seek friendships with the enemy. By "the enemy" I mean the devil, the world, and its lovers. For to leave the world and follow God is nothing else than to provoke the devil to a fight,[12] and to seek for ties with men of the world is nothing else, too, than to give the right hand of peace to the enemy. But you know, lord, you know that it is worse to make peace with an enemy of the king than to turn your back. But if either the duke himself or anyone else rich in the world or any relative of yours seeks your company, say what the ancients used to say: "What is there between me and you [cf. Jn. 2.4]? I am dead; the sea does not keep corpses."[13]

7. But perhaps you do not know what that persecution is which all those who wish to live piously in Jesus Christ suffer [2 Tim. 3.12]? It is multiform, just as its author also is multiform. It cannot be described, it cannot be recognized, it is performed by visible enemies without and invisible ones within, and what enemies do is inestimably less than what friends do. The flatterer's persecution of the monk is worse than the reviler's, the praiser's worse than the critic's, the relative's worse than the foreigner's, that of the man who gives him a tunic worse than that of the man who takes it away. To be brief: if anyone urges you to do whatever displeases God and pleases the devil, he is calling persecution upon you. Whatever the adversary does, be it interior or exterior, with the object of attacking the virtue of patience or brotherly love in you, is persecution. Whatever there is that causes pride or vainglory or (what is worse) envy, to flare up in the heart, is persecution; whatever stains the integrity of the mind and the chastity of the body is persecution; whatever tends towards gluttony or drunkenness is persecution.

On the other hand, unless a man competes according to the rules [2 Tim. 2.5], he will not be able to receive the crown, though he may aspire to it.

"But," you say, "David competed and fell."

He rose up again, I reply, and thereby hurled more powerful missiles at his enemy. Also relevant to the lawful contest, since it is said to another, too: "When you have once been converted, strengthen your brothers also" [Lk. 22.32].

4

Weigle, Epist. 27–29   Provence 939–944

[Rather writes to the monks of Lobbes, enclosing a *Life of St. Ursmar*[14] which he has corrected.]

⌒∽

To the most reverend lords, beloved fathers, and most learned teachers, also to the whole flock of Christians residing in the monastery of Lobbes, Rather, once a poor monk of the same, now bishop of Verona, by God's gift though utterly unworthy of both appointments, sends in the Lord's name this, which the Lord himself prepared from the beginning for His faithful [1 Cor. 2.9].

1. While spending time recently in exile, by God's just judgment, with the venerable bishop [Azzo] of the holy Church of Como, I found a book containing some few things about the virtues of a lord and especial patron of ours, namely, Bishop St. Ursmar. Its contents are more valuable than gold or precious stones [Ps. 118.127], but so filled for its small size with solecisms of language that it was difficult to understand whether this happened by the carelessness of the scribe or the ignorance of the writer. Since this offended me not a little at the time, I undertook to correct only those faults of the work which could cause the reader's understanding to miss the sense or which would alienate the listener with their grossness. But although the whole august text of the work can seem to the learned to be simple and, if I may say so, almost rustic, I emphatically thought that the changes should be minimal, because we know that even the authors of the sacred Scriptures ignored the rules of the grammarians,[15] and we everywhere see in the salvation of converted peoples that God was more pleased by the simple learning of the fishermen than the hair-splittings of philosophers.

The preface of a certain scribe called Anzo, a holy man as can be believed (though not very learned), which he attached to this work of his, should be quite left out, it seems to me, because it is so muddled that even the author's intent was entirely lost.

2. Receive kindly then, beloved holy fathers, from your—I do not dare to say son but—servant, and even runaway servant, this fruit of your instruction, small as it is, and compare it with charity with the works which are read in your company, and if they harmonize, well and good, but if not, decide with your most prudent and urbane taste whatever in this is better and more elegant,

carefully drawing it to the attention of those less learned (along with me), thinking that as one of the wise puts it, language that is simple, agreeable, and producing the appropriate response in the listener,[16] is good, and that a history should not contain anything obscure, since it is published for no other purpose than to convey the causes of the past or present to the notice of the future.

Meanwhile, I pray that the anchor of your prayers may hold me, wretchedly tossing among the shoals of this world, while you expect me to founder from my incapacity; only let not God's pity disdain to hear the sighs of a sinner.

Now may the God of Peace, who brought again from the dead our Lord Jesus Christ, the great Shepherd of the sheep, by the blood of the eternal covenant, equip you with everything good that you may do His will, working in you that which is pleasing in His sight, through Jesus Christ our Lord [Heb. 13.20–21], to whose mercy we may ever merit to find as pious intercessor saintly Ursmar, whose life I have herein undertaken to bring to light, for the praise and glory of the omnipotent Trinity and the edification of the people assembled.

5

Weigle, Epist. 29–31   Provence 939–944

[Rather writes to Archbishop Rotbert of Trier, who had raised some questions on literary topics with him; he answers that he is now studying not literature (i.e., the pagan classics) but Scripture.][17]

〰

Rather, faithful servant: to the most reverend Lord Rotbert, most noble of archbishops.

1. The fullest thanks—but still not sufficient to match the gift—do I render your lordship for the privileged benefits which your Claritude has promised me, insignificant though I am, desiring as I do that He who inspired you to make a promise may also inspire you to fulfill it, so that you may forthwith merit to receive from your humble servant the prompt return of service and from Him the eternal reward.

To reply to your lordship's question: since leaving,[18] I confess, I have studied no secular books; I regret that I have forgotten too much of what I did know. And so I admit that I am rather in need of teaching than fit to teach. Though in the very beginning[19] I was not lightly pressed by the questions of certain men of Milan, I think I have already discussed some of the things which you are un-doubtedly asking; yet honored with this burden which I bear by God's mercy, I at once ceased working at it, thinking that this office required me to meditate on the law of God night and day [Ps. 1.2].[20]

2. So making light of what "lying Greece"[21] and the garrulity of poets, ever ornamented by falsehood, may hand down, I gave attention to discoursing upon what pure Latin and the devout honesty of apostolic men has published. Despis-ing "the Hippocrene fount and twin-peaked Parnassus,"[22] I believed that I could attain both knowledge and salvation, if I could know the Fount of Life [Rev. 7.17], that is, Jesus Christ crucified and set on the cornerstone of the Church [Mt. 21.42]. For even though we are not prohibited by the Old Testament from marrying a foreigner,[23] yet, unless it is a lawful marriage with the head first shaved and—in full mystery as you well know—the other superfluities cut off [Dt. 21.10-14], we are bound to fear Phineas, the striker of the Lydianite wom-an [Num. 25.7-8], since the Israelites were ordered to steal the gold or silver vases from Egypt[24] not so that they would serve the same functions but so that the wicked race would be plundered and the Hebrew people would be enriched with the same wealth and later decorate the Lord's Temple with it [Ex. 12.35]. That wicked servant of the Gospel [Mt. 25.24-30] was addressed with the words of eternal damnation just because he chose to put the talent of his intelligence in the earth rather than wholeheartedly devote it to heaven. This parable, I think, besides other things, warns me as a sinner that I must rather exercize the little bit of talent that I by God's gift possess in the field where Christ sits on the right hand of God [Col. 3.1][25] than commit it to earthly vanity and take noth-ing else from it than empty wind along with the greatest harm to my soul [Mk. 8.36].

3. But to whom do I say this and for what purpose? Let my idle chatter final-ly be silent and my rusticity—excused, I hope—yield to your great urbanity. The hardness of the task, besides, prevents me from offering any book but this one,[26] which, lord, I entrust to you to read and send back quickly to me: to read so that the errors of the same may be corrected by you; to send back, so that I can have it to accompany my return [to Lotharingia]. For the rest I desire to have the fullest trust in your clemency. Instruct and advise me fully, I pray, how I may be of service. Know that I am ready to the best of my ability to do everything you may choose to require of me. If you deign to render any help and support to your humble servant's destitution, my lord well knows whom he ought to hope for as Rewarder thereof.

We desire your Claritude to fare blessedly and remember us till death, to the praise and glory of Him who is blessed for ever; may He preserve your honor eternally. Amen.

5A

CC Opera Maiora 279–83 (ed. F. Dolbeau)[27]   Reims, ca. 944

[A sermon delivered at Reims in praise of St. Donatianus.]

With the inspiration and support of the Holy Father and Son, there
follow some few facts about the life and deeds of saintly Bishop
Donatianus, written by a certain bishop of Verona and monk of
Lobbes.

1. Solemnly remembering that the most reverent Donatianus has been given
by God to you, glorious city of Reims, as your seventh bishop, I pray that the
seven-formed Spirit attend me, as I try to apply the same sacred number to the
sum of his praise, a number that is often commended in the volumes of Scripture. Though "small talents cannot sustain mighty bastions of matter and things
attempted beyond one's powers fail in the actual attempt,"[28] yet I am confident
that He will not be lacking who once turned the senseless braying of an ass into
human speech [Num. 22.28],[29] who unbars the mouths of the mute and makes
the tongues of infants eloquent [Wisd. 10.21], if I try to compose this speech,
crude though it be, for the praise and glory of His name and for the enlighten-
ment of His people. I do not rely on my own powers but trust in the virtue
of Him who is held the more glorious, the weaker the creatures in whom He
does His many glorious works. For His pity shines forth more widely and His
power appears more effective when weak people progress to virtue and inarticu-
late ones exceed the sophistication of even the most eloquent speakers. And so
he who places his hope in man, that is, in himself, is called by the prophet *accursed*, but he who trusts in the Lord, on the other hand, is pronounced *blessed*
[Jer. 17.5–7]. Because this one's trust is the Lord Himself alone, and he lives—
that is, unmovably remains—in the help of the Highest and dwells in the protection of the God of heaven [Ps. 90.1], he is for that reason freed from the
snare of the hunters [Ps. 90.3] (which we can with good reason interpret as,
among other things, the chatter of abusers or flatterers) and will remain untouched by that bitter word which the company of the damned is going to hear
in the coming judgment [Mt. 25.41]. For the man who in this world has not
been puffed up by any flattery nor depressed by any abuse will not in the next
be terrified by any bitter language. Like the most beautiful tree "planted over
the waters of refreshment, whose roots reach down to the moisture" [Jer. 17.8;

Ps. 22.2], because it is irrigated by the stream which the Lord promises in the Gospel—or rather by the rivers flowing from the heart [Jn. 7.38] (that is, the abyss of the soul) on account of the varieties of gifts [1 Cor. 12.4]—he stands ever youthful and joyful[30] through God's virtues, not his own. He also will not fear when the heat comes [Jer. 17.8]—that is, the final conflagration of the objects of desire of this world—when He comes with the army of angels [Mt. 24.30] who will render to each one according to his works [Rom. 2.6]. For a fire will burn before Him and a mighty tempest round about Him [Ps. 49.3]. By this fire he will not be terrified because, though we all have to pass through the fire [Job 23.10], yet he who will have within himself here the fire of charity will not there fear the fire of Judgment. For why should one who is unburnable fear fire? Why should gold fear the furnace? Though it can certainly be purified, it cannot be consumed. Therefore, dear brothers, let us burn in charity and we will not fear the heat of the Judgment. But let me now return to my theme and praise blessed Donatianus, as I promised.

2. Beloved, though it was the congregation's felicity to have merited such a man, yet it was not without some presentiment of God's gift that one of such stature and quality came after the sixth. For since the seventh number is also acknowledged to be rest for the creator of all things [Gen. 2.2], in so glorious a city, as we rightly think, no seventh ought to have come after a sixth bishop, but one who was going to be the sort of person in thought, word, and deed that God would deign sometime to rest in as in a dwelling [Dt. 33.12]. He was, as we see in his actions, most pure in heart, serene in countenance, eloquent in speech, perfect in action, a generous distributor of alms, a most fair possessor of things to be distributed, most gentle to the humble, severe on the arrogant, a man in fact over whom it may be certain that the Lord said: "To whom will I look if not to the man who is humble and quiet and trembles at my word?" [Is. 66.2]. Truly *humble* since no worldly ambition drove him. Truly *quiet* since he was free and disengaged from all the bustle of worldly desires. So unfailingly *trembling at* the word of the Lord's commands that with blessed Job he could say to the Lord: "For I always feared you like swelling waves above me, knowing that you would not spare the sinner" [Job 31.23]. "You would not spare," he said; for it is certain that the Lord does not spare the sinner if the sinner has spared himself in punishing his own sin. Therefore let us punish with weeping the wrongs we have done, if we do not want to be severely punished by Him.

But let me return, as I promised, to the celebration of that infinitely praiseworthy number, and show by God's grace that the bishop was granted this privilege of Christ also, namely that he was the seventh in order of succession to be honored with the bishopric.

3. As I said, the seventh day is taken to be rest in the Lord when everything has been properly done; God assigned a septiform face to man instead of one;[31] the whole man is formed from sevenfold matter.[32] In the seventh generation the fratricide was avenged for his crime;[33] in the seventy-seventh the guilt of the whole world was expiated.[34] The seventh man was taken to better things;[35] the septiform dove[36] brought back to the ark the gifts of mercy, pity, and reconciliation [Gen. 8.10–11]; in the seventh month the ark came to rest on the mountains of Ararat; and on its twenty-seventh day the dry land appeared [Gen. 8.4, 14]. Abimelech received seven lambs from Abraham [Gen. 21.28–30]; Jacob served seven years for Rachel [Gen. 29.20]. For seven years the world's Saviour saved Egypt from famine [Gen. 41.29, 47]; on the seventh day we are commanded by the law to cease from servile work [Lev. 23.8]. Seven candelabra were placed before the brazen altar.[37] In the seventh month the sons of Abraham were commanded to fast and to offer to God seven yearling lambs with a calf and a ram [Num. 29.2]. Seventy elders were given to Moses by the Lord to help him [Ex. 24.1; Num. 11.16]. Blessed Job had seven sons and three daughters [Job 1.2]. On the seventh day of the seige the walls of Jericho fell down at the blast of seven trumpets [Jos. 6.1–20]. The Seventh Well [Bathsheba] produced Solomon for us, the wisest [2 Sam. 12.24].[38] Seven times Naaman was washed in the Jordan and was cleansed of his leprosy [2 Kg. 5.14], and seven times the arrogance of the proud king was chastised [Dan. 4.16].[39] Seven lions kept Daniel unharmed [Dan. 14.31]. After the passage of seventy years the repentant people were freed from their captivity through Christ [Jer. 25.11–12]. In Isaiah's prophecy the flower of the royal shoot is going to be filled with a septiform Spirit [Is. 11.1–3]; and the septiform dove was seen to descend over Him in His baptism [Mt. 3.16; Mk. 1.10]. The crowd of five thousand was fed by Him with seven loaves [Mt. 14.19–21; Mk. 6.41–44]. Seventy times seven our brother is to be forgiven, He decreed [Mt. 18.22]. At the end of the seventh week after the holy Pasch the Holy Spirit came down from Heaven onto the apostles [Acts 2.1–4]. Seven Epistles of the apostles have come down to us, and he who "worked harder than all those others" [1 Cor. 15.10] took in hand to double that number, making fourteen.[40] Why do I protract it further? The levite Stephen, the seventh, was put in charge of the six deacons of Jerusalem [Acts 6.3–5]; with six preceeding him, Donatianus became the seventh bishop of Reims. Do we think this was fortuitous? In no way, beloved, in no way. This happened, I believe, because of the grace of the Holy Spirit, which abounded in both of them, so that what they were to receive in the gift was predicted in their very order.

4. Do you wish to know more fully why I ascribe this number to the Holy Spirit and say that this order of succession came to blessed Donatianus deliberately, like a kind of privilege? Pay attention, please, and listen not to me who am insignificant but to the prophet Isaiah: "There shall come forth a shoot from the root of Jesse and a flower shall rise out of his root, and the Spirit of the Lord shall rest upon him, the spirit of wisdom and understanding, the spirit of counsel and might, the spirit of knowledge and righteousness, and the spirit of the fear of the Lord shall fill him" [Is. 11.1-3]. You have there the seven gifts of the Holy Spirit working miraculously in Blessed Man and flowing like separate tributary rivulets into one channel. For since we know that the beginning of *wisdom* is fear of the Lord [Pr. 1.7; Ps. 110.10], as Solomon testifies, just as no one was more filled with the fear of God, no one appeared wiser in his days. And since "to depart from evil is understanding" [Job 28.28], he was that much the fuller in *understanding* the more he always kept himself from evil. Who ever found more salutary *counsel* than he did, who ceaselessly yearned to follow God with his whole heart? Greater *might* no one had than he did, who kept the same constancy in good and bad times alike, receiving prosperity with caution and adversity with patience. He was so filled with *knowledge* that he especially could say: "The anointing of God teaches us about everything" [1 Jn. 2.27]. His *righteousness* we cannot describe more vividly than by showing that he kept close to his heart and pursued in action the words of blessed James: "Religion that is pure and undefiled before God and the Father is this: to visit orphans and widows in their affliction" [Jas. 1.27]. He had became all things to all men [1 Cor. 9.22], by accounting their losses as his own and rejoicing in their gains as his own. What he could possess he gave away so gladly that he was confident that he lacked for nothing so long as he possessed Him who made everything. And all this he unfailingly did with *fear of the Lord*, that chaste fear which lasts for ever [Ps. 10.10]; for he had long been quite free and emancipated from that fear which perfect love casts out [1 Jn. 4.18]. So could the privilege of being seventh in the succession have happened fortuitously to a man endowed with so many blessings of the seven-fold Spirit? Let him say so who can be persuaded that those things mentioned above happened by chance and without divine providence. But we who know for certain that God established everything in measure, number, and weight [Wisd. 11.21], and that none of His actions is without mystery, will never be able to be persuaded that neither St. Stephen's nor St. Donatianus' succession happened without great presage of future deeds. For the supernal Disposition appointed to each thing before time its bounds which can in no way be passed or surpassed [Job 14.5]. "Nothing happens in the world without reason" [Job 5.6]; still less could the election, so glorious and worthy of God, of the holy bishop have happened by chance.

5. So now that we have heard, beloved, what kind of a life the blessed bishop led, let us try to fit ours to his by imitating him and as far as we can to use what he did as an example for our own pious action. Let us imitate the invinci-

ble strength of his faith, so worshipping One God in the Trinity that we may undoubtingly believe that the Trinity stands inseparably in Oneness.[41] And because that faith, though most constant, if it has no works is dead in itself [Jas. 2.17], let us drill our hearts with the works of charity, showing to our neighbors the behavior of which God approves, so that we too with undimmed hope may rightly aspire to those rewards which have been promised us by God in the future life. Let us scorn the goods of the world out of love for heavenly things, knowing full well that the former will sometime pass away, whether we like it or not, but the latter will last forever. Thus we will merit to have the blessed pontiff as supporter of our prayers if we try to imitate his way of life, since anyone who is drawn to love of this saint by his devotion, ought also to be inspired by his pursuit of the virtues. For one cannot arrive at the gathering of the Blessed except by like pursuit of good works. You will not be able to buy the fellowship of the saints there, if your vices have lost it for you here.[42] By works of piety, therefore, let us try to succeed in meriting to have him as an interceder for us in this life and as a consort in the next, with the help of the Holy Spirit, by whose name the blessed bishop was honored in his very beginnings[43] and by whose defense he was fortified in all things, and of our Lord Jesus Christ, to whom with the Father and the same Spirit there is one glory, equal praise, and equal power for ever and ever.

6

Weigle, Epist. 32–33   Provence/Lobbes 942–946

[Rather writes to Otto I's brother Bruno offering his service and enclosing a copy of his *Praeloquia*. He uses a grand style in his letter in order to impress Bruno with his rhetorical and intellectual capabilities.]

∾

To the most honored lord Bruno: the most unworthy servant Rather offers his service more faithful than the most faithful, with unceasing prayers.

Being unable to find among men of my order [the clergy] nothing at all worthy in integrity, at all distinguished in clarity, at all sharp in the wit of rational intellect, I direct this work to your lordship's inspection, desiring to have it back with improvements and to bring myself to your generous lordship's notice by

means of it. Observing in it the mark of my quality in some way, you can best
understand what I can and cannot perform in your service, a foreigner to you
though I am. Wherefore, if the work pleases, may the author of the work also
please as your servant and may you not disdain to get to know him a little.
For perhaps he too will obtain his place among the thousands of your fitter attendants. You can, if you desire, have him into your service. For I have heard
that ungenerosity is far remote from you, since you enjoy those habits of propriety which Divinity has always looked for in those rich in this world's goods
[1 Tim. 6.17]. Put aside the difficulty, therefore, and use your power, knowing
that this is what I earnestly yearn for. For my prescient heart seems, as it were,
to divine that my destitution will be relieved by your Claritude, if I can only
pay worthy and fitting service to your lordship, as a servant faithful to your
honor in everything and a most trusty aide.

My desire and prayer is that He who has conceded that the fine genius[44] of
your grace is strong in royal heritage may ever deign also to forward it to the
point that both among today's clergy everything be no less totally beneath you
and in the future nothing can be found above you.

I have attached no poem to this, as some are wont to do. For, believe me,
I am no poet, though I am not totally ignorant of the rules of metrics,[45] For
I have always cherished a more diffuse style, avoiding the epigrammatic as I hate
obscurity.

[Nos. 7, 8, and 9 are *commutationes* to the individuals named Leo, Garimbertus,
and Ursmarus, relating to property in Verona (947–948).]

10

Weigle, Epist. 33–43   October–November 951

[Rather writes to Pope Agapet II; he summarizes the dispute over the see of
Verona since 931 and seeks a public decision according to the canons whether
he or Milo is rightfully bishop of Verona. This letter provides much autobiographical detail for the years 931–951.]

∽

To the highest Lord Pontiff of the first — that is, Roman — seat, the
most reverend Patriarch Agapet:[46] Rather, sinner and exile.

1. My pitiful insignificance, wearied for twenty years now by every kind of calamity and unhappily blown from the shores of boyhood to the shores of old age through countless reefs of troubles, I offer to your sight, father, reverend lord, archbishop of archbishops and—if it can rightly be said of any mortal man—universal father, and I pray in love of the Almighty that you hear the complaint of my misfortunes patiently and kindly and, even though late, help me in the cause of Him whose seat you hold for a single purpose: never to let the gates of hell prevail against the Church [Mt. 16.18], as far as you are able to fight against it with the help of God and of Christ.

But if you ask about the person who is complaining, shouting, and crying in his troubles: I am, my lord, that poor wretch who, given to the Veronese as bishop, was on that very day, in a manner of speaking (and not absurdly either), given over to the destruction which I here bewail; in whose persecution almost the whole world so seemed to conspire that, wretched and destitute of the help of everyone, even of my own relatives, I often thought that there was no one so righteous that he was not wicked to me, so generous that he was not niggardly, so pious that he was not cruel, so humble and submissive to others that he did not seem a second Tarquin to me, so truthful that he deigned to give me even a single word of truth in his promises, from the highest of the nobility to the lowest of servants.

2. But if any can be excepted, let my brother bishops be excepted, but only with great difficulty—seeing how their wickedness is abundant and their charity cool [Mt. 4.12]; if they bore me any goodwill, I think, they did so out of fear of the great Pope Alexander's decretals, who said: "Any of your college who refuses help to them"—the bishops, that is, and the deprived—"will be judged a schismatic, not a priest."[47]

3. I am that one, lord, whom Greece can tell the East and Spain the West[48] that it has seen either pale with sorrow or red with shame, who now to his disgrace is seen everywhere as an itinerant[49] and is called that by everyone. It would be surprising if what was on everyone's lips could be hidden from your Apostleship. Add this also to the sum of my perdition (a perdition merited by my sins): I have never been able to find anyone to intercede for me either at your most holy seat or with any of the princes or potentates. But as once Paul appealed to Caesar [Acts 25.11], so I appeal to the seat of Rome.

To clarify what I have briefly touched on as succinctly as I can: when Bishop Notger[50] of happy memory moved on to a better state (as we think), the bishopric was given to my lord Hilduin[51] with right of stipend, with the promise of the king [Hugo], who at that time, as was believed, was very fond of me, that when an opportunity for promoting him was offered, I would be given as bishop to them if they so requested. When he was enthroned at Milan,[52] the king decided far otherwise than he had promised (such is often the instability and fickleness of the world), desiring instead, as the story has it, one of three: either one Aquitanus or one Garafridus[53] or Manasses, archbishop of Arles, against the canons though it would be.

4. While this was happening, I arrived back from the Roman seat, where I had been sent as legate, bearing the privilege granted my aforesaid lord [Hilduin], together with the archbishop's pallium. Along with these I also brought a letter from the lord pope of that time, John [XI] of glorious talent, in which were contained his prayers and those of the whole Roman Church that I be given to the Veronese as bishop. This was very displeasing to the king, who was working towards something quite different, but the apostolic request prevailed, on the insistence and request of my aforementioned lord [Hilduin], as well as the leaders of the realm. Now I was very ill, almost on the point of death. The king was persuaded, I think, by those who loved me, that I would not survive. Enticed by this hope he agreed, trying to satisfy as much the elder pope as the others, whom it seemed inexpedient to offend by refusing their requests. I survived; I was ordained. He was infuriated, he swore by God—and he did not lie—that while he lived I would take no pleasure from that ordination.

He sent me, therefore, in a missive a certain amount of stipend for me to keep for the affairs of the church, demanding for the rest an oath that I would not ask for more in the days of himself and of his son [Lothar]. I refused to give it, realizing what an absurd situation this would lead to. What more? He brought in from all sides persecutors and enemies either to frighten me into flight or provoke me into reaction against him, whereby he might find occasion to expel me. He found it; he arrested me; he had me locked up under guard in the fortress at Pavia.[54] I do not claim to be entirely without fault—for whoever in such a position "does not offend, even in word, this is a perfect man" [Jas. 3.2]—but he acted thus against the law and without giving me a hearing.[55] Let each say what he wishes about it—for according to St. Augustine "all things are full of rash judgments."[56] But I confess that from the time that I first saw him until the day he died I always wished for him the felicity of the emperor Theodosius and still at his memory I am greatly affected with grief.

5. For two and a half years, if my memory is correct, I suffered the former persecution[57] and for the same time the punishment of imprisonment. Released from here I spent the same period of time in exile also. But when by God's mercy I had been released even against his wishes and he by God's justice had been stripped of the honor of ruling,[58] it entered my mind to approach him and give him daily comfort for his calamity with my service. For there was one present who reported (too late, I fear, and this may God not hold against him, I pray) that the king regretted the incident and often wished that God would allow

that I would come to him, and that if he could he would gain my restitution for me, but if not he would give me sufficient money so that I would no longer be destitute. I came; Berengar arrested me on the prompting of Manasses,[59] a most holy archbishop, one who would justly hold the place of Ambrose. Held under guard again for three and a half months and then released and brought to Verona, I was treacherously received by Milo [count of Verona]; for he was hoping to expel Manasses, to prevent him in penitence from helping his uncle, the king [Hugo], whom he had greatly damaged (so the story goes).

6. Were I to try to tell of the martyrdom which I suffered for two years by the wiles of the same Milo, you would think it a history. To tell only a summary as briefly as possible: since he stirred up all the clergy, nobles, farmers, and serfs against me, I did not dare to call a synod or attend any assembly of the clergy, nor even to mention anything that had to be corrected, or to decree anything or prohibit anything. Nowhere could I say anything which he wanted to know which he did not know immediately. For he extorted it from everyone under an oath of allegiance, I think. And when all his people abused me in his presence, he alone pretended to take my part against all, so that under provocation, of course, they would exaggerate their complaints against me; so that you could believe him a second Antipater, son of the wicked Herod.[60] For any good or evil it was in my power or licence to do, even the very thing I did on his own orders (for I did not dare go against his instructions) he would turn to blame, secretly abetting the clergy's abuse of me while very treacherously promising me their punishment.

This continued to the point that one day, when I was holding a synod of the ecclesiastical orders, the archdeacon with all the clergy walked out, leaving me alone in the church, and appropriated another church for himself against me. O times, O attitudes![61] An open conspiracy against canon law! O abomination of desolation [Mt. 24.15] (so to speak)! O deed, done in Israel, at which the two ears of all that hear it will tingle [1 Sam. 3.11]! The archbishop of Arles [Manasses][62] laid an ambush for the bishop of Verona and ordained a man as bishop of his own diocese in the title of the church of Verona!

Who is not astonished? Who is not dumbfounded? Where is right? Where law? Where the secular arm that apportions certain fixed boundaries to each single province? Where the respect for Him who sees all things? Where: "Thou shalt not cross the boundaries which thy fathers have established for you"?[63] Those who do not know how far Verona is from Arles do not understand the relevance of this. Where the words of the law: "If any metropolitan tries to do anything beyond what pertains to his own parish alone, it will lie to his peril"?[64] And where: "Let the archdeacon hold his place established by the canons in humility and not go outside it"?[65] These canons refer to those who are archbishops of a single seat. But for the one who is allowed to oversee five bishoprics and benefit none of them, what will not be possible and allowed?

Though Milo was the author and prime mover of all this, yet he strove to appear and be called my supporter and protector. And he so cunningly attacked me that there could scarcely be found in the kingdom a man who did not think that he was my greatest friend in everything. But I, wretch, was so distraught day and night that I wearied of my life [Job 9.21] and would rather have sat as before in Walbert's castle [in Pavia] than in the cathedral of Verona, have rather hungered under Hugo than feasted under Milo.

7. This imprisonment I bore also for two years, the worst of all the miseries I suffered before and after. Then, as I was going to perform the evening offices, a messenger came from King Lothar[66] with instructions that I should leave the city and give Manasses the chance to usurp my seat. He added very friendly advice: it was better for me that I should withdraw than be mutilated or killed by Milo's machinations or—what would be much easier than these but worst of all for me—be arrested and led off to where I did not want to go [Jn. 21.18]. I avoid accusing, though I am able, anyone in calamitous circumstances, so as not to add pain to any wound of his, for this the prophet faults and prohibits [Ps. 66.27].

What more? I did under orders what I would previously have done most willingly without orders, had it not been forbidden by what the Lord says in the Gospel about the hireling [Jn. 10.12–13].[67] But I could not have done so unpunished. Those wolves sought to attack not the flock but the shepherd [Acts 20.29], and persecuted in one city I could with pardon flee to another [Mt. 10.23].

8. Some time after this, when our most glorious and pious king [Otto I], celebrated throughout the whole world, had entered Italy, I attended upon his most honored son [Liudolf],[68] trying to be restored to my position if the chance arose. But this was prevented by the fact that the king found another established there, namely Milo's little nephew (so it is not hard to guess why he had imposed such troubles upon me) to whom Manasses had sold the seat.[69] But the supporters of this ordination claim to have received the permission from your lordship's apostolic seat.

Thinking it would be safer to yield to your apostolic authority, as well as his royal majesty, than to criticize any decree you had laid down, freed now by God's mercy from imprisonment and exile and exercising my freedom of will, I decided to seek the solitude of a monastery and there to wait for God to make me safe [Ps. 54.9] from feebleness of heart and the storms of my persecutors, and to exact penance of myself for what had caused my expulsion, and to judge myself lest I be judged, believing that what you had decided had been decreed by God [Mt. 7.1–2].

For the highest pontiff ought to be rebuked by no one, and the heart of a king is in the hand of God [Pr. 21.1]. These two statements give instructions to each, I think: to the pope not to do anything reprehensible, to the king not to remove his heart from God's hand, that is, from the helm, if he really prefers to *be* king rather than to be called king, in making the necessary dispositions of his kingdom. I believe that you, Father, neither wished nor dared to give anyone the license of doing anything against canon law, and that he wanted the kingdom of Italy for no other pressing purpose than by imperial power to force the kingdom that had been wracked by many instances of wrongdoing of this kind and other injustices into the justice of Christian law.

9. So I had decided, as I began to say, in this way unencumbered to seek a monastery, but took second thoughts about what rank I ought to hold: as bishop or priest or some other rank or no rank? For perhaps one of those who in their own arrogance are apt to say in their heart "like this publican here" [Lk. 18.11] would say that I should not even be admitted into the public section of the church with the good laymen, and perhaps another on the other side would say, "The more he has been chastised the worthier he is" [Eccli. 30.1]. Faced with these viewpoints, my heart does not know to which it would rather give assent.

Now, later, I see from true and unexpected report that rivals are making certain criticisms of me, in which they declare that I was deprived of my priestly ministry not by force but by *right*, and I am afraid that this acquiescence or sufferance of mine may be precedent for the demotion of someone else, either present or in the future, that is, from his rightful rank (for old Adam's seed is ever inclined toward the worse); and there being "no one who might oppose himself as a wall for the house of Israel, standing in the battle on the day of the Lord" [Ezek. 13.5], I fear that the wound may become much worse in the future, creeping like the fire which fastens on small sticks and, if by negligence not put out, often burns up great cities. There is also something else I want to avoid: since the decretals state: "He clearly confesses a crime, who summoned by the canon court shuns their judgment,"[70] when *summoned*, or rather, *provoked*, I do not want to be thought to be trying to escape judgment by becoming delinquent. So I prostrate myself at the feet of your Apostlecy and desire to hear which of us two is the bishop, since one seat of the church does not permit two holders of that seat. If I am, then I am Verona's bishop; if he is, then my expulsion should not be furtive but public, so that the Church's "land and its furrows with it will not shout against you,"[71] as Gregory says, because of the false rumor of contrary suspicion.

I wish also to learn from you, Father, whether it can seem right to any Christian for a bishopric to be taken away from a bishop before the outcome of his case is known.[72] For I, wretched and unlearned, rereading and searching through much in my own cause, have nowhere been able to find this. But if there is (or rather seems to be) such cause for blame that the downgraded bishop lose first his office, then his bishopric, take care that the action not seem to have been one of enmity, not of justice.

10. Therefore, to avoid seeming a self-confessed criminal or summonsed runaway, I ask for an audience, I demand an audience, and (together with Himself, the Shepherd of all shepherds) boldly calling the invader of my church "a thief and a robber" [Jn. 10.1], because he does not enter by the door but comes in by another way—for when the husband is alive, the woman cannot lawfully be permitted to marry another man—I summon him to a canonical suit at your apostolic seat, with, if it please your lordship, this stipulation: that whether the law holds for him or for me, you may give the bishopric in the Lord only to whichever one you decide. For I do not aspire to further leadership if I cannot, as before, be of any benefit to anybody.

11. Your chaste ears, Father, will no doubt have been offended, I fear, by my appeal, rather more severe than was fitting and like an invective against my enemies, but I ask that you pardon my tortured weakness. For if you look on my misery with an attitude that is compassionate and not disdainful, you will be able to see, most wise and pious lord, that I have herein touched on no other fault of theirs than what is damaging to my ministry. And I readily call God to witness that I would rather find the ways of Probus in one and the ways of Ambrose[73] in the other than anything wicked to carp at, especially any of the things which I have suffered.

To sum up in brief what I desire: I want to be established as the true bishop of the Veronese or no bishop at all. For it does not follow that I am a bishop universal[74] and I am tired both of wandering in this capacity and telling others the reasons for my wandering. For the more frequently I see any of the lay people presumptuously perform, or rather celebrate, daily masses, the more I am able to know how dangerous it is for one who is no pontiff to presume pontifical honors. Since even a child's reasoning—if he has any—can very clearly see that one of us two is not a bishop, and since you in your overview as pastor ought to decide which one of us it is, you cannot at all leave the matter undecided without the greatest danger (if I may dare to say so), since a conflict has arisen over the question.

11

Weigle, Epist. 43–45   October–November 951

[Rather asks the bishops of Italy, Gaul, and Germany to consider in synod the dispute between himself and Milo over the bishopric of Verona.]

༄

To the lord fathers and most reverend fellow-bishops throughout all Italy, Gaul, and Germany established in the Lord: Rather, sinner and exile.

1. When driven from my rightful seat, that of Verona, holy Fathers, I had decided to yield to the malice of my persecutors (for we read that some of the most righteous have done so), and to seek the solitude of a monastery, and there "wait for the Lord to make me safe from faintheartedness and the storm" [Ps. 54.9] of those prating impiously against right and justice. But I have heard by true report[1] that I am being assailed by the taunts of my enemies, wherein they declare that I was deprived of my bishopric not by force but by right. And since the Apostle says, "All things are allowed but not all things are fitting" [1 Cor. 6.12], I am afraid that this allowed action of mine may redound to the loss or calumny of someone else, in the present or the future; or, since Pope Julius said to the accusers of Athanasius, "If you trusted in your genuine innocence, in no way would you defy the canonical summons,"[2] I am afraid of being thought so desirous of peace that I do not dare to be present in the court (though no one is summoning me canonically). I therefore make this most earnest appeal to your sacred assembly. For the love of Truth, which is Christ [Jn. 14.6], I beg for counsel and help, which is now nothing else than a synodic convention and the law established by the Holy Fathers.

For I leave it to you, fathers, to judge whether "it can seem right to any Christian for a bishopric to be taken away from a bishop before the outcome of his case appears."[3] It will be your choice, not my silence, which decides whether, with Pope Callixtus and a vast crowd of bishops, his predecessors, to use his very words, "it seems best to strike with the spiritual sword the crimes of conspiracies and the dissension of a congregation against its bishop or allow it in sufferance to grow and multiply to the prejudice of our whole order."[4]

2. And so, to avoid appearing either a self-confessed criminal or a summonsed runaway, I appeal for a council, I demand a council. With the Shepherd of shepherds I call the invader of my church a thief and a robber, because he climbs

in by another way and does not come in by the door [Jn. 10.1]; I challenge him to a trial in the court of the canons. And if he shirks it, by the most hallowed laws he is justly damned with everlasting anathema, as is clear to all wise men in their right minds; and unless he retracts in penitence, I declare "so be it."

I will also remind you, Fathers, of that chapter of the blessed Alexander which acts in my behalf: "Whoever is of your college and withholds help from those bishops" — that is, those unjustly deprived — "will be judged a schismatic not a priest."[5] And I do not leave out the words of the prophet chiding in the same manner: "You have not gone up into the breaches or built up a wall for the house of Israel, that you might stand in battle in the day of the Lord" [Ezek. 13.5]; and: "Mute dogs not able to bark" [Is. 56.10]; and that also of the Lord: "Whoever has blushed at me and my words, the Son of Man will blush at him also when He comes in His glory and in the glory of His Father and of the holy Angels" [Lk. 9.26].

This I demand and desire, wisely I hope; and you, Fathers, should all take note of the Apostle's words: "May the God of Peace crush Satan swiftly under your feet" [Rom. 16.20]. May the grace of our Lord Jesus Christ ever be with you.

12

Weigle, Epist. 45–48   October–November 951

[Rather writes to all believers in Christ bewailing the wrong done him and seeking charitable support so that he can travel to Rome to make his appeal.]

The same wretch, most unhappy, most deceived, glutted enough with the shams and ambiguities of promise-givers, and now, too late, prevented by the teaching of experience from giving credence to them any longer: to all those wishing to fulfill Christ's law.

1. Deprived of the tendance of the bishopric conceded to me, that is, that of Verona, and thrown onto the pity of all good men, I am no longer able as heretofore to dig, since labor is fruitless and I lack any kind of remuneration or income [cf. Lk. 16.3; Mt. 20.2]; and because I have always been ashamed to beg, whether from the sin of pride or from confidence in my recovery — because everything seemed tolerable if compensated by the hope of ultimate fruition on that one day at least, were it given me — finding no third course to fol-

low, I am compelled to ask your charity, wheresoever it is, and redoubling my cry, I implore you to look upon my trouble.

For nowhere do I have even the rest of lodgings, nowhere any refuge, except the place of men of charity, those, that is, who take to heart the words of the Gospel: "When you make a meal, call the poor and you will be blessed because they have no wherewithal to repay you; for you will be repaid in the resurrection of the just" [Lk. 14.12–14]; and also the fearful example of the rich miser, who, not realizing why Lazarus had been permitted to lie before his door [Lk. 16.19–31], a fact from which he could take the greatest refreshment, did not, unhappy one, foresee that he was lighting his own everlasting fire. Because he did not turn a righteous ear to the poor man's cry, he experienced for himself what was most truly said: "Whoever turns his ear from the cry of a poor man himself will cry and will not be heard" [Pr. 21.13]. And so, when the wretch later asked for the drop of water, he was not heard because he had not given.

This example shows the truth of the saying: "Whoever turns his ear lest he hear the law, his prayer is an abomination" [Pr. 28.9]. But it has been the law from earliest times to give to someone else what one would want another to give to oneself; and secondly, not to deny anyone any natural good; for the Decalogue declares: "Thou shalt love the Lord thy God with all thy heart and with all thy soul and with all thy mind and with all thy strength and thou shalt love thy neighbor as thyself" [Lk. 10.27]. And there is a third law, given in time of grace, to be sure: "Carry each another's burdens," says he who was taken up to the third heaven [2 Cor. 12.2], "and so you will fulfill the law of Christ" [Gal. 6.2] — of Christ, of course, because He himself, when asked by a man what was the great commandment in the law, after stating the first great commandment, declared that the second was like unto it [Mt. 22.35–39]. To distinguish His own from the rest, He said, "By this, all men will know that you are my disciples, if you have love for one another" [Jn. 13.35].

2. But every man, when asked, even the worst villain of all, even some despot, says "I love God"; for alas, today hatred of one's brother has spread so far that no class of person is more glorified in the world than the murderer. But one who lay close to His breast as He preached [Jn. 21.20] says: "If anyone says, I love God, and hates his brother, he is a liar. For if he does not love his brother, whom he has seen, how can he love God whom he has not seen?" [1 Jn. 4.20]. And again: "Every man that hates his brother is a murderer. And you know that every murderer has no part in the kingdom of Christ and God" [1 Jn. 3.15; Eph. 5.5]. *Every* murderer, He says, that is, every one of those damnedly glorious ones whom I deplored a little above and every hater of his brothers.

Another says: "I hate no one who is a Christian." Then you *love* all Christians; there is no third alternative. And this is that love which the apostle puts even above martyrdom [1 Cor. 13.3]. Since I undeniably lack the aid of this love, I hear nothing sweeter than the words that are read—and I would heartfully desire you to do the same: "If anyone has the world's goods and sees his brother in need, yet closes his heart against him, how does God's love abide in him?" [1 Jn. 3.17].

And elsewhere: "Little children, let us not love in word or speech but in action and truth" [1 Jn. 3.18]. And the psalmist's words: "Blessed is he who considers the poor and needy" [Ps. 40.2]. When I read Gregory's interpretation of this described in nine separate ways,[6] I take consolation, and even more when I read the words of Aurelius Augustine of august memory: "Pity is rightly due to all the poor, but a greater feeling of charity affects us for those who have come down to the lowest state from one of wealth or nobility";[7] and Jerome agrees with him, noting that one should give rather to those who blush when they receive.[8]

Inspired by this thought, I beg your purest charity (which I seek) to consider— and all righteous men to note—how hard and shameful it is for a man who has undertaken the office of distributing alms to cry that he is destitute of means, who groaning with both inward and outward need can say: "All day long my disgrace is before me and shame has covered my face" [Ps. 43.16], and—along with those like me—"Have mercy upon us, O Lord, for we have had more than enough of contempt; too long our soul has been sated with the scorn of those that are at ease, the contempt of the proud" [Ps. 122.3–4].

3. Since it is recognized that those who have more take more to satisfy them [Num. 35.8], and those who have little are satisfied with less, I fear that one of you in his wisdom may wonder what is the great pressure I am under to beg for money, since by my own admission above I do not have my household. To satisfy your curiosity: you should know that when I had lost my bishopric and hope of recovering it had vanished, I wanted to go somewhere where I might rest for good. But my enemies, carefully—so they thought—amassed material for suits and litigation and, though I had decided to spare them with my peace, challenged me with various charges, not indeed to my face but behind my back. If I do not reply to these in the court of the canons, I am judged either a deserter or a criminal, and I infamously brand the office which I hold with the mark of foul suspicion.

But I lack the resources for doing this; I am far away from Rome, yet the Church there must be addressed on this issue if my suit is to be allowed; and the generosity of emperors long ago dropped the custom of providing public vehicles for bringing bishops to councils (as in the former days of Constantine of blessed memory). Since I do not want to abandon this essential trip without even attempting it, and since I am not able to make it, I beg the help of all good men, soliciting nothing from wicked men as I ask only the assistance of love.

13

Weigle, Epist. 48–49   after September 953

[Rather writes to an unknown addressee asking for copies of works on medicine.]

Dearest Father: I beseech your lordship that for the love of God and the salvation of your soul you have what is written about medicine in your scroll transcribed into this book; you know that in this country[9] there is a great poverty of it. In return I will have ten masses sung for you.

14

His Decision

[Rather failed in his attempts to retain Verona; Otto confirmed Milo's nephew, also called Milo, in the see. Rather became a wanderer again. But his letter to Bruno (no. 6 above) had been well received.

In 953, two episcopal sees in Lotharingia lost their bishops: Cologne, whose archbishop Wicfrid died in July, and Liège, whose bishop Farabert died in August. Both bishoprics were important political posts for Otto's security. He had appointed his son-in-law Conrad to the duchy of Lotharingia, but Conrad had broken with him, and even though Conrad had been ousted earlier in the year, Lotharingia's loyalty to Otto still must have been in doubt. Accordingly, he appointed his brother Bruno to Cologne as its archbishop, and Bruno in turn appointed Rather to be bishop of Liège. Bruno was an enthusiastic churchman as well as statesman and he must have chosen Rather not so much for political reasons but because he wanted a man of Rather's integrity and doctrinal zeal to bring the Church back to a state of discipline.

Canonically, the bishop had to be elected by the clergy and people of the church, but it had become the practice for a pre-election to be held under certain clerical and lay magnates at which the king was present or represented; the candidate selected would then be "elected" by the clergy and people. In *Phrenesis* c. 1 Rather distinguishes two elections, the first at Aachen palace on September 21, by "those whose special interest it was," the second at Cologne on the following Sunday, "by the people of the Church of Liège," that is, presumably, lay and clerical representatives of that church. Rather is so insistent that due process had been observed in his nomination and election that it is clear that his election could be—and was—challenged on legal grounds: could a bishop expelled, as he had been, from one see (Verona), legally be appointed to another, even though that see was vacant? Whatever the arguments that took place, both Bruno and Rather were formally installed in their bishoprics at the Church of Cologne on the same day. Details of the ceremony can be gathered from *Conclusio deliberativa* and *Phrenesis*. He was then accompanied to Liège and formally installed there.

His first weeks seemed tranquil enough, as no. 15 shows. But by Christmas there was already formidable opposition to him, either through enmities which his acid criticism of the behavior of certain powerful figures both lay and cleric had aroused, or as part of a wider attempt by counts Rudolf of Haspengau and Reginar of Hennegau to undermine Otto's power in Lotharingia. Rather's position was challenged on the grounds that he had been expelled as bishop of Verona and could not therefore hold Liège. He tells us how Rodbert, archbishop of Trier and Baldric, bishop of Utrecht, hatched a plot to replace him with Baldric's nephew, a young man of the same name. Rather would not give in; he appealed to Bruno for support. But Bruno by now perhaps realized that the choice of such a controversial figure as Rather had not been conducive to peace in the see and he accordingly gave in to the pressures to have him removed. Two other uncles of young Baldric, Reginar and Rudolf, sent their troops and he was forcibly ejected. But before leaving Liège Rather issued a statement of forty articles of decison called *Conclusio Deliberativa*.]

⟨∾⟩

The Decision which he made at Liège: *or* Rhetorical Climax of the same not so lowly person who wrote the above.

Because it seems an impossible task to satisfy everyone with the propriety of my answer, I lay aside all circumlocution and declare clearly, and as openly as I can, to all who deign to know, what I have unshakeably decided.

Let everyone know that I have prayed, do pray, and will pray to God:

1. that it may never happen to me because of my sins that, seduced by some gain or in fear of some loss, I should by my own mouth expose to the wolf the fold which was publically entrusted to me in the presence of, and to the applause of, the whole church[10] whose interest it was;

2. that I may never, to the detriment of the flock entrusted to me, shelter within the same fold by my acquiescence and silence (by yielding to his wickedness, that is) a thief and robber[11] condemned by the mouth of God himself [Jn. 10.1] — a thief because by theft he usurped my seat, a robber because by force and the use of public power he twisted it out of the hand of my ordainer, a

curse and leprous plague because he mortally deceives those who think him to be the bishop and pollutes those who take communion with him;

3. that in fleeing this wolf I may not bring on myself the charge of being a mercenary or hireling [cf. Jn. 10.12–13];

4. that in shunning the thief I may not deserve the name of thief myself;

5. that I may not cease appealing for help from my fellow shepherds and servants;

6. that I may not cease stirring up my household watch-dogs[12] to confound him with the barking of the canons;

7. that I may not be shown to have "thrown in my lot with an adulterer" [Ps. 49.18] of such patent and sacrilegious assault, prostituting to him the church committed to me;[13]

8. that I may not "sit and speak against my brother" [Ps. 49.20], that is, the people of my native country[14] joined to me by the kinship of neighborliness, deprived of the office of their bishop, by urging them to become wicked with the wicked [cf. Ps. 17.27];

9. that I may not cause a scandal against the son of my mother [Ps. 49.20], namely, the congregation of that Church whose son I also am by baptism, so monstrous a scandal that it is apparent even to the little children. If I forget myself and do cause a scandal, though God may be silent (but only for the time being) for me who is deaf to Him, as He is for many today, alas, He will not be silent, I fear, when He comes made manifest, that is, when "the fire will burn in His sight and in His sight the storm will be mighty" [Ps. 49.3];

10. that I may not become part of the Nicolaitan sect, which God himself declares that He hates [Rev. 2.6];

11. that I may not be judged to have exposed (like the ostrich [Job 39.13–14]) those whom I ought myself to have protected to those who would trample them down;

12. that I may not be charged with having deceived by my continued absence those whom the canons do not allow me to leave for even a three-month period.[15]

13. that that same Church may not cast in my face the spit of lawful expulsion, as a result of my first having shown her the scorn of rejection;[16]

14. that I may not be wrongfully accused of having been the first to say, "Put me in one of the priests' places, that I may eat a morsel of bread" [1 Sam. 2.36], which was once said in the prophets;

15. that I may not foolishly count as unimportant the fall of a thousand oath-breakers;[17]

16. that, if the whole country should also be subjected to the mortal plague of excommunication, I may not argue that it is of no danger—or perhaps very

little—and so be accused of taking the Lord's name in vain [Ex. 20.7] or, what is worse, causing many others to take it in vain;

17. that by my example, if wretchedly I yield, I may not destroy what those Fathers, in whose hearts God has always lived, in whose lips Christ—because He is the Truth—has always moved, have conceded in the canons with all brotherly love and mercy not only to be lawful but even necessary in the common interest or necessity, which will daily increase, the more the world is placed in the power of the evil one and deteriorates as the end nears [1 Jn. 5.19];

18. that I may not myself, wretchedly to my own peril, be the first to deprive other wretches, who will like myself be destitute and thrust out from their sees as the AntiChrist's persuasions grow stronger, of the one asylum thus proclaimed by God: "If you are persecuted in one city, flee to another" [Mt. 10.23]; though I am well aware that those who are persecuted by the Babylon of worldly confusion ought by this commandment to seek most of all the refuge of Heavenly Jerusalem;

19. that I may not heartlessly block the way, conceded by this commandment to those who are unable to keep their bishoprics in their own churches, of recovering one in other churches that have a vacant seat, as allowed by the canons;[18]

20. that I may not myself come to contradict the declaration that God prefers mercy to sacrifice;[19]

21. that I may not decide that something which has been publically done by decree of the prelates, with the testimony of decrees, with the sanction of the canons, in the presence of the whole Church, by the lawful archbishop, with the agreement of the clergy (which the laws also require), can in any way be invalidated;

22. that I may not declare, nor even seem to believe, that what the most pious king [Otto] mercifully and truthfully conceded was either irregular or— what is even less befitting—fraudulent;

23. that I may not darken the dignity of the kind act which obtained it for me with the blackness of ingratitude;

24. that I may not myself brand it with the stigma of irregularity;

25. that I may not condemn the hand of the great authority which granted it;[20]

26. that I may not declare that my own ordainer [Bruno] was himself ordained with such ominous auspices (if it is proper to say so) that on the very same day on which he made the customary declaration that he would always obey the commands of the canons and was ordained, I should accuse him of decreeing something contrary to canon law, that is, by supporting the madness of those who do not realize whom they are really attacking, when they foolishly

criticize my incardination solemnized on the same day and by the hand of the same person;[21]

27. that I may not myself seem to belittle by lack of praise the ever-glorious privilege conceded in our time (by God alone and not by happenstance) to him and to his nephew,[22] most worthy of primates — the privilege whereby the latter on the day of his own ordination merited to ordain another, an act which in my case is as laudable as it is charitable;

28. that I may not accuse him[23] of having placed God himself beneath the persons of men — and those far inferior to himself — by declaring that he inflexibly yielded to their wickedness and quite destroyed what he had himself done in accordance with canon law, while confirming what was done against canon law;

29. that I may not set at naught the dignity of the great seat where this was done;

30. that I may not wretchedly make light of the reverence (worshipped throughout the world) of St. Peter, the foremost of the apostles, before whose sacred altar I merited to receive the pastoral staff;

31. that I may not despise — as though ignorant of the honor in which it should be held — the venerable pulpit on whose eminence I was that very day appointed to the congregation looking on;

32. that I may not despise the dignity of the one [Rodbert] who summoned me, since he also was an archbishop,

33. nor the acclamation of so noble a congregation,

34. nor the hymns of praise of the most noble clergy, along with the sounds of the trumpets;

35. that I may not forget without consideration the most holy, sweet melody of the hymn which was played;

36. that I myself by my secession may not be shown to have condemned the signatures of seven so eminent prelates, of whom two were also archbishops;[24]

37. that I may not seem to be spurning the persons of the *legati*,[25] since they were also bishops, who put me in charge of the people committed to me, one of whom was also the Metropolitan;

38. that I may not dare to call or believe false their report, which obtained the concession of the most pious king [Otto] in my interest, since, as the proverb says, the words of a bishop are either true or sacrilegious;

39. that I may not be slanderously accused of having been ungrateful in receiving so spontaneous an acclamation, so joyous, so devout, so wholehearted, so vociferous, filled with such praise of Christ (for I had been given to Him) from a congregation very devoted to me;

40. finally (what any wise man will think as much exceeds the above as earth is distant from the sky or east from west), that I may not dare to commit a

sin of such profane wickedness—by yielding illegally when it is possible to resist—
that I can be shown to be joining those who deny my ordination and to be condemning everyone who is known in the past to have been transferred for certain
reasons from their own seat to another by the same authority as I have been
(though not in the same condition of merit);[26] even leaving out those shining
examples of our own[27] (since no mention is made of where the action took
place), such as Dionysius, finest champion among the martyrs, and holy Cassian
of the Aedui, along with countless others whom either ignorance has hidden
from us or oblivion snatched—without these, I say, there are still very many
proven cases in the testimony of books. Peter—not any Peter but the one to
whom we know God said in His own voice, "Feed my sheep" [Jn. 21.15]—
stands at the head of this triumphant line. Close behind him come Felix, Eusebius, Perigenes, Gregory of Nazianzus, Meletius, Dositheus, Alexander, Reveren-
tius, John, Palladius, Alexander again, Theosebius, Polycarp, Hierophilus,
Optimus, Silvanus, Martin of Corsica, John Squillacenus, and a certain Terracinen-
sian. Their supporters are Pope Calixtus, Pope Antherus, and Gregory[28] our esteemed theologian (but only if there is no doubt about the testimony of so great
authority); if these men are damned, I consider it most fortunate to be damned
along with them.

But if the authority of these great precedents is scorned and I am expelled
by public force, let the wielder of that force look out for himself. I would rather
have force used on me in need by someone than be judged to have struck "a
pact with death and made peace with hell" [Is. 28.15].[29] I do not ungratefully
withdraw my hand from anyone who offers me help of charity, with the exception of that robber.[30] O blind hearts of the sons of old Adam! O darkness of
Egypt,[31] so dense still that it can be touched! For among the thousands who
seem, as it were, to acknowledge the crime, saying in complaint, "What a shameful
sin it is that that bishop seems to be deprived so unjustly," there is scarcely one
found who more rightly says, "What a terrible sin that so large a congregation
of the Christian name should be so deceived!"—since my destitution can be lightened by daily bread, but no one can tell how final is their perdition. If anyone
whose business it was deigned to think about it, he could easily decide whether
a person who is called in reproof and damnation by the shepherds' Prince and
Source, by God himself the Shepherd and Creator, "thief and robber" [Jn. 10.1],
can be a shepherd of the Church in the blessing and consecration of anything
mortal; again, whom can *he* bless, who has rightly been damned with the curse
of anathema? Whoever wishes may try to tone this down if he can; no man's
declaration will ever be able to persuade me that it is not absolute.

Therefore, the reader should know that I am replying to my wicked expellers
with these forty—unless my counting is wrong—points for the bishopric of Liège,

more earnestly than I, Rather, stood up to my most importunate urgers with those sixteen points for the bishopric of Verona.[32] May he besides be damned with Judas Escariot (unless he be helped by penitence) whoever further exhausts me—excepting the censure of the sacred canons and the imperial power of most pious Caesar [Otto].[33]

15

Weigle, Epist. 49–54   April 955–May 956

[Fragments of a letter to Bishop Baldric, his successor in Liège.]

∽

1. . . . which happened to the same acclaimed and praised individual.

I was enthroned [in Liège], I took my seat, I hastened to begin what had to be done, I set out with my soldiery against the king's [Otto I] enemies [Conrad], so as to show worthy service to him too; I returned, I welcomed my ordainer [Bruno] in my house, I offered my service, I gave him presents; when my guest departed, in good health and most affectionate to me, so I thought, I attended him with fullest service as far as Maastricht; I parted from him blest with his fondest kiss of farewell; I returned, I made the rounds of my see; with the leaders of the Church, both cleric and lay, I managed what had to be done, I allotted their several tasks to each; I decided with God's help to benefit many, obstruct none, lighten many, oppress no one. If I was perhaps a little hard on some, yet I had determined never to keep being an Olybrius[34] to anyone. . . .

2. All this I decided both to do and to conduct so equitably that I would leave to my critics (of whom I did not doubt that there would be many) no ground for malicious attack. For there was also present one [Rodbert of Trier] who, in a perverse opinion,[35] was not ashamed to blame what had been particularly commended by his own mouth at my ordination, when he regretted what he had done; he obstinately wanted the self-willed "I want and don't want, and now I don't want and want" of Terence's boy[36] to be part of ecclesiastical business, not fearing to "cast a sure opinion in a case of doubt" contrary to the command of the canons,[37] not understanding that when it says that no one should be condemned in his absence, this too is also equally contradicted. . . .

3. Yet if he had read the letter written by Gregory to Martin of Corsica and had not ignored it, he would have been able to see clearer than light that when another seat is conceded to a bishop who has been expelled, if he rejoices that

he has won his desire, he avoids the criticism of this theologian of such great authority. . . .[38]

4. While this was peacefully being handled, it was unexpectedly announced that Count Rudolf [of Haspengau] — not indeed as a friend, as befitted a fellow-priest and one treated with much kindness (in my opinion), but as an invader — had entered the city [Liège] of the seat I had received. This worried me a little, and while I was looking for a proper solution, you yourself [Baldric] the next night entered the city like a brigand. The archbishop [Bruno] (who, trying to give me the swift help he had promised, arrived three days later) asked you in the language of Terence, as he himself told me, "What are you doing in Athens, insolent one?"[39] You said that you had come to talk with your uncles. The second of these, Reginar [count of Hennegau], had arrived in the evening, as the archbishop's cape, torn by the bite of his [Reginar's] prancer, testified, an unfortunate incident that proved ominous. At dawn, when they found him [Bruno] there, since he could be preyed upon more advantageously, with a few retainers they put into action their long planned treachery, excited beyond words by the opportunity offered by the upheaval, vigorously assaulting the aforesaid [Bruno] with flatteries and violently exhausting him as he resisted with all the daring he could muster. . . .

5. So as not to nauseate my listeners with too much detail: for a year and a half he [Rather] was constantly tormented, wracked, dismembered, and un-sinewed,[40] while he looked more to the perils of the king's brother [Bruno] than to his own, as they [Rudolph and Reginar] forced him into a corner so that either you [Baldric] would be promptly ordained in his stead or, as rumor had it, they would make a complete break with the king. In that situation, his fear of the temporal danger was more compelling than God, the helper in trouble, his forced breaking of the law more compelling than the rewards awaiting those who persevere or the torments awaiting those who give in. . . .

6. And so that savory nectar turned into the bitterest poison for me, when, in a complete reversal, alas, my defender [Bruno] turned into an adversary, my benefactor into a tyrant, my savior into an oppressor, and one and the same hand gave me both help and hurt, while "former sweets became bitter, soft hard, white black, right left."[41]

As if I had muddied the stream which in the old fable flows from me down to you,[42] you have pursued me for a whole year with standards raised and colors flying. Cast your eyes on the whole kingdom, which you have not blanched to fill with slaughter;[43] is there any damage which you have *not* inflicted on your country. . .?

7. And so, after a year's occupation by the invaders, after the devastation of the whole province, after catastrophes of fire and famine, after numerous riots

and brawls, after violent deaths, after many tears of widows and babes, after the anguished cries of the whole oppressed family of the Church—after priests and clergy of every rank had been robbed of their substance, after the care of monks had been entrusted to lay persons, after the chastity of widows and virgins had been prostituted—after conflicts within families, after indescribable rampage both by your own troops and by your opponents. . . .

16

Phrenesis

[After leaving Liège, Rather went to Mainz where he stayed for some months with Archbishop William, a natural son of Otto. It was there that he wrote the work *Phrenesis*,[1] lit. "insanity," which he says he called by this title because Rodbert and Baldric had called him *phreneticus*, the madman; most of it is addressed to Rodbert, whom, though an enemy, he seems to acknowledge as a man of learning and erstwhile friend.[2] In fact, much of the work would have been unintelligible to all but a few *literati*. As a polemical tract defending the rightness of his position it is a total failure. But perhaps he was trying to make his peace with Rodbert (who had after all been one of his supporters in the election) by appealing to him as a man of learning, showing off his own learning by many abstruse allusions to a wide range of classical, patristic, and biblical literature. He ultimately hints that *phrenesis* is literary madness, which all literati share in the eyes of lesser men who lack their higher wisdom; the suggestion must be that Rodbert is one of his own kind, an intellectual, and should not be allied against him with the likes of Baldric, who only understands force.

In *Phrenesis*, he also tells us that he collected twenty books of his works but later reduced this collection to twelve out of respect for the king. Some of the twelve have survived but most are lost. *Phrenesis*, he tells us, will serve as the preface to the collection.]

≈

Here begins the preface to a book by Bishop Rather which he has called *Phrenesis* ("Ravings"), on the grounds that in it he has very harshly criticized certain individuals.

1. It is a great impediment to the students of any writing if they do not know its background—that is, the author, the author's objective and the circumstances which gave rise to it. All the books[3] for which this appears as a preface are called *The Ravings of a Man Called Rather* [*Phrenesis cuiusdam Ratherii*]. Why did they deserve such a title, when some of them should rather have been called *Invective* [*Invectiva*] and some *Self-justification* [*Apologetici*]? This is the reason for the name: After Rather had been driven from the see of Verona in Italy where he had been ordained, he applied for support to the most glorious king Otto [I], but he failed to achieve his restoration despite the efforts of that most pious monarch. Then, when an opportunity arose[4] at Liège, by the means and intervention of the king's brother, Archbishop Bruno, he was not only elected in the king's presence at the palace called Aachen by the proper representatives, but was also nominated by the bishops, abbots, counts, and leaders of the whole realm, on the fourth day of the solemn fast of the seventh month [21 September, 953]. And on the following Sunday [25 September] he was again elected by that congregation, that is, of the Church of Liège, by seven fellow-bishops, of whom two were archbishops, Bruno [of Cologne] and Rodbert [of Trier], and the rest bishops, Baldric [of Utrecht], Hildibald [of Munster], Druogo [of Osnabruck], Berengar [of Verdun], and Folbert [of Cambrai], in accordance with the decretals and following the precedent example of several to whom this had happened in times past. He was acclaimed with great applause by the whole congregation which was present and solemnly enthroned; and then afterwards, by the intrigue of the above-mentioned Baldric and at the instigation of Rodbert, archbishop of Trier, who in particular had praised him in front of the whole congregation from the pulpit of the church of Cologne, he was expelled by the men-at-arms of Counts Regener [of Hennegau] and Ruodvolt [Rudolf of Haspengau], so that their nephew, a boy also called Baldric, might be appointed—he was also the son of Baldric's brother, so it is not difficult to guess why it happened. To bring the matter to light in every detail (without showing partiality to individuals [cf. Rom. 2.11]): Because of the timidity of the king's brother [Bruno], who was afraid that those two counts might now defect from the king to Conrad[5] (who was at that time moving against him) and might join Conrad in opening hostilities—or (as [Bruno's] apologists more correctly declare) because the archbishop could find no one among Bishop Rather's friends and retainers to help in opposing this action, as he had earnestly hoped—Rather was expelled; and now, enjoying at Mainz the generous kindness and abundant hospitality of Archbishop Willihelm,[6] the king's son, Rather has been given this opportunity for leisure, and has taken in hand to put down on paper what had been done to him, endeavoring that the circumstances of his time would not be hidden from those interested. Hearing this, those two particular enemies of his, Rodbert and Baldric, said that he was *Phreneticus.*

2. Rather's ardor for writing, which had been dormant for a while, was rekindled by this taunt, and he hastened to write the present tract against them for all to read; he calls its title *Phrenesis* according to their phrase and himself the *Phrenetic*, because, in a manner unusual in this age, he took refuge not in money at such a crisis, but in books, in archives, in the ideas of the ancients. In this preface, he inveighs more fully against Rodbert, but more bitingly against Baldric; hence, right at the beginning, as though despising him [Baldric] more than himself, he calls him immune to the vice of *phrenesis*—for which he wishes *madness* to be understood—which in the poets of old would be purged by hemlock.[7] He also calls Baldric a fellow standard-bearer to Rodbert in their attack on himself, though in a different battle-line, that is, not with the same skill at speaking which Rodbert aspired to, but with greater cunning and deceit. Rather would appear to spare none but those defended by their own integrity, though like a second Lucilius he is often least sparing to himself.[8] The interested reader can see how he does not leave the archbishop [Rodbert] also untouched in his writings.

3. The books which he has written are also made difficult to understand by the fact that he very frequently inserts parentheses and, to make his style fluid, often adopts an astonishing order of words, which makes his prose very hard to construe, though it is the best order for men of understanding. Many may be deceived by a careless consideration of his eloquence, as they have been in judging his character; to forestall this, I admit that his abilities are due more to native talent than to training, and his fluency of writing (though not of speaking) more to practice than wide knowledge. He has learned to write from studying and researching the ancients, rather than from the rules of rhetoric. He has learned few things from his teachers and more on his own, attaining by rash presumption what others would hardly have learned with great toil from the finest masters. For this reason, a certain wise and equally religious man, after reading certain of his works, was afraid that, as the Apostle had warned, "knowledge that puffs up without the support of Love" [1 Cor. 8.1] would confound him, and said that in him grace seems stronger than wisdom, and that he should be an object of amazement rather than praise. But praise and admiration should rather be given to the merciful Grace, which has not abandoned him who had abandoned It, but has conferred such blessings on him who ought to be abandoned.[9]

4. To touch on some of his habits without either praising or chastizing them:[10] he would be more likely to say than to do any good, depending in both on a deliberate hypocrisy which entirely deprived those seeing him of any sure evaluation. He was more often led to avoid sins by his timidity and weakness than attracted by the pleasure of them, and his motives for not doing something were rather unconstructive idleness than obedience to the dictates of probity (to call it that). He often seemed to be angry when most glad and to be glad when he hid huge grief within him. He would give when not asked, but would be irritated if asked; he would often seem hurt, as though harboring some unknown rancor. He acted in this manner in much of his business, so that his mood was hard to assess. He would be happy, perhaps, if he lived the life of a monk, as his monk's habit shows. He would never have left the monastery at Lobbes if he had been true to his vows. He was wellborn, but rather from the antiquity of his family, it seems, than from living relatives in high position. The white hairs which he had when he wrote this were not premature, but had been brought on by the approach of old age.[11]

In short:[12] he would almost have been guilty before his critics, if some blameless person had not hurt him by his example,[13] or if "not to help" were the same as "to hurt." He was, as I have said, so inconsistent in his actions that a proper evaluation of him can scarcely be attempted. For though he was in the opinion of many hot-tempered, he had a strange habit of being irritated by the very slightest annoyances while being amazingly tranquil in tolerating the greatest. Therefore, let no one compare him with those he *seemed* to imitate, lest quite deservedly he hear the prophet cry to him: "Woe to you who say that bad is good and good bad" [Is. 5.20]. His right actions I praise; let no one gnaw at them in jealousy, lest blessed Job seem to challenge him with: "Envy has killed the little one" [Job 5.2].

5. This book would perhaps have been greater in size if it had not been cut short—as the shuttle is cut off when the weaving is finished [Job 7.6]—when he heard of the death of the aforementioned Rodbert,[14] though it was a false rumor which reported his death earlier than the fact. He touches on this too quite bitingly in the beginning of his preface and deals with it more openly at the end.

He has sown his work with quotations from Cicero, Vergil, and Horace, and various other poets, compelled by the fact that people of today, alas, like himself, are more delighted with the husks which are the feed of muddy swine [Lk. 15.16] than the feasts which are the life of blessed souls. Therefore, he surely inserted such quotations so as to acquire a wide readership for his work, because he knew that no one like himself would touch even with the tip of his lips a cup containing the nectaral essence of the heavenly gift, unless the worldly application had tainted the liquid, or because what is easily discovered is soon despised.[15] Such affectations show how little concerned he is with true simplicity and pure wisdom, when a man struggles to *appear* wiser to others, not to *be* wiser, by inserting as he does other people's ideas among his own, only so as to persuade more people that he is well-read; this is rather to purloin the rags of the arts, not to attain the arts themselves, to attach the ancients' glory to himself, not to follow their lead. "O imitators, servile flock,"[16] says one of them accurately, a flock which our Boethius[17] did not fail to criticize.

People who deceive people and so make them deceivers of others are, in my opinion, non-beneficial to themselves and damaging to every one else. My critics have superficially examined only individual items of my knowledge and they think from this that the whole or greater part of my knowledge is less than their own, and they make others think the same by telling them so. This is what God seems to me to mean when He forbids us to put a stumbling block before the blind [Lev. 19.14]. For if someone cannot see something put right in front of his face, how can he not be considered blind? It is clear that the apostle earnestly cautions against this [i.e., this kind of affectation] when he desired people not to think any more about him than what they saw in him or heard from him [2 Cor. 12.6]; yet the writer is horrified if anyone is deceived enough to build him up as knowledgeable, or noble, or—what's worse—righteous, when really he is not, and makes others tell lies about him through writings especially (in that writings speak after one's death when the writer is silent); thus he makes himself a hidden stumbling block to those who are blind in ignorance. It would have been much more felicitous to have been as obscure at death as at birth than to have won the acclamation of a false reputation for knowledge. Thus it comes about that hypocrites do not stop sinning even when they die, as they make themselves falsely praised after their death. Let this then suffice about the knowledge of the writer; let it be a summary of his whole character and endeavor, neither diminished in envy nor exaggerated in falsehood.

Index of His Books

6. I set down here the list of his works by title: though this first book is but the preface to the rest, yet its size necessitates that it be a book. One volume.[18]

There follows the work which contains the writer's creed, together with two letters, of which one continues to exhaust the Roman Pontiff with its complaints, the other the flock of his fellow-bishops. One volume.[19]

The third has a complaint made to the king [Otto] together with some letters. One volume.[20]

The fourth contains only two letters, both to bishops: a short one to Bruno, and a very long one to Rodbert. One volume.[21]

The fifth, though full of general material, has a complaint addressed specifically to Archbishop Bruno. One Volume.[22]

The sixth, seventh, and eighth are addressed to the usurper [Baldric], yet in many ways they criticize the actions of Rodbert and—briefly but bitingly—of the elder Baldric. One volume.[23]

The ninth—in acrimony masquerading as humility—makes amends to Bruno, to whom the writer had been much attached, complaining in mournful style. One volume.[24]

The tenth is addressed to the congregation [of Liège] which had been led astray, telling them of the solace of penitence. One volume.[25]

The eleventh is his Decision, small in size but great in ideas. One volume.[26]

The twelfth is a dialogue made for the attention of a certain individual, but it is not entirely inapplicable to himself. One volume.[27]

The books are not deliberately arranged in this order so as to make them coherent in effect, as they are in historians, essayists, poets, and writers of other works, or to make the matter of each relate to the preceeding one, but each book stands on its own account, regardless of the order of composition, because they are all composed about one subject only, though containing different ideas, and each is allotted its own place. The items in the individual books are linked not by rhetorical considerations but by logical ones; they will bear the same weight if the first should be placed last or the fourth eighth. This is required by their great dissimilarity; some of them are nothing but a collection of letters, some have a continuity like the minor works of some authors, some of them, though coherent in sense and theme, seem to have separate sections; one of them is even separated into six-line divisions of ideas, because the author arranged it in verses, as is seen in Martianus Capella, Fulgentius, and Boethius,[28] again with ideas taken from the same subject.

If anyone thinks it wrong to call a collection of letters a *book*, or that a single one should have the same name because of its length, he should note the *book* of Maccabees known as the "Second" and he should consider, besides others, the *books* of the Epistles of the Apostles, those of Augustine, Jerome, Gregory, and many other Christian writers. He should also note that among the pagans, Cicero, Pliny, and Seneca wrote works which they called *books* of Epistles, and in metre—to counter the barking of my critics' objections with Juvenal's rabid animosity[29]—Horace, supreme among satirists, and Ovid in the books called *Ex Ponto*.

They could have been said to be twenty, as was the original intent, but they were somewhat abridged out of respect for a certain individual and condensed into twelve, and they are to be called and to be treated as twelve separate books, from the diversity of their style, despite their single content. The first book serves as a prologue and has earned that title, though it was the last to be composed, and it is the victim's answer to the abuse of others, showing amongst other things how manifest is their author's *phrenesis*.

8. There is a story[30] that Nero, when the whole Senate had formed a general conspiracy against him, sent for one whom he thought his friend to ask advice about saving his life; when that one refused to come, he sent again for a member of the conspiracy, his hated foe, to come and kill him, not wanting to die in ignominy before the eyes of the whole city, as the Senate had decreed. When that one also tarried, he said, "Now I have neither friend nor enemy." The story bears a close resemblance to me and to my books. For since Scripture attests that a man's hatred is directed towards his friend and neighbor [Mic. 7.5–6; Mt. 10.35–36] (rightly, for an Indian does not really hate a Briton nor a Frank a Parthian), if we remove almost all the feelings in which the books were written which are contrary to God's command, there only remains pity, which has no part of hatred; and you may often see that he who sympathizes with the misfortunes of others is frequently intolerant of their good fortune.

But though, my trifles, you desire the favor of all, not even A. L. D.,[31] I think, close friend of mine though he is, will even deign to undertake to see what worth you hold in your pages, offended by the indignity of the title, saying, "They are too obscure," or thinking that my work abuses a proud man. As if any writer could ever be found who could so speak that he would be understood equally by everyone, witness St. Augustine, who says that the Holy Spirit has grandly and to our salvation so tempered its Scriptures that in the obvious passages hunger might be satisfied, but in the more obscure ones boredom might be swept away.[32] These obscurities are that much the less distasteful to the perspicacious, the more they are trusty guardians of the mysteries, meaningful only to the worthy, as Boethius attests.[33] Also, as St. Augustine points out in the book entitled *Concerning the Ways of the Church* [c. 1], it can happen, in fact it often does happen, that many things seem absurd to the uninitiated which, when they are explained by the more learned, seem gloriously praiseworthy in proportion as they did seem abjectly despicable, and the harder it was to unlock their mysteries, the sweeter they are received when revealed. I would like the person who judges that because some things are obscure the rest should be rejected to explain to me just this one thing (to leave out an infinite number): why in the gospel do we read that a certain man was beloved of the Lord who was not chosen to follow him [Mk. 10.21 ff.]? Or what made the Evangelist note this so carefully? What in my work can seem comparable in obscurity to this which is right before us, namely, the aforesaid Boethius' preface to his book on Arithmetic, apart from all the others?

9. O envy, ever greedy to find fault and, if there is no opportunity to do so, ever ready to find reasons at least for not keeping quiet, or for not being able to see what is shown!

> He burns with his own brightness, [says Horace] who presses down the arts by his own superiority; he will be loved after his death.[34]

Let the critic of them as much as their creator, the despiser as much as the reader, know that in the matter which we have taken on they can find no books today more beneficial to a bishop in difficulties; nor are they yet so lacking in the other arts and benefits also that, given study on the part of the reader, there cannot be found in them most pertinent teaching on certain topics found elsewhere with great difficulty. Any bishop to whom this does not bring valuable help in winning the victory over his opponents in any question of the canons will not be able to find help, I say, from any book anywhere in the world he may be (to say this obscurely too). Let him be done with seeking a knot in the bullrush,[35] often feigning sheer ignorance in his hatred; he should know that I have purposely placed obscurities in my work, but he will speedily be able to unravel them if they are carefully and industriously construed—except that, as often in other books, ignorance of the material here causes difficulty in comprehension. It is clear that he is utterly ignorant of construing if he claims that he does not understand my style; and he also admits that he is utterly ignorant of period, conceit, and parenthesis, if he fails to observe these in my books; he cannot claim to be versed in Latin, if he complains that he lacks the ability to comprehend them.

The Book Called *Phrenesis* Begins:

10. A little of the *Phrenesis* of a certain person,[36] a streamlet, as it were, drawn from the vast ocean of its complaints, I direct to you, my lord [Rodbert], so that it might come before your eyes, should heaven grant that you see it; it pleased you to call it *Phrenesis*[37] and to tell others to call it that, including the reverend Baldric (who is far immune from the fault of *phrenesis*), who is not only a supporter of your faction against me, but even a fellow-standardbearer, though in a different battle-line. Haste has caused it to be sent to you unpolished and somewhat shorter and in parts less stylish than the same book (the one which I commend in this preface in this fashion) would be if corrected in its place. This haste was caused by two things: first, because I had thought to escape the persecution of my enemies by my precipitate departure;[38] second, because a persistent rumor (though a false one) had recently continued to report that those who had been oppressed by your tyranny were now released by your demise— an omen perhaps not entirely without foundation (if it really is an "omen" which those who act with the specific aim of attacking another[39] attribute to diviners). I have taken care to attach no names of persons to it, thinking that your examination can easily determine whether it is done with just cause or from some slander born of hate, since the illwill of certain individuals has accumulated. Even a person who knew about the crime could not help but see why you have given him [Rather] a name like that, seeing that in such imminent peril, when people

would generally rush to their horde of treasure, your *phrenetic* chose to turn for
aid to books; when they go to arms, he went to the archives; when they go
to the resources of their friends, he rushed straight to the thoughts of the ancients. And it is not owing to his *phrenesis*, as you assert, that he replies with
a sentence of one familiar to you, "We cannot all do all things."[40] For he had
noted that he had many precedents from earlier writers, whose "negligence" —
to quote the words of the comic playwright — "he preferred to imitate rather
than their clever industry."[41] Indeed, since the sons of this world are wiser in
their own generation than the sons of light, as the Lord himself says [Lk. 16.8],
it is not surprising that everyone joins you in considering him mad.

11. With the gracious approval of the king [Otto], with the support of the
archbishop whose particular province it was [Bruno], with the vote of the clergy and the congregation [of Liège], with the sanction of the decretals, with better men as precedents[42] in no small number, with the consent of the canons,
with the voice and counsel of the compatriot bishops, on the announcement[43]
of a speaker of such power as you, and announcing it so convincingly from the
high pulpit of that splendid church that none could be unaware of it, with the
support of so pious a clergy and so vast a multitude, with the blare of trumpets
accompanying the melodies of the hymns — with all this, Rather was hailed, ordained, and installed as bishop, one who had no church, for a church that had
no bishop. Why after all this he was expelled, he could in no way find out — or
so he insanely asserts. Persuaded by his friends, in fact by his very ordainer [Bru-
no] (which ought then to have been kept secret), he trusted in right and in the
authority of those ordaining him; what was he to say in asking for help, *he* especially (as he told you) whose wisdom seems to have been widely acclaimed rather
by some Gnatho-like flattery[44] than by the true report of reality? And what
could the firmest of his friends find to say, except that if something had perchance been spoken or done against your wishes by the very person who is here
reciting all this, then it was done through negligence (as often happens), not
deliberate deceit? The sin of ill will in some degree of guilt he has confessed
so that he could wholly excuse it; that is, so that he might delete it by cautery —
your sentence of severe punishment — and afterwards rightly cultivate you as a
single patron and never cease from unlimited enjoyment of that cultivation, though
in such a way that he should not confuse gratuitous service, which in this matter particularly he knew would be worth more when you repaid it, with that
which should and must be handled wholly in consideration of God alone.[45]

For, he says, the appended precedents[46] of the saintly Fathers (which he
brings to your notice, learned father, by way of reminder, not for your information) show by their very clarity that it will be quite unnecessary for him to keep
wearing down the ears of one like you without success, since you are a knowledge-

able upholder of right. From these examples it is quite clear that if anyone lawfully promoted from anywhere, lawfully appointed, not coming on his own account but sent by one who has authority to send him, has in any way once undertaken the office conferred on him of residing somewhere as bishop (though unworthy), so long as his appointer and committee are in a state of salvation (if I may venture to put it this way, though my illwishers may rave enough to murder me), he cannot legally be removed from his position, while the defense of the order stands secure—unless perchance it is the civil code rather than the precedents of the saints which is stronger, or the mill-house has more authority than the office of the pontiff. For once he has accepted it, a bishop cannot be driven from his position, unless there has been a prior, uninterrupted, hearing. By this precedent, there is no force strong enough to dislodge a bishop; reason, the praise and censure of Christians, the demands and prohibitions of the law, agree with equal weight and equally protect him.

12. Confident of this argument, he goes on to say that everyone who fears God and is afraid of men's vituperation, everyone I repeat, will feel the same, if, putting aside all pretence, a person acts for himself and takes thought looking to his own good; and you in particular, to whom has been granted a greater capacity for knowing the truth and a stronger ability to avoid any endeavor against it, will forget in your accustomed manner to say with mouth, hand, and heart, "Zeal for thy house has consumed me" [Ps. 68.10], and will go up into the breaches and build a wall of defence yourself for the house of Israel, that you may stand in battle in the day of the Lord, that is, at the waters of Contradiction, where the strength of your devotion will be put to the proof [Dt. 33.8; Ps. 80.8; Ezek. 13.5].

Greatly encouraged and trusting in this expectation, I think it quite inappropriate to exhaust any of you with my urgings, since I know that you are well aware of the trenchant remark of Pope Alexander, who said: "If anyone fails to give help to one of these, he will be judged not a priest but a schismatic."[47] These arguments are the supports of my position, unworthy though I am (I bring them up not of my own accord but in obedience to command), and I submit them to your most holy hands for appraisal, beseeching you by the Lord to deprive no bishop who was a party to the proceedings of knowledge of them, but to show them and publish them to all, so that there can be no excuse for not defending me.[48]

This *phreneticus* labored to prove by the decretals of the saintly Fathers, namely, Antherus, Calixtus, and Gregory, and by the precedents of several saints, that he was legally enthroned in a vacant Church. After inserting these precedents below, he added: "No one can in any way invalidate what has been legally done, but should somone want to make it undone again by the charge, true or false, of some crime, these again are the supports on which I rely, thanks be to God. But I do not know if they will do me any good; these are times (for shame!) that do not recognize law."[49] And having proved conclusively that he had been instituted according to the precedents of the saintly Fathers, and particularly by your pronouncement, and, as Pope Telesphorus says,[50] had as it were fortressed himself in by building a wall of these arguments around him, he continues as follows, beginning where it says "from your announcement": there are many such instances scattered throughout the sacred fields of divine dogma, easy to find if need be (as the holy wisdom of your Lordship does not need to be told); but we believe that these are sufficient, nor does anyone even need to be reminded of them, except for him for whom[51] "the king of Babylon took out the eyes of Zedekiah the king of Jerusalem at Reblatha" [Jer. 39.6] — which is translated as *this much*, which we know from Gregory[52] (who explains it) to be immoderate care for this world, which draws those ensnared in it into the Stygian pit of Phlegethon — and not merely in myth either — and therefore it has happened to some that "seeing they do not see and hearing they do not understand" [Lk. 8.10], so that what was said about "those who turned aside their eyes so that they did not see the heaven nor remembered the judgments of the just" [Dan. 13.9] can rightly be applied to them. We desire that these be so tended by your care that they do not need to be warned that it is them whom the psalmist is addressing in his terrible voice: "Understand this, you who forget God, lest some time He seize you and there be none to deliver you" [Ps. 49.22].

13. O insane *Phrenesis!*[53] O phrenetic insanity! — in the judgement of a wise man! You were not capable of deploring your own wretchedness, yet, fool, you were not ashamed to bewail the sorrows of King Zedekiah justly inflicted more than a thousand years ago! But perhaps it[54] seemed to you, Phrenesis (and in this not entirely phrenetic) to have been playful fooling? But you went on that with Gregory you deplored many Zedekiahs[55] of this day and age, not this one alone, since it has unfortunately happened to many that, like him, seeing they do not see and hearing they do not understand, by whose blindness you thought it could come about that in such clear defiance of the divine law [the canons], he who had been ceremonially enthroned was so wickedly expelled from the bishopric lawfully entrusted to him (which you deplored so much); and he was expelled by none other than his own ordainers. But the obstinacy of him whom you were addressing, which could not be softened by such considerations, was remarkable, if indeed there was any integrity in him.

More remarkable, phrenetic one [Rather], are you who said such things to such a man [Rodbert], unaware as you were that you were telling a tale to that deaf one who, as our mythographer tells us about the envious miser,[56] had chosen not only to neglect his own soul for the time being, but, as you saw, to ruin it utterly,[57] rather than tolerate, still less work for, your restitution, you madman (in his estimation); unless perhaps he [Rodbert] was trying to entice with his words a man who was greedy for praise[58] (led on by this fine saying of Aurelius of august memory: "Often a man is said to be good not because he is good but so that he might be encouraged to be good";[59] in the manner of him who deliberately praises the fraudulent, because, realizing that he holds their loyalty, he fears himself to be branded with the infamy of their fraud), when he was appointing you as bishop, to those who had forgotten the Lord,[60] so that he might be careful not to forget God's commandments and realize that he too, like those Zedekiahs, could be snatched off to the place out of which he could in no way be delivered [Ps. 49.22].

14.[61] But it is very easy to see why he [Rodbert] conceived this hatred for you [Rather], for even one less gifted could uncover such secrets. For they affirm that he does not hate you yourself, but rather your insolent loquacity, just as you hate his; and just as someone stated that Demosthenes forestalled Cicero lest Cicero be the first orator and Cicero forestalled Demosthenes so that Demosthenes should not be the only orator,[62] you two strove in the windy war of words spurred by envy, which is the most just avenger of pride and the most accurate accuser of folly. For quarrels always arise among the proud, and if you had really been what each of you desired to be called [eloquent], you could not have kept apart from each other, because nature prevents the like from separating. In this contest he [Rodbert] seemed to win, as he always does, in that when he had driven you out of the episcopate in which you were honored, a throne for which you had long yearned and in which you took great pride (as he could not fail to see), he tried to deprive you also of the respect of the office which all should venerate.

For when the story was repeated in his [Rodbert's] presence that you [Rather] had publically excommunicated for sacrilege someone who scorned penitence, he brazenly shouted out that no notice should be taken of your excommunication of another. (For him to say this, of course, would not have been so surprising if he had been as aware of your lack of worth as you are. The whitewashed tomb[63] is wont to deceive the onlooker; no less than it were you foul within, and your heart and character were foul, "though fair-seeming with a decorous skin"[64]—as somebody's satire puts it.) But it is surprising, as I said, that he dared to make so sudden a judgment against your inner being, which he had never seen—against the apostle too, who says with Christ's authority, "Sitting, to speak against his brother and the son of his mother" (that is, the people standing round) "to raise such a stumbling block" [Ps. 49.20]—saying that you were not bishop because you had been expelled from your bishopric—though according to Aurelius, it is not the punishment that determines guilt but the facts,[65] and the punishment of the guilty should be their absolution; for, as Isidore happily puts it, the guilty man is not one who is *accused* but one who is justly and lawfully *convicted*.[66]

15.[67] "If your sons," the Lord promises David—and forcefully, to be sure—"break my law, I shall visit their iniquities with the rod and their sins with blows; but I will not restrain my mercy from them" [Ps. 88.31–34]. And Malachim also says the same thing, but in the singular: "When your seed does anything, I will chasten him with the rod of men, with the stripes of the sons of men, but I will not take my steadfast love from him, as I took it from Saul whom I moved from my face" [2 Sam. 7.14]. So you can understand how much difference there is between the practices of the state and the rites of the Church and how different are God, who himself bestows them, and the honors which wretched men can often confer, that is, when He permits them; or, to put it better in the words of Augustine: "All the earthly heights which totter in temporal motion are topped not by the peak that is usurped by human pride, but by that which is given by divine grace."[68] Anyone can therefore make up his own mind whether the presulate should be an empty shadow and a name without honor, or whether it should carry some authority which bishops will wield with a power which is too strong to be overwhelmed by earthly material in its resourcelessness.

"Sing to the Lord," Scripture says elsewhere, "with hammered trumpets" [Ps. 97.5–6]—that is, praise the Lord with souls hammered by the discipline of blows, or, corrected by blows yourselves bless the name of the Lord along with His elect. Yet it must not be forgotten that when the trumpet is forged, the hammer is blunted, so that the damage done hurts the wielder more than the victim, or so we should believe.

Not to go on indefinitely: the wise man should also ponder what we are warned by the altars of the sons of Levi which were saved by God's command when the men themselves were damned—and not to utterly forget what was meant by the words, "I will move your candle from its place" [Rev. 2.5]. It is worthwhile considering how beautiful (besides being very true and pertinent to you) is a sentence of a certain cultured person quite well known:

> Our troubles are increased by the fact that most people judge an action by its outcome, not by its merits, and think that only the action with a happy outcome has been providently[69] done; hence it comes about that their good repute is the first thing that the unlucky lose.[70]

And:

> I would add only this, that it is the last straw of adverse fortune that,

when some sin is imputed to unfortunate people, they are believed to have
deserved what they suffer.[71]

16. But so that my garrulous book may return at once to your *phrenetic*
[Rather]:[72] who is there who does not judge that it passes all insanity that,
though bishop and though with good reason, he dared to excommunicate an
archbishop [Rodbert] even after first invoking the Lord's words from the gospel?
For in the fifteenth book of this *Phrenesis* (as you call it), when in the Feast of
the Lord's Supper (than which in my opinion there is no more important feast)
you [Rodbert] received the offerings of the young women as is customary, his
equally phrenetic audacity (perhaps thinking that on so solemn a day—which
he did not cease to lament in pained complaints—you had put on the chasuble
which you had obtained through his expulsion, as was the story), his audacity,
I say, had this challenge made to you: "If you offer your gift at the altar and
there remember that your brother has something against you, leave there your
gift before the altar and go first to be reconciled to your brother and then come
and offer your gift" [Mt. 5.23–24]. Here, lord, I am in doubt which of the two's
madness I should be more astonished at. Allowed that *he* was insane under pressure of grief, where, I ask, was *your* sanity? And where were you present, my
lord, who had there been so absent to yourself? The repute of him who had
passed on those words [Rather] had justly decreased; but the commandment of
Him who commanded it ought to have been considered. His lack of merit prevented the petitioner [Rather] from obtaining his request; but the Majesty revered
by all compelled obedience. Perhaps you did not have the means to do what
was asked? Could you not then in humility have replied: "Pray thee, have me
excused" [Lk. 14.18]? To top it off,[73] after affecting, as it were, many types
of madness over the course of the years, often blabbering as is the habit of the
insane, the inclination of your eloquence would be so witless that you would
have been unable to hear with your intellectual hearing that terrible thunder
of the Gospel and to apply to yourself what he who had been wronged by you
kept warning himself; and because without his explaining it to you you would
have been unable rightly to understand how you ought to be reconciled to him
as the Lord commands, he hastened at once to provide this.

Another man who is sure of his salvation can properly show a person the
peril of his hidden sickness, O Father once so dear to me; but it should not
be improper for me to offer you some remedy of advice—the former generosity[74] of your Lordship to me prevents me from denying you advice (though
your subsequent ill will continues to press me to deny it). The Gospel message
just given you warns that it is you who ought to be reconciled to the wronged
one rather than I whom—and how greatly!—you have wronged. As you are

shrewd in wit, you can easily understand this (since Scripture says, "Understand thy neighbor from thyself" [Lk. 14.18]), if your mind is not lacking in that properly dominant force which was lacking when I decided to remind certain of the bishops, who "had turned their eyes so that they saw not the heaven nor remembered the judgments of the just" [Dan. 13.9], of the sentence, "Understand this, ye who forget God" [Ps. 49.22]. May the ancient Serpent keep far from us, who does not cease trying to do what he has continually done in his words from the beginning, striving to root out from the hearts of men, and to make light of, the threats of God.

17. But on the other hand, let the exhortation which is read today attend us, that is, those pertinent words of the Apostle. Mount the pontifical tribunal, I beg you, where you will receive fair judgment. Let your conscience confessing the truth attend there; assess my motive from your own. And since you have found two injured parties to whom you can be reconciled — myself not lightly wronged and God wronged most gravely, the one absent,[75] the other ever present in his majesty — remember Gregory's very salutary words of advice: "We ought to go in our minds to him we have wronged though he be far away, to make amends to him with goodwill and respect."[76] If you do this, and if you undertake to give me help in proportion to the hurt you did me, you can properly offer your gift to God, at least as far as I am concerned. If you fail to do so, sometime, I believe, you will be able to find out — though too late — how difficult it is[77] to break a threefold rope [Eccle. 4.12] and that that rope was the whip with which the traders of the pigeons were driven from God's temple [Jn. 2.15]. Don't let this happen, I urge you, begging you by the ministry of today's feast. If you scorn to be reconciled to me, be reconciled to God, striving by any means or remedy you like[78] to repair the open breach made on your part in particular (to tell the truth — saving your grace). Notice please (you easily can) how clearly the decree of Pope Antherus upsets your Eloquence's firm judgment against me, just as it also upsets the more distant judgment of all the same authority. For Antherus first says, most favorably to my cause:

> But to both — that is, to those suffering hunger of the Word and to bishops in need when they are enthroned in other cities — a great amount of pity is shown. Those who deny this, though they have the appearance of piety, yet deny piety's essence.[79]

Then he immediately adds, just as if he were addressing you specifically and as if you were in front of him with his finger pointed at you:

> For in such a case I do not acknowledge nobility. Yet if any storm of this tempestuous world has allied any of the wise with other foolish leaders,

he is besmirched by participating in their sins; yet the splendor of the wise man, though incurring the same charges as them, cannot offer itself as leader to the errant.

18. You will find me very obedient to every instruction you may wish to give me, if you do not scorn to pursue to the fullest what you know to be just; as far as this business is concerned, act justly. For since his [Rather's] insolence in these strong words has not been nipped by any reply from the addressee, he has felt free in his madness to reach such a point of brazen impudence (for, as Chremes says, we are all quite wicked)[80] that in the wordy garrulity of what is now twenty volumes[81] (which in his very fickle way he is trying to condense into twelve of equal size) he continually attacks everyone, particularly people whom you will have no difficulty recognizing if you choose to read; he spares no one's dignity (so that you seem to have been justified in calling it *Phrenesis*), no one's power, which does not have probity as its patron. There is a rumor, however, that he later destroyed the greater part of those works, compelled by the grace of the pious king [Otto] out of love for a certain person; yet in his madness he is quite ready to admit that he has done this. What he had not expected has now monstrously happened. As though you had given spurs to a galloping horse, you seem to have stung his insolent pride and provoked him[82] into criticizing certain individuals, yourself in particular, by saying that he was mad from his learning (just as Festus once thought that the apostle was mad from his learning [Acts 26.24]) — though it is rather to be believed that you thought him far otherwise.

19.[83] Ah, hush, quiet, I beg, quiet. For the person [Rodbert] you [Rather] are addressing is now gone, so they say. Stop wasting your substance in buying parchment and hiring secretaries. Your impudence is truly insane. Give up your phrenetic scribbling and say with threnetic wailing what blessed Job said: "For what I was afraid would happen did happen" [Job 3.25]. For he whom you pursued has gone, has gone alas, never to return; he has won his eternal departure. The wailing remains, alas, like this tolling of the bells. He has passed away, rather than gone away, moved ahead rather than moved away. You were raving with the people like one demented, pouring out trifles on a trifling trifle; be careful that you have not insulted the dead. Do not let your foolish chatter and the worthless stuff it has composed exhaust anyone any longer, but rather repent and say with the starveling satirist,

Who will read all this?[84]

because now (as another satirist complains)

the greedy rich man has learned to admire and praise the learned;[85]

do not yearn to be the talk of the town.

Not all admire and love the same things.[86]

Give up vainly trying to catch the favor of all, I beg. Do not curse the deaf
[Lev. 19.14] nor rail at the dead, a man of integrity at other times and (consider-
ing the times and place) not so very inhuman to others, though cruel to you.
But cry out, rather, within, raise your voice within.

20.[87] Some verses composed by the same [in hexameters]:

If perchance you want to know what my books contain, careful reader,
then take them up. The writer endeavors with just retribution to shake
up, lay low, raise, comfort, unite, solace, refresh, restore, reshape, and
dress up his friends, who bear, alas, my friend, a heavier weight than Etna.
For just as gout draws and vexes someone and a hump sitting misplaced
on his back presses him down, and just as a ferocious beast tears his mother's
ribs and aspires to be thought the avenger of its dead father, just so does
the crowd detested by God strive in internal strife to rend itself with ca-
nine fangs, snapping at each other, each decreeing on each other's head
wicked sentences which will be turned onto his own head also, while the
one who cares that the will of God be done toils in madness[88] so that the
hearts that serve a wicked god will fear. Each foolishly teaches that great
things are small, when he joins right with left and admits that crooked
is straight, and is delighted to have changed white for black, square for
round, savage for kind,[89] and to find fault with the righteous and delight
in their opposite, whereby he brings onto himself hellish woe, confusing
what Nathan by the Lord's gift established as right and once fixed with
firm bonds in those times, and what every teacher imbued with God's nectar established in fine order. Thus honor rushes downhill and headlong
the respect conferred by Heaven on the holy orders, and thus Ephraim attacks Manasses and Manasses Ephraim, and at the same time they both
strive to attack Judah [Is. 9.20] standing ready in dense array, forgetting
the Lord and starting civil wars which will have no triumphs,[90] knowing how to turn their own whip onto themselves; since my hand here has
contrived not to leave them untouched, it will be thought to have rendered great help to the afflicted, unless someone in hatred brand these words
while it composes, and prove that he, rather than our cause, should be
mocked by all, while he raves more strongly and care stimulates his fury.
Therefore, may He be present in His power on the right and may He bear
me, willing to avoid Syrtes with its shallows and Scylla and savage Charybdis,
pitying me; and may I be able to find help swiftly in the sacred coffers

of venerable dogma, help that may justly benefit many; may He sustain these with His help and check those others with His reins, so that held in they will not be able to fulfill their will. But I pray that the weary squadrons of priests long oppressed by wicked laws will find great strength in this gift; and that the wall of the Lord's teaching will remain firm and unbroken, which pious Pope Telesphorus said was built for us.[91] This group bewails no one expelled from the fold, except the man who could break the wall, for whose defense it was clearly built. Let each one of us, therefore, not disdain to bear our many burdens and to help each other, because he certainly will be able to, unless perchance he who would care for such concerns is missing. For it is well known that this type of person is increasing these days; may the kindly Lord turn them, I pray, and grant that those who are too heavily oppressed by the powerful be lightened. While I seem to speak my piece especially for you, holy group of men, lot and minister of the Lord, I am ready to give you arms with which each of you can protect your rights and under Christ's leadership show yourself as victor when the treacherous phalanx assails you with woes; for soon God himself will triumph, and his constancy victorious in its own right will ever overcome and, accompanied by His supporters, will trample down all hostile, noxious enemies, I pray, and will defeat them, rout them, and tear them asunder, I beg. And may the Universe, I pray, resound, "Amen, so be it."

21.[92] [In elegiac couplets.]

Spare, O God, your redeemed servant Rodbert, pity him, be merciful to him, mercifully giving him merciful pardon as well as peace. His sin (that is, his sin of wanting to sacrifice the flock of another) is not against me, because I am nothing, but against you; for he is held responsible not to the flock but to the Lord—this law is one and the same in all lands. You alone can quickly give him pardon and remission if you are willing to spare him. I ask you, O God, and ask it with all my heart, to grant that he be able to travel the starry paths in freedom.

Let him be blessed and despise Porthmeus the ferryman; and let no worry for the fare bring anguish to this man worthy of your lot.[93] Let him not reach the slough of Erebus and the black marshes, let Cerberus stand back, let the Gorgon shun him; let him not chance to swim the Stygian lake nor see foul Tartarus; the right hand road is his choice; let not Chaos or Phlegethon, dwellings for black monsters, be places which he must undergo or weep that he must undergo. Let him not see—command it, I pray—either the rocks or deserts of Cocytus, him whose hope it was to have

heaven as his city. Prevent him from seeing the chambers of the Eumen-
ides; let him see the ranks of the pious and let him see himself among them.
Let the path that leads to Tartarean Acheron's waters[94] know him not;
let heaven know him and want to keep him. May your hurts to me not
harm you, you who are known to have benefited many, you who carry
only your good deeds with you. Good deeds speak; their opposites are silent, lest wickedness prevail. Consider these good deeds of his, I pray; do
not let a single wickedness overcome a thousand good deeds; though the
wickedness be great, let it not stand in his way, O God. Almighty, you
can grant it, however small his good deeds may be; when your right hand
glorifies the right, then assuredly the left [wicked] vanishes, as the fiery
northwind scatters chaff. Here may the trumpet, when it utters its sound
so terrible[95] to those who have no hope as it gives each his rewards according to his merits, at least allow him to avoid *depart* if it denies him
well done [Mt. 25.41]; for many catch the former but only the most excellent catch the latter. "Do not fear, my flock," He says, "for I have decided
to ennoble you with the throne of my Father's Kingdom." Yet happy is,
was, and will be the man, who, blessed with the lot granted him, hears
Come ye [Mt. 25.34]. Hear this, immeasurable God, do not, pious one,
withhold this blessing from our friend but number him with the righteous. May your mother Mary, kind Christ, make this request for us, may
the heavenly cohorts ask pardon for him, and may St. Peter unbar the gates
of Heaven; then may all the saints come forward to give him succor. In
this way does my *Phrenesis* hound you, in this way: it asks that you be
blessed and stay blessed.

22. Leaving the absent one [Rodbert, now dead], I thought to deal with you,
Baldric, still present, in publishing the works which I had composed against
him (or rather *for* him) in particular. For he had excepted you as being immune
to that vice under which both of us were said to labor, that is, literary madness,
since you rely instead on money rather than books, on arms rather than armoires,
on political connections rather than the wisdom of our ancestors (for, as Horace
says, the word once spoken knows not how to return).[96] For in the meantime
there developed within me both practice and a surer awareness of myself.

[There follow a chapter addressed to Baldric (c. 22), which the Ballerini found
so textually at fault as to be both beyond correction and beyond comprehension,
and a statement of his faith that is more or less identical to that found in *Praeloquia* 3, c. 31.]

17

Weigle, Epist. 66   Alna December 955–January 956

[Account in an anonymous *Life of St. Bruno* of a letter of Rather to Bruno.][1]

∽

"There is also extant a letter of this bishop sent to Bruno, very finely written, in which, addressing him as *Patronus* and thanking him profusely, he declares that surrounded by God's mercy and guided by Bruno's spiritual wisdom, he has been transformed into a new man and by renewal of mind and spirit has been changed into a better condition, and that the love of all his people has been consolidated towards the success and increase of his honor."

18

Weigle, Epist. 66–69   Alna December 957–January 958

[Rather answers certain criticisms of his behavior made by a priest named Patricus.]

∽

Rather, most wretched, to Patricus,[2] wretched:

1. Recently—namely, when our lord Conrad[3] marshalled the ecclesiastical orders in the place called Horna—you asked someone in your usual way (that is, not out of affection for me but inquisitively) whether I had sung a mass during that week. I answer you myself: Would that neither you nor I had celebrated mass on our Lord's nativity. For I do so rarely and then, alas, unworthily, but you do so every day and then in white surplice [cf. Jas. 2.2; Eccle. 9.8]—which, I think, the Lord values on no one's body when their mind like yours, I fear (and mine too, believe me), is blacker than soot.

For I know that you zealously serve that seventh vice[4] which His soul detests—and would that I alone knew it! Let us leave it to the Apostle to judge which of us receiving the Eucharist unworthily [1 Cor. 11.27–31]—the one rarely, the other every day—takes it with the greater peril. If we should earnestly read, each of us, John Chrysostom's sermons on the apostle's letter to the Hebrews,[5] they would discourage us from celebrating masses—me from any kind of mass, you from daily ones.

2. When I also hear that you were shocked by my taking a bath on the eve of our Lord's circumcision, I cannot contain my admiration for the cleanliness and purity of your most chaste body, you who have no inkling what the flesh, which is subject to the law of sin [Rom. 7.25], suffers even when the mind is unwilling! Or perhaps it is allowed by your authority for a polluted man to handle the holy vessels without a double washing in the bath.[6] But Scripture says, "Be ye clean who carry the Lord's vessels" [Is. 52.11]; and "Be sanctified" [Lev. 20.7] is often commanded when anything holy is stipulated to be done in the Old (and also prefigurative) Testament. And to David, about taking the bread of proposition owing to his need, it says, "If the young men are clean" [1 Sam. 21.4].

3. But perhaps you do not take it seriously, and even think that you are speaking figuratively, when you say to the one receiving it: "The body of Our Lord Jesus Christ lead you to eternal life"? If this is so, the blindness of your understanding is more to be deplored and corrected than wondered at and derided, in that you do not know how to avoid the net of presumption and do not cease from falling into it because you do not know what power it has.

But, brother, believe that just as in Cana of Galilee, on God's command, real — and not figurative — wine was made from water, so by God's benediction this wine and this bread are made the true, not figurative, Blood and Flesh. But if the fact that the taste and color remain the same persuades you that this is not so, I offer you another proposition: Do you believe the authority of the Scripture, which says that man was formed from the mud of the earth [Gen. 2.7]?

I have no doubt you will reply, "I believe it."

And do you know besides that it says, "You are dust and will return to dust" [Gen. 3.19]?

"I know it," I think you say, "and I believe it is so."

Therefore, the man whom you see before your eyes is dust and ashes [Gen. 18.27]?

"Yes indeed," you say, "because he was made out of mud" [cf. Tob. 8.8]. What then is this figure of mud?

"No figure, but I call it rather earth."

Any earth?

"Not *any*."

Yet man is earth?

"Yes."

What about the figure of mud?

"It was transformed by the wisdom of the Creator."

Yet the substance remains?

"Yes."

Then here also believe that it is true flesh and blood which you receive, with the color and taste remaining, by the action of the same Creator, just as you do not deny that the substance of mud remains, though changed in form, in the creation of man.

4. But perhaps you importunately ask (since such is the vanity of man's curiosity) whose body this is the flesh of, and whence and from whom it has been cut, and if the bread, perhaps, has been invisibly removed and is substituted or if the bread itself has been transformed into flesh. For these, I think, are the stones by which the beast—that is, the carnal heart and animal man who does not perceive those things which belong to God the Spirit [1 Cor. 2.14]—is stoned if he presumes to touch the mountain of God's mysteries [Heb. 12.20]. So let us ask the Gospel: "Receiving the bread," it says, "Jesus gave thanks and gave it to them saying, Take and eat, this is my body. Likewise He took the cup after He had eaten saying, This is the cup of my blood and of the new and eternal covenant, the mystery of faith, which will be shed for you and for many for the remission of sins."[7] There you have it, the owner of the body to which this flesh and blood belong, with that much the more certainty since you are told by the actual words of truth himself. Do not ask about the rest, I beg you, since you hear that this is a mystery and a matter of faith. For if it is a mystery, it cannot be understood; if it is a matter of faith, it must be believed, not debated.[8]

19

Confessional Dialogue

[Rather enjoyed William's hospitality in Mainz till late in 955, then moved to the monastery of Alna, which, being subject to the bishop of Liège, had been given him as a benefice. It was here that he composed the work known as *Excerptum ex Dialogo Confessionali*, but which he himself refers to as *Liber Confessionis*.[9] The interpretation of this work has aroused some discussion; the imperfect state of the text, the lack until 1984 of an edition which indicates the form of the dialogue, Rather's habitual use of obscure allusions, the difficulties of his syntax, and his constant striving to appear learned and eloquent, all have compounded the problem of interpretation.

The Ballerini limit their discussion of the work to remarking on its possible authenticity as a confession. Could a man who had really committed such a catalogue of sins claim in his epitaph to have been "of good moral character for the time" [*pro tempore morigeratus*]?[10] Would his contemporaries have commented upon his "outstanding integrity" [*eximia probitas*]?[11] They conclude that this is not a true and genuine confession but an unusual work of criticism, in which Rather attacks the faults of others by attributing them to himself and confessing them as his sins; so when he describes his own sins, he is in fact censuring others.[12] This is clear particularly from c. 22 when the "confessor" says, "While you do not spare yourself, you sharply bite at me, or rather at all of us." Some of the sins he exaggerates to appear serious, when closer examination shows them to be negligible or non-existent. For instance, he confesses himself an adulterer through the actions of those whom he drove into adultery by his neglect, where the "adultery" of his flock is no more than their having Manasses and Milo as their spiritual leaders, and his own "neglect" is his having yielded the see of Verona to the pressures of the same. No sin this, surely! They further point out that the list of sins confessed in c. 4 is a formula only, not to be taken literally.

Another view sees the dialogue form he uses as a means for Rather to bare his soul in the manner of St. Augustine's *Confessions*. This view, espoused by Vogel, received support from both Manitius and Misch. More recently Klinkenberg has suggested that the work is not so much confession as invective, where Rather in his acerbic manner criticizes the monks of Alna for faults which he applies to himself.

I think, however, that it is a mistake to try to make this extraordinary work fit into any recognizable literary genre. As my translation shows, both the nature of the work and the character of the listener change from section to section, so that even the title *Dialogus Confessionalis* is misleading. The work is lacking in formal structure or development; it is as inconstant and fickle as Rather's own temperament (an inconstancy of mood which he readily acknowledges in other works also), and can perhaps be understood only if seen as an experiment in a new type of literature, a stream-of-consciousness flow of ideas. It is useless to try to establish the persona of the listener or to identify him, as Klinkenberg would have us do, with the simoniacal monk Oderad. This listener has several personae: at times, as in c. 33, he is any model observer of the Rule, any good monk; at other times, as in c. 37, he is a particular monk with sins on his conscience; again, and even in the same chapter, the listener becomes Rather's *alter ego*, or the voice of his conscience; and finally, he appears as the abstract voice of right, a true confessor with an authentic exhortation.

We need not be surprised at this variety or multiplicity of addressees; much of Rather's rhetorical work turns into a kind of inner conversation with himself, in which he answers imaginary objectors. He seems incapable of a straightforward exposition; in almost every work a *cavillator* appears to put forward an obstruction to the flow of argument and be answered with a retort that continues the argument or redirects it. This kind of dialogue can be very effective in the hands of a master. But Rather is too fickle a personality to carry it off, at times too impetuous and unrestrained, at other times too humble and self-critical, and at all times too intent on appearing learned, on preserving a flashy mystery of syntax and rhetoric. This work cannot be examined according to any of the canons of criticism by which we usually evaluate classical or medieval works; the lack of discipline in his writing forbids it as does his refusal to make his meaning clear.

This work does, however, merit study, not only as an oddity in literature—a new style which, fortunately, his contemporaries did not try to imitate—but also because through it we can see into the mind of a very unusual church leader of the tenth century. We see some of the turmoil in his psyche caused by the contrast between the high ideals of the Rule and the shallow reality of most monks' observation of it. Here is an abbot who has struggled for honor and authority and who now realizes that the responsibilities of his position give him little rest, one who in his old age would like to be a monk again according to his vows, but cannot abdicate the responsibilities of his rank. This leads him to question his own worthiness to perform the offices and offer the Eucharist, and to fear that his doing so will lead to his own damnation. He even doubts his own rhetorical skill and volubility (cc. 38–39) and questions his own motives, seeing his eloquence as windy sophistry and a source of pride, that most heinous sin. This is a theme that appears in no. 16, *Phrenesis*, and no. 41, *Qualitatis coniectura cuiusdam*, also and it is clear that in his conscience he is disturbed by that very reputation for being learned for which he has ever striven. His inner *cavillator* frequently accuses him of vainglory—seeking the vanity of men's praise of his intellectual achievements instead of the humble worthiness of God's service. In his old age—he is now almost seventy—he knows he must soon stand before God's tribunal and account for himself and for others in his flock; he knows he must try to find that proper humility of spirit which he has ever preached but never practiced, but the habit of rhetorical bombast is too deeply ingrained; it is now more than a style, it is the man himself. This conflict between the bombastic ideals of the rhetorician and the simple humility of the pious believer is, I think, unique in medieval literature; at any rate we do not have any other autobiographical works where such conflict plays so prominent a part in a writer's self-analysis.

The dialogue begins by addressing the confessor who had urged him to make confession, a confession which Rather implies will be a "perjury" (are we to take this to mean "false"?) and one which the confessor will have to bear responsibility for extorting—the inciter to sin (perjury) is as guilty as the sinner (perjuror) himself (c. 1). He confesses his sins, in particular the political troubles for which he has been responsible and the two broken marriages—by which perhaps he means the two Churches (Verona and Liège) from which he had been removed (Ballerini),[13] though in some of the phrases in this section "church" can hardly be substituted for "wife" (c. 2). He then notes his failures as a primate (c. 3) and proceeds to a "summary" of his sins, a summary, which, as the Ballerini point out,[14] is a formula for a general confession (cc. 4–9). The dialogue with the confessor now begins. "Have you confessed this before?" He tells why he confesses now and why he never did so earlier: he was afraid of being told like a runaway to return to his master and abandon the ambitious course he has set for his life (c. 10). He tells of his early vows as a Benedictine monk, vows which his career has forced him to abandon. The confessor reminds him of two other incidents in his life for which he bears guilt, and he says that they are slight compared with his own turning away from God (c. 11). He feels that mere confession of a sin is useless unless it is accompanied by cessation of that sin, but he has been unable to give up his sin of inconvertibility (by which he seems to mean his not returning to his Benedictine vows) (c. 12). The confessor asks how, if he felt himself such a sinner, he could continue to say the offices and take the Eucharist. This leads him to discuss the taking of the Eucharist worthily and unworthily (cc. 13–15). After some observations on who is worthy to receive (and to offer) the sacraments (cc. 15–16), he returns to the importance of ceasing to sin—confession and penitence are not enough. For him, ceasing to sin would require his return to God; otherwise he would remain a runaway (c. 17). One way for a runaway to return to his master is voluntarily to send messages of reconciliation—which on the spiritual level means prayers and endeavors to do God's will. The devil will try to obstruct these messages, by means of pride, sloth, apathy, and idleness (cc. 17–18).

At this point there is a break. Rather now returns to an earlier topic, his reluctance to perform the offices because he feels unworthy (being a sinner) and his fear that taking the sacraments will lead to his damnation. He wants to be demoted, to step down from his position of authority, but he feels constrained by necessity to keep the rank given him. The confessor points out that a carnal sin, or a blemish of any sort, is fit cause for demotion, so one can be deposed merely by confessing guilt in such. But, Rather argues, that does not happen in reality, because the Church is lenient to sinners who confess and amend. We then have a digression on sin, penitence, and absolution, whose point seems to be that the bishop seeking demotion by confessing carnal sin will not be demoted because his own confession coupled with the prayers of others will bring absolution of that sin—and nullification of the reason for demotion (c. 19). Should we then respect a sinful priest? Yes, because he sits on Moses' seat, a seat conferred by God, so his words are to be respected though his acts must not be imitated (c. 20). Rather returns now to his blemishes as a priest, and admits that since all-powerful God could effect his conversion from sinner to penitent but has not done so, he is totally damned. He concludess that his messages of reconciliation are the result not of love of God, but rather of fear of hell. He cannot hope for reconciliation (c. 21); he has confessed now in order to bring his listener out of a false sense of security. His own negligence has infected all the brothers; witness the monk who embezzled from the common fund, imitating Simon (c. 22).

This leads to a general condemnation of simony and of monks' greed, which Rather then turns against himself as part of his confession, even taking responsibility for the embezzlement committed by one placed under him. He admits that he has robbed the abbey of twenty-two pounds of silver (through the agency of this other old monk), and that his sin of negligence in not preventing the theft is worse than the other's sin—the abbot is responsible if he allows a sin to be committed. He then asks another abbot, nephew of the old monk, why he did not prevent the old man's simony (c. 23), and he muses on the precarious position of authority, bearing responsibility for sins committed by those in one's spiritual charge (c. 24).

Since this "secret" sin (simony) has been uncovered, he does not hide his others, hoping that God will free him as though from Babylon. He urges his listener not to be so infected by his sin as to become unable to examine himself by the standards of the Rule, for one not bound by the Rule is a son of Belial, the devil (c. 25). Rather returns now to his own sin of inconvertibility and the difficulty he has in turning to the Lord. Again, it is the fear of hell, not love of the Lord, which is making him turn to Him; prayers should be his messages of reconciliation (c. 28). There follows a digression on the Pasch (which means "crossing-over," but not from fasting to self-indulgence) and a discussion of the meaning of "exult and be glad," all familiar topics of his (cf. no. 31 and no. 43) (c. 29). Returning to the blemishes itemized in Leviticus, he finds them in himself, including lust and other vices (cc. 30–31), and admits that his prayers are blocked by his lack of reconciliation with his fellows (c. 32). The confessor remarks on Rather's fickle nature and hypocrisy and asks why he confesses: for himself. Augustine and Paul also wrote confessions, but Rather is troubled by his own pride in his humility, exhibited in his striving to appear eloquent instead of practicing good deeds (c. 33). His hypocrisy, his pious-seeming recitations and vigils are hollow; instead of praying, his wandering mind speculates on an abbot's prestige and responsibilities, on Bonito's handling of the store; the abbot is responsible—but why buy, as Oderadus did, such responsibilities? For honor? He contemplates his own ambition, the glory and luxuries of such honor—and the simony and sacrilege needed to win it, and the desertion of poor people who needed him (c. 34). He wonders at such ambition: it is futile, against Christ's command, and appropriately the cause of future execration (c. 35).

The confessor now returns to the subject of Rather's lust, inconvertibility, inconstancy, and spurious humility. He suggests that the object of the Confession is to demonstrate his eloquence and talent for literature (c. 36); "your confession is the product of your instability and love of your own fictions, not the result of your prickings of conscience. It is not accompanied by real tears of penitence. And after preaching to everyone in Lent on the necessity of abstaining from sin, after Easter you have reverted to sin yourself." He lists the many reasons for tears and he tells Rather that his eloquence is only rhetorical bombast, not true eloquence; his volubility does not give him any importance. His claims of enlarging the Church's structure only make him like Nebuchadnezzar. The confessor's last hope for Rather is to have everyone pray for him, but it would be better if he would truly convert (cc. 37–40) and weep real tears for his sins. He adds another sin to the list: receiving money to allow men to become members of the monastery, then neglecting their souls (c. 41). He tells Rather that his faith in Christ's mercy is misplaced unless he converts *and* repents, and he offers him some excerpts from Paschasius Radbert's work, *On the Body and Blood of the Lord* (c. 42). Next follows a further exhortation in the mouth of the confessor and some appropriate prayers, which Dolbeau has identified in earlier sources.][15]

∽

Excerpt from the Confessional Dialogue of a certain sinner, strange to say, Rather, bishop of Verona but a monk of Lobbes.

1. I beg and beseech you, by Him who lives for ever, to read this work through in its entirety, if you begin it and if He grants it. For because, neglecting your own sins, you have so much desired in mortal curiosity to know of mine that you recently urged me to perjury[16] and forcibly extorted from me a perjured confession (a sin which is generally agreed to be noxious enough on its own, but when combined with others to be most vile), I am willing to accord with your desire and to tell about myself such monstrous and unheard-of acts and thoughts (but only if it should be granted you to consider their madness), as to render you burdened with my sins, even if you had none of your own, so that in this Lent you may have something to weep for, since you are almost always remote from such sins. Do not think that this perjury which you have forced upon me is not a sin of your own; consider Eve and the devil in the serpent [Gen. 3.4]. The serpent it was who counselled, Eve it was who sinned, but the sinner earned pardon where he who counselled did not. The Jews cried "Crucify Him" [Jn. 19.6], but the crucifiers drank the blood of the crucified to their salvation.

2. But to do now what I have promised: —

A worse one than me from infancy itself, and one more involved with the vices of that age, you need not look for. When by God's gift I had come to puberty, from then I so began to wanton, to indulge in sloth, games, and buffoonery, that, even if there had been some benefit in your hearing of them, yet it would be quite impossible for me to enumerate them individually. In saying what I will now say,[17] I am most wretched in my conscience of what I now deservedly suffer (to be sure, he did not lie who said, "If a man returns evil for good, evil will not depart from his house" [Pr. 17.13]—which in me has been patently fulfilled): for my perjured loyalty to Hugo, for the crime of ambition and worldly earnestness, or rather forgetfulness of God, for the building or rebuiding of fortresses, you need not wonder at how much murder, blinding, mutilation, rape, burning, devastation, and pillaging has occurred.[18] Norica, Italy, Germany, and France are better able to acknowledge that I was such a wretch as I was or could be said to be. By my own fault I have broken up two marriages[19] [as bishop "married" to a church], one [Verona] as if with good reason, the other [Liège] through my pitiable vanity alone. Let him ponder who can the weight of just this, let him measure the sin, let him consider the enormity of it. What, alas, did the poor wives [churches] say, what grief and tears did they show, when one of them saw her rival sitting on high and enjoying kisses due rather to herself, saw the other mistress of the house, arranging what was to be done and scornfully holding her of no account, while she herself clung to the ashes, and the other, though from further away, heard that her successor was rich but saw herself poor?

You say: "What did they say, do you ask? That perhaps you got your just deserts, you wretch. For you took husbands from two women; two sees lost you, their man — and may nothing worse happen to you for this!"

3. Concerning also the shameful act of Warner's brother, the former Duke Conrad:[20] what is said in the psalm, "You took your lot with adulterers" [Ps. 49.18], happened to me. Do not ask, I beg, about the places put under my supervision, their resources ruined, their souls neglected; look at this matter alone and draw your conclusions from there. But because memory fails when there is a vast store of horrible things to be said, let this summary (too condensed though it may be) suffice, I pray; it will contain nothing which is not relevant to me, though put together by someone else.[21]

His Confession

4. I confess to Almighty God, and to all His saints, and to you, priest of God, whoever you are that shall read this, all the sins which I have committed from the beginning of my life right up to this wretched hour, conscious or unconscious, deliberately or under compulsion, waking or sleeping, in thought, word, and deed, in seeing, hearing, tasting, smelling, and touching, and particularly those committed out of pride, the mother of all vice: to wit, the sins of hate and murder, slander, undermining of any brother, perjury, false witness, theft, fornication of every kind, adultery, rapine, fraud, various unclean acts and pollutions, drunkenness, overeating, extravagance of every kind, vainglory, apathy, gloominess, avarice, quarrelsomeness and aggressiveness, hot temper, envy, dis-

cord, greed, ambition, hypocrisy, idleness, cowardice, laziness, sleepiness, gossip, ribaldry, and mockery of others.

5. In addition, I, a sinner, have sinned in that I have not kept Lent and the other required fasts, nor have I fasted as I ought. I have violated saints' days and Sundays, for shame, and I have not celebrated them with proper observance, as I ought; their days of preparation also I have wantonly abused, in that I have too often violated them in person, wretch that I am. In addition, if you have become a perjurer by urging the aforesaid to commit perjury, just as Saul stoned Stephen by the hands of all those whose garments he guarded,[22] so I, while sleeping or eating or holding Mass or matins or doing anything else, have committed adultery through the motions of those whom through my neglect I thrust into adultery. I have become a "bastard born of a whore" [Dt. 23.2], a wretched stepfather who has left an eminently noble marriage for a trollop.

6. I further confess to Almighty God that, fouled with all these and more sins of sensuality, and begrimed with all kinds of contagions, I have unworthily received the sacrament of the Body and Blood of the Lord, ever without remorse in my stony heart, ever without any sincerity of mind, without azyma [Ex. 12.8–11] and bitter herbs, with the ferment of malice and wickedness [1 Cor. 5.8], ungirded, without sandals and staff, dawdling not hastening to the country of everlasting promise, taking the Paschal Lamb of God, who takes away the sins of the world [Jn. 1.29], to my damnation, most wretched alas, and have become guilty of the same Body and Blood of the Lord, in eating it and rashly consuming what is forbidden; and I have sinned by making offerings before the altar impudently against the Lord's command, when many—you, sir, in particular—had much against me [cf. Mt. 5.23–24]. I have sinned in my exhortations, in evil flattery, in ignorance, in negligence, in embezzlement, in giving and taking bribes. But I acknowledge that I am not so guilty of usury, and I do not deny it; for I have rather been a prodigal, which little befits a usurer, and this I do confess and grieve.

7. I have sinned in taking the alms of the poor, in abusiveness, and in the gruffness of my responses, in unworthy hospitality and entertainment of the poor; and in that I have not loved or honored as I should my parents and neighbors, and too often when I did love them I loved them for the wrong reasons; and I have sinned in bullying the household and subjects entrusted to my charge. I have not visited the sick nor those in desperate straits, and I have not ministered to them. I have not buried the dead nor had them buried as was necessary. I have not clothed the poor, nor refreshed the hungry and thirsty. My elders and teachers and princes, my friends and benefactors, I have not honored nor loved with due affection; and their goods, their services, their counsels and their instructions I have not observed as I ought.

8. I, a sinner, have sinned in kissing and wanton embraces, in wicked caresses and fondling. And in church, standing or sitting, when the holy readings or sacred offices were going on, I have given myself over to otiose tales or wicked thoughts, and I have not considered what I ought to consider, but rather what I ought not to consider, and I have not lent my ears to those things which are holy; and I have sinned in unrighteous and wanton contemplation and (what is still worse) in fantasizing the mating of men, animals, and beasts, and other obscene things.

9. Besides these, I have sinned in frivolousness, whether riding, walking, standing, sitting, or lying; and in these and all other vices, in which man in his frailty can sin against God, I confess that I am guilty, to Almighty God and all his saints, and to you, priest of God, whoever and wherever you are.

10. But seeing the infinite extent of my sins, perhaps you say: "Have you ever, I ask, confessed these excesses to anyone?"

No, I answer, except to Him who could not be unaware of them even if I did not confess them. For I was enslaved to my lusts with such hypocrisy and concealment (as wretchedly I still am) that before you I never found anyone who could catch me properly, that is, with proof. Only they shared my guilty secrets who supported me in them, and though I was most befouled (as, to my grief, I still am and I do not deny it), I was thought and spoken of as most chaste, like many; and what is worse, I was glad I was spoken of in that way, wretchedly deceived by that saying used by hypocrites, which many people often say in deceit: "Though not with purity, at least with discretion." The reasons why I made confession to no one were many: one was so that others would not fall by following my example; a second, so that others would not grow proud by comparing themselves to me—and both groups would perish as though by the infection of my corpse; then, I was very afraid that my sinfulness would make people despise me; but the third reason, a more serious one, in fact the most serious of all, was that I feared that the confessor would say to me what the law prescribes should be said to runaways: "Return and be reconciled to your lord, because, just as the doctor's care does no good to a wounded man if the steel is still in him, so your confession and penitence do you no good if you do not abandon the sin which you confess."[23]

11. For when I was a child, a wellborn kinsman came and holding me on the altar of St. Peter and St. Paul,[24] together with bread and wine, offered me to God as a sacrifice, and promised irreversibly that I would serve Christ's name in a pact that would hold good forever. At a mature and legal age, I took the pen myself and wrote in this wise, and placed my statement upon the altar, upon nothing else than the altar: "I Rather promise my steadfastness, and conversion of my ways, and obedience according to the Rule of St. Benedict in the presence of God and of his saints." Infinite are my sins which could be set down in this confession, and unspeakably heinous are those which have been set down.

"Among them you should not have kept silent (since it is very pertinent to you) about the damnable crime of a certain courtesan, who secretly killed her child for fear of you, and about the death of him who suffered a fatal fall under the wheel of a mill because of your foolish pride."[25]

You should also remember, I say, the spectacle you saw of those who fell and those who caused their fall, as a result of which, don't forget, those three lost their eyes; but these are mere trifles compared with this single one, if, that is, this one is not left out.

"Which one?" you ask.

My turning away from God, I reply. For if I had been able to escape from this one thing alone, namely, apostasy, that is, denial of God, and to return reconciled as a fugitive to the Lord and to confess it to my advantage and do penance, I think that I could earn pardon for my other sins also. But if for that one sin alone I do not listen to the counsel . . . [26] in hoping for pardon. . . .

"But what counsel?" you say. . . . what the words of the Scripture show for all: "He who hides his sins will not prosper" [Pr. 28.13].

12. "You do not hide them," you say, "since you confess them to me even, or rather, to both friends and enemies, and even in writing."

I do, I say, I do.

"But don't deceive me, please. Let us rather hear the Scripture together: 'Whoever has confessed . . . '[27] Do you hear?" you say.

Don't hurry, wait, I say, and see what follows: "*and has abandoned them.*" This let us do both for the many sins and for the one sin [inconvertibility], but most of all for this one sin; and then we may joyfully hear, "Mercy shall follow." This, this had ever been my reason for not confessing any of these sins, because it was not yet my intention to abandon this one. To abandon those others was easy, just as I have already abandoned some few of them — but would that I had done so not uselessly but with perseverance. But in this one the vanity of the world had hardened me, and now a kind of compulsion, as it were, out of my inability prevents me. May God's pity break these bonds; for I will not otherwise "sacrifice to Him the victim of praise" [Ps. 115.17]. Just what the *victim of praise* is, hear in the book of Psalms: "Let us come into His presence in confession" [Ps. 94.2]. But what good is confession unless it is followed by the abandonment of the sins which you confess? What good is the runaway's making amends — or deciding to return — if it is not followed by his return to his master — provided that he is not prevented, which God is well aware of? Let him who wishes come and console me, or rather seduce me, with "empty words, for it is because of them that the wrath of God comes upon the sons of mistrust"

[Eph. 5.6]—that is, of the devil, who is called *mistrust* because, by making wretches now put their trust in vain things, he makes them despair utterly of salvation at the final hour. Now let him who wishes urge me not to abandon what I have confessed and still hope for pardon by confessing every Lent or when impelled by fear of death. Though able to urge it, he will in no way be able to persuade me of it, believe me.

"Then why have you confessed now?" you ask.

For two reasons, I say. First, because, having abandoned many sins by compulsion and some few by my own free will, I think that now I am beginning to bring pressure on myself to confess; for I am a little weary of my former way of life. And secondly, I think I am willing to abandon this one sin—and the abandonment of all the others was worthless without the abandonment of this one; may God grant that my willingness be not pointless, for wretched and hardened I do not find myself able. Also, though my sins are so great, so innumerable, and so far from trivial, I would myself forget them as the pile of them grew, and under the devil's influence it might come about that I would not even remember that I had once written them down, and thus I would be reminded to my consternation that I wanted to abandon them for God and had not implemented the wish. For you could know by experience how prone to all these faults the human race is, if you had not, sinner, also forgotten your own. For because I cannot even see with my eyes the sins which I ought to have unceasingly examined in my mind, it seems to me somewhat useful to reveal them, so that another seeing me should see himself in me and from my actions check and correct his own.

13. "Well," you say, "when you felt yourself such a sinner, how did you dare to celebrate Masses or such in the presence of Him who said to the sinner, 'Why do you recite my statutes?'" [Ps. 49.16].

I admit it, I admit it; some people celebrate them the more faithfully the more they feel themselves sinners. For it behooves a man humbly to *feel* that he is a sinner but not to be one; for the judgments of God are like the great deep [Ps. 35.7], in whose foreknowledge—or better, knowledge—already exists what will certainly be in the future.

"So such saying of the Mass has some validity then?" you ask. Very much indeed, I say, but would that it were not a problem for me alone—for it is not a problem for others at all (only provided that the offices are said faithfully), inasmuch as the sacraments of God belong neither to the one nor to the other, that is, neither to the righteous man nor to the sinner, but to Him about whom it is said: "He on whom you see the Spirit descend and remain, this is He who baptizes with the Holy Spirit" [Jn. 1.33]. It is enough that, if you are a righteous man, you should be, as it were, ignorant that you are what you are; if you are a sinner, that you should regret that you are what you are. Both sinner and righteous man should listen to the advice of the psalmist: "Sing praises in wisdom" [Ps. 46.8].

"Why?" you ask.

Because it is not any man you praise with a psalm but the "King of all the earth, God" [Ps. 46.8]; and elsewhere: "You (God) will destroy all who speak lies" [Ps. 5.7]; and another says: "Cursed be he who does the Lord's work carelessly" [Jer. 48.10]. If you are cursed for acting carelessly, what happens to you for acting hypocritically?

14. But[28] perhaps you are making some charge or accusation about my taking or not taking the Eucharist?[29] If so, you should be aware, I suggest, that the Gospel reading of yesterday should be taken with the apostle's words which will be read on Friday: "Unless you eat of the Flesh of the Son of Man and drink His Blood" — that is, taking the bread and wine not figuratively but in reality as His Flesh and Blood, the dwelling-place of His divinity through the incomprehensible working of the Holy Spirit — "you will have no life in you" [Jn. 6.54]; as if he were saying: "You will not receive eternal life but death of the soul, that is, the punishment of hell." Eat then, I say, lest you lose your life.

"What life?" you ask.

God; for He says himself, "I am the Life" [Jn. 14.6] — of the soul, of course.

"I do, I do," you say.

Very good, I say. But hear Him in His law: "Justice and only justice you shall follow" [Dt. 16.20].

"How?" you ask.

I will tell you: "Thus shall you eat it" (that is, the Lamb); "Gird up your loins" (that is, live chastely, if you wish to eat it); "have sandals on your feet" (that is, guide your actions with the examples of those who mortified their bodies so as to make their souls live), "hold your staff" (of discipline and reason), "in your hand" (of action), "and you will eat it in haste" [Ex. 12.11], hastening towards the glory of the supreme Solemnity, which means, of course, not to seek the reward for good deeds in this world, but to hasten in heart's desire to where the eternal reward is. Eat in this way and you will have life in you. But if you eat it otherwise, hear the words of the apostle: "Whoever eats the Flesh of the Lord and drinks His Blood unworthily, eats and drinks judgment for himself" [1 Cor. 11.29].

"How is it *judgment*," you ask, "if it is flesh and blood?"

Taken worthily, it is flesh and blood, I say; taken unworthily it is *judgment*.

"Who is worthy?" you ask.

You have read it in the apostle, I reply; it is he who eats it just as He prescribed. For he speaks about one who is in that condition in the present, not about one who had once been ungirded, had not held his staff, and preferring to roll in the mire of sin and to hurry into wickedness, had thus eaten judgment for himself. He will not have life, if he eats with these not corrected or not in the process or desire of correction.

And I think that this is what the apostle subsequently urges, when he says, "Let a man examine himself" [1 Cor. 11.28] — that is, determine in what state he is: if one of sinning, he should cease; if of correction, he should eat in fear and trembling. But no one should take lightly the sentence in Kings: "If only the young men have kept themselves clean since yesterday and particularly from women for three days" [1 Sam. 21.4], speaking, that is, of eating the holy bread; and the words of the Law frequently heard: "Be sanctified," that is, abstain from sexual relations. The examination which the apostle urges consists above all in letting drop all envy, in cleansing one's conscience of sinfulness, in correcting hatred and all disputes with one's brothers, in purging extravagance or any unchastity; and what you ought, wretch, to have constantly remembered (as the apostle knew how to distinguish the holy bread from other loaves), that the loaves affected the body only, while the holy bread when granted, effected the salvation of both body and soul, and that the latter should not even be handled, still less consumed, with the same haste or carelessness as the former.

15. Nor should you listen perfunctorily when "the body of the Lord" is said; but you should consider what is being said, about whom and to whom.

What is being said? The *actual* Body of the Lord.

About whom is it said? If you say, "About the Lord" — He who in the flesh which He assumed for you and in which He suffered much for you, was crucified, died, and was buried, rose again, and was raised into heaven, now enters into you to whom the words are said — see that you have the hostel for such a Host cleansed and decorated; for if He is pleased with it, He approves and blesses; if not, because He does not approve, it follows (which is greatly to be feared) that He also curses, unless speedy confession and penitence — together with His pity, which may He mercifully grant you — avert this.

To whom is it said? Take care. For if you are the one who has fulfilled the command, or rather the commandments — namely, "gird up your loins, have your sandals on your feet, hold your staff in your hands, and eat in haste" [Ex. 12.11] (that is, not saying "tomorrow, tomorrow") — you can rejoice in the great virtue of your sacred office, that is, not in yourself but in the Lord. Otherwise the words of the Gospel are greatly to be feared: "When He had dipped it, He gave it to Judas Escariot" [Jn. 13.26]. See that you be not the same in imitating him.

Let us therefore not be deceived or deceive ourselves: God it is who is received, yes, God; but just as then He was hidden in the flesh, so now in very reality

He is hidden in the bread turned into flesh. So it is expressed more accurately in the Greek when the prayer to God says, "Give us this day our consubstantiate bread" [Mt. 6.11], that is, what you yourself are because you have been invoked and have entered into us, ineffably, indeed, but not incredibly; for this is to "discern the Body of the Lord" [1 Cor. 11.29], to be able to distinguish it from other corporeal foods, in dignity and divinity, beyond everything which can exist and be seen. But great care must be taken with God's help that no "utterly dead person" dare to hazard such mysteries, that is, one who is known to have no charity in him; "for he who does not love remains in death" [1 Jn. 3.14]. So if you feel that you have no charity in you at all, either towards God or towards your neighbor, be fearful of hazarding such holy mysteries. The less charity you see in yourself, the more fearfully you should approach, I say.

The return from taking the sacraments should be considered just as much as the approach, because there is as much grace in receiving the Lord as in having Him with you. It says: "Satan entered into him after the mouthful" [Jn. 13.27]. And of the manna and heaven-sent food (which mean the same thing) it says: "Still were their morsels in their mouths and the anger of God came upon them" [Ps. 77.30–31]. Therefore, the hostel of the heart must be cleansed before taking the sacrament and kept clean after taking it. Note also that it refers to the Spirit not only *descending* over the Lord [Jn. 1.33], but also *remaining*, so that you should know that this is not the case with the rest of mankind, but that the Spirit comes on people through Grace but retreats for an offense.

"What of it?" you say.

This means both fear and comfort, I say. Fear if, after the Holy Spirit has been upset by our evil ways, we reject it from us—for we must fear that it cannot be recalled. But comfort, because it can be recalled by our making satisfaction. We can also understand from this, that if the Holy Spirit has been given to someone after proper self-examination and consecration, by a true invocation not tainted by the fault of priests,[30] and has been expelled again by his evil actions, it has still not so totally abandoned its lodging that it cannot re-enter him again when reconciled; and therefore he ought to put aside his fears of desperation and steadfastly presume for its return, and recall it with continual prayers, especially since He has promised, "Turn to me and I will turn to you" [Mal. 3.7]; "Don't kill us," it says, "since we have treasure buried in the field; and he did not kill them" [Jer. 41.8]. The treasure hidden in the field is hope in repentance.[31] Find the rest in the source from which I drew this.

16. "He says, 'What right have you to recite my statutes?'" [Ps. 49.16], you say.

I answer (if reply is appropriate): "Because Thy mercy is better than life, my lips will praise Thee" [Ps. 62.4]. For after the severity of His justice there follows the comfort arising out of His pity, proclaimed most holily in the same

psalm: "With sacrifice of thanksgiving he will honor me; there is the way by
which I will show him the salvation of God" [Ps. 49.23]; however, this sacrifice
is more one of action than of words, though it is also one of words. If you
want to know why or whom He forbids to recite His statutes, if what follows
there is not enough, listen to what had been set down before: "Offer to God
a sacrifice of thanksgiving" [Ps. 49.14].

"I am forbidden?" you say.

You are forbidden, I say, if you neglect to do what follows: "And pay your
vows to the most high." If, Christian, you have perhaps forgotten and ask what
your vows are, remember what you promised to God in baptism. If you, monk,
ask, remember, I urge, what you also promised later. That is what you should
pay. The Creator promises: "Call upon me in the day of trouble and I will deliver
you; and you shall glorify me" [Ps. 49.15].

17. You say: "'Why are you sad, O my soul?'" [Ps. 41.6].

Hear your consolation: "Hope in God."

"Why?"

"Since I shall still praise Him" [Ps. 41.6], I still live, breathe, walk on my
own two feet, it is still my day of salvation, the time is still acceptable [2 Cor. 6.2].

Likewise you say: "You flatter yourself too much. As Jerome says,[32] 'Let us
be ignorant of penitence lest we sin too easily.'"

Let us not sin at all, I say; why sin further? We have sinned more than enough.
This is a plank after the shipwreck, not a solid ship. If we cease to sin, we can
be carried by it to the haven of salvation, from which we have drifted away by
sinning. But — to venture an assumption — even earthly things often show us what
to hope for from the Heavenly. For, as the Apostle says, "His invisible nature
is understood through the things which have been made" [Rom. 1.20]. If a runaway is apprehended by his master against his will, what can he hope for? There
is no doubt that he must reply, "Due punishment." If he return of his own accord, what? Mercy, since otherwise one will be able to infer that he ran away
not from his master but from vicious cruelty. This mercy is justly and firmly reinforced as long as he does not begin to grow proud or slothful in his service as
a result of the security of his return and pardon. But he should ever ponder on
the wickedness of his running away and serve day and night with the greatest
humility, so that he can also repay the service that was neglected by his running
away, and add something for which he may receive the merit of just reward.

18. "Do you think," you say, "that you have yet reached this stage of this
servant?"

I would think so, I say, if I had returned to the intention of my vows.

"So now what?"

It seems to me, I say, but as it were dimly in the dark, that I am like the servant who, running away, is absent from his master for a long time and is finally compelled back by the terror of his master's threats, fearing lest he be suddenly apprehended (that is, when he is unaware) and handed over to the rack or torture, and who sends deputies hoping for some measure of mercy.

"Who are your deputies?" you say.

Any effort I make, I reply, but only if the effort happens to be in God's service; and if nothing else, then at least my desire of speaking with the Lord—and would that it were my true desire and that of others who are invoked in prayers for this purpose. For the psalm says, "The Lord has heard the desire of the poor" [Ps. 9.17], as if to say: His master knows well the desire of the runaway. Hear also what it says about preparation, as if for some kind of journey: "Your ear has heard the preparation of their hearts" [Ps. 9.17]. For don't you think that it is a kind of deputation from a fugitive escaping from an alien master, when you hear him crying from the bottom of his heart: "Snatch me from the hand of the sinner" [Ps. 70.4]? For he wishes to escape but cannot, unless he be helped, or rather snatched, by his true master. Cannot he also be seen as preparing his flight [from the hand of the sinner, i.e., the devil] who cries: "My heart is ready, O God, my heart is ready" [Ps. 56.8], but only if he cries it sincerely? For if not, he doubles his offense. But just as any tyrant or unjust possessor prevents the runaway from returning to his master and snares him lest he have a chance of escaping, so also the devil, as I too recently found, piles up divers obstructions so that he either does not want or cannot or despairs, or even is ashamed, to return, or at any rate makes him so abominable (which is much more serious) to his true Lord, that He chooses to seize him unexpectedly and hand him over to everlasting tortures, rather than to have him reconciled to His Grace by penitence.

This generally happens when he becomes proud of it and of his messages of prayer and adopts a sense of security about getting his desire, either some of it or a little of it or a lot of it, or becomes overconfident of good or becomes lazy or slothful without any security. For there are some (such as I myself now am), who in their apathy and idleness so much neglect their whole selves by neglecting their free will (for God demands this too) and, as it were, give themselves up to His mercy, that they choose to give loose rein to sloth, and even to stand in church gaping and dozing, to wander in every direction both physically and mentally, to sit and to lie down rather than to send a messenger to God's mercy, either by means of some good deed or reading or prayer or at the least by the contemplation of some good, so that sometime He may deign to rescue them more completely from the devil's snares.

Again, after a space:[33]

19. That's how it seems to me; you think as you please. For just as no one can promote himself to any ecclesiastical rank by his own efforts, so no one can demote himself at all, even if he wants to, from whatever station or rank he has been ordained into or lived in. Also, he seems to be compelled by the same necessity by which he holds his rank to do the things which befit that rank, however unworthy he may be—or do you think otherwise?

"I would think nothing truer," you say, "if it did not happen to be written in the Neocesarian Council, chapter nine, that 'if a bishop, priest or deacon should confess that he has carnally sinned, he should not consecrate the offerings, though for his good zeal abiding in the other offices.' I do not venture to question the holy Council, particularly when I hear the same judgment also given in the Law by the Lord, when He says, 'A priest who has a blemish shall not offer the bread to his God nor shall he draw near to His ministry' [Lev. 21.17–18]. But why shouldn't someone accuse himself of such blemishes in the council? He should also be deposed if he is afraid to do the offices which go with his rank."

Because it is very hard to do, I say, and for that reason you find no one who does it. If anyone were to do it, even though not thinking of his own good today, he would fear that at once there would be thrust at him what was once thrust at the Pharisees about the woman taken in adultery [Jn. 8.4].[34] For we read that even Gregory, beyond compare among all men under heaven, was so lenient to men like this that he took Maximus back into grace, who against his edict had usurped the bishopric of the city of Salona from Honoratus, who had been elected by the congregation, using military force and by means of the Simoniac heresy also, and had for seven years been a rebel ignoring his excommunication.[35] He allowed him to remain bishop when the case was brought to trial. For just as we ought to be strict with those who persevere in sin, so ought we to be lenient in granting pardon to those who amend.

"A serious condition," you say, "as far as his soul is concerned. Of such a man it could be said: 'He has put his foot in the net and walks in its spots' [Job 18.8]. Yet is there any remedy for him?"

None, I say, none, except only God's pity. For he has put his foot very far into the net, if he has also been ambitious. But what will we do? Will we despair of him crying from the deep? Where then will be the merciful omnipotence of Him who promises, "I refuse the death of a sinner" [Ezek. 33.11], and makes men out of stones [Mt. 3.9]? Will He not likewise be able to make watchmen out of thieves, guards out of robbers, shepherds out of bandits, sheep out of wolves, living out of dead, sweet-smelling out of fetid, free men out of prisoners, and movable out of the immovable? How often He has done this is a long tale

to tell. Make Him want to, you will see at once that He can. "Have I not told
you," He said, "that if you believe you will see the glory of God?" [Jn. 11.40]
What glory? A resurrection after four days. Let the supplicant sisters[36] come
and importune Him, pouring forth sisterly tears (that is, the weakness of humility) and telling Him of the death of their brother. Let them pour their prayers
to the Lord, the one signifying pious action, the other contemplative speculation and most holy prayer.[37] Their number and rank are also significant in that
they show that there are two orders in the Church that look to the salvation
of those dying: the first by preaching and doing; the second by praying to the
Lord with constant prayers, interceding for the dead and making supplication
so that they can be raised. Let them admit that the death of such a one happened
in the absence of God's protection as a result of negligence; for it is strange that
both of them said, "Lord, if you had been here, our brother would never have
died" [Jn. 11.21–33]. Let despair be far off, let the constant faith of hope be
present, that a man dead four days and fetid, blocked in by the massive boulder
of habitual sin, tied, immovable, even after a long sleep can be raised up, resur-
rected, can overcome the weight placed on him, be released and walk forth. You
will again see Christ "deeply moved in spirit" of compassion and prayer; you
will hear Him cry, "Come outside." You will see the man you despaired of at
once come forth, show himself alive though bound, and not conceal but confess
it, hear the command that he go away absolved, that is, that he should adjust
his life to the dictates of reason, so that by his resurrection others even more
deadened in sin should return to life and believe in Christ, that is, the Savior of all.

20. "What should we do," you say, "if none of these things happen? Should
we respect him as living whom we know to be dead [i.e., in sin]?"

As I deduce from this, I reply, you do not yet know what you should respect
in anyone, the fact that God made him or the fact that he as a man has reached
awareness of himself. But because you are ignorant in questions of this kind,
I think you will be enlightened more by teaching and examples than by reasoning. "The scribes and Pharisees sit on Moses' seat," He said, "so practise and
observe whatever they tell you but do not do what they do" [Mt. 23.2–3]. In
other words: Respect what God has conferred; tolerate what they do, not for
themselves (who are wicked) but for the honor which they have received—which
of course is good because it was bestowed by the Good Bestower. Take a mangy
ass carrying the finest wine: the ass is worthless but you admire the wine. A
deformed finger often wears the most precious ring: admirers covet the ring with
greed and longing, but their gaze is repelled by the finger.

"You state that honor is therefore good," you say, "because it has been bestowed by God; what about the honor which God has not conferred?"

What honor of that sort is there, I reply, since the apostle has testified: "There is no power except from God" [Rom. 13.1]? Or do you want power to be one thing, honor another? But power is weak without honor, and therefore it is not even power.

"'Kings have ruled,'" you say, "'but not from me; there were princes but I did not know them'" [Os. 8.4].

"Not from me," I say, means: "they have not ruled according to my statutes, they have not done right as I commanded; I did not recognize them, praise them, approve of them; yet they have ruled in my sight." But if you cannot be persuaded to want bishops of no other kind (may God's Pity grant it) than those whom the apostle describes—"A bishop should be without sin" [Tit. 1.7] (which is, for shame, a rare bird on earth today)—think of Caiphas, whom Peter seemed to obey; yet when he said this, he was not separated from Moses' seat; think, I say, it is not very long ago, it was read yesterday: "He did not say this of his own accord" [Jn. 11.51]. What is "of his own accord?" Of his own ill will by which he wanted Christ put to death; for he did not want Christ put to death so that the whole race should be delivered (which was quite impossible because of their wickedness), but so that He immediately might be removed from his dominion. Though this was his intention, yet even so what Moses' seat uttered was true (just as the sound made by the plucked string is the player's). For we read as follows: "Since he was High Priest that year he prophesied." Pay attention at this point. "Of that year," it says. Had God commanded thus through Moses? Far from it. Look at the strange indignity of it. This is not power bestowed by the law, yet still allowed by God, but power given by the wicked Herod. But if a man with power thus granted by such a one as Herod could prophesy, what could he have done if the power had been given him by God? Much more, namely, the wish to say good *and* the ability; but Caiphas's power has only the ability. For it was not because Caiphas wanted it that the people were delivered; he said it because the dignity of the seat made him say what was going to happen. Can you find a more unworthy man? And yet you hear that Caiphas prophesied, and so you can realize the power of the office and the dignity of this kind of rank, no matter what kind of life the holder of it leads. Do not be in doubt if power that was merely *allowed* could reach a state of prophesying effectively, since I have said that the office was good simply because it had been *conceded* by a good God.

To humor you in something: we must observe, I acknowledge, that when the Apostle said, "There is no power except from God" [Rom. 13.1], by not being specific he left room for understanding both *allowed* and *conceded*; particularly as he adds below: "Those that exist have been ordained by God"—not like that one of Caiphas which was far from *ordained* but still must be respected with the attention which we showed above. But let us make an effort, I say, and

see that our effort is not useless. For this whole argument is an indication of
my unworthiness and wretchedness, and while I try with it to twist the Scripture (all-unbending) to my aid, I show what the situation *could* be, not what
it actually is.

21. Therefore, so as not to deceive myself further, I admit that though the
all-powerful mercy of God can effect all this (just as He could create the world
out of nothing), if He has not done so it is quite clear that I am utterly lost,
along with all those like me, and that I falsely bear the name of bishop or abbot
in peril of eternal damnation, even though I be allowed, as Caiphas once was,
to prophesy; and from this damnation I cannot at all be freed unless I totally
abandon the vanity of the world — and may Christ's pity allow this. For it is
surprising that I can bear that name, when I hear Him crying against me and
my like (for I consider that all of those faults figuratively apply to me, alas):
"Whoever has a blemish will not offer the bread to the Lord nor approach to
His ministry, a man who is blind or lame or with a small or large or twisted
nose, or with a broken limb, or one who is a dwarf, or has a defect in his sight,
who has scabs or an itching disease or crushed testicles" [Lev. 21.17–20]. Caught
with all these faults, I have no confidence even in my family's[38] interceding for
me with God.

"You are in despair," you say, "it is clear; why do you strive to no purpose?"

I am neither in despair, I say, nor in hope; I hope in God, I despair about
myself, and the more I consider that I ought to despair about myself, the more
I hope in Him. For I despair that I have not even started to do what I know
I ought to do; but I do not despair that it will be done if God quite decides
it. But whether I strive to no purpose, I do not know; and therefore I do not
see why I still try to achieve it. But if there is a reason, it is not the one which
is appropriate, but the one which I mentioned above, remember, about the rebel, the wicked runaway servant. For I make my effort (if I ever do) not out
of love of the Lord or of religion (which I have rejected) or of the place (which
I wretchedly fled)[39] or, finally, out of desire of eternal life, but out of fear of
hell; and even if I dared to dismiss this fear, I still would not do so, and for
this reason I cannot think why God should care about such a servant. For I see
that I must be worthless even in my own eyes, when I read what true words
were spoken by a pagan, no less, in scorn of me and my like:

The good hate to sin out of love of virtue,[40]

since I observe that I (and they) am afraid to sin rather than love to be free of
sin. The reason for it is this: if I had been a lay person and sought penance for
all those sins, if I were sentenced to two hundred and sixty-five years of penance,
who would give them to me? What would I do, since I am already a septu-

agenarian?[41] The confessor would say, I know (if he was any worth): "You cannot do this as the time is too short; hand yourself wholly over to God and abandon the world; lo, all is forgiven you, because you have committed everything to God who is merciful." But I am a monk, both in habit (only barely) and in law (but a runaway from the rule to which I made my vows); even if I did fulfill so many years of penance, even if all were to be dismissed, there would still remain this one fact, that I irrevocably ran away from my rule. Don't you think that for this alone I will be damned?

"Yes, for this alone."

I can atone for all those other sins with all these years, but I cannot atone for this single one.

Again, after a space:[42]

22. By these steps of the mind, I arrived at the point where it seemed to me that unless God granted that I end my life as a monk as I had promised, it had been pointless to have abstained from this and all other sins, since I was destined for eternal punishments for this sin alone, even if I had no others. What benefit would I have had from abstaining from all these sins and to have done without the sweet enticements which the world offers, when I still did not escape eternal punishment? I want to impress the certainty of this on you who boast of a sort of chastity (acquired more by age than virtue) after many lapses from it, it seems to me, and to bring you back from this sense of security to the necessary tears and fasting and most of all to the duty of a monk (which along with me you honor only in the name and the habit); I chose to tell all my faults rather than remind you of yours (or at any rate some of them). Anyone considering the joy of security which you all have even during this Lent,[43] and not knowing the reality, could think that there is no sin in any of you. Alas, some infection, of false hope or deadly despair or wicked obduracy, has so taken you by my fault[44] (who neglected to warn you) that it has made you insensible also, and this is acknowledged to be more dangerous in all kinds of failing.

"While you do not spare yourself," you say, "you savagely gnaw[45] at me, or rather at all of us."

How otherwise? I say. For in taking care for myself and neglecting others, particularly you who have been entrusted to my care, what greater sin could I either have or confess? Yet I am — I do not deny it — by my own fault a person of such a kind that in my prayers I say "Have mercy on *me*" more intensely than "Have mercy on *us*." And even when I say "Have mercy on us" I am thinking of myself rather than anyone else, forced to do so by the heinousness of my sins. In this I show that love is cold in me and I have further doubts about the absolution of my sins. But O, would that sometime your sins would be as clear to you as mine are to me while I write this. For they would then temper your joy a little and indicate your desire to escape from them as soon as possible. They would also remove the lethargy of those wallowing in sloth, particularly those most affected, the priors or elders, whom the greatest danger threatens, you should know, as me also—which may God avert! For these, and they include me, have rather, as the prophet says, "broken their yoke and burst their chains" [Jer. 5.5], as lately one of them (note how cheerfully) served the devil. For though he had kept arguing that it was because of the poverty of the common funds that he and others neglected the precepts of the Rule, he suddenly produced coins long hoarded from those common funds, so that he was clearly shown to have served mammon long and faithfully, and not so lazily to have attended to the worship of idols—a fact which you knew before I did. Even at his age he did not fear the example of Simon [Acts 8.18–24], though he had heard that his predecessor, a petty thief of the same age, I think, had hoarded money for the same purpose and had died in a suitably wretched manner of judgment before he had been allowed to enjoy it even for a day.

23. From this it is very necessary to consider how backward a step we are taking, alas, we who ought to guide laymen on the path of righteousness, as our predecessors did. "Any unattached priest, if he obtains a church, is allowed to sell, give or delegate in any way to anyone as he wishes whatever he had previously owned; but whatever he acquires afterwards he cedes to the Church's right." But a monk, who should not even have his own will in his own control,[46] for whom should he amass funds? To whom give or leave what he has amassed, particularly if what he appears to have has been amassed from the monies out of which he ought to have been clothed and fed—and perhaps out of the funds for some office? And if this happens to some wretch—where will he be and what will he say to himself in his heart when he hears it read it in the text: "Let them always remember Ananias and Saphira, lest those who have kept something for themselves or all who have embezzled the funds of the monastery suffer in the soul the death which those two suffered in the body."[47] What ornaments there could have been in that church from so many pounds of silver (as they declare), out of which that money was embezzled and hoarded! I heard someone muttering in the sacristy: "They say that we should have nothing of our own; who then bestowed these ornaments and books here if not the monks of this place?" To this I say: it would have been better, I admit, for him not to have owned them than to have bestowed them; yet, in extenuation of the wrong, it was better to have left them here than to have dissipated them elsewhere.

"Good," you say; "I am satisfied." But turn to yourself, examine yourself, lest it be truly said to you: "Hypocrite, remove the beam first from your own eye;

for why do you see the speck that is in your brother's eye, but do not consider the beam that is in your own?" [Lk. 6.41–42].

I do consider it, I say, I do, and to the beam I also add this guilt: as though what I have done on my own account were not enough, I gave him[48] the chance to do it, being fully aware and not preventing him. "Not only those who do, but also those who approve of them doing, are worthy of death" [Rom. 1.32]. But, from the human viewpoint, do you think that it was more tolerable and natural that a foreigner, pauper, exile, beggar, and most deceived stranger did such a thing under stress of poverty, than that a citizen, native, rich, and — to tell the truth — lawful servant of this same church did it out of pride and ambition (lawful in that he had been legally handed over and bound for ever into service, by his own hand and vows), breaking the yoke, abandoning the service and bursting the bonds of the Rule, without his abbot's permission?

But — to humor you once again — so as to criticize him in such a way as not to spare myself, I admit that we both acted very inconsiderately. For if, since I am almost decrepit (as he is too), I meet with death or depart before I have returned the sum of twenty-two pounds to the holy place which I robbed[49] of this amount, I must fear the punishments of hell. And if he too, being no less in debt to this place and being of the same age as myself, as I have said, has not made this good and has not faithfully guarded that which he bought, none can doubt (except he who has lost his inner sight) that eternal punishment awaits him, along with Ananias, Saphira and Simon. But it was Peter, remember, who by his words struck down Ananias and Saphira for their fraud and sentenced Simon to die in perpetual damnation for his pride and ambition [Acts 5.1–11; 8.18–24], Peter whose money this was, Peter whose abbey was fraudulently plundered.

But let us consider both beams, mine, that is, and his; for there is no "speck" here that I see. You will today perhaps more clearly see with eyes open that both beams threaten my neck, in fact, that of the two, one will be impossible for me to carry. "If you do not tell the wicked man of his wickedness, I will require his blood from your hand" [Ezek. 3.18], He said. This is corroborated by him who said: "Where the students fail, the teacher is to blame,"[50] and also by him whose Rule we have both clearly transgressed and rebelled against in this one fact at least, even if there were nothing else — he because he did it, I because I did not speak against it, since it says: "Let the abbot know that whatever the Father can find fault with in his flock lies to the blame of the shepherd." But I shrank from telling him out of respect for his age.

"You are lying," you reply. "You are certainly lying and you are deceiving yourself. For it was not his age that you respected but rather his pride — which was to make cakes for the queen of heaven [Jer. 7.18], to worship the devil, just as the devil also strove to tempt Him to whom the angels ministered [Mt. 4.11]. But if you had so much respect for the devil (whom I call pride) in him, that you did not dare—when he ventured to tell you of his wicked fault—to tell him what God has commanded, how would you have behaved if you had stood before Diocletian? Had you ever heard, 'Whoever is ashamed of me and of my words, of him will the Son of Man be ashamed when He comes in His glory and the glory of His Father and of the holy angels' [Lk. 9.26]? Consider your cowardice and weakness. For I knew that you had often hated his pride so much that you had almost reached the point of hating him. This being the case, you should continually weep for your cowardice and the lack of love in your heart, even if there were nothing else to weep for. When you spared him, you denied, yes denied, God."

Remarks of the same to a certain seemingly religious abbot of another place.

Someone says: "O imitators, servile flock!"[51] O wickedness found, alas, even in angels! [Job 4.18]. What did you as a nephew do, when you saw your uncle (or, better, as the Italian puts it, *barba*) so raving for I know not what reason? Where was "Whoever hears, let him say, I have come" [Rev. 22.17]? Where even "Love your neighbor as yourself" [Mt. 19.19]? You scorned all transitory things, but you did not correct the man who panted after transitory things, though he was very dear to you (this also against the Rule).[52] One of two things is quite clear: either you were not what you wanted to appear or be called, or you hated him rather than loved him. For if you loved him, why did you not strive to draw him with you where you were headed, that is, towards God?

"Look, I advise," you say, "'He who falls even so are his eyes opened'" [Num. 24.4].

But look, I exclaim, to the place where they went as if to pray, containing the money given for such a purpose. O den, turned (if it is as they say) from a holy house of prayer into the wickedest den of thieves [Mt. 21.13]! "Were these, these, the many comings and goings to Lemnos?"[53]

24. Attend, please, you who yesterday tried to cast out a speck of the beam, and presume no further to compare denial of God and devil-worship with any other sin. You should know that I am guilty of none of the things which, you remember, I confessed above [c. 2], that is, of homicide, blinding, mutilation, arson, pillage, or many others, more than of this one; in fact, I did none of these things nor wanted them done nor ordered them, but I did do what resulted in these things being done.[54] But there is something to be added to this: though in fact I neither ordered nor wanted it done, yet I am to blame for allowing it to be done,[55] by not forbidding it, which at least I was able to do.

But you should know that I am glad that it was done without my permission, if that seems to be any mitigation. "Who can discern his errors?" [Ps. 18.13-14] says the psalmist, duly adding: "Clear thou me from hidden faults, O Lord, and spare thy servant from the faults of others," further adding: "If they"—that is, the faults of others—"have not dominion over me, then I shall be blameless and cleansed from the greatest sin," the *greatest*, I repeat. Does it not seem to you to be the greatest sin, that he who by his own crime is twenty-two pounds in debt has by someone else's crime joined to it a debt of eighty in addition?[56] What a wretched state of responsibility! Who except one confident of his own virtue would not rightly run from such a danger? Another man sins without your knowledge and you are bound to pay the penalty!

But to excuse the nephew[57] mentioned a little above for his failure to join me in restraining him, as he ought to have done: it can be seen that I too followed the example of the doctor who does not forbid the dangerously ill patient to take anything he wants. Jerome in a similar cast says: "Doctors say that the more serious illnesses are not to be treated but left to nature, lest the treatment worsen the condition."[58] If Jerome had seen him irrevocably hardened in obduracy against his own prescription, what good would it have done to forbid him any worldly pleasure? To suffer loss in this life and punishment in the next (especially as he well knew that he himself was no less establishing the pit of his own perdition)? Was this what it was to sing every Sunday, even while meditating such sins, "We must despise the world," and to add, "so that we may be able to follow the Christ of the Lord,"[59] as if we cannot follow both the Lord and the world together? And adding still again: "Lest we lose the life eternal because of the vainglory of this world," was he not afraid someone would answer from the side: "Out of thine own mouth I judge thee, wicked servant" [Lk. 19.22]?

25. To show that it must now be time to return to us, I want you to know, I say, that I get great comfort (and may it not be empty) from the prophet's words, "You shall go to Babylon; there you shall be delivered" [Mic. 4.10]. For as I said, in God's house, with no one knowing except my accomplices, under the guise of deceitful sanctity (like many), I shamelessly committed many sins; but since in this one I have been uncovered and caught by you, I have been thrown into so great a panic that with the one uncovered I do not trouble to hide any of my other crimes any more, thinking that what I could suffer without any gain for that one, I could better suffer with gain for all of them, and so I can be thought to have been brought by you into Babylon, so to speak—and may I be truly delivered by God's mercy. For the iron pan is present too, in which my bones also are roasted, perhaps making claims about themselves, though quite pointlessly.

"A great benefit," you say, "I did you when I opposed you, and little benefit when I supported you. But what benefit did I get?"

As much, I say, as the salvation of the world benefited Judas. But I beg you by Jesus and our hope, remove from yourself the infection of my sins, or you will increase my own grievous pain by making me believe that by joining the infection of mine to that of your own you have perished because of me. I beg and caution you not to fall further than you have already fallen, being so engloomed by my darkness, that you are unable to examine yourself or to know where to put your foot of action. Let us therefore cleanse our mind's eye with the salve of the Rule, and direct our gaze rather at the most splendid light of the saints as though at the brightest stars of the ether, and there each of us will see what he ought to think about himself and about the other.

"Are you bringing up the Rule again?" you say.

What else is there, I say, if you ignore that? Run through all the Scriptures, including the Gospel, you must still return to it, willy nilly, if you want to look out for your soul. But tell me, I ask, have you ever heard of the son of Belial on the side of the good?

"Never," you say.

But who is worse than a heathen? I say. For "Belial" is translated "without a yoke."[60] But there is no human condition which can be governed without any yoke; each man's yoke is the restraint of the law under which he lives, as the lay Lombards under Italic law, the clergy under canon law, the monks under monastic law. Throw that out and what yoke coerces you to avoid any crime or allows you to do something? If none, not only are you the son of Belial—that is, the devil—but you are Belial himself. If then you have ever heard the son of Belial or Belial himself obtaining pardon through penitence without conversion, persuade me if you can; if not, persuade yourself, that without the yoke of the appropriate law anyone benefits at all from the labor of penitence.

"I claim," you say, "that the yoke is the same as penitence."

Who imposed it? I ask.

You say: "I see, you deceiver, what you are aiming for. As usual, you are calling me back to the abbot and the Rule."

Right, I say; for what is done by a monk without the abbot's permission will be deputed to presumptuousness and vanity, not reward.

"While I listen to your assertions," you say, "I never stop being tripped up; for in some things you are very strict, in others quite remiss. You appear to boil the kid in its mother's milk, which is forbidden" [Ex. 23.19]. For when you relate your many wicked sins, you block the door of penitence for yourself (which was necessary) and you open it at will. What then do you want to do?

You complain that you are without a yoke; you admit that you are also a son of Belial. What, I say, are you asking for?

What is said in the psalm, if only God's mercy concedes it.

"What is that?"

It says: "Listen, daughter, and see and incline your ear and forget your people and the house of your father" [Ps. 44.11]. Attend: He who calls you shows that he is your Father, so as to call you away from your father. Let us therefore leave this father with his hard yoke and follow Him whose yoke is sweet and whose burden is light [Mt. 11.30].

"Why do you not do so?" you ask.

The fact that we are speaking is to that purpose, I maintain. "If you offer aright and do not divide aright, you have sinned," it is written; and elsewhere: "Justice, and only justice, you shall follow" [Dt. 16.20]; and the apostle says: "All your things should be done decently and in order" [1 Cor. 14.40]; and [Gregory] the theologian of Rome: "We must take care that our goods be not non-existent nor small nor unexamined."[61]

26. While I am examining what I must do in my wretchedness, there occurs to me the advice of the runaway, which is superior to every type of advice in this alone, even if not in anything else: "Charity extinguishes all sins" [Pr. 10.12], and: "Her many sins are forgiven, for she loved much" [Lk. 7.47]. For though my sins are infinite, yet I have not committed every sin. There are in fact many others into which our human weakness falls of which my sinful nature is guiltless; and even if I had committed them all, it would be very easy to wipe them out with charity.

"Then have such great love toward God," you say, "that leaving all the others you may wish to enjoy Him alone, and such love towards your neighbor that you want to consider his good as far as possible and beyond, and laugh secure at the parade of your sins."

Although, I say, this is very necessary for me, know that it will be very difficult for me in every respect, unless, following the example of the runaway who returned of his own free will, I make haste to return to my vow while there is yet time; until this happens (if it only would happen sometime with God's mercy), even if you go up to heaven and return again, you will not be able to persuade me that I can hope for my soul's salvation for any other reason.

"Try," you say, "keep trying."

I will try, I say, if God helps me, but not as those desire who in their illwill find my presence irksome (to speak calmly, and would that it were truly calmly). Yet I will try. It is not with physical steps that one approaches or withdraws from God, but with those of the mind—though when I was trying to escape from what I fear, I tried it first with mental steps.

"That would have been satisfactory," you say, "if I were not still greatly troubled by the violation of the sanctuary. You have twice brought up the statement that 'the judgments of God are a great deep' [Ps. 35.7], and I think that you are denying me and hiding from some other sin."

Yes, yes, I say; for I did not promise to tell you all the sins I was aware of but just to load you up with my offenses; if they are not enough, add your own and you will not go away with an empty sack, believe me. One thing, however, I will say, and if you cannot fish out from it what you are looking for, I refuse to toil with you further: "No man knows whether he deserves hate or love but all is kept uncertain for the future" [Eccle. 9.1]. But—to pick up where I left off a long way back—if the only reason for refraining from this sort of thing is so that I should not be rewarded with temporal joys alone and thus have to hear anything else on Judgment Day than "Remember what goods you have received in this life" [Lk. 16.25] (a very ominous charge to be sure), what use are these goods to me without the license of enjoying them? But if the refreshment in the next life would be the greater in proportion as the evil done in this life is less, this too would be an unhappy gain of mitigation; for if this were the case, it would have been better (to speak in the voice of desperation) to have been in the next life long ago than to be here daily amassing the grounds for future torment. Yet if one clearly should expect the punishments of hell though never having committed these sins, or having had them all absolved through penitence except for this one alone; whereas either never having committed this one alone or having had it wiped out by returning to God we do not need to fear any future punishment however monstrous or manifold all of these others might be; then reason shows that this should not be overlooked but should be done without any delay when one is conceded the means.

"But what if effective means are lacking?" you say.

Then hope for God's mercy and implore Him that it should not be denied, with good thoughts as your messengers and continual prayers as your interceders, so that your yearning heart may be able to win the desired outcome.

27. "But," you say, "what of the fact that you do this not willingly but compelled by fear, like the wickedest servant?"

Don't say *wickedest*, I beg; enough to have said *wicked*; for *wickedest* rather is he who makes his conversion neither drawn by love nor compelled by fear. For many who have long been rebels return through fear of punishments and afterwards wholeheartedly love their masters and are even loved by their masters up to the point of being freed. But hear briefly what our Master has said about Himself to those returning to Him: "You have not chosen me but I you"; and about them, "because you have loved me" [Jn. 15.16; 16.27]—that is, because they merited it through the prevision of His love. What, even so, do you think is the source of that fear of hell which leads to the desire to return, if not the gift of His pity going before you, since He himself first causes the fear in you with His threats, inspires the course of action which you should follow out of fear, and promises gifts if you return?

"On what grounds," you say, "do you persuade yourself that despite the enormity of your sins you can still merit escape from eternal torments merely by your conversion to your vows as a monk?"

Because, I say, He who cannot tell a lie promises this in the Gospel: "Every man who leaves everything for my name will possess eternal life" [Mt. 19.29].

"But you do not claim to leave anything *for His name*, but for fear of hell."

And what power, I say, does hell have to punish me without the authority of His name? For unless God hurls me there, hell does not receive me. So we should fear God himself rather than hell, because he alone can pronounce hell; or rather love Him who, by threatening hell, postpones pronouncing it, so that He may confer the Kingdom of Heaven on those who fear, care, and return to Him. But take note of His name also: Jesus He is called for our sake, that is, the Savior, and whoever is converted so as not to be sent to hell, does he not desire to be saved? And by whom is he saved if not by the Savior? Therefore, he is converted for the name of Jesus if he is converted so as to be saved; and he is saved if he is taken from hell; therefore, for the name of Jesus is he converted.

28. "Why then," you say, "do you weave delays?"[62] Why do you not hasten to return to the Lord?"

I think I am doing so, I say; is it not so?

"What?"

What I have already told you about the runaway servant, I say. Any effort I make is a kind of prayer, as it were, that is, a message of my return, unless I am led astray in this also, as in many things. But I see how lukewarm I am in doing it and therefore don't even do it, for it is not the actual return to God, even if I dare to presume it; now in my mind I begin to return but I am greatly hindered.

"By whom?"

By myself; for I refuse to accuse anybody else or I will seem to be imitating Eve. I am held by toils in which I myself have bound myself, and the net's mesh in which I have thoughtlessly put my foot. Also, the tyrant whose bondage I have preferred to the service of my Lord is that much the more vicious in stopping me the more he hears I want to leave him; he sees me not only making confession but even writing it down. Yet in one particular I fear he makes himself many promises about me.

"What's that?"

What you yourself have said more than once: *that* I fear, nothing as much as that, you should know; if that one thing remain, I fear there will be no perfect return. And I am terrified by the fact that even now I still consider myself in prison and for that there is need [*opus*] to cry from the deep without yawning [Ps. 129.1].

"There is need," you say, "if by *need* you mean necessity [*necessarium*]; for I think that the ancients rather made it mean use [*usus*], that is, benefit [*utilitas*]. I agree, it is *necessary* to shout from the depths (where I see you lying) of the lake, and not yawning, as even you think. But I see that you are constantly yawning and are gradually interrupting the message of your effort, and I am afraid that it will one day come about that in this way you will return to Egypt."

Return, I say, return? Would that by God's gift I had even left it! Do you think that I do not sit over the pots of flesh, stand in the mud and straw, even sometimes groan and sigh gasping under the bundle of my labors, do you think that I am not bound by the thongs of my own tying, not restrained by the bars of ingrained habit, not caught in the mesh of a tightly-woven net, and not miserably changing my course of action from one hole to another? Do you think that horrible demons do not come and go over me, swoop down on me with unfurled standards as I cross over; that my enemies not hear my soul and watch me, that is, attend my ways, and deride my sabbaths [Lam. 1.7]?

29. But perhaps when you were set up on high[63] and heard me singing our Pasch along with you, you thought that I had made a passing-over from the lowest to even worse? I did, I confess it, I did make a passover, alas, a shameful one and one that I ought not to have made; for I passed from fasting to self-indulgence, from tears to laughter, from the lowest not to the highest but to the very lowest, from noxious to even more noxious, from night vigils to sleeping even in daytime, from ill-observed silence to ceaseless chatter and, what is worse, depraved and foul chatter, from psalm-singing to idleness, from scripture-reading to sloth and laziness, from healthful gravity to the empty joy of this world.

"But surely," you say, "one should relax those austerities for the joy of such a feast [the Pasch, Easter]? Surely one should exult and be glad?"

Relax them, yes, I say, but not utterly discontinue them. Exult and be glad, yes, but not so as to give in to vice, but to have even more time for the Lord. For the psalmist says, "My heart is glad" not merely to relax and play but "to fear thy name" [Ps. 85.11]. And elsewhere likewise: "Serve the Lord in fear and exult" not in yourselves but "in Him with fear" [Ps. 2.11], not with unconcern, which leads to the downfall of the soul. If you do not understand this, I will briefly explain: in eating out of sensual indulgence of the flesh rather than out of need, I confess that I have touched forbidden food and have indulged in overly elegant food and eaten beyond sufficiency, and therefore I have made licit eating into illicit. In Lent we must abstain from food and vice, in the Pasch from vice alone, which I confess I have in no way done. In Lent we must weep and lament, in the Pasch exult and rejoice in the Lord. When I ought to speak helpful words, I have mixed in purposeless and, what is worse, damaging words; I have spoken jests instead of gravities. I have not taken good note of the promise of "woe to them that laugh" [Lk. 6.26], and I have even raised up my voice in laughter, which is proper to fools. I have wretchedly exulted, forgetting that I will have to render account to God, with heaven and earth watching, not only for my acts but also for my thoughts. Furthermore, such lethargy and sloth have overcome me that I have scarcely been able, wretch that I am, to fulfill the very offices of psalm-singing prescribed and ordained for these days, let alone add others; wherefore I grieve for my utterly neglected attempts at the necessary litany (but not as much as I should). From this arises the great difficulty I have—as I in my state of deception see it—in obtaining return.

30. "It seems to me," you say, "while urging you to pay to the Inspirer the continual debt of thanks (something at least you see is necessary), it seems to me that you ought, if only you could, to enquire further into the causes of such dereliction. For it is possible that the law's prohibition [i.e., Lev. 21.17–18] (which, touching on it summarily, you have said you can bear—extraordinary!) is the source of such a difficulty."

It is indeed so, I say; it is as you surmise; and so that you may know, in fact so that all my readers may know, I will clarify for myself as far as I can how I feel all the requirements there noted apply to me, though in a single blemish there specified, my unworthiness in receiving the sacrament can be recognized. Well then: the Lord spoke to Moses saying: "Speak[64] to your brother Aaron and say to him: A man who is a priest from the seed of Aaron *who has a blemish* may not approach to offer the bread of his God nor come to His ministry." Concerning the blemish, let what I have said suffice; would it were the only one.

But there are some items subscribed: "If he be blind," which I cannot deny that I am, if you consider how those seeing God's light proceed; "If he is lame," which I cannot deny since through weakness of the will I cannot follow even what I see to be good; "If he is mutilated in the nose," which I confess I am, since I cannot hold the breath of discretion, as it were, in all my excesses; "If he has a small, large or twisted nose," which I admit, because under the pretense of discretion I often do wrong actions; "If with a broken hand or foot"—who does not see this in me? For unable to pursue the Lord's way (as you heard a little earlier), I slothfully and lethargically refrain from good work like a man with a broken hand; "If a hunchback"—would that I were not so weighted down, Lord, with the yoke of iniquity nor with the weight of worldly concerns! "If he is a man with a defect in his sight"—who is there who does not see that even though some light of knowledge shines in me through divine grace, my carnal works wretchedly obscure it? "If he has a film in his eye"—I cannot tell anyone how blind my pride has made me, known to God alone (and to myself in part), though I count it as the root of all evils, and keep calling it the invasion of the spirit of vainglory. "If he has scabs"—I do not deny that this particularly fits me when the above items are weighed, that is, from the beginning of my wantonness as long as I have endured in it, if you know that *scabs* is taken to be self-indulgence, and that scabs are caused most of all by the onset of pride, since we are told to be fully aware that where there is pride, there also will be abuse; and I see that not even the weakness of age can overcome it. "If he has any rash on his body"—I do not deny that this particularly fits me; would that I had been free from avarice also, as this is what *rash* seems to me to be. "If he is weighed down"—woe to me wretched who, even when I did not physically practise my wicked ways, have felt—and still do not cease to feel—weighed down by them in my soul almost all the time, even up to my present old age, in fact. Though blemished with these spots along with countless others, I confess that I have up till now offered bread to the Lord against His commandment; and I have turned into the judgment of eternal damnation for myself that which is the panacea of salvation for those offering worthily; which can seem to be a most certain indication of the difficulty I experience in returning to the Lord, as you have said can be done.

31. But I do not see what I can do. Almost all the time up till now it has been my habit to ask the Lord to give me pardon for my sins and to take from me the concupiscence of the world and desires of the flesh, in which I have tossed and turned like a three-year-old all night long, both waking and asleep; and even today at almost seventy[65] I feel myself titillated by them, even as I write. I pray also that He may take away my appetite for the praise of men, which you can see is strong in me; and that I long for it is apparent even to me who fight against it—even in these writings, which I feel are the product of a vainglorious spirit.[66] I pray that He also take away the vice of lethargy and sloth, which makes me procrastinate both physically and mentally, and inconstancy and fickleness also, and obstinacy and hypocrisy, and obscenity of heart and mouth—all of which I rightly reprehend in myself, as you do, and conjecture that they arise from pride, because, though I properly implore God's mercy and grace that I be saved from these, stupidly I do not compel my free will, as I ought, to co-operate in bringing it about—which hurts me rather than helps me. And while neglecting to blame myself for my part, I pat myself on the back for falsely seeking what is God's part. For example: after the shipwreck of my chastity, I beg God for the haven of continence, but I am not willing to straightway lay on myself either maceration of the flesh or abstinence from fornication.

32. There is also something else which not a little, I confess, blocks the path of my prayers. Nothing is so important, for all that is necessary for a man, as that singular sacrifice which daily represents our Pasch for us, namely Christ truly sacrificed for us. But if I were worthily to offer (which, however, does not follow) my gift, if not daily, at least frequently, it still would not be able to win, as many say, acceptance for any prayer, I think; the words I hear, "Go first and be reconciled to your brother" [Mt. 5.24], get in the way. If we are all brothers in Christ the head, the more we ought to fear Him, the less should we offend Him—whom less?—lest He have something against us. But He has two things, I confess, against me: first that I hurt His members, second that I do not stop hurting Him. And since days and nights are not enough for reconciliation alone, when, I ask, will it be proper to offer my gift? But the time would come, I presume, since reconciliation would be the gift, if satisfaction had been made to my brothers. I have harmed them in many things, I confess, but nowhere more than in what the Savior censures heavily, saying: "Whoever causes one of these little ones who believe in me to sin, it were better for him to have a great mill-stone fastened around his neck and to be drowned in the depths of the sea" [Mt. 18.6].

Again, after a while:

33. "You seem to me," you say, "to shift about too much, and like the neck of Ennius' peacock to change your colour as you move.[67] For at times I wonder at your great energy, at times at your excessive weakness; sometimes at your seeming fervor, sometimes at your apathy; now I note your constancy, now your instability; now you seem to tell me everything candidly (and would that it were so even some of the time), now hypocritically (as, for shame, you always do), and in making your miserable confession, even to hide certain things, such as that first thing which is so hidden even from me who read it (who know it as well as I know you) as if it were never said."

Yes, I confess it is so, I say, and I show it also by my actions. But about the thing which you mention: I realized it would be worse if it were known to all and therefore I thought it would be sufficient if in some way you alone could be better informed of it. But while I address you, I am looking at any person with eyes in his head, the sort of person that the Rule which we have transgressed requires, one, that is, who can cure his own hurts and not reveal and publish the hurts of others. For you ought not to forget what you heard above about confession too long neglected.

"To whom and for what reason do you confess, if you are anxious to conceal it?"

To God and myself, I say.

"Why to God?"

Not so that He should know—He cannot be ignorant of anything—but so that He should deign to forgive; for this is the presumption of the prophet also, I hear. I confess to myself, so that sometime I may be able to say more truly and with less anxiety, "My sin is ever before me" [Ps. 50.5]—which it would not have been if I had not happened to have written it down—and to rejoice in the words, "Happy is the man who is ever in fear," and "The heart knows its own bitterness and no stranger shares its joy" [Pr. 28.14; 14.10].

"But it would have been better," you say, "to have written it in the pages of the heart."

Yes, better, I say, and more valuable, both in this world and in the next. But along with Augustine's example of confession in writing, we have the apostle confessing, "I who once was a blasphemer and persecutor and insulter" [1 Tim. 1.13].

"In this you have been mastered by some temptation of pride," you say, "or vainglory, or certainly a false sense of security."

Yes, I say, almost to the point of mortal despair. For when I hear that "Just is the accuser of himself in the beginning" [Pr. 18.17], my wretched folly or foolish wretchedness whispers to me that I am in this the unhappy imitator of one of these just people, and if it continues thus, I see myself lost and wretched, being treated in such a way that no more despicable monster has ever been seen on earth. For since pride, that is, ambition, has ever been the cause of ruin, it seems to me that that ruin was worse in me than I had thought, because my humility is born out of pride. For I am proud of the fact that I see myself most surely despised and beneath others, while other people are usually proud of that in which they see themselves excel others. I would clarify this for you by an apt citation from the Apostle, did I not avoid wicked speech in this command at least. But because I am lacking in eloquence and I cannot say what damage I do to myself, and because I see that externally you know me very well, I direct you to the inspired words of Gregory, so that you may know me internally as well. Ask him; read what he says about wicked, proud hypocrites, and there you will be able to see me in my entirety.[68]

"But," you say, "in avoiding solecisms of syntax rather than of reason, of words rather than of actions, you show more clearly that you are what you say you are, since you strive (if only you could!) to *seem* eloquent instead of practicing what you preach so well. You would willingly plant, I see, a stand of trees in the house of the Lord [Dt. 16.21] (against His edict though it be), you who are so studious in the siting of shrubbery."

I say: You will soon see more clearly what sort of a man I am; but the tumor of pride in one's eloquence, once grown, will not be suppressed.

34. The psalmist says: "If I have cherished iniquity in my heart, the Lord will not hear me" [Ps. 65.18]. Though this can be taken at will in this sense or in that (for the Lord says, "If you do not forgive men their sins, your Heavenly Father will not forgive you" [Mk. 11.25], and again, "Whoever turns his ear from the cry of the poor man himself will cry and will not be heard" [Pr. 21.13]), hypocrites, like Herod, because they seek God speciously, never merit to find Him. None more continually spend their time in psalms, more often celebrate the solemnities of the Mass, give essentials to the poor, preach more sermons; and in all these things it is clearly apparent to me (I confess in knowledge of myself), that the iniquity which the psalmist mentions is the very same thing which I see in myself: hypocrisy. For with two different tongues, as it were, I say two different things: to those who hear me I recite psalms or something else, but to the Inspector of my heart I say countless other things far dissimilar. For instance, this last night, the one to which this morning belongs (it is the vigil of the apostles Philip and James), I kept vigil under attack (as often) from the devil (it would have been better to have slept in my bed), and, moreover, the thing that had happened against my vow was swelling within me. For your Bonito had been reported to me as having dispensed the wool to the brothers without orders from me; and while I was counting this up along with the other illegal goings-on here and, though at vigil, was conjuring up fantasies of them in my mind, I came in my thoughts to the item in the Rule (which we have wretchedly ignored) to which we abbots cling fast, but with love not of God but of our own interests: "Let him do nothing without the abbot's sanction."[69]

Alighting on it, therefore, and seeing it as the cause of future punishment, I began to consider if there was any other reason why we yearned so avidly for such a quasi-honor. I could find none at all. Then when it came to matins, I said the psalms with my lips, but in my heart I cried: "O foolish Oderadus, was it this that you bought for eighty pounds without a second thought, though you had been considered so thrifty?"—for thus we wretches often err in our judgments of people. But at once I silenced myself and scolded myself for being a hypocrite: "Hush, look at yourself, you hypocrite, and leave him alone. Cast the beam from your own eye and then, if you wish and are able, remove the speck from your brother's. For to tell the truth, in comparison, his folly which causes you amazement is the tiniest speck, while yours is the mightiest beam."

And then,[70] lo, in the middle of the mellifluous singing of hymns, that great escort[71] which recently accompanied me from Liège broke in upon my thoughts, a vast multitude of attendants and such. The infinitely discordant whinnying of thoroughbred horses, the most diverse possible collection of fleeces and other attire, of table-ware, couches, vessels, and other fine stuff; the sound—sweeter than the honey-toned swan—of clerics and noble monks; the vast crowd of noble relatives, handsome and resplendent, and some weeping and crying too (to remember the poorer ones), because they saw themselves left behind—all came into my mind; and when I considered my thoughts on abandoning them, the countless hardships and dangers of the march, the sickness and losses, which I suffered for this goal alone, the huge amount of money spent on my part for gifts to obtain that goal—when I turned to this alone considering those gifts and remembering the most costly item among them, a cloak brought here which I had obtained by the clearest sacrilege, well, if nature had allowed me to die in gloom, I could have expired in the most violent grief. Conjured up before my imagination in this way, it made me sigh in sorrow, so that if anyone had chanced to stand outside the door, he could have thought that I was being tormented by the pain that was quite usual for me.[72]

Finally, putting those thoughts aside for a little, I began to ponder: "What reward will you have in the future life that has been bought in this life at such cost (as you consider it)?" And lo, again before my mind's eye came that dove for sale in the temple, Jesus with the whip of cords in his hand, the fearful expulsion from the temple [Mt. 21.12], Simon's curse [Acts 8.20], the repulsive leprosy of Gehazi [2 Kg. 5.27], and the sentence of Ananias and Saphiras and the curse of the recipient [Acts 5.5], because it ought to have been given and received for free. "Without the order of the abbot," the Rule says, "let the monk do nothing."[73] Look at what you have acquired, unfortunate man, at such cost not only in money but also in troubles. Listen carefully, I urge you, when you hear: "Let the abbot himself do everything with the fear of God and under the ordering of the Rule." And again: "Let the abbot know that the shepherd is responsible for whatever fault the Lord can find in his sheep; and therefore he ought to teach or establish nothing outside God's command (heaven forbid it), mindful always that he will have to make account in the terrible Judgment of God for both his own teaching and the obedience of his disciples."[74]

35. So you rejoice that without your orders nothing is done? Then look at what orders you give. You demand obedience? Then examine what you demand; they must obey you, but you must obey the Rule. They sin if they act without your wish and order; you sin if you require or order anything outside the statutes of the Rule. The Rule says: "He should eschew doing in his own actions everything which he has taught his followers is irregular; and he should know that whoever undertakes to govern souls must of necessity be prepared to render account himself. And let him surely know that for every single one of the brothers he has under his charge he will render account on the day of Judgment to God for all their souls"[75]—"and for his own as well" is surely added.

O foolish, windy vanity! To have bought, with so much toil, with such distress and trouble, with such pain and such anguish, at such cost in this world, with such torments in the next, only the privilege of being called *Rabbi* by men, when the Judge-to-be himself has cautioned us, "Wish not to be called Rabbi" [Mt. 23.8], as though to say: Do not desire that honor in the world, for which, if you are deprived of that spirit which the apostle tried to describe but could not, saying: "What no eye has seen nor ear has heard nor the heart of man conceived" [1 Cor. 2.9], you suffer in hell great torments equally indescribable. In all this, when I consider the violent storms of curses (like squalls of the Euxine Sea)[76] rushing over me, they on their own, not to mention added to others, force me most wretched to live in no confidence of my salvation. The first of these curses that comes to my mind, though it was uttered later, you should hear in the words of Gregory who uttered it:

> Just as he who refuses when invited and he who runs away when sought will be promoted to the sacred altars, so he who is overly ambitious or acts too importunately will undoubtedly be kept away. For he who strives to climb higher, what does he do but decrease in his own growing? Why does he not consider that the blessing is turned to a curse on him who moves ahead to the point that he becomes a heretic?[77]

What a fatal curse these people chase after (though they ought to forestall it), attend: "Cursed are those who wander from thy commandments" [Ps. 118.21]. "Cursed is he who announced to my father, A male child has been born for you" [Jer. 20.15]. "Cursed is he who keeps back his sword from bloodshed. Cursed is the man who places his trust in men"—so that his heart turns away from the Lord; "Cursed is he who does the Lord's work negligently" [Jer. 48.10; 17.5]. And there are many other curses which cannot be recorded now; among them nothing is more to be wondered at in me than that I can with dry eyes even remember them, let alone write them down or tell of them. In this you can see the obduracy of my heart clearer than light, I confess.

36. "It is as you say," you remark. "For as I do not cease to wonder at your fickleness and inconstancy, I am no longer surprised that such a thing as that which I know of could happen to you physically at this age, when I see you still being so wanton spiritually. For from your own writings and words I surmise that you do not feel with a very sincere heart what you pretend to feel. For if you had really considered returning to the Lord, that is, converting from bad to good, you ought not to have valued so cheaply what has been granted you in whatever way; for I see that you regret as lost anything that you spent or gave away to achieve this goal, as though it had been Arabic gold; it would be quite safe if you had been allowed by heaven to live henceforth in the way which you have touched on with a few words of the Rule, no matter what you were before. But as Scripture says: 'He who watches the wind sows not,

and he who gazes at the clouds reaps not' [Eccle. 11.4], I see you so weak-witted, pusillanimous, cowardly, timid, fickle, deceitful, soft, and slothful, that I would be compelled to despair utterly of your escape, if I did not know the ineffable riches of God's omnipotent mercy, goodness, and pity, gratuitously bestowed on thousands since the beginning of time even against their own expectations.

"Consider, please, that I am applying the words of the Prophet to you, and ponder them: 'How cheap you have become repeating your ways' [Jer. 2.36], and when you write in truth that you are the most heinous sinner, note that you have been warned, 'Do not repeat a word in your prayer' [Eccli. 7.15]. Note what good it does the washed sow to wallow in the mire, and remember how offensive the dog returning to its vomit [2 Pet. 2.22] is to the eye of the beholder. Recall with shame (as you should) that in those vices in which you still toil (alas), you have already made many wallowings of conversion to and then aversion from the Lord.

"Even now, as you stand at your last hour in fact, fix your heart on a firm base; 'For the fool changes like the moon' [Eccli. 27.12] — which you were wont to do — which doubtless can be seen to fit you closely, whether or not it was said about you. All the land this side of the ocean, so to speak, now tells through how many changes of fortune and misfortune, of conversion and aversion, you have gone; you have become engloomed in them, then enlightened, only to be engloomed again. 'We have cared for Babylon,' says the Lord, 'and she is not healed' [Jer. 51.9], for your sake, it seems, while your confusion, wretch, yet sprouts resurgent. 'You have a harlot's brow, you have refused to feel shame' [Jer. 3.3], was said of you, as you would have been able to see if you had not been, by your own admission, blind in mind, since you could relate about yourself, without shame and sorrow, such numerous grievous faults, and tell of ones that, as the Apostle charges [Eph. 5.3], ought not to be mentioned — and stylishly also if you could — as though they were honorable.

"But I see what your scheme is, shameless one; like your many accomplices in this, you see everyone embrace the saying, 'Just in the beginning is the accuser of himself' [Pr. 18.17], and prefer to boast in the confession of sins that should be wordlessly regretted than to humble yourself; and therefore, though you say with all truth that you are a sinner, cunning one, you would if you could persuade the listener that you are saying all this out of humility rather than out of truthfulness.

"For if you really wanted to be called and seen as a sinner as much as you write, you would not have been so upset that I have shown you up. But if you cannot persuade anyone that you are just (because no one with eyes can fail to see that you are not), at least you might persuade some that you are lettered. And so I am assured that you do not test your life by examples of better men, nor do you consider the foulness and deceitfulness of your fickleness, nor do you feel that you are being reproved when you hear, 'The man deceitful in his heart is inconstant in all his ways' [Jas. 1.8], and that what Sallust said of Cicero,[78] that he had loyalty neither to the one nor to the other—neither to Caesar nor to Pompey, that is—pertains to you; for you are shown to keep your loyalty intact neither to the Lord nor to His adversary whom you court.

37. "To pay you back for starting on my sins when you undertook to tell of your own (or so you pretended), I will finish up on yours. I will reveal how cunningly you have acted, though you pretend that the trickery is not at all clear to you. For to prevent me showing you up (as you feared I would), you very cleverly (or so you thought, but in reality very deceitfully) injected my faults for me to attend to and so leave your own. And as for your charging me with violating the Rule (in most wordy vanity arising out of your pride or instability, I think), you seem to me to have done it solely so that you could somehow mitigate what I had recognized in you with the gravity of that sin."

Yes, I say, I am caught like a thief in this too, and I do not immediately know what to reply. I am aghast; yet if it is right for me to do anything, I do it in bewilderment, not being able to comprehend why God has permitted or wanted me to do it.

"I think you have forgotten," you say, "what you read in Gregory's Dialogue about a very proud rich man called Chrysarius;[79] at the point of death he saw the adversaries of the human race gathering around him and asked for a stay until morning; but he did not receive it and was unable to hide from those around him what he was suffering. We know from this, on the authority of St. Gregory, that he saw all this while alive not for his own benefit, since he could not enjoy the fruit of it, but for ours. In the same way, then, you can form conclusions about that astonishing act of yours, so that if it does not happen to benefit you, it can perhaps benefit your readers, when they recognize in themselves things which they think you sincerely confessed about yourself. For since Scripture says 'His friend comes and will examine him' [Pr. 18.17], (though speaking about a better man than you and not of the future), you can be sure that they realize you have done all this out of ostentation and love of applause and out of your mental instability, as I have pointed out, and habitual love of your own fictions, all of which is known to be native to the arrogant.

"Therefore, you ought not to have said so confidently a little while ago[80] that you were surprised that you could relate this with dry eyes. For what warmth of charity could melt that icy coldness of yours into flowing tears? Actually, since you are all wax, it is not surprising that sometimes a droplet of a tear is elicited from you, one which obviously arises from your Balaam-like [Num. 23] instability rather than from the healthy prickings of conscience; this is clear from the fact that you cannot produce any tears unless someone is watching you or you see another weeping in your presence; and the fact that you frequently change at once to excessive cheerfulness[81] proves this to be the case. Hear what value the inner judge attaches to such weeping: 'Daughters of Jerusalem, do not weep over me but over yourselves' [Lk. 23.28]. He weeps over another, not over himself, who, moved by the good of another fails to imitate the good by which he too is moved. For we can count as wasted those tears which appear when the heart of the weeper does not care.

"You are missing, I see, the voice crying within, the one essential for you, the most friendly one: 'Let the tears stream down like a torrent day and night, give your eyes no respite' [Lam. 3.48], so that you would rightly be able to say in your last hour, 'Let my eye flow with rivers of tears,' even against your insistent accusers, who will certainly revile you on the grounds that, though you have written them down, you have not adequately wept for nor emended nor repented of any of your sins, nor have you ever inwardly wanted to. 'Who will give me water for my head and a flood of tears for my eyes' [Jer. 9.1] so that I may weep my own contriteness, let alone that of my people, that is, the flock committed to my charge? For when you sang yesterday, 'Weep, shepherds, and cry, sprinkle yourselves with ashes' [Jer. 25.34], and, 'Weep like a maiden, my people' [Joel 1.8], who saw in your face any gravity even, let alone sorrow? Who saw tears in your eyes to suit such sinfulness as you had written of? Who heard even a sigh fit for your own many sins, foul and heinous, let alone for those of your charges, since, wretch, to your damnation you were falsely ranked as a shepherd?[82]

"Then in respect of that three-day feast, you were, like many, abstinent; you wrote down your sins in silence, as if making preparation for the Paschal unleaven; but the field-lettuce [Ex. 12.8], so it seemed, you had carelessly ignored, without which you ought not to have believed it proper to eat the Paschal Lamb sacrificed for you. Even then you showed in advance that you would forget—as of course has happened—what you felt about the servant who returned; even then you gave certain indications that after the Pasch you would not even say, let alone think, what you had exclaimed to me: 'Let us not sin; why should we sin further? We have sinned more than enough already,' as if you had decided not to sin any more. But now like Balaam you are beginning to revile those very virtues you espoused, to return like a dog to its vomit, to roll in the same mire where you lately had been [2 Pet. 2.22]. You are no longer concerned with that which you said from the pulpit during the Pasch should be avoided, that is, that we should not senselessly destroy after the Pasch is over the house constructed during Lent or burn it down by applying fire, lest the unclean spirit, driven out of us by our penitence, we should recall, along with his seven colleagues, no doubt [Mt. 12.45].

"For now you are growing fat, with the result that it is possible for all to see how and on what you are feeding. Now you can scarcely be restrained from wantonness, you wander lethargically in all directions; you who were silent now throw out insults and slanders; you are beginning to be reconciled, so to speak, with that negligence which has ever been close to you ('reconciled' because in concern you had abandoned it for a while), and lest it lose strength you provide for it by mixing obscenity with falsehood. You who in Lent happened to avoid saying *racha* (though not deliberately) and feared to say *fatue* [Mt. 5.22], are now not afraid to transgress, making up thousands of insults and not even hesitating to resort to fisticuffs. Now you are retreating backwards with the very steps (as it were) with which you pretended that you wanted to return to the Lord on high. And you who lyingly told me that you wanted to rise are clearly falling; while asserting that you are escaping from the net of your former way, you betray how much you still value it.

38. "What more? Others can think about you what they may; to me you seem on the evidence of such a confession to have become worse than the worst, if you do not continually engage in the inner weeping to be given by God's mercy and to be sought from him incessantly, which (as you admit and I observe) you do not have. For if the sleeping man sees nothing, that is of course quite natural; but it is accepted that, just as the wakeful man sees, so also it is his own fault if he neglects to thwart his slayer placed before his eyes. You see how many are the subverters of your soul in front of your eyes and you neglect to thwart your end (by tears at least, if you cannot do it by true repentance) — and you pressure me not to despair of you? What, wretch, do you think is the use of having seen that they are threatening, if you do not happen to evade them?

"You see yourself prevented, though you are a priest, from offering bread — and you do not grieve? You see yourself the object of the Lord's curses — and you cannot weep? Christ calls you a thief and a robber [Jn. 10.1] — and you want neither to return the stolen goods nor to relinquish the plunder taken by force, nor even in anxiety of heart, to mix tears (even a few) with sighing not only for that theft and plunder but also for the obstinacy of not correcting it? You see that you are without a marriage garment [Mt. 22.12] — and at the marriage of Christ and the Church, not fearing that you will be thrust out ignominiously to be sent to the fire of hell with feet and hands tied, do you yet dare to recline without tears? You hear a curse on the receiver[83] — and weeping is impossible for you? You hear Peter the apostle saying to Simon Magus, 'Let your money be with you in perdition' [Acts 8.20] — and you do not ask me to pray for you to be saved from damnation? You see Ananias and Saphiras expire for a sacrilege which you also have committed [Acts 5.5] — and you cannot weep at all? You see the leprosy of Gehazi [2 Kg. 5.27]—and you do not wash out your leprous soul with tears? You have violated the temple of God in yourself and in others, you have taken away from the Lord your father's offering—and serving in a position of trust in the house of God's Church, do you without tears, without anxiety, place on his altar the offerings of the faithful? You see that you are without field-lettuce [Ex. 12.8]—and do you still dare to eat the Lamb of God? That you have no unleaven [1 Cor. 5.8]—and you still dare to presumptuously take the Pasch? You feel the ferment of wickedness and evil in you—and you dare to feast in the Lord (or at any rate believe that you do)? You are well aware that many have much against you—and you bring your gifts to the altar [Mt. 5.23–24]? You hear that what you are rashly doing is forbidden—and yet you do not give up doing it? If you give up doing it, you face the charge of disobedience; for since you have somehow obtained the ministry, it is incumbent upon you to fulfill it, lest you should appear to have obtained it to your own damnation rather than for fulfilling it.

"Caught in this dilemma as you are, I therefore beg you in earnestness to consider how desperate and grievous is your plight. If you had not anticipated judgment by your confession (though cunningly, I fear), I would suggest that what Gregory in the *Moralia* [23.11.18] says against the reprobates, the proud, and the hypocrites, fits you exactly. In fact, when I consider your arrogant wordiness, I think I hear Elihu saying, 'I am full of words, the spirit within constrains me; behold, my heart is like wine that has no vent, like new wineskins it is ready to burst. I must speak that I may find relief' [Job 32.18].

"You ought to have been much afraid—you and all those like you who, while striving to emulate the eloquent, imitate windy philosophers instead and follow the lovers of vainglory, without considering that you are being branded as a group when you hear it said, 'A fool puts forth all his feelings' [Pr. 29.11], and (if I may add), 'A man without self-control in speaking is like a city broken into and left without walls' [Pr. 25.28]. But as I said, you ought to have been afraid that you would hear it said of you (and of him you try to imitate); and to have been afraid also of hearing the words spoken out of the whirlwind (though you are not going to be reconciled through any sacrifice): 'Who is this that darkens counsel with words without knowledge?' [Job 38.2]. How far you are beneath him whom you follow you can comprehend when you see that you do not have the spirit of prophecy as he had it. But if such criticism can be made of a prophet, what can be said of a vain and (worse) lying compiler and sycophant who, as is written, 'like the seer and soothsayer guesses what he does not know' [Pr. 23.7]?

39. "That you may know how vile to wise men is this vanity of yours, consider that the reprobate Saul and Caiphas, among others, prophesied [Jn. 11.51];

recall to mind that the ass received words of reason from the vision of the angel [Num. 22.28], that the demon said, 'We know who you are, O Christ the son of God' [Lk. 4.34], and you can understand that though you may be more voluble than others, you are of no moment on that account. For a man 'who allows the discharge of his seed' [Lev. 15.2] is 'unclean' according to the Law, not 'eminent' as you long to appear.[84] So also about the works of your restless instability, by which you claimed to your intimates with haughty neck and arched brows, that the Church, diminished for a while, had been enlarged and extended by your merits (of mean structure though it may be compared to thousands)—but with no improvement in religion (though may the Almighty grant that it has not deteriorated)—in the manner of your Nebuchadnezzar: 'Is this not Babylon which I built in the strength of my dignity and courage?' [Dan. 4.27; cf. Ps. 48.13].

"So see how worthless what pleased you monstrously has been to everyone, since those who you thought would sing your praises after your death have in your lifetime formed up, from the greatest to the least, as revilers of your achievements, to such an extent that they demanded that the edifice which you longed to be praised and celebrated by everyone as most sacred, be sacrilegiously torn down by the soldiers on the king's command.[85] 'They have done you well, it has turned out well for you, ashen one,'[86] who, though you are not even a man in that you are without reason in many things, and do not understand your position of honor, 'compared to foolish asses' [Ps. 48.13] and become like them, still strove with the trickery of an adulterer to have yourself extolled with the praises due to God alone, if you could. This, of course, was why you were unable to weep—because by this kind of deception you thought you were something. But you were truly caught out, thanks be to God, as you deserved, by those who used the eye of a mole on themselves or on others, but the eye of a she-goat on you.[87]

Learned and unlearned, we keep writing poems[88]

—see what a complaint you call forth even from the pagan orators when you presume to compose books without any experience of learning! How many beasts you listen to when you think so highly of yourself! For if you had listened to men, you would have said, 'I have sinned.'

"If you saw the light, you would not think so highly of the dark. For when you note that you excel the beasts and see more clearly than the blind, what pride can you take from that, fool? For what is so great about a fool excelling a beast or a seeing man one who is blind? But since you cannot compare yourself with a wise or righteous man, what are the grounds for your pride? the fact that at least you are not the same as the damned and the stupid? See that in this you are not judged by the Inner Arbiter as more damned and more stupid. For with the same sharp sentences with which you lay low (as it were) the enemy, you kill yourself, following Eleazar's example,[89] when, in what, perhaps correctly, you think about God, you seek not God's glory but your own, as though rejoicing that 'your hand had gotten much' [Job 31.27], instead of rather grieving as you ought that you did not make it; and as though impudently 'kissing your hand with your own mouth' [Job 31.27], you do not even hesitate to praise what you do yourself and on the testimony of your own words attribute the virtue of the Maker to yourself. But remember, I say, that on holy Job's assertion [Job 31.28] this is the greatest sin and denial of the Almighty, and do not deny that you are one of the foremost of the proud, when, passing up words that require courage, you fall back on empty inanities.

"'Consider,' said the Preacher, 'the works of God, which no one whom He has looked down on can correct' [Eccle. 7.14]. For if you considered what was more appropriate for you, you would desist from writing so much. For recalling your scattered wits (which I see you are unable to do), you should rather have groaned inwardly and given way to prayers and weeping to wash away the sins you describe, than have indulged in such vanity. For while often you think you are praised for this, more often, believe me, the opposite of what you desire occurs and you are mocked and reviled.

"There is a story that once an unfortunate wretch on his deathbed saw a great book offered him by devils, written on the inside and outside; to imagine you in this position, they will have no need of any other to offer you than the one you wrote yourself, and they will conclude from it (you should know) what you aspired to also. But beware, I caution you, lest you chance to hear, 'Out of thine own book do I judge you' [Lk. 19.22]. And since you often rise from the due office and even (as now) from the Mass in a state of vicious restlessness, where, I ask, is what you wrote above, namely: 'Everything which he has taught his student is wrong he should eschew in his own actions'?[90] That is, the students of that religion which he often yearned for should be told that no one, nothing, is to be preferred to God's work. If *nothing*, how, then, the pomp of vainglory?

40. "But why do I labor when I see that nothing avails me? I see that one thing alone remains, otherwise I do not cease to despair of you, and this I make bold to try on the urging of the Law which you do not at all cease breaking (though you have regretted—or so you pretend—that you broke it). 'If he has applied the poultices, the medications, of the Holy Scriptures, if he sees that the one or the other, nor his own energy, avail not at all, let him apply a stronger cure, namely, the prayers of himself and everyone for him, so that God who can do all things may bring the sick brother to salvation.' Let the Canaanite mother of old [Mt. 15.22] come, I beg; that is (unless I am mistaken), the one converted from the curse of Cham to Christ's blessing [Gen. 9.25].[91] May she merit to hear, 'Great is thy faith' [Mt. 15.28]; may the Lord's disciples implore Him for her. And may the holy congregation of all the saints cry, 'Pity me, Son of David, my daughter is sore vexed by a demon' [Mt. 15.22], that is, the soul of this sinner (I speak of you) begotten of me through baptism and nursed on the milk of my teaching; his soul assuredly is sorely vexed by a demon since it is also (worst of all) obdurate. Pity me, even if you disdain him. For the perdition of anyone baptized is (as it were) my failure, just as his salvation is my success. May the family of Christ keep asking the same with prayers to the point of importunity. May they obtain what seems to me impossible to obtain from Him to whom nothing is impossible, by their merit or at least their voice, because it cannot be won by yours and mine. Since, as I do not doubt, you embrace the ancient saying that 'a pure confession frees one from death' and rejoice that you have made one, remember, I pray, the words 'he who curses his father or mother must die' [Ex. 21.17]; remember that yesterday you called your father *fello*, which is much stronger than *fatue* and that you have often called your mother *puta*, which is monstrously worse than *racha*,[92] in addition to a host of other sins. Adam and Eve (as Reason teaches us, I think) have been established in the Heavenly Kingdom which they lost through sin but recovered by the saving hand of Christ and have been reconciled to God (though they cannot be to you).

"Remember that as a youth you offered verses about the purification of Mary, the holy Mother of God, brilliantly composed for your family by I know not whom, and since lost, to a certain king[93] in commendation of yourself; in these you can understand that many things remain to an accuser which you have left out from your past actions contrary to your vow—but I can promise that it will be sufficient for him to observe what you will do hereafter, if you persist as you are now (which I consider is greatly to be feared)—which, however, may God grant to be otherwise—since you have confessed that even what you have frequently heard sung is not fulfilled in you, that is: 'For a fire is kindled by my anger and it burns to the depths of hell' [Dt. 32.22].

"In one other thing too, I think you are grossly deceived: when the Lord truly says in the Book of Wisdom (which is Himself who cannot lie), 'Him whom God loves He seizes' [Pr. 3.12], you think that therein you have been described because of the many things you have suffered in this world *by your own fault* (do not be wrong in this, I caution you) and you hold yourself secure as though having suffered the whole penalty, not remembering that there are four kinds of blows; if you do not recall them, you should go to Gregory, I say. To speak with his authority in summary: 'Temporal blows free from eternal punishments only those whom they change.'[94] For though you have been 'called from the thoroughfares' [Mt. 22.9–12], that is, from the failures of your efforts, yet because you are without a wedding garment, you can surely fear that someone will say to you, 'Friend, how did you get in here?' Make sure that what is written in this passage does not apply to you, since not even blows restrain you from wickedness; for, as the apostle James said earlier, unless you correct the forwardness and looseness of your tongue, 'vain is your religion' [Jas. 1.26] (even if there were any), that is, the religion of your confession. What is *vain*, it follows, must equally lack the substance of reward.

"But as I said, you should understand yourself addressed in these words and be ashamed to be branded thus, I earnestly suggest. 'Crush a fool in a mortar with a pestle,' says the Scripture, 'along with crushed grain, and still his folly will not desert him' [Pr. 27.22]. And the prophet also says, complaining against you and your like (read it thoroughly, I urge): 'Thou hast consumed them, but they have refused to take correction' [Jer. 5.3]; and the Lord, the Inspirer of prophets, says: 'I have bereaved them, I have destroyed my people and yet they still have not turned from their ways [Jer. 15.7]. The house of Israel has become dross to me; all of them, bronze and tin and iron and lead in the furnace have become dross' [Ezek. 22.18]; no one is gold and silver, purged in the fire of tribulation, as you think you have been. And again, against you and about you in particular: 'There has been much toil and sweat, but its rust has not gone out of it, even by fire' [Jer. 24.12]. And again: 'In vain the refining goes on, for the wickedness'—that is, yours and your friends'—'is not removed' [Jer. 6.29].

41. "Had you not earlier[95] chastised yourself with that verse of Horace, I would point out the worthlessness of that conversion of yours (if indeed it exists), avoiding sin not from love of virtue but from fear of punishment.[96] But because I see that even in this description of your sins you are so beholden to the external senses that you remember what you know very well only when you see it, I urge you to see that you do not have the Spirit of the Lord if you lack liberty; for 'where there is the spirit of the Lord, there is liberty' [2 Cor. 3.17]. Therefore, you should know that you are a wicked servant not a son, an enemy not a friend, if pressure of punishment makes you act or refrain from acting. For (as I know from your own statement) if you did not fear punishment, you would be doing worse things even than you are doing. You could have learned, in the works of Cicero[97] at least and of others like him and of Horace recently mentioned, if not in the Scripture, that good was to be loved for its own sake and not to be pursued under compulsion of punishment. Remember: 'Be ashamed, O Sidon, for the sea has spoken' [Is. 23.4]. It is certain that innocence of the body is lost in the presence of God, who sees when one sins in thoughts of the heart. 'If the hand is held in hand'—even doing nothing, you should add—'the wicked man will not go unpunished' [Pr. 11.21]. Anyone who

wishes that God had not created torments so that he would be able to sin freely is also rebelling against Him to the best of his ability. Both from your words and by my own intuition I have perceived that you are unable to weep for your sins; I see that you do not sufficiently understand why the showers of tears, as the prophet reasons [Jer. 3.3], have been withheld from you, which now at least, late though it be, would wash away your sins and make in you the seed of the Word grow (when the aridity which is apparent in you has been irrigated and the hardness of your heart moistened) and bear fruit from the Lord and be stored in the granary of heaven—if only your sinfulness and obdurateness did not prevent it, wretch.

"For what do you think of the guilt which you have contracted by this one sin alone, in that hearing that vigils were being kept by the brethren, as is customary, for a man's soul, you said impetuously in your fashion that you would not pray for him because you knew he was in hell, reasoning that though he had promised a long time ago that he wanted to become a monk and so, having given an offering (of which one libra came to you), acquired entry into the monastery, procrastinating like a raven,[98] the unfortunate (as he seems to you) died in the habit of a cleric? Who next to himself is to blame for his damnation (if he is damned) more than you and the brothers, who, taking what was his, did not care for him but dismissed him with the devil? For you ought continually to have advised him to hasten to render to God what he had vowed, before that which he knew would soon happen happened. Because you did not do so and he died in his own sin, ask the prophet at whose hand God ought to require his blood [Ezek. 3.18], since, though it was possible for you to do it, that sentence of the Lord's restrained you as follows: 'Woe to you, Pharisees, hypocrites! for you traverse sea and land to make a single proselyte, and when he becomes a proselyte, you make him twice as much a child of hell as yourselves' [Mt. 23.15].

"Therefore, I pity you, wretch, because you cannot weep for your own sins, who ought to weep for others', since this is required of you also. The less you are able to weep for yourself, the more all good men must weep for you, considering also the blow which you gave today to the rustic appealing to you; you should perceive and know also how far you are from those about whom the apostle James says, 'If anyone thinks he is religious and does not bridle his tongue but deceives his heart'—that is, in thinking that he is religious—'this man's religion is vain' [Jas. 1.26], since, wretch, you cannot even bridle your hand, let alone your tongue.

42. "I also see that you are deceived by false hope in words of the Lord like these: 'You have sinned, cease; I do not want the death of the sinner' [Eccli. 21.1], and: 'At whatever hour the sinner is converted, he will be saved' [Ezek.

33.12], and: 'Turn to me and I will turn to you' [Zech. 1.3], and this from the Gospel: 'There is more joy in heaven over one sinner than over ninety-nine just men' [Lk. 15.7], and by many sayings like these sprinkled through the fields of the divine books; all of which, though uttered both mercifully and truly, are corrupted by the carelessness of him who misconstrues them by giving less than just attention to their contexts. To illustrate them all by one instance: He promises more joy in heaven over one sinner than over ninety-nine just men; but if you take heart at the words solely because you know that you are a sinner, mark over what sinner He says there is this joy in heaven, and strive yourself, if you cannot be just, at least to be such a sinner, the kind, as He says, 'that repenteth.' How long 'repenteth'? I do not tell you, because I do not hear it said there. But when I hear it said in the Law about the faults cleansed through various sacrifices, 'He will be unclean till evening' [Lev. 15.11], I confess it seems to me that every single sin, even the absolved ones, should be wept until the last hour.

"'You have sinned,' He says, 'cease' [Eccli. 21.1]. You have dismissed one sin, cease from doing the same or a similar or perhaps even a worse one. It is a worse one if the one you have committed you do not weep for, in that you do not cease to sin if you do not repent of it. For you have not wiped out what you wrote, even if you have ceased to write it; nor when you have abused someone, have you corrected the insults merely by being silent. Perhaps at times you have bewailed some sin, have made your heart contrite. But if you have not abandoned the sin nor repented of it, because you have not also humbled your heart, you can fear (appropriately and with good authority) that you are despised by God. With what face do you dare to enroll yourself among the ninety-nine just men (even if they could be found), so that you think no more is required of *you* (who ought like them to have remained just) than of them? You ought to repent because you have not done so, and give to the angels in Heaven at least some joy, that is, according to the measure of your penitence. You can understand that with God's grace this is in your power when you consider the freedom of the will. With what mind should you neglect to weep for the sins committed since baptism, when St. Peter, the supreme shepherd, trying to urge people terrified by the consideration of their own wrongs to be baptized, began his words with 'Repent ye' [Acts 2.38], though he did not doubt that all sins could be cleansed by the sacrament of baptism, even if no penitence preceded it? Though drumming into you such words as would even soften steel (so to speak), I do not see you pricked to tears and therefore I do not cease to suspect that the words, 'I have struck thee the blow of an enemy' [Jer. 30.14], were spoken to you.

"But lest I seem to add venom to my savage sword, that is, to put despera-tion into the hardness of your heart, now that I have ended my accusation of you, I take care to leave you to God, to be cared for perhaps in a manner beyond words and beyond belief. I pray that His omnipotent mercy and gratuitous clemency may achieve what I see no attempt or threat of mine can do.

"Concerning, then, your not rashly taking the Eucharist: seeing my emotion you chattered on impossibly long above, trying, vain one, to throw up what you had not yet drunk, not thinking this sin to be serious and citing the example of Jeremiah and the psalmist; because I am now compelled by some unavoidable necessity, contrary to my intentions, to tell you what I afterwards learned and to show you how much less you have thought about them than certain others, allow me, I pray, without envy to sneak in under various headings some excerpts from the works of a certain Paschasius Radbert over this. For I owe you a debt also in this. Perhaps you will feel in this too how much my importunity has conferred on you."

[There now followed in the Lobbes MS Paschasius Radbert's *De Corpore et Sanguine Domini*, edited by Martene and Durand (PL. 120.1346–50), after which came the following Exhortation and Prayers. The Exhortation itself and the first twenty-one lines of the second paragraph of the Prayers are identified by Dolbeau[99] as Rather's personal meditation. The other prayers are dated anterior to Rather; I have included them here since they are not readily available in translation.]

20

CC Opera Maiora 269–73   Alna ca. 960

Exhortation

"What the Rule requires of you, beloved, you have now read and reread. What you have decided I ask you now to show. Indicate whether you are deaf or dumb: I see both. When I see you so bemused and remember what is written in the prophet [Mic. 7.16] about such people, I am not a little afraid. I advise you, however, if you find nothing else to do since trust from any other source is entirely destroyed, to surrender yourself wholly to God's clemency and not, as before, to complete sloth and cowardice. But continue your discourse, dismissing from your heart the sins which on the apostle's authority you do not doubt to be mortal. And because that is not enough, 'decline from evil' (he says) 'and do good' [Ps. 36.27], if you are unable (I know that you are unable) to do penance in proportion to the measure of your guilt; for you are short of time, age, bodily health, mental alertness, and the chance of fulfilment; if you cannot do full penance, at least do some and continue at it. If sometimes lawful pleasures are available, remember that you have too often enjoyed the unlawful. Beg from any source—or extract by force—a supply of field-lettuce, cook azyma, cast out the ferment of wickedness, gird your loins, put the staff of discipline in your hand of reason, hasten to go in desire to the place which you cannot aspire to reach through merit [cf. Ex. 12.8; 1 Cor. 5.8]. Be reconciled to men: to some by making satisfaction, to all in love, making sacrifice with fear in proportion to your rebelliousness. Because you cannot extort quittance from your heart (as would be better), promise it with tears, if you can; if not, with inner sighing. You must in your perilous position give something of yourself, sending messengers of prayer to the ears of the most pious Redeemer. For who knows if He is moved and pardons you and is turned from His furious anger and you do not perish eternally? You have indeed perished as far as sinning goes."

Prayers

Behold, Lord, I who have not been worthy (wretched and unfortunate) to approach the porch of your Church nor to enter your house through the sacred doors, I approach to minister at your holy altars, and I stand guilty and a sinner before the sight of your divine majesty, without any ornament of good work and without any worthy fruit of penitence and without even a single pure thought. I am very unworthy and sinful. But confident of your ineffable mercy and piety and of the merits of your saints, I presume, though trembling and afraid, to advance to offer sacrifices to your holy name. Therefore, most pious Lord and Creator, most merciful Redeemer, who would rather correct than destroy every confessing and penitent soul, and who was willing to be incarnate not for the righteous but for sinners, and who not only spared the robber hanging on the cross and confessing your majesty, but even promised that he would enter paradise with you [Lk. 23.43]; do not reject me, a wretched sinner who confesses and is penitent (though slothfully) for my sins, from your piety and mercy; accept the faith, hope, and trust which I have in your inestimable clemency; but just as you have spared all the wicked sinners who believe in you and trust in your mercy, so deign to be indulgent and sparing to me, a wretch fleeing to you and after my many crimes and sins renouncing the devil and returning to you, and to support me and make me worthy by your Father's piety to celebrate the office that is my duty.

And though I approach more importunately than is proper (for I am fully aware of what is forbidden me by the strictures of both the Old and the New

Law and I know with full belief that the angels who are destroyers of the wicked and guardians of your altars are ever present at your holy shrines holding the weapons of destruction in their hands [Ezek. 9.1]), yet I have trust presumptuously in your real mercy from long ago, because, that is, right up to this old age which I have reached, grown old in wickedness [Dan. 13.5] and ever angering you, those angels that avenge wrongs done to you have not slain me, which would have been fitting, since perhaps they knew that your kindness patiently waited for me to be penitent (though storing up anger for the day of wrath and the revelation of your just judgment [Rom. 2.4–5]); furthermore, many of my brothers have much against me [Mt. 5.23]. Because, Lord, I stand, though fearful and trembling lest suddenly I be struck down, as is just, you being present in your Body and Blood (since in your divinity you are present everywhere), yet spare me, most pious one, spare me, still presuming I pray; put off the blow, postpone the punishment; and looking not to my wickedness, the sins and faults of my youth and (as is worse, I confess) of my old age too, but to your many acts of mercy and pity, by which you have ever been accustomed to pity the human race, take up my prayers and offerings, which for my sins and the sins of your faithful both living and dead I presume to offer to your majesty. Remember that we are flesh made from fragile material. Even the heavens are not pure in your sight [Job 15.15] and your angels have been found delinquent in your presence [Job 4.18]; how much more are earthly men unworthy and unclean! For we cannot be clean unless we daily merit in heart and body to be cleansed by your pity and mercy. Wherefore, Lord, you who wanted to arouse my thoughts and my sluggish, wretched, and tainted devotion to take up the holy mystery of your altar, and permitted me, an unworthy sinner, to minister to you (shamefully however), withhold yet the anger which I deserve, merciful one, show your gratuitous clemency, and favorably allow that the celebration of this holy mystery, to which I come forward fearful and unfervid, may turn out not to my judgment and damnation but to the remission of my sins and my eternal salvation.

Lord, being guilty of monstrous sin as our conscience attests, we are so disturbed that we can come to your office neither without anxiety nor free. For who weighing his sin would not wish to hide himself from your face (if it were possible to avoid the eyes of such majesty), to see if he might escape notice and get away, or get away by staying hidden? Or who would not rather desire to see you, if he were not more afraid that you are watching him sinning? Therefore, because you find us everywhere, we flee to you from whom we can never escape.[100] Our one hope, wretches, is to interpose not hiding places but tears. May your indulgence nurture us whom, having erred, it frightens. Your power threatens but let your mercy comfort. From you comes the one who is to free us; through you comes the one who is to excuse us. Spare us, omnipotent Father, and deign to raise and reward those whom you see humbled in guilt; and those whom you know by their confession to be wretched, do not throw into terror by your inquisition.

Dismiss, O God, any chastisement and tongue-lashing my headstrong mouth has given to inferiors from failing to control my biting tongue. Forgive anything we have said that is not the means to a good end; pardon any words that have been out-of-place or excessive. May my presumption not punish me heedlessly, but may the piety of your mercy absolve me as I recognize my iniquities. And because I have no trust but in your mercy, both fortify my mouth with words of truth and sanctify my work with fuller harvest, so that you may make me worthy of salvation, and the flock committed to me righteous, for your piety. Heal any fault you see in them; any vice you find in me, cure. If they have contracted or are contracting any damage by the fault of my coolness or lack of care, remove it. If they have fallen into any sin, whether I know of it or not, and if they have come into guilt from the fault of following my example, pardon them and do not for such faults transfer your vengeance onto me. May those to whom my scolding has seemed deserving of rebuke profit by that scolding to their salvation, and may this prayer accost them and recall them from the sin they have committed so that they do not undergo the tortures of hell. Being mortal, I have imposed on them rules of penance, so that you, God, being charitable to the failings of both them and me, may give pardon to their wrongs and wash away any offense of mine caused by improper exercise of my authority. Offer your ear to our sacrifices, God, and write my name and the names of those committed to me in your pages, so that I and the flock entrusted to me may both be cleared of all sin and merit to come to you in peace. Pacify, God, the dwelling of our hearts by expelling vices of the flesh; and may I who now try to instill the sum of the virtues into my flock, and soothe the tensions of minds and bodies, merit in peace to be crowned with the angels in your judgment. Make us then, we ask looking piously to you, God, enflamed in your sight with the gift of your grace, so that the zeal of your house may consume us and we may so rule and govern the flock with the strength of the Holy Spirit, that they may obtain their reward under the discipline of our guidance and their stubbornness be broken and their life sanctified. Accept Lord, the offering of our vows, so that through them, whatever we communicate to our flock by corrective word or merit may not be a source of discord but may profit them and us and bring us the perpetual joy of sweetness. Absolve us, God, both from our own sin and that of others, so that in both we may receive the action of spiritual grace and the more faithfully worship your name.

The Host of salvation urges me to the office of ministering the sacrament for the sinfulness of the people; my conscience terrifies me for the guilt of an improper priesthood. If the sacrifice is offered by me, the dog's body of all the priests, the sin of a tainted conscience is increased; if it is not offered to so great a majesty, the Judge of all flesh, the guilt of omission is added on. In such a scale, Almighty, I implore the balance of your piety, whose day of vengeance I fear while my conscience accuses me, so that you may not judge me unworthy of your mercy, I pray, whom you do not shut off from the time of penitence. Withhold the axe until the tender of the vineyard brings the basket of dung to the root of the unfruitful tree [Lk. 13.6–9].

Spare me, a penitent, O Lord who mercifully recalled to pardon David after his fall; who mercifully looked on the tears of Peter weeping bitterly; who brought the light of God's grace on the robber on the cross who was guilty of so great a crime, whose confession at once obtained a clear sight of the Son of God, whose faith obtained its reward, whose pain obtained its pardon, whose cries obtained his eternal joy, since he was a confessor on the cross, a possessor of paradise after the cross. But since my words, being smeared by the works of an unworthy priesthood, fail to win the pardon of your piety, receive at any rate the prayers of those standing by so that their sacrifices may bring pardon to me by their prayers in your presence and also by their merits may they healthfully bring the medication of our wounds to us so that as Christ, Savior of the world, you have been made a sacrifice for all for our sins, you may be present to us in our sacrifice as a sanctification for our faults, who with the Father and the Holy Spirit live and reign as God, world without end.

May he who wrote this live in peace, and he who reads it rejoice forever.

21

Weigle, Epist. 69–70	Alna December 960–February 961

[Rather writes to Bruno, Otto I's brother, thanking him for his charitable gifts and begging him to reconsider his decision to convene a synod about Rather's restitution to Liège, since he no longer wants it.]

෴

To Bruno most worthy lord, Rather most unworthy servant; to the most holy pontiff, Rather the most persecuted sinner:

Even if everything which lives, feels, and is conscious in the senses of my body and soul were to shout out in unison, I would be unable to give you worthy repayment of thanks for those gifts of alms which during this time I have received from your holiness, very beloved father, even if they had not been preceded by any of those in which you previously showed me your lordship's most kind and generous love.

Now, my lord, because your love and the authority of lord Archbishop Frederick [of Salzburg] compel me, though I am unwilling and working towards ends far different from this, to be present at a synodal council for the sake of my restitution (which I no longer want), I urge you to deign to reconsider; otherwise, often trying, often repulsed, I may seem to be attacking God and to be struggling against Him who said, "Give place to this man" [Lk. 14.9], with the vain toil of violent attempt. May I rather be allowed to "take the lowest place" (which I hold)[1] though "with shame," lest my shame be doubled[2] and my enemies have further cause for laughing at me. But if, dear father, your most kindly sweetness presses me with inflexible will to execute what you command, then let the most generous munificence of your bounty deign to succor my will, which is quite unprepared to consent, by bearing me aid. For otherwise my obedience without any resources will be inefficacious to perform what you command.

22

Weigle, Epist. 70–71

Alna 955–961

[Rather threatens G. with excommunication if he does not redeem the pallium, belonging to the Church of St. Peter, which he has made over to someone else.]

∞

Bishop Rather to G.

I beg and beseech you in God's name, brother, acknowledge, if you have not previously acknowledged, ponder, if you have never deigned to ponder, that God is not what man is; for God is Creator, man the created; God is Redeemer, man the redeemed; God is Judge, man the one to be judged—and judged according to what he has done not by the law which holds in the courts and, to say it more openly, folkmoots[3] alone, but by the far different Law, without witnesses, without any advocate or lawyer, without any sworn retainer. For there no brother will redeem you nor any man another [Ps. 48.8]. Know most assuredly that there St. Peter presides, whose pallium you hold[4]—unjustly, according to the law which pertains there—St. Peter who also "holds the keys of the kingdom of heaven, and what he binds on earth know that it shall be bound in heaven, and whatever he looses on earth will be loosed in heaven" [Mt. 16.19]. I beg and beseech you, by the fear or love of them both and of all the dear faithful born or to be born, and along with you I beg him also who holds the pallium received from you in token, that since you have received three more *solidi*[5] than is your due, you return to God and St. Peter what is theirs. If you refuse, know that you will be excommunicated, with that same terrible, mortal, excommunication with which all wicked men and killers of saints and sacrilegious men and violators of the temple of God, from Cain the fratricide to that last vessel of perdition, the AntiChrist, have been excommunicated.

23

CC Opera Minora 11–29   Verona after February 962

[In 961 Otto came into Italy for the second time to oust Berengar. He secured Verona, putting Counts Ernest and Bucco in charge, and restored Rather to his bishopric.

Rather's first extant work after being reinstated was a pamphlet in answer to those criticizing his participation, or acquiescence, in the removal of the body of St. Metro from the Church of St. Vitalis on January 27, 962. C. 14 seems to indicate that Metro's ashes remained in Verona while his bones had been removed elsewhere, but that the circumstances of the removal—or theft—were only known to him from rumor. The work is highly rhetorical, with many biblical and patristic allusions. He bewails the dearth of good writers in Italy and the lack of devotion in the upper classes, who had neglected St. Metro's tomb. He attempts to supply a grandiose narrative of the saint's self-punishment and concludes with a paean of triumph over the devil.][6]

∽

On the Removal of St. Metro

A mournful account, very abusive of certain individuals, by a man called Rather, once of Lobbes now of Verona, who from being a monk became an exile, and from an exile became a bishop; then, following the example of poor Attalus,[7] who was made bishop, unmade, remade, and deposed again (for what purpose only the Maker, Unmaker, Remaker, and Deposer knew), being made bishop, he was unmade and then remade bishop: concerning the removal of the body of a certain St. Metro, whose anniversary is celebrated on the eighth of May and whose removal is bewailed on the twenty-seventh of January [962], though to no purpose; no one on earth now knows whether it happened or not, but it was certainly believed to have been close to the truth at the time that it happened.

1. As the most sacred, ancient, and true chronographer of former times[8] relates, when God's pity mercifully disposed to free the long-afflicted people from the hand of the tyrant of Memphis [Pharoah, king of Egypt], or rather, from the jaws, so to speak, of the monster of the Nile, He gave instructions [Ex. 11.2, 12.35], among other things relevant to that work, that every man of that people on his departure should borrow gold and silver vessels from his Egyptian friend, so that, we can suppose, the impious race, most justly about to be swallowed up in the depths of the Red Sea for their own personal guilt and for that of their master, might be despoiled of their wealth and of their goods long unjustly possessed, and so that the God-worshipping offspring of Abraham might be enriched by a gift from heaven. The matter of this mystery might seem quite similar to the fraud[9] which is everywhere condemned by the law of nations; yet if we consider the puzzle to be beyond human understanding (which God confounds), we miss thereby the greatest comprehension of the wisdom and knowledge of God (whose altitude wise men should praise [Rom. 11.33] with the divinely inspired apostle rather than disparage and criticize with the insane catalogue of heretics), and we miss the understanding of God's disposition — yet it has been made clear to us by those [i.e., the twelve apostles] to whom was given, as we read, the authority of filling the twelve baskets with the remains of the fragments [Jn. 6.12–13].

When we are moved, therefore, by the zeal for proper inquiry and consider the manifold mysteries of this Incomprehensibility (as far as that most merciful bestower of graces deigns to offer to our slow wits), there often occurs what the incomparable Wisdom of that time was not ashamed to admit to all, saying: "I sought out wisdom and it receded far from me" [Eccle. 7.24]. But no matter. For these twelve baskets were filled with fragments of the two fish acquired with labor and skill from the waters of the shore of Zabulon [the Sea of Galilee] and Nephthalim (where the venerable patriarchs of the apostolic seed happened to be bidden to dwell [Num. 34.13–29] — all of which details doubtless have inner significance but need a studious investigator to interpret) and with the fragments of the loaves to the number of five [Mt. 14.17], again not without mystery. If we care to regurgitate this, as it were, from the stomach of memory and return it to the molars to be more finely ground in the gullet of recollection, we shall find that it was most truly spoken that "he who takes on knowledge takes on also labor" [Eccle. 1.18]. For the loaves are not *wheaten* so that the meaning can be easily grasped,[10] but *barley*, to whose kernel even the most laborious study can hardly penetrate. So when the upper millstone is set turning and the lower is stationary (and as it were inactive—not without mystic significance),[11] the barley mass, which we have taken in hand to interpet, is of necessity ground up, and, when offered to our taste, it shows to the palate of our mind that Egypt stands for the world in evil, Pharaoh for the devil, the chief of this world; the people oppressed by mud and bricks signifies the human race, to free which the Lord came down on His mission; the Red Sea tinged with blood signifies baptism; the drowned signify our sins, the freed those washed with baptism and redeemed by Christ's blood from the soul's death through our Saviour.

But what about the gold and silver vessels fraudulently borrowed and stolen on the instructions of the Deliverer? They are, I say, the ornaments and trappings of secular books,[12] which, as we see, have been completely taken over from paganism and have now, by Christ's disposition, long since passed into the use and adornment of the Church.

And if a shrewd questioner asks, "To what purpose is all this?" obviously it is so that I may point out that the words of the Apostle, "Where is the wise man? Where is the scribe? Where is the debater of this age? Has not God made foolish the wisdom of the world?" [1 Cor. 1.20], are quite applicable to us today. Now, of course,

Now, a second Joshua had destroyed Cariath-Sephor,
And had razed utterly to the ground the walls of Jericho,
With the saints triumphant through all the paths of the world.[13]

2. Our historiographers undertook to describe the trials of the martyrs who had gone before, the merits of the confessors, the chastity of the celibates, virgins, and widows, and the penitence of the converted, with no less study, style, and elegance than those inventors or propagators of the liberal arts, produced most of all by lying Greece,[14] who were conspicuous in the beauty of their eloquence and were admired throughout all the world; no less also than those deceitful poets who never stopped extolling their earlier heroes and falsely exaggerating their achievements. But now, alas, in our grandfathers' time and in our own (and we are therefore driven to conclude that we are not far off from the coming of him of whom the prophet said, "Want will go before his face" [Job 41.13]), such a dearth of writers has come upon the world that, if any either from our own time or from the time of those mentioned above have shone for their good works, their praises have been sung more by the crowd than by any man of letters. Tell us then, writers, to what purpose have you

borrowed from the Egyptians those gold and silver vessels which you possess, if you do not show any embellishment from them in the Lord's tabernacle or temple? You should be afraid that what happened to Achan in the story [Jos. 7.19-26] will happen to you (referring to the measure of gold he had stolen and had not revealed to Joshua) — unless God's pity spare you against your deserts. "The Lord Jesus was throwing out a devil and it was dumb; and when he had thrown out the devil, the dumb man spoke" [Lk. 11.14]. Let us pray to God to repeat this miracle, so that our mouths may speak the Lord's praises.

3. How rightly, then, should I be angry at the scholars of our father's time and of our own! But now to tell a sad story: recently — that is, at the time when the most glorious, just, and pious emperor Otto Augustus, praiseworthy everywhere, had entered Italy[15] to his happy triumph — the people of Verona incurred a most serious loss, the fault not only of the bishop who was then most unworthily in office there,[16] but also of those who had preceded him in the previous sixty years. For the body of a certain man, namely, St. Metro (I hesitate whether to call him martyr or confessor) had been taken from a suburb of that city (the Church of the Blessed Martyr Vitalis had kept it), a laudable theft but a damnable loss, as the uneducated crowd said. For because countless miracles had been performed there, the vulgar throng visited this saint's memorial with religious love, to the sorrow only of the prelates and of those who, in vainest toil, were given to eating the pods of the pigs rather than those sweet wheaten loaves which in the Gospel the prodigal son, before returning to his father, complained that the crowd of hirelings had in abundance while he was dying of hunger [Lk. 15.17]. This place had become so little valued that, since the revenues due to that church had been given to knights, there was not even a priest there to look after the place containing so precious a treasure.

Alas what grief! Eyelets in mourning, weep ye, I pray![17]

For in the universal degeneracy we could bewail that the world was daily rushing down to perdition if we were not rather instructed, "When these things begin to take place, raise your heads" [Lk. 21.28], that is, lift up your hearts (lest, of course, God in His divine justice think that we are more kindly disposed to this present world which passes with its pains and desires [1 Jn. 2.17] than to that which approaches with glory and felicity on the passing of this one, and lest by being contrary in anything to the will and disposition of the Creator we be thought to have destroyed His image in us and to have cavilled at His word).

To single you out, poor Italy: who could sufficiently criticize you, or rather weep for you (which is more salutary and rational)? You most unworthily abuse the leading apostles, you walk over martyrs, confessors you trample on with your feet, the venerable tombs of virgins you tread on with impure steps, and, like dogs keeping others off their spoil with jealous growling, those whom you had refused to venerate when they were present, you pursue with curses when they have gone, or rather have fled from you (which is closer to the truth) to visit others. Are you not most envious and avaricious in this? Should you not have rejoiced at the honor of those saints, who became cheap to you because of their numbers, instead of envying the desire, devotion and salvation of those who, since they had no saints of their own, deserved to receive a few from the Lord? Why, in this at least, do you not care to remember the apostle's words, "If anyone has the world's goods and sees his brother in need yet closes his heart against him, how does God's love abide in him?" [1 Jn. 3.17], and, "You will love your neighbor as yourself" [Mt. 19.19]? Why are you so upset at losing that which, when you had it, you did not love so much? You are not genuinely upset but craftily pretend to be upset on the instigation of certain people.[18] For if you really were upset at their loss, you would attend those who are left with more devout worship and veneration.

4. But though you can rightly criticize your prelates, as you try to by enviously abusing them, yet take note, I urge you, that you have not deserved better ones. For it has been truthfully said, as we read, that "God makes the hypocrite rule because of the sins of the people" [Job 34.30], and God Himself has said, "I will give them kings in my fury and in my anger" [Os. 13.11], understanding by "kings" not only those who are normally called kings in this world but also all those of any rank set over others to govern them.

If you loved your martyr so much, why did you look after him so badly that your bishop [Rather] did indeed consent (as you are trying to charge) to a higher plan and one more conforming to God's disposition? You were horrified at such an action. Why? I want to know. "Because it was wicked," you say, "in that thus we lost our saints." True; but you would more appropriately say that thus our saints fled from us. Though no one greedy of foul gain is a saint, no saint is found to have refused honorable gain; honorable gain is that which enriches heaven and despoils hell. If every one of your saints decided at all costs to flee from you and go to where he would be treated with the reverence shown him in the love of Christ, a reverence which he did not have with you, ethereal paradise would be filled with devout souls and infernal hell emptied. Since none of your people has in the course of so many years merited paradise for this kind of devotion, beware lest you seem to be distressed by heaven's successes and glad at its losses. By the example which you show, you want the saints to have honor neither here nor anywhere else.

5. But you, great Verona, admired for the number of its wise writers as second only to Plato's Athens, why did you not extol your saint in high-sounding praise? Why did you not publish the miracles which God performed through

him, in prose at least if not in verse? You would have handled with more esteem what the untaught crowd sang, believe me, and you would have decorated
this tabernacle of God with Taphnitic [i.e., Egyptian] bronze at least and decked
it out with the silver and gold which the cultivator of the land of Gessen [i.e.,
the Israelites] had borrowed. For, to your shame, when someone who knew
the value of the theft asked your bishop about that blessed one's sanctity, the
bishop did not go to a book of the saint's *gesta* written by one of your eager
students but to the truthful word of those who could sing with the psalmist,
"God, we have heard with our ears, our fathers have told us" [Ps. 43.1].[19] From
them he learned that the saint in his youth had been involved in such acts of
this world as the divine book mentions thus: "But those who desire to be rich
fall into temptation, into a snare of the devil" [1 Tim. 6.9]. When such entrap-
ment by the devil happened to Metro by the just Lord's merciful concession (as
often happens to many others), he was moved by consideration of his own guilt
and was not slow to correct himself, to abandon all the stuff of this world, so
that unimpeded and free he might have leisure for the Lord alone. And so like
Zacchaeus he climbed his sycamore [Lk. 19.4], that is, the Cross, so that he
might see Jesus and be freed.

And so as not to carry his cross under compulsion like Simon [Lk. 23.26;
Mt. 27.32],[20] but to be mortified by it along with his vices and desires like
Christ, and not on one occasion, but every day, nay, every minute, he chose
for himself, so it is said, a kind of punishment that he could in no way get out
of, if he should be overcome by the flesh's insistence and want to escape it. Judging himself publican and sinner beyond all men, he blocked the threshold of the
church with his body and brought it about that standing afar he might be able
to cry along with that other one mercifully justified, "God, be merciful to me,
a sinner" [Lk. 18.13].

6. But why do I say *standing*—which does not fit the situation at all—as though
I have heard of any Christian, before or since, who brought on himself so worthy a martyrdom? It would be more appropiate to say *rolling*, for *standing* does
not apply. For omitting those who undergo internal agonies in their stomach
or abdomen (I leave these to those who review other martyrdoms), as far as
externals go the pain which he inflicted on himself was unprecedented. For as
though he were addressing himself in the voice of the most cruel, most vicious
torturer—"When you were in a position of honor, like foolish beasts you did
not understand and became like them; so I will tie you with beasts' thongs so
that you cannot wander any more in your foolish way" [Ps. 48.13]—he put a
chain on his feet, fastened it in lead in a great stone (which still stands before
the door of the church), anchored the leg-irons in the doors and locked them,
and threw the key in the current of the well-known river Athesis close by, on

whose bank the aforesaid church stands (I speak somewhat crudely the better to be understood), perhaps asking God never to let him see it again till he had with His mercy expiated the sins which he had undertaken to repent. I have used the word "perhaps" because, though my sources did not say that he asked this of God, yet the miraculous outcome showed that what happened to him was conceded by God.

And so for seven years he is said to have stayed in the open like this, chained to the stone. Then, since God mercifully wished to put an end to the agonies accompanying such a punishment and to crown His martyr with supreme honors, fishermen brought to the bishop a fish in whose stomach that holy key was found; this revealed that all his sins had been remitted. For when the key was recognized, the chained fetter was unlocked by the city prelate and the saint was washed, clothed, brought back to the church and refreshed with the sacred participation of the Body and Blood of the Lord. And when on the expiration of his spirit that most acceptable sacrifice of the Lord passed from this world and was brought to heaven on angels' wings, no one endowed with even a child's intellect can doubt that the saint received in heaven the crown of martyrdom as well as the palm of victory; for he had overcome one who, wrestling with him, had vainly boasted too early that he had won him over. The remains of his body entrusted to the earth provide further testimony to this by the working of miracles. But, as I have said, this has been hidden by the inertia of those who have received from God some talent of knowledge but have kept it buried under the cloth of earthly vanity [Mt. 25.25], preferring to lend it to secular pomp for pleasing the world than to deposit it, as though with a banker, with the people who desire the glory and praise of God for the edification of those who will listen.

Lo, what a glory, what a heritage, what a treasure you have lost, Verona (if indeed you have lost it), unfortunate in this at least! If you had been aware of this by reading it, or even had known it by hearing it from some learned man, you would not, I think, so easily have lost so important a patron. If only those to whom he was given by God would take this to heart and not neglect so precious a jewel bestowed on them by God! Be angry, then, I say, be angry at those poets and writers who, in longing for vain glory, have filled your walls with verses but have not committed this saint's deeds or miracles to paper. For if you had known of him, you would not have looked after him so badly.

7. Now I turn my gaze on those who, though encumbered with great sins, like me pay little attention to those true words of the apostle: "If we were to judge ourselves, we would not be judged" [1 Cor. 11.31]. Assuredly, if you do not remember him and the many saints like him, and if you do not ponder why they underwent such great sufferings, you will get perdition. They suffered because, without a doubt, they took seriously the Psalmist's words: "You have

commanded your precepts to be kept diligently" [Ps. 118.4]. Why "diligent-ly"? you ask. Surely because, as has been truly said before me, "One cannot come to great rewards except by great labors."[21] For, as the apostle says: "The sufferings of this present time are not worth comparing with the glory that is to be revealed to us" [Rom. 8.18]. This all the apostles, all martyrs and saints certainly meditated upon. He who has not meditated on this has entirely neglected himself. Let us focus our attention on anyone you like, one who also has in-curred the same sin as this saint merited to atone for with such pains, and much more guiltily, inasmuch as he is well aware of it (for the saint had fallen into it unawares). If he were to lie before the saint's tomb and strike his breast and cry, "St. Metro, intercede for me, a wretched sinner," don't you think that that saintly martyr could reply to him to his face: "Do what I did and you win what I won." What answer can we make, we who are involved in worse sins, and, what's worse, in the habit of them, sweating over our pillows and murmuring psalms (though even this is a rare bird), futilely promising ourselves pardon for this kind of penance,

if winter by the fireside, if summer in the shade,[22]

groaning and hoping for indulgence, deceived by presumption alone?

For seven years that saint wallowed half-naked day and night on the bare and rough ground. We sinners, when we come to ask pardon, so as not to catch cold put a wool cap on our hair—which we ought rather to have torn out in grief. His hat was snow, hail, and windy rain, winter's harsh discomforts, which were to wash away the sins he had committed. With us it is the custom for penitents, even those weeping for incest or many other sins of like gravity, to wear a cap inside exotic furs; but his head was covered with the winter's hoar. Instead of the straw parasol of the Saxon fashion[23]—which they put over their heads to ward off the heat of the sun—he had scorching Phoebus himself. His tent was the aereal sky—so that he would not be shut off from that ethereal one. The sun served as his shade, the heat as his cooler; the moon's rise and fall reproached him with having fallen from his rise and rushed into ruin. The infinity of the stars—if ever the Orderer of the constellations lit up the starry sky with golden-tailed luminaries—reminded him unceasingly to think on his own countless acts of guilt and endlessly charged him with ingratitude. What did the crashes of thunder do, the squally storms, the stones of hail, the bolts of lightning, if not sound in his heart that terrible judgment of God's anger? His roof was the sky, often starry, sometimes stormy, usually cloudy, calm if God willed it so (the alternations of which make mortals think of shelter), his roof, I say, was for ever that variable sky of heaven, not warding off the show-ers but pouring them down, giving snow like wool, scattering frost like ashes

[Ps. 147.16–18], casting forth ice like morsels on him not escaping it, before whose cold he stood patiently alone, until the power of God should melt it on command, till His breath should blow and the waters flow, to wash away both the internal and external mire from his saintly head. If ever storm clouds covered the pole with inky darkness, threatening thereby some imminent loss for poor farmers, he thought that it was his own sin which had so offended God that it brought that disaster not on himself alone but on the land in which he lived. For thus saints are wont to feel themselves responsible for such disasters, thus to take others' guilt on to themselves, not in false devotion but in respect and fear of God—not that servile fear which love displaces, but that chaste fear which lasts for ever [Ps. 18.10; 1 Jn. 4.18]—and not because they fear punishment (which they presume that by their conversion they have escaped, since God so promises), but lest basking in security they become unworthy to see the glory of God's clarity. In love of sanctity, they not only avoid vices at the Lord's command, but also abhor and hate them; as the most diligent verse-writer of his age [Horace] says:

From love of virtue the good hate to sin.[24]

8. Behold in what school you were brought up, most obedient and modest disciple of Christ, in what field you exercised, athlete of the Heavenly King, in what fire you were sacrificed, victim most acceptable to Christ. What did you think, holy one, what did you say against the devil, who, envying your salvation, had impelled you to that sin for which you were forced to undergo torments like a thousand deaths? You certainly called down on him the torments which you were ordered to suffer, when you fired him with unspeakable envy for the victory about to come to you out of God's mercy. What of the fact that, bound with a chain in the open like some bear, lion, panther, or Hyrcanian tiger, made a spectacle for angels and men, you saw around you or heard a multitude of people, laughing, being merry, often celebrating weddings and banquets, enjoying the delights of parties and social gatherings, the laughter and fun of a life far different from your own? You were deaf to all this, I believe, as that other hero was deaf to the song of the Sirens. For all this what were your feelings? Your sufferings? Your martyrdom? I know what you did, I know it, and do not hesitate to tell it at once so that others may know. Without a doubt with tears and prayers you summoned the angels and archangels to help, you called on the apostles with weeping, you implored martyrs, confessors, and virgins to join battle for you with the hated enemy.

What of the Queen of them all? You supplicated her, I think, helped by modesty, which undoubtedly leads pious men to success in achieving their prayers; the more modest and humble your supplications to her, the more successful were your efforts. For I think that no one who is polluted (as our group) with carnal delight appeals to her inviolate ears without shame, unless he be mad. For she merited to become the Mother of God clothed in man in unity of person in two natures for this reason, that her unique and incomparable humility, which alone is able to safeguard the most persevering state of good, was respected by God, and so she could remain a virgin, as before giving birth, so in giving birth and no less after giving birth.[25] It is usual for all men to hate the opposite of that which they most love. So the holy Mother of God, because she loved chastity more than anything, most hates its contrary, lust, in all Christians.

With what shameless temerity, then, do the lips that are polluted with wanton kissing and the tongue befouled with obscenity dare to mouth the name of the most chaste virgin—not to mention that she is also the mother of the inner Judge? How can the heart that is dirtied with lascivious thoughts presume even to recall a name venerated by the very angels? But what guilty conscience shrinks from doing, the pity of her most merciful Son and the fact of His Incarnation contemplated with faith makes us presume to do. For He mercifully denies that she is angry, I think, even with her most sinful servants, when He shows her the flesh which He assumed from her for the cleansing of the sins of the guilty. And therefore, O martyr, now secure for yourself, using the same modesty humbly intercede for *us* for your part before the same Mother of God.

9. But why so clumsily do I make these vain attempts?

I am lacking in eloquence and cannot extol thee.[26]

For even if I had the talent of Cicero, such is my excitement I would be unable to tell what I feel about you. But I will try again, though having no gift of eloquence. My will does not let me be silent.

You tried, I say, daily to make sacrifice to the Lord, to offer a victim, not from someone else's flock, but from your own body. You were the priest, you the victim, the slayer, the martyr, the torturer, the tortured, you were the throat, you the slitter of the throat, the avenger of crime, the saviour of your protégé, the neglecter of the flesh, the champion of the mind. You greatly hated the person you thought you were, when you tortured yourself so viciously. You tried to subject your flesh to reason, and for that purpose you savagely crucified it; but in reality by hating it you loved it, since thus you reconciled it to the Lord. For what the apostle says is true: "No man ever hates his own flesh but nourishes it and cherishes it" [Eph. 5.29]. *His flesh*, he says; and by that we should understand that it is the vices of the flesh that should be hated (a fact that did not escape you), for they proceed from evil, as you were aware, while the flesh was made by Him who "saw everything that He had made and it was exceeding good" [Gen. 1.31]. It was vices, therefore, vices, not the flesh, good martyr, that you did persecute when you tortured it in so many different ways, just as the doctor wanting to heal a man treats sickness with cautery, though it is painful to his flesh. How severely did you torment and cauterize yourself, good doctor, in love of health! What bitter medicines you took each day to heal the inner organs of your soul! With what essential nourishment did you cherish your flesh along with your soul, that it might receive immortality and live through eternity! The tale is long to tell.

10. But, crafty Devil, I still cannot see what success *you* achieved by that temporary victory of yours against the soldier of Christ. For we rejoice more exultantly that you have been worsted by his *fall* than if you had kept your hands off him, you fool, at that time. Perhaps you had forgotten, reprobate, that the merciful Saviour said that there is more joy in heaven over one sinner that repents than in ninety and nine just men that need no repentance [Lk. 7.20]. For this saint, living too slothfully (perhaps confident in his own righteousness), like many, had to presume for pardon only for innumerable faults rather than for serious sins; but in hatred of the crime into which you had driven him, he exerted his whole strength and seized the sword of God's help against you; covered by the shield of the Lord's protection, he did not hesitate to rise up most fiercely and wear you out with the blows of an Entellus,[27] to hurl his shafts unceasingly, to cast his javelins, to wrestle constantly with you naked (God's grace making him naked so that no part should be left to you on which you could get a hold), to keep assailing you by shooting from a distance the arrows of Jesus' quiver, and (by praying to God for help, so as to be inaccessible for ever) to surround himself with the wall of God's protection. You did not know — or perhaps had forgotten, wicked one — as is asserted by Job, that erstwhile noble victor in your mire, or rather by God, who had exposed him to you to be tempted but in no way overcome, speaking to him out of the whirlwind, you did not remember, I say, that there is a hole in your jaw [Job 40.21 ff.] caused by the band of God's mercy embracing us, through which he could escape the crunching of your teeth, as can all people who enjoy the worthy fruits of penitence.

For how, wretched Devil who forget your past defeats, how did Peter, or Paul once Saul, or many others, escape your gullet if not by that hole? And see what happened to you. For when you assailed his breast with fleshly lusts, you drove him (though this you did not want) more determinedly to the love of God. As a result, by placating the most pious Judge with penitence, he had a stronger peace with Him and in that peace he resumed the fight with you more staunchly. Rightly, therefore, are you called *follis*[28] in rustic Latin, since, empty of truth, packed with falsehood, and therefore most foolish, you deceive yourself so often. Thus you caused Abel to become the first martyr, thus you caused Sem and Japhet to be blessed, thus Joseph to be glorified. And — lest my invective against you proceed forever—you lost the sovereignty of the whole world of the faithful, when you urged the disciple to sell his Master, Lord, and God, and the buyers to cry, "Crucify Him, crucify Him" [Jn. 19.6]. Yet you at once regretted doing this, when you visited Pilate's wife in a dream and made her send a messenger to ask her husband to change his mind [Mt. 27.19]. But the celestial Disposer, who mercifully knew how to profit even from your wickedness, brought damnation for you and all your associates for so great a crime, but for all the blessed He arranged redemption, as happily occurred for this saint also.

To give an example from more recent times to reproach you with, ancient serpent: look at the most famous of hermits, namely, Moses and Macharius,[29] and see what damage you did yourself in inciting the one to robbery, the other to murder. Blush then, blush (though uselessly) in the shame of your many defeats and cease your vain attempts on God's elect. For, as a certain brilliant orator elegantly says, the Heavenly Doctor knows how to do much good even by means of the wicked,[30] when He converts to His own advantage their plans to damage Him. But you would not now know, cunning Folly (to call you so), that the Lord had exposed one of His own to you in order to overcome you, if you had been able, darkest one, to comprehend that light in you with which He out-blinded you, when He handed over to you everything which Job had (you had demanded that he be assailed) but told you to "save his soul" [Job 2.6]. For how would you "save" his soul, you who wish to destroy all that has been and will be saved? But when He said "save," He meant it to be understood as "do not touch." For unless you touched his soul by your suggestion, how would you, O most deceived in this at least, seduce him to agree to curse God?

And so you can believe that the sentence, "Woe, you who deceive, will you not also be deceived?," was most truly said of you (and of any of your associates as well). For you are often deceived, I say, O violent serpent, you are "formed to deceive yourself" [Ps. 103.26], as the psalmist says. Between your malice and God's kindness, there is this gulf, that the souls which He loves above you, you hate most of all. Why did you not consider that you were being given nothing which you valued, when you were permitted (though not granted) to afflict for a while a corruptible body but were commanded not to damage his incorruptible soul, you who swallow the river of paganism and are not surprised, having confidence even though the Jordan of Christianity rushes against your mouth [Job 40.18]? Why so, if not for swallowing down the souls who are washed with the water of baptism, for whose fall from salvation into perdition you insatiably thirst? So it is surprising that you have not realized that you were deceived in this grant, O especial deception of the deceived. If you exacted from your own people the tribute of your once invaded dominion, we should not have had to ask why you invade the rights of another—and indeed of a greater One (which is more surprising) who has thus reassured His own with the promise from His own mouth, "Father, I have not lost any of those whom you gave to me" [Jn. 18.9]. But, foolish one, you thought that as He used the past tense, He did not care for the future, so you do not stop undermining them, I think, to this end. But listen, detestable one, you and your court as well: "Lo, I am with you all days up to the end of time" [Mt. 28.20]. Believe it, He will not expose to you any weak one of His own, for you to fully exult over. Those whom He permits to be seduced for even longer by the malicious deception of your hatred (though they are innumerable) the Merciful One will promote to the palm of victory, even after their fall, as also He has promoted St. Metro.

Finally, there is this distinction between power and omnipotence, that the former is powerful over some things, the latter over everything. It follows from this distinction that power can do nothing when omnipotence forbids it; and so it is an unassailable fact that God can draw to Himself despite you those of your followers whom He wishes and however He wishes. But you cannot even venture to tempt any of His if He does not permit it; this you most clearly discovered, wretch, when you did not dare to enter even the herd of swine except with permission [Mt. 8.31]. His embrace is salvation, yours is perdition—from which He has also been wont mercifully to free countless numbers. For even though "your young lions roar for their prey" [Ps. 103.21], as the psalmist says, yet "from God do they seek their food," that is, they seek that God's watchfulness may overlook some whom their wickedness can enter. But though we read that with your tail you swept down a great part of the stars of heaven to earth [Rev. 12.4] (or are sweeping or will sweep), yet do not be deceived, I advise. For this is not said of those who "will shine like a sun till everlasting and like the brightness of the firmament turn many to righteousness" [Mt. 13.43; Dan. 12.3], not about those, I say, who truly gazing on the true light truly shine, but about those who imitating you are not afraid to transform themselves into hypocritical angels of light [2 Cor. 11.14], outwardly stars, inwardly darkness (so to speak), doomed with you to fall into the pit of hell. For I cannot see how those who "shine like the brightness of the firmament" (who of course are the ones who try to the best of their ability to imitate the integrity of those who, when you fell, held to the grace of their unchanging form) can ever be wrapped in your eternal darkness, for their names are written in heaven. Believe me, blackest Lemur,[31] they will never be found in the roll of your perdition (though you try to infect them with a thousand plagues of sin), since they have escaped from your gullet, like this saint of ours, through the hole in your jaw [Job 40.21].

11. But you, blessed martyr, who bore such tribulations, we cannot praise enough, while him who drove you to have to suffer them we cannot revile as he deserves nor can we persecute him with hatred equal to his hatred for us. We are very wretched and unblest trying to praise you, martyr, with our voices, when we are opposite to you in our ways, and glorifying you in our talk when we are different from you in our actions. You are glorified by your blessed crown, whereas we are accused by our guilty consciences, which fear and dread that He may say to one of us:

"Out of your own mouth do I judge you, O wicked servant [Lk. 19.22]. For if you had such a man, why were you so unappreciative of him? Why did you allow such a pearl to be stolen from you? Why did you not tenaciously guard a coin of such brightness? Why do you not make haste to do for innumerable sins of like damnation what you claim that he did even for one? If he by penitence, as you credibly assert, merited to receive not only pardon but the crown of martyrdom also, why do you unrepentant store up anger for yourself and a fire that will never be extinguished [Rom. 2.5]?"

But our weakness and frailty does this, pugnacious athlete, we confess; may your strength and constancy help us, I pray.

12. Someone may be surprised that I call you martyr so often, when you did not come to a bloody end, most saintly confessor. But he should rather be surprised, I say, that he does not remember that the Lord said to the sons of Zebedee, "You will drink my cup" [Mt. 20.23], though only one of them passed from this world with shedding of blood for Christ [Acts 12.2]; but the other underwent many sufferings for God,[32] as also did you, most blessed one, and, though summoned in peace, did not lack the glory of martyrdom; the same happened to not the least among Christ's excellent, the Levite Vincentius, unconquered before death, during death, and after death, as the tale of his sufferings shows, and also to many others. The tyrant's sword did not drive his soul from his body. But having eagerly surmounted terrible tortures and pains for Christ and having stalwartly undergone the trial of the blessed fight, as the beautiful poem about him tells, he was finally released into precious death and triumphantly gave up his soul to heaven, as also did St. Agathes.[33] "A sword shall pierce your own soul also" [Lk. 2.35], the just Simeon said to the blessed Mother of God, prophesying by this that she would undoubtedly undergo the martyrdom of grief, though not of death.

13. Rejoice therefore, martyr, rejoice, I say, be glad and exult and ever intercede with God for our wretchedness, we pray, though we do not deserve your intercession. If you spare your guilty servants gratuitously, you imitate the gentleness of Joseph, who once pardoned his brothers, who had sold him, with such mild yet true address [Gen. 45.5] — although we have not yet been able to apprehend any seller of your holy body; to have sold it was to imitate the crime of Judas the betrayer or the sacrilege of some criminal villain. But we weep, holy one, that you have so far been neglected by us (for shame!), that your venerable sepulchre could have been robbed in some way; such neglect also we do not deny was a nefarious crime. For who but a madman could neglect such a patron, even if he had the bodies of a thousand saints as well as yours nearby. Therefore, kind father, since we honor you with more devout love now you are absent than once we honored you when you were present, consider us (because this often happens) degenerate sons, or rather wicked servants, and forget our wickedness; do us this favor in return, we pray: do not desert us with your protection (though you deserted unworthy us in your removal), but being very present for us in Christ your head, do not cease by your merits to reconcile Him to us, not only for this guilt but also for every kind of guilt. This happened to you through our fault and negligence (and it would be wrong for us to deny it); but we cannot deny that it was done by the will and disposition of Him who moderates both the world and the heavens, whose arrangement no upstart has ever been able to oppose. For when you were pressed down by the mound of the sepulchre, He wanted you, we think, to be raised from the ground and placed in worthy state. For the crowd worships the bones of a celestial spirit more devoutly if they are not covered by the earth, but are beautified with the adornment of a mausoleum.

But if it really happened as is believed, there is no doubt that you are like the example of Joseph and his brothers, which I mentioned a little earlier; for he said to them in their fear: "Do not be afraid, for can we resist the will of God in anything? You meant evil against me, but God meant it for good, that he might exalt me" [Gen. 50.19]. Let not your exaltation then be our damnation (avert it, we pray), nor your removal our perdition. But, we ask, may your exaltation rather benefit any of us who with simple heart did not stand in the way of your exaltation — though perhaps he was so engloomed by the darkness of his own sins that he was driven by a sudden impulse, not remembering the admonition, "Let your gaze be straight before you" [Pr. 4.25], and forgetting the statement, "There is a way which seems right to a man, but its end is the way to death" [Pr. 16.25]. But since the Lord strengthens such faint-heartedness by saying, "If your eye is sound, your whole body will be full of light" [Mt. 6.22], may he be allowed, relying on your guidance, to come to one of the three cities of refuge [Jos. 20.2–7], between hope of pardon and fear of hell, so that, if there is need, he may be able to cry — and be heard — in the words of the psalmist: "Evils have encompassed me without number; my iniquities have overtaken me till I cannot see; they are more than the hairs of my head; my heart fails me; be pleased, O Lord, to deliver me" [Ps. 39.13–14].

Further, when this sun visible to mortal eyes goes on high drawn by its flaming horses, it gives mighty blessings to the earthborn. But of your light, O celestial star, Christ himself the Sun is the infusor; listen, let Him tell of His own doings in His own words: "I am going to him who sent me; let none of you ask me, Where are you going? But because I have said these things to you, sorrow has filled your hearts. Nevertheless, I tell you the truth; it is to your advantage that I go away" [Jn. 16.5]; and also: "When I am lifted from the earth, I shall draw all men to myself" [Jn. 12.32]. Rightly thankful for this, the Apostle said: "Even though we know Christ in the flesh, now we no longer know him" [2 Cor. 5.16]. Therefore, it is certain and cannot be doubted that, if faith in the saints does not suffer loss in death, much less does it suffer loss in absence; for this reason we unwaveringly trust that, if we follow your steps, your absence has benefited us and that though we know that we no longer have your dead body in our neighborhood along with countless others, yet we realize that God has granted that you, being truly holy, have been most gloriously transported to the place where the martyrdom of your trials is glorified night and day with due veneration.

But we believe that there is some little mitigation of blame, because we have now, late though it be, ceased treating you so unbecomingly, and have grown accustomed, on the teaching of others at least, to venerate you with worthy honor as we ought to have done before, to weep for you as a lost father, in weeping to love you more ardently, in loving you to honor you more often, in honoring you to pray to you more reverently. You have drawn us, martyr, so to speak, to you as you merited when you were exalted by God; you have drawn us, and though leaving us, holy one, you possess us the more securely, the more devoutly we venerate you. For every sensible man now frequents the remains of your ashes more religiously than he once revered the place that kept your entire saintly body along with the rest; and therefore, where our devotion to you, martyr, increases, the watchfulness of your piety towards us must increase also—nor should we despair of it. Those who dared to violate the sanctity of your relics, I urge to address their inner counsellor and earnestly ask of it what impulsive intention they acted upon in so great a crime, and to censure their own action in endangering him. For if in this action the "eye was sound" [Mt. 6.22] in pursuing their desire, they can rejoice, I say, that they have found an essential guide. But if otherwise, we can fear not a little, I think, that they are struck by the authority of him who says, "If anyone destroys the temple of God, God will destroy him" [1 Cor. 3.17]. In this case I rejoice at the words of whoever said (and how finely he spoke!): "Have charity and do whatever you wish."[34] For, as the other Apostle says, "Charity does not do evil" [1 Cor. 13.4]. Then it does nothing? Far from it. Listen to these true words: "Never is the love for God otiose. For it does great deeds if it exists: but if it is unwilling to act, then it is not love."[35]

14. These then, martyr, are the dispositions for the worship and veneration of your bones in the place where they are said to lie, and of your ashes where they are believed to rest; what sort of a reward any of those who took you away or who allowed you to be taken away can hope for from God can surely be conjectured. But we pray that you yourself will forgive both groups for their excesses against you, most holy protector, and that you will be an unfailing intercessor for us with our Lord Jesus Christ, the merciful Redeemer of the world and most just Judge not only of our actions but of our thoughts as well, who with the Father and the Holy Spirit lives and reigns as God for ever and ever. Amen.

24

CC Opera Minora 33–35   Verona Lent 963

[Rather preaches during Lent to the congregation of Verona.]

∾

Sermon I on Quadragesima

1. I urge and advise you along with me—if there are any in this congregation like me—to turn the ear of your mind to the words of the prophet, who says, "Recall it to mind, O transgressors" [Is. 46.8], and to ponder, each one of us, why he was created, why born, why reborn, why redeemed and at what price, whether he has given due thanks to his Creator, Maker, and Redeemer, and whether he has obeyed His most wholesome commandments worthily. If in this he does not find himself at fault (as I would desire), then, giving thanks to his Protector, let him rejoice *humbly*, not in pride attributing it to himself, and let him ceaselessly desire from Him a good end in this, and let him continually pray that he may never justly be called a transgressor.

2. But those who have done otherwise, I advise not to despair, but, remembering the countless examples of God's mercy over sinners, to speedily turn from their sinfulness while they are safe and sound, lest, if they are unwilling, while they can, they should be unable when they want to. Yet, if they do this, without a doubt they will at once raise up that old adversary against them, who, showing himself in his full strength against them, will try to embroil them in worse sins. But the apostle says, "Every man that competes in the contest abstains from everything" [1 Cor. 9.25]. Therefore, being about to compete against so vicious, cruel and cunning a tyrant, since these days in particular have been chosen both as a group and individually for doing this with God's help, let us abstain from all things which make him at all stronger and us at all weaker.

What these are, let the Apostle Peter say better: "I beseech you as strangers and pilgrims, abstain from fleshly lusts which war against the soul" [1 Pet. 2.11]. Lo, there is what makes us weak and him strong: fleshly lusts. If we do not abstain from these, we make our souls vulnerable. For since no one wars except *for* someone and here it is not expressly stated *for* whom fleshly lusts wage war, while they are said to war against the soul, clearly they are shown to war *for* the devil. For there is no other adversary of our souls than he who immediately enters them when God abandons them with good reason; God abandons them with good reason if they first have abandoned Him, though countless numbers who have abandoned Him He has in no way abandoned—though this more from mercy than from justice.

3. Since, then, fleshly lusts war for the devil against our souls, to prevent their commander from triumphing over us, let us oppose them with abstinence and with God's help we shall win the victory. And so, brethren, "let us be converted to the Lord with all our heart, with fasting and with weeping and with mourning" [Joel 2.12]. But from whom to whom do we urge you to turn, do you think? From the enemies of our souls, of course, fleshly lusts, to their ally, abstinence: from the devil, for whom they war, to the Lord, who night and day fights against him for us, if we are willing. If we wish to fight against him, let us strive to drive him forth far from us and to cast him from our hearts and not ourselves foster him within us. "He lieth under the shady trees," as the Lord says, "in the covert of the reed and fens" [Job 40.16].[36] The *shady trees* are the cunning, the *reeds* are the hypocrites, outwardly smooth, inwardly empty, the *fens* are the fornicators and their lustful desires. But we know, by the Lord's assurance, that no one is able to cast out this kind, either from himself or from another, except "by prayer and fasting" [Mk. 9.28]. But how can a man cast off the devil from him *by prayer* if he is one about whom it is said, "Whoever turns his ear from hearing the law, his prayer shall be abomination" [Pr. 28.9]? O, may our prayer, even if unheard, at least not be abomination! And likewise elsewhere, "Whoever turns his ears from the cry of the poor, he also shall cry himself but shall not be heard" [Pr. 21.13]. Here, in addition, something even deeper is meant, namely, that unless you help the poor man appealing to you, God does not hear you when you pray. How do you *fast* except by abstaining from sin, since the Lord says, "Ye shall not fast as ye do this day" [Is. 58.4] and the rest that follows?

In order, then, to expel the devil from our hearts, let us fast, let us pray, let us give alms, as far as we are able, but let us have God as witness that we have wanted to give alms beyond what we are able. For thus, with His help, we will be able to overcome our fleshly lusts together with him for whom they make war on our souls.

4. But someone says: "If we abstain from everything which our flesh desires, how do we live? Does not the hungry man desire to eat, the thirsty to drink, even if not extravagantly or to excess? Does not the man lacking sleep (to offer only these examples from the countless just and necessary needs) desire to sleep?"

To which we must reply that this injunction bans not the necessary needs but the extravagant, the unwholesome, the shameful, and those forbidden by God. Wherefore also the other apostle, Paul, says, "Make not provision for the flesh, to fulfill the lusts thereof" [Rom. 13.14]—by which surely we are commanded so to serve the necessities of the body that we do not subject the heart to any pleasure; otherwise, while the reason should be mistress and the flesh the handmaid, we are in danger of destroying the mistress for the sake of the handmaid and having the part that should obey give the orders and the part that should order obey.

But unless our abstinence is three-fold, it is altogether useless for perfect fruition: we should cease, first, from wicked thought, second, from foul word, and third, from perverse deed, for the love or fear of God, so that, cleansed with God's mercy and loving kindness, from all pollution of flesh and spirit, in these sacred days [Lent] at least, we can celebrate with joy and gladness the most holy Pasch which is to come after them, with the help of Him who with the Father and the Holy Spirit lives and reigns God for ever and ever. Amen.

25

CC Opera Minora 39–43   Verona Easter 963

[Rather makes an Easter address to the clergy of Verona, urging them to replace their malice with sincerity and truth.]

❦

Sermon I on the Pasch

1. Today, dear brothers, we are about to take up and serve to you, as is due, the Paschal Feast, that is, the sacred refreshment of that Lamb which His precursor

John pointed out with his finger, exclaiming, "Behold the Lamb of God, that takes away the sins of the world" [Jn. 1.29], (assuredly because he as a forerunner could only prefigure Him, not truly remit sins, because only He in the Godhead which is unique to Him, together with the Father and the Holy Spirit, is able to do this). Being about to solemnly handle today the Body and Blood of this Lamb and to pledge it to you, beloved, I ask that none of you take it amiss if we slip in some small quantity of field-lettuce [lactucae], since this too we do by God's command [Ex. 12.8; Num. 9.11]. Though, of course, it does no one any harm to be ignorant of the physical appearance of these herbs, or rather vegetables, it is a great impediment if one cannot recognize their spiritual quality and hold it in one's mind. The nature of this vegetable is said to bring tears to the eyes and to scour the teeth of anyone taking it, but the nature of what it signifies causes the inner eyes of the heart and body to be roused to a healthful grief. Those who lay claim to scientific expertise say also that if an eagle by some misadventure loses the sharpness of its sight, which is its greatest attribute, it recovers it with a taste of this herb.[37] The analogy is most pertinent: anyone who has contracted blindness of the inner vision by the persistency of his faults may strive to recover it by tasting such lettuce.

2. But now let us decorate the table which we have promised. Dear brothers, the most holy prophet said, "This day, which the Lord has made, let us rejoice and be glad in it" [Ps. 117.24]. But surely, brothers, the Lord likewise made yesterday also? Of course, but that day He consecrated to fasting, this one to joy; that day brought grief to his disciples, this one brought the greatest gladness. What then must we do, brothers? As reason shows, if yesterday we mourned with the disciples, today let us rejoice with them and all the saints. Nor should we fear that it will be said to us, "Woe to you that laugh now, for you shall mourn and weep" [Lk. 6.25], since because of our past fasting and mourning we are revived by the comfort of His words (spoken to the apostles before His Passion, just so spoken to us before the day of His Resurrection): "And you now therefore have sorrow, but I shall see you again and your heart shall rejoice, and your joy no man will take from you" [Jn. 16.22]. This was said to the apostles; it is also said to us. The apostles mourned the death—though very necessary for them—of Christ, for whose Resurrection they rejoiced with inestimable joy and immeasurable festivity. Yesterday we imitated their grief, today let us imitate their joy.

But if we wish to imitate them, let us take from them, I advise, the pattern of our joy. Tell us then, blessed apostle, summoned indeed after all the others but divinely caught up to the third heaven [2 Cor. 12.2–3] in a way which you know best, tell us, I say, satisfy our asking, on what grounds we ought to rejoice. "Christ our Passover," he said, "is sacrificed for us" [1 Cor. 5.7]. Not for any other reason? For we thought that that *sacrifice* was the same as that which the apostles had mourned as a death, whose mourning we imitated yesterday also. We ask, then, tell us, what we ought to do today and how we should act. He continues: "Therefore let us keep the feast"—that is, eat the flesh of the Lord and drink His blood—"not with the old leaven, neither with the leaven of malice and wickedness, but with the unleavened bread of sincerity and truth" [1 Cor. 5.7]. *And truth*, I repeat; why this? Because the same apostle also says elsewhere: "We have been buried with Christ by baptism into death, that just as Christ was raised up from the dead by the glory of the Father, even so we also should walk in newness of life. For if we have been planted together in the likeness of His death, we shall be in the likeness of His Resurrection also" [Rom. 6.4–5]. So, dear brothers, if in our actions we keep to what we believe, in this sense we are reborn in Christ, suffer in Christ, are raised from the dead in Christ, and for this we have the greatest reason for joy. Therefore, because the Lord made this day not for Himself alone but for us also, let us rejoice and be glad in it [Ps. 117.24].

Behold, this most proper meal, which I promised you, of the Paschal Feast has now been explained to you and in a while is going to be served to you. But what do we do about the promised field-lettuce, my sons? Let it be there too; let it clean the tartar from our teeth, that is, the blockages from our minds caused by the accumulation of our sins. Let it cause floods of tears to flow from the eyes of those that come to eat the Lamb. "Not in the old leaven," he says— in other words, not in the guilt of previous sin nor in the desire of committing the same or another, that is, that you should not be in the same state of sin today as you were yesterday—"neither with the leaven of malice or wickedness"— as if he were saying: "Change your past evil for good, abandon your wickedness if you wish to eat the flesh of the Lamb of God and to drink His blood." He continues: "But with the unleavened bread of sincerity and truth." Understand it, I urge, understand it, brothers, if any of you here are perhaps like me, sin-ners, that is, and full of evil. If you wish to rejoice wholesomely, rejoice in the Lord [Phil. 4.4], not in extravagant wantonness, not in lustful sensuality, not in gluttony and drunkenness, not in worldly songs. If you wish to rejoice, "Serve the Lord with fear, with trembling rejoice in him" [Ps. 2.11]. If you wish to celebrate a proper Pasch, celebrate it with unleavened bread. If you ask what is *unleavened*, I reply, "The unleavened bread of sincerity and truth." For the worst leaven is the hypocrisy of pretense, the most poisonous leaven is deliberate falsehood; for since leaven is derived from the word meaning *ferment*, we can suppose that that malice, that wickedness, that moral state of old Adam (since we can know that all evil is meant), is nothing more than the opposite of sin-cerity and truth, namely, deceitfulness, which leads men to cheat their neighbor, with which the hearts of the fraudulent rage inextinguishably. Since, therefore, the desire to do something evil is a strong one, abstain, brothers, I urge you, from it, that is, deceitfulness, in proportion as it offends the majesty of God and stains the divinity of the Pasch. For if it were not so, the apostle would not have commended these two virtues, sincerity and truth, so highly by condemning their opposites, in the Feast of the Paschal Festival, repeating them in different words and saying: "Therefore let us keep the feast, not with the old leaven, neither with the leaven of malice and wickedness, but with the unleavened bread of sincerity and truth." For the man with ill will in his heart in no way celebrates the Paschal Feast, since no one has glory in the highest with God or true peace on earth with men except he who has goodwill in his heart [Lk. 2.14].

4. This most tart truthfulness and truthful tartness, dear brothers, I call the field-lettuce; I pray that it may change the qualities of our hearts and bodies when tasted by the spirit; while it stirs the heart to sighing and the body to tears, let it stir both of these to abandon the objectives of ill will. Without doubt this will come about, I believe, if what the Lord commanded us concerning the celebration of the Pasch through His minister in the Decalogue, we strive to apply also to the properties of this lettuce. "And thus you shall eat it," he said, "with your loins girded, with your shoes on your feet, and your staff in your hand; and you shall eat it in haste" [Ex. 12.11]. What stricter or sterner words could be said to him who, understanding these things, remembers that he has in no way observed them in celebrating the Pasch that is past? For anyone who has not given ear to the words of the psalmist, who says, "Gird your sword upon your thigh, most mightily" [Ps. 44.4][38] — that is, most bravely — but effeminately giving himself up to wantonness has dared to come forward to take the body and blood of the Lamb of God, whoever has not followed the examples of the saints who have passed on in Christ, whoever has not defended himself with the *staff* of discipline against the roaring lion [1 Pet. 5.8] (that is, the devil seeking to devour him), whoever has not *hastened* with pious longing — that is, desired to be dissolved and to be with Christ [Phil. 1.23] — how today he can presume to take the Body and Blood of the Lord without wailing and sighing, I do not see, unless I am to believe him hardened by deadly despair or deceived with false hope of this sort. But I urge him not to do so; I tell him not to despair, I beg him not to deceive himself with false hope any longer. Let him hear what follows and sigh and wail, "It is the Lord's Passover" [Ex. 12.11], as if He had said, "He passes over from the devil to Christ who *girds up his loins* against wantonness, who *strengthens his steps* and actions with the examples of the saints, who *with the staff of discipline* defends himself against the devil, who with his prayers *hastens* to reach the Heavenly Kingdom." And so this man alone is allowed to celebrate the Pasch of the Lord, and not even he is allowed to celebrate it without field-lettuces, that is, the remembrance of past sins and the most beneficial outpouring of tears.

5. But now we must return to the apostle, to let him conclude the great undertaking which we entered upon, forgetful of our own inability (though he is quite able to): "Christ, our Passover, is sacrificed for us" [1 Cor. 5.7], which was to say, so we think, "To this end was Christ sacrificed for us, that He himself might be our passing-over to Himself and himself might be our only joy." Let Him therefore be so; let each one of us pray for it, I advise. "Let us rejoice and be glad in Him" [Ps. 117.24]. For He himself is our peace [Eph. 2.14], our light, our leader, our day, our sun, our salvation, our life, our resurrection, our true joy, our everlasting blessedness, our eternal happiness, our unceasing gladness, and finally He himself is the day which the Lord has made [Ps. 117.24] — not truly made but begotten — and this in a way that cannot be described. "Let us rejoice and be glad in Him." Let the joy of our table also reach to the poor people of Christ; let their needs be supplied by our abundance. Let the poor also help each other in turn; what is lacking to one, let another give, if he has it; if he does not have it, at least let him want to have given it, so that Christ our Paschal Lamb who was sacrificed may rejoice for us in all our doings. And let this day of ours be one which the Lord has made, so that we may be able to rejoice in it now and for ever, and also be able so to take His Body and Blood, that this may bring us, not to judgment, as, alas, happens to many, but to eternal health, as happens to the blessed. And may He assist in our desires and bless our actions, Who gave His only Son in death, Who with Him and the Holy Spirit lives and reigns for ever and ever. Amen.

26

CC Opera Minora 47–53   Verona Ascension 963

[Rather addresses the clergy of Verona on the Feast of the Ascension.]

Sermon I on the Ascension

1. I would like you all to remember, dear brothers, that my work has reached this point at this time, that borrowing matter for my speech from the testimonies of the orthodox Fathers, I recommended to your brotherhood the actions we should take, the reasons for those actions, and the behavior we should observe, in the forty days preceeding the Lord's Resurrection.[39] I recommended to you how we should rejoice and be glad in the Pasch,[40] and how after the Pasch, or rather in the fifty days of the Pasch, we should stop our fasting and sing "alleluia" day and night. But we absolutely must not return to the vices which have been overcome by fasting, prayers, and alms, with the grace of God helping us so that we ought not to despair; otherwise, to be sure, it would be that, having left Egypt, having eaten the lamb, having crossed the Red Sea, having tasted of the manna from heaven, we would be seeking again the Egypt we left behind, in longing for Taphnitic[41] meats and pumpkins and onions, cheating ourselves of the promise of the land flowing with milk and honey, and, together with those of whom many thousands perished in the desert, undergoing the damnation of eternal perdition [Num. 11.4–6, 26–64]. With a view to this I have been able to find nothing better to recommend than that we should day and night sing "alleluia," that is, that we should cry "Praise the Lord" to each other, and all try to do this without ceasing. For truly, what room is there for sin when there is no letting up of God's praises?

St. Gregory first, and afterwards St. Mamert, archbishop of Vienna, thought it advisable from like necessity to institute certain litanies [*letanias*] within this Quinquagesima. Since the Latin language translates *litanies* as *prayers,* does this in any way clash with that remark of the Lord's, "Can the children of the bride-chamber mourn as long as the bridegroom is with them?" [Mt. 9.15]? At what time is God prayed to more solemnly than during days of festivity? If one lives soberly, justly, and piously [Tit. 2.12] in the Pasch, does this in any way clash with what the apostle urges when, after saying that Christ Himself is our Pasch, he continues, "And so let us keep the feast"? For he adds, castigating those who are enslaved to drunkenness, gluttony, and other vices, "Not with the old leaven" — that is, not in the guilt of unshriven offence and the desire of repeating crimes that have been committed or of perpetrating others — "neither with the leaven of malice and wickedness, but with the unleavened bread of sincerity and truth" [1 Cor. 5.7–8].

If, then, we cease from gluttony and drunkenness, if likewise we abstain for the love of God from even licit intercourse during these three days, if we refrain from frolic and wantonness, from worldly songs and amusements, if, finally, ceasing from all servile work (that is, service of the devil) as we have rightly done during the Lord's Days of Quadragesima, we are careful to serve God on these three days, then what harm do we do to the joy of the Pasch, since, in these days of the Lord's Resurrection also, we have not neglected our worship in any detail (but only if we have done what we ought)?

But since, as I have often said, it is necessary for those who are to be refreshed by the Body and Blood of the Lord to make a *Parasceve*—that is, some preparation—lest they assume the gift of so great a sacrament unworthily, and we can think that the glorious vigils which precede the ceremonies were invented for this very purpose, what harm does it do if, in so great a feast, in place of vigils we use these three days to atone for any sin we have committed in the joyous days of the Pasch and at no time cease from singing "Alleluia" and ever rejoicing and being glad in the Lord? For since the Apostle James says, "For in many things we all offend" [Jas. 3.2], who would dare to boast that in so many days and nights he has done nothing which needs to be atoned for so that he can worthily take part in the celebration of so great a feast?

2. Now that the struggle for our common salvation has proceeded this far, dear brothers, we have arrived within this Quinquagesima with no letup of singing "alleluia," of being glad also and rejoicing, at the day of Our Lord's most glorious Ascension which does not allow us to be silent. How can we be silent when we remember the most wonderful miracle of all miracles, if we look at man alone, that a man, not in an angelic vehicle as Elijah once was [2 Kg. 2.11], nor in winged flight as our hero of poetry,[42] but in the full solid body of a grown man—that is, of about thirty-three years of age (as the apostle vouches will happen to us sometime, saying, "Till we all come . . . unto a perfect man, unto the measure of the stature of the fulness of Christ" our Lord [Eph. 4.13])—is raised up while speaking and taken up into a cloud, in the sight of worthy witnesses, with angels standing by and saying that so He will come again to judge all the quick and the dead left here from the beginning to the end of the world [Acts 1.9–11; 2 Tim. 4.1]? Who can communicate this with sufficient praise or praise it with sufficient communication? For we fail in our wonder if we try to picture God remaining within carrying the man, whom He took from us for us. We ought to give fitting thanks—if that were possible—for His Mercy alone; for the rest cannot be spoken because we utter them better in silence than in speech. Let us turn the service of our mouth to the great promise of His ineffable clemency, the promise which we heard just now in the Gospel, "Whoever believes and is baptized shall be saved" [Mk. 16.16]. Thanks be to God, shouts everyone; for we believe and have been baptized in the name of the Father and of the Son and of the Holy Spirit. We all say this, we all hope that we will be saved by means of this, we truly believe and confess that without this no one can be saved.

But about whom is Peter, to whom this was spoken, speaking—Peter, to whom particularly the instruction had been given with the others to "go into all the world and preach the Gospel unto every creature" [Mk. 16.15]—about whom, I say (if it is so), does the Apostle Peter say: "It had been better for them not to have known the way of truth, than, after they had known it, to turn from the holy commandment" [2 Pet. 2.21]? About those, we can very rightly suppose, of whose faith let us hear what the Apostle James feels: "Faith, if it has no works, is dead, being alone" [Jas. 2.17]; and again, "Those who confess that they know God, but in their works they deny Him" [Tit. 1.16]. These, to be sure, are those who destroy with their actions the faith which they support with their words. We have greatly to fear that the Lord also speaks of such when He says: "When the unclean spirit is gone out of a man, it walks through dry places seeking rest; and finding none, it says, 'I will return to my house whence I came out.' Then it goes and takes seven other spirits, more wicked than itself; and they enter in and dwell there; and the last state of that man is worse than the first" [Lk. 11.24–26].

If these truths did not pertain to those who confess that they believe and are baptized, where would be that sentence of the Lord's in which He said, "For many are called but few are chosen" [Mt. 20.16], and also, "Not every one that says unto me, Lord, Lord, shall enter into the kingdom of heaven" [Mt. 7.21]? For who are the *called* if not those who have entered the Church through baptism? Who are the few *chosen*, if not those who in their lives have held to the sacrament which they have received in faith? Who are the not-chosen, if not those who have not kept the promises they have made? What did they promise? Let each of you go over in his mind that which he promised, or which was promised on his behalf, before he was baptized. It is short, it can easily be recalled. If he observes it, he can rejoice secure in his salvation; if not, he has sinned. First let him desist, that is, cease sinning, then let him make his penitence. "For the kingdom of heaven is at hand" [Mt. 3.2; 2 Cor. 5.17] should be said to him too: that is, with the crossing over, or rather flight, of all earthly things, the heavenly kingdom is at hand, but only for those who, with the help of God's grace, have merited by their energetic actions to reach it.

3. Who these are, our same most pious Promiser shows as He continues: for when He had said, "He that does not believe shall be damned" [Mk. 16.16], in order to separate by some indications the believers from the non-believers, He added: "And these signs shall follow them that believe: in my name shall they cast out devils; they shall speak with new tongues; they shall take up serpents; and if they drink any deadly thing, it shall not hurt them; they shall lay hands on the sick, and they shall recover." What does this mean, brothers? For who literally and materially does these things today? No one, beloved, no one. Then does no one believe? Far from it. For as many believe as the psalmist's words indicate: "I have announced and have spoken it, they have multiplied beyond number" [Ps. 39.6]. How then do they believe, since only those are said to believe who do these things, but these do not do them?

Well, they certainly do them, some do them, but not materially and literally, but that much the more beneficially in proportion as the spirit is separate from the body. For they *cast out devils* in the name of Christ who in His virtue drive out from their hearts the vices which devils put into them; they *speak with new tongues*, when, abandoning blasphemy, their mouths resound the praise of God and their speech utters things of benefit; they *take up serpents*, when what that ancient Serpent tempts them to do, they in no wise do; and when they feel the devil's temptation within them, but do not do what he tempts them to do, then indeed *deadly is their drink* but it will not harm them. "For we shall all stand," says the apostle, "before the judgment-seat of Christ, so that each may show the attributes of his body, according as he used them, whether for good or ill" [Rom. 14.10; 2 Cor. 5.10]. They *lay hands on the sick* so that they recover, who hasten to make up for the sins which they have committed by zealously pursuing good so that they may progress to a better state.

Lo, there is the revelation, there is the indication, there is the distinction, of believers and non-believers, brothers. Let him who recognizes any of these signs in himself say that he believes; whoever does not, I urge him rather to make himself ready for believing than to boast that he believes.

4. Also the Lord says to the blind man, "Do you believe *in* the Son of God?" [Jn. 9.35] with a preposition, and to the Samaritan woman, "Woman, believe me" [Jn. 4.21] without a preposition; but here it is used absolutely, "He that believes," and no *God* or *in God* is added; so it can be assumed that two things are demanded, that we *believe* God and that we *believe in* God. He *believes in* God who believes catholically: he *believes* God who obeys His commandments. To do both, and to be baptized in the orthodox manner, brings us, thanks be to God, the greatest security. "For he will undoubtedly be saved if only he endure to the end" [Mt. 10.22, 24.13]. O, may no one be found in this our people who does not believe the truth of what he hears in St. John's Gospel, that is, "All things were made by Him, and without Him was not anything made that was made" [Jn. 1.3]. For they are non-believers in the rest so long as they do not believe this one thing and think that the weather can be made by a man, though the psalmist proclaims quite clearly, "Fire and hail, snow and vapors, wind and storm fulfilling His word" [Ps. 148.8] (that is, the word of the Lord), and in another psalm about God: "He gives snow like wool, He scatters the hoarfrost like ashes. He casts forth his ice like morsels; who can stand before His cold?" [Ps. 147.16–17]. How then does he believe in God who does not believe that God is the creator of all things? How does he believe God who gives a deaf ear to Him when He proclaims, "See now that I am alone and there is no other god but me; I will kill and I will make alive; I will wound and I will heal; neither is there any that can deliver out of my hand" [Dt. 32.39]?

Pay good attention, beloved. For against those who say that a wicked man or devil makes the weather, scatters hailstones, destroys vineyards and fields, sends lightning, kills herds and flocks and even men, against those is directed what He says: "*I* kill and *I* make alive" [Dt. 32.39]. Against those who claim that they themselves change the weather by their incantations is directed, "Neither is there any that can deliver out of *my* hand" [Dt. 32.39]. But even though we read that Elijah for three years stopped the rain by prayer and by prayer brought it back again when he wished [1 Kg. 18]; that he sent fire from heaven over the impious prophets of the impious king; that Samuel made thunder to crash in the summer time against all nature [1 Sam. 12.1 ff.]; and that many other saints either of the Old Testament or of the New made signs appear from sky or earth or sea: even so, they did not do these things of themselves, but God did them acting through them. Faith itself did this, about which the Lord Himself speaks to the Apostles thus: "If you had faith as a grain of mustard seed, you would say to this mountain, Remove hence to yonder place in the sea, and it would obey you" [Mt. 17.19]. The devil cannot do this, nor any evil follower of his. But God does this through His servants when He so decides, and since He is supremely good, He does it beneficially in proportion as He is good.

5. But let us return to the Feast of the Lord's Ascension. "When He had spoken these things," says the excellent narrator of the great occasion, "while they beheld, He was taken up; and a cloud received Him out of their sight. And while they looked steadfastly toward heaven as He went up, behold, two men stood by them in white apparel, who also said, 'Men of Galilee, why do you stand gazing up into heaven? This same Jesus, which is taken up from you into heaven, shall so come in like manner as you have seen him go into heaven'" [Acts 1.9–11].

Here, listener, pay attention for a while, please. In Galilee first Christ is seen arising, to men of Galilee alone Christ is shown ascending, to them He is promised to return [Mt. 28.7, 10.16]. But who are or have been or will be men of Galilee except those who have lived or do now live or will live in Galilee in future ages? *Galilee* is translated as "a crossing-over," as we have it from the Fathers. How do we know this? Twice, or rather four times, this was done. Omitting the first, let us speak about the other three. The sons of Zebedee crossed over from their father to Christ [Mt. 4.21], Christ crossed over rising from the sepulchre to them, and finally they crossed over when they went to the mountain where He had directed them [Mt. 28.16], and in their sight He was raised from there into heaven. Let him who desires to follow Him to that place cross over from the devil to Him; let him consider that He died and was buried for him; let him rejoice that by His Resurrection he has been restored and by His Ascension he has been carried into heaven, but only if he anchors his desire most surely on Him.

Therefore, let each one of us, beloved, strive that, just as Christ today with our body ascended heaven, so, in whatever way we can, we individually may ascend in our hopes, cross over in our longing, struggle to reach there in our action. Wonderful to relate, we can ascend heaven even through our vices, if we strive to trample them down, that is. In fact, we make a sort of ladder for ourselves out of them, if we overcome them by correction. They raise us if they are under us; they overcome us if they are over us. Our flesh ascended heaven in Christ; let our soul follow it in desire. The soul of Christ desires our souls to be transferred there; let us work together with His desire. It is God who moves the soul; the Omnipotent has abundant mercy and grace; let us not doubt about the possibility, if we are not wanting in the will. Our virtues alone He wishes us to carry in place of scrip; our vices, like deadly want and constant hunger, the noxious opposite of our ascension, we are to leave here. While remaining here, also, let us never cease from hastening there. For without a doubt we will come to where Christ is with our flesh, if we never cease from longing for Him, with the help of the mercy of Him, who with the Father. . . .

27

CC Opera Minora 57–61   Verona Pentecost 963

[Rather addresses the clergy on the day of Pentecost.]

Sermon I on Pentecost

1. Alas, brothers, what am I to do? If I am silent, I cheat myself in the very duty I should have discharged, I am guilty of cheating you in it, and I also hide from myself the meaning and importance of this day. But if I proceed to speak, I am afraid I may fail before the magnitude of the thing about which I want to speak. But I will do what I can, for I believe there is no one more bound to do so.

Today, the Pentecost is fulfilled, brothers. What have I said? Today, the fifty days of the Pasch are ended. So what? Let him who knows say: "Better is the end of prayer than the beginning thereof" [Eccle. 7.9]. Let him attend who can. "For he that endures to the end," said the Lord, "shall be saved" [Mt. 10.22, 24.13]. Happy are they who have observed these fifty days as they ought to be observed, and have never ceased from spiritual *alleluia*, and even in sleep have not neglected it. But if these desire to be saved, let them today show their devotion and endurance, I urge.

Today is the fiftieth day from the Resurrection of the Lord, the tenth from His Ascension. Great mystery and ineffable gift [2 Cor. 9.15]! Today is the fiftieth day from that on which we arose with Christ, the tenth from that on which we ascended heaven with Him. Of whom am I speaking? Of those, to be sure, whom the apostle forthrightly addresses: "If you have risen with Christ, seek those things which are above, where Christ sits on the right hand of"—that is, in equality with—"God. Set your affection on things above, not on things on the earth. For you are dead"—that is, immune from sin—"and your life is hidden with Christ in God. For when Christ who is our life shall appear, then you also will appear with Him in glory" [Col. 3.1–4]. Happy are those who belong to this group, unhappy are those who fall forever from their company, for they will appear not with Christ in glory but with the devil in everlasting damnation.

2. Assuming, however, that we are still of their company ("For man," says someone, "does not know whether he is worthy of love or hate, but everything is kept uncertain for the future" [Eccle. 9.1–2]), let us say without despairing of ourselves that today is the fiftieth day from that on which we arose with Christ, the tenth from that on which we ascended heaven with Christ. What do we expect today? Gifts, to be sure, allotments of blessings [1 Cor. 12.4], the joys of all the beatitudes. What are those? Let the apostle set it forth: "The love of God is shed abroad in our hearts by the Holy Spirit which has been given to us" [Rom. 5.5]. But to what purpose has it been given? As a pledge, without a doubt. For just as here "we have no continuing city" [Heb. 13.14], so neither do we have a sure beatitude. But how do we know that we have received the Holy Spirit as a pledge? Because the same apostle says: "Who also has given to us the *pledge* of the Spirit" [2 Cor. 5.5]. Lo, there we have the knowledge of the receipt of the pledge. How do we know that we have received it today? Let Luke, the physician and historian, testify: "And when the day of Pentecost was fully come, all the disciples were with one accord in one place" [Acts. 2.1]. In what place? "And while they looked steadfastly toward heaven as He went up," he had previously stated, "behold, two men stood by them in white apparel, who also said, 'Men of Galilee, why do you stand gazing up into heaven? This same Jesus which is taken up from you into heaven, shall so come in like manner as you have seen Him go into heaven.' Then they returned to Jerusalem from the mount called Olivet which is from Jerusalem a sabbath day's journey. And when they were come in, they went up into an upper room, where abode both Peter and James, and John, and Andrew, Philip, and Thomas, Bartholomew and Matthew, James the son of Alphæus, and Simon Zelotes, and Judas the brother

of James. These all continued with one accord in prayer and supplication, with the women, and Mary, the mother of Jesus, and with His brethren" [Acts 1.10–14].

So, when they were all in that place, "Suddenly, there came a sound from heaven as of a rushing mighty wind, and it filled all the house where they were sitting, and there appeared unto them cloven tongues like as of fire, and it sat upon each of them. And they were all filled with the Holy Spirit, and began to speak with other tongues, as the Spirit gave them utterance" [Acts 2.2–4].

O, how the mystery of the Old Testament here calls to the mystery of the New [cf. Ps. 41.8]! How the older agrees with the newer! On the fiftieth day after the sacrifice of the Lamb and the crossing of the Red Sea, the Decalogue was given to Moses on Mount Sinai [Ex. 19.16–20]. On the fiftieth after the Resurrection of Christ the Holy Spirit was sent upon the Apostles. The fiftieth is the year of release [Num. 36.4]; our fiftieth day is consecrated to grace. On that day, God the Son of God descended on the mountain; on this day of ours, God the Holy Spirit of the Father and the Son was present in full sight in the tongues of fire. Both these miracles were fulfilled by the Trinity. In the former, the Father promised the Son to Moses; in the latter, the Holy Spirit sent by the Father and the Son and proceeding from them, flowed over the Apostles with spontaneous power. There, the thunder and the voices and the smoking mountain [Dt. 5.22]; here, the men inflamed with different tongues, the Apostles, that is, burning with the flames of divine fire.

Finally, this is the fiftieth day of the Lord's Resurrection, the day which all the patriarchs and prophets, while decreeing that all the other days of Passover should be revered, singled out in particular for celebration. Tobias shows this, most clear-sighted in his blindness [Tob. 14.1]. The apostle shows this, summoned to the sublime reaches of the third heaven [2 Cor. 12.2]. "I went," said the former, "on the festal day of Pentecost, holy day of the weeks" [Tob. 1.6, 2.1]. Blessed Paul is said to have hurried to celebrate this day at Jerusalem [Acts 20.16], because he knew it outshone all other days. "Holy day of the weeks," he said. Count carefully, I say, and you will find that from the Pasch to this our most holy day of Pentecost is just *seven* weeks, if I am not mistaken. Read the prophet and you will find that the *seven*-form Spirit rested upon the branch growing out of the root of Jesse [Is. 11.1–3].

4. And who is that Spirit if not the one who descended over the Lord in a dove, over the apostles in a fire [Mt. 3.16]? And why did he appear over the Lord in a dove and over the apostles in a fire if not because the gentle Lord in His coming wished to be shown to men by a gentle sign, but in the sending of the apostles to announce His judgment He shows with what terror He comes to judge and, lest He be thought mild, comes with a mightier sound? And why

did He show the tongues of fire if not in order to show that His servants would have to be both burning in their love and most ready in their speech, so that they might preach (as we recently heard in the Gospel reading) with the truth with which they knew it had been spoken? And what is this, brothers? "Jesus said to His disciples," says the Evangelist, "If a man loves me he will keep my words" [Jn. 14.23], and the rest. Who having a fiery tongue would dare muddle that command with sophistic subterfuge? It is clear; let it be plainly put: There is no compromise; either we love God or we do not. If we love Him, we do what He commands. If we do not love Him, we do not keep His commandments. If we love Him, we are loved by Him. If not, even though we may fear Him mechanically, let us not presume to suppose that He loves us. But let us not despair of its happening. For it is said of Him: "Thou hast mercy on all things, Lord, and hatest nothing that Thou hast made" [Wisd. 11.24–25]. There is no truer word. God does not hate what He has made in you but He hates what you yourself do to your own detriment, and for this reason He is so benign, so merciful, so ready to forgive those who have been converted, that we know that He does not hate our substance, which He has made, but rather abhors our wickedness. If, with His help, we try to imitate Him in this, then clearly, when we are angry with one another, we should not hate each other for that reason but rather hold in hatred the evil which we recognize in one another.

And so, since our love can turn to hate and our hate to love, we love God that much the more fixedly and determinedly the more we recognise that His will is the same as Himself. Wherefore no limit is put on our love for Him, but on our love for each other there is this condition imposed, that we should love our neighbor as ourselves [Mt. 22.39], that is, that besides other things we should desire them to be such as we ought to be ourselves. Let it be enough that I have said only this concerning the Gospel reading.

Let us turn to the announcement of today's feast. Just as, brothers, we speak of a Song of Songs and of a King of Kings, so this day is the Feast of Feasts, in fact, the cause of all feasts. For Christ was born that He might suffer; He suffered that He might die; He died that He might rise from the dead; He rose that He might raise up to Heaven the flesh which He had taken from us for us; He carried it there that He might make it immortal and ever-blessed. Because this could not happen except by the gift of the Holy Spirit—for unless we were made new men by being regenerated by baptism, we could in no way be saved remaining in our old state; but in no way could we be baptized except in the Holy Spirit and with fire [Mt. 3.11]—He sent the Holy Spirit to us today in tongues of fire, so that, baptized and speaking about God and burning with love of Him and of our neighbor, we might at some time be transferred there where we could in no way be transferred without love.

"Now if any man," as the apostle says, "has not the spirit of Christ, he is none of His" [Rom. 8.9]. But whoever is none of His must not share, it follows, in His kingdom. But since the possession of the Holy Spirit itself is an indication of His love—the same apostle says, "For the love of God is shed abroad in our hearts by the Holy Spirit which is given to us" [Rom. 5.5]—we can recognise the more certainly whether anyone has the Holy Spirit the more we see him burning in his love. "But whoever," says the apostle, "has this world's good, and sees his brother in need, and shuts up his bowels of compassion from him, how dwells the love of God in him?" [1 Jn. 3.17]. This being the case, the proof of love without a doubt is the exhibition of one's work, as Gregory says.[43] The exhibition of one's work is the indication of the Holy Spirit, which we received today among the apostles, as is said in the psalm thus: "When He ascended on high, He led captivity"—that is, our flesh once held captive by the devil along with our souls—"captive and gave gifts to men" [Eph. 4.8; cf. Ps. 67.19]—that is, gave the joys of the Holy Spirit to the apostles on this day, Who with the Father and the same Spirit is blessed for ever and ever. Amen.

28

Weigle, Epist. 71–106   Verona November 963

On Contempt of the Canons

[Rather writes to Bishop Hubert of Parma, discussing the authority of a bishop as laid down by the canons and showing how the strife between some of the clergy and himself is due to their rejection of those canons. He recounts some of the abuses not only of the lower clergy but even of his fellow-bishops — gaming, licentiousness, dissension, and pride. The Ballerini call the work *De Contemptu Canonum* from the title in the index of the Laon manuscript.][1]

∽

To his fellow-bishop Hubert, venerable lord in Christ, Rather, a sinner.

1. Your urbane lordship knows, I think, that sentence of the orator: "To strive in vain and to pursue only that object to the point of exhaustion is the height of madness."[2] Though I agree that it is so, I do not stop doing just that. When the rebellious clergy once rose against me[3] in their folly, they left me no part of that office, about which Christ once said to a certain person, "Feed my sheep" [Jn. 21.17], except the rights of ordination and consecration, going so far as to expel me in public.[4] I therefore undertook to assemble the following relevant matter from the sacred canons as an aid to the memory, little though it is and culled from other sources, though to no purpose. After you have seen it, you will be able to know my intentions in attempting so great a labor, and to judge to what extent I have been successful.

2. The beginning of these trifles is as follows:[5]

In the canons of the apostles, chapter 39: "Let the bishop have care of all Church business, and let him manage it as though God were watching."

Item: "We instruct that the bishop have the property of the Church in his control. For if the precious souls of men have been entrusted to him, it is much more obligatory for him to take care of the finances in such a way that under his direction everything is dispensed to the poor by means of the priests and deacons, and administered with all respect and attention. From these funds let him take for himself what is needed for his necessities and for the use of itinerant brothers, so that he can lack nothing at all. For God's law commands that those who serve at the altar be fed from the altar [1 Cor. 9.13], because not even a soldier takes up arms against the enemy with his own resources."

Item: "Nothing should be done without the permission of the bishop."

From the letter of Pope Clement: "All the faithful, and all priests, deacons, and other clergy in particular, must note that they should do nothing without the permission of their own bishop. That is, let not any priest in his parish conduct masses without his order, nor hold baptism, nor do anything without his permission. Similarly, the other orders, both greater and lesser, should do what must be done with his approval; they should not leave their parish without his permission, nor on arriving in it presume to stay. Their souls are entrusted to him; for that reason they must do everything with his consent and nothing without it."

Again, in the Antioch Council, chapter 9: "Let each bishop have control of his parish, to govern according to the respect befitting individuals and to supervise all the possessions which are under his power."

Again, chapter 24: "All Church property should be kept with every care and good attention and faith in God, who sees and judges all things. This also is to be handled at the behest and direction of the bishop, to whom are committed the people and the souls which are congregated within the Church."

Again, chapter 25: "The bishop should have control of all Church business to make dispensation to all who are in need with the highest respect and fear of God. Let him take his share of what he needs — but only of what he needs — to meet his own necessities and those of the brothers whom he supports, in such a way that they be not deprived of anything by any circumstance, according to what the holy apostle says: 'Having food and clothing, let us be content with these' [1 Tim. 6.8]."

In the decretals of Pope Gelasius, no. 27: "Just as it will be the priest's business to pay out to the ministers of the Church the full amount that is laid down, so the clergy should know that they must not insolently demand more than the sum delegated."

In the canons of Gangra, chapters 7–8: "If anyone wants to take or give away the offerings of a church with baptismal right outside of it without the knowledge of the bishop or him to whom these offices have been committed, or does this without his consent, let him be anathema."

Again: "If anyone gives the offerings of the Church excepting the bishop or the person who has been appointed by him to dispense them, let both the giver and receiver be anathema."

In the canons of Chalcedon, chapter 26: "Since certain persons are handling the Church's resources besides the bishops' appointees, let those who do so be punished with the rebuke of the canons."

Again, chapter 8: "Concerning the clergy who are in hostels, monasteries, and martyrs' shrines, which are under the control of the bishop of single cities: Let the clergy who are put in charge of almshouses or who are appointed to administer monasteries or martyrs' shrines, remain in the control of the bishops of the individual cities according to the traditions of the holy Fathers and let them not in insolence break away from their bishop. Those who dare to depart from this structure in any way and do not obey their proper bishop, if they are clergy, will be liable to the rebuke of the canons, but if they are lay or monks, they will be deprived of communion."

Again, from the letter of Pope Urbanus: "The Church's resources in the past were in the control of the bishops who hold their place in the Church of the Apostle and they are still so today and must be in the future."

Concerning monasteries and convents both of monks and nuns from the decrees of Pope Eugenius' Council, chapter 24. and again in the same words from those of the Fourth Council of Pope Leo, chapter 23: "Let the resources be managed by the attention of the bishops to whose diocese they belong to be put to the use for which they have been established, so that the due food and other perquisites are rendered to those who want them, so that those who give their time to God may not be in want or necessity, but with all worries removed may be able to remain in God's service with pure hearts."

3. While I barked these out rather indiscretely (inasmuch as I was chattering to no purpose), I began again to argue with myself like this: But why like certain fools do I labor to emphasize the point with a thousand testimonies when one would suffice? For ask anyone the source of that old tradition of calling bishops of the Church "shepherds" [*pastores*]. Was it not the usual practice of the patriarchs and prophets to *tend the flocks* and they applied the word to the spiritual aspects of this world of ours? And did not the Supreme Leader of shepherds say to the man who tried to question Him, "I am the good shepherd" [Jn. 10.11]? And so that you may know that he who is shepherd of the Lord's flock is consequently the *bishop*, listen to the words of him who says: "For you were straying like sheep but have now returned to the shepherd and bishop [*episcopus*] of your souls" [1 Pet. 2.25]. Our Lord is followed in order by Peter, whom, when meaning

to establish him as bishop (if I may say so), He carefully asked if he loved Him more than the rest [Jn. 21.15–17], obviously to make it clear that the chief criterion for feeding a rational flock is the strength of charity, the love, that is, of God and the love of the neighbor committed to him by God. Three times He asked and three times Peter said that He knew that he loved Him, and three times also the Lord said to him, "Feed my sheep." That is to say: be the shepherd of my intelligent sheep, that is, bishop of the people that believe. Whether that tendance is single or multi-formed, bodily or spiritual, or both, no one should expect to hear from me. One should ask those eminent teachers who have written truthful holy books on the Gospels. If they agree that any physical responsibility attaches to those who in the churches hold the place of him to whom this was first said, let them show how anyone can feed those committed to them in body if he is not even allowed to know from what source he ought to feed them. And since the guardians of the Lord's tabernacle, that is, the clergy of the Church, ought to live from the oblations and tythes of the faithful, if the bishop does not know how many tythemen, how many farms, how many bushels of wheat, how many barrels of wine in such or such quantities suffice the clergy for victuals and clothing, is he not shown either to be no shepherd or certainly to be a foolish shepherd, in that he does not know where those pastures are to which he ought to lead the flocks committed to his charge?

4. To return to our business, that is, alas, the secular one: since you very rarely see people associated together without the compulsion of either fear or love, how will that person fear you from whom you can take nothing, how will he love you on whom you can confer nothing? If, then, the bishop has no responsibility for the means whereby the clergy ought to live, or he himself does not have to give them their physical as well as their spiritual measure of food at the proper time [Lk. 12.42], and if it is not distributed, as the Acts of the Apostles hold, to each according as any has need [Acts 2.45], by the bishop or by somebody else appointed by the same for that office, but the clergy themselves divide it up among themselves according as any of them is stronger; and if they ought to distribute what has been collected for the Church of Verona not among the whole clergy of the Church according to the custom of other churches, but only to the deacons and priests according to their own will—with the result, of course, that being enriched they have the wherewithal to rebel against their bishop and to dominate the rest of the clergy and to be able when they want to compel them by force to their aid and to force them to make an oath of loyalty to another bishop,[6] one whom they have brought in, forsooth, and if they do obey, to be able to expel them from the Church; and so that they have the wherewithal also to get wives for their sons and husbands for their daughters, and vineyards and fields, and finally so they can serve the mammon

of iniquity [Mt. 6.2] without intermission—what ought the deacons, acolytes, and other clergy in order do, where get their living, with what reward fight for the Church, keep their vigils, even submit to the rod for learning their letters, when, to the apostle asking and saying, "Whoever serves as a soldier at his own expense?" [1 Cor. 9.7], still no one answers "This person or that"?

This quarrel of mine against those who scorn the canons in this matter does not entirely please even those for whom I make suit,[7] but there are two reasons for their attitude: first, they think that they can use this as an excuse for retracting from God's service; second, each hopes that he too will eventually live in such a way that he can himself impose on others what he now suffers from his superiors. Deluded by this expectation, many of them have both suffered the greatest hardships in this world and have to fear that perhaps in the next they will suffer hell. My enemies' whole mad deceit and perfidy takes its source from this fact, that (not unlike those about whom it was said that they abandoned God's commandments and held to the tradition of men [Mk. 7.8]) they utterly flout the canonical law and they hold to the tradition of their predecessors—kings to that of murderers or mutilators, bishops to that of those who either compel men to live disgracefully or, if any of them like this one of ours [i.e., Rather himself] cannot patiently acquiesce in it, most deceitfully like Judas make him suffer from others for what they had themselves done. No one prefers custom[8] to the sacred laws except he who is not terrified by the words spoken to King Josaphat: "You offer help to the wicked and you join in friendship with those who hate God" [2 Chr. 19.2] and the rest; and the words of the apostle also: "Not only those who do, but also those who consent to those doing, are worthy of death" [Rom. 1.2]; those of Jerome too: "Whoever defends the wicked should be destroyed and the defended and defender should be condemned with like punishment." Again: "Do not defend another unjustly or you may be justly bound and subject to another's punishment; for whoever strikes the wicked in the area of their wickedness, is a minister of the Lord." Again: "To punish murderers and violators is not a shedding of blood but the ministry of the laws."[9] Note that he did not say "kill" but "punish," carefully choosing his words; for another says this: "Strike the flanks of your son when he is still a child, but do not make your soul responsible for his killing" [Pr. 19.18].

"Leave the dead," says the Lord to someone, "to bury the dead" [Mt. 8.22]. Trying to explain this, a truthful interpreter says: "The dead bury the dead when sinner defends sinner and buries him under a heap of falsehood, so that he cannot revive for correction."[10] "Woe," says the Lord to these too through the mouth of the prophet, "to those who sew bands for every wrist" [Ezek. 13.18]. These are the same as those of whom it is said elsewhere: "Woe to those who say good is bad and bad good" [Is. 5.20].

5. The quibbler says on the other side: "'As long as I am apostle of the people,' says the egregious teacher, 'I will honor my ministry' [Rom. 11.13]. Well then, consider how egregiously you honor the ministry of this ideal bishop of yours,[11] when you contend that he ought to measure grain and wine and divide coin and the rest among the clergy in the manner of the famous Sardanapallus, who, when he was (or rather ought to have been) king of that great and famous empire, was found apportioning jobs among the servants."[12]

To which in return I make reply: if you had received in your inner vision the articles set forth here as a basis for my case, you would have been able to understand that the method of feeding the Lord's flock was here most honorably depicted with the dignity of the pontiff's position left unsullied. For these jobs must be done by the bishop through the agency of priests and deacons (if only trusty ones can be found), not by the bishop in person, as has been shown.

If necessity, though, compelled him to do these tasks in his own person, pride would not prevent him, and in doing so he would in no way offend Him who said, "He who would be greater among you, let him be servant of all" [Mk. 10.43–44]. But let such an one not scorn to reread the Acts of the Apostles and Paul's letters to the peoples; there he will find it put most clearly who ought to do this and who ought to give the instructions [Acts 6.2–6]. Also, review the passions of the blessed martyrs Sextus and Laurentius, in which one of them is shown to have said to the other: "Take and distribute the resources of the church"; and the other, having faithfully distributed the same, cried: "Do not leave me, holy father, because I have now expended your treasure."[13] Note and take to heart that the one said "resources of the church," the other "your treasure," the one asserting that the treasure was the church's, the other that it was the bishop's, just as, for example, what is a husband's is a wife's and what is a wife's is a husband's. But if you are shocked at such a statement, listen to something similar from a letter of Pope Evaristus: "A church may not dismiss its bishop to take another while he is still alive, lest it incur the charge of fornication or adultery. For if it has been adulterated, that is, has joined itself to another bishop or has taken another bishop over itself or has caused or desired this to happen, let it either be reconciled to its proper bishop by means of the strictest penitence or remain unmarried."[14] What is "married" if not husbanded, what "unmarried" but given to no husband? Therefore, from these words of a pope most truthful in this matter, you can recognize (if you did not understand the rest) that the husband and wife (by the law not of fleshly but of spiritual marriage) are the bishop and the church betrothed to him, and following the same law you can see—if you have those ears of spirituality which the Lord demanded of His listeners [Mt. 11.15]—that what belongs to the one belongs to the other.

And this also the civil laws established of old seem to imply, unless I am mistaken. For how would damages apply to a bishop with immunity if that against which something has been unjustly done or, as is said there, some malice has been done, were not *his own*? Be wise, therefore, cease, you empty verbiage, from struggling further against right and law, and as you have have not found any just response, put a finger on your sacrilegious mouth [Job 21.5].

6. While thus railing furiously with swelling mouth like a second Chremes,[15] I began to consider deep within me to see if I could perhaps discover the source of this general contempt of the divinely published canons in these climes,[16] a contempt so general that I can find no upholder of them, from the lowest in the Church to the most eminent, from the dumbest fool to him who yearns to be called most wise, from the layman to, alas, the Highest Pontiff.[17] While I bewail and deplore this state of things and can find no other reason for it at all, there occur to me the Gospel commandments (contempt of which is contempt of Christ Himself), and its threats and acts, as for instance that which I mentioned above when I complained that I was being opposed by the clergy most of all, namely: "If you love me feed my sheep" [Jn. 21.16–17]; for it is obvious that that person is no shepherd of souls who clearly does not love Christ. The man who does not follow His commandments is said not to love Him, since we read that He said in the Gospel: "The one who loves me is he who hears my words and does them" [Mt. 7.24; Jn. 14.21].

If I attempt to note all the threats on the wicked, I must needs turn over every page of the Gospels, but particularly that place where He inveighs against the scribes and pharisees and hypocrites [Mt. 23.13–33]; when He criticizes their faults, He criticizes the ministry, I say, of all false prelates of today as well, unless they cease to imitate the former. The acts are those which He demonstrated in person, both when He made a whip of cords [Jn. 2.15], and when He is said, by means of a parable, to be a king coming to his son's wedding and says that whomsoever He finds not clothed in a wedding garment will be rebuked and sent with feet and hands tied into outer darkness [Mt. 22.11–13], that is, hell. He shows that He will condemn in particular the whole catalogue of false pontiffs, those who without charity—that is, without love of God and love of the people committed to their charge—have thought that they could enjoy what was conceded to that first bishop [St. Peter] because of that same charity, namely, "Feed my sheep"—though there it was preceded by: "If you love me" [Jn. 21.17]. This they are shown not to have done and thus to have rather been wolves and hypocrites than shepherds.

7. After these harsh requirements—such an impossible barrier for the man who is unwilling to do them—passing by what is contained in the law of Moses and the prophets and psalms and is read by these with no benefit, such as, "Woe,

why do you devise wickedness?" [Mic. 2.1], and "Woe and a thousand times woe to the shepherds of Israel" [Ezek. 34.2; Mt. 23.13–30] (and to those modern ones as well), and "Cursed are they who do not abide by thy commandments" [Ps. 118.21], and "Cursed is he who has done the Lord's work negligently" [Jer. 48.10]; along comes the apostle, like a second stern Cato,[18] and as though trying to take away every bold ambition to be bishop proclaims, "A bishop must be without sin" [Tit. 1.7] and—what is even more impossible—"above reproach, the husband of one wife" [1 Tim. 3.2], which today these people hear with deaf and obstinate ears. This indescribably harsh rule for choosing a bishop the Fathers have not cared to relax; more than once they have decreed that no bigamist should be elected or received into the clergy (and if not into the clergy, how into the priesthood? O would that in their ranks there had never been born nor seen nor heard nor spoken of any centigamist, for shame, or any infinitely promiscuous person). A large number of these lawgivers, namely, the crowd of 318 gathered at Nicene, in the presence of God himself, as history reveals, as though their purpose were to thoroughly terrify every single one of those who heard it by the very forcefulness of their statement, decreed as follows: "The great synod totally forbids any bishop, priest, deacon, or anyone else at all in the clergy, to keep a woman in his house, except perhaps mother or aunt or only such as escape suspicion."[19] Inflexible also is Augustine, who says: "I refuse to let my sister be with me since my sister's companion is not my sister."[20] So since the Scripture says that "when the wicked man comes to the depth of evil he becomes contemptuous" [Pr. 18.3], if he lies in the depth of transgression of such great commandments and hears the psalmist crying, "Thou hast commanded thy precepts to be kept diligently" [Ps. 118.4], but realizes that he has kept them not even a little, does it seem surprising to you if he is hardened in desperation? Particularly if he does not know how to observe James' sentence that "Whoever offends in one particular will be guilty of all" [Jas. 2.10].

8. There's the case, there's the pretext, which lovers of this world, transgressors of the canons, hold out, saying that it is impossible to observe all the items which are contained in the canons. And there are so many madmen driven by the demon of desperation that quite recently with these very ears I heard a certain member of the episcopal rank, in view of refuting all the scriptures which promise hell, say about the Gospel itself: "What is written on sheep-skin is read too,"[21] as if falsehood as well as truth can be contained in the Gospel. I too once, when we were pressed to attack the castle of Garda on the emperor's command,[22] and the bishops and clergy of this province maintained that this was not proper for the clergy (not out of love of religion indeed, but in hatred of hard work) replied with angry words (as I often do): "Just as the canons do not allow a cleric to fight, so they do not permit him to visit brothels either."

"For woe to you," said one who cannot lie, "Scribes and pharisees, hypocrites, for you tythe mint and dill and cummin, and have neglected the weightier matters of the law—justice, mercy and faith" [Mt. 23.23].

9. When I was arguing with a certain person[23] about my enthronization at Liège [953] and I tried to justify it with the authority of Pope Antherus, he attacked me with these two chapters of the Council of Sardis: "1. Bishop Osius said: We must totally eradicate the evil practice and vicious corruption whereby it is allowed to a bishop to change from one city to another; for the reason he tries to do this is clear, since no bishop has been found to change from a larger city to a smaller. Hence it is apparent that they are inflamed by the ardor of avarice and serve ambition and seek power. If it pleases all, let such a scourge be strictly and severely punished so that such an one should not even have lay communion. All replied, 'Agreed.' 2. Again, concerning the same bishops, that if they change their seat out of ambition, not even in death should they receive lay communion. Bishop Osius said: 'And if such an one should be so impertinent as to affirm by way of excuse that he received commission of the people, since it is clear that some few who do not have a pure faith could have been bribed with money and gifts to acclaim him in church and appear to seek him for their bishop, I think that this kind of fraud should be so utterly condemned that such a one should receive not even lay communion in death. If this pleases you all, so decide.' The synod replied, 'Agreed.'"[24]

This was my rebuttal: I was troubled and pointed out that I had not been enthroned [at Liège] for reasons of avarice or pride, but I had been expelled from my proper seat [Verona][25] and forced by necessity to approach the then pious king, now most glorious emperor [Otto I]; he had consulted on this matter with a council of bishops[26] and they in their mercy had chosen me and in brotherly spirit had enthroned me [in Liège] with the people assenting. This course of action they chose out of self-interest and expediency.

When I was not able to reduce him to silence even with such arguments, but finding by report (though whether a true one I did not know) that he was married to a wife, I puffed myself up with authority (though not with action) and rendered him this reply: In the canons of the Apostles—if you do not reject those as apocryphal—chapter 17 and the Laodicensian Council, chapter 1, in the decrees of Pope Siricius, chapter 11, in the decrees of Pope Innocent, chapters 11, 12, 13, and also 29, in the decrees also of Pope Leo, chapter 2: it is commanded that "twice-married persons be not admitted to the clergy," and—woe is me—if not to the clergy, how to the priesthood, since priests may not even eat at the wedding of one twice-married, because, since the bigamist lacks penitence, who is the priest that can offer consent to such a wedding in order to eat at it? For what the same canon says about multigamists, look in chapter 3.

10. When he tried to make other answers, he blathered like a madman; and when

his veins as ever swollen with yesterday's Bacchus[27]

he played at the dice-tables as well, in anger again I said: If you did not reject the canons of the Apostles, together with the apostles themselves, I would tell you that in the canons chapters 42 and 44 it says that "a bishop, priest, and deacon must not be dicer and drunkard" as you are, and "if he is he should either cease or be deposed." And the Sardis Council also says that you are not allowed to be absent from your church more than three weeks.[28] To proceed from greater to smaller: whether it is allowed for you to have hunting dogs or hawks for birding (of which you have many), see there also. Whether you are also allowed to engage in secular business, that is, any business to be engaged in only by secular people, consider in the apostle [cf. 2 Tim. 2.4] as much as in the canons, and stop criticizing the brotherly tolerance of those wiser than you. Let these words — or rather thoughts — of mine suffice.

11. To tell what I have heard: I have found two of this rank [bishop] criticizing each other, one for having a mistress, the other for wearing arms. The Apostolic canon answered one: "A bishop, priest, or deacon, who has borne arms in any sedition must be removed from all gatherings of Christians."[29] To the other, the canon: "A bishop, priest, or deacon, who marries, must be expelled."[30]

I know of two men, one who committed adultery before his ordination and afterwards lived as though in continence, the other who took a wife after his ordination, and the one criticized the other and vice versa. To both of these the teacher of the Gentiles cried (though as if to one person), to the one because of the empty boasting of his continence, to the other because of his illicit marriage: "Do you not know that the patience of God awaits your repentance? You lay up anger for yourself on the day of wrath and retribution of the just judgment of God" [Rom. 2.4–5]. To this one: "Do not become proud" [Rom. 11.20] because of your present continence, but fear for your past incontinence, which, though ended, cannot certainly be deleted by any satisfaction. And to the other: "Adulterers will not possess the kingdom of God" [1 Cor. 6.9–10]. And it could be that both of them, brought up at the same time, equally educated in puberty, were wanton in their knowledge of their respective practices and when they had been brought forth to the presulate without examination,[31] one of them affected philandering, the other warmongering, and perhaps neither abandoned the foulness of a practice that should not even be named [Eph. 5.3]. In one chapter the canon gives each his due separately, when it says to one: "The priest who takes a wife after his ordination should be deposed";[32] and to the other: "If he has committed adultery, he ought even more to be expelled."[33] But it condemns both in one chapter, that is, chapter 9, of the Nicene Council: "If any have been brought forward without questioning or when examined have confessed their sins, and people in anger against the canons have tried to lay hands on those who confessed, the rule does not admit such, because the Catholic Church defends what cannot be criticized." Again, in the Neocaesarian Council chapter 9: "If a priest confesses that before ordination he sinned in body, he may not consecrate the offering though remaining in the other duties because of his good zeal." Great is the strictness of the law, I say. For why (alas for me), if he has lived continently after ordination, will he not be able to consecrate the offering for his good zeal—of pleasing God, that is?

12. The second is doubly referred to, when besides the above he sees himself condemned by this heading also: "A bishop, priest, or deacon, who has taken up arms in any sedition, should be expelled from any gathering of Christians."[34] But of all the lighter faults (such as dicing, drunkenness, hawking, or hunting) this today is considered the lightest, so that a priest would rather, it seems, fight in arms for the loyalty due his patron than be called a perjurer—though perjury exacts a heavy penance but taking up arms is said to be inexpiable by any penance.

But perhaps they belong to the number of those here mentioned—that is, those to one of whom the Lord seemed to say, "If you love me, feed my sheep" [Jn. 21.15] (though he did not say it to them since they are shown not to love Him)? Them the apostle seems rather to expel from the priesthood than choose for it, when he says, "A bishop must be without sin" [Tit. 1.7], or, more expressly, "faultless, a husband of one wife" [1 Tim. 3.2]. Following him as a standard-bearer, that legion of Christ's soldiers instructs that no bigamous person be admitted into the clergy.[35] If no bigamous person, how can any centigamous person be admitted? And if not to the clergy, how to the priesthood?

13. But let us suppose one of them, perhaps a bigamist before his entry into the clergy, perhaps wanton as a cleric, then after a priesthood of many wives, wars, perjuries, and the damages of hunting, hawking, dice, and drink, summoned by some circumstance to the apostolic see of the Roman seat,[36] where it is customary for the one who is to be duly ordained to be told, "Take care that you have not made any promise to your electors; know that that is simony and contrary to the canons."[37] If this man, then, by some open illegality—in the face of the strong opposition of the Osius just mentioned, together with all those voting with him in that Council—should perhaps be placed in the Apostolic seat—which of course magnanimous God can tolerantly permit as He permits much—and if I approach him like a wronged party to a minister of law, and he, striving to vindicate my wrongs—or rather, the wrongs of God who prohibits such things and of the holy Gospels, the apostles and apostolic men, the

canons and decretals—were to send [Milo] a letter of apostolic authority, will not he who wronged me so sacrilegiously [Milo]—if not as much as the other [Pope John XII] wronged God and all rights both human and divine, in that Milo only wronged me a mere man while he wronged almost the whole world, Milo adulterated one church, while he adulterated both it and all those spread throughout the world—but, as I said, if on my behalf he were to send Milo even a moderately strict injunction, would not Milo be able to write back to him that stricture from the Gospel: "Why do you see the speck in your brother's eye but do not see the beam which is in your own eye?" [Mt. 7.3]; and also that reply which a pirate captured on the river Ganges is said to have given Alexander the Great,[38] who had looked at him fiercely and said: "Foul thief, why do you not leave us in peace?" He gave a great laugh, and the king, astonished as were all those standing by, said, "You laugh?" He said, "And rightly so." The king: "How so?" "Because," said the other, "though you are the thief of thieves, the greatest robber of all, the most cruel bandit of all who have ever despoiled any kingdom from the ocean to the lands of the East, the chief of all robbers, you call me a thief, who carry my bark on my back and put it into the river and steal some tittle from the shore, somebody's cloak or a mere bridle." The king burst out laughing with them all and admitted that he spoke wisely.

But he [the pope] will not do it, he will not send him [Milo] a letter containing any stricture, he will not condemn him, he will not excommunicate anyone for such an action. For disparity of wills does not separate hearts of like disposition, since likeness of desires ever generates equality of action and human friendships seek out equal hearts and not dissimilar dispositions. For of them it is written in the description of the members of the head of the devil or Antichrist, "The limbs of his flesh adhering to themselves" [Job 41.14], and of the devil's followers also in the form of scales: "One is joined to another and not a breath goes between them" [Job 41.7]. The more compact and allied the wickedness of the wicked, the more strongly is it armed against God's justice. For, as St. Gregory says, just as it is very damaging if good men have no unity, so it is very noxious if wicked men have it.[39] This was proved by the case of Paul the apostle; when he was attacked with one mind by both the Pharisees and Sadeuces, he caused division among them by saying, "Fellow men, I am a Pharisee" [Acts 23.6], and was helped by the Pharisees and defended from the assaults of the Sadeuces, and by dividing the pack which united was harrying him, his innocence came through undamaged.

14. There is also another reason why I have no confidence of receiving any help in this matter; the Lord says: "The thief does not come except to steal and slay and destroy" [Jn. 10.10]. Who is that thief if not the one about whom He says, "He who does not enter the sheepfold by the door but climbs in by another way, he is a thief and a robber" [Jn. 10.1]? What is the "door" other than that about which the psalmist sings, "For the lawgiver will give blessing" [Ps. 83.8], the lawgiver who also says of Himself, "I am the door" [Jn. 10.9], who only bestows His blessing on a pontiff being ordained when he is chosen by the law passed by Himself. That "the sheepfold" is the congregation of the faithful is shown by what He said to Peter: "Feed my sheep" [Jn. 21.17]. "To climb in by another way" is to enter illegally. That person is shown to have climbed in rather than entered of whom the canons say: "If any man uses secular powers and by them obtains a church, he should be deposed and those who communicate with him should be segregated."[40]

15. Let your lordship then in your wisdom (which—as is said—has seemed worthy to have charge of the universal Church)[41] consider whether this *climbing-in* is clear and evident, when such an one is said to have "used secular powers" but is judged to be deposed on the decision of Him who said in the Gospel, "Every man who exalts himself will be humbled" [Lk. 14.11]. But note that He does not say, "Every man who is exalted is going to be humbled," but "he who exalts *himself*," that is, raises himself or thinks himself worthy. *By another way* is to rise by simony or some other illegality. *Thief* he is called because of his character, *robber* because of his violence and rapine. The specific purpose of a thief or robber can easily be learned, again from the same authority: "The thief does not come except to steal and slay and destroy" [Jn. 10.10]. What, then, does he *steal*? First, the words of the law of God, by hiding them and not promulgating them in his decrees, then the property of the Church which belongs by right to another. He *slays* the souls that will be stored in the devil's maw (just as, on the other hand, another is told, "Rise, Peter, slay and eat" [Acts 10.13], that is, take from the life of paganism and store in the maw of Christianity). Whom does he *destroy* rather than himself first and his followers second?

Anyone, therefore, who approaches a man like this for help, must watch out, I advise him, that he is not rather hurt by him. For if he is perhaps of gentler disposition and he is accused before that one [Pope John XII] of being invader of someone's church or wife,[42] the pope, remembering that he has done the same, is afraid of hearing, "Let him who is without sin be the first to cast a stone at her" [Jn. 8.7]. O, how is he not without sin who is struck with the leprosy of Gehazi [2 Kg. 5.27], who is damned along with Simon the magus [Acts 8.20], who is multigamous, who—since all the women of his diocese are his spiritual daughters—is perhaps polluted by the corruption of one of them, who is reproved by the sacred canons on many points and not corrected in any way![43] If he fears to rebuke anyone guilty of a trifle, do you think that that one is going to be reproved? "Greater sinner, spare the lesser,"[44] as our Flaccus finely puts it.

16. What of the fact that such a man is not allowed to call God himself *Lord* by His own stipulation when He said, "Why do you call me 'Lord, Lord' and do not do what I say?" [Lk. 6.46]; or to call God *God* since He thus complains through the prophet: "If I am God where is your fear of me?" [Mal. 1.6] nor *Father* since He adds, "If I am Father, where is your love of me?"; when he is restrained from announcing even His commands since the psalmist says: "What right have you to recite my statutes?" [Ps. 49.16], and, besides, he can sanctify nothing, since the Scripture says: "What the unclean man has touched will be unclean" [Num. 19.22]. Since a priest seems to have a name composed from the words *sacred* and *given* [*sacer/dos*]⁴⁵ how can what is unclean be—or even be thought to be—sacred? How can anything even be thought clean which the unclean man has touched, against the assertion [Tit. 1.15] of Him who is uniquely clean and without whom no one is clean? Yet here there seems to be help from what the Lord's Baptist testifies was divinely revealed to him, namely: "Over whom you see the spirit descending and remaining over him, that is he who baptizes in the Holy Spirit" [Jn. 1.33], that is, who bestows the Holy Spirit on the baptized. Yet what will we do if that was said uniquely about that mystery? But let us assume that this was said about all baptizers. [. . .]⁴⁶ How is the ministering of the sacrament to others conceded to a man who is not allowed to taste of it himself? For you have the apostle saying: "Whoever eats and drinks of the Body and Blood of the Lord unworthily, takes damnation to himself" [1 Cor. 11.29]. The saintly teachers define as unworthily receiving the Eucharist the man who presumes to take communion at the time when he ought to be doing penance;⁴⁷ clearly, this is ignored by the man who receives what follows with a deaf ear, namely: "If we judged ourselves, we would not be judged" [1 Cor. 11.31]. For when we spare ourselves too much in the present, we bring it about that we are not even spared a little in the future.

17. Lo, there is the cause of the general contempt which today's world has for the canons, or rather for the Gospels and all the Lord's commandments, when a man says that it profits him nothing if he observes the smaller points knowing that he has ignored the larger. For on this principle what does it matter if a man does not have dogs for hunting but has numerous mistresses for whoring, if he takes no arms for his own and others' defense but does not cease from doing criminal acts to his own and many others' damnation, if (a neglect also forbidden by the canons)⁴⁸ he does not strike the faithful who are delinquent with fist or stick but kills them with the rod of his adulterous absolution or obligation or even blessing of adultery or with the example of foul acts? But since, as the Scriptures everywhere assert, silence on the part of those ordained to that office is condemned, and their preaching is required and praised (to such an extent that it is even said through the prophet's mouth to everyone, not even secu-

people excepted, "Let him who hears say 'Come'" [Rev. 22.17] and through
nes the apostle, "If anyone wanders from the truth and someone brings him
ck, let him know that whoever brings back a sinner from the error of his
ay saves his soul from death and covers a multitude of his own sins" [Jas.
19-20] — where no one is excepted but it declares that whoever does this is
ing to be rewarded with such remuneration that he is said to have both won
e salvation of his brother's soul and secured that of his own — and other exam-
es also show that the Lord not only ordered His words and decisions to be
read abroad [Ps. 49.16] but even promised rewards to those doing so and strongly
uked those not doing so and threatened that the blood — that is sins — or souls
those whom they did not correct with their advice would be demanded of
em [Ezek. 3.18]), what sort of a sin, how grave, can we think his to be whom
e assesses to be so unworthy to recite His statutes that he is forbidden with
rebuke to do so?

Therefore, so as not to be in doubt and make a mistake, let us see what fol-
ws; there we find the cause: "You," He says, "have hated discipline" [Ps.
.17] — which nothing prevents us from interpreting as canon law — "and have
it my words behind you" — that is, you have preferred your own judgment,
actice or will to my law. How? "If you saw a thief," He says, "you ran with
n" [Ps. 49.18] — that is, you did not observe what I commanded through the
postle, namely, "Do not be hasty in the laying-on of hands nor participate
another man's sins" [1 Tim. 5.22]. "You kept company with adulterers" [Ps.
.18], by defending them, that is, and giving them privilege (would that I had
ver experienced it)[49] so that they could steadfastly endure in that adultery.
our mouth has abounded in wickedness" [Ps. 49.19] — by accumulating false
thorities so that you would be allowed what was never allowed anyone —
nd your tongue" — by declaring this — "has compounded treachery." "Sitting,
u spoke against your brother" — a fellow-bishop lawfully established or any
ristian — "the son of your mother" [Ps. 49.19] — that is, of the Catholic Church,
which no greater scandal can be put than to obtain an adulterer for a bishop
d receive a wolf instead of a shepherd.

18. When men do this, they recite God's statutes not to the benefit of their
eners but to their perdition, corrupting the words of God, by false interpre-
ion, that is, and twisting a reluctant Scripture to their own purpose. They
this and God is silent [cf. Ps. 49.21], that is, He permits no opponent to
em to oppose such a course. But they should listen to what follows and then,
andoning such action, "glorify God with the sacrifice of praise" [Ps. 49.23],
oclaiming first by their example, then by their words, that the words of God's
v are to be embraced, revered, and followed. For "there" — that is, in the sa-
fice of God's praise — "is the way to God's salvation," that is, Jesus Christ

Our Lord, because, of course, we find in God's praises, which the pages of Scripture contain, what we must follow, do, avoid, and hope for. Anyone, therefore, though a sinner, may recite God's statutes without worry if he does not hate God's discipline (that is, the edicts of the canons), if he does not prefer his own decisions to God's commandments, if seeing a thief (by His definition) he does not run with him [Ps. 49.17–18] — that is, does not make agreement with him or defend him — if he does not take the side of those adulterating God's word and scorning the requirements of the canons, if "his mouth has not abounded in the wickedness" [Ps. 49.19] of speaking against the rightness of divine law and his tongue does not compound the treachery of deceiving anybody, if "sitting" — in the seat of judgment — he does not "speak against his brother" nor put any stumbling-block for him in the way of the Lord [Rom. 14.13].

For if anyone does such things, though God may be silent towards him — that is, permits to be silent those who either do not know how to or cannot or dare not contradict him — let him not think thereby that he is like Him in will, that is, that God approves his doings. For he will "be rebuked" sometime and his works and thoughts will "be charged before His face" [Ps. 49.21].

From these incontrovertible arguments, besides others which can be said here, we should know that a man is not restrained from reciting God's statutes for the purpose of keeping them quiet but so that they be said sincerely and be told by one who loves them and strives to keep them to the best of his ability. Every day we hear, "Jesus said to His disciples" [Mt. 16.24]; only he who loves Jesus' discipline truly is a disciple of Jesus, and Jesus speaks to him. For of him He says: "Whoever is of God hears God's words"; what He feels about the others, He adds: "You do not hear because you are not of God" [Jn. 8.47].

19. The shrewd reader can see how far these words of the psalm mentioned here [Ps. 49] are from him who is backed by no power, or how applicable to him who is preeminent with the fullest authority [John XII]. What kind of a man is he who is guilty, perhaps, of such sins but still is not afraid to hold the highest seat of apostolic dignity — as has now happened, alas! For you should not be surprised if the authority to teach is denied to a man who is supported neither by the legality of his ordination nor the purity of his ways and (what would be more becoming) who lacks integrity of mind and body, since the power also of ministering to the Lord is denied him. For the Lord says to Moses: "Speak to your brother Aaron and say to him, No priest of the seed of Aaron who has a blemish may approach to offer the bread of his God nor draw near to His ministry," adding also: "Nor a man blind or lame or one who has a mutilated face or a limb too long, or a man who has an injured foot or an injured hand, or a hunchback, or a dwarf, or a man with a defect in his sight, or an itching disease or scabs or swollen testicles" [Lev. 21.17–20].

Consider, most wise and urbane lord, the sort of stupor, insensibility, or madness which hardens the heart of anyone who, when Gregory interprets all these as spiritual or moral faults,[50] understands them in that way and is not pricked to the quick, particularly if he sees any of these in his own soul. What does your lordship think about the man who is afflicted by all these plagues and is not restrained from either desiring or retaining the priesthood? For if a man is *blind* in his mind, if through weakness of will he is *lame* and cannot walk the path of life with an even stride (even though he may see the path), if he has a *small nose*—that is, with little discernment he equates good with evil or perhaps gives preference to evil—if he has a large and *twisted nose*—that is, he is so subtle and twisted in his decisions that he is deceitful enough to be called "crooked" in popular parlance—if he has an *injured foot or hand*—that is, cannot go from strength to strength (like those who will see the God of Gods in Zion [Ps. 83.8]) or effect any good action at all—if too much *pressed with the hump* of earthly cares he tries to turn only towards the things which are trodden underfoot—if his eyes are *clouded with a blear* which prevents him from seeing in the mind what ought to be done, if he is *blinded* with the defect of pride in thinking that he is wise or righteous, if he is chronically afflicted with the *itch* of carnal wantonness, if greed possesses him like a *scab*, because, though he monstrously dishonors his soul if he obtains on earth what he desires, he feels no pain about that which he loses in heaven, if he is so crushed by wantonness of the *genitals* that, even though he does not practice it in action, yet he never abandons it in his thoughts and never is at rest, in the manner of one with swollen testicles: how does this man presume to offer his bread to the Lord, who daily hears that he is prohibited by Him to whom it ought to be offered?

20. To set down here only three of these reasons for disqualification, omitting the rest so as not be burdensome: if he has a defect in his sight, if he has an itching disease or scabs, or if he has swollen testicles, is he not sufficiently disqualified? For since these three signify both a spiritual defect and a physical defect—spiritual, that is, the pride which God opposes [Jas. 4.6], and the physical corruption of one whose fire is said to be kindled in the Lord's anger [Dt. 32.22]—who recognizing them in himself is not appalled, who hearing them is not terrified? For about these two kinds of defect it is said to blessed Job that "the devil sleeps in shadow under the covert of the reeds and in the marsh" [Job 40.16]. One of them God is said to oppose (as I said above), the fire of the other He declares to be kindled in His own anger. The spiritual defect—pride—turned an archangel into a devil; the physical defect made him who, since he was a son by grace, should most readily have called God "Father" by His command, be called the son of the devil because of the impurity of his life—to use here the authority of St. Zeno, who said (in the sermon which he made about the patriarch Judas and Thamar, his daughter-in-law, most brilliantly, as was his wont): "The devil is father of all those living viciously."[51]

And O how fearful[52] is this consideration: The man in whom the devil rests by means of these three vices—that is, pride, hypocrisy, and lust—though he may seem to take communion with the faithful, does not eat the flesh of the Lord nor drink His blood, since the Lord says: "Whoever eats my flesh and drinks my blood, remains in me and I in him" [Jn. 6.57]; this can be turned around and put this way too: "Whoever remains in me and I in him eats my flesh and drinks my blood." For the man in whom God remains and he in God, how the devil can sleep in him I do not see. But the devil does sleep in the man who because of his hypocrisy and pride is shady and empty and because of his lust is damp (marshy [cf. Job 40.16]). What then does he eat when he takes communion? If you say, "Judgment upon himself" [1 Cor. 11.29], you echo the apostle and urge me too to understand that he will be judged—that is, condemned—because, though unworthy, he dared to eat Christ's flesh and drink His blood, and for that reason what ought to have been his salvation is turned into his damnation. Concerning the bodily substance which he takes, since that is now my question, I now give in to myself, so to speak. For to him who takes it worthily, it is true flesh and blood, though it may seem to be the bread and the wine that it had been once; what it is to him taking it unworthily—that is, not remaining in God—I confess that I cannot even ponder, let alone say. The words "Do not ask things too high for you nor seek into things too deep for you" [Eccli. 3.22] apply to me, at this point, I think.

21. But let us hear what John Chrysostom says on this question; for perhaps we shall be able to understand something from him.

> Let there be no Judas at the table. This sacrifice is spiritual food. For just as when bodily food enters a stomach occupied by adverse humors, it hurts it further, harms it more, gives it no help, so also this spiritual food, if it finds anyone corrupted by wickedness, will hurt him more, not of its own nature but by the fault of the receiver. Let everyone therefore have a pure heart, pure thoughts, because the sacrifice also is pure. Let us then ready our souls in holiness for such a sacrifice.[53]

Augustine also says:

> What Judas received was good, but he received good to his own hurt. It is not then surprising if Christ's bread was given to Judas so that by it he might be delivered to the devil, when you see in reverse that the devil's angel was given to Paul, so that by it he might benefit in Christ.[54]

In this sense, therefore, it seems to me that this sacrifice is the same to the good man as to the bad, to the worthy as to the unworthy, but it does not confer the same, in that to the worthy it gives life, to the unworthy it gives death, to the worthy grace, to the unworthy wrath. For thus also the psalm says, "Still were their morsels in their mouths and the anger of the Lord came upon them" [Ps. 77.30–31], referring to the manna that was abused—which there is no difficulty in understanding as the Lord's sacrifice unworthily taken, since Judas' damnation also shows that something must be understood in addition in the Lord's words, namely: "Whoever eats my flesh *worthily* and drinks my blood *worthily* remains in me and I in him" [Jn. 6.57]. If this is so, we must see to whom is said "Come to Bethel"—that is, the house of God—"and transgress and offer a sacrifice of thanksgiving of that which is leavened" [Am. 4.4–5]. For concerning the worthily offered sacrifice, I do not doubt that it is flesh. Yet Christ's apostle, when he had said of it, "And so let us eat," added "not in the old leaven nor in the leaven of wickedness and evil" [1 Cor. 5.8]. In these words, clearly, every evil thought is forbidden both to those taking and to those offering the Body and Blood of the Lord. But since the sacrifice to be offered to the people is consecrated with that particular prayer where God is addressed as "Our Father, who art in heaven" [Mt. 6.9], what the man who is by his corrupt life a son of the devil (as St. Zeno declares)[55] should think, how he should assess himself, I leave to another to consider, for I am not up to it.

It can easily be seen in the psalm how interconnected these two are, that is, pride and lust, when the psalmist prays, saying: "Let the foot of pride not come over me" [Ps. 35.12], (that is, let not the demon of boasting trample my life to the ground [Ps. 7.6] in urging me to desire only the things of this world); where there also follows, "nor the hand of the wicked drive me away," that is, the spirit of fornication which, when the spirit of vainglory has seized the heart of any religious person, at once stirs up his body with the motions of lust. Why the one who is stirred up does evil is shown when it adds: "There the evil-doers lie prostrate" [Ps. 35.13]. Where? In pride first, and then in the pit of lust. Why? "Because they are thrust down," it says. From where? From the grace of God. And they are unable to rise, being unworthy to taste the Eucharist, because the Lord forbids it as follows: "Whoever eats of the flesh of the sacrifice, which is the Lord, and his foulness is upon him, that soul shall perish from his people" [Lev. 7.20].

22. But since it is written that "Nothing happens in the world without reason" [Job 5.6], I think I see, I admit, the reason that this can often happen. Take a scion of the nobility handed over to the schools, which today seems to happen more from ambition of the episcopate than from the desire of serving the Lord. There's one *foot of pride*—the ambitious will of the parents. When he matures, he begins to wax insolent, either because of that very nobility or

from some acuteness of intellect, or perhaps from physical good looks, or because he has a voice (as Jerome says of someone) "sweeter than the songful swan."[56] Trampled then by these devil's feet of pride, he weakens and because of his conceit he is cast down into fouler wantonness, just as that first one was cast down into ruder air.

From that point he becomes not so much bigamous as multigamous and is brought forward without examination[57] to the priesthood; this is certainly the source of all subsequent evils, up to the point of damnation of the soul. For when those of the secular number who are not utterly uneducated hear that on the second day of Pentecost Jesus said to His disciples (that is, both those who then were his disciples and these today who do not hate His discipline, that is, His teaching, correction, and commandments): "He who does not enter the sheepfold by the door but comes in by another way, that man is a thief and a robber" [Jn. 10.1], they are not unaware that Truth cannot lie and also that it follows that he who is a thief cannot also be a shepherd; and they understand that the sheepfold is the Church, in that it contains those sheep who will be set up at the right hand in judgment (though therein are also mixed those who will be placed on the left who will never be free of everlasting woe), that the shepherd is the lawful bishop, and that the thief is the false bishop. What then do they care about the supervision of one who they know was not put there by the lord of the estate but who put himself there like a thief? What do they care about the blessing of one whom they know to be accursed, since Gregory says that the blessing is turned into a curse for him who is promoted so as to become a heretic?[58] But of what sect is he a heretic? Of that one to whose author we read that Peter said, "Your silver perish with you because you thought you could obtain the gift of God with money" [Acts 8.20].[59] And since anyone communicating with a heretic is himself also a heretic, what, I ask, should be done, what should be considered, what thought, about pastors like these? How can their excommunication be feared by a person who is well aware that they have been excommunicated by canon law not once but a thousand times? How can their blessing be embraced, since the Lord says, "What the unclean touches will be unclean" [Num. 19.22]? How can their damnation be feared when Christ urges, "Let whoever of you is without sin cast the first stone at her" (i.e., the courtesan) [Jn. 8.7]? For these especially are the ones who order the whores to be tied to the stocks for excoriation.

23. I remember that once on the "forked Rhine"[60] when the waves piled up like mountains, such a panic took hold of me, that I thought none had been more frightened even on the Euxine Sea; but when I saw the sailors confident in their seamanship and joking among themselves, I took heart and lost my fear. Let it not be thought irrelevant to use this as an example here: if the laity saw us [clergy] aroused to these great thunderings of God's terror which I have described here, when we read them and understand them (as we cannot deny we do), they too would yet be afraid to some extent. But when they see us often reading them in jest and so obstinately and so brazenly opposing them and hardening ourselves in open rebellion against God, can it be surprising to anyone if they too pay no heed to such warnings? They do not even know what is said, still less understand if it is truly said. Therefore, they make light of our excommunications and our absolutions, because, as far as they can understand, they know that we have been excommunicated by the sacred canons and they understand that on our own judgment we can bind no one nor absolve anyone when bound.

Since we have arrived aimlessly at the subject of preaching: though the Lord, remember, said, "What they say do, but do not do what they do" [Mt. 23.3], yet the apostles in collecting their thoughts did not think they were short of material to say: "While you preach against stealing" [Rom. 2.21], in robbing the poor so as to become rich, "you steal far worse. You who say that one must not commit adultery" at all, doing it in a thousand ways "you commit adultery" worse, not even fearing to be polygamous. Yet what the result of this is, do not ask to learn from me, but listen to Gregory: "The cause of the people's ruin is bad priests."[61] If they did not despise the sacred canons, or rather, if they did not set at naught the words of the prophets, Gospels, and apostles, then no lay person would be mad enough to take these words lightly, but all would know that they ought fully to respect the commands that were so studiously respected by us. These commands would be respected by us in some way if they were loved; but they would be loved if the opposites of lust and accursed wantonness, whose hatefulness no literate person is allowed to be ignorant of even if he wished, had not been drilled into us so severely. As Christ attests, all hate lust, but they love the pleasure of it (though many shun it out of fear of hell) and for this reason God's commands are unpopular among us in the way of the present time.

24. But like it or not, we shall have as our judges those very books of God's law which we now so obstinately hate and ignore; we ought to have had them as our defenders, but we shall have them as our accusers. For it is written: "The court sat in judgment and the books were opened" [Dan. 7.10]. Though this can also be understood about the consciences of individuals, yet another prophet shows that all men will be judged according to what is contained in the books; for he says: "I turned and lifted up my eyes and saw, and behold, a flying scroll and he said to me, What do you see? I answered, I see a flying scroll. Its length is twenty cubits and its breadth is ten cubits. Then he said to me, This is the curse which goes out over the face of the whole land, for every one who steals shall be cut off henceforth according to it and everyone who swears falsely shall be cut off henceforth according to it. I will send it forth, says the Lord of Hosts,

and it shall enter the house of the thief and the house of him who swears falsely in my name; and it shall abide in his house and consume it, both timber and stones" [Zech. 5.1–4].

"Hear," says another (to pass on to other things), "Hear this, O priests; give heed (O house of Israel), for the judgment pertains to you; for you have been a snare for spying" [Os. 5.1]. What is clearer to understand, what, I ask, more obvious? For that the *spy* must be the bishop is shown when it says, "I have made you a spy, says the Lord of Hosts, O House of Israel" [Ezek. 3.17]. Hence also *episcopus* in Greek is translated *superintendens* [over-seer] in Latin.[62] If the bishop either does not know or neglects to do it, or, what is more serious, presumes to do it when not ordered to, he without doubt is turned into a "snare for spying," that is, a snare for the episcopal rank, and a cause of damnation, particularly if he does this not ignorantly but in full knowledge. For the foremost of the Apostles says this about such people: "It had been better for them not to know the way of truth than after knowing it to turn back from the holy commandment delivered to them" [2 Pet. 2.21]. Heartily assenting to this and dismissing what others may feel about themselves as their own concern, I cry out along with him who uttered the same words before me: "Would that I had not been a man with breath, and would that the Lord's words had not been addressed to me!" [Mic. 2.11]. For what is the Lord's word to me living in my fashion other than an indication of my open rebellion against Him and the mountain of my perdition? For when He promises rewards to the good and pardon for those abandoning evil, He deceives none; He says to all: "The Son of Man will come in the glory of His Father together with His angels and then will render to each according to his works" [Mt. 16.27]. Following Him the apostle says: "We will all stand before the tribunal of Christ, so that each may receive good or evil, according to what he has done in the body" [Rom. 14.10; 2 Cor. 5.10]. Also someone no less truthfully (yet whose words the clergy of Verona refuse to sing) says: "To His advent all will arise with their bodies and will render account for their actions, and those who have done good will go into eternal life, and those who have done evil into eternal fire."[63] But, we must pray, may Christ then help him who can there expect to hear: "Out of your own mouth"—and writings—"do I judge you, wicked servant" [Lk. 19.22], who can there expect to be charged with having used the blind eye of a mole on himself but the sharp eye of a she-goat on others.[64] Amen.

II

1. That the second part may respond to the first: the attentive reader should here observe that to my astonishment I have been unable, even after a careful

search, to find any other cause for the contempt of the divine canons, which is, alas, so general, than the fault of pseudo-bishops, a fault spurred by the hand of the wicked [Ps. 35.12]—that is, the devil, because of the punishment of his pride—by means of the weakness of lust [cf. 2 Pet. 2.18]. Lust "burns today in the world in the fire of God's wrath [Dt. 32.22] and will burn to the depths of hell, devouring the earth"—where the vineyard of the God of Sabaoth is planted—"together with its increase" [Is. 5.7] of the good works which it ought to have borne, either when some wretch makes it return some profit to himself by burning it temporally so that eternally it should not unceasingly be burned along with the soul; or "it devours the earth with its increase," when, as another says, "he leads to perdition all the good deeds he has ever done, so that it profits nothing if he has done any good at any time." However, I think that this was said about that *perseverance* in lust about which God himself declares complaining in a passage in the prophets, "The herds have putrified in their own dung" [Joel 1.17], and which "burns up the mountains' (i.e., bishops')[65] bases (i.e., the very beginnings of learning God's law) with pestiferous lust."

This has happened to such an extent that almost no one suitable to be chosen, though there has been need, or totally worthy to lay his hand on one lawfully chosen, alas, can be found. This being so, since these men most embrace what the sacred canons most eschew, while they refuse to avoid these sins, they do not hesitate to make light of the rest. Seeing this, all the sons of the Church also despise everything which is contained in the Scriptures, depending on the examples of such alone and entrusting themselves to God's pity which He himself has promised, and turning their backs on His justice; and thus without fear all men everywhere are slaves to their own pleasures and mortal passions. And since ecclesiastical law is so despised, there is an easy answer why secular law is so feared: because men are more afraid of losing their money than of losing their souls, they fear temporal pain more than everlasting damnation.

2. Someone may also ask why there are more despisers of canon law and more scorners of the clergy *in Italy* than among other nations reborn through baptism. The answer to this, I say, lies in what I related above: Italian clergy more frequently use potions[66] which nurture venery; and the continual drinking of wine and the negligent discipline of their teachers makes them more libidinous. Habit and the example of their elders has long ago brought them to such a point of laxity that you see them differ from the laity only in the trim of their beards and the bare patch on their heads, together with some tiny dissimilarity in dress, and the fact that in church they play (with negligence) a not insignificant role (yet in this too they aspire to please the world more than God). For this the laity despise them and hold them in execration, and rightly. For thus God promises them in the person of His servant, rebuking the insolence of the sons of Eli:

"Those who honor me I will honor, and those who despise me shall be lightly esteemed" [1 Sam. 2.30]. In the person of Malachi also, after saying first about the good, "The lips of a priest should guard knowledge and men should seek instruction from his mouth, for he is the messenger of the Lord of Hosts," see what He says about the reprobate: "You have turned aside from the way; you have caused many to stumble in the law. You have corrupted the covenant of Levi; and so I make you despised among all the people" [Mal. 2.7–8]. And in another's voice: "They have provoked me in him who was not god, and they have angered me in their idols. So I will provoke them in that which is no people, and I will anger them in their foolish nation" [Dt. 32.21]. And He adds this worst fate, touched on here more than once, from which I have now said that all these ills have proceeded, namely: "A fire"—that of lust as is well known—"has been kindled by my wrath and it will burn to the depths of hell and will devour the earth and its increase and will set on fire the foundations of mountains"—that is, the bases of Christianity when apostasy follows. For is it not a clear indication of recession from God and the traditional faith when someone does not fear in His presence to commit such acts against Him (acts which He threatens to pursue with inextinguishable fire [Lk. 3.17], acts so heinous that he can derive no benefit from any good that he has done, even including the very baptism which he has received), especially if he does it not in ignorance but in full awareness?

3. I learned recently that a certain person (he told it to others with his own lips—for shame) in almost the very hour in which he had most wretchedly sung the offices—though he remembered the words in the story of Job, "There is a fire devouring to the point of perdition" [Job 31.12], and was fully aware of its interpretation, and though he remembered also what the apostle said about God, that "all things are open and bare to His eyes to whom we have converse" [Heb. 4.14] (that is, our very thoughts speak to Him, still less do our actions escape His notice)—was so burned up with this deadly fire that to his own damnation in lust and wantonness he caused "the pleasure that scratches the itch within"[67] to be stimulated to the point of obscene discharge. And others have acted even more vilely—if only there could be anything mentioned in such vileness which is not the most vile. What, I ask, was his participation in the morning lauds if not the declaration of his open rebellion against God, since the Lord's service which he had done was nullified? It would have been incomparably better for him to have slept on and missed matins than to have attended them and then done such iniquity.

For, on Gregory's authority, wickedness displeases God to such an extent that no goodness which is diluted with wickedness pleases Him;[68] still less should we be so led astray as to think that He is pleased by those good deeds which will in turn be compensated for by subsequent wickedness. For Isaiah says: "The garment rolled in blood will be burned as fuel for the fire" [Is. 9.5]. Another likewise: "I will change their glory to ignominy"; and so that you are not in doubt about whom he is speaking, he adds: "They feed on the sin of my people; they are greedy for their iniquity. And it shall be like people, like priest. I will punish them for their ways and requite them for their deeds. They shall eat but not be satisfied; they have played the harlot and have not ceased because they have forsaken the Lord in not keeping His way. For harlotry and wine and drunkenness take away the understanding" [Os. 4.7-11], that is, destroy the reason. And again: "They shall not pour wine to the Lord nor will they please Him; their sacrifices shall be like mourners' bread; all who eat of it shall be defiled, for their bread shall be for their hunger only" [Os. 9.4]. A most fearful sentence! But if anyone argues that this only refers to the priests of the Jews, let him hear the apostle refuting him: "Whatsoever is written is written for *our* learning" [Rom. 15.4]; and the same apostle also says: "How will they preach unless they are sent?" [Rom. 10.15] (if *sent* and not rather *permitted*); that is, if they had been legally brought forward, elected and ordained, and did their duties for the salvation not only of themselves but of countless numbers, they would earn the everlasting crown, as on the contrary now they earn — alas for them — everlasting ignominy together with the pain of continual punishment.

"Coming to Babylon there you will be set free" and there "I will redeem you" [Mic. 4.10], says the Lord, who speaks through another's mouth, saying, "You have a harlot's brow, you refuse to be ashamed" [Jer. 3.3]. Would that these two sentences would warn us, wretches that we are, and make one of us say to the rest with King Josiah, rending his garments: "Go, enquire of the Lord for me and for my people and for all Judah" (which by God's declaration we can understand as the excellent Catholic Church) "concerning the words of these books" (of the canons, that is, and decretals which are contained in the archives of the churches); "for great is the wrath of the Lord, that is kindled against us because our fathers have not heard the words of these books to do everything that is written in them" [2 Kg. 22.13] — understand that "our fathers" are the bishops of the churches. So that He may deign to reply to one of us at least: "Thus says the Lord, the God of Israel: Regarding the words which you have heard, because your heart was penitent and you humbled yourself before the Lord, when you heard how I spoke against this place and against its inhabitants, that they should become a desolation and a curse, and you have rent your clothes and wept before me, I also have heard you, says the Lord. Therefore, behold, I will gather you to your fathers and you shall be gathered to your grave in peace, and your eyes shall not see all the evil which I will bring upon this place" [2 Kg. 22.18-20].

4. "What is the point of all this?" envious rivals eager to criticize may ask. Obviously, so that what the earlier part of my treatise was unable to make clear, this part next to the end might show, namely, that anyone looking for it should clearly see the source of this (that is, today's) general contempt of the canons. My investigation and enquiry have come to this conclusion: that it has come about without a doubt through the fault of those who read and understand the canons but hold them worthless. Why do they hold them worthless? Because these people willingly do the things which the canons strongly forbid and they quite refuse to make an effort to do what the canons command. What is that? Two things: the Church teachers' womanizing so often prohibited (or their manifold and God-hated wanton sensuality) and their neglect of the chastity beloved by Christ. Since these three vices of theirs make the other things which are contained in the divine books quite despised, clearly the despisers themselves in return are reproved by God and this reproval is followed by everlasting punishment, not for their own sin alone but also for the bad example by which they damn others.

5. Since I have found no remedy for this pestilence, I admit that I have failed, unless we remember the three things set forth above. What are they? "They have fornicated," says the prophet, "and have not ceased" [Os. 4.10]. When I put this alongside the verse, "You have sinned? Cease" [Gen. 4.7], and alongside "Let the thief no longer steal" [Eph. 4.28], it would seem to me that the fornicators would benefit if they earnestly tried to cease their fornicating. Also, when the psalmist says to God, "The residue of thought will make a festal day for you" [Ps. 75.11], he seems to me to mean that abandoning wicked thought we should strive to prevent the poison of deadly sensuality, like a foul itch deep below the skin, from bursting out to produce sinful deeds, and that that day will be holy for us to God if our action does not follow our evil will. When I also read, "Coming to Babylon, there you will be freed" [Mic. 4.10], the words seem to me to be of great benefit to the person who is disturbed about things he has previously done. Also, the example of King Josiah [2 Kg. 22.10–20] pleases me much, when I compare it with what we read in the Pentateuch: "He who feared the word of the Lord among the servants of Pharaoh made his beasts and cattle flee into the houses, and the hail did not fall upon them" [Ex. 9.19–20]. And this too: "Blessed is the man who is always in fear, but the man of obdurate heart will rush into evil" [Pr. 28.14]. "Do you see," says the Lord, "how Ahab has humbled himself in my presence? Therefore, because he has humbled himself before me, I will not bring the evil in his days" [1 Kg. 21.29].

6. These sentences lighten my desperation some little bit, I admit, though they do not offer security. For I am greatly worried when I read elsewhere that just as the application of any medicine does not profit the wounded man if the steel is still in him,[69] so penitence does not profit him who does not abandon the sin which he bewails, as compunction benefited Balaam [Num. 23.10] and tears Esau [Gen. 27.34]; and the Lord supports this also when He says: "How vile you have become repeating your ways" [Jer. 2.36].

And when I read or hear that Gregory said that one cannot come to great rewards except by great toil,[70] and then consider my own ways, I really must be mad not to be terrified. For if one does not come to great rewards, it can be understood that without a doubt one will come to the greatest punishments. For what is there given in heaven which is not great reward, what in hell which is not great damnation? How delighted I am with those sweet-sounding words of the Lord's in which He says: "There is more joy in heaven over one sinner," but how it terrifies me beyond words when He adds "Who repenteth" [Lk. 15.7]. When I consider what *repentance* is, either in the sacred canons or in the examples of those who did it worthily, and at the same time mark my own failing, I am compelled to cry out only "Woe." For if we abandon our sins, we have the most true and holy promise of Him who says, "Turn to me and I will turn to you" [Zech. 1.3].

But I stand in doubt about what to think, let alone say, of those things which cannot be abandoned. For I know that it has been written of God: "If He shuts in a man, who can say to Him, Why do you do thus?" [Job 9.12] And also about such a man: "For he has put his feet into a net and walks in its spots" [Job 18.8]. Whether He may deign to absolve him (He of whom we sing, "Who opens and no one closes, he closes and no one opens" [Rev. 3.7]) or not, it is not for men in this world to judge. For it is written: "Man does not know whether he is worthy of love or hate, but everything is kept uncertain for the future" [Eccle. 9.1]. But just as this sentence takes away desperation from the sinner, so also it causes worry for the righteous man, even if he does not cease to do what is fitting; so that, to be sure, no one should be without worry in this life; but he who hopes in the Lord [Pr. 28.25] should keep hoping, but in such a way that, as He himself promised, he should not vainly hope in anything else, and he who glories should not glory in himself, that is, his own works and virtue, but if he glories he should glory in the Lord [2 Cor. 10.17].

7. Let this now suffice to show fully the source of the contempt for canon law. For Scripture declares that it is the part of a fool to pour forth all his feeling [Pr. 29.11]; and at the same time I must be cautious lest I be justly reproved for carrying logs into the wood[71] and senselessly pouring water into the river when the gardens are parched.

But your urbane lordship once deigned, if you recall, to advise me in my laxity how I should pray; what I should urgently pray for, I confess, in my lowliness I have found in the book of Hubert,[72] your friend of the same name and ally in persecuting me; this I have thought it worth while to put down here too.

Collect: "Lay low, Lord, with the strength of your right hand those conspiring against the foundation of your rectitude, so that iniquity should not dominate justice, but falsehood always give way to truth."

Offertory: "We seek to please you, Lord, with these gifts and offerings: mercifully free us from our enemies."

Post-Communion: "Let this communion, Lord, both free us from all our sins and defend us strongly from the attacks of our enemies."

29

CC Opera Minora 65–89   Verona Lent 964

[In a Lenten sermon, Rather discusses alms, fasting, and prayer; he moves on to love of one's fellows, and then to deceit; he then attacks the heresy of Anthropomorphites, which has appeared close to Verona.]

⸏

Sermon II on Quadragesima

A very long-winded sermon on Quadragesima: or, chattering ineffective in his [Rather's] lifetime (as it seemed to him).[1]

1. Everyone steeped in divine doctrines is well aware that these forty days, which we firmly believe should be duly observed with fasting and abstinence, have been set at this number for two reasons: firstly, they were prefigured by the cataclysm [Gen. 7.12] and they were devoted to continuous fasting first by Moses [Ex. 34.28; Dt. 9.9] and Elija [1 Kg. 19.8], ministers of the law and prophecy, and then by the Lord himself [Mt. 4.2], the inspirer of the prophets, the founder and stablisher of the law, the bestower of grace, the creator of the Gospel; secondly, they bear a certain mystical force which is not at all to be despised. So I cannot help but wonder at the superstitious practice of those who, though tasting nothing at all for, not forty, but twenty separate days, yet in the remaining twenty, starting early in the day, give themselves up to gluttony and drunkenness in the solemn feasts and still do not scruple to call the observance of this sort of irresponsibility *Quadragesima*, though they should rather call it *Vigesima* [twenty days].

Do not think, listeners, that when I begin my address in this way, I am trying to censure the religious devotion of those who, above what has been lawfully ordained for all Christians, impose on themselves some stronger degree of
abstinence for three or two or at any rate one day of the week, remembering
to be sure the words of Gregory, "Whoever has committed unlawful acts must
abstain from what is allowed";[2] and not forgetting that it has been set forth:
"These you ought to have done, and not to leave the other undone" [Mt. 23.23]
and "Whatever you spend more, when I come again I will repay you" [Lk. 10.35].
I do not reprehend them, I say, but I praise and approve. Only let them take
care that it is not said of them also, "Verily I say unto you, They have their
reward" [Mt. 6.2].

2. We should regret, rather, the madness of those who on one day taste nothing,
on the next surrender themselves to high living, as I frequently remember having seen people do, to such an extent that even on the most sacred Sabbath,
on which no priest is allowed even to celebrate a mass before the evening hour
(since, unless we protract our fast to the evening of that Sabbath, we cannot
fulfill the Quadragesima in the rite of the western church), I have seen individuals at the third hour of the day staggering from drink and excess [Lk. 21.34].
What else must they be said to have done than to have fasted through Good
Friday as if for the Lord, but on the Sabbath, as recompense for this fasting,
to have taken this drunkenness from the devil? Unless perhaps someone is mad
enough to think that Lent has earned this special privilege, that, contrary to
the constitution of other times, there is some day in it that does not begin in
the morning and end in the evening.

3. The violators of Lent find a similar occasion for being delinquent over the
Lord's Supper also, though we read in the sacred canons, "If anyone says that
fasting should be broken on the fifth day of Holy Week, let him be anathema,"[3]
and though those duly celebrating the day of the same feast may rightly have the
greatest joy after the ninth hour of the day. For they claim that the fast has not
been broken by a person who, fasting until the same hour as on other days, comes
to church, sups with the Lord, that is, receives the sacraments of His Body and
Blood first instituted on that day, afterwards in great joy eats soberly, washes
the feet of the poor, drinks in moderation abiding in God's name, gives thanks
to God, and proceeds to bed, blessing the Lord and fortifying himself with His
sign. But since no people has ever been in the habit of naming any meal before
the ninth hour a "supper," I do not cease to wonder how anyone dares to celebrate
in any way a mass before the same hour, which reflects nothing else than the
Lord's Supper itself celebrated at evening, just as also the rites of the Sabbath reflect
the Lord's Resurrection. Both of these considerations, of course, nullify the reasoning
which some people advance in adding two extra days on to the forty.

4. I add, besides, that, if we follow the advice of St. Gregory,[4] we cannot give a tenth of the days to God unless we are willing to extend Lent up to the evening of the blessed Sabbath.

5. It should also, of course, be known, that, since under the one faith the practices of the churches are different, the eastern church keeps a stricter and longer Lent than we do, and therefore begin their Paschal joy at the third hour of the blessed Sabbath, so it is said—which is not at all permissible for us. They are said to celebrate baptism, not on that day as we do, but at Epiphany and Pentecost alone, contrary to the practice of our canons though it be.

6. I castigate also the quite absurd foolishness of those who go against the licence open to all of taking something at the ninth hour of the day, and choose instead to prolong their fast each day till nightfall, so that they can gorge their stomachs at night as though it were allowed. For since the holy reading of the Gospel says of the Lord, "And when He had fasted forty days and forty nights, He was afterward an hungred" [Mt. 4.2], but refused the devil tempting Him to eat, a person clearly does not fast following the Lord's example, who hungry after his fast does not overcome the greed of his belly as He overcame the devil tempting Him.

7. They also fast ignobly who do not give to the poor what they deny to their own bodies, but while abstaining save it either for their own belly, or, what is worse, for mammon, that is, the evil spirit of greed and avarice.

8. God also does not approve of the fasting of those who give over the fast-days to brawls, lawsuits, or criminal acts. While they abstain from wine, they are ever drunk with the poisons of hatred; while they do not eat meat, they continually gnaw at the ways of others; while they refrain from the sweetness of their cups, they are tormented by the noisome bitterness of their evil intentions. Therefore, against the folly of all these, I approve rather what wise Jerome said: "It is better to have too little every day than occasionally to have too much."[5] Truly, truly, it is both better and a safer protection against vainglory. For observing you with the others at the lawful hour eating too little, who can tell whether you do this from love of God, or, as with many, from an inability to eat? A two- or three-day fast, as Jerome says, often is sure to militate not for God but for vainglory.

9. On the other hand, this is the usual defense of gluttons—though not entirely false: "It is better," they say, "to abstain from sin than from food." But how does he abstain from sin, I ask, who is a slave to his belly? Is not three-headed gluttony one of the eight principle vices? And since man lost paradise by eating the forbidden, how will anyone gain heaven who occasionally does not fast and who always sins? "What is the harm," they say, "if I eat before the ninth hour, when I am doing my fasting by only eating once in the day?"

To which I reply, What good did it do Adam that he only ate the fruit of the forbidden tree once and afterwards abstained from it? Did not that disobedience of the divine command make him guilty for all time? But God, who forbade him to eat the fruit of that tree, has commanded you on days of fast to abstain from food up till the ninth hour. If in disobedience you dare to ignore this command, what kind of fasting do you think you made?

10. But why is gluttony called *three-headed*,[6] if not because its first fault is to eat before the hour, its second is to eat on time but to excess, its third to seek over-elegant or sumptuous delicacies? For, as someone says, God rightly despises the whole day's fasting which is compensated for in the evening, or even on the next day, by cramming of the belly or by quantities of rich foods or even by overly sweet foods.[7]

11. "Make alms," they say, "and eat what God provides." Better were they to say, "Make alms, fast, and pray." For unless our fasting is borne on these two wings—that is, the help of prayer and alms—it cannot reach heaven. For these three so help each other with mutual support that alms and prayer carry fasting, fasting and prayer carry alms, and alms and fasting carry prayer to Him who without a doubt rewards those doing them, but only if they are done in sincerity. But if fasting, alms, and prayer do not unceasingly help each other with mutual support, but any one of them is lacking to the other two, they cannot at all win over God, who demands all three, the just judge and lover of perfect goodness.

12. This being the case, let me not be silent also about prayers, which inspire our heart. I do not cease to censure in like manner those (including myself) to whom the apostle James says: "You ask and receive not, because you ask amiss" [Jas. 4.3]. He asks amiss who does not ask for what the Lord requires but rather for what He forbids. For He bids us seek and desire heavenly things; we on the contrary seek and desire earthly things. He bids us pray for those who persecute and slander us [Mt. 5.44]; we on the contrary pour curses on our enemies and slanderers. And what of the fact that some people devote their nights to psalms and prayers, but leave the days free for slanders, blasphemies, idleness, and sloth, though rather the night has been given for rest, the day for work? This he knew best who, after saying, "At midnight I rise to praise you" [Ps. 118.62] and "In the morning I will meditate on thee" [Ps. 62.7], (consecrating only two Hours to the night, to be sure), said, "Seven times a day do I praise thee" [Ps. 118.164]. Let us, dear brothers, avoid with God's help all wicked actions and remember the words of the apostle, "Whether we wake or sleep, we should live together with Christ; in the night we should lift up our hands"— that is, our actions—"in the sanctuary and bless the Lord" [1 Th. 5.10; Ps. 133.2]. Rising after rest, let us consider that we ought to pray even when silent (in

the words of the same Apostle [1 Th. 5.17]), and let us remember at all times the text, "He that turns away his ears from hearing the law, even his prayer shall be abomination" [Pr. 28.9]. But on the other hand, the Lord Himself says to us, "The true worshippers shall worship the Father in spirit and in truth" [Jn. 4.23].

Let us also ask from God, not what He forbids us to desire, but what He orders us to desire, so that He may deign to reply to us what He replied to Solomon asking for wisdom [1 Kg. 3.11]. That reply of course agrees with those words in the Gospel, "Rather seek the kingdom of God, and His justice, and all these things"—that is, bodily necessities—"shall be added unto you" [Lk. 12.31].

13. Of what kind, of what effect, are the prayers of those who, at the time of prayer, are fantasizing—if we may call it such—every kind of sin, robberies, assaults, murders, adulteries, fornication of all sorts too, and are planning a multitude of sins like these, remembering neither God to whom they "pray" nor the thing for which they pray? What do they pray for, I ask, whom do they pray to, for whom do they pray?

14. But because this happens through the treachery of devils (who of course envy the success of prayer), since our secular involvements and what we frequently see, say, and hear are too much an obstacle to prayer, we must in addition to our other interests keep doing what the blind man in the Gospel is said to have done: though the passers-by railed at him to be silent, he kept shouting all the more, "Son of David, have mercy upon me" [Mk. 10.48]. Most truly—to use the words of the truest writer—"our mouth is that much the less heard in prayer the more it is polluted by foul speech."[8]

15. So, since I have said enough for the time being about prayer, let us proceed to alms. Since alms [elemosina] is derived from the word for mercy [Gr. elemosyne], no alms, it seems to us, can more fittingly take priority than those about which the preacher admonishes us in these words: "My son, pleasing God have mercy on your soul" [Eccli. 30.24], admonishes us, that is, to apply that exhortation of mercy first to ourselves, so that we strive to do what pleases God; and because we are ordered to love our neighbor as ourselves [Mt. 19.19], let us direct him into the way of the Lord with just counsel, where it may seem advantageous, whether by remonstrating with him or beseeching him or rebuking him [2 Tim. 4.2]. If he lacks bodily necessities, let us offer him from our just works according to what we can. We have a text to be sure, "Whoever offers a sacrifice out of a poor man's substance, he is as one who sacrifices a son in the sight of his father" [Eccli. 34.24]. But as we do this let us remember the Lord's words: "When you give a dinner, or supper, call not . . . your rich neighbors, who can recompense you, but call the poor . . . and you will be recompensed at the resurrection of the just" [Lk. 14.12–14]. No one, however, is rich

in that thing in which he needs support, and therefore what we give to God, we give not to the rich but to the poor man only, for the reverence of God, and let us do this in love of our neighbor, following the authority of His command, "Do unto others what you would they do unto you" [Mt. 7.12; Lk. 6.31].

When we are urged to "make to ourselves friends out of the mammon of unrighteousness" [Lk. 16.19], it does not mean that we should take away from one person what we give to another (since it is better, as St. Augustine says,[9] to give to nobody than to take from somebody else), but that we should know that riches, being given for common use for all time, can in no way be amassed by an individual without the sin of avarice. "For," says St. Jerome, "every rich man is either unjust or the heir of an unjust man."[10] And because the psalmist says, "Blessed is he that considers the poor" [Ps. 40.2], let us take care that he who is the more needy receives more, who less, likewise less. And as we are also instructed to give rather to the good person than to the bad, let us do so provided that we can distinguish them; if not, let us follow him who says, "Do not choose whom you will pity."[11]

Let us be careful also not to treat anyone with sullenness or derision, even though he ask importunately; "for God loves a cheerful giver" [2 Cor. 9.7]. And because, as St. Ambrose says,[12] the distribution of alms has often caused offence by being put off, let us carefully incline our ear to Solomon saying, "Say not to your neighbor, Go, and come again, and tomorrow I will give, when you can give at once" [Pr. 3.28].

In all this let us be careful that we strive to do the good which we are doing not for vainglory but in obedience to God's command and in consideration of our common nature, since the Lord orders: "When you give alms, let not your left hand know what your right hand is doing" [Mt. 6.3] (although this saying can also be interpreted to mean that in our alms there should be nothing which has been acquired by left-handed work — that is, unjust labor — what follows shows that it is ostentatiousness in giving that is censured in this remark, as He says, "That your alms may be in secret; and your Father who sees in secret Himself will reward you"), and as the apostle also says, "He that sows sparingly shall reap also sparingly" [2 Cor. 9.6].

And because "alms extinguish sin in like manner as water extinguishes fire" [Eccli. 3.33], let us consider the effect of a little water thrown on a large fire. In addition to this consideration, there is the forceful advice which Tobias gave to his son of the same name: "Son, if you have much, give much; if too little, try to give of yourself also" [Tob. 4.9]. For nothing is dearer to God than goodwill (in fact, nothing at all is dear to him without goodwill), since even a cup of cold water offered with goodwill does not lack the reward of remuneration, as the Lord Himself says in the Gospel [Mt. 10.42], to which the pious psalmist adds, "Your vows are upon me, O God" [Ps. 55.12], that is, the goodwill which I offer to you who sees all things.

For which reason, if someone is so poor that he has absolutely nothing to give, if he give himself, let him believe it is enough. For it is said: "Give yourself to every man that asks" [Lk. 6.30],[13] that is, give yourself both to the man to whom you give something and to the man to whom you give nothing. For example, if someone asks for a gift of bread and you have no bread to give, give yourself, that is, your goodwill with which you would most willingly give him bread if you had any. And because "a good word in addition to the gift is best" [Eccli. 18.17], strive with all your energy that, though food is lacking to your hand to give, a good word is not lacking to your tongue to reply.

16. But (strange to tell!) all these things if done without charity will profit nothing, witness the apostle, who says: "Though I bestow all my goods to feed the poor, and though I give my body to be burned, and have not charity, it profits me nothing" [1 Cor. 13.3]. Therefore, in order to keep the terms of this charity unbroken, let us offer the ear of our heart to Him as He says: "If you bring your gift to the altar and there remember that your brother has something against you, leave there your gift before the altar and go your way; first be reconciled to your brother, and then come and offer your gift" [Mt. 5.23–24]. But if the man who has hurt and damaged his brother in anything has not disdained to act in accordance with the Lord's advice, then he who is damaged and has something against his brother should not offer a deaf inner ear to Him advising also this: "When you stand praying, forgive if you have something against any, that your Father also which is in heaven may forgive you your trespasses. But if you do not forgive, neither will He forgive you your trespasses" [Mk. 11.25–26].

17. But on the other hand, there are those like me who are very lenient in dismissing what is done against God, but would pursue with everlasting hatred, if they could, what is done against themselves, although charity rather demands that they lightly dismiss the things done against themselves but most rigorously punish what is done against God, while still remembering that He said: "He that is without sin amongst you, let him be the first to cast a stone at her" [Jn. 8.7]. Let us believe, besides, that no good should be done to compensate for evil; you should not fast, you should not give alms, you should not wear out this air with your prayers, you should not dismiss what is done against you, only with this end in view, that you may believe you can commit adultery or fornication or something similar as if with impunity; for pardon of sins is promised to no one except to him who has abandoned his sins and been converted.

18. Since such fastings, prayers and alms of ours, alas, are just as contemptible, we can fear that Jeremiah was referring to us when he said: "The adversaries saw her and did mock at her Sabbaths" [Lam. 1.7], and that the Lord in the mouth of another was speaking to us when He commanded: "You shall not fast as you do this day" [Is. 58.4].

19. Since, following the apostle, whatsoever action is not of faith is sin [Rom. 14.23], but faith itself without works is idle or dead [Jas. 2.20], we ought not to pass over those deceivers of souls, who, wretches, against the affirmation of the Catholic faith, in which it is held that the "Lord will come again to judge the quick and the dead and the world through fire,"[14] and "They that have done good shall come forth unto the resurrection of life and they that have done evil unto the resurrection of the damned" [Jn. 5.29], promise impunity of their sins to all who are baptized. God is so benign and merciful, they say, that He permits no Christian to enter into hell. Yet they would speak the truth, if they could believe that only he who does Christ's will is a Christian. But when they hear the apostle Peter say: "It had been better for them not to have known the way of righteousness than after they have known it to turn from the holy commandment delivered unto them" [2 Pet. 2.21], about whom, I ask, do they suppose he was speaking?

20. Sacred authority holds that there will be four orders in the Final Judgment: one which judges with the Lord, a second which is rewarded through the Judgment, a third which is condemned through the Judgment, and a fourth which is neither condemned nor rewarded through the Judgment[15] — since in the Gospel it is written, "He that does not believe is condemned already" [Jn. 3.18], and in the Psalms, "Therefore the ungodly shall not stand in the judgment" [Ps. 1.5], as though to say more clearly: "Even if they do rise, they do not rise in order to be judged because they have already been judged, but they rise in order to receive bodies and go where they are destined for ever" (by *ungodly* we ought to understand only those who are unbelievers and unbaptized). Of whom then does the third order seem to you to consist if not the believers, that is, the baptized, who, because they had faith but lacked the works of faith which are demanded by it, have justly been condemned to go to the eternal fire which without a doubt will be below?

21. Therefore, it is certainly established that it was for one purpose that the Lord urged a man as follows: "Behold, you are made whole, sin no more lest a worse thing happen to you" [Jn. 8.11], and in another place said: "The last state of that man is worse than the first" [Mt. 12.45], namely, so that you may know that we who have been redeemed by the great humiliation of God descending from heaven to earth for men, by the many indignities and insults He endured, by His hunger, thirst, and exhaustion, by the spittings, derisive kneelings, false testimonies, by the vinegar, gall, and crown of thorns, and at the end, the yoke of the cross, the piercing of His side, the pouring of His blood and water, the nailing of His hands and feet, the insult of an ignominious death, so that you may know, I say, that we who have been washed by His sacred baptism, enriched by the illumination of the Holy Spirit, prospered by the recognition of the will of God, long tolerated though evil-doers, improved by the scourgings of His fatherly hand, encouraged by the sweetest promises, crowned with both secular and ecclesiastical honors, drawn onwards by the enticements of inestimable good, enriched by innumerable other privileges and benefits, that we justly deserve greater torments than those to whom none of these things have been conceded. "For to whom more is entrusted, from him more is demanded,"[16] as one of the blessed, not the least, said; and "The servant who knows his master's will and does not do it shall deservedly be beaten with many stripes" [Lk. 12.47].

22. But because God is omnipotent and His pity is nothing else than God Himself, and His pity is omnipotent just as His justice is also (even to doubt this we believe to be apostatic), let us throw ourselves on His pity while we live. For dead, we shall do nothing at all, but shall receive what we have done. But if someone does something good for us, even if it does not profit us, it will profit him. Let no one deceive himself about those purgatory punishments after death, I advise, for they have not been ordained for sins but for lighter faults, that is, those defined by "wood, hay, and stubble" [1 Cor. 3.12].

Since this is established as certain, what am I to do, who know that some people have been so bound by noxious habits, by evil service, by wicked deeds, or by other things that are unavoidable, so they claim, that they can in no way be turned to correction? What can I say to them, what advice can I give them? Whatever I say to them, they undoubtedly will reply—if not in actual words, yet by their subsequent actions—just what those in the Gospel invited to dinner replied [Lk. 14.17–20], and we must fear that, abandoned likewise by the Inviter, they will perish hardened like Pharoah in obstinacy [Ex. 7.13].

23. For these of course are the ones who, though they could be free, of their own accord have put their feet in the net, poor wretches; walking in its mesh [Job 18.8], while they free themselves from one danger, they fall into another, and we must fear that they will be inescapably enclosed by God. But let us try, let us say something to them. Let us urge them in no way to throw themselves into the pit of despair without knowing what is destined for them. "For no man knows whether he is worthy of love or hatred, but all is uncertain for the future" [Eccle. 9.1]. Let them think on Lazarus raised after four days [Mk. 10.47]. Let them cry importunately with the blind man in the Gospel, fasting and praying and giving alms, not, however, so that they should have licence to sin, but so that it may come about through God's mercy that they be freed from their sin. Let them cry with the woman of Canaan, saying, "Have mercy on me, son of David, my soul is grievously vexed with a devil" [Mt. 15.22], and, "Be not overcome, Lord, with my evil, but overcome my evil with your good" [Rom.

12.21], and, "Deliver me, O Lord, from the evil man, preserve me from the violent man" [Ps. 139.2], yes, *me* indeed; and "Restore me to you, my Maker and most Holy Redeemer"—which to be sure you most mercifully do if you make me not do, whether I will or no, what I meditate against you. But if you permit my death-bringing efforts to prosper, what hope of abandoning them do you leave me?[17] And if I do not cease from my present wickedness, what pardon do I hope for for my past ones?

Let each of these groan incessantly in a kind of complaint until he should merit to be heard, and cry out: "How long shall my enemy be exalted over me?" and "Consider and hear me, O Lord my God" [Ps. 12.3–4], and "Shew me a token for good, that they that hate me may see it and be ashamed because you, Lord, have helped me and comforted me" [Ps. 85.16]. If he tires with heart, hand and mouth the ears of the Lord most ready to hear with these and similar cries, and if he continues right up to the end of his life, then perhaps His pity (Who when He wishes is able of these stones to raise up children unto Abraham [Mt. 3.9], Who does not wish the death of the wicked but rather that he may turn from his wickedness and live [Ezek. 33.11]), pressed by the prayers of the saints, will reply to him, too, what He replied to the woman shouting insistently, "O woman,"—for not up to now acting like a man but with womanly softness succumbing feebly to vices—"great is now your faith"—that is, your perseverance in prayer—"may it happen to you even as you wish" [Mt. 15.28], and his soul will be made whole from that very hour; which may the mercy of our Redeemer deign to bestow on us all.

24. There[18] is another clear indication of those perishing everlastingly: when we read in the Gospel that three people were raised from the dead, He refused to raise a fourth reported to Him, but on the contrary said, "Leave the dead to bury their dead" [Mt. 8.22]. Those three dead signify the three kinds of death of the soul, namely, one in secret, one in public, and the third in habit (which is said also to *reek*, that is, to infect one's fellows with despair of recovery).[19] But because nothing is impossible to God and all have been in His eyes from the beginning such as He foresaw that they would be in the end, He is shown to have loved them since their unhoped-for correction is visible. The fourth type of death is that about which the psalmist says: "For the wicked is praised in his heart's desire and the unjust man is blessed" [Ps. 10.3]; and the prophet says, "O my people, those who call you blessed cause you to err" [Is. 3.12]. For when a man both himself defends the evil which he does and in addition is raised by the praises of flatterers, never returning to knowledge of himself, just as the dead man is pressed by the weight of the sepulchre, so is he, unblessed, pressed by the false praise of flatterers. He, to be sure, never revives who never recognizes that he has died, nor does he return to salvation who does not believe that he needs salvation. Therefore, it must not be doubted that he who comes to such an end has perished everlastingly. Let us strive mightily with God's help to avoid this type of death, if we desire to receive remission of our sins, that is, that we neither defend the evil done by ourselves nor believe the lies of flatterers about us, but both point out our sins ourselves and not be angry with those who point them out to us. Let no one think that he is committing only a small sin when he exalts an evil-doer with false praises, when in the Lord's words he hears it said of him that the dead should bury the dead. For he kills irrecoverably a man who perhaps would rise to a life of correction, did he not continually bury him with his flatteries.

25. There are eight kinds of lie, as St. Augustine states,[20] but that of *flatterers* is, I hold, the worst of all. For they most of all are the slayers and buriers of souls, particularly those of kings, of dukes, of counts, of bishops, of abbots, and of the powerful of this world. They do not fear that terrible curse of the Lord in the prophet: "Woe unto them that call evil good and good evil" [Is. 5.20]. Their deadly laudations Job, and afterwards Jeremiah, symbolically are said to have cursed: "Let the day perish wherein I was born and the night in which it was said, There is a man-child conceived" [Job 3.3], and the other: "Cursed be the man who brought tidings to my father, saying, A man-child is born to you" [Jer. 20.15], and the psalmist, invoking the help of the Lord against them: "Let them be turned back at once in shame that say to me, Well done, Well done" [Ps. 69.4].

26. We ought the more to abstain from every lie the more certainly we can see that it proceeds from the devil, since the Lord says of him: "When he speaks a lie, he speaks of his own, for he is a liar and father of it" [Jn. 8.44] — of lying, that is —, and since the psalmist says to the Lord: "You will destroy them that speak a lie" [Ps. 5.7]. But if we are to understand this about every lie, we judge no one to be free of perdition, for the psalmist says elsewhere: "Every man is a liar" [Ps. 115.11]. Are you, then, who say this [i.e., the psalmist] a lying prophet? "By no means, for there [i.e., Ps. 5.7] I called a 'lie' that certain something which only the sons of perdition speak, while here [i.e., Ps. 115.11] I called *a liar* every man in ecstasy, that is, in contemplation of God's truth, just as Ecclesiastes [3.19] and after him the apostle [Rom. 8.20] call him 'subject to vanity.'"

How noxious is every lie, another, moreover, warns us, saying, "The mouth which lies kills the soul" [Wisd. 1.11], and "A false witness shall not be unpunished" [Pr. 19.5].

27. How far the leaders of the church ought to be from lying can be seen by someone's invective sentence, habitually quoted by both leaders and congregations: "A priest's words," they say, "are either true or sacrilegious." But on the other hand how beloved of God is truth, God the Man Himself speaking of Himself shows when He says: "I am the Way, the Truth, and the Life" [Jn. 14.6], and by the prophet: "Love peace and truth, says the Lord God" [Zech. 8.16], whose Pasch the Apostle urges us to celebrate "with the unleavened bread of sincerity and truth" [1 Cor. 5.8]. And after reproving certain acts of his people, he adds: "These are the things that you shall do, speak every man the truth to his neighbor, execute the judgment of truth and peace in your gates" [Zech. 8.16].

28. See, brothers and sons, mercifully looked upon by Him (God grant it!), see how many true evils I have noted, how many false goods, and also how many evils mixed with good. What should we do about these, except (as I said before that the Lord has commanded) that we should not so fast, pray, and give alms as we have fasted, prayed, and given alms up till now, or we will offer occasion to our enemies, malignant spirits, that is, for further mocking us. But consciously serving the Lord in simplicity of heart, let us first see that our goods be not false, then that they be not few, then that they be not irregular.[21] And never forgetting that advice which we read was given—though fruitlessly—to a man: "Thou hast sinned, cease" [Gen. 4.7], let us equally remember the very clear statement agreeing with it of one of our own: "Be not a doer of evils but a slayer of them,"[22] that is, of course, of evil deeds; and mindful of this too: "Son [he said], do not add sin on sin saying, The mercy of God is great" [Eccli. 5.5–6], and what follows. Let us not so underestimate Him in our thinking as to believe that we can delude Him—who though invisible to all penetrates the universe with His gaze—with prayers made up to placate Him and fastings, prayers, and alms, all as insincere as up to now, and vigils contrary to reason. But if we wish to please Him, let us strive to serve Him as He ordains, so that we may merit to receive remission of sins and recover His grace, by the pity of Him alone, which we deservedly lost by the freedom of our will.

29. I had thought that at this point I had reached the end of my address, but on the contrary there comes to mind every kind of reason for not being able to stop. For here among us, a certain heresy of the ancients, which was thought defunct everywhere, has appeared rather to be dormant; this heresy Latin has customarily called that of *anthropomorphites*, a word borrowed from the Greek. The day before yesterday, one of our priests reported to me that the priests of the diocese of Vicentia, our neighbors that is, think that God is corporeal, led on presumably by such readings in the Scriptures as: "The *eyes* of the Lord are upon the righteous and His *ears* are open unto their cry" [Ps. 33.16], and: "Your *hands* have made me" [Job 10.8], and: "Let us make man in our own image after our likeness" [Gen. 1.26]—although, to be sure, this likeness or unlikeness is relevant not to the body but only to the soul, which is of course spirit (though circumscribed), just as God also is spirit (though that much the more

unlike in proportion as He is an uncircumscribed, and incomprehensible, spirit) —
and other passages of this sort in the scriptures, not understanding, fools, that
God is so inconceivable, so inscrutable, so ineffable, so incomprehensible, that
the practice of human speech can say nothing appropriate about Him.

30. For who would dare (to take this one example from many) even to imagine that Christ was in His nature a worm or a beetle? Yet by a certain analogy
He Himself says truly of Himself: "But I am a worm and no man" [Ps. 21.7],
and: "The beetle will cry from the wood" [Hab. 2.11]. I was much angered
by this shameful report, but then I found that this same heresy is so deeply rooted in the flock entrusted to me, that, though a sermon about the same danger
had been made to the people and it had been shown by scriptural testimony that
God is a spirit, incorporeal, invisible, untouchable, and inconceivable, some of
our priests,[23] even (for grief!), have been murmuring: "What will we do now?
Up till now we had thought we knew something about God; now, it seems
to us that God is nothing at all, if he has no head, no eyes, no ears, no hands,
no feet."

To which I offer this reply to one of them: You dullard, does your soul or
mine seem, then, to you to be nothing, just because you cannot see it? What
sort of head does your soul have, what hands, what feet, what other limbs?
Show me at least its color, if you can; if you cannot, I will show you its power.
Set me up here two bodies, one with a soul and one without. Which of these
two will see, hear, speak, walk? That which is with a soul, or that in which
there is none?

"No doubt that which has the soul," you will reply.

I will then say: Why not that which does not have a soul? Obviously because
it is lacking the very force, the very power, the very something inestimably better and stronger which directed it to do something, without which it could do
nothing at all; for reason shows there is no visible thing which is not directed
by an invisible.

31. See how much more powerful the invisible soul is than the visible body.
What do you think about the life itself of the soul. Is it not much more invisible
than the soul itself? What would the soul itself be able to do, nay, what would
it be, without life? Nothing, without doubt; for it is written: "The first man,
Adam, was made a living soul, the last Adam was made a quickening spirit"
[1 Cor. 15.45]. If, therefore, the soul, which of course is spirit, is so much more
powerful than the body that without it, it cannot even move, the life of the
soul, which is of course even more invisible, is so much more powerful than
the soul that without it, it cannot even be a quickening spirit — and this is, of
course, God — and in proportion as God is more invisible than it, by so much
could the spirit be called the invisiblest (if the regular rules of grammar will

allow such an expression) spirit of all spirits, and the spiritest spirit of all spirits; and the more it is less visible than all spirits, so much the more is it interior than all, and the more interior, so much the more to be believed as the ruler, inspirer, mover, life-giver of all spirits, just as the soul is of all bodies, nay as life is of all living things, and by so much the more excellently as the more ineffably and powerfully.

32. For just as the soul would be nothing if there were no life, so every creature, whether visible or invisible, whether material or immaterial, would be nothing at all if there were no God, animating everything surely (to put it thus) like the quickening spirit which, the more interior it is than everything, so the more invisible it is, just as also the spirit is more interior in bodies in proportion as it is more invisible, the more invisible in proportion as it is more interior, up to the point where it can no longer be expressed, and therefore the more efficacious at moving bodies. So, to clarify by repetition: God is the more interior in proportion as He is the more invisible, the more invisible in proportion as He is the more interior, up to the point where it can no longer be expressed, and so much the more powerful (up to the point of omnipotence) that whatever exists, exists through Him, whatever lives, lives through Him, whatever moves, moves through Him, again up to the point of inexpressibility. I have added "up to the point where it can no longer be expressed," because I remember the movements of homicides, thieves, adulterers, who indeed have the very motion which, wretches, they so foully abuse from no one but from God, though they have the vice of evil motion from themselves.

33. Such a force, therefore, such a power, so inestimable, so impenetrable, a nature, so inscrutable a substance, so incomprehensible a deity, so immeasurable a size, such a beauty irradiating the universe itself out of itself, such a glance piercing everything with penetrating look, so invisible a hand containing all things, such a clarity illuminating the universe, such a height pre-eminent above everything, such a depth enclosing everything, such an action doing everything, such an immobile motion unapproachably leaving nothing unapproached, such a succulent sweetness nourishing everything, such a breath able to distinguish everything, so subtle a hearing able to know from afar not only voices but even thoughts, to whom Moses is said to have shouted in silence, and (lest we extend to infinity Him whom the words of all who have ever lived, are living, or will live, have not been able, are not able, will never be able, to make finite by saying that it is ineffable and inconceivable to all) finally, He is uncircumscribed, everywhere whole, nowhere less, nowhere greater, who holds the thrones of heaven and surveys the abysses, weighs the mountains, holds the earth in his palm, to whom all things celestial, terrestrial, and infernal kneel: a spirit who is surely Father, Son, and Holy Spirit, a spirit in every point, indivisibly a spirit, who

is over, in, and through everything, blessed everlastingly God—does He seem to you to be nothing just because He does not have a body which you can see?

You have not taken the trouble to learn by reading, or to inquire from those who do read, what are those "eyes of the Lord upon the righteous," what are "His ears open unto their cry," what is "His face against them that do evil, to cut off the remembrance of them from the earth" [Ps. 33.16–17], what are His hands, what His feet. But pondering all these things with the intellect of a blacksmith, you have most unwisely said, not only in your heart but much more senselessly with your voice: "God does not exist," or worse, "God is nothing if He does not have hands and feet," though, rather, with that very quality by which you were made rational, from reason you ought to perceive that He who made you is that much the more God the *less* you can see Him. As St. Gregory says,[24] it is possible to see Him when you see His reason by use of your own reason. We know something of Him as though in part, at that time when we feel that we cannot worthily know Him; we see Him as though in part at that time when we fully know that He can be seen by none.

34. They say: "We have considered and there was not an aspect from which we did not ponder Him" [Is. 53.2–3].

This is what those confederates of yours are said to have said about the wisdom of God made incarnate for us. But you rave the more insanely about the whole Trinity, imitating to be sure those who, when Moses tarried on Mt. Sinai, said to his brother Aaron: "Make us gods, which shall go before us, for we do not know what is become of Moses" [Ex. 32.1]. Just so, you too, grown tired of being led out of Egypt, that is, out of the darkness of ignorance into the light of recognition of the invisible God, foolishly began to make idols of a sort for yourself in your heart and, forgetting the immensity of God, to depict Him as a sort of great king, sitting, of course, on a golden throne, with an army of angels, like some winged men just as you are accustomed to seeing in murals, attending Him clothed in white garments; and since they too are spirits, they appear both invisible in their nature and with men not in their own nature but in a form which God wishes to give them, either from this corporeal, though very thin, air, or from whatever He wishes, or, if He so choose, from nothing, as He did in the first beginnings of all creation, so that they can be seen with bodily eyes: they are apparent and return voices from the same air, with lips and jaws and throat made of air (so to speak), to us incomprehensibly, though to those to whom it is divinely conceded to see or hear this, recognizably.

35. They say: "The Archangel Michael celebrates a mass to God on the second day of the week."

What blind madness! What do you think is the cause that gives us a first or second day of the week? Is it not the rising of the sun and its setting? And what other sun is there in the sky except the sun of righteousness [Mal. 4.2], together with the Father and Holy Spirit, Christ? Or are you so mad as to think that there is night in heaven, whose light makes tomorrow's day? Then how can there be eternal light there, if any darkness interrupted it? In what sort of temple does St. Michael sing the mass, since John in the Apocalypse says: "I saw no temple therein" [Rev. 21.22]?

"The Lord is in His holy temple," you say, "the Lord's throne is in heaven" [Ps. 10.5].

Would you like me now to tell you what comes into my mind about that temple? The Lord in the womb of His virgin mother, not leaving behind the Father in heaven, —for thus He says: "No one ascends into heaven but He who descended from heaven, the Son of Man who is in heaven" [Jn. 3.13]—at one and the same moment, to be sure, was both in heaven and in the Virgin's womb, but in heaven timelessly, in His mother temporarily.

"But," you point out, "The Psalmist says, 'You sit on the throne, judging right' [Ps. 9.5]."

We also have often sung, "You that dwell above the cherubim" [Ps. 79.3], and have understood that the cherubim are translated as the fullness of knowledge and that the throne is also called *cherubim*, that is, the angelic *spirit*, in fact, both these are the legions of angels. Above which of the angels does the Lord *not* sit, since we also read about the soul of the just, that it is the seat of wisdom and that "The wisdom of God the Father is God the Son" [1 Cor. 1.30]? Where sits wisdom without Him who is the essence of wisdom?

36. But heretics are of such a character that they can be refuted at once but not easily overcome. If, therefore, with this whole argument we can persuade you, not what God is, but what He is not, that is, that He is neither corporeal nor visible nor conceivable, inasmuch as He is the spirit of spirits, the most invisible of all spirits, then we may rejoice that the enemies of truth have been refuted. But you, my sons, whom I am addressing, this I urge, that you reject nonsense and lies of this sort, remembering the admonition of the preacher: "Seek not the things that are too high for you nor search into things above your ability" [Eccli. 3.22] (for there are many who, while scorning to become disciples of truth, become masters of error, not understanding either what they say or whereof they affirm [1 Tim. 1.7]); and that you betake yourselves to that Angel of Great Counsel [Is. 9.6] who says, "I am the way, the truth, and the life," and, "No man comes to the Father except by me" [Jn. 14.6], for it follows that he does not come to the Holy Spirit either. For in answer to Philip who asked that He show them the Father, He said: "He that has seen me"—meaning with the inner eyes with which God can in some way be seen (for "Blessed are the pure in heart, for they shall see God" [Mt. 5.8])—"has seen the Father" [Jn.

14.9], and added: "Do you not believe that I am in the Father and the Father in me?"

All of this cannot stand up unless you apply it to the invisible deity of Father and Son; for it does not mean that he who saw the Son in the flesh which He assumed for us therefore saw the Father also. Otherwise the Jews persecuting Him would also have seen Him, to whom the Lord replied: "You know neither me nor my Father. If you had known me, you would have known my Father also" [Jn. 8.19], that is: "If you had recognised my invisible and incorporeal divinity hidden in me and had had a pure heart for contemplating it, as a consequence you would know my Father remaining in me and me in my Father." So He himself, who by an introduction of this sort made us know that the Father and himself and He who said, "Go therefore and teach all nations, baptizing them in the name of the Father and of the Son and of the Holy Spirit" [Mt. 28.19], were one God, Son and Holy Spirit, He, I say, who instructed His disciples like this with lips of flesh moved by the inner God, let Him tell us what is God: "God is a Spirit" [Jn. 4.24], He said, and after the Resurrection, when the apostles were in doubt, He said, "Handle me and see, for a spirit does not have flesh and bones as you see me have" [Lk. 24.39].

37. If, therefore, a spirit does not have flesh and bones, how can He have a head, which is certainly made of flesh and bones? How hands? How arms? How the lips, tongue, throat, lungs, arteries, how the hollow of the palate, the four front teeth, with which in every person voice is undoubtedly formed and speech made, with which Michael is said to sing the mass?

But you who answered above say, on the other hand: "Who was the first to sing 'Glory to God in the Highest' [Lk. 2.14]?"

"Angels," we reply.

"How [could they sing if not corporeal]?"

Since it pleased God to endow angels with what shepherds could hear and understand, since angels in their spiritual nature could in no way do this, and this in the air (which when struck makes a sound, and which is also called the sky, of course—wherefore birds also are said to be of the sky), not in the ether, not in heaven, where no one needs the sound of voice to know anything, least of all God who knows everything. For the angels' voice in heaven is nothing other than the perpetual admiration of the clarity and ineffability of God, without movement of tongue, without sound of voice. On earth, too, this is more pleasing to God, who, as we mentioned a little earlier, says: "God is a spirit and those that worship Him must worship Him in spirit and in truth" [Jn. 4.24]. Also, since at the celebration of the Mass he who celebrates it is refreshed by sharing in the Body and Blood of Christ, show me the bread and wine with which Michael is refreshed.

"'He gave them of the corn of heaven,'" you reply, "and 'Man did eat angels' food' [Ps. 77.24]."

Here let St. Augustine answer: "What other bread of heaven is there except Christ the Lord, from whom the heavenly beings receive spiritual food and enjoy inestimable delight?"[25] And the angels' food rightly is called Christ because truly they feed on His praise; for we must not think that the angels eat material bread. (Since the prophet said this figuratively, you should know that though that food came from heaven, yet, because it was material, it was not appropriate for angels, but the manna of course stood figuratively for Him who descended from heaven, who gives life to the world, so that, whence angels take their life, thence may man too take spiritual life, by worthily taking His Body and Blood.)

What will you do about the *wine*?

You reply: "'I will not drink henceforth of this fruit of the vine until the day when I drink it anew with you in the Kingdom of God'" [Mt. 26.29; Mk. 14.25].

There is still no help for you. By "the Kingdom of God" He means the Church, and He had already begun to reign there, as the psalmist says, in the cross [Ps. 95.10] and to refresh the inhabitants of His kingdom with new wine—that is, His blood—together with the bread of His flesh, when He was seen by the apostles forty days after His Resurrection, and, speaking of the things pertaining to the kingdom of God, and eating with them, He cannot therefore be doubted at all to have drunk with them also [Acts 1.3].

But you, wretch, who must be thought more stupid than the priests of Belis [Dan. 14.1–21], you who fed on that bodily God of yours from the middle of Lent one year, our God is the true one, invisible, immaterial, untouchable, immeasurable, undefined, unspeakable, creator of all who ever have been, are, or will be, ruler of all, disposer and moderator of all, everywhere whole, everywhere present, nowhere greater, nowhere less, the Head of the Universe, His eyes surveying all things, His ears penetrating even into our innermost hearts, His arms embracing all things, His hands managing all things, His feet motionlessly coursing through everything, in all of which things He is to be sure a *spirit* [Jn. 4.24], God the Father and Son and Holy Spirit, whose unity stands in Godhead, whose Trinity stands in three persons—our God, I say, is to be worshipped with great trembling and reverence, to be embraced with the greatest love; now at last see the source whence such a God of ours as this feeds His angels eternally, convinced if not by us, then at least by St. Augustine—and would that you were converted! Concerning the communication of God to the angels and of the angels to God, Gregory fully teaches you, if you look in the *Moralia* [2.42].

38. And because, as is apparent, you cannot be separated from carnal intellect, keep yourself at least to that carnality which the wisdom of God deigned to assume for us. For without a doubt that [carnality] sits, with bones which a spirit in no way has, in heaven at the right hand of—that is, in equality with—the Father [Col. 3.1], who everywhere is right, nowhere left, inasmuch as He is an unbounded spirit. To His divinity the incorporeal spirits attend incorporeally, the holy angels, that is, and also the blessed souls, the bodies of the saints, also, as some have thought, which arose with the Lord, together with the souls of the just [Mt. 27.52]. For you are not of such merit that you can say with the apostle: "Though we have known Christ after the flesh, yet now we know Him no more" [2 Cor. 5.16]. But if you wish somehow to investigate His divine substance, listen most intently to Him: "He who has seen me, Philip, has seen the Father" [Jn. 14.9]—that is: "no one has seen either Him or Me in divinity, which if you could see, you would not say this; for I and my Father are one; you see me in the flesh which I have assumed for you; you do not see me in the divinity in which I am one with the Father [Jn. 10.30], and therefore, if you wish to see the Father, cleanse that eye of your heart so that it can somehow contemplate an invisible God, and, looking at me, you will see Him too, not by touching Him with a corporeal eye but by contemplating Him with the spiritual eye."

If you are curious about His *food*, hear Him: "My meat is to do the will of Him that sent me" [Jn. 4.34], and: "Man shall not live by bread alone but by every word that proceedes out of the mouth of God" [Mt. 4.4], and: "I was hungry and you gave me meat" [Mt. 25.35], speaking of course about the poor.

39. Because I have said all this in complaint of our priests, I advise them together with myself that, meditating on the law of God day and night [Ps. 1.2], they should examine the Scriptures better than they have done up till now; for "If the blind lead the blind," as the Lord says, "both shall fall into the ditch" [Mt. 15.14]. Let them ever ponder what God has ordained, continually having this instruction above all before their eyes, since it greatly helps them; for necessity compels them to celebrate the Lord's Pasch not once in the year but every day: "You will gird up your loins" [Ex. 12.11]—that is, you will strive to be chaste—and "Be you clean that bear the vessels of the Lord . . . for whatsoever the unclean toucheth shall be unclean" [Is. 52.11; Num. 19.22], says the Lord, and He does not lie. "If the young men have kept themselves at least from women," as one says, speaking of course about the hallowed bread which stood figuratively for our sacrament [1 Sam. 21.4].

This being so, what can we wretches think of ourselves, what self-opinion can we have, whereby we who have such unclean hearts may call ourselves priests? Can what we give even be called sacred when it has been handled by our polluted hands? Is the word which we utter from a mouth polluted by wanton kissing even (besides other things) a benediction? "Woe to us wretches, and pg 32-33

96-198

398-399 — N. Bollettino

Ruthen (end of it?)

The Complete Works of Ruthen of Vuovra

ed. & trans. P.I.D. Reid

Binghamton, 1991

m Diana, 26-34

a thousand times woe" (for such offences of course) it was once prophesied, and "It shall be as with the people so with the priest" [Is. 24.2]. If only, just as some in the people of God are more righteous, so there were also some priests of this sort!

I urge them, besides, not to be so estranged from God, that mortally deceiving first themselves, then others, they think that the Holy Spirit could have lied saying through the apostle's mouth: "Neither adulterers, fornicators, nor drunkards, shall inherit the kingdom of God" [Gal. 5.19–21], and: "Know this, that no whoremonger nor unclean person nor covetous man who is an idolator has any inheritance in the kingdom of Christ and of God" [Eph. 5.5]. But, so that this very true statement should not drive them to despair, they should know that this does not refer to those who were once whoremongers, adulterers and covetous, but it brands those who, enduring to the end in such sins, have failed to be converted to God; who, to be sure, if they were permitted to live forever, would not cease from sinning forever and therefore justly ought to pay the penalty forever, because they merit it.

I have learned of a person of our time (whom, if he is destined to die such, would that no man had ever known) so inextricably ensnared by these vices which I have here deplored, that, though he has almost reached old age, poor wretch, bitten by his conscience, he dared to kiss neither the book of the Gospel nor the priest who was about to administer communion, thinking that the priest would be contaminated by his own kiss, remembering, to be sure, the text "Whatsoever the unclean touches shall be unclean" [Num. 19.22]; he judged himself so unworthy, particularly in that his mouth and hands and arms were polluted by wanton embraces, that he was afraid even to touch the sacred vessel which had touched the mystery of such solemnity, yet was there no trace of correction in his obdurate heart. There seem to be two reasons for mentioning him: first, that we should strive to avoid his example, second, that we the more pray for God's mercy on him, the more we know he needs it.

40. For such a man, though he may irrationally *fear* God, is in no way persuaded to *love* God, who, he wretchedly feels, is so opposed to his ways.

41. Nor is that promise of the Lord's contrary to this, in which He says: "He that believes and is baptized shall be saved" [Mk. 16.16], for certainly, though one of this sort *believe in God*, he does not *believe Him*, because he does not keep His commandments nor in his life keep the sacrament which he has received in the faith, but tears down with his ways that faith which he builds up in his words.[26] Only by the Lord's concession does he say with the faithful, "Our Father, Who art in heaven" [Mt. 6.9]. "But the devil is the father of all corrupt livers,"[27] the blessed Zeno says, to the contrary. May His pity deign to keep the devil far from us, who came into this world to save sinners, Lord Jesus Christ, who, made a hostage of salvation for us, bestows everything which He wishes, with the Father and Holy Spirit living and reigning God everlasting. Amen.

30

CC Opera Minora 93–94   Verona Lent 964

[This short piece is in answer to those who had misunderstood his sermon on Lent above, particularly cc. 29 ff. on the anthropomorphite heresy, and were now criticizing him for it.]

Of the Same Against His Critics

1. Rather, bishop of Verona, does not say that God the Son of God, our Lord Jesus Christ, that is, the wisdom of God made flesh for us, does not have head, eyes, hands, and feet, and the other limbs of a human body, full of God with the body together with a rational soul, since he truly believes that with body and soul He ascended into heaven [Acts 1.11], whence He had never been absent in divinity, and has learned that, as the angels teach, in that same body He will come again to judge the living and the dead [2 Tim. 4.1]. But Bishop Rather says that God, that is, the substance of divinity, does not have a body, nor is His body such as can be touched or seen, because "God is a Spirit" as our Lord Jesus Christ said [Jn. 4.21], and "A spirit has not flesh and bones" [Lk. 24.39], as Christ Himself says in the Gospel.

2. Bishop Rather does not say that he does evil who goes to the church of St. Michael or hears a mass of St. Michael, but he says that anyone who says it is better for someone to go to the Church of St. Michael or hear a mass of St. Michael on the second day than on any other day is wrong. Bishop Rather says that anyone who says that St. Michael sings a mass, is wrong, since no other created thing can sing a mass except man alone, because he as well as being rational, has flesh and bones, without which a mass cannot be sung. But a spirit has not flesh and bones, as the Lord says [Lk. 24.39], though he who is an angelic spirit (and not a rebellious one) hath a stronger reason than man. But Michael is a spirit and an angel-spirit always attends in the sight of God without flesh and bones, and praises Him unceasingly without a book, with which the mass is usually sung, without bread and wine, out of which the Body and Blood of the Lord is usually consumed in the mass.

3. But if you ask what St. Michael sings, strive, says Bishop Rather with God's help to ascend heaven after death; there you will hear what he sings. But if you wish to go to the church of St. Michael, you should know, says Bishop Rather, that St. Michael hears you no more willingly on the second day than on any other. If you wish to ask him, you should know, says Bishop Rather, that St. Michael hears you no more mercifully on the second day than on the first, third, fourth, fifth, sixth, or seventh. Since this is what he feels, let Bishop Rather say and add: he who wishes to ascend heaven and can and dares, him Bishop Rather does not forbid, nay, he demands that he try [to reach heaven], for he may thus refute Bishop Rather [by experience].[1]

31

CC Opera Minora 97–105   Verona 964

[Address to the congregation on the Lord's Supper. It is a time of public penitence, when all show on their faces their grief for their past sins; so his main theme is penitence and absolution. C. 4 refers to his enemies' hatred, a motif that will dominate all the works to come.]

∽

Sermon on the Lord's Supper

1. If, brothers, turning to God with your whole heart, you keep this humility in your heart which you show in your appearance, there is no one of the faithful who can doubt that there is greater joy today amongst the angels of God over one of you than over ninety-nine just men who have no need of repentance, as attests our very truth and redemption [Lk. 15.7]. But mark what I said, I beg you, when I began, "If turning with your whole heart." For if we do not turn with our whole heart from those sins for which we seek God's indulgence, in vain do we pray to God to take away from us what we are unwilling ourselves to remove. Rather, we kindle God's anger against us the more violently in proportion as we not only persist in our sins but also hypocritically feign among men a turning from our sins. For most blessed Job says: "Pretenders and dissimulators provoke the wrath of God" [Job 36.13]. *Provoke* he said. How serious it would still be if he had said only *deserve*. But since he said *provoke*, who is there who does not tremble? Who does not almost gasp out his breath at this thunder? Rightly he does not tremble in whom there is no guile; but the man in whom there is any guile or all kinds of guile, how can he face the sound of such rumblings? Is it because he lies dulled not only in sleep but even in death? Let him bestir himself, I pray; let him arise, I demand—and perhaps I am addressing myself. Let him listen to Him saying: "Girl, I say to you, arise" [Mk. 5.41], or—because habit like a massive rock is hard to shift—"Lazarus, come outside" [Jn. 11.43]. For in the former Christ is telling you to arise from the death which your thoughts bring upon you, in the latter from the death brought on by constantly practicing evil ways. Let him come out of doors, bound though he is, for the benign mercy of the Lord will release and absolve him if he opens his heart to the Lord in confession; and He will reveal the light of His countenance, the light which he lacked while he did not see how gravely he was offending, or rather, *provoking* the Lord.

2. And I ask you, brother, whatever kind of man you are, like me to be sure, if you had an enemy very antagonistic to you, a wicked schemer against your whole honor, even against your life itself, and if I should take away your coat and give it to that enemy, wouldn't you be more bitterly angry for the fact that I had given it to him than for the fact that I had taken it from you? Just so, believe me, the Almighty is more angry if what is God's is paid to the devil than if it is given neither to Himself nor to the devil. Fasting, prayers, alms, and the rest are due to God alone; they ought to be done in love or fear of Him alone. The man, then, who hypocritically does these for the praise of men or for the empty glory of this world, what else does he do but bestow God's due on the devil?

And so I urge and beg you again and again, that what you show in your face you keep rather in your heart, so that you can gain the remission of your sins. But hear what that remission is and how we may win it: "When a wicked man turns away from the wickedness that he has committed and does what is lawful and right, he shall save his life; he shall surely live and not die" [Ezek. 18.27-28]. *He shall surely live*, He said. What life? A temporal one? No, for the just die in the same way as the wicked, but only a temporal death, whereas the wicked die eternally—though of course they do not die eternally in the flesh for they will rise again at the last day. He dies in the soul eternally, who dying in sin in the present does not deserve to rise again through confession, repentance, and the mercy of God.

Do you then turn from your wickedness? Do what is lawful and right and you will live and not die, that is, you will not be damned in sin. What is this I say? "Depart from evil and do good, so shall you abide for ever" [Ps. 36.27]. For if you depart from evil but do not do good, listen: "Every tree that does not bear good fruit will be cut down and thrown into the fire" [Mt. 3.10]. And of the unclean spirit He said, "And when he comes, he finds the house empty, swept and put in order; then he goes and brings with him seven other spirits more evil than himself and they enter and dwell there; and the last state of that man is worse than the first" [Mt. 12.44–45]. For the recurring fever is more often wont to kill than the first attack. If you begin living a good life but do not persevere in living it for ever, beware lest unexpectedly you hear, "How have you fallen from heaven, Lucifer?" [Is. 14.12]. Since, indeed, if anyone has persevered in good deeds right to the end he will be saved [Mt. 24.13, 10.22], without doubt he who has not persevered will be lost.

3. Standing, therefore, in God's sight asking and waiting for His mercy and the remission of your sins, think carefully on these two things, I urge you, on the one hand what you have done, and on the other what you ought to receive for your deeds did not Christ's pity intercede for you. Let each question himself; let each see in how much he will be able to find himself guilty. For since, to every man with a healthy mind, it is most certain that everything which it is agreed pleases the devil *dis*pleases God, we should know that we can never better understand what a man subject to any fault deserves than when one considers whose partner in the deed he is held to be. For truth says that in the final time of harvest the farmer will say to the reapers: "Gather the weeds first and bind them in bundles to be burned" [Mt. 13.30]. What else is He saying than: "Join those equal in wickedness for punishment that is also equal?"

Whoever, therefore, puffed up in pride despises others, what else does he do than strive to compare himself, if he could, to him with that original pride [Satan], whom the Lord and Creator of all things rightly surpasses in all things? The man who wastes away in envy, does he not acknowledge the devil and his followers, the traitorous Jews, to be sharers of his jealousy? The man who gasps in the fevers of greed and avarice, what else does he do than imitate in his actions both him who strove too greedily to be like the Most High [Is. 14.14] and Judas drunk with the venom of avarice—imitate them the more closely in proportion as he hungers for riches the more greedily? The man who burns with the fires of passion, what else does he do than prepare for himself the pyre of future and perpetual conflagration, together with those who played the harlot with the daughters of the Moabites [Num. 25.1] and perished with the punishment of heavenly vengeance? Those who openly rave in such acts are attempting to join in the cry of the Sodomites, but those who hide their lust from the eyes of men under the cloak of chastity are like the Pharisees, about whom it is said: "Woe to you who are like whitewashed tombs full within of dead men's bones" [Mt. 23.27]. In those in whose mouth lying is more frequent than truth, as alas in the majority of men today, in them is the devil's deceit most closely equalled, the devil who was always a liar and father of lies [Jn. 8.44]. Those who slander their brothers, don't they make themselves like the Pharisees about whom it is said: "The arrows of infants are their blows" [Ps. 63.8] and: "They have stretched the bow, a bitter thing, so as to shoot in the dark" [Ps. 63.4–5]?[2] And those who attack with the persecution of their hatred men of good works for no cause other than the fact that they exist, and prevent them from good as far as they can, what do they do but harmonize with the treachery of those about whom it is written: "When I talked with them they attacked me for no cause" [Ps. 119.7]? For those who find that good action of theirs intolerable are the same ones who say to themselves in the book of Wisdom: "He is hard for us even to see" [Wisd. 2.15]. But those who also speak against men of good works, who are they if not the persecutors of Christ? For they strive, as it were, to wipe out the name of Christ when they speak against the man who preaches or praises the name of Christ.

What am I to call thieves but Philistines, what robbers but Babylonians? Though such a man be God's rod, yet woe to him as the rod is shattered when the son is chastised.[3] Whoever is a murderer, what should he be considered but another Cain, the most evil killer of his brother [Gen. 4.1–25]? For if what has been said is true, that "we are all brothers in Christ" [Gal. 1.2], no murderer of a fellow Christian can be released from the charge that he has killed his brother unless he has been able to deny that Christ, the Father in one, is a brother of the Christians. But if Christ is the head of the Church and any Christian is a member of it [Eph. 5.23, 30], let him who can plead that he has not cut off a member from the body of Christ who has dared either bodily or spiritually to kill one of the Christians.

4. Beloved brothers, in atoning for the countless vices into which human frailty slips, you can clearly enough deduce from these few words how much vices are to be eschewed and how much the commands of God are to be embraced. For just as by doing evil we enter the society of evil men, so also by doing good we acquire the fellowship of the saints, nay, with the deed we are named with the sons of God; for thus He says: "Be merciful, as also your heavenly Father is merciful" [Lk. 6.36]. Wherefore, because you have gathered here today to earn the release of your sins, consider, I beseech you, what you are asking, and, the more gravely you acknowledge that you have sinned, that much the more carefully endure in your prayers. Shout with your voices, shout with your hearts, saying, "We have sinned against you, O Lord." Let none plead that he has no sin, let none be evasive. "For God," as Job declares, "suffers nothing to go unavenged" [Job 24.12]. Hear the apostle in today's reading: "If we judged ourselves truly, we should not be judged" [1 Cor. 11.31]. And so let us judge ourselves, here and now, and let us condemn ourselves, lest we be judged in the future. Let us be our own chastisers, that below we may not feel the torturers.

What further shall I say? This day is called the feast of the Lord. It is called a feast from the communion of the partakers, but there is no communion where there is division and discord. And so whoever retains in his heart the poison of hatred, let him not come to this feast of love. Whoever has not washed away the corruption of lust through some little penance, let him not receive this feast in his unclean mouth. The Pasch is almost here, in fact it begins today. *Pasch* is translated as "crossing-over." Let us therefore show in our actions what we understand by the name; for if we have been buried with Christ in the mortification of our sins [Rom. 6.4], then we will also rise again with Him in the demonstration of our virtues. But if we do not bury any vice in us by correction, what Pasch, that is, crossing-over, do we make? And if there is no cleansing of the old leaven, how will there be a fresh dough in us [1 Cor. 5.7]? Hear me, I beg you, as I instruct, and I think that you will not despise my advice or — to speak more accurately — my admonitions; for what I seem to be advising you, I am also addressing to myself.

The Lord says: "Thus you will eat it, you will gird up your loins, you will have sandals on your feet, holding your staff in your hand, and you will eat in haste" [Ex. 12.11]. To *gird up your loins* is to curb your sensuality, to *have sandals on your feet* is to fortify yourself with the examples of the saints who have died in the flesh, lest any *splinter* of vice lame the carriage of the mind or the soul be tainted by the taste of poisoned works. For the man whose heart is goaded on by sensuality, just as the splinter forces the foot to limp, so in him sensuality compels the desire to act piously to become faint. The man whose heart is eaten out by envy, does he not pale with the jealousy of raging poison? To *hold a staff in the hands* is for us to control illicit appetite with the power of heavenly discipline and to use a support in the form of the fear of God in our hand of action, lest in the hazards of the present way we meet with any damaging fall, and to control ourselves also in our pastoral duties, to put God in charge of our souls, our souls in charge of our flesh.

5. If we are careful to do this, we are properly celebrating the Lord's Pasch, *hastening* to reach that point where we know that Christ sits on the right hand of God [Col. 3.1], that is, in equality with Him. For this is called the Lord's Pasch, that is, the Lord's *crossing-over* [Ex. 12.11]. And if we cross over from vices to virtues, we are crossing over from earthly things to heavenly things in a most wholesome conversion; it is meet to do this at all times, but at this most holy time I urge that it be done that much the more attentively in proportion as this mystery should be the more worthily celebrated. (Most unfortunately, it usually happens that if people begin anything good in Lent it is interrupted when the Paschal ceremonies take place and thus afterwards they return to their old vices, just as though it were not for the veneration of God but only for

the veneration of this day that they have departed from their vices, or rather not even departed from but only interrupted for a while.) To do this (that is, cross from vice to virtue) is nothing else than to want to show some consideration for the eternal day. For how far the Pasch of Christians ought to extend, the psalmist declares in Psalm 117 (which is sung complete in the service of this day), saying, "Set up this solemn day with thick foliage" [Ps. 117.27], or, as another version has it, "In gatherings up to the horns of the altar."[4] "With thick foliage" [in condensis], that is, in the secret recesses of the mind; but "in gatherings" [in confrequentationibus] means by custom or habit or practice. For our Pasch, that is, Christ, should never recede from our hearts; the Pasch we should observe in constant veneration, right up to the horn of the altar. But what is this altar? Christ, to be sure, who at the same time is priest, altar, and sacrifice; and let us never cease from searching for Him until we see Him.

But what kind of a thing is it to fast on the eve of a festival but in the festival itself to be gorged with surfeit? In the feast of the Lord to wash the feet of the poor but in His eight days to scheme for the death of some Christian? To give a denarius on the day of Preparation but after the Preparation to steal a hundred? To continue through Lent with psalms, hymns, and holy songs, but in the Passover feast to give one's mind to sloth, or rather, what is worse, to brawls or slander? In Lent to be continent of one's own wife, but in Passover to be stained even with fornication? In Lent not to eat even one's own bread, but after Passover to make off with someone else's? What could be thought of worse, what more inappropriate? For this is merely to rest a while in order the more violently to serve the devil with renewed strength; to give up one day to betterment, in order to be able to sin on all days; in Lent to advance with Christ, in the Passover to defect from Christ.

6. Today is the released day, they say. How, I ask, is it released when it was never bound?

"But men are released," you say, "on this day."

For what? To serve the devil? Hear the words of release: "You shall do no servile work on this day" [Lev. 23.28]. By servile work He means the wickedness which takes away the liberty Christ has conferred and puts in the servitude which the devil has invented. "Rest" [Ps. 45.11], said the Lord. But for what? For leisure? For sloth? For games? For entertainment? For brawls? For slanders? For drunkenness? "Hear and see," He said, "that I am the Lord" [Ps. 45.11], as if He were openly saying:

"While you are at leisure from your work, you do not know what to do. Think on the fact that there is a Lord and consider who the Lord is. You are compelled to serve me the more attentively in proportion as you are the more kindly raised from your necessities by my grace. For you have the greatest provision, but whose is this gift, do you think? Consider the giver and repay equal return of service. Remember the powerful torments prepared for the neglect of this for those in positions of power, and don't neglect, I urge, the safeguards of humility and the fear of God. If you enjoy a moderate sufficiency, rejoice for your advantage, bow down for what is given you, and use your labors as though you used them not, remembering that the time of the present age is short [1 Cor. 7.31]. Or if you perhaps stand in almost total need, rejoice greatly and be glad; for if you shall bear it patiently for the fear or love of God, a very large treasure is laid up for you in heaven."

In contemplating along these lines, brothers, at leisure we will not be at leisure, nor will any day, in fact any hour or minute, seem to us to be released. For we shall meditate on God's law day and night [Ps. 1.2], than which nothing is greater work, nothing has more appearance of leisure; for it is work, but not servile work but the work of freedom of the Lord's day, of the day of Resurrection, the work of the Passover, the work of everlasting festivity; and when you hear "everlasting," I ask you not to take it lightly but to understand the distinction between eternal and everlasting: eternal has neither beginning nor end, whereas everlasting has a beginning, to be sure, but no end. Take note that I call this a work of everlasting festivity for this reason, that since it begins with someone acting thus in this present life, it will last the same, though more perfectly, for ever, just as truth itself says: "Mary has chosen the good portion, which shall not be taken away from her forever" [Lk. 10.42]. This is against the ignorance of those who think that you should not plough on the Lord's day but dance, and that because you do not have to fast, you are therefore free for self-indulgence and surfeit.

The apostle says: "The grace of God has appeared for the salvation of all men, training us to renounce irreligion and unworldly passions and to live sober, upright and godly lives in this world" [Tit. 2.11–12]. *In this world*, that is, as long as one lives on this earth, and so at all times, that is, all days and nights, if none is excepted of all days and all nights. But if any day is to be excepted from living soberly, uprightly and godlily, it would be more fitting for what is called *everyday* (but much rather should be called *work-day*) to be excepted. But as I have said, if some day is to be excepted from following the commands of God, then it would be more appropriate for other days to be excepted than the Lord's day, than a feast day. For it is called the Lord's day for this reason, that it has been sanctified by the Lord, that it has been allotted only for rest from labor or from work, servile work to be sure, that is, sin, for the service of the Lord. But if we are released from fasting on that day, it is done not so that we can lapse into the vice of drunkenness, but so that our virtue be gratuitous and not the result of some penance, and so that God may be glorified the more graciously as our worship is the more freely given.

7. But since I have addressed particularly those who have gathered for the sake of absolution, *the penitent* in other words, let the end of my sermon be aimed at the same people as was the beginning. Something is called a *regimen* by physicians which is so much more important than cures by medicine that, they say, the essence of natural or recovered health depends upon it. Regimen is the precaution or care in taking or rejecting things, that is, you may take this, you may not take that. Let us see, then, the regimen of our Physician, that is, our heavenly Physician. "You shall not kill, you shall not steal, you shall not commit adultery, etc., honor thy father and mother," and the rest. The same, too, from the Gospels [Lk. 18.20]. If we transgress, our soul, alas, perishes. But by necessity a cure is available so that our life should not utterly perish. The Physician has come with His bandages. "Repent" [Mt. 4.17], He says. "As I live," says the Lord, "I have no pleasure in the death of a sinner but rather that he might turn from his wickedness and live" [Ezek. 33.11]. We have heard, we have rejoiced, we have approached, we have received the medicine, the oil and wine has been poured into us, thanks be to God, our health has been recovered. So again a regimen is necessary, as once of recovering our natural health, so now of keeping our recovered health. "Lo," says the Physician, "you have become well. Now sin not, lest something worse happen to you." From that worse something may we be protected by that Healer and Physician who was sacrificed for us on the cross, who with the Father and Holy Spirit lives and reigns for ever and ever. Amen.

32

CC Opera Minora 109–13   Verona Pentecost 964

[Rather's guilty conscience for something wicked (*turpe quid*) spoken and done in God's presence (i.e., in church) has brought gloom into the festal joy of Pentecost. No. 41 *Qualitatis coniectura*, c. 7, and no. 46 On Otiose Speech also refer to this incident and to his subsequent confession of guilt for it. There are also verbal echoes here of no. 27 *Sermo 1* on Pentecost and no. 29 *Sermo 2* on Quadragesima.]

On His Own Sin[5]

1. "Blessed is the man who is ever in fear" [Pr. 28.14], said the Old Testament preacher, while another, later, said, as though to the contrary, "The conscience of the guilty is ever in punishment" [Wisd. 17.10]. Yet since the double pipe sounds with but a single breath, how *blessed* and *guilty* are reconcilable I cannot see. But while the former is asserted to be ever in fear and the latter in punishment, each of them seems almost equally to be denied the blessed state. In fact, *fear* and *punishment* refer to that mental anguish of which it was said, "These are afraid." Whoever is afraid fears, whoever fears is punished. Therefore, how is he who fears blessed, since anguish is far from blessedness, and no blessed person fears punishment? So I take it that if before sinning a man is afraid— that is, anxious not to fall into sin—he is blessed (though in hope rather than in reality) in the very fact that he is careful not to fall into sin, nor when standing firm to take a fall; but becoming a sinner he draws punishment on himself and rushes into evil. This is proved by the corollary, as the text continues immediately: "But he who hardens his heart will fall into evil," the evil, namely, in that having become a sinner, he is ever punished by his fear. How do we conclude this? By the fact, I say, that we know that these two sentences distinguish three types of people: (1) those of the group referred to by the saying, "He who hardens his heart will fall into evil"; (2) those of the group to which belongs the man who is happy specifically because he is ever in fear; and (3) those of the group referred to by "His conscience will ever be in punishment."

2. Would that I knew this last type rather by report than by personal experience! But since this is not so, I wish that the pain mentioned were only temporary, and that they were not both eternal—that is, both this one and the pain that lies in the expectation of punishment. For when someone ignores that fear which makes a man blessed and hardens his heart, he does fall into evil: the evil of thinking himself so guilty in the monstrosity of his sins that his conscience is continually haunted day and night (as mine, alas, is now) by the fear, not indeed of God, but of the things which God in His power can inflict. Scripture tells us what often happens to a man like this: "The wicked, when he comes to the depths of evil, becomes contemptuous" [Pr. 18.3]; but what St. John the Apostle says always applies to him: "Whoever fears is not perfect in love" [1 Jn. 4.18]. And would that at least the words of the psalm were applicable to a man of this sort: "God's eyes have seen my imperfections" [Ps. 138.16]. For since the same apostle says, "There is no fear in love" [1 Jn. 4.18], it clearly follows that there is no love of God in the man whose conscience is not refreshed by His love but is forever tortured with hell's punishment. Therefore, however much he may fear God for the wrong reason, he never loves Him if he feels that God is always opposed to his ways, as He of course indicates in the text where He says that the word of God is adversary to us; and He has mercifully urged on us our obligations to follow His ways while we tread the path of this life, lest after all we be sent to the pit of hell.

3. To condense just these points from an infinite number: how can he love God, I ask, who knows that God has said of him, "What the impure has touched will be impure" [Num. 19.22]? How can he love Him who hears, "A priest from Aaron's seed who is stained shall not offer bread to the Lord" [Ex. 21.17]? And how is the man with the stains which are listed in that text required to dedicate a sacrifice to the Lord, that is, in that office which he unworthily performs? Is it surprising if a man is forbidden to make an offering since he is not permitted even to taste of that offering, the Lord thus completely prohibiting it in these words: "The person who eats of the sacrifice which is the Lord's while an uncleanness is on him, that person shall be cut off from his people" [Lev. 7.20]? Finally, how can you say that that person loves God when you know that God has denied him even the authority to speak about Him, since He says: "What right have you to recite my statutes?" [Ps. 49.16] For men of this sort, the only consolation that occurs to me, I admit, is this: "No man knows whether he is worthy of hate or of love, but all things are kept uncertain for the future" [Eccle. 9.1]. For other comforting words about God's incomprehensible mercy ("charity wipes out all sins" [Pr. 10.12; 1 Pet. 4.8]) apply only to those who fully meet the standards of *charity*.

4. And so it seems to me that we ought rather to lament that any of us has dared to hurt so merciful a Father (and especially to weep within with many tears) than to despair of His mercy or to stand in fear of hell without hope of salvation. For He hates no sin more than despair; it surely is the only sin that cannot be forgiven because it also amounts to apostasy. Rather, he should be ashamed that he has yielded to the devil than fear that he will be damned with him; he should be ashamed that he has not abstained from carnal desires as the apostle instructs [1 Pet. 2.11], but has made them wage war against his soul as the devil instructs, most wretchedly allowing them to triumph over him as well.

So such a man should rather repent because he has offended so pious a Redeemer than fear because he will have to meet Him as the terrible judge. He should repent because he has taken His body and blood unworthily, rather than fear because he knows that he has taken it to his damnation; he should repent that he has celebrated the Paschal Quinquagesima without spiritual joy because his joy is broken by the gloom of the sins he has committed, rather than fear that he has brought on himself the punishment for those sins; he should repent that he has not even persevered to the end of the feast, though the end is now at hand;[6] that when the feast is over, he has not been able to resist his bad habits, but has returned to the vomit of noxious evil [2 Pet. 2.22]; that he has celebrated Pentecost in gloom, a feast more joyous than all others, whose joy ought to be celebrated even more than the Pasch, as he certainly knew and did not deny; that in it he could not exult with profuse joy but was forced to wail with profuse sadness; and more than all this, that in God's very presence and sight he did not fear or blush to say or do something wicked in some corner,[7] and this, surely, was an indication either of lack of belief in God or of open rebellion. And since the Lord says, "Take away the evil of your thoughts from my eyes," to what degree do we think He is offended by horrible *actions* done in the very presence of His majesty, when He says this even about evil *thoughts?*

5. In fact, it is less serious for someone to be self-deluded out of ignorance than to be a rebel against God out of pride. A wrong done out of sight, however great, is more tolerable to bear than a lesser one done face-to-face. Offences and premeditated contempt of God are not weighed equally, nor is an act forced on us by circumstances weighed equally with one done in free will. Would that the narrator of all this had taken thought beforehand, so that as a result of his guilty action his conscience would not undergo so grave a punishment — which of course in no way would have happened to him if "the fear which makes a man blessed" had possessed his conscience before he fell; that fear, namely, which, when replaced by love, leads to the reverence which stays pure through eternity.

And indeed, our very nature shows us that there is a great difference between the wicked servant's fear and love and the good son's fear and love. For the former's love depends on his fear of his lord, the latter's fear depends on his love of his father; this the Lord himself shows when He says: "No longer do I call you servants but my friends" [Jn. 15.15], and the apostle also when he says: "You did not receive the spirit of slavery to fall back into fear, but you have received the spirit of sonship in which we cry, Abba, Father!" [Rom. 8.15] Whoever, therefore, calls the Lord *Father* professes himself free, not a servant. He should therefore be ashamed, rather than afraid, to offend Him whom he presumes to call *Father.* But if he has offended Him, let him not despair of reconciliation, however serious his offense against Him. For He is the Father, is merciful, is good; not good alone, but also kind, which is indeed greater. As the Lord's mercy is inestimable, so also is it omnipotent. Only may He deign to instill in us some particle of His love (that is what we should unceasingly pray for), which I have certainly been lacking; without doubt it will make us abandon our evil ways and turn to good in compensation for them. This God himself is able to bestow, so that no longer is there need for us to fear hell but to hope for Heaven with sure constancy, so that with the psalmist we may be able to cry: "According to the many cares of my heart, thy consolations have cheered my soul" [Ps. 93.19]; and: "Why are you cast down, O my soul, and why are you disquieted within me? Hope in God for I shall yet confess to Him" [Ps. 42.5]; and by apostrophe to him to whom it behooves us to confess: "my face and my God" — by *face* meaning that He who is God and Lord has put on our flesh, assuredly Jesus

Christ, who with God the Father and Holy Spirit, consoler of the faithful, is inseparably one, blessed for ever and ever. Amen.

33

Weigle, Urkunden 18–20   Verona late 964[8]

[A fragment of an invective against Count Bucco of Verona, who had been appointed by Otto I to keep Verona secure. The work is valuable to us for showing some of the difficulties Rather faced when he was restored to Verona in 961.]

༄

. . . the quality of a certain one who had been cheated of his church.

Returning from a distance, I was first promoted through Caesar's[9] graciousness, but was not received with fatherly love . . . far from there being any correction of those crimes once committed against me[10] there was not even acknowledgement of them, nor any plea to forget them. After the lunch which I began to eat on that day of pain, I fell from the staircase fifteen feet below . . . I broke my right arm, which has not so far mended. Confined, I spent the time in constant despair that I had returned, not for my resurrection, but to my own ruin, as I believed. I found no source of sustenance for that year, though it was the beginning of winter [December 961] . . . they said that up to a hundred measures remained in grain and wine. This another [Milo] took away, to whom I was also forced to give one of my best communities together with two small abbeys, so that there might be "friendship" between us, and that we might harmoniously keep our sworn pledge. The friendship was a dream, the gift was sure reality.

There came a man whose name [Bucco] echoes another full of horror [Pharaoh]—he is the subject of our enquiry—saying that he had been especially commissioned by the most pious emperor to take me under his particular care and to be my advocate, protector, and defender against all my enemies. Elated beyond words, as men usually are when they think some disaster has turned into a blessing, I depended on him as on some helper sent from heaven, until I realized that instead of being my advocate he was the despoiler of all my goods, instead of being my protector he was my chiefest adversary, and instead of being my defender he was my stealthy attacker,. . . so fanatic that, if he had been told to show the same vigor in thrusting me out as he had for the assault on Garda,[11] he could not have kept at me with greater determination. For he who should have cherished these properties for me against all my enemies attached every enemy to himself, either existing ones whom he could find or other non-enemies whom he could make into enemies, and has now for a full year been so constantly assailing me with treachery, entrapments, and ambushes, that this poor sinner is weary of life itself. All this he does or commands or allows to be done because he thinks that my rancor is so strong that in despair I will abandon the bishopric. But those who stress my rancor are wrong and do not consider how impossible for me abdication would be; for where could I go so worn out with pain, or where would I be received with my bodily strength so far gone? In fact, I would be afraid of becoming a Nicolaitan[12] in this, my old age.

In the first year of his reign [926], King Hugo, on the request of Bishop Notker, had by decree[13] given three farms to St. Mary and St. Zeno. They were afterwards owned by those who succeeded him, either lawfully or unlawfully or, like Berengar, by force. Well, this good supporter of the bishop [Bucco] either caused or allowed it to be hinted to the ears of the emperor that the ownership of these farms belonged to Berengar [king of Italy], and had been made over to the blessed Mother of God because of the wretched destitution of the bishop's person. Though I regret that this . . . [lacuna] happened in my own days, yet I patiently put up with it out of loyalty to the Caesar who graciously restored me.

Two young men were sporting on a bridge, one a cleric and the other a Jew.[14] The cleric drew tears from the Jew; the other slashed at the cleric and gave him a scar that will be visible for life. The case was heard before that "advocate" of the bishop [Bucco]. The Jew was dismissed without even being questioned; the cleric was fined six pounds of silver. In order to pay the fine, either from his own property if there was any or from the Church's if there were none, the bishop wanted to give what he had and to take the rest from the Church. That fine "defender" of the bishop replied that the bishop's property was worthless and that nothing at all could be taken from the Church's property—though canon law states far otherwise. What was to be done? The cleric saw that the bishop could not help him and betook himself to the clergy of the Church. With the bishop's knowledge, however, they took from the Church one red cloak. . . . An amazing loss, which the deacons did not have to contribute![15]

A young man of the Frankish nobility had followed this pitiable pontiff in all his dangers and countless necessities. It happened that one of his countrymen was poorly advised and refused to put himself and his vassal under the bishop's protection. The illustrious Count Ernest and that fine "advocate" of the bishop ordered that anyone who did not appear before the bishop before Friday, which it then was. . . .

[No. 34 is a fragment of a letter to an unknown addressee.]

35

Weigle, Urkunden 21   Verona 12 February 965

[In a decree he prohibits those clergy who had been ordained by his predecessor Milo (whom he sees as a usurper) from assuming their offices.]

Mitigating the requirements of the canons on those who have been ordained by the pretender to this seat [Milo], I hereby instruct them to abstain from the office to which he unlawfully appointed them until the coming day of lawful ordination, with the authority of God and of the Blessed Mary and St. Peter, first of the Apostles, and all the saints.

Given this second Sunday in February.

36

Weigle, Urkunden 21–22   Verona 13 February 965

[He moderates the previous day's decree.]

Rather, bishop of Verona, to all the clergy of his Church:

It is from Cicero,[16] not St. Augustine, that I have learned that in warfare the laws are silent. When I observed that yesterday's decree was not greeted with unanimous consent, it was quite apparent that it would lead to the opposition of many, rather than any statement of right or any fruit beneficious to the good of our souls.

I do not want to be thought an outrageous singer of my own praises or an avenger of personal injury rather than an administrator of the laws. I will not go so far as to call the usurper of my office [Milo] "bishop" lest I damn myself with my own words, nor will I recognize that those appointed by him could in any way be priests or deacons, lest I seem to have demoted my own appointees. Therefore, I moderate the canonic sanction against them which I announced yesterday, and repeated today, leaving them to God's judgment and their own conscience: if they have no fear in carrying out the offices enjoined by the usurper, I do not forcibly prevent their presumption; if they are afraid, I do not tell them not to be afraid. Let it be on their own heads whether they decide to follow or to defy the Lord's command; I will be quite without blame on this.

Concerning the bishops whom he is charged with having ordained to the priesthood, I can be content with taking no action only if I reply that "each will carry his own burden" [Gal. 6.5]. Would that the trespass referred to[17] could at least be a defence of these bishops. However, I claim that there will be people who have seen a deacon made a bishop without the rank of priest, though the perpetrators assert that a man who was a bishop must consequently be a priest, if he was indeed in holy orders. Only let those who have obtained the presulate by an ordination of this sort make sure that they obtained the deaconate from a *lawful* bishop.

[The letters listed under no. 37 are all fragmentary, with many textual problems.]

37a

Weigle, Epist. 106–7   Verona February–June 965

[Fragment of a letter to an unkown addressee. The first paragraph is so fragmentary that it defies translation or interpretation.]

∾

. . . the apostle's words in this wise had escaped his notice: "Though absent in body, yet present in the spirit, I have pronounced judgment: to hand a man of this sort over to Satan for the destruction of his flesh" [2 Cor. 5.3–5]. For any of us to be present in the spirit . . . to know perhaps . . . of the thing which he no less knows or remembers than if previously . . . he considers. And oh! how much is hidden from us by ignorance of letters . . . "Poles outside the rings of the ark" [Ex. 25.13–15] that man had (do not . . . I pray), that man, I say, who "though not knowing what to say" of these "yet could not keep silent."[1] But what is left? "Let us return," says Daniel [Dan. 13.49], "to judgment." Whoever wishes may keep sailing; I, by God's grace, stand in the harbor. I accused no one, I testified against no one, I judged no one. When asked, I told only things known to me. What was imposed, I have undergone because it was commanded legally or quasi-legally. It is not in my interest to act, if compelled [to do otherwise]. God's help alone I wait for, and the help of the holy emperor [*sacri imperii*] given us by Christ.

37b

Weigle, Epist. 107–8   Verona February–June 965

[Fragmentary letter to Ernest, count of Verona 961–964; Rather asks him to use his influence with the emperor on his behalf.]

∽

To Lord Ernest, eminently graced with the pedigree of nobility, Rather, a sinner, [gives] his faithful service:

I beg your most noble lordship to take great care that you and I be not dishonored of the benefice [*beneficium*], which your faithful servant Ecahard[2] happened to receive from the hand of the emperor [Otto I] and that he be not deceived in us. You must do nothing else, my lord, than say to our lord the emperor what you have seen and heard or done, and what you instructed me concerning Bernard,[3] and how I have been ready to receive him [Bernard] and give to him all those things which he came here seeking. But he did not want to be mine and, further, all those who ought to have been mine, for three months until you could arrive, he left in such doubt that no one truly knew whether I ought to hold the bishopric or not. I do not want to do anything disloyal to the emperor, yet I have learned such things about him that, if I offer any help to him, I am afraid of perjuring my oath to our lord [Otto]. Well, my lord, let it now be apparent who ... for you to keep him or for Bucco[4] to lose him [?].

37c

Weigle, Epist. 109–10   Verona February–June 965

[Fragmentary letter to Bishop Odelric of Bergamo: he regrets that gifts which he had sent the bishop to assure him of his loyalty had been brought back by the messenger. He hastens to send further gifts, hoping to mitigate the impression of enmity which he has caused by his candid criticism.]

∾

To lord O.,[5] dearest of bishops, worthy to be respected with awe
and love: R., a sinner, [offers] his most faithful service in all things
to the best of his ability.

After the many blessings of your goodwill, lord, which you have shown me,
and which I think it very necessary for me that you do not disdain to continue
to show me, not seeing what I can do (walled in as I am by a cloud of destitution), I recently dared to send you—rash, indeed, yet very loyal—a chestnut mare
[castaneam],[6] acquired by a loan, along with a bolt of material [pallium], not
such a bad one, from which you can cut out, if you please, a cloth of the right
size to fit it. Do not think, I pray, that I have sent them in place of the service
which I am mindful that I promised your lordship, but like the tokens [arras]
which those about to make a contract in some business are accustomed to give,
to put them under obligation so that they cannot change the terms of the contract. In return for so slight a gift, or rather the service which is to follow it,
if opportunity offers (since I have received from your generosity not just once),
I ask nothing else than that the unchanging grace of your pity never be lacking
to me, as needed, along with the love of God, which I know full well is strong
in your benign lordship.

But the stupid messenger, when he found your lordship absent, brought these
back to me and certain other things not so slight, though he could, witless,
have left them to be handed to your lordship by Ambrose, my dear friend and
your trusty servant. Realizing this, though it was not bad, I hastened to send
a Venetian cloak,[7] sweetening the gift with the addition of some valuables [?].

What, lord, am I to do? "Whoever speaks the truth will be an accuser. Is
it wrong for me to mutter?"[8] Or, as the wise man says: What does it profit
that he is the best smith if his tools [sc. servants] are the worst? "One man building
and another destroying, what does such labor achieve?" [Eccli. 24.38].

"My smallest finger," says that foolish divider of his father's kingdom [Re-
hoboam], "is stouter than my father's back. My father has struck you with whips
but I will strike you with scorpions" [1 Kg. 12.10–11]. Along with me let those
of our time . . . [heed this warning] . . .; though they hear by the actual events
more certainly than those to whom it was promised at that time, they do not
even dare . . . [to mention any of the truth] . . . . For they are those of whom
the Hungarians say that if a finger is put in their mouth, they do not dare to
bite it. Yet they have long been hiding, you should know, a fire in their bosoms
[Pr. 6.27] . . . I have now been branded as showing you disaffection [animositas].
If I, even though driven by the worst pain and in obedience to the Lord's com-

mand also, dare to bark [i.e., criticize you], I am shown to be doing this more out of disaffection than motivated by justice and necessity.[9] And therefore, what I really ought to say, I am afraid to say. "Whoever has ears to hear, let him hear" [Mt. 13.43] — and let him see that it does not obstruct me, but rather help me, by God I pray.[10]

37ð

Weigle, Epist. 110   Verona mid-965

[To Bishop Gauslin of Padua, answering his request for advice.]

Rather, a sinner, to his venerable fellow-bishop, Gauslin.

Your question is a large one, requiring no small amount of leisure, and no short answer can satisfy it.

The apostle says: "If possible, so far as depends upon you, live peaceably with all" [Rom. 12.18]. But it is not possible for you to live peaceably with a man against whom you have sworn a suit of war, compelled by a power which you must not resist any more than you can God's ordering [Rom. 13.2].[11] However, you have a course of action, I say, if you examine what the angels sang in the Gospel; for there is always peace to men of goodwill [Lk. 2.14], even when war threatens. Therefore, because you have sworn to attack the emperor's enemies, keep your oath, attack them, but with goodwill. Because they are brothers, love those whom you attack in the fact that they are brothers; that is, wish that they had been not such as they are, but such as they ought to have been. Briefly, my brother, I suggest: both love them *and* keep fully to your oath.

37e

Weigle, Epist. 115–18   Verona mid-965

[To the emperor Otto, abjectly begging for more material resources for his Church, and hinting that, if he does not receive these resources, he will be forced to resign his bishopric and become a monk again.]

≈

To the most serene and holy of emperors, elected by God and mercifully destined to the help of the wretched, lord to be addressed with the utmost reverence, Otto, unconquered, ever august: Rather, the lowest of his servants, renders the service of obedience most loyal and most wretched above all the rest, so that he may merit to obtain mercy.

If my lowliness, insignificance, and poverty, most clement lord, be compared with the abundance of your mercy, no one, even the most articulate, could be found able to express in worthy praise, try as he might, the great pity and favor you have shown in restoring at last, unexpectedly and with such honor, one who by his own just deserts has been deprived of his seat for so many years, and in mercifully confirming him with a decree of bishops so venerable as to be incontrovertible.[12]

But if, as rumor has it, the efforts of certain people have obtained their desired effect, even an intelligent man might think that, given the opportunity—that is, after the expulsion of the usurper [Milo]—it would have been better for the authority of the apostolic see rather to have placed in this seat (to which I have uselessly been restored) one whose lowliness would not be such a detriment to the Church as will occur from my insignificance (thus many people think and suppose, predicting the future from the present). Alas for wretched me! To cap my misery, if I happen to make any complaint, I seem to do it more from animosity than from reason. And so, putting aside all complaint, on bended knee I pray with all my heart that an unfailing stream will encircle your Amplitude's mercy, so that, because you have begun to bestow this favor upon me—or rather, because you deign to bestow it on the Church charitably committed to me—even though the Church cannot gain anything because of my lowliness, yet at least, for the love of God, it may in the days of your most holy rule not lose any of those resources which my predecessors and I have justly and legally held for thirty years.[13] If, because of my sins, this is not granted, it would have been better for me to die in Christ than to hold such an office. . . .

If these things, my lord, are not granted me by God's mercy, I am compelled to despair, no less for my temporal safety than for my eternal salvation. I see no other course of action open to me than to thank your majesty's clemency for the charity of my restitution, and, making light of the charge of fickleness, seek again the haven[14] which I left in my wretchedness, that of the monastery, so that I may give back to God—if He does not object—not a bishop, as that is not granted me, but at least the monk, such as he is, which I took away from Him.

38

Weigle, Epist. 111–15   Verona 1 August 965

[Letter to the pope: on behalf of the Veronese clergy, Rather refers to the pope and the Roman Curia for their decision concerning the question of the clerics ordained by the usurper Milo and dismissed from their offices by himself (see nos. 35 and 36). But it is clear from the number of canonical precedents which he cites that he is really seeking their support for his position as bishop.]

⌘

To the Apostolic Lord of the Holy Roman seat, whoever he is,[15] and to all the Senate, and to all the formulators of the sacred canonical law, and, finally, to the holy congregation of all those living in the Catholic faith: all the clergy of the holy Church of Verona send their respects of due devotion.

1. We know, holy fathers, that it is not unknown to you that an invasion[16] instigated by the devil once occurred here. Since in it, many of us were—not promoted indeed, but—established in diverse offices by open illegality (as is declared), here on bended knees (which we have done) we beg of you as suppliants to show us the course which we ought to follow; for your Holiness is acknowledged to have been granted the sole arbitration in such matters.

The obstacles which prevent us from standing in the office granted us, our lord bishop [Rather] here recites as follows, together with countless others. Along with the apostle, he declares that "whatsoever is written is written for our learning" [Rom. 15.4].

In the Antioch Council, c. 13:

If on one's petition someone moves unusually fast in settling any ordinations or church business not in his province, whatever is done by him must be invalid. And he must undergo punishment for his inordinate haste and unreasonable presumption, being condemned by the holy Council for this.

In the Constantinople Council, c. 3:

Concerning Maximus the Cynic and his improper ordination at Constantinople: We have decided that Maximus neither is nor ever was bishop, nor are they who were ordained by him in any rank of the clergy in office, because everything which was done by him is seen to have been invalid.

From the letter of Pope Innocent, c. 53 and 54:

We agree, and it is surely true, that he could not give what he did not have; that is, the condemnation which he had done he did by a wicked laying-on of hands. And we cannot find how a man who was made accessory to the condemned ought to receive any honor. But the true and just benediction of a legitimate priest is said to take away every fault which a sinful person may have contracted. If this is so, let the sacrilegious, the adulterers, and those guilty of every sin apply for ordination, because faults or vices are thought to be removed by the benediction of ordination. Let there be no place for penitence because ordination can offer the same as what a long correction has normally offered.

From the letter of Pope Nicholas to the see of Constantinople:

Excising the love of power by the roots, inasmuch as it is an evil source of scandals arising in the church, we condemn with just decree him who rashly and falsely and irregularly leapt into the sheepfold of Christ like some dangerous wolf, namely, Photius, who filled the whole world with a thousand disturbances and tumults. We declare that he never previously was nor is now bishop, nor can those who were consecrated or promoted by him in any clerical rank remain in the rank to which they were promoted. Furthermore, those who received from him the regular benizons for promotion to archdeacon, we restrain from exercising this privilege. The churches which, as is thought, either Photius or those who were consecrated by him dedicated, or, if their altars were moved, established, we decree must be rededicated and enthroned and established, since everything which he did in the way of ordaining or defrocking priests has been rendered invalid.

From the same:

Those whom Photius the neophyte and usurper of the see of Constantinople has promoted in any ecclesiastical rank, since it is clear that they have participated in all the iniquities of their consecrator and communed with him after his usurpation, we deprive of all clerical office, and by our canonic and apostolic authority and synodal decree we sequester them.

2. If it please your lordship, our bishop says that he has found no greater support than this alone.

From the Council of Lord Stephen III in the Third Actio:

After this the holy bishops said: Since everything which pertains to the salvation of all at fault has, God willing, been dealt with and decided, it now remains for us to declare before all what we have unanimously decided about the ordination of the bishops, priests, or deacons which the aforesaid Constantine, usurper of the apostolic see, directed: First of all, we decree that the bishops whom he consecrated, if they were previously priests or deacons, should revert to the same former rank, and afterwards, the decree of their election being made in the customary manner, should come with the congregation and decree to the apostolic seat for consecration and receive their consecration from our apostolic emissary, just as if they had not previously been ordained. But all the other things which Constantine did in the same sacred offices, excepting only baptism, must be repeated. But those priests or deacons whom he ordained in this holy Church of Rome must return to their former rank of subdeacon or other office which they performed, since thereafter it is in the power of your most holy protection either to ordain them or dispose of them as so you wish. As for the laity who were tonsured and consecrated by him, we decide and decree that they should either be kept in the monastery or reside in their own homes leading a spiritual and religious life.

3. The above-mentioned bishop of our Church also says in addition that, since the Lord says that "The disciple is not higher than his master" [Mt. 10.24], whatever you decide on this question he will take as decreed. But he would wish that your decision, which he thinks should follow in this, would not totally differ from the authority of the canons. He says that it is up to you, holy fathers, whether you choose to follow your own judgment or that of your predecessors. But if you deign to help us in such danger of our souls, you do not need to be told whom you should expect to have as Remunerator in this. And, venerable Romans [*Quirites*], whom we particularly address in this prayer, since we are many, we promise that one will not fail to return to your Holiness to give in you glory to God and a worthy remuneration.

Given this first of August.

39

Weigle, Epist. 118   Verona late 965

[In a letter to an unknown patron, he complains of the persecution of his enemies and begs him for the horse he had promised as a gift.]

⌒∾

. . . I learned long ago to suffer poverty. I admit that daily bread is not lacking to me, since God mercifully nourishes me according as He pleases but not
as my voracity demands, nor do I lack clothing fit for my lowliness. Now I
ask for nothing else, therefore, save only that those whom the lady duchess
[Judith][17] instructed to help me, at least not harm me, and to grant my earnest desire—the peace to meditate on God's law day and night [Ps. 1.2] (since
now the latest hour of life is upon me, as my age proclaims), so that I also may
seem to make the same complaint that the comic playwright once did.[18] Let
them cease for a while from false accusations, at least out of fear of God, even
if they will not do so out of love of anyone.

If your generosity decides to send me the promised horse, know that my poverty
will receive it most gratefully; only let it be a saddle-horse and look at the ground
rather than the sky, and not be overly thin nor exceedingly high but fat and
long, not a mere expectation as up till now but in bodily reality. However, though
I like nothing less in a horse than impacted feet, be sure that I will readily take
whatever kind you give me; only see, as is right, that you do not break your
promised word—that I will not have.

[Added in margin in Rather's hand]: If you find any faults in this letter, be
sure to impute them to the scribe rather than to the one who dictated it, I say.

40

Weigle, Epist. 119–24   Verona December 965

[Letter to Milo, by whom Rather had been displaced as bishop of Verona (948)
and whom he had in turn displaced (961): he accuses Milo of spreading false
accusations about him, assures him that he will not be forced out of office again,
that the canons are on his side, and that Milo will have to answer to God for
trying to destroy the flock.]

❧

To the violent attacker Milo of Vicenza: Rather, bishop of Verona,
the violently attacked, the ejected to the ejector.

1. The feast [Christmas] is upon us, which ought to be observed more strictly than the others which have lately passed. The high point of its celebration
is the mystery of giving and taking the Sacrament, at which point the declaration is made that "the Lamb was born to suffer for us." I am doubtful in my
mind (as often) whether I can venture to do this safely, since I know that God
himself (who is also the Lamb) said to the disobedient: "If you offer your gift,"
and the rest [Mt. 5.23-25]. I know full well that you have something against
me. Since I have to offer to God the gift of this feast, I desire to find the point
of blame so that I can be reconciled, but I find none, except that I ventured
to admit myself to the episcopacy of the Church of Verona for consecration [931],
before you yourself were able to be born. But even if I could have known you
would be born, why should I have been concerned, not knowing whether you
would be male or female? This indeed is an earlier fault of mine against you,
for which you arrested me, led me off, robbed me, exiled me—all of this to
the shame of the emperor and (though they pretend otherwise) of our dukes
[Judith and Henry of Bavaria], and against the command of Him who prohibits
every wicked deed. But that is your concern.

2. But it is a more recent fault of mine, or rather a most immediate one,
that I do not die or take to the flight to which you are goading me. But who
can die when God preserves his life? How dare he flee who is well aware that
he is addressed in God's words: "The hireling flees because he is a hireling,"
that is, "when he sees the wolf" [Job 10.12];[19] and "He who dismisses his wife,
excepting the reason of fornication, makes her commit adultery" [Mt. 5.32]?[20]
Does not whoever makes anyone commit adultery consequently kill his soul,
since it is written, "The soul which sins itself will die" [Ezek. 18.20]? He forbids me to do so who says, "Do not put your soul to the killing of your son"
[Pr. 19.18]; and if not to the killing of a son, much less to that of the many
sons of the Church to which I am legally wed. But if *you* are not ashamed to
be called here a wolf, as elsewhere a thief, I know that *I* am afraid to be called
a hireling. For I desire to be found in the ranks of the shepherds when everyone
rises in his order [1 Cor. 15.23]. Since in that division, as the Gospel says [Mt.
25.32-33], even kids will be so sternly damned, consider if you can what wolves,
the devourers of lambs, will suffer, and beware, I urge you, the stigma of such
a name. These analogies indicate two things: that he who unjustly suffers anything from an attacker is a sheep (though a sinner); and that he who attacks

is a wolf. When you hear that "he who marries a wife who has been dismissed commits adultery" [Mt. 5.32], if you do not fear to commit adultery, know that *I* fear to be called a Nicolaitan.[21]

3. I put all this down in order to show how my fault against you is impossible to correct, but I'd rather you consider your fault against me than that I offend Him who says, "To me" (understand "leave") "your revenge: I will repay, saith the Lord" [Rom. 12.10]. In this *repayment*, I urge you to consider how to prevent anything worse happening to you and consider how you are acting against yourself (since you swore, as I did, an oath of loyalty to the emperor) when you try to undo the emperor's action[22] and force men who swore the same oath (which you are dragging to your aid in this) to perjure themselves. Consider, I say, how you are acting against yourself, when you make bishops[23] become such transgressors of the canons when they help you, and when you make a father suspect his sons[24] and sons hate a father without cause: when you cause perjury to be overlooked, when you make anathemas[25] despised, when you do not refuse to promise rewards to anyone who says, "What will you give me and I will hand him over to you?" [Mt. 26.15]. Since you do this and similar against me, or rather against yourself, consider this: just as I cannot die on my own decision, so I fear to abdicate, which I could not do regardless of you.

If you decide never to make amends, try to achieve what you have begun by another route, by acquiring the command of the emperor and of our dukes for me to retire, a clear and open command, not one whose meaning is debatable. For you work at everything else to no purpose—unless, perchance, God has permitted you to do what He permits the wolf to do with the lamb, and this to your own loss more than mine, believe me.

I am "ready for the whips" [Ps. 37.8], acknowledging my faults: what the just Judge [Ps. 7.12] thinks of you who calls for a whipping for me who have done you no wrong, see for yourself. If you are unaware, hear what the prophet says to Nebuchadnezar in a similar situation: "I was angered over my people, says the Lord, and I have handed them over to your hand. You did not have mercy upon them, nor did you remember your own end. Therefore, evils will come upon you from which you will be unable to flee; disaster will rush over you and you will not know its rising" [Is. 47.6–11].

Those who help you in this mischief should note this: "You offer help to the wicked and you join in friendship with those who hate God" [2 Chr. 19.2]; and the words of the psalmist too: "For they persecute him whom thou hast smitten and to the number of my wounds they have added more: add to them punishment upon punishment" [Ps. 68.27–28], and the rest which you well know. Nothing obscure need be said to those who do not restrain you from these attacks when it is in their power; the apostle very clearly says to them: "Not only those who do but also those who consent to those doing are worthy of death" [Rom. 1.32]. Those who refuse me help against you cannot claim that they have not heard Pope Alexander the Martyr, since he still lives in his decretals, saying: "Whoever is of your college and witholds help from them will be judged to have been a schismatic rather than a priest."[26] If you are unaware how both you and your supporters and those who do not give me help are acting, not only against me but also against those who from the beginning of the world have suffered persecution for Justice's sake [Mt. 5.10], listen to the Gospel: "That upon you may come all the righteous blood shed upon earth, from the blood of innocent Abel to the blood of Zechariah, the son of Barachiah, whom you murdered between the sanctuary and the altar" [Mt. 23.35]. But if I am wrong in this I do not mind being wrong along with Jerome who makes this interpretation,[27] provided that you tell me how the scribes and pharisees could kill Zechariah whom they never saw. "He who has ears to hear, let him hear" [Mt. 13.43] — and justly contradict what he will.

41

[Early the next year, Rather defended himself against the continued attacks of his enemies in a remarkable work entitled *Qualitatis coniectura cuiusdam, Ratherii utique Veronensis*. In this he puts into the mouth of an imaginary opponent the worst possible accusations against himself. Gradually he turns to self-justification, and concludes by appealing to the emperor to make a full enquiry into the situation in Verona and not to rely solely on the reports made to him behind Rather's back. The work is an interesting experiment in autobiography, in which he ironically seems to be blackening his own character through his enemies' mouths, but is in fact making a strong statement of his values and defense of his position. Most of the items which his enemies accuse him of *not* doing are censured in the *Praeloquia*[1] as behavior typical of worldly bishops.]

∾

Examination of the Character of an Individual, Namely, Rather of Verona

1. For all my actions, words, and thoughts as well, I am forced to answer to the criticisms of those who hate me, just as though I alone did not have to come to that Final Judgment where all unatoned actions in this world must be reviewed, but had to answer for everything to men in this world; as though I were the only man not allowed to speak without previous permission, nor even to go from one room to another without rendering an account for it—though I do have many blessings thanks to God's mercy and the charity of him [the emperor Otto] who has conferred them upon me, and I do have the licence to enjoy them. Of course, if they were growling their complaints of me to each

other, it would not be surprising. But it *is* surprising that they should dare to tire the ears of the emperor with such tattle. For what need is there to tell the man who has to think about the whole government of the realm, if some starveling shifts from one bed to another or if someone turns from one side to the other? Therefore, I will myself provide material for my critics for what they are bent on doing, and will combine true with false and moot with certain, collecting here all the idle slanders that I can, enough to satisfy you all; forestalling and anticipating what you do say or what you can say about me, and in what sense, I will attempt to offer an unprecedented explanation of myself. Let him who wishes, then, read on, and let him say something worse about me if he can.

2. They say: attendants whom he does not dare to whip he does not cease calling wicked servants. He says that because he is hot-tempered and very poor, he refuses to have anyone whom he dare not call *fello* [knave] as his minister or agent.[2] He constantly charges that his vassals are no help to him, and even that they had let him be seized and led away.[3] He criticizes the habits, reading, and singing of his clergy; he calls unlawful marriage "adultery";[4] he declares that [canon] law should be observed rather than custom.[5] He forbids servile work on the Lord's day. He orders those committed to God to serve Him in an unusual, and even unprecedented, way. He never stops quoting St. Gregory: "One cannot arrive at great rewards except by great labor."[6] Where, then, do kings go? Where all the wealthy? And where all those who live for pleasure? For by this saying he promises the kingdom of God only to the afflicted.

He always keeps his nose in a book and never stops chattering about it. He charges everyone: "Don't be a friend to anyone whose ways are pleasing to the devil." But whom does he praise, this man who is always castigating himself? Perhaps he is deceived by that most true sentence of the apostle, wrongly interpreted: "If we judged ourselves, we would not be judged" [1 Cor. 11.31] — as if it were enough for one merely to confess oneself a sinner without abandoning the sins confessed (though if another were to say this to him he would be very angry). What he says, he writes and tries to leave it to posterity to read, so that it might put his contemporaries in poor light. He calls this writing the *Chronography*[7] of his time (using a Greek word in his vanity, though he is not even Latin),[8] containing as it does the life of his contemporaries. Beginning, middle, and end, he gnaws first at himself, then at all those who live after his fashion; he does not stop sinking his jaw-teeth in them,[9] leaving none unscathed. And so, since his tongue is against everybody, everybody's tongue is rightly against him. His scurrilous tongue could, perhaps, be tolerated; but his slanderous fingers, writing such things for future generations to read, someone would be justified in breaking.

What more? His life is unlike all those who care for honor; his clothes are not cared for, his shoes are dirty, he does not collect tapestries, he lacks for tables, he is content with moderate couches and other furnishings, he does not look for valuables. Nothing pertaining to glory or honor is seen in him. He only washes his hands and lips when about to eat, and also after eating, his face rarely. Perhaps in his own country he had been a *bacularis*[10] and therefore all honor is cheap to him—though we have been told far otherwise, that he is the son of a carpenter. That is why he is so expert and eager to build and restore churches, and that is why he is ever handling and turning stones and often carries them himself.

3. He is not ashamed to behave like a servant; the habits of a lord he so disdains that, scorning the pontifical couch, he more often sleeps on the floor, and, like a second Epicurus who thinks that the highest good lies in pleasure, is content if all is well with his stomach, his side, and his feet, and if he is sufficient to himself alone and his friends. When he is eating, he does not care if he has company; his table is devoid of riches; appropriately, he does not reject mean company, insisting that a poor table disdains rich diners. He makes no distinction between noble and churl in furthering the highest good, asserting that many nobles have done ignoble things and, citing Sallust, that nobility depends on one's own abilities and actions more than on someone else's.[11] Perhaps in this way he is trying to buy the honor which he thus pretends to eschew. He grasps for the show alone, it is evident; true glory he exchanges for vainglory.

He has become a very Labeo,[12] we think, because of this, and has perhaps fallen into those very actions which he is almost always deploring in his sermons, "moved by the hand of the sinner, inflamed by the breath of Behemoth" [Ps. 35.12; Job 41.19], expelled from God's grace, unable to stand upright, perhaps doing something unclean and therefore perverse. He has so often sinned in looking at his own image that he can truly say of himself what the prophet in Lamentations could once say about others: "My eye has damaged my soul" [Lam. 3.51]. For if this were not the case beyond a shadow of doubt, he would not have conceded that he too has done, or is doing, acts for which he must atone with punishments in hell. He would have dined at the same hour as others dine at, however ravenous he might be; he would have eaten meat occasionally, as others do all the time; he would not have shouted so often "Woe is me," as he is reported to do when all alone. For there are plenty of people who have often heard him alone arguing as if with another and sometimes saying: "What do you want with me now, Satan? Have you not already grown old with me in such exploits? Why do you still tear these worn-out limbs and this strengthless frame? Am I not sufficiently delivered over to you? Have I not bought my way into hell enough? What prize are you still seeking? Eternal life could be bought for less. If my writings in my book of *Confession*[13] are not enough, go back, evil one, to your own book, where I know that none of my evil deeds is omitted. But, I confess, the wicked deeds which Italy, France, and Norica sing, which Burgundy acknowledges, which Provence remembers, which Septimania records, Saxony utters, and Suevia recollects, could suffice on their own. You could justifiably be satisfied, evil one, that I can be called 'grown old in evil days' [Dan. 13.52]. Yet I know, you cunning devil, I know you are not seeking *me*—whom, alas, you already hold in your clutches—but are striving *through* me to acquire others."

4. When we hear this, what are we to think that he is worth? We know that he is displeasing to God; how can we hold him pleasing to us? Since these are words of desperation, what can our estimation of him be, when even his own self-estimation so censures him? And since, according to the apostle, "a bishop should be above reproach" [1 Tim. 3.2], who could tolerate that such monstrous reproaches can be found in one? Most surprising of all is his loquacity,[14] since he is backed by no talent for speaking nor by the authority of a master nor by the full voice of a reader. So if God is to be admired in His holy men and works [Ps. 67.36], He is more to be admired, let us say, in granting what He has conceded to a man like him and in a manner like that. We can compare him to Balaam's ass [Num. 22.28] or to that impious idol-worshipper [Balaam], prophesying and deceiving, blessing and cursing, conscience-stung and hardened. We can liken him to Elihu (though he is believed to be the same as Balaam), who surprises even the Lord himself as he rolls out sentences in unskilled speech [Job 38.2]—which this one never stops doing. He is like the lamp that illumines others but burns itself up. And so if any goodness at all appears in him, it is to be thought of as hypocrisy rather than true goodness. Even if he restores or constructs churches (they say), he does this from the vice of vainglory—would that they lied or rather were wrong! Yet when the apostle says: "Do not pronounce judgment before the time, before the Lord comes, who will bring to light the things now hidden in darkness and will disclose the purposes of the heart" [1 Cor. 4.5], it is just this kind of criticism of others that he is condemning. (However, even I have to admit that they are not entirely wrong.)

5. How then (they say) does a man like this handle the office of bishop?[15] He does not serve the emperor, nor the duchess [*dux*];[16] he never takes the field, he rarely goes to court, and even then only under pressure. If he does do so, he waits at least four days before going to the palace; as soon as he can get away, he heads for an inn and picks up a book. He never appeals to the emperor on any matter, never importunes him for clemency for any of his people, and seeks nothing from him. He acquires nothing for his Church, but allows it to lose much.[17]

With the leaders of the realm he has no dealings; he does not use their hospitality, makes light of their discussions; he never invites any of them to his own table. He does no favors to any of them and seeks no favors in return; he always goes back home empty-handed. He pledges his loyalty to no one nor seeks it from any. He does not follow the example of others in choosing worldly glory. He says that he detests glory because, when he wanted it, he was unable to obtain it; now, when he will not have the years to enjoy it, it would be very foolish to desire it. If any man tries to kiss his foot, he thrusts him back with an exclamation. If allowed, he would sit alone all day, would read books or reread them. A crowd he hates, solitude he loves; he does not join in play, shuns dice, cares naught for hounds, naught for falcons. At times, he is very wordy, at times almost dumb; dissolved in laughter one moment, the next morose and quick to pick a quarrel.

In his language he can be slanderous or frivolous or ribald at any hour, whatever his mood. He might give generously or not at all, but he will have no one beg him; he is mostly impatient, but often very long-suffering. Even if he gives to someone, he allows promises to no one. He can be very deceitful, but he despises lying; he would be crafty, if he did not himself hate (and believe God to hate) the cunning. He is ambivalent to all, and thereby in agreement with none. Furthermore, from being at one time most generous — or rather, to be more accurate, a prodigious spendthrift[18] — he has recently become as miserly as if he had changed into another person; and from this you can clearly see his unstable temperament.

He says: "Eat"; should you refuse, he would not pressure you. "Then have a drink, at least," he says; but he does not twist your arm if you refuse. He does not invite you to sit down, but he never fails to jump on you if you do not sit. If you ask him for anything at all trivial, he is annoyed; if for an essential, he is silent, then becomes quite irritated; if you ask subtly, he begins to rave. If he wants you to do something, he tells you not to do it; if he wants something not to be done, he tells you to do it. His word cannot be trusted, though sometimes he asserts that in reports he always tries to appear trustworthy and in promises he wants to appear so. He has never begun anything good and brought it to a conclusion.

6. He habitually denies the Lord the tail of the victim,[19] and thereby most wretchedly deprives himself of salvation. "For whoever perseveres in good up to the end," says the Lord, "will be safe when others are removed afar" [Mt. 24.13]. But, conversely, he who perseveres in evil, as he seems to be doing, will without doubt go to perdition. Alas, unfortunate wretch! Why is he not converted even at his life's very end,[20] where he now stands? But he has reached desperation, we think, because he has put his foot in such a net that walking in its mesh [Job 18.8], he can in no way be released. For since he has been a monk and is now a bishop, if he abandons his flock and goes back to the monastery [Lobbes], he is afraid he will hear: "O shepherd, abandoning his flock!" [Zech. 11.17] If he does not, he is afraid that the apostle was referring to him when he said: "Having damnation because they violated their first pledge" [1 Tim. 5.12]; and the Lord also: "No one putting his hand to the plough and looking back is fitted for the kingdom of heaven" [Lk. 9.62]. Thus, when he was arrested,[21] he foolishly began to chortle: "Lo, I now see what I desired." For he thought (he admits) that he was then going to be expelled once and for all, and rejoiced that he had not abdicated his bishopric but that his bishopric had abdicated him. By this device he wanted to go back to the monastery (he says), promising himself that it was for this that the Lord had said: "Turn to me and I will turn to you" [Zech. 1.3]. Since this has not happened, he thinks, most desperately, that the words, "If God shuts in a man, who can say to Him, Why do you do this?" [Job 9.12] apply to him. For he says that, far from making penitence for past sins, we do not let him even abstain from perpetrating new ones, since, even if he had no sins of his own, he could fear perpetual damnation for ours too, in that he neither checks our sins with his words nor corrects them by example nor lessens them by his merits.

Found wanting in these three ways, he is compelled in another work to cry out to God: "If you permit my damning attempts to prosper, what hope of avoiding them do you leave? And if I cease not from present evils, what pardon can I expect for past ones?"[22] This then (he says) is that shutting-in of a man, in which he will perish eternally, as God shuts him in but does not open. And he will perish justly, for Justice can do nothing unjustly, as he declares; and he cites the apostle: "Who was made Justice for us by God" [1 Cor. 1.30]. Deceived by this gloom of his, some of us think that he wishes to resign his office, as he himself states that he would like to do, but refuses; he would like it if it were allowed; he refuses because it is not allowed.

7. Furthermore, he claims that we make up such monstrous fictions about him as alone could make him abhorrent to everyone, and that since he is very sensitive they cause him sharp anguish. But he cares so little if someone speaks ill of him, that he recently paid a man twelve coins to abuse him for a whole day. He claims that he is so preoccupied with fear of hell that there is no need for him to fear anything further. One otiose word — and (he would have us believe) a wicked one — he confesses[23] he spoke in such a place that, when he remembers it and hears that he will render account for it on the Day of Judgment, he belittles every shame in this world in comparison with it; he asserts that there is no way that a man rendering account for a word like that, uttered in such a place and on such an occasion, will join the throngs of the blessed

and hear addressed to him the words: "Come, ye blessed of my Father, receive your kingdom" [Mt. 25.34]. For since blessedness has no wretchedness in it, whereas shame for such acts goes hand in hand with the greatest wretchedness, how will a man who, in the sight of all rational creation, both men and angels, renders account for such a word, how will he ever be able to be blessed?

8. What more? Whoever wants to know him, let him read through the whole of his book of *Confession*. For if he really is such as he tells there, no one in this world is worse. But if in claiming that he is such he tells fictions, he is proven to be a thorough liar. There is, besides, no book of his, no sermon, no history, in fact nothing which he has ever dictated to be read by posterity, which does not, if properly understood, confirm his wickedness. He says that he sings psalms not because he knows that they are listened to (since he always believes otherwise), but because (since he knows that he sings them very unwillingly) he thinks that that strength which he puts into reciting them against his will has some effect towards the end of acting willingly *against* God, or because he is forcing his lips to serve God, but his heart is not in it and his other limbs are rebelling against God (since also in none of them is he more inclined to anger God than in the excesses of his tongue).

About fasting and all the things which he *seems* to do well, he says the same; for, apart from all his other vices, he is so slothful that, were he not always working, he would slumber in lethargy—though he could not last in sleeping, which, however, he does quite willingly either on a couch or on the floor. He claims that he makes penance for the sins of others when he fasts till the ninth hour (though afterwards he gorges himself), but really he is making penance for his own sins (insufficiently however).

9. At one time he is so kind to people, at another so mean, that he amazes everyone. But the surprising thing is that he dares to tell those who are amazed why he does this. For he claims that there is no one on earth whom he dare not or will not stand up to, even someone who has some authority over him in any sphere of his activities or who is his friend. He says, to be sure, that he will obey the unavoidable commands of secular power; yet for all the time that the receiver of the favor thus given keeps it, he will ever bear him a grudge. This he said to the renowned duchess [Judith] to her face, and this he has shown in the case of Lanzo and Sikerus.[24] For (first) after the countless wrongs which Sikerus had done him in those three years, though Rather had been most friendly and had allowed him to keep for four years a castle from which he could draw (not counting other service) a yearly income of six librae of Venetic denarii, and in addition was willing to let all the land which belongs to the Church of Verona across the lake be shared between Sikerus and his son-in-law, on the day on which Milo had intended to displace Rather in the bishopric, this Sikerus sent to Rather a note of all the money which he had given him as a friend, asserting that he gave it not in payment of any fine but for acquiring land. The bishop answered him — as of course he is so miserly — that he would give him nothing further except from the diocese of Milan[25] and that from the diocese of Verona he would not give him even half a manse — as he did not want him to keep a manse — and that the fort [*castrum*] which he had himself given him must suffice him; and when Sikerus had replied that thus Rather was claiming to have given him the fort as a favor, as though he was some kind of vassal, when in fact he already held it as a gift from the emperor and empress (this was a lie), this holy bishop so flared up in anger, this preacher, this ascetic (but really hypocrite), that he at once took the land from him.

As for Lanzo's case: when Counts Earnest and Bucco only after much toil and many promises had won from him as if from some fierce adversary what they had acquired from the glorious emperor, namely, that Lanzo should thereafter give his son a fine benefice, Lanzo kept the whole of that fine benefice for himself and allowed his son to have none of it, though he was a fine knight and beloved of the bishop, and compelled him to serve his seigneur [i.e., Rather] in unbecoming poverty. For that little fault this maniac devil bishop held him in such hate that he could not even look him in the face. He did this also to both Grimald and Conrad, who wanted to hold that one's land in defiance of him, and he is merciless on all those who try through someone else's authority unlawfully to hold any land which belongs to his (episcopal) right; it is a wonder that such a devil is even allowed to live! Who then could love such an adversary? If he happens to find favor with anyone, it is more for his clownishness [*scurrilitas*] than for any good quality, since his clowning is amusing even to his enemies.

10. He does not like gifts if they demand a return. If a poor man gives him something, he calls him a fool either for not keeping it for himself, or for not bestowing it on a better man. He would rather have enough than be rich, rather be in want than be pressured to give at all generously; he would rather let everything in this world go to ruin than that another after his death should come to enjoy the abundance of his goods. He keeps telling everyone to remember the breastplate of Dr. Galivertus,[26] the fraudulence and dishonesty of the executors, and the wealth of bishops deservedly handed over to the power of kings. Therefore, let kings hear, let them consider what kind of thanks they should render to a man like this. He says that he wants to die such a beggar that his cadaver would be buried by another's charity (for he calls his body "cadaver" to show how cheap it is to him). Greedy of acquiring anything and then generous of it, continently weak and weakly continent, he shows that it would be his wish to receive no good rather than embrace the Lord's words restraining

us from sin. In affectation, he shuns worldly glory to a prodigious extent and in fleeing it he wins it for himself. Showy himself, he does not stop criticizing the empty show of this world; wicked, he does not stop reproving wickedness. He would deceive many with his cleverness, he admits, if he knew that they would not force him to swear an oath,[27] which he greatly fears, or if he did not fear that the devil would say to him in the end: "Like a sharp razor have you worked treachery" [Ps. 51.4].

11. Though he is evil to all, to the Jews he is worst — not because he whips them (because he does not dare to), not because he seizes their goods, but because he never stops reviling them. He abuses their rites, he criticizes all who extol them above Christians and permit them to blaspheme the Lord Jesus Christ and His holy Mother. He gives an example: would a king want to have as a *fidelis* a man who heard someone say something blasphemous or wicked about his lord and kept his peace with him? He reproves the man who even greets them or returns their greeting, let alone embraces them or eats with them. He cites as his authority the apostle's words: "If any does not love Jesus Christ, with such an one you ought not to take food" [1 Cor. 16.22, 5.11], and: "Who says Hail, shares his wicked work" [2 Jn. 1.11]. He reproves all those who would rather do business with them than with Christians; he cites as a text the curses on them mentioned in the Pentateuch where even their business is called accursed. But he does not reprove if they are defended by Christian kings and princes; for, he says, it was of them that Isaiah said to Christ: "Under your shade we shall live among the nations" [Lam. 4.20],[28] and the psalmist: "He caused them to be pitied by all those who held them captive" [Ps. 105.46]. He only censures the fact that they are allowed to revile the name of Jesus Christ and to state that He is not God and that His holy Mother was not a virgin before birth, a virgin in birth, and a virgin after birth, nor did she bring forth God. "For who," he says, "would bear this patiently except the devil himself? For no one can bear to hear anyone speak ill of his patron except he who is shown to be the greatest villain. The son of the devil says that Jesus Christ, who created me, redeemed me, holds me, feeds me, defends me, and finally promises me eternal life, is not the Son of God — and should I not be angry with him? The malicious villain says that His Mother did not bear a Son of the Holy Spirit, to whom I never cease to cry: 'Lord, my defender and redeemer' [Ps. 18.15] — and should I not be angry, or rather, furious? He says that the soul of St. Peter is in the same place as his father's — and am I, who am a servant of St. Peter, to be a friend of his? He says that I worship idols — and am I to presume to offer him a kiss, even if I do not dare to give him the cup?"

The person who is not naturally angry at such a one is worse than the Jew himself, is equal to the devil. He who loves the Jew who denies God, denies

God. He is not a Christian who likes the Jewish blasphemer of Christ. He is not a friend of God who loves the enemy of God. He is not loyal [*fidelis*] to the king who loves the king's infidels. If kings judge thus about themselves and their disloyal subjects, why do they not judge the same about Christ and His enemies? Since He is King of Kings and himself has given them the kingdom, which they ought to possess and rule under Him, why do they allow a race hostile to God to bark against Him within the kingdom committed to their charge? It would be enough to allow them to live at all, not permit them so openly to blaspheme Jesus Christ. "Under your shadow we shall live" [Lam. 4.20], says the prophet about them—*we shall live*, not *shall be loved*—and "He caused them to be pitied" [Ps. 105.46], not *to be extolled*, not *to be befriended* or *honored with office*.

What sort of a thing is this, when a cleric fights for Christ and a Jew blasphemes Christ, the cleric strikes the Jew and the Jew strikes the cleric,[29] or rather strikes Christ in the person of the cleric (for this is what Saul was told [Acts 9.4]), and Erimbertus, our verbal contortionist and legal distortionist,[30] says that for the cleric's striking of the Jew a triple fine must be paid to the king, but for the Jew's striking of the cleric no fine must be paid to anyone? O holy Josaphat! King best in other matters, would you had been so in this! You would say to Erimbertus what the Lord once commanded you through the prophet to say: "You offer help to the impious and join in friendship with those that hate the Lord" [2 Chr. 19.2]. What is this? For these same words [*lord* and *impious*] kings usually use of themselves and those who are friendly to their disloyal subjects. What then, I ask, do they think about Christ,[31] about themselves, and about the Jews who are enemies of Christ the King? And though they know for very truth that the Jews always speak ill of the Lord, even so they do not stop them; what then do they think about the apostle's words, "Not only those that do but also those that agree with the doers are worthy of death" [Rom. 1.32]? This sentence, considered, just, and God-pleasing, refers to the Jews, though to Erimbertus it seems, or rather *is*, empty chatter.

12. To return again to the criticism of his ways:[32]

He says that individually he loves no one in this world excepting only the emperor and himself, that "generally" he hates no one. What this means we cannot fathom. He does not trouble to care for his relatives, either because he thinks that they lack nothing and knows that only he and his brother are poor, or because he knows that he is forbidden by canon law to give them anything, or because he thinks that being so old he has none, since even those he has are already in their sixth age[33] and a series of grandsons has taken the place of his brothers (though he says this garrulously and falsely—and he is a garrulous fellow!). When someone greets him, he does not return greetings but is instead angry, saying that if the other had met an enemy he would have greeted him in the same way. Since you often hear him groaning, or wailing rather, but rarely see him weeping real tears, you can tell that he labors under obdurate pride and terror alike, and since he oftens sings, "The sacrifice to God is a contrite heart" [Ps. 1.19], he must think that gloominess confers the same grace as weeping.

While he remembers also that Augustine said that "there should never be prayer without groaning,"[34] he must believe that *groaning* is different from *weeping*, and that groaning can take place without tears but weeping can never do so. For at the place where the Gospel says, "And going outside Peter wept bitterly" [Mt. 26.75], he [Rather] says: "Happy indeed are your tears, Peter."

13. If anyone says to him: "Go to the emperor; petition to have restored to you the Church's property which has been taken away in the days of your tenure,"[35] he replies:

"Why should I do more as I shall die within the next three years?[36] Or now that I am an old man should I begin to enroll an army for the conduct of wars, to plunder and loot, to pile up wealth for others to enjoy when I am shut up in hell, to enlist supporters for my successor and to build up a legacy as if for a son? I would be the stupidest person in the world to do so; for as I live within the bounds of sufficiency, what do I lack—except integrity? I do not seek to be better clothed; I have daily food enough for my modest needs. Even if I had more, the rich would not allow me to use it for the redemption of my soul; rather, they would force me to waste it in vanity. Yet I do not deny that I would dearly have loved to be very rich if I knew that I was given time to enjoy it, or even, as I would like, time to spend what I had. It is now almost forty years[37] since I began to be ambitious for power. I have never been able to hold it, or if I ever held it, I could not keep it for long. If it were given me now on my deathbed, what, I ask, would it confer, since I would not be able to enjoy it for even a year—particularly if it turned out that for this alone I heard in hell: 'Son, remember what goods you have received in life' [Lk. 16.25], and so lost the rewards which, says Gregory, no one can come by without great toil.[38]

"But in this country a man cannot without great sin reach the heights of pomp and power which they look for, let alone find the great wealth which is needed as a consequence. Would I not then be out of my mind (he says), if I were to acquire riches for others at the cost of my own soul? Indeed, when I consider the messenger now summoning me to render my account for my long office wickedly administered, ought I not to be afraid of foolishly piling up for myself more to answer for? I know that Age itself cries out to me, 'You can no longer be steward' [Lk. 16.2]—and should I then want to be given even more estates to administer?"

And at the same time, this hater of all the rich claims that he would be satisfied if at least he were given back those properties which were illegally removed from the jurisdiction of the Church [of Verona] to the king's jurisdiction in such a way that the Church can only recover them if they are given back.

"I would also ask the emperor," he says, "to deign to defend against the counts, viscounts, and *sculdascii*,[39] the properties which his predecessors by their mandates conferred on the Church [of Verona] or ratified as belonging to the Church. If anything has been done either by these two aggressors[40] or by me against God or equity, either under pressure or by some fraud going by the name of *Commutatio* or *Libellarium* or what they call *Precaria*,[41] he should decree that it all be rescinded; I would not ask to have them returned to me, but granted to any tenant he wishes; only let them not be removed from the Church.[42]

"As for my own position I would ask nothing else than that his pious Lordship deign to answer my humble questions:[43] (1) Who ought to restore the destroyed churches[44] in our diocese and with what funds? (2) What funds should I have with which to feed the flock entrusted to me by God and himself?[45] (3) What person should administer, and where and how dispense, the offerings made to the Holy Mother of God? For I know for myself that I ought to despise worldly things and love heavenly things. Would I not have enough for my livelihood if I held at least the land which my parishioners, and even enemies of mine, hold without my permission?"

All of this he admits he would not even say if he were not compelled, by the oath of fealty which he solemnly swore to the emperor, to care greatly for the emperor's life. In his madness he never stops saying that he has no hope that in the days of the emperor it will ever be well for him. But if he happened to hear that by his own neglect the emperor had died—which heaven forbid— he says that he would thereby expect to be killed, but he would not care; for he has no useful friend in this world except the emperor, though even he [the emperor] continues to offer his enemies help against him [Rather] and to take away his property and give it to them. So since he is a man of this sort, loving none and loved by none, as he does not deny, what in the world can he do, they ask. Nothing, I say, nothing.

14. [Rather now speaks in his own person.]

What if they had known my inner thoughts and the reasons for my attitude? But so that I may not leave them suspicious about my coming up to the top of this hill[46] and my lengthy stay on it (and I hear from a reliable source that they are now further pained by it), let them come here, I say; I beg them to. The Lady Duchess [Judith] finding me inclined this way (and with many enemies as a result and without any friends as I am a foreigner)[47] and fearing that even worse would happen to me than actually happened, commended me to the protection of a well-known count [Bucco]. What more? I accuse no one, I excuse no one; I revile no one — I also do not praise anyone. I was arrested,[48] removed, brought back.[49] The aforesaid count said that it had happened through my own improvidence; he said that he had bid me come up to the fortress called the Palace,[50] but that I had refused. He warned me not to trust myself any longer to that house[51] in which I had suffered the other troubles, but that I should live in the High Court,[52] which was more protected. I believed him; I did so; from fortified, I made it *very* fortified. Again he told me that if I left there and came up into the Palace it would be safer. I obeyed. It was thoroughly destroyed. I quickly had it restored.

That done, he asked a second time that I allow his wife and children to live with me there; he himself would stay in the Circus, called the Arena, to protect the city — which is what he did. It seemed very absurd, as everyone knew well except the most stupid of them. Again, I do not accuse or excuse the motivation of anyone; however, I came down and went back again to the house,[53] perilous though it was. Not daring to stay in it long, I began to head for Garda,[54] but I changed my plans again in deference to Easter, which was imminent. I chose a little corner in the city; I asked the count's approval; he even gave me help. I put up a building there; it was immediately set on fire; who did it, no one asked. I rebuilt it better, but he told me not to. I was again given permission to rebuild,

when the lyre in greater prosperity sang praises after the insults.[55]

This began to make me suspicious. Again in my fear I pondered flight to Garda. While I was thinking it over, Lord John, the deacon, arrived and began telling me of the deplorable state of the portico of St. Peter's, which threatened to collapse (he said) unless speedy relief was brought to it. I[56] promised help and did not delay in providing it. I went up, reviewed the situation, and prepared my shoulders for the assistance. Though my desire for helping was strong, I saw that there were many other particulars more in need of correction (and I am not sure that these can be implemented in my lifetime). I have no trusty agent to whom I can assign this; the man to whom I had entrusted one pound of silver the previous year for buying beams had cheated me of it (I realized) in a most monstrous way. I do for myself what I can; when I have done it, I will return home[57] if you instruct, O enemy[58] who are provoked by my absence [from the episcopal palace]. As for you, move into your own oven,[59] if you like and when you like; I do not stand in your way.

15. [Milo is the "you" in this section.]

There are eight reasons for staying here a while, but one particularly cogent one.[60] Your malicious intentions must not be hushed up. I know full well that you would rather I had stayed in such a place as to make me accessible to my enemies, and that you are upset not because I was suspicious of the house and left it, but because I placed myself in a safer one; and I know that for this you cannot escape the charge of being my murderer—though God's providence still preserves my life. And do not think that you are not killing me daily with your schemes, though you see me alive despite your efforts, when you hear that God said about another crime: "Whoever looks at a woman lustfully is already an adulterer in his heart" [Mt. 5.28]; and Jerome: "Woe to us wretches who commit fornication as often as we have desires."[61] So you could also say: "Woe to me, poor wretch, who murder this caitiff as often as I lay a fatal trap for him." You could say that I lie, did we not read that the beloved of Christ said of a lesser offence: "Every man who hates his brother"—that is, any Christian—"is a murderer" [1 Jn. 3.15]. But I will be avenged, I say; know it surely, I will be avenged. "For vengeance is mine, says the Lord" [Rom. 12.19]—"when I permit the guilty to be whipped," we can add—"for I will repay, says the Lord."

For if it is about us that the psalmist says: "If his children forsake my law and do not walk according to my ordinances, if they profane my judgments and do not keep my commandments, then I will punish their transgression with the rod and their iniquity with scourges; but I will not remove from him my steadfast love or be false to my faithfulness" [Ps. 88.31–34]; then in this sense I could say that a bishop driven from his office for his faults is most blessed in comparison with those of whom the prophet truly said: "They spend their days in prosperity and at death they go down to hell" [Job 21.13]. About the scourgers[62] of those ones I will put down (with your peace, please, O object of my examination) what the Lord says through another: "I was angry," says the Lord, charging impious Babylon, "with my people; I gave them into your hand; you showed them no mercy nor did you remember your end. And evils also shall come over you for which you cannot atone. Ruin shall come over you and you shall not know its rising" [Is. 47.6–11].

That I am such, then, as I have set down, I do not stop you saying if you wish; if you like, say that I am something even worse—but only if you can. Yet I think that I have left nothing more foul or abusive for you to say about me. I am well aware, though, that you can now cast at me: "Your own confession proves you worthy of damnation since the Scripture says, 'By your own words you will be justified and by your own words you will be condemned'" [Mt. 12.37]. I neither confess nor deny it, I say. But that the person who can truly condemn me is far away He ever promises me who, we are told, writing with His finger on the ground, mercifully said to a group of accusers: "Whoever of you is without sin be the first to throw a stone at her" [Jn. 8.7]. But alas, because many fear that this verse will be cast back at them in return, many faults are left uncorrected in this world, reserved for perpetual fire—that is, while a man is conscious of his own sin he spares others'. But what estimation we should have about such a sacrifice[63] is very much a mystery to me, I admit. We can deplore that "from the sole of the foot even to the head there is no soundness in us" [Is. 1.6]; and that today "he who does good is missing, down to the last one" [Ps. 13.3].

16. Though it is right to understand this "one" as God himself, the Head of all good, together with some of His members, yet consider how few of our people attain to that One. Would that we could at least think that the one specifically mentioned was the most glorious person of the present time, the emperor; since he is singularly rich—more than all those who have governed the Roman Empire (though with division of the kingdoms) through this cycle of three hundred years—in nobility, power, energy, industry, courage, prudence, wisdom, kindness, constancy, fortitude, mercy, fairness, wealth, largesse, and the abundance of all means to achieve this, would that the omnipotent grace of God deign to concede this to him alone, that he should set about turning first himself wholly to the good, then the empire committed to him to the same good.

All those of the Christian name, alas, especially the leaders, have become corrupt and abominable; thus the worship of God has now completely vanished, and we see that what the Lord commanded and what everyone does could not be at more opposite poles. Though we try, with God's approval, to except him (that is, the holy emperor) alone from this, we should be doing everything, if we dared, to suggest to him, that to the other qualities in which he is strong, he should add this one virtue in particular, namely, that he should apply to himself the words of most holy Job: "I searched out the cause which I did not know" [Job 29.16].[64] For since Gregory says, "What is surprising if we who are human are sometimes led astray?," nothing thwarts those who have been set in power over others more than the deceit and treachery of those counsellors who, according to the prophet, "say evil is good and good evil" [Is. 5.20]. One philosopher says that there is never a shortage of informers if anyone is willing to give them an ear. "Flee the teller of tales," says another, "for he is a gossip."[65] Since poor Italy is packed full of these "tellers of tales" more than all other kingdoms,[66] and treacherous advisors are ever ready to follow up on their information, they should be treated with that much the more caution and suspicion the more they are by nature perverse and prone to this kind of action.

To offer one example from countless: when Hubert of Parma[67] pressed me to accept a large payment[68] and yield the bishopric to that rival of mine, one of my closest political allies (but no personal friend) approached the duchess[69] and, though having promised me the fullest help in this, deliberately made her understand that the most just emperor wanted it that way—perhaps he added "had commanded it that way." What an extraordinary thing! That the great emperor, so just, so God-loving, so God-fearing, should indicate that he wanted what was contrary to God! It could indeed have happened that the emperor was led astray by someone falsely telling him that that is what I wanted. My arrest, expulsion, victimization, removal, and reinstatement, and the plundering of the Church, the destruction of the episcopal palace, the termination of the emperor's alms, the undoing of the reinstatement, the invasion of the city, the disrespect shown to the emperor, and much else relating to these things, were at issue (they still are), yet, without making good on those points, they charged me with perjury,[70] a capital charge!

One should be particularly careful about people like this for this reason: those who protest to authority before those who have suffered the injustice are usually considered to be the ones at fault. This we know was very recently done by one of the leaders of the group who once arrested me; and though constantly planning and carrying out innumerable attacks on me and my friends, when he was promoted, against all law and right, to the Deaconate by the usurper of my office [Milo] (despite his many thefts and sacrilege which those who claim to know charge him with), and though violently taking over property of my jurisdiction and plundering it, he came running—though not pursued—to the feet of the emperor and falsely swore that I had made off with the emperor's gift to him!

What monstrous crimes of this sort do such people do! Who can avoid them except the man who tries most diligently "to search out the cause which he does not know" [Job 29.16]? What king can be in harmony with the King of kings other than the one who tries to do so industriously? What judge can discern the just man without Him? This may the King of kings himself deign to concede to our most pious lord [Otto] to do, we pray, and to grant in return, if he does it, that both in this world he may rule blessedly with long-lived leadership and in the next he may reign with Christ for ever. Amen.

42

CC Opera Minora 135–36   Verona early 966

[The following is a decree on the little abbey of Maguzzano: the abbot here had abused his privilege by spending on a wife the revenue of a property charitably given to the monastery, by ignoring his priestly duties, and by trying to bribe the bishop to overlook what he was doing. By this decree Rather appoints three priests to serve there and fulfill the proper functions, and he provides for their support. He also recalls the monks there to their monastic vows.]

⧼⧽

Decree

1. Since "all the issues are so full of rash judgments"[1] (to use the words of St. Augustine of august memory) that I, hounded viciously at this time by the smears of my ill-wishers, even I am so in doubt about myself that I sometimes do not know myself what my intentions are in some action I take—when, that is, I compare their true or false reports about me with the events which are known to me more than they should be—in this written decretal I intend to clarify my recent decision about the abbey called Maguzzano [*Magonzianus*] and to publish it for present and future generations so that all may be advised of it.

This little abbey, a small monastery of a few souls, came under the control of our cathedral [Verona] in this way: when its abbot either passed away or committed some unpardonable sin, another was put in charge by the bishop of our diocese to make those serving in it live under the monastic rule. When this did not turn out as the bishop intended (the task was extremely difficult) and the refectory was burnt by the Hungarians, it came to such an unfortunate pass that the man who alone wore the cowl under the false title of abbot was quite unable even to abstain from a wife, still less could the others renounce their own wills as the monastic rule prescribes.[2] Then in all my attempts I was unable to make a certain one of them do what was required at the time in the way of devotions; he three times went into hiding and tried by intermediaries, moreover, to infect me with the leprosy of Gehazi [2 Kg. 5.27] (that is, he tried to bribe me into allowing him to hand over to the devil what had been offered to God, as he had previously done). I refused what he wanted and he kept asking for what I kept refusing in respect of God. When both sides had parted, I was quite at a loss what to do. For if I retained for myself the property offered to the Mother of God on the grounds that I would administer it better, or if I gave it to one of my household, I was afraid that one of my successors would do the same following my example and would nullify the charitable alms of those good people. But if, because of one false monk called the abbot, that is, a false father but in truth a very stepfather, I allowed him to spend it on his wife and carnal sons, brothers, and nephews, I was afraid of incurring the punishment of a negligent, disloyal minister [Lk. 12.42]. Now, since the monk's vow is very strict and quite inappropriate for such people (for just as there is nothing more sacred than a monk, so there is nothing more criminal than a hypocrite), I have abandoned the impossible and take care to apply myself to the possible.

2. Therefore I have ordained that at least three—if more should not be available—priests familiar with their office should at all times serve there so that there will be a Mass every day, one deacon, one sub-deacon, and several clerics. Each of the priests is to receive ten measures of grain and rye, ten measures of legume and buckwheat, ten measures of millet, twelve measures of wine, and for clothes the priests are to receive five solidi, the deacon two, and the sub-deacon one. None of them is to wear a cowl; remembering the ancient practice they are to sing hymns with lauds at matins, prime, tierce, sext, nones, vespers and compline, which, I have decreed, are all to be held at the proper hour. And because I have little hope that this can happen without any authority, I have put in charge there a priest with full honors, who will practice his ministry in addition to the other three, and I have decreed that if that one dies or scorns to do what is decreed, another is to be appointed in his place by the bishop of Verona. When all those items specified above have been dispensed to each, not in vineyards or fields but in measures, he is to have what is left over, but he is to invite those five to eat with him on the great feast-days, generously sharing with them the same food and drink to the best of his ability. On these days they are to have a reading at table and after eating the monks are to sing.

43

Weigle, Epist. 124–37   Verona Lent 966

[Rather addresses in synod the clergy of the diocese: he instructs them generally on their duties and behavior, requiring them to know by heart the three creeds.]

∽

Synodica

Address in synod to the priests and all orders within the Church,
that is, established throughout the whole diocese:

1. I know that you are surprised—or rather (which is worse) I know that you grumble [cf. 1 Cor. 10.10]—that I have summoned you three times now and yet seem to have done nothing with you. So that you should not think that I have done this to no purpose, I admit that I have done it in order to examine you, and I have found you to be such, alas, as I thought that I would find you to be. The words from the Book of Wisdom at once seemed to apply to me, unfortunate that I am: "Do not make light of your foolish sons if they should multiply, nor delight in them if there is no fear of God in them" [Eccli. 16.1].

Therefore, I advise you as a father and instruct you as a pastor, that you remember the words of the apostle: "It is impossible to please God without faith" [Heb. 11.6], that is, without believing the creed which has been passed on to us by the apostles and by their successors, and: "He lives righteously from faith" [Rom. 1.17] — that is, his creed — "and whatever is done without faith" — that is, without belief in God — "is sin" [Rom. 14.23]; "but faith" — that is, belief in God — "if it has no good deeds is dead in itself" [Jas. 2.17]; and that you hasten to take this faith — that is, belief in God — to memory in three forms, namely: according to the Symbol (that is, the collation of the apostles as it is found in the corrected psalteries), and that which is sung at Mass, and that of St. Athanasius which begins, "Whosoever wishes to be saved." Whoever wishes, therefore, to be priest in my diocese or to be made one or to remain one, must recite those three by heart to me, when next he is summoned here by me.

2. I also ask you to meditate on why the Lord's Day is so called, or if you do not know how to meditate, to ask. For in daily use we call those things "lord's" which properly belong to their lord. So in that sense the day is called the Lord's Day because it properly belongs to the Lord, that is, Jesus Christ. But since every day is His, just as is everything which is in the heaven and the sea and the earth and the abysses [Ps. 134.6], we should ask why this day alone is said to be *His*. Obviously because He rose on that day. Do not worry about what day of the month; think only about the day. On the night of the fifth day He was betrayed, He was crucified on the sixth, on the seventh He rested in the sepulchre, on the eighth He rose from the dead, and after three days in part, or two whole nights — a triduum, as He had promised — "from the heart," or interior, "of the earth" [Mt. 12.40], He returned to His disciples. Hence this eighth day, or first day of the week, is called the Lord's, and on whatever day of the month it occurs, it is always the Pasch, that is, the passing of the Lord from death to Life, and it must be preserved from one thing whatever you eat or drink. From what should it be preserved? From servile work [Num. 29.35]. What is servile work? Sin; for whoever sins serves the devil [1 Jn. 3.3].

If then there is a Pasch on every Lord's Day, we should ask what we must do on it. Let the Apostle say: "Christ, our Paschal Lamb, has been sacrificed" [1 Cor. 5.7]. Why is Christ the Pasch? Because He was sacrificed for us. Why was He sacrificed? So that He should die for us. Just as that first lamb, by whose blood the people were cleansed just before being freed from Egypt, was sacrificed, so also He was sacrificed so that He might die, He died so that we, freed by His blood from the destroyer of the world (that is, the devil) might be snatched out of Egypt (that is, hell) and led through the Red Sea (that is, baptism reddened by the blood of Christ) across the desert of our present life, and so could come to the land of promise (that is, eternal life). There you have the Pasch (that is, the good crossing), there you have the lamb killed for you; you have crossed the Red Sea, you are going across the desert [cf. Ex. 12.4–20]. Look where you are going. Be sure to arrive at your proper destination. Strive with God's help not to return to Egypt or perish in the desert, but to arrive at the heavenly fatherland. Know that you return to Egypt if you repeat the sin which you have left. You perish in the desert if you do not persevere in toil and good work.

3. But let us return to the apostle: "Christ, our Paschal Lamb, has been sacrificed," he says. And then: "And so let us feast" [1 Cor. 5.7–8]. Do you think that he means: "Let us have time for gluttony and drunkenness"? By no means! For this follows: "Not in the old leaven"—that is, in blowing up the stomach or in the swelling of previous sin or the desire of returning to past sins or of perpetrating others—"nor in the leaven of evil and wickedness, but in the unleaven of sincerity and truth"—that is, that we be righteous in our action, pure in our thoughts and truthful in our words. When? At all times, but especially in the Paschal Feast, that is, on every Lord's Day of the whole year. For if *the Lord's* means "of the Lord," the day is not ours. If it is the Lord's, the Lord's reverence must be respected. But of which lord? Truly, the Lord who made us when we were not, who restored us when we were lost, who governs us, feeds us, nourishes us, defends us, who gives us our life here as long as it pleases Him, and when it no longer pleases Him will change it from here and turn it into a better or worse according to our merits, and finally who will judge us and either damn us eternally in hell or give us an everlasting crown in heaven. Since this is properly the day of a Lord of such power, let it be honored as befits such a Lord. It cannot be honored except as ordained; for unless a *parasceve* [preparation] precedes the sabbath (i.e., the Lord's day), the day is in no way the Lord's.

4. But what is a *parasceve*? Let the Apostle tell: "Let a man examine himself and so eat of the bread and drink of the cup" [1 Cor. 11.28]. Of what bread? Of Him who says, "I am the living bread, who descended from Heaven" [Jn. 6.41]. Of what cup? "Your cup overflows, how fine it is" [Ps. 22.5]—that is, Christ filling us with His blood, how fine He is, i.e., "the fairest of the sons of men" [Ps. 44.3]. So He who is the bread is himself the Lamb, who the Lamb is himself the Christ, who the Christ is himself the Pasch, who the Pasch has himself been sacrificed for us. He is "the day which the Lord has made" [Ps. 117.24]—not by action but by creation co-eternally—"let us rejoice and be glad in it." He is the day, I repeat, the Lord himself, whose day this is. What do we do about His sabbath? "Be still" [Ps. 45.11], the Lord says through the psalmist, "and see that I am God." The sabbath, then, is called a *stillness* or "rest," that is, that we should rest from evil works and *be still* for God's commands.

Parasceve means *preparation*, that is, that we should prepare the dwelling of our hearts for Christ coming to us through the substance of His Body and Blood.

If, therefore, every eighth day is the Lord's, and the Lord's is so-called for the resurrection of the Lord, or, as we find it finely said by someone, "Because the Lord made every day by His command, but He made the Lord's day by His blood and dedicated it by His life," every Lord's day needs a preparation day or sabbath. The *parasceve*, or preparation, is nothing else than what I have said earlier, that is, that every man should examine himself [cf. 1 Cor. 11.28], that is, should investigate what his desire is: namely, if he stands with God's grace in the desire of improvement or in the obduracy of deterioration. If he finds the former in his conscience, presuming for God's mercy let him gird up his loins and eat the lamb along with bitter lettuce [Ex. 12.8], that is, with contrition of his heart and the bitterness of tears; but if not, I dare not advise him to do so. Let each man look to what he does.

5. Every Lord's day, therefore, is a Paschal day for the reason that it is honored by the Lord's resurrection. And Christ is our Paschal Lamb because He was sacrificed for us. On every Lord's day, therefore, the apostle calls to us, "And so let us feast" [1 Cor. 5.8], that is, let us eat the flesh of the Lord and drink His blood.

But where are those who daily celebrate the Mass, daily make the Pasch — that is, eat the flesh of the Lamb and drink His blood — and yet frequently beget sons and daughters by adulterous intercourse (not to mention the rest), where are they who belch yesterday's drunkenness or excess [cf. Lk. 21.34] before the Lord's altar over the very flesh and blood of the Lamb, who are busy with continual suits, who burn with greed [cf. Gal. 5.19–21], who waste away in hate or envy, who never cease to set the snares of fraud for those whom they ought to have loved as themselves? When did any of these make the preparation or sabbath we are talking about? I fear for them — and would that they were not like me! — I fear that when they think that they eat the Lamb, they are eating rather a goat[3] — and would that it were not that goat which was taken out into the desert (which in Latin is translated *emissarius* but in Hebrew is *Azazel*, that is, the *cruel one of God*; he who sent out *this* goat into the desert is not worthy to enter the Lord's camp till he has washed his body and all his garments), but rather the kid which was sacrificed by all the people on the fourteenth day at evening [Num. 9.10–11]. Woe to those in whom such good is turned to so much evil [cf. Ex. 12.6], that is, the gentleness of God into cruelty, when eating the flesh of the Lord and drinking His blood unworthily, they eat and drink judgment for themselves [1 Cor. 11.29]! Woe, I say, to us wretches and a thousand times woe! For since we are called priests for no other reason than that we ought to consecrate the sacrifice and give it to the people, and the holy Scripture says: "Whatever the unclean touch will be unclean" [Num. 19.22], how can anything handled by our unclean hands even be called "sacred"? And since

our especial teacher and patron St. Zeno[4] says in the sermon which he most eloquently composed about Judas, Jacob's son, and Thamar, his son-in-law, that
the devil is the father of all those who live corruptly,[5] what avails it that in the
sight of all who know that we live corruptly, that is, are slaves to wantonness,
we cry to God, "Our Father, which art in heaven" [Mt. 6.9], when He immediately replies to us through the prophet, "If I am father, where is your love
for me? For what do you do for love, what do you leave undone for fear, of
me?" [Mal. 1.6]? Because I grieve that you do not at all know this and things
like this, in fact, I lament that you do not care about them at all, as your pastor
I instruct you to hasten to learn them and earnestly try, I beg, to teach God's
people by good example, because you do not know how to do so by words.

6. "We[6] urge and beseech you, brethren, just as we find it written elsewhere, to think about our common salvation and listen to our admonition more
attentively, and to store our advice in your memory and be earnest to carry it
out in action.

"First, we urge that your life and habits be beyond reproach, that your cell
be close to the church, and that you keep no women in it. Rise to nocturns
every night, sing your psalms at the appointed hours. Perform religiously the
celebration of masses. Take the Body and Blood of the Lord with fear and reverence. Wash and clean the sacred vessels with your own hands. Let no one celebrate
the Mass who is not fasting, or who is not a communicant, or without amice,
alb, stole, maniple, and chasuble, nor with sword hanging without, nor with
spurs on. Let these vestments be clean, and used for no other purpose. Let no
one presume to celebrate the mass with an alb on which he uses for his own
use. Let no woman come to the altar nor touch the Lord's cup. Let the corporal
be clean; let the altar be covered with clean linens. Let nothing be placed on
the altar except reliquaries and relics or perhaps the four Gospels and a box with
the Lord's Body for a viaticum for the sick; let the rest be stored in a clean place.
Let each church have a missal, lectionary, and antiphonary. Let a place be prepared in the vestry or next to the altar, where water can be poured when the
sacred vessels are washed, and there let a shining vessel hang with water in it,
and there let him wash his hands after communion.

7. "Let no one celebrate Mass outside the church in homes or in places not
consecrate. Let no one celebrate it alone. Let no one celebrate Mass with spurs
on (which are called *sporones* in rural areas) or with a sword hanging outside,
because it is improper and against the rules of the Church. Bless the cup and
offering with a proper cross, that is, not in a circle with the fingers spread as
many of you do, but with two fingers straight and the thumb enclosed within,
which signifies the Trinity. Be sure to make this sign † correctly, for you cannot
bless anyone otherwise. Visit the sick and reconcile them, and according to the

apostle anoint them with holy oil and strengthen them with your own hand, and let no one presume to hand the communion to a lay person or woman to pass on to the sick. Let none of you ask for payment or reward for baptizing infants or reconciling the sick or burying the dead. See that no infant dies without baptism due to your negligence.

8. "Let none of you be drunken or litigious, because the Lord's servant ought not to litigate. Let none of you bear arms in sedition, because our arms must be spiritual ones. Let no one indulge in the sport of birds or dogs. Do not drink in taverns. Take care for the sick and orphans and strangers, and invite them to your table. Be hospitable, that others may take a good example from you.

"Every Lord's day, before the Mass, bless the water from which the people are sprinkled and keep the vessel for this alone. Do not give the sacred vessels and sacerdotal vestments to any merchant or innkeeper as a pledge. Let none of you bring to reconciliation anyone who is not worthily penitent for some consideration and bear witness of reconciliation for him. Let none of you engage in usury or be a lender of capital. Know that the substance and resources which you acquire after the day of your ordination belong to the Church.

9. "Let no one acquire a church without our consent and knowledge. Let no one obtain a church through secular power. Let no one usurp another's church by means of money. Let no one leave the church to which he is titled and move to another for the sake of gain. Let no one celebrate Mass in another's parish without the wish and request of the parish priest if he is present. Let no one take the tenth part belonging to another. Let no one invite a penitent to eat the flesh and drink the wine unless he makes alms for it in his presence.

10. "Let no one presume to baptize except on the eve of the Pasch and Pentecost, except when there is danger of death. Let each one have a font, and if he cannot have a stone one let him have another prepared for this which has no other use. See that you teach all your parishioners the Lord's prayer and creed. Tell your congregation that they must fully observe the fast of Ember days and of Rogations and of the greater Litany. On the fourth day before Lent invite the people to confession and enjoin penance upon them according to the nature of their sin, not from your own feelings but as it is written in the Penitential. Four times a year—that is, at Christmas, the Lord's Supper, Easter, and Pentecost—tell all the faithful to come to the communion of the Lord's Body and Blood. At the appointed times exhort married men to abstain from their wives. On feast-days after the Mass give the people a blessing.

11. "Let no one go on the road without a stole; let none put on lay garb. Let no one presume to sell or lend or make over in any way at all any property or possession of the Church. Teach them to celebrate the Lord's day and other feasts from evening to evening without doing servile work. Prohibit the singing and dancing of women in the churchyard. Forbid those devil-songs which the crowd is wont to sing over the dead in night hours and the laughter which they practice—forbid them with Almighty God's admonishment. Do not communicate with the excommunicate. Let no one presume to sing a mass for them; tell this also to the people committed to you. Let none of you go to their nuptials. Announce to all that none may take a wife without the public celebration of nuptials. Prohibit rape in every way; see that no man marry a blood-relative or marry the wife of another. Make swineherds and other shepherds come to Mass on the Lord's day. Let fathers teach their sons the creed and Lord's prayer, or have them taught. Let the chrism always be kept under lock or seal because of certain infidels.

12. "We wish to know about any priest: if he is born from free parents or of servile condition or if he is born of our parish or ordained or titled to some place. If he was a slave, let him show his card of liberty, if from another parish let him show the letters of commendation which they call *formata*. Concerning the ministry committed to you, we take care to instruct that each one of you have the interpretation of the Lord's prayer according to the orthodox tradition in writing in your possession and understand it clearly and if he knows, instruct in it the people committed to him in thorough lessons, and if not, at least keep to it and believe it.

"Let him understand well the prayers of the Mass and the canon, and if not at least let him be able to quote them from memory clearly. Let him be able to read the epistle and gospel well, and would that he could explain its meaning, at least its literal meaning. Let him know how to pronounce the words of the psalms regularly by heart, along with the usual chants. Let him know by heart, as I said above, the sermon of Bishop Athanasius about the creed of the Trinity, whose beginning is 'Whosoever wishes.' He must be able to utter distinctly and individually the exorcisms and prayers for making catechumens, for blessing the water also, and the rest of the prayers over male and female. Likewise, he must at least know how to say well the order of baptism for helping the sick, and according to the manner canonically reserved for it the order of reconciling and of anointing the sick, and the prayers also relating to that necessity. Likewise the order and prayers for making the obsequies of the dead, likewise the exorcisms and benedictions of salt and water he should know by heart. He should know the day and night chants. He should know the lesser compute, that is, epacts, and Easter chronology and the rest, if possible, and he should have a martyrology and penitential," and the rest.

13. Concerning ordinands, know that they will in no way be promoted by me unless they have lived for a time in our city or in some monastery or at the house of some wise man, and are educated in letters a little, so that they seem suitable for the ecclesiastical dignity.

14. Also, since ecclesiastical authority holds that there ought to be four divisions of ecclesiastical resources, one for the bishop, one for the artisans of the church, one for the clergy, and one for the paupers and pilgrims, if you have your full portion you should have no envy of what belongs to the bishop, the artisans, or the paupers, remembering that the Lord instructed: "You will not lust after the property of your neighbor" [Ex. 20.17]; and: "Do not be concerned about property which does not belong to you" [Eccli. 11.9]. About the property which does belong to you, have trust among yourselves and divide it communally whether it be great or small, knowing that the apostle said: "Let no one outwit his brother in any business" [1 Th. 4.6], that is, in any thing, since the Lord is an avenger in all these things, as I solemnly forewarned you. Know also that it is better for every Christian to suffer wrong than to perpetrate it.

15. Treat the days of Lent as equal, except for the Lord's days. For if you fast on one day and stuff yourselves on the next, you make a *vigesima*[7] not a *quadragesima*. In the Advent of the Lord, know that for four weeks, unless a feast intercedes, you must abstain from meat and coitus. At Christmas you must cease entirely for twenty days and nights even from licit coitus, and likewise in the eight days of the Pasch and the Litanies of Pentecost and the eves of all feasts, and also on the sixth days, but especially on all Lord's days.

I also advise you, beloved, since the authority of the Paschal feast compels me, purely loved brothers in Christ, that on the second, third, fourth, and fifth day of Holy Week you should fast till the ninth hour, excepting infants and the sick and those afflicted with great age. On the fifth day at the ninth hour, all must come to the Mother Church to be reconciled. On the sixth day fast till the ninth hour or (whoever wants to) beyond. On the seventh day let no one presume to sing a mass before the tenth hour or to hold a general baptism. But if someone cannot fast because of infirmity, let him take benefit from the fast which the universal Church makes. "For we are all one body in Christ" [Rom. 12.5]. Only let no one by his importunity compel the universality of our Church to sin against the Lord and violate so glorious feast in any point.

Know that you may give penance for private sins, but for public sins you must defer them to me.

Let none of you make a cleric without my permission, nor one who stammers or is too badly wounded nor one who has little feel for letters.

If a feast, other than that of the holy Mother of God or of the apostles, should fall in Lent or the fasts of Ember days, the fast should be kept rather than the feast celebrated (unless perchance it is the feast of a saint buried in the same parish), because God is pleased by no celebration more than that fast in which there is abstinence from both food and vices. Also, leisure is inimical to the soul.[8]

Without a knowledge of these points which I have set down you cannot make your ministry and lead the people committed to you to eternal life and offer them to Christ.

44

CC Opera Minora 139–42   Verona Lent 966

[Rather is distressed that a priest in the diocese has held the wedding of his son, who had also been ordained, on the Lord's night. He sees this as a source of future sin without end.]

Concerning the Illicit Marriage of a Certain Person

1. Since the psalmist proclaims, "Over my back have the sinners built" [Ps. 128.3], and also the apostle says: "Not only the doers but also those agreeing with the doers are worthy of death" [Rom. 1.32], I am weighed down not only with my own abundant burdens but also most wretchedly with the excessive burdens of others. So subject to this double responsibility, I am distressed that John, a son of our Church,[9] is reported to have affianced his son to a girl during Lent and to have had them married on the Lord's night — with a double illegality (as also had been done previously by our Pedrevertus).

When a man brings his son to the ministry, he takes him, both apparently and actually, out of the secular world and hands him over to the Lord, so that, where previously the son had to live under the same law as the state lives by, he now begins to live under canon law and, as first he obeyed the governor of the state, so now he obeys the prelate of the Church — that is, the duly ordained bishop. This being the case, it is quite clear that he who hands over his son to the Church to fight for the Lord under canonical law, and who later arranges a secular marriage for him, takes him away from the Lord with the same hand with which he had himself given him to the Lord and removes him from the Church's administration to give him (for shame) back to the civil administration.

Therefore, let him who does this not be angry at God, I suggest, if He takes from him some of the things which He has mercifully granted him, either by force of storm or by some affliction of his faculties, either in this world or in the next. For if God, in a manner of speaking, did not know otherwise how to do this, He would be able to learn following his example — as if He should say: "You have taken away from me what you had given to me: following your own example, I am taking away from you what I had given to you."

2. O insatiable greed of the human race, what illegal, foul and dishonorable deeds you [greed] are not ashamed to commit! And against God even. For since a man is called a cleric for the very reason that he is of the Lord's lot (that is, attends to God's part), what a good father is he, what a lover of his son, who, taking his son from God's lot for the price of three vineyards, returns him to the power of this world and consequently to the power of the devil also. For the Lord calls the devil "the prince of this world" [Jn. 16.11]—not of heaven and earth and sea and all that is in them, but of evil mankind, who, loving the world more than God, enjoy it temporally, to lose what they ought to possess in heaven eternally, serving the devil, that is, rather than Christ. Perhaps each of them did it with this in mind, that in comparing the evils each thought it was better that his son be married to one woman than that he should sin with many and thus more mortally. But John, the object of our distressing sermon, exceeds the other in sin for the reason that he began it during Holy Lent and completed it on the Lord's night, and that whereas Pedrevertus managed to do it in secret, John did it so brazenly, for shame, that everyone in the city knew about it.

Therefore, it seems to me that this matter should not be hushed up, because if it remains unreprimanded, it will be taken as done quite properly; for no one will hesitate to take as a precedent that which he finds that no one has reproved.

3. Incredible to tell, there is also another person [Erimbertus] who is said to have done this, who is called in another work of mine (without mentioning his name) "our verbal contortionist and legal distortionist"[10] because he could often have heard it said to him with other law-makers: "Love justice, ye who judge the land" [Wisd. 1.1], and no law, so I think, allows that something once legally given to someone should be taken away from him without just complaint. But since reason shows that "a just complaint" is either some fault or some necessity, it is clear as we ponder and meditate on this whole question, that it is God to whom that injury appears to have been done and of course in Him no blame can be found nor necessity adduced. For He feeds everything, so that in no way could the life specially dedicated to Him end in starvation. He [Erimbertus] would certainly have done better if he had helped his son serve the Lord out of his means, as a father ought to do. Yet he is afterwards said to have driven his son out, refusing to give him this charity.

4. And alas, how grave the crime which has no end even when the criminal dies. For example, if someone unjustly attacks the estate of another (as often happens) and continuing the same wrong leaves it to his son, and his son again to the son who follows him, and so on up to the end of time all do who by

succession of each generation descend from the first wrong-doer, when does the injustice of him who first sowed that field have its end, except at the final end of all creation? In the same way, since, as everyone knows, every man who lies with any woman but his lawful wife commits either fornication or adultery, and since a priest or a deacon cannot have a lawful wife, if the son born from that fornication (or, what is worse, adultery) the father makes a priest, and he likewise makes the son born to him a priest, and he again his, and so on, likewise continuing it till the end of time, whose is the adultery unless his who first sowed it? Wherefore you should be urged and implored, brethren, because you cannot, alas, be restrained from women,[11] to dismiss your offspring at least to be lay men, and to marry your daughters to lay men, so that at least with your decease the adultery will be terminated and not last till the end of time.

5. You quote, against this: "The son will not carry the wickedness of his father," and the rest [Ezek. 18.20]. I say, on the other hand: "I am God, He says, all-powerful, who visit the wickedness of the fathers on the sons" [Ex. 20.5], and the rest. St. Gregory, dealing with these two seemingly contradictory statements of the Lord, reconciles them both from what follows in the second, namely, "In those who hate me," asserting that if the ill will of the sons does not accord to the ill will of their fathers (just as, to be sure, the will of the apostles did not accord to the will of their fathers), the malignity of the evil fathers does not obstruct the goodwill of the good sons.[12] But if the sons do the same as their God-hating fathers have done, they will be damned not only for their own wickedness but also for their fathers'. And their fathers will be justly punished not only for their own sin but also for that of their sons, who, following the example of their fathers, have not desisted from doing the same as their fathers did. O would that you, therefore, O mistress,[13] to whom your good brother gave so many goods, had considered this earlier and had given his daughter, blessed with his goods, to a good lay man only and had put an end to his sin; for as long as it will last, it will hardly be expiated, you should know, with infinite alms. But since the Lord says to certain people: "Woe to you, scribes and Pharisees, hypocrites! For you tithe mint and dill and cummin, and have neglected the weightier matters of the law, Justice and mercy and faith" [Mt. 23.23]; would that over the body of your brother day and night the rain would fall, which you earnestly took care not to let happen, and that this noxious, filthy, and foul moisture would not so gravely afflict, befoul, pollute, and torture his soul.

6. So I urge these people—and all who know that they have violated in such sin either Lent or a particular fast or the Lord's night or any feast-day—to do forty days' penance, together with me, who have been an accessory inasmuch as I did not oppose it, a penance, namely, in that where other faithful are refreshed

at the third hour, we be refreshed at the sixth; if they at the sixth, then we at the ninth; if they at the ninth, then we keep fast till vespers. Let us not stop making alms to the best of our ability; but let us not think that by these means we have been cleared of the offense. For it is not the kind of sin that can easily be expiated. However, let us not despair of God's mercy; "For no man," says someone, "knows whether he is worthy of love or hate, but all things are kept uncertain for the future" [Eccle. 9.1–2]. But if you reject this penance, as I suspect (or rather am certain) you will, and are not willing to fast with me, and either I excommunicate you temporally or God damns you eternally, let it be your concern and no blame of mine. The mistress I addressed a little above I also invite to penance for it likewise; for that is your duty, and it will perhaps help your brother.

45

CC Opera Minora 145–53   Verona August 966

[A sermon on the active and contemplative roles of members of the Church, which develops into a self-analysis of his own position; he acknowledges that he ought to be fulfilling both roles and giving leadership to his flock by haranguing and rebuking them till they follow the correct way.]

∝∾

On Mary and Martha

1. I would have you remember, brothers, that on the past Feast of the Blessed Mary, Mother of God, I performed the service of preaching to your college, and on that occasion I showed from the Gospel reading that what was said at the end of it, namely, "Mary hath chosen the good part, which shall not be taken from her" [Lk. 10.42], no less fitted the Mother of God than it fitted her to whom the Lord Himself said this. And though my poor eloquence offered your brotherhood what it could in treating this passage of Gospel reading, yet when I examined the expressions of some, I saw you all unmoved (for shame!), as though I had said nothing of moment. I saw no tears there, heard no sighs or beating of the breast. It was then clear that what we read that St. Augustine said more than once, "Unless he who teaches burns, he cannot fire the listener,"[14] was very true. And when at the same time I saw from your faces that I was not well loved and for that reason despised, I found that the saying

of Gregory was quite true: "It is difficult for a teacher who is not loved to be heard, however right his preaching";[15] and again: "Whose life is despised, his preaching also is scorned."[16]

On the other hand, I realized that the words spoken to the prophet, though far from comparable, fitted this situation of mine: "The house of Israel will not hearken unto thee, for they will not hearken unto me" [Ezek. 3.7]; and those of the Lord: "If they have kept my saying, they will keep yours also" [Jn. 15.20]. And also the words of Moses, to whose worth we cannot aspire: "What are we? Your murmurings are not against us but against the Lord" [Ex. 16.7–8]. For though I am, for shame, at fault in innumerable things, while any of you does not abuse what should properly be criticized in me but faults what should properly be praised, he shows that he does so, not in love of justice, but in hatred of those words which he would not hear. O, would that those of you who were like that would pay as critical attention to the serious things I say, as you pay greedy attention to words that are not only unbeneficial but even dangerous, and would that you would attend as much to the good of your souls as to the damnation of them caused by my acquiescence in their faults as I speak.

2. But now I must repeat what I said on that occasion. As many have pointed out before me, these two women stand for two qualities of life, one which takes its name from action *prakthiken*—or practical—the other from observation or inactivity *theoriken*—or contemplative.[17] For obviously the more one ceases from labor, the more one widens the scope of one's inner view. As I said, quoting others, these two blessed sisters signify these two kinds of living, and their devotion has shown the statement to be true, since one was said to be *cumbered* (that is, busy or working hard) *with much serving* [Lk. 10.40]—that is, she did not then begin doing it for the first time, but had turned it into a habit by frequently doing it, namely, serving the Lord from her means, as she had done in many ways. The other is said to have preferred to sit at the feet of the Lord, not, however, with that idleness which is inimical to the soul,[18] but with that tranquillity about which the Lord Himself enjoins in the psalm: "Be still and know that I am God" [Ps. 45.11]; she was as earnest, indeed, in hearing what proceeded from the Lord's mouth as the other was in serving. In fact, no one in the Church does anything but these two things, when he does what he ought to do. Here is no room for fornication, adultery is afar, drunkenness is distant, falsehood nowhere, and, lest my address go on for ever, all evil in its entirety is utterly absent. But one of these descriptions applies to the secular members, the other to the spiritual: one applies to those who are going to hear: "Come, ye blessed of my Father, receive the kingdom which has been prepared for you since the beginning of the world" [Mt. 25.34], for "I was hungry, thirsty, a stranger, sick, and in prison"—but all of these *in my members*—"and underwent

many similar sufferings, and you comforted me"; the other applies to those who among the Apostles and with the Apostles have heard in person: "Verily I say unto you, that you who have left everything and followed me, in the regeneration when the Son of Man shall sit in the throne of His glory, you also shall sit upon twelve thrones, judging the twelve tribes of Israel" [Mt. 19.28].

3. Well, brothers? If this is so, will no one be found within the confines of these four walls, who rightly ought to beat his chest, sigh, and groan? Where then are those like me? Here, no other lot, no other condition, is mentioned for those who do otherwise (and this is what we must expect for our sinful nature) than, "Depart from me, ye cursed, into the everlasting fire prepared" — not for men, but — "for the devil and his angels" [Mt. 25.41], that is, either those angels who fell from heaven with Satan or those who have attended him in this world (for *angelus* is used like *aggelus*, that is, "standing near"); they most wretchedly did for the devil what these now called blessed did for God, ministering to him what he wanted, that is, every kind of abuse, ever attending him and most willingly embracing his suggestions and carrying them out in action. None of these imitated Mary, none Martha, none Lia, none took Rachel to wife, none of them loved one of these and supported the other, that is, in love of seeing God did what good he could.

Therefore, let him who wishes come and persuade me, if he can, to hope for what God has not promised, that doing evil I will receive good: and that, neither like Martha serving God in action nor like Mary attending Him in contemplation, I may expect the reward promised only to those who have done one of these two things. On the contrary, He proclaims: "Every tree that does not bring forth good fruit" — that is, one of those good actions of either Mary or Martha — "will be hewn down and cast into the fire" [Mt. 7.19]. For iniquitous thought alone He himself promises woe for us, but for otiose talk He has further said that we will give account on the Day of Judgment [cf. Mic. 2.1; Mt. 12.36]. And since, as I look round the multitude in this church, I find here no imitator of these women at all (so that it is quite proper for me too to change my mode of speaking to be more applicable), since, as I have said, I can find here no imitator of them, and I see myself more than everyone to have no part in them, let the same try to persuade me to ignore the fear which vexes me, albeit uselessly. For I am quite sure that I will not thereby find salvation if I do not leave off any vice because of this fear, even though my conscience be ever in punishment, as the Scripture says the guilty man's will be [Wisd. 17.10].

4. Alas, in this position how like I am to the famous Sicilian tyrant![19] I am aware that in the office to which I am unworthily raised I am obliged to live both kinds of life, that is, that I should both minister to the Lord in His members (i.e., the sons of the Holy Mother the Church) and yet never cease from

contemplating Him but meditate on His law day and night [Ps. 1.2], and I see
that I do neither of these things, but, on the contrary, by corrupting not only
myself but also all those entrusted to me, and particularly those of my brotherhood, provoke Him day and night to anger (though no passion affects Him).
What then can I say of myself (to omit the shameful acts and put down only
the honorable, though forbidden, ones), what can I think of myself, if I do not
meditate—as I am well aware that I ought—day and night on the law of God,
when I now sometimes read Catullus[20] not read before and Plautus long
neglected, when often asked I expound music (though quite unable as I lack
the first help of mathematics), when I marshall my soldiers for war following
Caesar's orders, and send men out hunting? For here in the text, no amusement
is allowed, no rest, but it categorically states that he is blessed who meditates
on God's law *day and night.*

But O, most wretched in such activities and even (for shame) more detestable
ones, how I descend into hell living [Ps. 54.16], that is, aware that for such
offenses I will certainly go into hell, if I be judged without God's pity. But when
I see neither my laymen nor my clergy being busy about the frequent, that is,
habitual, service of the Lord [Lk. 10.40], when I see the former not pursuing
the works of Christianity, the latter so thoroughly opposed to canonical law
that they openly marry, and when I see my monks in no way willing to make
themselves alien to the ways of the world in the love of contemplating God (in
fact I do not think that this anchorite standing next to me has left the ways
of the world at all), when I consider all this, where, alas, is my Martha, where
Mary, where Lia, where Rachel, since the Lord on the Day of Judgment is going to demand of poor me a reckoning of you all, as of sheep entrusted to my
care? Where, finally, in this church, is that tripper of the devil, who, though
desiring one way of life, the contemplative, follows both, that is, in his ministry
for Christ handling worldly goods in such a way that he does not lose the things
eternal?

5. This could seem to my critics, who are abundant, too stern and of my
own invention, had I not mentioned sterner stuff in the quotes today from
Gregory. Would that our insensitive intellects could have beneficially understood
and appreciated his words. For he speaks as if indicating our group. When recently I was trying to teach what I had learned more by meditation than by
action, and was looking for a text to help me, I came across that sermon of
his about the Gospel where our Lord is reported, on seeing the city of Jerusalem, to have wept and to have foretold its fall [Lk. 21.6–24]. Anyone who is
willing to run through the whole of it, will be quite able to weigh whether
he need grieve or not, so let him stop being angry with me. I, indeed, examined
the whole text of this sermon, and while pondering that it had "more aloe than

honey,"[21] I began to investigate whether some consolation could be found there which might refresh a heart reeling in fear, a fear, though, that is unbeneficial because it cannot be changed.

All the same, I came trembling to that place where he writes:

> Wherefore we must take care and ponder with much daily weeping how severe, how free, how terrible, the prince of this world will be when he comes seeking his works in us on the day of our death, if he came even to God dying in the flesh and sought something of his own in Him in Whom he could find nothing. What then are we wretches, who have done so many evils, to say, to do? What will we say to the adversary who seeks and finds in us much of his own, except only that we have a sure refuge in the firm hope that we have been made one with Him in Whom the prince of this world has sought some of his own and has been able to find nothing, since He alone is free among the dead? And we are now freed in true liberty from the slavery of sin, because we are united with Him Who is truly free. For it is certain (we cannot deny it but admit it truthfully) that though the prince of this world has much in us, yet at the time of our death he is not strong enough to snatch us because we have been made members of Him in whom he has nothing.[22]

And when I had digested it, I thought that it gave me considerable support, quite wrongly, since he said this more about himself and people like him. But when I read what follows, the same thing happened to me as often happens. For when I hear that joy shall be in heaven over one sinner more than over ninety and nine just persons [Lk. 15.7], if this should be said absolutely as here written, I would think that it applied to me. But when "who is repentant" is added, I see this applies to me as much as black does to white, as I never make penitence yet am wretchedly ever heaping up faults that I have to repent. So also here, when the same most saintly teacher says:

> But what profit is it if we are joined to him in faith but separated from Him by our ways? For He himself says, "Not everyone that says to me, Lord, Lord, shall enter into the kingdom of heaven, but he that does the will of my Father who is in heaven" [Mt. 7.21].[23]

I see that I have every cause for fear.

6. But what is the will of the Father if not what either Martha or her sister Mary was doing? We are given no third choice; we are told either to serve Christ in His own members or to sit at Christ's feet contemplating His will. If we neglect any part of these instructions, we should sigh, wail, beat our breasts, do penance, and we should either look for the frequent service of God or, give

our time to prayers and heavenly longings, and never be torn from the feet of kindly Jesus, until we come to "that one thing which alone is necessary" [Lk. 10.42], that is, God Himself, Who alone suffices us.

You say, on the other side (for this is man's way of speaking): "Maybe I do not do as much good as I ought to do, yet I do some, and believing perfectly in God I hope for what God instructed His faithful to hope for." O, if only I was sure that you, brother, did both of these (that is, that you both believed perfectly in God and hoped only for those things which He instructed us to hope for), then I would be sure of your salvation.

The psalmist says: "Hope in the Lord" [Ps. 36.3]. You reply: "I do." But he says: "Do good." If, therefore, you hope in the Lord, do good, I urge you and your hopes are not empty, I promise. For when James says: "What doth it profit, my brethren, if a man have faith, and have not works? Can faith alone save him?" [Jas. 2.14], you can take it in this one sense only: if you perfectly believe in God and do not hope for anything else than what He instructed you to hope for, that is, if you have good works, then there is no need for you to doubt about everlasting reward, if only you have persevered [cf. Mt. 10.22].

But what are good works if not those which proceed out of love? If you do not have this one thing, I tell you, you may neither trust in faith nor hope for what God has promised His faithful. For "Faith, if it has no works, is dead, being alone" [Jas. 2.17], and "Hope does not disappoint us, because the love of God is shed abroad in our hearts by the Holy Spirit which is given to us" [Rom. 5.5]. If, therefore, you do not have love in your heart, your hope is useless. If you do not have the Holy Spirit, you are not of Christ. For it is written: "If any man does not have the spirit of Christ, he is none of His" [Rom. 8.9].

But what love towards God does a man have who is not afraid in His presence to commit adultery (to name one sin out of many)? Clearly, far from loving Him, he does not even respect Him. For if he does not believe in Him in His presence, how does he believe in Him, not to say perfectly, but even a little? But if he believes even a little, is he not clearly a rebel to God in Whose sight he has presumed to commit such foul sin, wretch and self-destroyer? Can we argue against this? He perishes, I say, he perishes, unless perchance he at once take refuge in His mercy by truly repenting. For experience teaches us that more recent wounds are healed sooner than older ones, which he evidently means to show who says: "Do not let the sun go down on your anger" [Eph. 4.26]. If anyone should say that these are merely *my* ideas, are they mine, brothers, when they are voiced by James and Paul?

7. Now, in case perhaps you say that I am trying to drive you to despair, you can, if you want and whenever you want, imitate with God's help not only Martha but also her who chose the best part, Mary. For you know what she

was before, if only you know what you ought to know. But what she became through God's mercy, you can know if you wish, and you should not in any way despair that this cannot also happen to you. Do then, I say, what she did and hope for what she merited. But, O, how I would be in the utmost despair thinking that I was not one of these, if I did not have His promise: "Lo, I am with you always, even to the end of the world" [Mt. 28.20]. For in what people is He *with us*, if not in those whom He has of His own *with us*? For if He is not with me for my evil, He is with me for the goodness of Him who is with me; for this He promised, saying: "Where two or three are gathered together in My name, there am I in the midst of them" [Mt. 18.20]. If only the devil had not been able to say this about his own who are living with us; for then God would not have said to any of us: "You therefore hear not God's words because you are not of God" [Jn. 8.47]. And, to be sure, those to whom He said this were neither deaf nor absent, but were absent in will, were deaf in hatred, when they refused to conform to what was said.

But though God in His long-suffering patience should be admired, embraced, and glorified, yet He should be revered for what the Apostle says about Him and not vexed or provoked to wrath, but besought and continually supplicated. For that man measures God by his own standards, who after grievously offending Him (as we wretches often do), fears to come forward to praise Him; for no doubt he also would not like to be praised by him who had dishonored him in the same hour. But the preacher urges us not to fear to come forward to praise God when he says, "If the spirit of the ruler rise up against you" [Eccle. 10.4]—that is, the spirit of the lord who harried Saul, with his most cunning suggestion prevailing over you up to the point of fatal consent—"do not leave your place"—that is, don't abandon that state of goodness in which you then were when you fell into the sin which he suggested to you, adding the reason, "For deference"—that is, by penitence or by the mercy of God—"pacifies great offences." Wherefore also St. Augustine brilliantly says, "Everything which is feared is rationally avoided. But God alone is so to be feared that we should flee from Him to Him,"[24]—since, to be sure, if God had been of the same impatience as we are, the earth would once already have opened up and swallowed us wretches, alas, or fire rushing from heaven would have devoured us.

The man who thinks that God is so kind that He does not care how much He is hurt by anyone, but without any satisfaction being made gives out not only pardon but even rewards to the undeserving, measures God in a most childish way. For if it were so, one could think—though wrongly—that God is a lover of evil; but that a just Being can love injustice is against logic.

8. But we have a very useful counsellor against this view, who says: "Do not be without fear about the forgiveness of sin, and do not add sin upon sin,

saying, 'The mercy of the Lord is great, He will have mercy on the multitude of my sins. For mercy and wrath quickly come from Him, and His wrath looks upon sinners'" [Eccli. 5.5–7]. And again: "Give mercy to the just and do not uphold the sinner, for the Highest hates sinners and has mercy on the penitent and will repay vengeance to the ungodly and to sinners, and keep them against the day of vengeance" [Eccli. 12.3–4]. And again: "Do good to the humble and do not give to the impious man; forbid bread to be given him, lest in it he become stronger than you, for you will find two-fold evil in all good things, since also the Highest hates sinners and will repay vengeance to the ungodly" [Eccli. 12.6–7].

If it is even partly so, O!, how then no sinner, especially one like me ought to be without fear. The book which contains this is by itself called the Book of Wisdom: can there be anything in it which does not have to be believed? And He is wisdom who in the Gospel says, "I am the Truth" [Jn. 14.6]. Since we must concede that wisdom cannot have any untruth, let him who wishes to contradict so great a truth advance what arguments he can. Can anything be more marvellous to relate? Let him show it who will. For though almost all of you are objecting and exclaiming openly against me, yet there are some among you who say: "Why does the bishop allow this to happen?" To this I am not slow to give a reply, since the apostle in the person of Timothy [2 Tim. 4.2] instructs us and says, "Reprove"—that is, *criticize*—"Rebuke"—that is, in the love of God *argue* and question—"Exhort"—that is, wear down those committed to you even with *censure*, excommunications, and, if fitting, strokes also—but not neglecting charity. So long as the *criticism* which I make of people who ought justly to be criticized has no efect and as long as my *arguments* win no respect from you for either God or me, when it comes to *censure*, they will be sorry, though too late, that they did not once listen to the advice (which proved very useful to another, I admit) of him who said: "Do not seek to be made a judge, unless you can extirpate the strength of iniquity, lest you fear the person of the powerful and lay a stumbling block for your integrity" [Eccli. 7.6].

9. But I will keep this for another occasion. What I have already said must be repeated, that this reading has, of course, been read today because what this Mary did at that time when she sat at the feet of the Lord, her namesake, the Mother of the Lord, had begun to do from the day of her birth, that is, choose the best part, namely, what is best among existing things, in other words, longing for God with all her heart: because she loved Him with all her heart more than anyone, she merited to enjoy Him more than anyone, to such an extent that she conceived Him first in her mind, and afterwards in her mind and womb. This part, to be sure, has never been taken from her, since she was a virgin

before the birth, a virgin in birth, and remained a virgin after giving birth. May she deign to make us reconciled by her prayers to her own most Holy Son, our Lord Jesus Christ, who with the Father and the Holy Spirit liveth and reigneth for ever and ever. Amen.

46

CC Opera Minora 157–61   Verona August 966

[In this short work Rather refers to an incident also mentioned in no. 41, *Qualitatis coniectura* c. 7 and no. 32, On His Own Sin c. 4, from which we surmise that he said something foul in church.]

◅◦▻

Concerning Otiose Speech

1. I have worn out a certain passage of Scripture by quoting it four times now, because I could say that only by it am I consoled against despair when I consider what I have done and what those like me have done; to show briefly that it still has not satisfied me, I quote it again in the same words: "No man knows whether he is worthy of love or hatred but all is kept uncertain for the future" [Eccle. 9.1–2].[25] Unless I add something personal to this, of course, I must admit that I do not know why I have mentioned this so often.

For I know, I know, that I am truly worthy of hatred if I do not cease from my ways. But whether it has been given to me to cease entirely from these before the end of my life, I admit that I am in no way sure. For I try to improve and am overcome; I toil and I fail; I rise and I slip back and never remain in a state of any good. For, unblessed and wretched, I persist in my ways, like the proverbial dog returning to its vomit and the pig to its wallow [2 Pet. 2.22]. In this sentence alone I take comfort, finding nothing else. Doing so, I despair while I hope, I hope while I despair, I am confident while diffident and diffident while confident—that is, I am confident that everything that God has promised, He will give, but I am diffident that I can be found worthy of receiving His promised blessings. But though He promises pardon to none unless converted, while I see myself unrelenting, I do not despair of His compassion, but fear for my own obstinacy. What further? I know and admit that I am more worthy of hatred than of love if I die now such as I am. Whether I am destined to die in this condition, I do not know; but if I do die in this condition, all can be sure of my damnation, I do not deny it.

2. Many people put off conversion till the end of their life, when a sudden death may strike them completely insensible, seizing them unfinished, still less worthy. I do not know what I should feel about them, but I am almost desperate about myself, in case it should happen to me. Some on the verge of death have made many promises to God which they have not fulfilled upon getting well again. What, therefore, will these do when they fall sick again? If they do not make promises again, they are clearly shown to perish in despair; if they do promise and, getting well a second time, are false to their promises, what will they do afterwards? Well? The pity of God will reach them somehow. It seems to me, nevertheless, that, because it is by the workings of the devil that they happen to do this even a thousand times, they ought not for that reason to despair of the Lord's pity, though they can have no trust in such insecure promises.

No man knows whether he will be worthy of love or of hate in the future, though he knows that for the present he is worthy of hate, since the Scripture says that the Omnipotent hates the wicked and pities the righteous [Eccli. 12.3]. For they could not become righteous after being sinners unless, protected by God's mercy, they had been converted from evil to good; and they would not have endured in sin unless they had been permitted by God's justice to become obdurate. Therefore, this sentence of the Scripture is full of fear for people like this also: "If God takes away a man," — that is, permits him to pass away — "who will say to Him, What are you doing?" [Job 9.12].

3. O, then, O the inscrutable judgments of God, O His untrackable ways! [Rom. 11.33]. For who of those like me is able to have no fear that he will inescapably be taken away and so be worthy of hatred? For surely he seems worthy of hatred (not to mention the rest) about whom the apostle says: "For this you know, that no whoremonger, nor unclean person, nor covetous man who is an idolator has any inheritance in the kingdom of Christ and of God" [Eph. 5.5]. But since very many people are converted from such sins and cease to be whoremongers, unclean, or covetous, this has clearly been said, of course, about those *persisting* in sins of this sort. He persists in sin who, as far as age or health is given him to commit it, does not eschew committing it, or, if he does eschew it, is not earnest in atoning for it by penitence. Whoever is prevented from committing it by old age or debility clearly has not abandoned sin, but sin has abandoned him, and, therefore, not even if he ceases from fornication does a man cease to be a fornicator unless, as far as he is able, he both ceases to fornicate and strives to wipe out the fornication he has abandoned with fastings, alms, and tearful sighings.

When, therefore, we read or hear: "No man knows either love or hate," unless we add *in the future*, so that the sense is that a man does not know whether he has been allowed to be converted before his death or left to endure in his sins right to the end of his health, I confess that I am quite at a loss what it means.

4. Though one must not despair that debility itself can also purify a man from previously committed sins — but only if it is accepted with joy, which I think happens only after a prolonged sickness patiently borne, as I said — and though one may lightly agree that "a short punishment here puts an end to noxious sins, so that due punishment will not hold the guilty eternally,"[26] still, Gregory says that temporal scourgings only free from eternal scourgings those that they change. So while I await these two, that is, either salvation-giving conversion or God's punishment of scourgings, relying on the sentence which says, "No man knows either love or hate" [Eccle. 9.1], if I do not stand in awe of the third choice, that is, certain damnation, I really believe that I am mad, and I do not know where to direct my longing, what to desire or what to embrace.

For though I fear that a sudden death hangs over me, if I deserve a long life (as I would like, I admit), I hear the words of the apostle though I am deaf to them: "Do you not know that the patience of God leads you to repentance? You are storing up wrath for yourself in the day of wrath and the retribution of the righteous judgment of God" [Rom. 2.4–5]. O unblest long life of this sort, which is followed by so great a catastrophe, O despicable time which piles up such a treasure, O pitiable extension conceded to amass the punishment of sins ! It had been better for the wretch, I say, to have received the just sentence for his first contempt of God rather than, having waited so long, to have contracted so many offenses, certain to be punished eternally for any one of them.

5. This being so, brevity of life seems to me more blessed than longevity. "Woe to you," says the prophet, "that draw iniquity with cords of vanity" [Is. 5.18]. God is indeed full of pity and ineffably kind, but He is nevertheless truthful and indescribably just. He promises pardon, He assesses punishment, He deals out pardon to those perfectly converted, He reserves punishment for those hardened against Him. For is not the assessment of the punishment clearly evident when He says: "I say to you, that every careless word that men shall speak, they shall give account thereof in the Day of Judgment" [Mt. 12.36]? Was anything more terrible ever spoken? Let others see what they feel about this; to me it seems that it would have been more bearable if He had said: "They shall merit punishment for it for thousands of years."

Alas, since nothing is more useless than what is foul, if, in the same place, and perhaps even in such a place as one would shrink even from eating in, someone doing some foul act said something very foul,[27] if he afterwards did penance for the foulness he had committed, what, I ask, will be done about the foulness which he had spoken? If, in the judgment, he shall be upbraided for saying such a thing in such a place for such a reason, are we to think that he can in any way hear with the rest, "Come, you blessed of my Father" [Mt. 25.34]? After such a shame in the presence of the whole human race, can we expect that he will have, not celestial, but *any* glory? Won't also what he did be equally made manifest, since perhaps he has spoken the same as he acted and has acted the same as he spoke? He will have punishment worthy of a rebel; since he did not respect God nor what, as a Christian, he has learned about God, and in His sight, in such a place, did not fear to dishonor Him so foully (well aware, too, that He was present, even remembering Him), he will perish dishonored in the sight of all creation.

What are we to say, alas, about very frequent perjuries, about constant disparagement, about continual falsehood, about words of deceit and mockery, about false promises, about numerous curses? If for "Racha" we shall undergo judgment, and for "Thou fool" [Mt. 5.22] we shall undergo eternal fire, what account will we render for careless words? "Consider this (with me), you that forget God (with me), lest we be suddenly snatched and there be none to deliver" [Ps. 49.22].

6. "I do consider," you say,[28] forgetting God (for shame) more often than you should, and fearing (as of course you admit you do) lest you be suddenly seized and there be none to deliver [Ps. 49.22]. "But when I compare that message of the apostle [1 Cor. 11.31] about judgment of our own accord meted out to ourselves by ourselves with that which I remember hearing very recently, I confess that I am greatly worried. For the reading was: 'If you have considered your sins rightly, you have judged them; if you have ignored them, you have fallen.'"[29]

To better elucidate this: though many texts could be cited, one must say that this divine sentence which you have offered is enough: "Every careless word," the Lord says, "that men shall speak, they shall give account thereof in the Day of Judgment" [Mt. 12.36].

"What is *a careless word*?"

A useless one.

"But nothing is more useless than what is foul, as you said; to which we might add, harmful, abusive, mocking, deceitful, perjured, fraudulent, slanderous, lying, sacrilegious, heretical, rebellious, blasphemous, bearing false witness, raving, revolutionary, litigious. Putting forward only one out of all these in that earlier mention, you concluded that he could not be believed to be safe, who, on that final Day of Judgment, will be reproached for what he said in such a place for such a reason."

But though God allows us most firmly to believe that nothing can be done temporally against right and the law which cannot be expiated temporally, we must despair for him who spoke that foulness, unless we give him counsel what to do before he come to that reproach. Let us, therefore, say first who they will be who are to give account on the Day of Judgment for every careless word which they have spoken. They, surely, are the ones to whom will be said, "Depart from me, ye cursed, into everlasting fire, for I was hungry and you gave me no meat," and the rest [Mt. 25.41–42], and, "Verily I say to you, you shalt by no means come out thence till you have paid the uttermost farthing" [Mt. 5.26].

"And why," you ask, "will this be said to them?"

Because they have not listened to Him saying: "Repent and turn yourselves from all your transgressions, so iniquity shall not be your ruin" [Ezek. 18.30], and: "Turn to me and I will turn to you" [Zech. 1.3]; and finally because they hardened the ear of their heart when the apostle cried: "For if we would judge ourselves, we should not be judged" [1 Cor. 11.31], Augustine also adding: "If you have considered your sins rightly, you have judged them; if you have ignored them, you have fallen."[30] For as it was to be understood in this sense for the other abuses, so is it also to be understood for foul speech; that is, that you who spoke it should make for yourself a day of judgment for it here; as the fairest critic, you should condemn it according to its quality; having condemned it you should punish it; having punished it you should kill it, that is, by discarding it you should not carry it forth into eternity, considering the foul expression equal to the foul deed and *vice versa*: from similar vices also you should strive with your whole might, with Christ's aid, to abstain. For this being the case, it seems to me that if the foul deed which you have done has been perfectly expiated by penitence, then the foul word which you spoke on the occasion of it will be equally eradicated, with the help of His pity who with the Father and Holy Spirit lives and reigns for ever and ever. Amen.

47

Weigle, Epist. 137–55 Verona December 966

[Rather to the clergy of his diocese: he tells the clergy why he is planning to go to the synod in Rome. Among other things he wants to find out what the synod thinks about clerics living with women.]

⁓

Itinerarium

1. I know full well, my sons, that your fraternity is aware that I wish to go to Rome in the near future but is entirely unaware of my purpose. I am going there not for prayer, since I read in the Gospel: "Woman, believe me that the hour comes when you will worship the Father neither on this mountain nor in Jerusalem" [Jn. 4.21], and the addition: "God is a spirit and those that worship Him must worship Him in spirit and in truth" [Jn. 4.22], which of course everyone can do at home. Nor am I going by command of the emperor, because there is no such command, since I have been ordered by him only to send my soldiers. I shall not learn there what is good and pleasing to God, since I know that people have very often sung at this time: "I will show you, man, what is good or what the Lord requires from you: act justly and righteously and take care to walk with your God" [Mic. 6.8] not only when we go to Rome, but also wherever we are. For the man who never leaves the path of God's commands always walks with Him. Everyone is urged to do this attentively, that is, "serve Him with fear and rejoice in Him with trembling" [Ps. 2.11]. For, as Gregory says, "in the heart of the sinner hope and fear ought constantly to remain."[1] What is *to act justly*, if not to observe what the law prescribes, which

of course is what you lately heard urged upon Peter and Andrew in the Gospel: "Follow me; for this is the law and the prophets" [Mt. 4.19, 7.12] — so that at all times we ought to follow Christ in our thoughts, words, and actions. What is justice, which we are enjoined to do, if not the condition of right, that is, the law? Whose law? Christ's, of course. How do we do it and fulfill it? "One carry another's burdens" [Gal. 6.2], said one who knew, "and thus you will fulfill Christ's law." But what heavier burden does a man have than when he is stooped under ignorance of those things which he ought to have known?

Since we cannot fulfill it unless it has been started, and we cannot start it unless it has been recognized, and since we see that in many, when it is not understood, there is some leaving of the path of God's commands; so that I may be able both to lighten myself of this burden and in some way to help you in carrying yours, as the apostle tells us, I intend to go to the council of all those who are going to attend the apostle's seat under holy Caesar's escort, primarily to investigate certain inconsistencies in the canons to see if they can be reconciled.

For example: we read in the canons of the Apostles: "A bishop or a priest should not leave his wife, whom he ought to govern chastely";[2] but in the Nicene Council we see it sternly stated thus: "The great synod entirely forbids that a bishop, priest, or deacon, or anyone at all among the clergy be allowed to keep a woman living with him, except perhaps a mother, sister, or aunt, or only those persons who escape suspicion."[3] The canons say that if anyone communicates with one who is excommunicate, he should be equally excommunicate;[4] but as though to the contrary, Augustine gave instructions to an excommunicate named Classitianus.[5] Since I see that none of my people cares about the excommunication of any of us, whether it is just or unjust (though I am not entirely unaware of what St. Gregory says on this),[6] I very much want to discuss this question with that sacred council.

2. I also want to know what that sacred convention feels about the chapters here subjoined, which are almost universally ignored, with very few exceptions. When one fears to correct in another the faults which one sees in himself, because of Christ's prohibition, "Let whoever of you is without sin be the first to cast a stone at her" [Jn. 8.7], and "Hypocrite, cast first the beam from your own eye" [Lk. 6.42], and yet the canons instruct with great authority that such faults cannot be left uncorrected, they make me (who am falsely reputed by some to be well-lettered) quite ignorant concerning what I should even think, still less say, about them. Where better can I be relieved of this ignorance, where more aptly taught, than at Rome? What is there which is known about ecclesiastical doctrines somewhere else which is not known at Rome? For there the most renowned teachers in the whole world and the most eminent leaders of the whole Church have blossomed; there are the decretals of the pontiffs,

the universal congregation, the examination of the canons, the approval of those to be accepted and the condemnation of those to be rejected; and finally, nowhere shall something seem ratified which is there invalid, nowhere shall anything seem invalid which is there ratified. So where better for me in my ignorance to consult than where the fount of understanding is seen to be?

But the greatest of these benefits is the fact that the Creator has mercifully given us a most just, pious, and wise emperor, our lord most glorious Caesar, who is inestimably superior to all who are under heaven in the aforementioned and other qualities of royal privilege; and the most holy pope, the lord bishop [John XIII], whom the grace of God (appropriate to his name)[7] has established as most worthy father of Romulus's city by election to that task, father and careful overseer of the whole world. May God concede, I pray, that the universal synod which they will convoke will be good for His holy Church, as is right.

3. So I will attend it, if I can with God's approval; and "checking my lips with my finger,"[8] I will try the more humbly to listen to those who will be there, the more I see that it is essential for me. For I know that the most learned men, both of this kingdom and of our august lord's court,[9] will attend it; I wish to learn their explanation of these points, which I have here abbreviated under headings because I am sure that the full texts are contained in their codices. They are points which could be observed by all if they were willing to be obedient to God; they are neither out of date nor irrelevant to this country (if we omit those which seem to apply only to the ancients or to those across the sea, not to us). Just as physical remedies are gathered in certain books of medicine, so those of the soul are collected in the sacred canons; as he who heeds what he reads in books of medicine is freed from sickness and he who disregards it dies by his own fault, so I desire to find out how he who scorns the remedies of the soul can avoid death by other means. Of this I am still ignorant, indeed stupid. Also, the apostle says: "If we would judge ourselves we would not be judged" [1 Cor. 11.31], and just as secularly we ought to be judged by civil law, so ecclesiastically we ought to be judged by canon law; whether, therefore, he who refuses to be judged by canon law temporally can in any way escape that judgment where each will perish in damnation eternally [Job 4.20], let someone else say; for on this point I am totally silent.

Indeed, how do we act justly if we neglect the law imposed on us by God through the holy Fathers [Mic. 6.8], how do we keep justice if we do not keep canon law, how do we walk with God if we leave the path which He instructed us to follow? Any task which is not done with the integrity of those doing it is noxious, since it can be very clear and certain that each man will "receive in accordance with what he has done, whether good or bad" [2 Cor. 5.10]. So how can the man who goes beyond the line of canonical rectitude have any hope of salvation, I ask, when it is written: "Do not measure the court which is outside the temple, for it is given over to the nations" [Rev. 11.2]? To which "nations," if not those about whom we the psalmist said to the Lord, "My liberator from the wrathful nations" [Ps. 17.48]? For as the devil is elsewhere called "evil man,"[10] so the legion of devils here possesses the appropriate name of "nations." Therefore, he who is found in the outer court is handed over to the devils, because he who is outside the line of ecclesiastical rectitude, though physically inside the church, is seen to be inside in body but is shown in his soul to stand in the outer court; and certainly one who associates with non-Christians is "given over to the nations." For though he may be called a Christian, he who is contrary to Christ in no way is one. He who does not obey the sacred canons rebels against Christ. He is "given over to the nations," unless he gathers himself back inside the defined line, since he will not be able to dwell in the company of those by whose law he did not wish to be held, by whose discipline he did not wish to be corrected, and whose ways he did not wish to imitate. But woe to any of us who happens to be found outside the canonical line, when the congregation of the elect begin to be examined! For no one is elect who is not canonical, no one is canonical who is not elect.

4. One of you may say: "What does it matter to you when others, even those more eminent than you, make no effort to do this?" It matters, I say, in every way, and it is so important that I could say, "All you who pass by, look and see if there is any sorrow like my sorrow" [Lam. 1.12], if I did not languish in a stupor of insensibility. I will leave out the fact that I have been three times exiled[11] contrary to the canons, a thousand times wronged, my bishopric illegally taken away from me (and another [Milo, 950/51] adulterously brought in above me), then brought back to it again [961] by the mercy of most pious Caesar [Otto I] on the instruction of the apostolic father who then commanded the seat of Rome [John XII], restored by the decision of the bishops in synod [962 at Pavia], later arrested by the same usurper (and you were not so completely unaware of this action nor opposed to it; in fact there were thousands who believed that almost all of you had not only assented to it but had even instigated it), ejected, abused, robbed, given into custody;[12] but leaving all these details unexamined (just as if nothing could be found in them which could even lightly be reproved by the laws), once more by the Creator's mercy, by the pious emperor's clemency, with the help of the excellent duchess [Judith],[13] I was rescued and brought back; and I was received by you so coldly that it was not difficult to tell from your faces how unwillingly you saw me return.

From that time on you have never stopped provoking me and damaging me; as before, so also since then, you have never stopped denying me every privilege of episcopal rank, to such an extent that you leave me no privilege except the bestowal of chrism and the power of consecrating anything, along with the signing of documents. Also, I am so without honor among you that, though all my fellow bishops coming there will be honored by the attendance of their own clerics, I will not be attended by even one of you—though despite my poverty I have been so generous to you that I have enriched ten of you with knight's benefices, and that, gratis. Yet I will omit all of this in respect of him who said: "Do not resist the wicked" [Mt. 5.39].

5. What must we do about the synod recently held?[14] For you know that I have always put off holding one (though it is laid down that we hold one twice a year)[15] for this reason: because I said that I did not at all know for what purpose I ought to hold one. If anything is done against the canons, it is usual to correct it in the synods;[16] but if I had tried to do this going full circle through everything which is written in the canons, I would see that you did not care at all for any of them. To offer a few examples: if I were to read what I touched on above, namely: "The great synod entirely forbids that any who is in the clergy have a woman living with him, except a sister,"[17] and the rest which are mentioned there, which of you could I pick out as not having disobeyed this command? Again, if the words, "If any priest takes a wife, let him be deposed, but he must be expelled if he has committed adultery,"[18] were to be observed, who of you would go undeposed? Again, if the words, "We order that bigamists not be admitted to the clergy,"[19] were read, who of you would I be confident has been lawfully promoted to the priesthood? And—to come to lesser faults (no faults at all to you)—if we were to read that those who ignore the canons about conspiracies and conspirators, about perjurors, about drunks and those who drink in taverns, and those who are given to usury, all should be more sternly reproved, if I held a proper synod whom of you would I leave undamned? If I were to demand the penance required by the canons for perjurors even, whom of you would I permit to celebrate a mass? If I were to expel from the clergy those with many wives, whom would I leave in the church except boys? If I were to cast out the bastards [cf. Dt. 23.2], whom of these boys would I permit in the choir? "I looked for you to do righteousness," it says, "and behold, bloodshed, for justice, but behold a cry!" [Is. 5.7]. What cry? A foul report, a bad example. "The cry of the Sodomites came to me" [Gen. 18.20–21], it says. Briefly would I state it: The cause of the whole perdition of the people entrusted to me is the clergy remaining in it. For how would I have dared to summon any of the laity in synod about adultery, or perjury, or any sin at all, when I was denied righteousness in the clergy? There would be no cleric to whom the layman would not constantly say in his heart, even if he did not dare with his lips: "Hypocrite,"— that is, false cleric—"cast out the

beam first from your own eye and then you will see so that you may take the speck out of my eye" [Mt. 7.5].

6. Since, then, an open examination on these lines is not possible for me, for what purpose ought a synod or council to be held? For you remember, I know, that I gave instructions that for two days the arch-priest and arch-deacon along with the cathedral canons, all equally presiding, should visit the parishes without me and make examination, and on the third day report back to me all that had to be corrected. That was done. Taking my seat, I asked what had been done. The spokesman replied that you had made inquisition about the psalms and such, and, thanks be to God, had thus found no wickedness. What then would I have to say about such paragons but "Thanks be to God"? If they knew the psalms so well, they would be free of other faults — for what purpose, then, would a synod have to be held? Realizing then that this was the greatest deception of souls, I said one thing in my heart, and uttered another with my lips. In my heart I complained to myself thus: "Are you a bishop or a quasi-bishop?" With my lips I replied to the one who reported this: "If there ought to be in this council an inquisition or examination about the psalms and not about other things, lead *me* forth first to the scale. For I can be shown not to know those as I should. So for what purpose should a synod be held if nothing more to be corrected is found?"

Asking therefore about their faith, I found that many of them did not even know the creed itself, the one which is believed to have been the Apostles'. I was compelled by this discovery to write a synodical letter to all priests,[20] which began with this admonition:

Therefore, I advise you as a father and instruct you as a pastor, to remember the words of the apostle: "It is impossible to please God without faith" [Heb. 11.6], that is, without believing the creed which has been passed on to us by the apostles and by their successors, and: "He lives righteously from faith" [Rom. 1.17] — that is, his creed — "and whatever is done without faith" [Rom. 14.23] — that is, without belief in God — "is sin; but faith" — that is, belief in God — "if it has no good deeds is dead in itself" [Jas. 2.17]; and that you hasten to take this faith — that is, belief in God — to memory in three forms: first according to the symbol, that is, the collation of the apostles as it is found in the corrected psalteries, second that which is sung at Mass, and third that of St. Athanasius which begins, "Whosoever wishes to be saved." Whosoever wishes, therefore, to be a priest in my diocese or to be made one or to remain one, must recite those three by heart to me, when next he is summoned here by me.

7. I had given them this in mid-lent [966] to be written down and memorized. When I saw that they were not obeying and I enquired what I could do about it canonically, so great a fear took hold of some of them, that they promised me help in making the journey, and also promised that they would henceforth sing the creed of St. Athanasius and do the other things written therein to the best of their ability. I have found that all the priests of the city churches and all those of the rural churches are ready to do this (thanks be to God), but I see that you cathedral canons, who are sending all these into perdition, as once the scribes and pharisees sent their peoples [Lk. 15.1–2], still remain so rebellious against it that you would rather be damned forever with Arrius, the adversary of this faith, than be persuaded to your salvation by singing this in public, as the clergy of other churches do.

8. Pressed, alas, by such urgent necessity, do I not have to go to Rome where I might be able to find some advice on this problem? O evil chronicle [*Chronographia*] of Rather,[21] O truth that is hateful to him! For how much better it would have been that I alone should be a liar than that I should be able to say in full truth such things about almost all of you; and I myself can scarcely believe them, I who am compelled, wretch that I am, to say such things. Therefore, we must cry and pray without pause: "Turn us, O God of our salvation, and keep your anger from us" [Ps. 84.5]. For one who is not forgetful of his own charges is sternly straitened—and not undeservedly—by this sentence: "Evil habit must be thoroughly rooted out no less than damaging corruption"[22] (as Osius the very strict cries in the council of Sardis); and elsewhere another: "Let habit yield to authority, let law and reason overcome wicked practice."[23]

When I see you so utterly despise the authority of the canons and so obstinately lean towards the habits of your predecessors, who were likewise rebels against God himself, who is known to have established those canons, I find that you ought to cry to God along with me unceasingly, as much for them as for yourselves: "We have sinned with our fathers, we have done unjustly, we have done iniquity" [Ps. 105.6]; and also with the most holy king Josiah we should cry to one another: "Go, enquire of the Lord for me and for the people and for all Judah"—which we can understand by God's statement to be the excellent Catholic Church—"concerning the words of these books"—of the canons and decretals which are contained in the archives of the churches; "for great is the wrath of the Lord that is kindled against us, because our fathers have not obeyed the words of these books, to do all that is written in them" (you should understand by *fathers* not only the bishops of the churches but also their elders), so that God may at least deign to reply to any one of us: "Thus says the Lord God of Israel: Regarding the words which you have heard, because your heart was penitent and you humbled yourself before the Lord when you heard how I spoke against this place and its inhabitants, that they should become a desolation and a curse, and you have rent your clothes and wept before me, I also have heard you, says the Lord. Therefore, I will gather you to your fathers, and you shall be gathered to your grave in peace, and your eyes shall not see all the evil which I will bring upon this place" [2 Kg. 22.13–20].

"Run to and fro," says the Lord elsewhere, "through the streets of Jerusalem; look and take note; search her squares to see if you can find a man who does justice and seeks truth, and I will pardon them. Though they say the Lord lives, yet they swear falsely. Lord, your eyes look for truth; you have smitten them but they have felt no anguish; you have consumed them, but they have refused to take correction; they have made their faces harder than rock and have refused to repent. But I said: Perhaps these are only the poor and silly, not knowing the ways of the Lord and the justice of their God. I will go to the great and speak to them; for they know the way of the Lord, the law of their God. But lo, even more these had broken the yoke, had burst the bonds. Therefore a lion from the forest struck them; a wolf destroyed them at evening" [Jer. 5.1–6]—the lion of course "that roars, seeking whom he may devour" [1 Pet. 5.8]—that is, the devil, and the wolf is the same, who due to the negligence of the hireling shepherds, possessing them in name, not in right, and illegally usurping the position, "snatches and scatters the sheep" [Jn. 10.12], not only through himself but through his members who work with him and destroy the vineyard of the Lord of Sabaoth.

9. And alas, how fittingly all this applies to us wretches! For we ourselves are leaders, in repute though not in reality; we, I say, who abandoning the poor and those totally ignorant of God's law, are addressed by the Lord's words. By reading, we know the way of God which we do not choose to follow; by despising God's judgment of ourselves but despising ourselves more, we have, as it were, broken His yoke—which is sweet for the willing and a light burden [Mt. 11.30] for those not scorning to bear it—we have burst the bonds of canon law, caring nothing about it. Therefore, we must fear that worse will happen to us than to those about whom this was said then in their presence, inasmuch as we have despised not only those who then spoke, but also Him who now addresses us not only through them and their successors, but also through Himself: God. The lion that devours souls [1 Pet. 5.8] is much worse than the lion that ravages the flocks; the wolf that kills men in the spirit is much worse than the wolf that devours sheep in the body, particularly if this happens to us "at evening," that is, when we are about to end our present life. It is in fear of this peril that I am forced to undertake this journey, to seek the advice of others because I do not find any in myself.

10. I am not a little troubled by these thoughts, I admit, as I ask whether

any other road of salvation remains if this one is despised, and I do not even suspect that one does. For if the Catholic Church defends what is canonical, that man is wrong to call himself Catholic, I think, who presumes to fight against the holy canons.[24] But (as we sing) "unless each man keeps the Catholic faith pure and inviolate, without doubt he will perish for ever."[25] What a stern sentence: that he who rejects canon law is not a Catholic, and that none except a Catholic can win eternal life. Since this is unshakeably and certainly so, what can we think, what can we consider, about that so open contempt of canon law which prevails among us, when we do not only what is so sternly prohibited in the Nicene Council [c. 3] concerning cohabitation with women forbidden to ministers of the Church, but also that which is severely punished elsewhere, as stated above, and no less so in the Neocaesarian Council, where some such as this is contained [c. 9]: "If a priest confesses that before his ordination he sinned in some carnal offense, he may not consecrate the oblations, remaining in his other offices for his zeal"?

Recognizing these in himself, a man could drown in the whirlpool of desperation, had it not previously been said: "A man does not know whether he is worthy of hate or of love, but all things are kept uncertain for the future" [Eccle. 9.1–2]. For if the man who confesses that he sinned carnally before his ordination is so severely punished, what about him who is known after his ordination to have fornicated a thousand times? Though for these sins certain people, though very few, seem to go free, what must be said or thought about the seemingly lighter ones and those so customarily practiced that they are now not even faulted, as for instance these: "A bishop, priest, or deacon who takes up arms in any sedition is to be dismissed from all gathering of Christians";[26] and: "A bishop, priest, or deacon given to dice or drunkenness must either cease or be deposed,"[27] and countless others of this sort, which are struck by the sword of the canons no less severely than cohabitation with women and fornication and adultery and incest that is contrary to nature itself? When in pride these are neglected, how a man can be called, still less be thought, a Catholic, I do not see, when, as I mentioned above, the words in the Nicene Council are read [c. 9]: "The Catholic Church defends what is canonical."

11. The Lord says: "Leave the dead to bury the dead" [Mt. 8.22]. So the guilty either defend or hide those like themselves, and no one deposes those who ought legally to be deposed, and no one condemns those who ought to be condemned. But they will not for that reason be able to avoid the damnation brought on them through the Holy Spirit, nor will those whom the Lord calls thieves and robbers [Jn. 10.1–2] be able to be shepherds of His sheep. For the man committing simony will not be able to avoid the damnation of Simon [Acts 8.20–24], nor will the man who has done what Gehazi did [2 Kg. 5.20–27] be able to

escape Gehazi's leprosy. "So of you will be demanded," says the Lord as though speaking of the Jews alone, "the blood of all the prophets shed on earth from this generation, from the blood of innocent Abel to the blood of Zachariah the son of Barachiah, whom you murdered between the sanctuary and the altar" [Mt. 23.35], though of course those to whom He said this had themselves killed neither Abel nor Zachariah nor any of the prophets; but because they were similar in wickedness to those who had done so, they were to be struck with similar punishment. Elsewhere, the Lord says that some time it will be said: "Gather the weeds first and bind them in bundles to be burned" [Mt. 13.30], that is, join those equal in sin in like damnation. If, then, this is so, just as Maximus Cinicus was condemned,[28] so are condemned his accomplices in that crime; as Photius,[29] so also his imitators; as Constantine the usurper of the seat of Rome,[30] so also any imitator of him; and just as the ordination of those is invalidated, so also is that of these, and their damnation is similar.

Alas, purity of the Catholic faith, ancient sanctity and true Christianity, where have you gone? Do you ask? Let us make her reply as though present—for she is present though unseen for her small numbers. For not yet has that time passed which the Lord himself specified, telling Christians: "Lo, I am with you always, to the close of the age" [Mt. 28.20].

12. Let the Lord be silent about Himself, let Him speak about those pseudo-Christians: "As they go on their way," He says, "they are choked by the cares and riches and pleasures of life, and their fruit does not mature" [Lk. 8.14]. What fruit? That by which they would be fed in the kingdom of heaven. But they incur the wrath of the most high; for thus also the apostle testifies: "Whosoever wishes to be friend of this world makes himself an enemy of God" [Jas. 4.4]. Unless this is taken to be said in a figure of speech (i.e., that which is contained is shown by that which contains it), it seems to urge a kind of ingratitude for those things which God has conferred upon us. For if we little love this world which God made for our sake, we are, as it were, ungrateful to the creator and giver of it. "God saw everything," says the Scripture, "which He had made and it was good" [Gen. 1.31]. How should what seemed very good to God himself be hated by us?

Let us therefore understand that it is not *this world* which is called the earth—that is, the heaven, land, sea and everything that is in them—or those revolutions of the seasons owing to which this our life is called "the world" that anyone ought to hate, but what is wrongly done *in* this world: first the greed or extravagance of those things which this world ministers for our use, then pleasure, then every kind of vice. Therefore, whatever seems good to God himself, we should love as good; what bad, we should hate as evil, so that we may somehow be able to avoid God's enmity and be counted among those who are truly Christian. We can in no way do this unless we do what the sacred canons require.

13. But to return to myself and those like me, that is, those hitherto rebels against the sacred canons: how can we act this way, when to all in general the remedies of penitence after sinning have been made available, and when the Lord himself says to us wretches that "if salt" — which we ought to be — "lose its taste, it is good for nothing, not even for the dunghill" [Lk. 14.34–35]? This figure of penitence we have elsewhere, thus: "Lord, overlook it this year while I dig around it and apply manure" [Lk. 13.8]; that is: "bringing back to his memory the stench of his sins, I[31] will compel him to do penance" — which of course is denied us wretches, since after penance one is not allowed by canon law to be even a cleric.[32]

What then shall we do, wretches, hemmed in on every side? Unceasingly we are told: "Whosoever eats of the flesh of the sacrifice which is the Lord, and his uncleanness is upon him, his soul will perish from his people" [Lev. 7.20]. And again: "A priest of the seed of Aaron who has a blemish will not offer his bread to the Lord nor come forward to His ministry" [Lev. 21.17–18]. How then, most wretched, can we be cleansed of that uncleanness, how can we be cleared of these blemishes, who, after the cleansing penitence of our sins, are not permitted even to stay in the clergy, still less perform the rites of priesthood? Acknowledging that this one awful obstacle stands in our way, what are we to think about those committed to us? What about these vessels which ought to have been washed, cleaned, and blessed by us, which our touch, alas, must render unclean, since the Lord says: "What the unclean touches will be unclean" [Num. 19.22]? If we had been few (which, would that we had been) and there could be found, by God's Grace, others to take the place of those of us who are unworthy and expelled, there would not have been such peril. But as it is, alas, since the Lord cries in complaint saying: "Yet these have all broken the yoke, have burst the bonds" [Jer. 5.5], what remedy has the deceived Church, which we ought to govern, found, when the Lord's voice complains that we all at the same time have broken His yoke and burst the bonds? For since James says: "Confess your sins to one another, that you may be saved" [Jas. 5.16], and the Neocaesarian chapter [c. 9] written above has: "If a priest confesses that before his ordination he sinned in some carnal offense, he may not consecrate the offerings, remaining in his other offices for his zeal"; who is to sing the Mass, since that sentence prohibits almost everybody from consecrating the offerings?

See what contradiction is contained here: you are not permitted to consecrate the offerings if you confess that you have sinned, but you will not win salvation unless you confess that you have sinned. What then will I do about you, my brothers and fellow priests? If you do not confess your sins, I fear you may not be saved; if you do confess, you consecrate the offerings in defiance of the prohibition; if you consecrate in defiance of the prohibition, you light up unholy fire [Lev. 10.1]. Therefore, you must fear that you perish like those whose example you follow.

14. I would therefore be compelled to despair of you as well as of me, if I did not remember again what we have often read: "No man knows whether he is worthy of love or of hate" [Eccle. 9.1]. Who knows if it has been conceded to any of us to be converted before dying? For by this law those are fortunate who have been deposed, expelled, robbed of their property, and deprived of their bishoprics, if only something happen to them like that which we heard happened to the two Scots [*Scottigeni*]:[33]

A certain powerful bishop attacked a weaker one, drove him from his seat, and usurped it for himself. The latter had charge of a poor man who was quite paralyzed, who addressed him thus as he was departing: "For whom are you deserting me, father?" "For God," he said. "Will you ever return?" "Not unless you lead me back," he answered. So he went away on a pilgrimage to the Lord's tomb. After a time a great plague overwhelmed the province from which that holy man had been driven, so that scarcely a tenth of the population survived. These besought the Lord with fasts, litanies, and alms, and He replied in the way in which it pleased Him, showing by the confession of that usurper that the people's ruin had come about because of his sin. He was moved by the consideration of his guilt and left the bishopric which he had usurped, and departed, and went to an island to do penance till the end. He had wanted to remain a solitary hermit, but the neighbors in their generosity visited him often. Then suddenly a famine swept the country which caused the generosity of those feeding the holy man to be checked a little. There happened to be a large boat on the beach. The boys whom he was teaching climbed on board after their play and fell asleep because of their hunger.

While they slept, the boat was rowed by angels and came to the shore of an unknown country. The king of that country, while out riding, was astonished to see a boat without men aboard approaching on a straight course and to find only boys in it asleep. Waking them up, he asked them where they came from. So when he had been told by them (as their age allowed it) about the hunger which the man of God suffered, he refreshed them first with food, then ordered the skiff to be loaded with grain. So the boys were put back on board again and fell asleep immediately at God's command; and with no one rowing, the boat returned to the other shore, and God's servant, together with the whole island, was freed from the danger of starvation. The people besides, who had been deprived of their pastor, began to seek him back, but it happened that no one knew where he had gone. While they were looking for a plan, a man came to them who said that he had heard the holy man say that he would never return unless the poor invalid led him back. So they adopted a plan among themselves and trusting in the merits of their bishop they commanded the paralyzed invalid in the Lord's name to rise and hurry straight after him. Wonderful to relate, he rose, he went forth, he found him in Jerusalem, he brought him back; and the bishop was received back and placed again on his proper seat. [. . .]³⁴

15. Let him estimate who can which merits were the stronger: those of the expelled or those of the expeller. The one by his penitence made the angels help him, or rather serve him (if I may say so); the other made the invalid run half way round the world. But since the fulfillment of penitence can do so much, it would be surprising if canonical decree denied the clerkship to a holy man such as the latter one had become, though no one can seem to become a cleric more worthily than he who happened to become holy through penitence. The man to whom such a thing happens or something else relevant to punishment of such sin, or who of his own accord himself is the punisher of his sins, about him I have no doubts after his death. But the man who I see has suffered no misfortune in this world, let another feel what he can about him; I am apprehensive, believing in that sentence which says about such people: "They spend their days in prosperity, and in peace they go down to hell" [Job 21.13], and I fear that the words of John the apostle apply to them: "There is sin which is mortal,"—add, "lasting for ever"—"I do not say that one is to pray for that" [1 Jn. 5.16]. Why? Because, as St. Gregory explains, "the beasts rotting in their manure" [Jl. 1.17] are the carnal ones finishing their life in the stench of wantonness.³⁵ There is no reason why this should not be understood also for other sins, because, since the Lord says that "whoever perseveres in good will be saved" [Mt. 24.13], so on the contrary whoever perseveres in wickedness will without a doubt be damned. And (woe is me!) how can he not be damned of whom the apostle cries: "Be sure of this, that no immoral or impure man or one who is covetous, that is, an idolater, has any inheritance in the kingdom of Christ and of God" [Eph. 5.5]?

Woe, then, woe to us wretches! For who else is there in this multitude but men of this sort, alas! For it is clear that every illegal coition is either fornication or adultery. No law allows marriage to ministers of the altar. These *fornicators, impure and covetous men* are people who happen to *die* in those sins, since the Lord mercifully promises: "At whatever hour a sinner is converted and weeps, he will be saved" [Ezek. 33.12]. Behold your course, behold your remedy! Would that my own were so easy! For it is about me that the Lord addresses the prophet Ezekiel, as though in a question: "Son of man, what will become of the wood of the vine?" [Ezek. 15.2], and the other things than which there is nothing more terrible in the eyes of those who know Gregory's views of them.³⁶

16. What then will we do? I have found a prayer in certain psalters; if we offered it to the Lord every day and earnestly strove in our actions to win merit to be heard, we would be confident that it would benefit us. It goes like this:

Save us, omnipotent God, and by our merits and by the intercession of Mary the holy mother of God and all the saints, be propitious and merciful to us, and conceding pardon for our past sins, give us henceforth the desire and the ability to do the things that please thee and benefit us; give us solace in tribulation, help in persecution, strength in every trial; give us pardon for our past sins and correction for our present; and deign to bestow salvation on us for the future.[37]

But what are we doing, brothers? Lo, again the exact opposite. He cries to us: "He who turns his ear so that he hears not the law, his prayer shall be an abomination" [Pr. 23.9]. How much turning away from the law there is here among us is clear from the fact that, though the Lord in rebuke once said, "Like people, like priest" [Hos. 4.9], now our priests are much worse, for shame, than the people.

17. Caught then in such difficulty as to what to do, I am compelled to look for advisers; and since I find none anywhere, I am making speed, as I said, to go to Rome. May God's pity mercifully prosper my intent. And since I have found that many of you are glad at it, as though I may never return from there, I think it necessary to advise you to know that you and I share this common lot: that is, that if I were destined to die here, I could not pass away there, and if you had to finish your conceded time there, you could in no way have an end of life here. No matter what your disposition towards me is, I commend you to God's care and pity, as I leave here compelled by the love of learning.

48

PL 136.599–602   Verona November 967

[In November Otto and his court passed through Verona, receiving hospitality from the bishop. Rather seized the opportunity to secure his support and protection (*mundeburdis*), as well as revenues to alleviate his poverty.]

❧

Ottonis Privilegium

Privilege of the emperor Otto granted to Bishop Rather and the church of Verona:

In the name of the holy and separate Trinity, Otto, by God's mercy emperor:

Let the attention of all our *fideles*, both present and future, know that by the intervention of our dear son of the same name we have conceded to the church of Verona, which by our imperial clemency Rather oversees as bishop, for the love of God and of the holy mother of God and of St. Zeno, whatever is left of the revenues, which our predecessors have conferred on his predecessors, pertaining to the two gates of the city, namely one which is called St. Zeno's, the other which is called by the name of St. Firmus, along with the tolls from carts and all the revenue due to us from them. We have also granted him, or rather returned to him, the right to a market [*mercatum*] on the Feast of St. Zeno or Palm Sunday, just as our predecessors are said to have granted that church. We have also conceded him two parts of the riparian dues [*ripaticum*][1] and the entire due on the castle which is called Portus; whatever also our predecessors conferred on the same church up to our time and confirmed by charters we grant entire and confirm by this charter. Also, all the public fees [*functio*] on any properties which now belong or will in the future belong to the same church in perpetuity we so rescind and remove that neither count [*comes*] nor count's agent [*vicecomes*] nor officer [*sculdascio*][2] have any authority to stay in them or any judicial powers; but all those staying in them should remain in the power of this bishop or of whatever bishops will be in charge of the aforesaid church in the course of time, so that no power that is subject to us should have any license to prosecute them. But if anything wicked has been done by his manse-tenants [*mansarii*] or by his castellans [*castellani*] or by his homesteaders [*plectitii*] or by his manorial tenants [*incensiti*] or by his stipendiaries [*commodati*][3] or by his clerics or by his servants, let it be lawfully and justly punished either by the bishop or by his minister. Furthermore, let no one dare to fish in his waters unless there has been license from of old.

And because he himself is a needy foreigner[4] and lacking everything except what God and our help provide, he has already suffered many deprivations. We wish to relieve him with this device of help: beside the fact that he is, like others, a bishop of our kingdom, let him also be guarded by our protection [*mundeburdis*],[5] the privilege that is so especial that if anyone dares to harass him further, as up till now, or to rebel against him[6] or refuses to give due service to God: if he is a cleric, all his possessions are to be put in the bishop's control and he is to be driven from the church until lawful and condign satisfaction has been paid; if he is a servant, he is to undergo what is proper to servants and remain in the bishop's control as is due; and let all our *fideles* and friends have license without any fear of punishment to help him as far as possible to take action concerning these things and everything else which affects him. If count, count's agent, or *sculdascio*, or any secular authority does this or imposes himself on anything subject to the bishop against the bishop's will, that is, that he holds the bishop's land without anyone's giving it to him or has received any cleric of his or any servant of his in protection [*commendatio*] without the bishop's consent or has attacked him in like manner, he is to pay us a fine of one hundred pounds [*librae*]; he is in addition to make good to the bishop by law any loss he has cost him. Let him not entice any castellan [*castellanus*] of the bishop away from the bishop's property [*castellum*] to put him on his own holdings, as this is most unjust; and if he does so, he is to be made to pay a fine for breach of immunity [*fractura immunitatis*] to him and a fine [*bannus*] to us. The same lawful penalty is to be suffered by anyone who refuses him on any matter pertaining to the same church which it is within his authority to do and is pleasing to God, and by anyone who dares to be protector, defender, and patron [*patrocinator*] of anyone guilty of such a crime.

If any fraudulent deeds [*libellariae, commutationes, precariae*][7] have been drawn up since the time that he was ordained bishop, we wish and require that they be entirely rescinded and corrected according as is pleasing to God, so that, free from all those obstacles which we with Christ's support are able to remove from him, he may be able to serve God without anxiety and so that you all may be able to pray to God's mercy for the safety of us, of our wife and of our dear offspring, until the end.

I, Ambrose the Chancellor, *vice* Bishop Hubert [of Parma] the Archchancellor, acknowledge and here subscribe.

Dated the fifth of November in the year 967 of our Lord's incarnation, the sixth year of the emperor Otto, at Balsemate.[8]

49

Weigle, Urkunden 25   Verona November 967

[A decree redistributing the revenues of some of his enemies among the more deserving of his chapel priests.]

❧

Judicatum

Rather, by the Grace of God bishop of Verona, to all his successors:

1. While the practices of the wicked are gaining strength against the commandments of God and the decrees of the saints, I have been quite unable to

ensure that either in the apostle's words "each" in our church "receive due reward according to his labor" [1 Cor. 3.8] or, as we read it in the Acts of the Apostles, the offerings be divided among the clergy "according as each has need" [Acts 4.35]. But they pervert the meaning of the Lord's sentence, "To every man who has it will be given in abundance, but he who has not, even what he has will be taken away from him" [Mt. 25.29; Mk. 4.25; Lk. 8.18], when they take it to mean that whoever had more ought to receive more of what is offered to the Church. In fact, He intended it to mean that to the man who has love the other virtues are added, but the man who does not have love gets no credit for other virtues.

So that the sympathy I feel for those who have been hard pressed by poverty and have withdrawn from God's service may bear some fruit, I have decided to bestow on them something of my own. "My own" I call that which has been conceded to me to administer at my discretion and to enjoy, should I so please, for my livelihood.

Another reason which has driven me to do this is that from infancy I have been, alas, so slothful in God's service that wretchedly I have never merited to gain the place of myrtle or of cedar or olive wood [cf. Is. 41.19] or other trees of this sort in the Church. So henceforth by helping some who bear good fruit [Mt. 3.10], that is, those who attend to the duties of the Church, I may be able to gain the office at least of elm, while there is yet time. Thus I may have a share in all their work as a collaborator and, just as "he who receives the prophet in the name of the prophet will receive the reward of the prophet" [Mt. 10.41], so I too by helping them and their successors in God's service may ever receive the same reward as they do — as though I could do by their hands after my death what I alas had neglected while alive to do with my own. In the same way it was said of him who was then called Saul but was afterwards by God's gift called Paul and was later the great teacher of the gentiles, that he stoned Stephen by the hands of all [Acts 7.58], because he guarded their cloaks while they stoned him.

2. I observed that those who took on the greater labor in the Church were also beset by the more pressing poverty, so much so that they constantly grumbled and even out of need rushed to be ordained unlawfully [cf. Tim. 5.22], to find in holy orders some sustenance even though at great damage to their souls [cf. Mk. 8.36] — for their age did not advance them nor their knowledge commend them nor their righteousness illuminate them. I have therefore bestowed certain property recently confiscated from ingrates[9] on some of the chapel priests, subdeacons, acolytes, and doorkeepers of our cathedral, namely, those currently in those positions, and after these on seven subdeacons of the sacristy, seven choristers, seven acolytes of the sacristy (and five choristers and six doorkeepers though they too were ingrates — on the grounds that they were

either led astray by the seduction of their elders or frightened by their threats or infected with the poison of their conspiracy), all in addition to what ancient custom has laid down that they should normally receive from righteous, God-fearing, and charitable people, namely, the revenues of the Church of Sta. Maria Consolatrice, together with all that belongs or will belong to it, except for the income of the priest serving there, but with this proviso: that it be in their power, if he should die or move on, to appoint another but to take nothing away from what he has a right to have. If they so decide, the chaplains themselves may sing the Mass in the Church by turns or they may choose some of their number to sing full-time; let them take for their own what it was customary for the priests who served there to receive. The rest let them share equally with the subdeacons, acolytes, and aforementioned doorkeepers, not in vineyards and fields, but in measures and barrels, in such a way that there be no cause for quarrel or envy, but that all may rejoice in it in that peace which the Lord has conferred on men of goodwill [Lk. 2.14].

I have given them also another church of the Blessed Mother of God, the one called In Stelle, so that the candle money which comes from it may be at the service of the aforementioned church and that of S. Giovanni in Fonte; the rest they are to share. For it is wrong that what is placed on the altars should benefit the taverns[10] and what is offered to God should serve the devil.

I have allowed them also something from the manse of S. Procolo in the Valpantena, in the area called Cuzzano, one homestead; in the valley of Sala two tenancies of S. Giusto at the walls. I have also bestowed on them the little manse called Paltiniaco with its serfs, servants, and all belonging to it, and tythes also from Castle Oppeano, and the property which is called De Forendanis, i.e., what belongs neither to Tombazosana nor to Roverchiara nor to Cerea, nor to any other parish, together with the Church of S. Pietro de Pressana with all its properties.

3. We have decreed and wish, both I and they, that they should have no one in authority over them except such as they should elect or appoint from their own number, who with his assistant is to collect it all and, as I have stipulated, divide it equally by measure and number. If they wish to give these something for an honorarium, it is in their power to do so, provided that it is not much. But if, as is human misfortune, one of them should neglect some of God's service or not make an effort to learn his ministry, the bishop or clergy are not for that reason to have the right to take away any of these privileges, but the above-mentioned superior whom they have themselves appointed is to summon him with all the others and, if he refuses to mend his ways, to take his share from him and divide it among the rest, or at any rate they should themselves settle on a penalty by which those who are so negligent or who will not learn

their letters ought to be corrected. If the superior himself should be slothful or fraudulent or non-productive or lax in correcting the negligent, he is to be removed and another from the same priests or subdeacons deputed to his place.

4. I have further conceded them whatever accrues from that contract which I made with John, son of Bertana, on the house near the forum, which is on precarial tenure to a minter named Dominicus, but with this stipulation, that the priest Galivertus and his assistant Martinus, while they live, should share it between them, over and above the share they are to receive with the others, and that afterwards it will return to the other common property, to be given thereafter to no one individual for his own but to be divided in shares.

But because I am quite unable in my poverty to insure that all this be divided among the designated individuals "according as each has need" [Acts 4.35], I have undertaken to give something from that same property to individuals so that "each might receive due reward according to his labor" [1 Cor. 3.8]. Therefore, besides what I have conferred on all to be divided in common, I have made over to the aforesaid priests and subdeacons and acolytes of the sacristy one house in Bonavigo, three fields in Porto Legnano, one garden in Cerea, one house in Roverchiara, together with three homesteads in Nichesola, from which the income is nine solidi, one cottage at Cavalpone, one house at Begosso, to hold as their own and not share with the others, but each to take home what accrues to each therefrom; but the rest are to be divided in common with the others. The supervisor of these properties is to oversee the Church of S. Giovanni in Fonte; he is also to appoint two doorkeepers there from the same prebend; they are to guard the church and always keep watch in the night hours over the treasury door, that is, either in watches or, if it seems better, on alternate nights. For I have decided that since these three orders toil in the bishop's service more particularly than all the others, in addition to what they do in their ecclesiastical ministry, they ought to receive something peculiarly theirs for the service specially rendered him. I have bestowed little on them for this reason, that I did not have much to give (for when others were in charge, I only "sang in grief" [Pr. 25.20]) and I thought I ought to avoid causing envy against them. If, as I truly am confident will happen, while they serve the Lord faithfully, one of the faithful should be inspired to add something for them, I wish that it be divided in common amongst them like the rest, so that no quarrelling or hatred prevail among them, but "the peace of God which passes all understanding may keep their hearts and minds" [Phil. 4.7].

But if, as often happens when the devil goads us, out of envy and hate one of them should be expelled from this Mother Church unlawfully, not for that reason is he to lose what he had been accustomed to receive from this Blessed Consolatrice, but he is to receive what the others do and give himself to the

Lord's service here, if he wishes and if it is granted him. It is easy to see that anyone who thinks that another has license to put a cleric in a church or expel him therefrom, other than he who can, if he wishes, make a cleric into an acolyte, is quite ignorant of canon law.[11]

5. But because it is ever the way of ill-wishers that they desire ill even if they cannot effect it, I set this warning on my action: if anyone, whether he be called bishop (he will not *be* one) or priest or deacon of our church, try either to thwart this or subtract anything from what the good predecessors of this church have justly and lawfully been wont to give the forerunners of these, as though they can say: "You have your stipend, let that suffice; or if you want to share ours, put what is given you in our common fund," let such have no part with any of the saints in the next life, but with Cham, Dathan, and Abiron [Gen. 9.25] or with those whom the flood has drowned or the earth swallowed up [cf. Ps. 105.17], and with Pilate, Anna and Caiphas, Judas the betrayer of Christ, and Simon the Magus [Acts 8.20], Ananias also and Saphiras, whom St. Peter damned for embezzling the church money [Acts 5.1–11], let them be anathema, marantha, and denied eternal life [1 Cor. 16.22] unless they amend.

But if, like those who "decline into words of wickedness for making excuses in their sinning" [Ps. 140.4], they say, "We cannot give them as much as our predecessors gave their predecessors," we reply, "Do not err; God will not be mocked" [Gal. 6.7]. *They* gave what they could; *you* too give what you can, if you wish to avoid the above curse.

6. Critics say: "You are making a schism when you turn them from the discipline of their elders." I do not turn them from discipline, but I am trying to save them from need and from the chance of neglecting God's service, if that were possible. I do not prevent wrong-doers being corrected, but I will not allow that they lose what I bestow on them under the rubric of "correction," and I therefore lay it down that they be fined of what I have given them only by their own minister. Let the elders compel them to their duty by discipline not by want. I would be making a schism if, on account of what I am adding to them, I allowed what they had always had to be taken away; that would not be an addition but an exchange and a split from your brotherhood; a schismatic is anyone who endeavors to be separated from God and from the company of the saints.

I further beseech my successors in the future that when they read what is written here they should be at pains to remember: "Son, if you are wise, you will be so for yourself" [Pr. 9.12]; so that they can note from the analogy that if they are good it will benefit none more than themselves. For, as St. Augustine truly says: "Every sinner sins against himself before he sins against another."[12]

And if for my worthlessness it is not granted *me* to receive the cherished reward from this, let *him* at least obtain the due reward from this in whose time

this was done, namely, the most pious emperor, who has also been a gracious
supporter of this church, establishing me in it for this purpose, that I might
conscientiously do what must be done and neglect what must be neglected; relying
on his help I have made this disposition and for that reason the work is more
his than my own. To him may He grant everlasting reward from it, I pray,
Who has caused this poor family of clerics to be supported in such a manner,
providing them their yearly stipend. May He make him govern with power in
this world and give him everlasting glory in the next. Amen.

50

Weigle, Epist. 155–56   Verona 1 December 967

[Letter to Martin, bishop of Ferrara: he criticizes him for his symoniacal ordinations and calls on him to cease from his uncanonical ways.]

∾

To his venerable fellow-bishop lord Martin, Rather, a sinner:

Though the Apostle commands that an older man should be respected [1 Pet.
5.1] and forbids that he be rebuked [1 Tim. 5.1], yet, compelled by the love which
I feel for you, I think it murderous to hide from you how much the sons of your
Church criticize you, particularly for the illegal ordination of boys; they add also
that you ordain them for a price—which is simony and damned with perpetual
anathema by the sacred canons.[13] So as a son to his father, as a servant to his lord,
as an old man to an older octogenarian, I beseech you to remember what was
said today to you and me in particular, namely, "Knowing that it is now the
hour for us to rise from sleep" [Rom. 13.11], and not fail to remember the apostle's
command to Timothy, "Do not be hasty in laying-on of hands" [1 Tim. 5.22];
and also Peter saying to Simon: "Your silver perish with you" [Acts 8.20]; and
many saying: "Let both him who gives and him who receives be anathema."[14]
    Now finally *arise from the sleep* of such open contempt of the canons and cease
from such ordinations, I beg you. Perhaps He who said, "You have sinned, cease"
[Gen. 4.7], and, "Turn to me and I will turn to you" [Zech. 1.3], will not despise
this your late conversion, since He is pious and merciful, and He does not want the
death of a sinner but rather that he should turn from his wickedness and live
[cf. Eccli. 2.13; Ezek. 33.11]. You should also know that none revile you for
this more than those whom you have so ordained or at whose prayers you did this.

51

Weigle, Epist. 157–59 Verona Advent 967

[His continued difficulties with the higher clergy are seen in the following "Address to his Rebellious Clergy." He had hoped by his *Judicatum* (no. 49) to establish a more equitable division of church revenues among the various orders of the clergy. The canons of the higher clergy had resolutely refused to go along with this and had found some support among the lower orders by pointing out that they would suffer in the long run as they would not in turn succeed to the formerly wealthy positions. It is apparent from the final paragraph of this letter that he had refused to meet with his opponents to discuss the question, not out of scorn, as they charged, but because of the pain which this feud was causing him. He sees the issue as much more than pecuniary; the canons are not only greedy in their demands on church revenues but are also failing abysmally in their spiritual duties.]

∽

Sermo Clericis Suis Sibi Rebellibus

Rather, bishop of Verona, to his rebellious clergy:

1. While I was listening to the nightly reading, I happened to hear something that applies to us (and I wish it were pardonable):[15] "They are a rebellious people, lying sons, sons who will not hear the instruction of the Lord, who say to the seers, See not, and to the prophets, Prophesy not to us what is right, speak to us pleasing things, prophesy illusions: leave the way, turn aside from the path; let holy Israel cease from our face." When I added to this text the things which I heard in the same prophet and in the other prophets, psalms, hymns, and spiritual songs [Col. 3.16], which you boast that you celebrate better than the other churches of Italy, and when I added to it the words of the Lord, in which agreeing with the prophet sent by Him He speaks thus to your antecedents: "This people honors me with their lips, but their heart is far from me: for in vain do they worship me, holding as doctrines the precepts of men" [Mk. 7.6–7]; and the words of the apostle also: "For the time is coming when the people will not endure sound teaching, but having itching ears they will accumulate for themselves teachers to suit their own likings and will turn away from listening to the truth and wander into myths" [2 Tim. 4.3–4]: well, reviewing these texts as a group, I was compelled, alas, to understand *us* as the people provoking the Lord to anger, since I know that, as the apostle truly stated, "whatsoever is written is written for our learning" [Rom. 15.4].

For who can "the sons who will not hear the instruction of the Lord" more appropriately be understood to be (excuse what I say) than these who, though they desire to be called canons and continually complain about the portion allotted to canons, so much refuse to *be* canons that, imitating the practices of the wicked only, they refuse even to hear, let alone do or read, what the holy canons require, saying in almost the same words to the *seers* (that is, those seeing the danger of their souls) "see not," and to those *prophesying* their wickedness "Prophesy not to us. Speak to us what is right" (that is, not what is *truly* right but what *seems* right to us), "say things pleasing to us"—not to God—"prophesy illusions" (that is, allow us to be deluded by our own inventions and the wicked practices of our predecessors). "Leave the way" (Him, that is, who says, I am the Way [Jn. 14.6]), "turn aside from the path" (the narrow and hard path that leads to Life [Mt. 7.14]). "Let holy Israel cease from our face"—that is: let the holy man stop harrying us by showing his holiness for us to imitate, revealing the vision of true and everlasting peace; and let the Lord's words, which you put upon us, stop disturbing us.

2. What then, my sons (in whom we are warned by God not to rejoice if you multiply [Eccli. 16.1]), what will it be, if, after listening to merciful God's promise "If you return and are quiet, you will be saved; your fortitude will be in silence and in hope," and, after a little, "the Lord waits to pity you" [Is. 30.15], you scorn that, replying in your actions if not in words: "No, we will speed upon horses!" [Is. 30.16]—which on the authority of Pope Gregory nothing prevents us from understanding as the powerful people on whose patronage you rely as you so scorn Church discipline.[16] What if the Lord happened to take you literally and reply: "Therefore you shall speed away. And we shall ride upon swift steeds. Therefore your pursuers shall be swift" [Is. 30.16] in punishing your monstrous rebellion temporally, lest He damn you eternally (as I do not cease to fear)? What, I say, of the manifest vastness of merciful God and the great assuaging of His just retribution?

And so for this reason, following the apostle, who says, "Be imitators of God, like the fondest sons" [Eph. 5.1], (whom He mercifully awaits,[17] I hope), I do not dare to chastize you harshly, while promising myself, though perhaps vainly, your conversion. Though I had stated that you, like rebels not only to lowly me but also to the power of the incomparable emperor, or rather to the omnipotence of almighty God (for it is rebellious both to the canons' and the emperor's decree), were ejecting me from the church from which you had already four times[18] ejected me, my heart refrained from "clothing you in the mantle of confusion" [Ps. 108.29]. This I would have done, if I had damned you eternally as you deserved, by excommunicating you and if I had undertaken to prepare an accusation against you at the court of his majesty the emperor (which I neglected to do since I did not send any representative for my position); if I happen to do this it will be quite apparent.

3. "Let the evil-doer still do evil" [Rev. 22.11], Scripture says. In that sense I commit to God's majesty whatever His providence wishes or permits me to bring upon you, and I give you license to serve the Lord in whatsoever church[19] of this diocese you please, until with God's approval a legate comes from most pious Caesar and hears what I have said and compares it with the remarks which you made to his imperial ears about me; then he can report back to the emperor as he sees fit and decide what I must do.

As to my avoiding negotiating with any of you on this matter, I do so not out of contempt for your fraternity, but, warned by the rustic proverb which says, "What the eye does not see, the heart does not fret over," it seems to be a kind of lightening of pain (and a necessary one), if my eyes do not see those who have done me and are still doing me so much wrong, and the memory of their wickedness leaves me for a time, while some little oblivion covers the authors of it.

52

Weigle, Epist. 159–69   Verona April 968

[Letter to Otto's Italian Chancellor, Ambrose. Rather tells of the origins of the quarrel between himself and the clergy: the clergy want to follow the tradition-al, though uncanonical, practices, while he demands adherence to the canons.]

◦~◦

Discordia

1. "A great quarrel," people are saying, "has arisen in these days between the bishop and the clergy of Verona."

But who are saying it? Certainly people who are utterly ignorant of the source of the quarrel; like those, for instance, who think that Judas perished for the first time when he wretchedly sold the Lord [Mt. 25.14–16] — although he had long since perished when he physically joined the apostles [Mt. 10.4], when, that is, drunk with the poison of avarice he did not stop thirsting after gain till he most wretchedly arrived at the noose [Mt. 27.5]. "In these days," they say — not entirely without truth though true rather in appearance than in fact.

After showing what the disagreement is, I will prove that there never was agreement between them and me, especially since they have already thrice[20] betrayed me and expelled me from here. For if, according to him who first said it, strong friends are those who like and dislike the same things,[21] or if, as another says, human friendships look for like minds and similar wills,[22] then our contrary habits cannot lead to strong friendships, and our friendship, that ever desires opposites, will never be able to stand firm on my side or on theirs, any more than it has been able to in the past. For they have always preferred the practices of their predecessors, who constantly rebelled against their bishops and the sacred canons decreed by God, while I have held that the sacred canons and God's decrees were to be put before habits invented by the devil. They openly and habitually keep women, which was forbidden in the Nicene Synod [c. 3], and they hold so lightly the respect of God and of men, and even belittle the very fear of hell, that they think that it not only *may* but even *must* mean that anyone who refuses to keep a woman must be engaging in that foulest sin which the apostle mentions in his Epistle to the Romans.[23]

Does not this seem to you to have been invented by the devil? O sacred and immaculate modesty of virgins, nowhere do you escape infamy amongst depraved men, if this is true. How damned is the whole order of clerics if there is none among them who is not either an adulterer or homosexual. For every man who womanizes contrary to the canons is an adulterer. Who then is a cleric? For if an adulterer is in no wise a cleric, that other is even less so. For if he is called "cleric" because he is "of the Lord's lot,"[24] what allottment can anyone have with the Lord, I ask, who practices one or other of these abuses? Heaven help the whole congregation of Christians if, according to the way these people think, there can be found no one among them who is not either a hypocrite with the pharisees or a publican with the gentiles [Lk. 13.10–13]! For the man who is an adulterer in public is a publican, and the man who under the cloak of piety is most impious, who under the cover of chastity is most unchaste, who under the pretense of justice is most unjust, is a hypocrite.

I inveigh against him in the superlative *most*, because I remember hearing more than once: "Cunning hypocrites provoke God's anger" [Job 36.13]. Therefore, though hypocrisy and unchastity far excel other sins in gravity, the remaining sins are more serious the more they are done in the open. For hidden sins kill only those who commit them, but public sins both kill the committers and injure those witnessing them. For hidden sins are not objects of men's judgements; all may speak about open sins but none about hidden ones. For instance, suppose somone (as could happen now) were to copulate with some animal in a corner before God's eyes alone: you censure him to the highest degree just for the suspicion of it; if you see it, what do you do but claim for yourself the right which is God's alone.

But anyone can make up any fictions he wishes about someone else. He tries to measure others by his own standards if he does not think others can be of any other kind than he is himself. The rustic proverb surely fits him: "A man in the fire seeks out those like him."

2. To make a habit of doing or saying things like this, of rebelling against their pastors, of dividing what has been allotted to all the clergy in common so unequally in terms of tenancies that some of them from being very poor become very rich, some receive a moderate amount, and some receive almost nothing at all, of sticking to the practices of those whom the pit has long held, and, finally, of disobeying all laws, both man's and God's—does this not seem to you to have been invented by the devil? But what is found written in the law of Moses, and in the Prophets and Psalms, in the Gospel and in the Acts and preaching of the Apostles, in the decretals of the popes and in the constitution of the canons—is it not clear that this, on the contrary, has been inspired by God? When you can find nothing in the latter which matches those habits of the former, under what law do you think that they live?

Therefore, between him who forbids such practices—or, if he does not dare to *forbid* them, at least *criticizes* and *censures* them and those practicing them—what agreement can there be, particularly when the Lord by His use of the word "sword" declares that He has come to bring discord. For He says (it is well known, it is clear): "Don't think that I have come to bring peace on earth. I have not come to bring peace but the *sword*. For I have come to set a man against his father and a daughter against her mother and a daughter-in-law against her mother-in-law" [Mt. 10.34–36], and—what He had already said through the prophet—"A man's foes will be his own household" [Mic. 7.6]. The reason why a man's foes are his household in particular is evident: that is, that though people are enclosed by one set of walls, they are divided from each other by opposing habits. For it often happens that a husband is sober but his wife a drunkard, he is mild, she is irascible, he has the fear of God, she is goaded by the devil. What agreement can there be between them, what peace, what friendship, when he refuses what she desires, since such a split proceeds from God Himself? For He commanded gentleness [Tit. 3.2], forbad anger [Eph. 4.26], and allowed no one to give assent to another in evil, saying through the apostle: "Not only those who do but those who consent to those doing are worthy of death" [Rom. 1.32].

2. So when you[25] act against the law of God, ought not I who have been appointed by God to correct you, ought not I at least to bark? When you prefer the practices of those who are undoubtedly held in the pit, to the statutes of those who stand in heaven with God, should I not even dare to mutter?[26] What then will I do when I am addressed along with other poor wretches (and you will be among them): "You have not gone up into the breaches or built up a

wall for the house of Israel, that you might stand in battle in the day of the Lord" [Ezek. 13.5]; and: "I tested you at the waters of Contradiction" [Ps. 80.8]? Will my friendship with you benefit me at all then, you who now urge me to have peace with you, so that I would be able to say with those others, "We have made a covenant with death and with hell we have an agreement" [Is. 28.15], though the most holy teacher says that it is better for a man to earn the devil's enmity than his friendship. For in you wickedness never stops fighting against justice, blindness against light, and falsehood against truth. I see you so rebellious against the Lord that you do not even deign to listen to His commandments but like the Jews you abandon them and cling so obstinately to the customs and ways of men [cf. Mk. 7.8] that the words, "The sin of Judah is written with a pen of iron" [Jer. 17.1], can be thought to have been said about you — and do you urge me to forget that I ever heard: "If you do not tell the wicked man of his iniquity, I will require his blood of your hand" [Ezek. 3.18]; and: "You offer help to the wicked and join in friendship with those who hate God" [Mt. 8.22], and the countless thunders of God's threats threat?

I read in one of St. Columban's books[27] that a priest has the same function in the Church as the stomach has in a man's body: it digests the food given it and ministers it to all its members, each of which turns it to his own nature, so that what the liver receives becomes blood, and what the gall-bladder receives becomes bile, what descends to the lungs becomes phlegm. By this analogy, if what I say happens to benefit some listeners to eternal life, but rouses many others to anger (just as he was roused who said, "He who sings songs with a heavy heart is like vinegar in alkali" [Pr. 25.20]), ought I from fear of the latter to have neglected even one of those who could have been benefitted by the words spoken to Ezechial by the Lord: "Son of man, do not fear their words nor fear their looks, for they are a rebellious house" [Ezek. 2.6]? What of the words: "Whoever is ashamed of me and of my words, of him will the Son of Man be ashamed when He comes in His glory and the glory of His Father and of the holy angels" [Lk. 9.26]?

4. If you argue[28] with me that a *scandal* to the Church ought to be avoided, I do not contradict. However, I counter you with two passages of the Gospel, one where the Lord is reported to have said to Peter: "Simon, from whom do the kings of the earth receive tribute, from foreigners or their sons?" When he replied "From foreigners," He said: "Then the sons are free; but so as not to give offence [*scandalizemus*] to them, go to the sea and cast a hook and take the first fish that comes up, and when you open its mouth you will find a shekel; take that and give it to them for me and for yourself" [Mt. 17.24–26]. The second, when the same Peter was saying to the Lord with the rest: "Do you know the pharisees were offended [*scandalizati sunt*] when they heard this saying?" [Mt.

15.12–14]; showing that He cared nothing for such offence [*scandalum*], He said, "Allow them"—understand "to be offended" [*scandalizari*]. Why? He adds the reason: "They are blind and guides of the blind; but if a blind man leads a blind man, both will fall into a pit"; as if He had said: "Because they themselves are blind and lead other blind men to fall into the pit of perdition, we should not care that they are offended." For it is better, as someone says, for offence [*scandalum*] to be given than for truth to be abandoned,[29] because, even though the declaration of truth be abandoned because of them, they will not for that reason be improved, but, as they began, they will grow wretchedly worse rushing into the pit of perdition predicted to them from the beginning. But let this suffice.

5. We should now, however, seek the source of this disagreement which has arisen between us. If anyone pays attention to what was said above about Judas, he will see that not only has this disagreement arisen, but that from the time of my inordination there has never been any agreement between us. There are a thousand indications to prove it, if one can remember the monstrous things that have already happened to me. Even though the authority of the emperor's presence and of the convened synod[30] has made public declaration, still there is cause for dispute between us, in that I have made clear the following points to them, not compelling them by force to obey them, but urging them with reasoned persuasion to take note of them:

In the Canons of the Apostles chapter 39 it says: "Let the bishop have care . . . put a finger on your sacrilegious mouth."[31]

6. Let him who wishes come and judge which of these courses was better or worse: that through fear of those who anger God I have now put up with this as though in acquiescence for almost thirty-five years; or that now, though too late, I have uttered these charges against them, having learned from Gregory, a truthful teacher, that "to tolerate an enemy while still hating him is not the virtue of love but the hiding of anger,"[32] and fully believing in Augustine's statement that "that man is unwilling to be in the body of Christ, who is not willing to take the hatred of the world upon his head."[33]

Besides finding fault with them for acting in this way against the canons, I was also particularly angered recently by the fact that, though his majesty's decision[34] had sounded against them on the question of removing their women, they almost all claimed that they could in no way do so because of their poverty, but they might perhaps be able to if they had the stipend due them from the Church's property. It seemed to me that they could have had it if either, following the apostle, "each one received his proper reward according to his labor" [1 Cor. 3.8], or, as we read in the Acts of the Apostles, the revenues were allotted to the clergy "according as each had need" [Acts 4.35]. By the term "revenues" I wanted to recognize everything which either had been allowed them by my predecessors or had been bestowed on them by God-fearing men. If that was enough, well and good; if not, I was willing to supply them in prudent measure with what I had foolishly given to certain ingrates and enemies.[35]

This idea they resisted so strongly that they said that they would sooner die than see it done. And with good reason: for their resources, though not, thanks to God, small, are so split up by *massaritia*[36] and suchlike divisions that some of them are really very wealthy from them, but the greater part languish in poverty, and, for shame, those who perform in the Church the greater service to God receive little or nothing, while those who hardly ever do anything for God's service become rich from the Church property. But if any of them tries even to murmur against this state of affairs, he is told: "Just as I waited for the death of my masters who preceded me, so you wait for my death; and the goods which I enjoy for the present, you also after my death look forward to enjoying"; as if to say: "When I am established in the place where those are whom I strive to imitate, try to follow me and fall into the same pit of the deep which I have fallen into," and so this is truly the blind leading the blind into the pit [Mt. 15.14].

7. "What then did you do in answer?" you ask. I showed them the authority of the canons for it against their usual practice. I sent to them some of their close associates, I implored them by the oath of loyalty which they had sworn to me more than once, that if they had any justification for their position, they should not hide it from me, lest when we came to the synod they cause me embarrassment if they proved that I was making unjust demands. And to show that I could never have had any trust in their oaths, they said, for shame, that they knew very well that they had sworn many oaths to many people which they could in no way make good, adding that it was foolish for them to try to teach me.

Again, I told some of them that they were at fault on both counts if they knowingly permitted either me to fight with them or them to fight with me. Their spokesman replied that it would be very foolish for him to presume to teach either his masters or "you who are praised throughout the whole world."[37] This achieved nothing. Trying in another way to bring them to the peace not of the world but of Christ [Jn. 14.27], I threatened, since some of them had benefices given by me, that I would take away what I had given them if they refused me my rights. They replied that they cared so little that, if I took away what I had given any of them, they would not for that reason be less loyal to me, so long as I stopped worrying them with redistribution of Church revenues. And truly, if they were never loyal to me for my having given them something, they were not less loyal—how they could be!—for my having taken it away. They never at any time stopped being disloyal to me—may the Lord spare them. Why? Let the apostle speak, for I am tired of repeating myself so often: "For the time is coming when the people will not endure sound teaching, but having itching ears they will accumulate for themselves teachers to suit their own likings and will turn away from listening to the truth and wander into myths" [2 Tim. 4.3–4]. You should understand that by *myths* he means open illegalities, for a fiction is properly called a "myth."

In all the sermons which I have made to the people this Lent, I have not stopped warning them along with me that we should not put off coming back to the peace—but alas a peace we never have held—of Christ; that is, those who have wronged others should remember the precept of the Lord (and this *I* have been quite ready to do): "If you offer your gift at the altar," and the rest [Mt. 5.23]. And those wronged should remember the words of him who says: "When you stand to pray, dismiss it if you have anything against anyone" [Mk. 11.25] — and this too I have continually promised that I would be quite to ready to do, if they deigned to ask me, so long as they are willing to do so in true peace.

But this only increased their pride and fanned the flames of their malice to the point of making such accusations against me that, far from allowing others to think anything good about me, they made even me believe worse things about myself than what I had put in the writing which I recently sent you, dear Ambrose.[38]

8. But because traitors always grow worse as a result of a favor and anyone who confers a gift on them only gives them strength to fight against him and works to propagate their treachery, I did not postpone putting into effective action what I had threatened. And following the instruction of him who says: "Give to the good man and do not support the sinner" [Eccli. 12.5], I took away from them two benefices, those of the Blessed Mother of God and of St. Stephen, the first martyr, and gave them, or rather gave them back (making moreover a written record which they call *Judicatum* [Decree, no. 49 above]) to the poorer clerics of this Church, for whose sake I had undertaken this great labor, namely the Cathedral priests, the seven subdeacons of the secretary, seven singers, seven acolytes of the secretary, five singers, six doorkeepers—not, however, so that they should become more loyal to me, but so that they should become more ready in the Lord's service and, now that the excuse of poverty was invalidated, more zealous in serving the Lord day and night.

Now that this disagreement, which has grown old over several years, has been brought to light (not "happened" as they say), they do not cease their efforts, as always, to entrap me; however, I am fully aware of them. And those that said that they do not care if I took away from them what they had had from me and would not be any less loyal to me because of it, provided I stopped harassing them on the points for which I had molested them, now, secure about my giving in, are trying to attack me with the patronage of certain powerful people[39] for what I took from them[40] for their ingratitude. But may the Lord deign to look mercifully upon me ready to be whipped for my sins and kindly defend me from their traps, giving them pardon and putting true peace in their hearts, so that we may all together merit the peace of Christ. But even if, through neglect of the words of Blessed Job, namely, "The cause which I did not know I most diligently enquired" [Job 29.16], I should in doing so meet with the fate of those wretches who, we read, would have been acquitted without blame even before a court of barbarians [cf. 2 Mach. 4.47] (for I am so ready to be whipped, as I have said, that "my pain is ever in my sight" [Ps. 37.18] — that double pain, the pain which I feel because I suffer all this for my own sin, and the fear that I may suffer even worse in the future), even if, I say, that happens, there is nothing else pertinent for me to do than to desire with all my heart and unceasingly to pray to God that he to whom I remember that I have sworn loyalty [the emperor] will never do something for which he would lose His grace irrecuperably, but may God's pity rather concede that he do what may both make him happily rule longer and in the future rejoice with Christ everlastingly.

53

Weigle, Epist. 169–78   Verona beginning of Easter 968

[In a letter to an unknown critic, entitled in the Laon manuscript *Liber Apologeticus*, Rather defends himself against the criticism that he should have used funds given him by the emperor to feed the poor, not to rebuild the Church of St. Zeno. His defense on this particular point is expanded into an attack on his enemies amongst the higher clergy, abusing their lack of celibacy, their commercial activities, their breaking of their oath of loyalty to himself, their appropriation of Church properties, their brawls within the cathedral itself, their arrogant treatment of the lower clergy, and the fact that one of them went to Rome and there "bought" a judgment that he, Rather, should not interfere in their affairs.]

Liber Apologeticus

Rather, touched a little with the fear of Jesus, ready to endure all this rather than yield to his enemies: to the unceasing critic not only of his actions but also of his thoughts, the chief supporter and defender of his enemies.

1. That great urbanity of yours, which you take from Martianus [Capella][1] and others like him, of whom I am the more uncaring and indifferent the more I fear that the words spoken to some people apply to me, namely, "Ever learning and never coming to knowledge of the way of truth" [2 Tim. 3.7] (as also they can apply to you), this inept, nay, pointless, urbanity and boastfulness of yours causes me such trouble that, when you send me little notes, or little non-senses, carrying "more of aloe than of honey,"[2] more of certain poison than of salutary antidote (so that I would now choose to forbid this wicked servant [Rather] even to speak to you, still less ask any help of you), I am made weary enough to want to exclaim about you in particular what the psalmist does about many: "The godless have dug pitfalls for men, men who do not conform to thy law, Lord" [Ps. 118.85]. But though I would like at least for now, in view of the season [Easter], to be at truce, you compel me to dictate something of a defense.

2. When our most glorious and august emperor was about to depart from here,[3] he entrusted to my charge a sum of money with which to rebuild the Church of St. Zeno,[4] (our particular patron, as is well known) — after, that is, everything from which I had to live (still less would there have been anything left over from which I might be able to make any alms if I abandoned this work which had been entrusted to me) had been licked up by his [the emperor's] — I do not say power, or rapacity, but certainly his — presence.

How true is the saying of Augustine that all things are full of rash judgments![5] For since his equal, the holy Gregory, declares that in obeying commands evil should never be done but sometimes good may be neglected,[6] who could believe that money entrusted by him to whom one has sworn so sacred an oath of loyalty should be spent in any other way than it was his will to command? "On the poor," says the critic, just as the betrayer of Christ once did [Mt. 26.9]. But where are those poor, I would like to know? For I find here none so poor in resources, thanks be to God, that for them the rebuilding of churches, even if it were done out of my substance as it should be, ought to be delayed, except, strange to say and incredible to hear, myself and those whom I had to feed in my own household. With you,[7] I think, the poor are fed only by the bishop. But here the generosity of all who inhabit this country shouts that that is not necessary, as they all in common observe the command: "Choose not whom to pity," and even stuff them to the point of gluttony and drunkenness [Lk. 21.34] — and before the ninth hour against God's commandment — though they ought themselves to keep solemn [Lenten] fast like the other faithful.

3. Would that he who, just like me, did not fully know the requirements of almsgiving laid down by St. Gregory[8] would learn them; would that he would approve of them and cherish them. He would doubtless find that those

whom you place above the need of restoring the Church as the emperor commanded, are entirely denied alms by divine decree. For it says, "Give to the just man and do not support the sinner" [Eccli. 12.4]. By this command also those who you claim should be given the emperor's charity are rejected each for his own sin, whereas St. Zeno, whom you are trying to deprive of his proper funds, qualifies by his justness to receive it. For we should rightly believe that Zeno ought to be called "the brother of Him who sits in the seat of majesty" [Mt. 25.31] rather than any of those who must be afraid of hearing "Depart from me, ye accursed, into the eternal fire which has been prepared for the devil and his angels" [Mt. 25.41]. A curse like this is obviously intended not for brothers but rather for enemies.

We are told to "make friends for ourselves by means of unrighteous mammon" [Lk. 16.9] so that "they may receive us into the eternal habitations"; since it does not say "send" but "receive," consider which group would rather be able to receive us, if we should make friends from our mammon: the Saint who will sit in judgment with the Judge over those who will hear "Come!" or those who will be told "Go!" [Mt. 25.34–41]? So by this authority the poor in spirit are to be chosen, for "theirs is the kingdom of heaven" [Mt. 5.3], and, I think, if they wish they can give it to us as it belongs to them. For who bestows on another what he does not have? And who is unable to bestow what belongs to him on anyone he wishes? I do not say this so as to urge that the ties of nature should be ignored in anyone, whether he is just or unjust, but so as to grind that saber-tooth of yours which mawls me so in a pestle of this sort.[9] For though I know that everyone should be given our goodwill because of our natural likeness, yet I think it should be given especially to the household of the faith [cf. Gal. 6.10], through whom it penetrates to the household of God also; and therefore I cannot believe anyone, not even an angel, who would tell me that it is more acceptable to God that our own property be given to those who will certainly be told "Go, accursed, into the eternal fire" [Mt. 25.41], rather than to those who will be told "Come you blessed of my Father, receive your kingdom" [Mt. 25.34], still less that what has been allotted to the latter by anyone else should, when entrusted to me, be taken away from the latter and given to the former—particularly as the Book of Wisdom makes a very clear statement about them: "Do not give them bread" [Eccli. 12.6]; and the apostle said of such people as they went around the houses, when they were able to lay their hands on any food: "If anyone will not work, let him not eat" [2 Th. 3.10–11].

4. What more? I see a great battle brewing for me on all sides. Urgently I must cry to the Lord: "Show me a sign of your favor that those who hate me may see and be put to shame because you, O Lord, have helped me and comforted me" [Ps. 85.17]. For certain individuals are hurling charges at me, either

believing them valid or more likely making them up.[10] Certain individuals are constantly blackening any good I seem to do with evil motives. But I think that those who, being undeniably perverse themselves, say malicious things whether fictitious or factual, are more tolerable than those who, while desiring to seem good, put a malicious interpretation on any good that appears in me and befoul white with black.[11]

But tell me carefully, friend, do you not think that the funds which are assigned to building or rebuilding (I do not say decorating) churches are in fact paid out to the poor? For who benefits from them? Not those who stand under the sky, are parched by the sun, are soaked by the rain, are chilled by frost? Which group comes into the church in higher proportion, the rich or the poor? Which do you think is better, to provide a house for thousands of people of both sorts, that protects them from all three elements, or to give a cheap garment to an individual? To offer to everybody tiles that grow old by centuries, stones as durable as the world itself, or to offer to an individual bread that will turn to manure? "May lying lips become dumb which speak iniquity against the righteous" [Ps. 30.19]; (but do not think that it is I that am here called *righteous* but He who said: "Woe to you who say good is bad" [Is. 5.20].)

Now, to demand from our friendship its due (a friendship which, I admit, you have always shown me better by giving than by counseling), I will advance a familiar argument (since I am sure that you well know what is to be advanced): since whatever is bestowed on the Church is sacred to the Lord's saints and belongs to the right of the priests, this I understand and interpret as follows: whatever is offered to the Lord, I say is sacred and reserved for the use not of any individuals but of the saints, those who either rest in our shrines or are especially venerated among us, and the "use" is the use of those who serve those saints, and because it is the priests who are most bound to serve them, whatever is bestowed ought properly to belong to the priests' right. The sacred canons command that it be divided into four parts:[12] one is allotted to the prelate's supply, another entrusted to his charge for the building or rebuilding of churches, a third likewise entrusted for the benefit of the poor, and the fourth reserved for the needs of the clergy. To whom do you think, pray, that it has been entrusted? If being a canon yourself you do not refuse to stand by the canonical rule, you will have to reply (I have no doubt): "The bishop has the power of disposing of all Church property."[13] And when it comes to alms for beggars, hospitality for travelers, and other duties of this sort, I think that Eugenius' opinion is quite clear where he says in the decretals: "All these are to be done by priests and deacons under the bishop's charge"[14]—but those are another matter.

5. To return to the point: leaving out the portion of the clergy and the supply reserved for the prelates, I want your advice on the two parts which remain.

Since he to whom Christ said, "If you love me, feed my sheep" [Jn. 21.15], has to feed his *whole* flock both spiritually and, if need be, in body also, and to this end the third part has been allotted; and since, thanks be to God, the country is not wracked by famine and there are more who can feed than need to be fed by charity, whereas the churches of this country everywhere have all been either utterly destroyed or in large part ruined either by the fires of the pagans [Hungarians] or by the neglect of pseudo-bishops; and since the third and fourth parts are to be buttressed by the first and second parts, if necessity requires; and since the second part greatly needs buttressing and such a necessity does require it of me, what, I ask, do you advise be done? Towards the third part I have countless helpers, to the fourth I have the clergy themselves looking out for themselves even beyond what is right and sufficient. To the second part I can use the words of Martha, saying, "Lord, do you not care" [Lk. 10.40] that all the parishioners leave me single-handed and without means to build and rebuild the churches of the diocese or, if that is not possible, to decorate them? Moreover, if I do anything, those who want to be thought my friends abuse me and declare that it would be better to squander it, which is like saying, "Vain is he who serves the Lord" [Mal. 3.14], or like preferring uncertainty to certainty, or favoring sinners above saints and affirming that God values the sinner's gluttony over the saint's glory—as you are doing when you say that it would be better for me to spend what I have in charity on those two, the poor and the clergy (who, thanks partly to their own endeavors, partly to the largesse of others, are not so very poor), and to neglect entirely that second part, the necessity of building and rebuilding churches—and that this is better you not only think but even say in public. What ears can tolerate to hear such wrong? This is not the advice of a friend but of an enemy.

6. Though, my friend, I rightly called you the chief supporter of all my enemies—the clergy who tear me apart are none other than rebels to the Lord himself—yet I am not angry that this is so since I well know that you are motivated by hatred not of me but of your own bishop. Except for those who aspire to the office of bishop, almost all the clergy agree that they would rather pay attention to the apostle when he says: "Not as domineering over the clergy" [1 Pet. 5.3], than when he says: "Command and teach this" [1 Tim. 4.11]; or to another who says: "Declare these things, exhort with all authority, let no one disregard you" [Tit. 2.15]; and: "Rebuke them sharply" [Tit. 1.13]; and other similar commands. If I quote them all, I know I can be countered with: "A fool puts forth all his anger" [Pr. 29.11]. For the privilege and honor of being bishop today is offered to none except the most powerful, the richest, the most aggressive—and therefore not a bishop but, so they murmur, a tyrant. All aim to have their bishops subject to themselves; all take it hard, when they

think of bishops, that the Lord says, "The disciple is not over his master" [Lk. 6.40]. Though they all find it very agreeable when they compel those below them to pay them honor, even honor that is not due, they do not listen closely to the words, "What you want men to do to you, do you do to them likewise" [Lk. 6.31], but love to hear "Fathers, do not provoke your sons to anger" [Eph. 6.4], and complain that I am not observing this when I demand of them what is God's or mine. They are deaf to the words: "Sons, obey your parents in everything" [Col. 3.20]. They hear "Convince" more readily than "Exhort" or "Rebuke" [2 Tim. 4.2]. They little care when the curse of Cham, who betrayed his father's nakedness,[15] is put upon them; they love it when any infamy, be it true or false, is attached to me. O woe is me (to apply the words particularly to myself), "Woe is me for the word spoken in Israel in my days, which shall make the ears of whoever hears it tingle deservedly" [1 Sam. 3.11].

7. After such accusations, so wicked, so foul and even contrary to my very age[16] (and I think you have been quite ready to listen to them), I shudder to say what heights of madness that rash Martianistic[17] rhetoric of yours has lately reached, or your pestilential group may be infected with this stench—as I think will certainly happen. For after all this, though the canons decreed that anyone daring even to go for service at court without my permission should be demoted, with unheard-of temerity he[18] went to that venal city (as Sallust calls it)[19] and buying there (as everything was bought in the old days) pseudo-apostolic letters of anathema, he used that sword to harry both me and my successors in such a way that if any bishop henceforth interfered concerning the property [res] of the clergy he would be damned with perpetual anathema (so they say). But since "properties" [res] are properly said to be abstract in substance, according to Donatus[20] who briefly defined a noun as "a part of speech signifying body or property" [res], what is there more particularly the property [res] of the clergy than their souls?

I have no doubt that here I will be challenged for using the testimony of a pagan author in a point of religion (for which, however, I rely on the support of the apostle, who in his letter to Titus used a pagan's words against empty talkers and deceivers [Tit. 1.10–13]), but you will not go unrebutted in turn. Though the persons of the clergy are body, yet the clerkship itself is incorporeal. If I abstain from all their property [res] I understand unwaveringly that just as I must neglect their bodies and the substance allotted for their expenditure, so also I must neglect their souls and the clerkship itself as well, since of course they are "property" [res]. Since, I say, the properties themselves, that is, their very persons, consist most of all in their souls, as I have shown; then, if their souls are forbidden to me by this anathema more particularly than their other properties, I take it that I have clearly been entirely deprived of any care of them, together with their property. So give me some advice here if you can. If I ignore the anathema of the apostolic see, I lay a bridge of bad example for everyone, a thing not to be thought unimportant; if not, in no way can I even sing a mass for them, since they are properties [*res*] and the singing of the mass means the greatest interference with their properties [*res*].

If I do not celebrate the mass for them, I clearly see that I am not even their priest, still less their bishop—if I am indeed bishop of Verona as was once proclaimed in the synod at Pavia.[21] For *bishop* is said to be translated "overseer."[22] Whom do *I* oversee, since I see myself underling to all? These? Who think nothing of being trigamous, though even monogamy would be open adultery since marriage is illegal, or even quadrigamous, for shame, and these are priests and deacons—though a layman who is bigamous cannot even become a cleric? These, who though they read that commerce is totally forbidden them, rashly engage in usury? Who have so forsworn their faith that they do not even bother to deny that they have many times perjured themselves? Who appropriate to themselves the revenues of the Church, both the general revenues and their own particular ones, so that all the rest excepting them, who stand above all in the manner of the Scribes and Pharisees [Lk. 18.11–12], toil dreadfully under the scourge of hunger, while I watch from below and can give no help? Who fight among themselves in the womb of the Church with their fists or even gloves (like Entellus' in Vergil,[23] so to speak) and do not fear to violate the temple of the living God [1 Cor. 3.17] (as recently happened on the instigation of your Martianistic rhetoric) to such an extent that, unless there is immediate reconciliation, the law will forbid the solemn mass to be celebrated in it, even in this very Easter that is upon us? One of them, a deacon, most arrogantly had a cathedral priest beaten like his own servant in his presence before the very doors of the Church. In sum, am I *overseer* of him who went to Rome without my permission and arranged that I be absolutely forbidden to question such behavior, with anathema hurled in my face?

8. To leave entirely uncorrected abuses like these, and countless others no less serious, because power to correct them is denied—is this, I ask, to *oversee*? To have no power to oversee, is that to be a bishop? For a bishop not to have a place in the episcopal cathedral, is that legal and commendable? If to this unprecedented situation I add something unexpected, though I am sure that you will challenge me, yet know that I will do this without delay (unless God diverts me), even though you may think it very foolishly done (for you are, after all, a man of flesh who does not perceive what belongs to God's spirit). But of course if God allows it it would not be foolishly done. So though you can boast that Rather has thus been vanquished, do not, I warn you, crow over Antony[24] thinking that he can be beaten in this way; for if it could happen it undoubtedly

would have happened already and everyone knows that there is a difference between a real man and a weakling.

But[25] lest, my good friend (as you would have it believed) my invective
against you go on forever, I wish to make an end of it here, knowing that it
is best to try to avoid the habit of long-windedness; otherwise I might happen
to incur the sin of abusiveness, which is a far worse fault—particularly if one
unpardonably overlooks the rights of charity and overleaps the bounds of truth,
by joining fact to rumor, by bringing in false slanders from every source, being
unable to find true ones; and since meanness of intellect prevents the making
up of quasi-probable fictions, changing white for black and black for white (for
which may God pursue him, Who threatens woe to him for such falsification
[Is. 5.20], as the psalm declares), thinking . . . and incurably burning himself
up as though with cautery in envy of another's happiness. This may the ineffable
pity of Christ deign to avert from both of us, who with the Father and the
Holy Spirit has both the power to do this and the majesty of reigning for ever
and ever.

54

CC Opera Minora 165–67   Verona Easter 968

[He urges his enemies to examine themselves and be reconciled to God. The
four sermons which follow all relate to his feud with the clergy.]

Sermon II on the Pasch

1. Though the prophet enjoins all on this day to rejoice and be glad [Ps. 117.24],
I do not greatly fear criticism if, after my own fashion, I interject a small amount
of grief into my address. But away with the critic, for an inner counselling voice
forbids me not to be sad. For as Tobias replied to the angel, so can I, to anyone
urging me to be glad, not inappropriately reply: "What sort of joy will I have,
who sit in darkness and see not the light of the sky?" [Tob. 5.12]. For it is
not inappropriate to call this feast *the light of the sky*, since the psalm says of
it: "Let the heavens rejoice and the earth be glad" [Ps. 95.11] (not that earth
which the serpent, persuader of evil, was told "You will eat all the days of your
life" [Gen. 3.14], but rather the earth mentioned earlier in the words, "Let the
earth bring forth green grass" [Gen. 1.11], and the other things which accord-

ing to the literal interpretation are good enough, but according to the mystical interpretation are assuredly better). With what temerity, then, do I state that I rightly share in the joy of this day, who, walled in by a cloud of sinners, am not able to see the light of the sky, that is, Him who lights the sky? For since we know that these forty days which have now passed were instituted for this purpose, that we might in them cleanse our minds and be able to see the Sacred Day of the new days itself and to celebrate it with joy, and since we have far from done this, what joy, what gladness can we have?

For the holy Apostle says in commendation of this same joy, as you have heard read: "And so let us feast" [1 Cor. 5.8]. What did he mean? "And so let us take up in exaltation the Body and Blood of Christ himself who was sacrificed for us." Then let us do so.

2. But what if we are unable to do so worthily and justly? He continues: "Not in the old ferment" — that is, the swollen state of previous sin — "nor in the ferment of evil and wickedness" — the evil of wanting to do harm to any Christian, the wickedness of even trying to do so. Then how? "In the unleavened bread of sincerity and truth." Sincerity is purity, that is, having nothing except what is visible. Truth, Pilate asked to be defined, but did not stay for an answer [Jn. 18.38]; for that he did not deserve to be glad about it. Whoever, therefore, has neither truth in his mouth nor purity in his heart, think how he has dared to eat the flesh of Christ, especially since the apostle quite openly forbids this, saying directly: "Whosoever eats of the body of the Lord unworthily eats damnation to himself" [1 Cor. 11.29]. And how can he rejoice today and be glad who is about to eat damnation instead of salvation and death instead of life?

This, I say, this is what has compelled me almost this whole Lent to exclaim that "laying aside all malice, and all guile, and hypocrisy, and envy" [1 Pet. 2.1], we should all strive to turn ourselves to Christ's peace, that is, true peace. And because very many do not know how to do this, I urged you, setting forth as it were a standard, that those who remembered that someone had wronged them should remember His words: "If you bring your gift to the altar, and there remember that your brother has something against you, leave there your gift before the altar and go your way; first be reconciled to your brother, and then come and offer your gift" [Mt. 5.23–24]. But those who have been wronged by someone, if he has sincerely asked for pardon, should not forget the Lord saying: "When you stand praying, forgive, if you have ought against any, that your Father, also, which is in heaven may forgive you your trespasses. But if you do not forgive, neither will your Father which is in heaven forgive your trespasses" [Mk. 11.25–26].

3. But, for shame! I have seen certain people (and would that it had not been those who ought in particular to set a good example for others) despise this ad-

vice to such an extent that they did not cease both to hold out the noose of destruction even for him who was putting the sacred bread in their mouths, saying: "The body of our Lord Jesus Christ benefit you for eternal life," and, like Pilate in the same days, to cry: "Crucify him" [Jn. 19.6], forgetting that He said: "Woe to the impious betrayer!"—and woe to their confederates today in His Church! Some of these today I have instructed, by our Lord's authority, to stop doing this; and if they continue to do it, they will do so at their own peril. For most learned Jerome says clearly: "Let it be chance to have sinned once. Why do you sin deliberately and often?"[1] For unless they watch out, they must fear that it will happen to them as happened to those of whom it is said: "But while their meat was yet in their mouths, the wrath of God came upon them" [Ps. 77.30–31], and as was said the day before about Judas, betrayer of the Lord, whose imitators that holy one whose words we just recalled did not hesitate to say are still in the Church: "And after the sop Satan entered into him" [Jn. 13.27]—that is, by the doing of the wicked deed which had been effected in him by the impetus of Satan's wicked will. For if they had listened to the apostle saying: "Let a man examine himself, and so let him eat of that bread and drink of that cup" [1 Cor. 11.28] (that is, let him decide in what state of will he is to be, whether of sinning or correction, of harming another or helping him, in hatred or in brotherly love), if, I say, they had pondered this with a view to their salvation, they would have avoided taking the sacrament, at any rate from the hand of him they hated, so as not to be such open imitators of Judas.

But because with God conversion is neither difficult nor slow, people like this should not despair, I advise, since to be sure the Jews' Pasch is at a definite time, but the Christians' Pasch at any time, but particularly on the Lord's day of sharing in the sacraments and conversion from the worse to the better. For since Pasch [Passover] is interpreted as a *crossing-over*, at whatever time, day, hour, moment someone crosses over from the devil to Christ, from vice to virtue, from dark to light, he truly observes a solemn Passover. For since the Lord says in the Psalms: "The remainder of wrath will make the feast day for you" [Ps. 75.11], someone makes a solemn Pasch in the Lord if he abandons the evil he contemplated and takes care to do that which the Lord himself enjoined.

[Nos. 55 and 56 are placed after no. 65.]

57

CC Opera Minora 171–76   Verona Easter 968

[An invective against his enemies leads to his account of the origins of their quarrel; he urges them to be reconciled with God and to make a true Passover.]

Sermon on the Octave of the Pasch

1. "For my sinning cometh before I eat," blessed Job is reported to have said, adding: "For the thing which I greatly feared is come upon me, and that which I was afraid of has happened" [Job 3.24–25].

To refer this to myself, who am as far distant from Job as the air is from the ethereal heaven: I am sorry, I admit, that what I feared and warned you about on the Lord's day[2] has happened to some of you. For I am afraid that there has happened to some of you, for shame, what the psalmist once said of the Jews: "But while their meat was yet in their mouths, the wrath of God came upon them" [Ps. 77.30–31]. For "after the morsel, Satan entered into them" [Jn. 13.27] through their evil actions (Satan, who for a long time already had been in them through their evil intentions), just as though he [i.e., Rather] who offered them the morsel had said: "What you do, do quickly" [Jn. 13.27]; and from that moment on they [his enemies] have not ceased to do as quickly as possible what they had already been planning, particularly throughout this Lent.

They had been earnestly warned by word and example to be reconciled to God and the brothers they had hurt and, in sincere desire to be reconciled, not to despise this warning. Yet they did not even care to imitate those who once said, "Not on the feast day" [Mt. 26.5], but instead, openly proceeded against him (would that no one knew that this was *me*) with all the endeavors of treachery and all the falsest accusations, through whatever agents they could, making up such lies about him as no one could believe except those who happened to have done the same or similar themselves. They have bribed two of the rulers of the state,[3] so it is reported. Would that one of them (I have often quoted "He hath delivered Israel out of the hand of Pharaoh" [Ex. 18.10] to refer to him, sufficiently recognizable because the names are declined with the same inflections), would that he were such in name and nobility that I could here and now claim quite openly that it is I who suffer all this: he, leading them round the whole episcopal palace,[4] fraudulently changing the meaning of my words, not scrupling to alter the passive to the active, fabricated a story that I was contriving what was, in fact, being done *to* me, as though providing them with a motive to keep shouting "Crucify him" [Jn. 19.6], though using other words.

For though in these three years I have spent almost forty librae (according to those who were in charge of the work) on the restoration of this episcopal palace, I have been expelled from it by them, and the house has remained without a tenant. Yet the same people who are upbraiding me for this do not stop looting it, while those visiting there[5] keep violently wrecking it, as the evidence shows, while I, to be sure, am not strong enough to resist either group, either the thieves because I am at a distance, or those visiting there because I am absent and seem far inferior in power, since they are known to be returning from the imperial army or on their way to it. Hiring inspectors, they lyingly accuse *me* of destroying it — as though it could be credible that I myself would destroy or willingly allow to be destroyed what I have built at such expense of my own! Lodging there, they abuse it, with such show of authority that if any of my staff, whose business it is, come there to inspect it, they at once seize him, beat him savagely, and lock him up.

2. Though I am the sorry *victim* of all this, these slanderers change the meaning of my words, as I have already said, and claim that I am doing what in fact I am having done to me, and throw in the most outrageous lies that anyone has ever been able to concoct about another. What senseless madness of the villains! What baseless lies! What devil's cunning, which knows even this day to speak through serpents! If the emperor [Otto I] were not my master and if I were equal in power to him, I would be able somehow to defend my house and property against his officers; and if these others in their treachery had not driven me from the house, I would be able to guard it against their thefts with my presence day and night. But as it is, the emperor is my master, and to fight against the officers of my master, even if I could, is not only disloyal but even, so to speak, apostatic — for he revolts from God who is a rebel against the earthly master appointed by God; for it is written that "whoever resists power" (that is, power put over him by God) "resists the ordinance of God" [Rom. 13.2].

Since, then, I cannot resist one group, and the other group follows the devil's example and keeps trying to do me some hurt and distress, even without advantage to themselves, what can I do about either? No action is possible.

When I was administering the sacred morsel to them with a hand which they, at the same time, wanted cut off, and was saying: "The body of our Lord Jesus Christ lead you to everlasting life," someone should have shouted at them what once someone had shouted at the stoners of St. James the apostle (who was called the brother of our Lord, as those close in kin are said to be "brothers" even today), saying: "Hold, what do you do? This righteous one whom you are stoning is praying for you" [Gal. 1.19]. For I have behaved righteously in my relations with them (though God knew my other offences which were unknown to them), since I planned good for them in exchange for evil; but they planned to requite me evil for all the innumerable favors I gratuitously did them. This would not have been so surprising if they were complaining of any injury I had done them — though for this too I ought previously to have been sued in all humility according to the decision of the canons.

3. But to dispute about things which are no business of theirs, to say such things about me as no one could believe without offence to God, to have me belittled in everything, to corrupt whatever is good in me by evil interpretation, to search out by studious investigation any faults of mine past or present and eagerly point them out to others — what else is this than publicly to bear witness that they are false not only to me but also to him who in his charity appointed me, most pious Caesar? Alas, "what a terrible state of madness," as someone once said; "he who suffers violence is bound the more."[6] For the stream of their evil action flows down from them to me, and I am accused of muddying it like the lamb in the story.[7]

A certain young king had a band of young men and a multitude of wise old counsellors. The young men were unable to do what young men would, as the wise kept repressing their folly, so they hatched a plot for each of them to kill his own father. So it was done; but one of them, who could not bear to commit so great a crime, said to his wife: "If I kill my father, I am very much afraid that we will die if the plot miscarries." His wife agreed to save the life of her father-in-law, and they hid him away secretly in a cell where they looked after him. The father told the son that if he should be asked by the king for advice, he should make no answer until he had referred the question to himself. Complying, therefore, the young man became so capable a king's counsellor that all his comrades began to envy him. So they approached the king and pointed out that unless he put him to death, he would surely destroy them all. The king was distressed, but agreed, and asked them on what pretext he could do it. "Tell him to come tomorrow," they said, "bringing none with him except one servant, one friend, and one enemy." Terrified by this order, the young man went to his father to ask advice. His father said: "Don't be upset, but prepare a very good meal for us and I'll give you some excellent advice." So after dinner his father said to him in secret: "You have a fine ass; take him with you laden with bread, wine, and meat. You have one little she-dog well-trained to defend your property; take her with you. Take also your wife along with you. Offer the ass for your servant, the dog for your friend, and your wife for your enemy."

The young man did so, took up the ass and brought the dog with him; nor did he leave behind his wife. He went to the unhappy king and asked him to view what he had brought, saying: "This one standing here loaded is my servant, that other is my friend, and this third is my enemy, than whom I hope I have no one more hostile to me." Hearing this, the wife flared up: "Do you pronounce me your enemy? Just deserts, indeed, for one who obeyed you and saved your father's life against the king's command."

The young man turned to the king and said: "Does it not seem to your majesty that this woman is my enemy?" "Yes, indeed," he replied, "but I want to know whether what she says is true."

"It is true," he said.

"Thanks be to God," cried the king in great joy. "Run then, quick, and bring him speedily back to me."

He did so. The king was given back his best counsellor, the young man was freed from the danger of imminent death, and the wife was exposed as not loving the young man, though she would have been thought his dearest friend were it not proved otherwise.

Applying the story to myself: if I had not stirred these people up a little, I would not have been able to know them with such proof, though I had always had this suspicion about them. However, may God yet deign to convert them and show them the true way of peace and charity and set them walking upon it, or it may happen that we too perish together at the same time for such offences, seized suddenly by vengeance (God forbid), as the kite in the story is said to have seized the frog and the mouse together.[8]

4. But this whole argument must be passed over, I think, as it may seem not so much a sermon as an invective against those plotting against my life and position. My pastoral address should now be aimed at counselling all in common, as much my supporters, that is, as my enemies.

But first, of course, I am bound to show both why and when this disagreement arose between us, though I have done so often enough already. To answer the last first, and in brief: it certainly did not start recently but dates from the day of my ordination. It has now been brought into the open because the support of the emperor's presence decreeing only what is just and the synod ... [*lacuna*].[9] Why our disagreement arose has frequently been shown by both sides, not only in speech but also in writing. Though the words are numerous, the sum of the matter appears to be this: that I lay down that the law of God should be followed, and they, that the lore of men and the ways of the wicked should be our guide. For is not he truly wicked who shares what has been given in common to him and to me in such a way that I become very poor from it while he becomes very rich? If I were to condone this by my silence, or rather by my approval, I would clearly be denying God by abandoning truth for no other reason than because of that friendship which they wanted to have with me. He who urges me not to worry about that must be an enemy of my soul; by no means should I be that one.

5. That is a brief summary of the matter. Now I urge each one of you with me to examine by himself how he has behaved in this sacred Pasch (that is, in these eight days), and whether he has acted in such a way that he could answer "Amen" without danger when the priest says: "Grant, we beseech thee, Almighty God, that we who have spent the Paschal feast in veneration may hold it in our ways and life as thy gift."[10] Therefore, let each ask himself whether the priest has spoken truly about him — that is, whether he has taken the Body and Blood of the Lord in the unleavened bread of sincerity and truth [1 Cor. 5.8]; and if, that is, in his heart he has planned evil for no one during the Pasch; and if he has not wittingly said anything about the behavior of any man, except what was true (otherwise, while the food of Christ's Body was still in his mouth, he has made the anger of the Lord God descend upon him [Ps. 77.30–31] through the vice of hatred or envy or greed or avarice or extravagance); and if, "after the morsel, he did not allow Satan to enter into his soul" [Jn. 13.27] (that is, if he did not rush to put into effect that evil which he had previously planned); and finally, if "on the feast day" (that is, in these eight days and up till the time when we sang: "This is the day which the Lord has made" [Ps. 117.24]) he has neither polluted himself by adultery or any uncleanness, nor wickedly harmed any of his brothers.

Finding none of these faults in himself, he may congratulate himself on having passed the feast of the Lord's Pasch reverently, and may humbly reply, "Amen." And he should not cease with hand, tongue, and heart to pray that God's pity deign to allow him to stay that way in his person and life.

But if he finds otherwise in himself, as I am afraid is the case, he should repent that he has not tried even to follow the example of those who said: "Not on the feast day" [Mt. 26.5] — that is, just as they feared a tumult of the people if they arrested the Lord, so he, fearing the anger of the Lord if he violated the most holy feast, should have earnestly tried with God's help to refrain, at least on these eight days, from wantonness of any sort, and to restrain himself from any hurt to his brother. So he should regret that he has followed the example of Judas the betrayer, and earned damnation; and he should turn, not as Judas to the noose of desperation, but as Peter to tears of repentance, and, abandoning the evil things he has planned, he should hasten to pass the feast day in the Lord, while there is yet time. For thus he will be able to recover the Pasch which he has lost and make a good Passover to be sure, and to placate the anger of God (for, as we have already said, the Jews' Pasch is at a fixed time, the Christians' at all times — or rather, at any hour at which each man is converted and crosses over from vice to virtue, from the devil to Christ; for this is what is called the *Pasch* in Greek, the *Phase* in Hebrew, the *Lord's Passover* in Latin, which we must never cease to do in crossing from death to life by His example), with the help of Him who, with the Father and the Holy Spirit, ever reigns as God, world without end, Amen.

58

CC Opera Minora 179–81   Verona after Easter 968

[Rather points out that his enemies did not, in fact, make a true Passover as he had admonished them to do in Sermon 2 on the Pasch, no. 54 above. He urges them to beware of Judas's example.]

෴

Sermon after the Pasch

1. The Lord says that at the Last Judgment He will say: "Out of your own mouth will I judge you, wicked servant" [Lk. 19.22]. But to whom? He shows by adding: "You *knew* that I was an austere man," and the rest. By this statement it can be certain that a greater penalty awaits the man who *knows* than him who does not know. Therefore, those who know the good but do evil have cause to fear, greatly fear, I repeat, particularly if they also preach that good. Some, while speaking the good, do not know what they are saying (and so they do not really say it). For instance, many read the Gospels and recite the apostles as a duty entrusted to them; fulfilling after a fashion what has been assigned them, they act the part not of a teacher, but of an obeyer. They are not judged out their own mouth, since they do not understand what they are saying, but they are only censured if they do not do it.

Therefore, wretched on both counts are the worldly teachers, wretched, I repeat, and accursed, if they either do not understand what they are teaching, or teach what they do not practice, and are judged out of their mouth alone. For if they know the punishments of hell and do not make others aware of them, they will be guilty for all whom they ought to have taught if those fall into sins out of ignorance. And if they have pointed them out to others but have not steered clear of them themselves, who is more wretched, who more stupid, I ask, than they? If, after showing others the fount of life, they themselves die of thirst, who ought to grieve for them?

I have just cried out with the apostle, I have cried out—if only I were not to be judged out of my own mouth for that as for much else, instead of freed as the prophet promised—I cried out for myself and for you; may God's pity grant that I did not cry in vain. I have cried out, however; I have cried out: "Christ our Passover is sacrificed for us" [1 Cor. 5.7]. Would that He had been sacrificed for *us* as for the apostle. For Christ was sacrificed for the apostle who gave Him worthy thanks; we must be careful that Christ was not sacrificed without — heaven forbid! — worthy thanks on our part for so great a blessing. This is what the apostle means by the words: "Whosoever shall eat the Body of the Lord unworthily shall be guilty of the Body and Blood of the Lord" [1 Cor. 11.27]; that is, the guilt of the pouring of the blood of Jesus Christ will be imputed to him if he dares to drink the blood that the Jews shed unworthily — that is, if he himself is such in action as they were in faith.

2. Then I continued: "Therefore, let us keep the feast, not with the old leaven, neither with the leaven of malice and wickedness, but with the unleavened bread of sincerity and truth" [1 Cor. 5.8]. I explained all this so that I thought I had satisfied even the young. But would that I, too, had done what I urged others, and had cast off the ferment of ill will and noxious act, which I had previously had, by genuine reconciliation and productive penitence.

I said ironically:[11] "How well can that person rejoice and be glad today, who is going to receive judgment instead of salvation, and death instead of life!" adding the pertinent testimony of the psalmist about the Jews then — and would it were not pertinent now! — "While their meat was yet in their mouths, the wrath of God came upon them" [Ps. 77.30–31]. I pointed out that Satan had entered into Judas (as the Gospel says [Jn. 13.27]) after the morsel through his evil action (and Satan had already been in him through his evil will), and we had to be afraid that something similar might happen to us — namely, that some sin that we had avoided because of the holy sacrifice which we had to consume in the Pasch, we would rush to do as soon as that sacrifice had been consumed — even before the eighth day — forgetting that the people trying to arrest the Lord had also shouted: "Not on the feast day" [Mt. 26.5].

O foolish, mad impatience, not strong enough to tolerate the wrongs of enemies nor the attractions of vices! For if you have driven us, deadly one, to excess in any of these, you have compelled us, alas, to violate the Lord's Pasch. We ought to have considered as witnesses of God against us those who have bravely borne both the terrible tortures of enemies and the extended temptations of their own flesh in either sex. What has stopped us from following their example is not God's grace on the point of abandoning us, but our own weakness, the lust that wantonly assails our body and the sinner's hand inflated by pride that excites us [cf. Ps. 35.12]. And we have fallen here by perpetrating wickedness of this sort, expelled from God's grace for our vainglory, unable, wretches, to persist in good. Therefore, I have to admit without hope of correction, that we are judged by God out of our own mouth [Lk. 19.22], since we both knew this as certain and yet scorned to eschew it, since our proud contempt overrode our fear of God. And so, handed over to perdition for our own just deserts (not from God's neglect), and damned by our own mouths, we must be doomed eternally, unless God's pity swiftly help us.

3. What are we to do if this is so, brothers? It is so; indeed, it is so, alas, it is. Give me your counsel in return, I beg. Say at least what I have said, expound what I have expounded, urge what I have urged (for I have found nothing else to do), namely, that because we are like Judas in this, we should from now on beware of his example, not rushing with him to the deadly noose of desperation, but rather with Peter to life-giving tears of conversion, asking for the Lord's mercy; so that, helped by his merits, we may do what he did and obtain what he obtained. And so, by the Lord's turning to us and regarding us with His mercy, we may be able to turn to Him with weeping, and thus be able somehow to recover His grace, and at some time to celebrate His Passover more truly than we have ever done, and be able to pass over with His help from the devil to Himself and not turn back again in the future. This may He deign to grant us, most unworthy souls, Who deigned to be our Pasch that He might reconcile us to God the Father by His blood [Rom. 5.10], and, wrested from the power of darkness, make us a people acceptable to Himself, pursuers of good works, Who with the Father and the Holy Spirit lives and reigns as God, world without end. Amen.

59

CC Opera Minora 185–89   Verona Ascension 968

[A homily on confession and abstaining from sin. "Brothers, abandon the evil to which you are inured."]

∽

Sermon II on the Ascension

1. In almost every detail the quality of our ways and of our doctrine falls below the standards of the ancient fathers; and there is a great discrepancy also in this point, that in feasts such as this, in making their address the fathers started with the matter of the Gospel and then turned the listeners' attention to consideration of the feast itself. Then, in a homily—at which they were more competent than we are—succinct in its opening, prolonged at its end, more ur-

gently than we do, they exhorted their listeners to refrain from evil and stand on what is well-pleasing to God.

Our practice, on the other hand, is to observe at the very beginning of our address what the psalmist tells us: "Let us come before His presence in confession" [Ps. 94.2] — of our sins, that is — and what Isaiah says: "Declare first your transgressions that you may be justified" [Is. 43.26]. *Justified*, I repeat, not *judged*. "For if we should judge ourselves, we would not be judged" [1 Cor. 11.31], says the apostle — that is: if we ourselves were truthfully to accuse ourselves, we would not be condemned by the Lord. That person truly accuses himself who says frankly what he remembers he has done and who does not get angry with anyone else for saying the same thing about him; he truly accuses himself if he execrates the evil which he confesses and strives with all his might to correct it; if he fears to repeat it later; and if he is wholesomely concerned about it. If he does otherwise, the Lord says to his soul: "How exceedingly base you have become going the same ways over again" [Jer. 2.36]. Going the same ways over again is also condemned in the sentence: "In your prayer do not repeat a word" [Eccli. 7.15] — that is, do not do again what you have confessed, so that it becomes necessary for you to confess that sin a second time.

For when we acknowledge and confess that we have gravely sinned, we acknowledge also the punishments to which we are liable for doing so. If even the fear of these does not deter us from committing evil, we invite the accusation: "Out of your own mouth will I judge you, wicked servant" [Lk. 19.22]. But as for carnal sin — if we are guilty of this in particular — we forbid ourselves to consecrate the offerings at all, unless we pretend that we do not know the contents of the Neocaesarian Council, c. 9.[12]

2. Since this is so, what can I say of myself, what can I even think? For if before speaking to you I come before the face of the Lord in confession [Ps. 94.2] — that is, if before I come to tell His judgment I truly accuse myself — by what licence do I consecrate the bread to be offered to you? If I do not, how do I ever start my speech? Or rather, what can I ever say to you as I ought? In fact, about having joy I can say nothing else than what Tobias replied to the angel: "What joy will there be for me, who sit in darkness and see not the light of heaven?" [Tob. 5.12]. For that I sit in darkness, I myself am witness for myself, who do not realize as I ought (my mind's eye being dimmed) that I am proceeding into the fire. The *light of heaven* is Christ in His clarity, by whom the angels are illuminated above, the saints below, the former in possessing Him, the latter in desiring Him, both in enjoying Him in communion with Him. Do you think, then, that anyone who is not now illuminated in desiring Him can then be illuminated in possessing Him? What joy can such a man have in any feast except an entirely empty joy?

3. This today, brothers, is the greatest feast, the greatest. But it is no feast for those who are either unwilling or unable to see the light of the sky, no feast, I repeat. However, since today truly is the greatest feast, the feast of the Lord's Ascension, how could the bishop, albeit lacking in eloquence, yet prating with a modicum of experience, be allowed to keep silent? To what lord does this feast belong, I ask? To Christ, of course, and to Christ for this reason: He deigned to be made man for us. For the psalmist sings of Him: "You love righteousness and hate wickedness; therefore, God has anointed you with the oil of exultation above your fellows" [Ps. 44.8]. What "righteousness"? That righteousness by which He thought it right that a creature should serve Him who had created it. What "wickedness"? That with which man served the devil, man who had been created to serve God. For that reason, therefore, God anointed Christ with the oil of gladness; that is, He endued Him with that mercy which would make the angels rejoice for the reconciliation of the human race, shut off from their company by the treachery of the devil. By that same mercy, some of the sons of the devil were going to be adopted as sons of God, that is, they were going to be fellows with Him who, not by adoption but by nature, was the Son of God, and so it is said that "He was anointed above His fellows," because to others the same grace of the Holy Spirit was given to a certain degree, but in Him "dwelleth all the fulness of the Godhead bodily" [Col. 2.9]—that is, fully— since God so totally filled Him, assuming body for us, that with both mind and flesh equally filled with God from two natures and in two natures, He is not two but one Lord, Jesus Christ, the true, as Father and the Spirit, God in everything, and with the Three not three but one everlasting God.

If God had not mercifully put on our flesh, He would not have raised our flesh to heaven; if He had not raised it to heaven, He would not have sanctified this day for us; and so this feast is Christ's, brothers, but not omitting His fellows. For these He took with Him to heaven, and also—wonderful to tell!— those not yet born on earth.

4. Therefore, since all the cycles of feasts have been instituted for Christ and for Christ's fellows, let anyone who wishes to have part in any of them strive to do what I, alas, have neglected to do. For though I had often exhorted you in the days preceeding these Feasts[13] to "endeavor to keep the unity of the Spirit in the bond of peace" [Eph. 4.3] and to forgive each other "if any man have a quarrel against anyone" [Col. 3.13], so that, coming to eat the flesh of the Lamb of God, we might be shown to have celebrated the Lord's Pasch "not in the ferment of evil and wickedness, but in the unleavened bread of sincerity and truth" [1 Cor. 5.8], this I myself who urged it have not done with the same earnestness with which I urged it.

The most sacred day of the feast of the Lord arrived; we read what the apostle said; I urged that this warning be observed, namely, that we should not take the Lord's Body to our own damnation [1 Cor. 11.29].[14] But for shame, there were some present who took the holy morsel from a hand which they were wanting cut off; there was one present[15] who wished he had deserted those to whom he was giving the morsel. And alas, with what deadly ferment both groups were swollen! Though I had told certain individuals to abstain even from legitimate intercourse in this Lent, so that, purified, they might merit to receive the Lord's sacrifice in the Pasch, some, after taking the sacrifice, were unable (woe to them) to refrain from adulterous intercourse even till the Lord's Octave. We can be certain that what we have often sung in the psalm applies to these, namely, that when after the morsel Satan entered into them, as into Judas [Jn. 13.27] (that is, the unclean spirit who was thought to be driven out only by fasting, with the other seven [Lk. 11.26]) "while their meat was yet in their mouths, the wrath of God came upon them" [Ps. 77.30–31], since they were most wretchedly detected to have been violators, not observers, of so important a feast. Let them choose, therefore, what to do. If they persist in their desperation, that is, in repeating the same sin, they are strangled by their own doing in the noose of Judas. If they imitate the tears of Peter, they win pardon; if they win pardon, they follow Christ in heaven, as now in love, so later in very reality. If they merit neither of these two, they should know that this feast is for God and for angels and for men of goodwill [Lk. 2.14] (as we sing), but that they are entirely without a part in it.

5. Don't let them flatter themselves by mentioning that sentence of the Lord's: "He that believeth and is baptized shall be saved" [Mk. 16.16]. They should know that, though most truly spoken (as uttered by the mouth of Truth), this is true only for those to whom it applies. "For these signs," He continues, "shall follow them that believe: in my name they shall cast out devils," etc. If anyone recognizes these signs in himself, understanding them figuratively,[16] he may safely rejoice for his salvation. Whoever does not, I suggest, should tremble and know that nothing will do any good unless he earnestly try not only to *believe God* but also to *believe in God*. But do not hasten, Christ, I pray, to utter: "Out of your own mouth will I judge you, wicked servant" [Lk. 19.22]. Put off the blow, I pray, merciful one, suspend the punishment, most holy one; say, I beg, merciful one, to the pruners of my life: "Let it alone this year also, till I shall dig around it and dung it" [Lk. 13.8]. For perhaps I will be able to improve sometime with the help of your grace. Still standing incorrigible in desperate ingratitude, while I do not wet my eyes with the tears of conversion, but throttle the throat of my mind with the cord of deadly procrastination and wicked deterioration day to day, I descend into hell living [Ps. 54.16; Num. 16.30], that is, not ignorant, as many, but in full knowledge and, moreover, not con-

cealing it. Hence, with good reason, I fear that I will hear the sentence, in company with those who say good and do evil: "Out of your own mouth will I judge you, wicked servant."

I tell others, Lord, about the severity of your punishments; I know that you are omnipresent, yet I do not shudder to say or do things that shame your sight. What, Lord, can I do? I would flee if I could flee anywhere; but this is impossible, and so, on the urging of your true mouthpiece, Augustine, I flee in terror from you to you, that is, from justice to mercy.[17] As you consider my acts that dishonor you, Lord, so consider, I pray, what is necessary for me, freeing me from deadly stubbornness, which compels me so monstrously to transgress your commands. For unless I am quickly snatched from it, I await eternal damnation, though ignorant of your intention about me. For the paths of man are not his own, but of your power alone, who does not condemn unjustly those whom you have created kindly.

Brothers, what you hear about me from my own mouth, fear for yourselves also. Abandon, post-haste, the evils to which you are inured. Turn yourselves to unaccustomed good while there is time; steer clear of hell; climb to heaven in your longing; strive to hurry there, where Christ is sitting at the right hand of God, relying on His help. Consider carefully that the hour has come for you either to ascend there or to fall downwards, but not to stay here any longer; otherwise it may unexpectedly happen (may heaven prevent it!) that you be seized and dragged where no one can help you [Ps. 49.22]. Which, may He deign to avert from us all, who came into this world to save sinners, Jesus Christ our Lord, who with the Father and the Holy Spirit lives and reigns as God for ever and ever. Amen.

60

CC Opera Minora 193–97   Verona Pentecost 968

[A homily on love and hate, with his enemies specifically in mind: "He lies who says that he loves God, if he hates his neighbor."]

⟨∿⟩

Sermon II on Pentecost

1. Again, brothers, what am I to do now? Shall I be silent or speak? If I stay silent, I am afraid that I may harm some of you. If I speak, I am afraid

that I shall be judged from my own mouth [Lk. 19.22]. But though this fear may discourage me from speaking, neither the duty of my office nor the consideration of the magnitude of such a feast allows me to keep silent.

For today is the Pentecost of the Pasch, the feast of feasts, to be sure, just as a certain song is called the Song of Songs, like a great sea into which flows the totality of feasts, in fact, the source of all spiritual joys. We shall therefore rejoice. How not? Let us rejoice, be glad and exult: but if we do so rightly, we rejoice in God, more especially in the Holy Spirit, whose feast this day is, inseparable to be sure from the Father and the Son. For who can refrain from rejoicing except one who is empty of that Holy Spirit? And who is that if not he who lacks the good of charity [caritas]? "For the love [caritas] of God," says the apostle, "is shed abroad in our hearts by the Holy Spirit which is given unto us" [Rom. 5.5]. Did you hear? I know that you heard, but would that you had heard it with the ears of your minds as well as the ears of your bodies. But you did hear, nonetheless.

Is there any other evidence which shows that whoever has charity has the Holy Spirit? Let your memory now run back to those words which a short while ago were recited from the Acts of the Apostles: "And when the day of Pentecost was fully come," he who wrote it says; and the rest, until you come to the place where he says: "And there appeared unto them cloven tongues like as of fire, and it sat upon each of them, and they were all filled with the Holy Spirit and began to speak" [Acts 2.1–4]. What? I ask. The greatness of God, the salvation of the multitude that were confounded, as it says there. And what else is charity [caritas] than the love of God, the love of one's neighbor? Therefore, out of love for God they praised God, out of love for their neighbor they urged people to believe in God. How? "As the Spirit gave them utterance," that is, as charity, which raged in their hearts like a fire, compelled them to speak. Why had they not done this before? Let the Gospel tell: "For the Holy Spirit was not yet given"—that is, not yet sent from heaven in such fullness (though it was not lacking to the holy men of the Old Testament, and when the Lord was upon earth, it had already been given to the holy apostles by inspiration)—"because Jesus had not yet been made clear" [Jn. 7.39]. What is *made clear*? He had not yet risen, had not yet ascended to heaven, had not yet led captivity captive and given gifts unto men [Ps. 67.19; Eph. 4.8].

When all these things were done, see what happened: "They began to speak," he says. "For never is the love of God otiose," he who knows says, "for it achieves great things if it exists: but if it is unwilling to act, it is not love."[18] Let your charity, if it exists, take note. "If love is unwilling to act, it is not love." And so if you love God, do good works.

2. But let us see whether the Gospel says anything further on this. "Jesus said to His disciples" [Jn. 6.12]—would He had done so to us! Happy is he who not only is called a disciple of Jesus but really is one. For *disciple* comes from *discipline, discipline* from *learning*; for truly, when a boy is whipped in school, he learns things good for him. Let us, therefore, love the discipline of Jesus, because Jesus, since He is called Savior, teaches nothing else than what pertains to eternal salvation. And if He whips you temporally, if you are His disciple, therefrom you grow stronger with a view to eternal salvation. If you are not, then at least you receive your due punishment. What Jesus says, would that now the disciples of Jesus would listen to. "If a man loves me," He said, "he will keep my words" [Jn. 14.23]. Lo, there is the sign, there is the test. "A woman either loves or hates, there is no third alternative,"[19] we read that one of the pagan wise said. Who is so mad as to dare to say that he hates God? But since there is no third alternative between love and hate, by this reasoning we are shown either to love God or to hate Him. We love God if we keep His word. Let us therefore examine ourselves, and if we keep His word, let us learn from His word.

This is His word: "Thou shalt love the Lord thy God with all thy heart and with all thy soul and with all thy mind. This is the first and great commandment. And the second is like unto it, thou shalt love thy neighbor as thyself. On these two commandments hang all the law and the prophets" [Mt. 22.37-44]—that is, he fulfills the whole law who does this, he complies with all the prophets who observes this. On the other hand it follows that whoever does not do these things does none of those things which the law requires, none which the prophets had commanded. For it is written: "Whoever shall keep the whole law and yet offend in one point"—that is, love—"he is guilty of all" [Jas. 2.10], because, even though he may not kill, fornicate, and steal, it is not for the love of God that he omits to do so, and therefore he receives no merit for it.

What is not virtue is vice, and what is unacceptable to God does not lack offence. For if it were not so, in no way would the Lord have said, condemning the vice of idleness: "Every tree that does not bring forth good fruit is hewn down and cast into the fire" [Mt. 7.19]. Nowhere is this taught more clearly than in the place where the apostle states that if he spoke with the tongues of men and of angels, and if he bestowed all his goods to feed the poor, and finally if he gave his body to be burned (which all, of course, seem to be very definite indications of charity, as it were), but did not have charity, it profited him nothing [1 Cor. 13.1-3]. Which surely means that if he did all these things without the love of God and of his neighbor, just as though he were observing all the law, and did not do that one thing alone on account of which the law was given, namely, that God should be loved beyond one's might, and one's neighbor with all one's might [Mt. 22.37], from it he would take no reward. For those who, having suffered or done all these things as if for God, happen to receive no other reward than that which those received who for their unfruitfulness were hewn down and cast into the fire—the reason being given thus: "Verily, I say to you, they have their reward" [Mt. 6.2], the reward, of course, which they sought for all this, namely, the empty wind of human praise—do they not seem guilty enough of transgression of the whole law, receiving no other merit for the fulfillment of it than those others received for the transgression of all the commandments which are in it? For how can anyone of these, most deceived, love God, since he neither does good nor avoids evil for love of Him, though he may *appear* either to do good or avoid evil? And if he does not love Him, how can he excuse himself by saying that he certainly does not hate Him?

3. Where do I see us now, brothers? There, for shame, where we see those about whom the psalmist once said: "Did I not hate them, O Lord, that hate you? And was I not grieved with your enemies?" [Ps. 138.21]. And again: "The haters of the Lord deceived Him: but their time will endure for ever" [Ps. 80.16]— that is, they will perish everlastingly. "For if a man say," says the beloved of the Lord, "'I love God' and yet hates his brother, he is a liar" [1 Jn. 4.20], and in consequence, an enemy of the Lord. For as it is said about those most especial enemies of God, that they are called Jews and are not, but are the congregation of Satan [Rev. 3.9], so it is to be feared that this man, too, may falsely be called a Christian, because a man is shown not to be Christ's if he does not have the spirit of Christ. He does not have the spirit of Christ who does not have charity, and he does not have charity who loves neither God nor his neighbor. He who neglects his neighbor does not love God; he neglects his neighbor who does not come to his aid in time of need. Let us, then, help our neighbors in any way we can: we need no other witnesses than I myself who speak. Would that, even if we were not willing to help, we would at least stop injuring our neighbors.

He lies indeed, who says that he loves God, if he hates his brother; he lies who says that he does not hate God, if he does not love his brother. If he who has charity has the spirit of Christ, but he who does not have the spirit of Christ is not one of His, it is established beyond doubt that he who does not have charity has no lot with Christ, and hence possesses the name of Christian falsely. And since the Lord Himself orders us to show an even greater earnestness of love to our enemies than we show to our friends, even those close in blood, why do we toil to no purpose? Even though we seem, as it were, to love certain people, the more we love them in the flesh, the more we do not fail to destroy them spiritually. Some of them we corrupt and destroy with talk that is both evil and, what is worse, continuous, some with evil deeds, many with deadly treachery, and in proportion as eternal death is more savage than temporal death, we kill them (let my *Chronography* mention this too) with a more savage murder.

Since, in what we take away from others unjustly, we enrich them in their future inheritance, what else do we do but cry with the Jews: "This blood be on us and on our children" [Mt. 27.25]? To whom, therefore, am I speaking; or rather, what am I, wretch, who do speak? I was afraid that if I said this, yes this, I would deservedly hear: "Out of your own mouth will I judge you, wicked servant" [Lk. 19.22]. For consciously and deliberately I am putting my hand into the flame, not ignorant that the danger of eternal damnation threatens me. For if the above be conceded, I love none of my brothers, none at all, nor yet any stranger, and consequently I do not love God who made me, nor in the end do I love myself; for whoever loves wickedness hates his own soul.

4. What, then, will we do? Shall we despair? No, I beg, no. "Whoever speaks a word against the Holy Spirit, it shall not be forgiven him, neither in this world nor in the world to come" [Mt. 12.32]. A word against the Holy Spirit Judas spoke in heart and action, who, weeping, did not wait for the Holy Spirit to be sent—through whom is conferred the remission of sins—but, pre-empting the remedy of conversion, hastened most wretchedly to put the noose around the throat of his intentions [Mt. 27.3-5]. Let us then avoid his example: let us wait for the remedy of salvation. Let us in supplication pray to God to create a clean heart in us and a right spirit to be renewed in our vitals [Ps. 50.12], that is, in the inner parts of our hearts; and, lest God cast us from His face, let us pray to be strengthened without intermission by the chiefest spirit. Let us prepare ourselves to keep His commandments while there is time; for we can obtain what we do not yet have, for those also who once obtained it had not previously had that which He deigned to confer on them when it pleased Him.

And because we have fallen into this evil by neglecting love, so that we ought rather to mourn without intermission than to rejoice, let us first be preoccupied with knowing what that love is, then let us pray with every kind of compassion that it be given us by the Lord. Love means always to love good and hate evil; not, however, those things which are falsely called good and evil, but those which are truly good and truly evil, that is, either approved or hated by God. It is love when, if you do some good, you try therein to please God alone and to profit your neighbor as yourself. It is love when, if you abandon evil, you abandon it with the fixed intention of no longer thereby offending God or damaging your neighbor.

This is that love which the apostle testifies some people do not have, even though bestowing all their goods to feed the poor [1 Cor. 13.3-6]; that love which "suffers long and is kind," which "does not envy"—that is, does not hate out of jealousy—"does not behave itself unseemly"—that is, does nothing shameful—"is not puffed up in pride"—or, to be sure, deadly anger—"is not ambitious"—that is, desirous of vainglory—"does not seek her own"—but that which is to God's or one's neighbor's good—"is not easily provoked, thinks no evil, does not rejoice in iniquity but rejoices in the truth," and the rest. In love there is no fear (though he who possesses it fears God) because a person does not fear hell if these conditions are observed. But he does consider that he does not know whether he is doing these things as they ought to be done, and so fears that he may incur God's offense and cries with the psalmist to the Lord (so as not to despair of salvation for his imperfection): "Your eyes have seen my imperfect substance" [Ps. 139.16]. We must most earnestly ask that this be given even to us also and we must yet continually strive for perfection, which may He kindly deign to bestow on us, allowing us pardon for our past offenses, He who deigned to come into this world for no other reason than because of the great love with which He loved us, who, with the Father and that Holy Spirit whose Advent we are now celebrating in gladness, lives, reigns, and is glorified as God, for ever and ever. Amen.

[No. 61 is a *commutatio* to Leudibertus, abbot of the monastery of St. Zeno. No. 62, his will, is placed after no. 65.]

63

Weigle, Epist. 179–80   Verona mid-June 968

[Letter to the empress Adelaide: he tells her that his enemies in Verona are saying that the emperor and empress no longer care about him, but he begs for protection at least until he has completed the reconstruction of a church.]

∽

To the Lady Adelaide the most gentle (to those whom she does not disdain): Rather, a sinner, gives his faithful service beyond what is due and possible.

If what Nanno[20] tries to persuade all my enemies is true, you desire nothing more than my death, and your husband cares for nothing less than the state of my safety. But if you are doing this for the episcopacy, try to preserve my life for a little with your power, until I have completed the Church of the Blessed

Mother of God. For I call the Lord to witness, I am very ready to do what you instructed me before, when reason was your guide. For I would rather wander far away in safety and lodge in the solitude of my monastery and there await the Lord, who makes me safe from the raging wind and tempest [Ps. 54.8–9], than uselessly put up with such things any longer to the detriment of my soul. But, O, how it would benefit all who are established in power [Dan. 3.3] (as I have more than once suggested to your ladyship) if they did not make such hasty decisions, but listened to the words of Job: "The cause which I did not know I diligently investigated" [Job 29.16].

The stomach that swells with aloe,[21] lady, does not belch forth the sweetness of honey, and he who praises what he hates tries cleverly to deceive.[22]

64

Weigle, Epist. 180–83   Verona end of June 968

[Letter to Count Nanno of Verona, asking him to stop supporting the rebellious clergy.]

To lord Nanno, eminently and necessarily conferred on us as *princeps*
for his merits: Rather, sinner and sufferer of what he deserves, like
it or not.

1. Your obedient servant has discovered that your lordship's excellency is threatening to cause me embarrassment before his majesty the holy emperor, though I was confident in thinking, foolishly, that no knowledge of my indiscretion [*impudentia*][23] had leaked out; but perhaps you have penetrated my household more deeply (I deserve it) and know those things which spoken in private rooms will be proclaimed (unless God spares us) on the housetops [Lk. 12.3]. I am confident that you are as ignorant about the other things as the world is now tired of giving ear to the lies of those who revile me. But what, lord, will you do? When words will cease, actions will speak. As I have urged the lady empress more than once, do not think that the wise emperor is quite forgetful of that sentence of blessed Job: "The cause which I did not know I diligently investigated" [Job 29.16],[24] or that he is so ready to believe you, that he cannot remember that "The mouth of an enemy does not speak the truth" [Ps. 5.9] was not only once said, but is also repeated in frequent use.

O what useless cloaks of vain Rather, which gave no return at all but this! O Venice, whose cloaks are so cheap to those who receive them that they cannot even buy this favor which does not achieve or confer anything![25] "The fact is that you lose old favors unless you back them up with later ones"[26] — how true and how applicable to today! For you waste a thousand of your gifts if you deny one thing to an ungrateful recipient unscrupulous in his demands.

2. But O how guilty of the greatest fault are those who fail to win what the psalmist prays for: "Cleanse me, Lord, from my own secret sins and spare your servant from those of others" [Ps. 18.13–14], and to enjoy it in security. I beseech you to stop threatening me, since you cannot terrify me, in the name of the emperor, who has always been very kind to me. I fear you a thousand times more than him.

Since good things are usually loved, while evil things are on the contrary feared, being unable to serve two masters, I love him, I fear you. Let a man consider why, but a man who is appropriate, I ask. The gospel reading for today said of John: "This man is a prophet and more than a prophet" [Lk. 7.26] (we sing it, we cannot forget it); see that you are not "more than an emperor" — for while the most glorious emperor consigns the bodies of his subjects to his bishops, you take their very souls away from the bishops when you forbid the priests to come to a synod[27] and to listen to a message from the pope [John XIII][28] himself about dismissing their wives. Quite forbidding them to obey their bishops, you keep them like soldiers in your control and do not fail to give them patronage in all the abominations which they do against the Lord; and as if you were the one who was told: "Whatever you bind on earth shall be bound in heaven" [Mt. 16.19], you make them laugh at *my* prohibitions. This is indeed to "be an emperor and more than emperor"; it is not, I say, to rule; for to rule is to do rightly or to rule — i.e., govern — what one possesses.[29]

3. Would then that you had governed me, as you possess me, and would that you had loved to rule me as much as you loved to be an emperor over me! For it would have been more tolerable to suffer your dominion in such a way that I would love the very one I feared, as I had begun to love him [Count Bucco] in reference to whom I turned Ovid's line to apply to me: "He who had earlier told of the wrongs of his Teraphnean spouse now sang her praises with more favorable lyre."[30]

For after I had said of him [Bucco]: "May He who freed Israel from the hand of Pharaoh [Ex. 18.10] now free Rather from the hand of Bucco," he began to improve just before his departure. Then I also began to prattle as follows: "If God wishes to bestow a better Bucco[31] on me, may He take you away; but if a worse one, I pray that He save you." I did not succeed in this prayer, and He bestowed on me a worse one with the same declension ending; so may the

words of the same prayer[32] be repeated for this one. Even if God despises me,
I pray that He may free—not indeed by destroying, but by converting them—
from your hands at least the souls whom you are turning into rebels against
the Lord out of hatred for me. I fear you for this a thousand times more than
the emperor, you should know; for he does not neglect the salvation of souls
the way you seem to do.

65

Weigle, Epist. 183–88   Verona early July 968

[Some weeks later Rather wrote to Ambrose, Otto's Italian chancellor, outlin-
ing what had transpired in his feud with the clergy since April. The long-fomented
dissension had come to a head in a public trial presided over by Nanno. Rather
now fears that not only can he not count on the emperor's support any longer,
but the emperor and empress are even against him. In this he must have been
right; shortly after the trial he left Verona for Belgium. He died in Namur six
years later, on 25 April 974, at the age of 84.]

Rather to Ambrose.

1. When I returned from the general synod at Ravenna in mid-April [967],
I summoned to a council all the priests and deacons of all the congregations of
my diocese to tell them what had been decided there[33] on the command of the
most serene emperor. But some of them refused to come, thanks to the treachery of the senior canons of the church who were ever rebelling against me and
making plots on my life; and some of those who did come declared with the
greatest arrogance that they would neither give up living with women nor resign their office. I ordered them to be arrested and held in custody till satisfaction was made. I decided that this satisfaction would consist in the restoration,
or rather decoration, of the Church of the Blessed Mother of God, hoping that,
because in their drunkenness they had been very lax in doing penance, through
her intercession the Mother of God might deign to win pardon for them, who
could not of themselves make any correction. But when they did not come and
I had had them summoned again and again, an officer named Giselpert appeared
and on behalf of his master [Count Nanno] issued a ban forbidding them to
come to my council at all.

2. And when some of the laity who had been charged with various crimes refused to come to make amends, I sent out my officers with the proctors of the church and had them arrested, as is the custom, and had them make amends in the same task.[34]

A certain priest called me "the mouth of the womb" [Pr. 30.16] and him likewise I had arrested; when he escaped in flight, I took from him what I could. I did not, however, offer it to the church because I did not dare to offer to God the vengeance of wrong done me, I who ought rather to have been a reconciler than an avenger.

A deacon whom I made a cathedral ordinary last year against his expectations (though he had a parish with a manse from my favor, when I had none) called me a felon, and deceiver and perjurer:[35] I took the manse from him and retained it for my own use, because there was need.

3. Almost four years ago I placed a pound of silver on the altar of S. Lorenzo. A certain priest took it on the understanding that he would repay it. He has not done so: he has come to no synod of mine, for which he has suffered no loss. He is reported to have gone to his majesty the emperor, appealed on I-know-not-what grounds and brought back a document making all my enemies happy and instigating them against me.

I had a lot, as much mine as my servants', in the middle of vineyards next to the river. Coming and going there people kept destroying the vines and wrecking the adjuncts, and still demanded a tax from me in addition. So when they had thoroughly gnawed at it, I had it ploughed up and planted with millet.

I have foolishly spent forty pounds on the restoration and enlargement of the bishop's palace. The Bavarians and the clergy living nearby, and particularly their servants, are wrecking it and putting the blame on me.[36]

Night and day the canons and their servants never give up seeking my demise and falsely accusing me since I will not stop attacking them. I commanded them on pain of excommunication to cease from servile work on the Lord's day [Num. 29.35]. When I could not make that stand, I ordered the gates to be locked against the wagons coming in. This "crime" they judge must be expiated either by my death or by my expulsion.

While Bucco was with us,[37] they plotted against him and me. When brought to punishment and forced to pay a hundred pounds of silver as a fine, they came to me and received a loan from the Church treasury of almost thirty pounds, but on this condition, that if it was not paid on time they would have to pay back double the capital. Three years have now gone by, and they have repaid nothing at all.

4. From this your Holiness can see how forgetful of great benefits they are and how ungrateful. For God's sake help me, I beg, as I will soon perish unless speedily helped.

Almost the whole city turned up at the festivity of St. Paul the apostle [30 June 968], when Nanno, sitting on the tribunal, stood up and said: "What do you think, townsmen, about this plot which you see ploughed up?" In one voice they all replied: "Terrible!" They could have replied, if they had wished, with more right and justice: "What does it have to do with us? [Mt. 27.4]. He who could justly collect the revenue from it could also legally plough it up."

Again he said: "What do you think about this house [the bishop's palace] which you see so damaged?" They all replied: "It is the bishop's fault." They would have done better to say: "Let an investigation be made to see if any of the neighbors did this, and force him by law to make the damage good. It was your duty[38] to provide for the outsiders, as the obligation to receive and entertain them is clearly yours. Who of us could prevent them when they were on their way either to or back from the emperor? The bishop, so it is reported, has spent forty pounds in restoring, enlarging and decorating it, six alone in repairing the doors, which had been removed partly by theft, partly by violence. He spent a considerable sum and got no profit from it. What more could he have done? It was very unwise for him to live in it, in case he either be arrested as once happened,[39] or if he tried to defend himself, fire be produced" (for what will the mob of Verona not dare?) "and the surrounding halls be burned because of him. And if neither happened, still what could he do, when on the departure of one captain from your people[40] another came in, and when he left, another? Could the bishop live in the same house with them?" They said none of this, but instead each voiced the worst thoughts he could.

He again: "What about these clergy who have thus lost their benefices?"[41]

They all cried: "Nothing could be worse." Yet if they had been good sons and not ungrateful for their benefices, they could have replied, as just now above: "What is it to us? Almost everyone does this, even God does this; He gave Saul his kingdom and took it away. He did not allow Judas to keep his rank of apostle, and He gave the devil first heaven and then hell. Since it was just for God to do this, then it ought not to be unjust for man to do it."

And again: "What of the fact that if a cleric or his servant, when summoned by the bishop, does not come of his own accord, he sends his proctors to seize him by force and bring him to him?" Though to this they could all have justly replied with Terence's words: "O, well done,"[42] they all to a man howled and squealed like pigs.

Then he: "I bring you word from the emperor and empress that if anyone henceforth dare to do this, all may resist him with all their strength." So saying, he gave back to them all the property that I had taken from my enemies and had given to the poorer clerics, in the document [*Judicatum*] which I sent you, and had confirmed by the signatures of the archbishop and my own and all the fellow bishops of our province. He did this, saying that the emperor had sworn that he would never let it be permanent.

5. But if this is true, you did wrong in not forewarning me of this. For if I break a promise signed by my own hand, you well know what I deserve.

What more? You see a conspiracy made against me, you can observe an edict of the emperor's condoning violent resistance to me, you see my danger. If you are able and do not help me, you kill me yourself; for it is a true saying that he who does not save a helpless man when it is in his power to do so puts him to death himself.[43]

If what Nanno keeps telling everyone is true, the empress desires nothing more than my destruction, and the emperor could not care less about my safety and survival, and none of them considers me even baptized. Unless what he is persuading everybody is quickly shown to be false, and unless this instigation, violence, provocation, and conspiracy against me are put down by a letter from the emperor, it is all over with me.

[I have placed at the end of the work the following three documents belonging to earlier in the year 968, as they are of little biographical interest and would interrupt the flow of the narrative if placed in their correct chronological position.]

55

Weigle, Urkunden 32–33   Verona 968

[Rather's bestowal on the clergy of S. Pietro in Castello.]

In the year of our Lord's incarnation 964 [968], in the seventh year of the reign of our lord Otto, in the first of his son, in the eleventh indiction, Rather, bishop of Verona, servant of the servants of God:

Since the church of S. Pietro in Castello is admired by all, but its clergy are very needy, judging this wrong and most inappropriate, I hereby give them by decree: whatever is offered to the Lord on the altar and around the altar and the cemetery also, and whatever below the castle of S. Pietro belongs to the church, four acres of vines, and near Fontana de S. Pietro two more acres of vines, two pieces of uncultivated land, in S. Giovanni in Valle three acres of vines, at Cadregule [?] a half-acre, at the Cross a half-acre, and two acres of ploughed land. I invoke the curse of St. Peter on Saphiras and Ananias [Acts 5.1–11] on anyone who tries to violate this decree, unless he amend; may he die struck with everlasting anathema, unless he try in repentance to atone for it.

In the name of God, I Rather, bishop of Verona, sign my hand to this decree of my bestowal.

56

In the name of the Father and of the Son and of the Holy Spirit,
Rather, bishop of Verona, servant of the servants of God:

Since by God's command we are required to spread the Church far and wide, so that the church which is entrusted to us pastors to govern may be known to have received some increase from me (and so that I may believe that the fullness of the heavenly kingdom will be given me by the highest king, when I enrich the Church, which is His spouse, with the largesse of property and great honor), I have therefore decided to increase the church of S. Pietro in Castello in Verona by my generosity, so that a church which is rich in many privileges through the bishops, my predecessors, may be increased by me also. For that purpose I make this decree, and add to its domain the chapel which is on the land of the castle called Poiano; I place it under the administration of the aforesaid church, together with all the possessions which it now has or will have in the future, and I concede it to the disposition and governance of the men of Holy Orders who are or will be in that church. Also, because my predecessor Ratold of blessed memory granted the same church of S. Pietro a tythe of the above-named castle and proclaimed it with his official sanction, I, too, hold it to be valid, and grant by this new document both the chapel and tythe of the same place to the aforesaid church. But if anyone enveloped in the mists of error or blinded by the hopes of his own ambition or greed should try to circumvent this, my disposition, and destroy the validity of what I have done, unless he amend, may he incur the penalty of God's wrath and of my wrath, may he be bound with the chains of unbreakable anathema and damned and fined one hundred pounds of gold, so long as our church remains in its own control.

62

His Will

✑

Rather, not only long tolerated by the ineffable mercy of the Creator but also still safe and sound, bishop in name alone, certain to be ashes at the preordained time:

(1) Because the instability of transitory life allows no one of right mind to stay secure, the resources which I appear to have I wish so to dispose in my lifetime that, after my death, those to whom I have given them may be able to possess them without legal dispute, so that those who will grieve at my departure may be able to take like measure of solace from it.

(2) First of all, I wish: if I possess something unjustly, that it be restored in full to its rightful owner. Next: whatever is found in my domestic furnishings, namely: the household goods, couches, furnishings and tapestries, should there be any, clothes or other things of this sort, are to be divided amongst my household, that is, the clerics who attend on me and certain lay persons. My money (if I should have any) I wish to be divided as follows: one libra (if there should be one) to be given to those responsible for my funeral; a second (if such there be) to the clergy of the church of Sta. Maria Consolatrix, along with the others specified in that decree [*Judicatum*]. Whatever remains, whether it be much (which I do not believe) or little or even nothing at all (which I do not doubt), Martin, the present curator of my estate, is to have, or whoever currently holds that position when I die. Whoever takes any of it away from him, eternal damnation and execration upon him. Any victuals that there are I would wish to be given to the churches which I began (too late, alas) to restore; may God give of it to each man according to his actions. My horses, and any other comforts for travel which I may have, or any arms perchance, should be given to any of my household who may have to move elsewhere, particularly if they are of my country or kin. Though these things and what goes with them will not be worth much, may the right hand of the Omnipotent and the curses of all the saints prevent all opponents from appropriating them and crush them. Amen.

(3) (Addendum) All this is done in suspicion of a sudden accident; whether it happens or whether, as I hope, a promised continuation of life is given me, I commend to your protection, highest Father, all who are written down in my *Judicatum* [no. 49], specifically asking you to defend them along with your

own against all in your see, and your own people against others, with all the strength you can; and especially the deed which I made with two clerics, Martin and Gisempert, namely one house called . . . which is now occupied by two men named Albo and. . ., which, because a deacon named Benedictus had fraudulently acquired it, I took away from him and gave to those two, on this condition (because I could not do otherwise), that while I lived they should enjoy it with me, and after my death they should possess it for a term of twenty-nine years, the usual term of a lease.

66

Weigle, Epist. 189–92   undated

Prayer

When one of the powerful comes to penitence and it is not known whether he does so with heartfelt sincerity or with merely the pretense of humility (as usually happens), this prayer should be said over him after the psalms and litany:

Lord God, Creator, Redeemer, Lover, and Savior of mankind, who wishes none to perish but all to be saved and to come to the knowledge of Truth [1 Tim. 2.4] (which you are): to show that the only reason that you came down from heaven and, in the flesh which you had taken on for us, suffered spit, scourging, blows, mockery, and crucifixion, the most cruel punishment of all, was so that by your death you might lead sinners back to life, you reclined more often with publicans and sinners [Mt. 9.10] and did not find it abhorrent to be touched, washed, and anointed by a sinful woman [Lk. 7.37], crying with your honey-sweet voice of pity: "I have come to call not the righteous but sinners to repentance" [Mt. 9.13]. And you have said that there is greater joy over one sinner—but only if he repents—than over ninety-nine just people who do not need repentance [Lk. 15.7]; and so that they do not rely on this security and, growing sluggish, put off making a fast return to the ways of Life, just like people who have had conferred on them by you some period of life and penitence, you have said in another place in the Gospel, "Watch, because you know not the day or the hour" [Mt. 25.16], offering as a precautionary example the fate of those who perished in Sodom and in the Flood, to show that you love sinners, not sins, and penitence, not faults.

Holy One, who are alone without sin, you have sanctified with fasting these holy days of Lent and have made them sacred for us, so that in them we may bewail the sins of the whole year and so that, purified by tears of repentance, by prayers, by almsgiving, by vigils, and by the other acts of piety divulged to us by your apostle [2 Cor. 6.4 ff.], we may be able to celebrate your holy Pasch and come forward to take your Body and Blood with worthy lips and a pure heart. If we do not, there is death for us. For thus you have spoken: "Unless you eat the flesh of the Son of Man and drink His blood, you will not have life in you" [Jn. 6.54]; but, alas, if we take it unworthily, we amass for ourselves, judgment and damnation. For so the apostle, filled with your spirit, warns, saying: "Whoever eats and drinks the Body and Blood of the Lord unworthily, eats and drinks judgment for himself" [1 Cor. 11.29].

We pray to you as suppliants by that sacred and ineffable name of yours, which you alone for eternity, Lord, possess with the Father and the Holy Spirit, that you graciously receive this your servant fleeing to the refuge of repentance. Offer him your merciful hand, inspiring his heart, so that the repentance which he shows in his body he may rather feel in his heart; for you know with what intent a person seeks you, with what devotion he flees to you. But you also have the power, when you wish, suddenly to turn the heart of anyone to whatever disposition you wish. Saul when he persecuted David suddenly prophesied, and Saul when he persecuted the Christians suddenly became Paul, the teacher of the Christians.

As one of your own[44] has said: "No one has rightly searched for you and not found you; and everyone has rightly searched for you whom you have made search for you rightly." Make this one too, we pray, O Lord, rightly search for you, chasten him from the errors which deceive his soul, be his Enlightener, routing the darkness of the vices which blind his mind. We too, pious Lord, if you grant us the power, though unworthy, can show him the light of life to follow. But unless you, Lord, open the eyes of his mind, the effort which we make for him fails; for thus the psalmist, inspired by you, says: "Unless the Lord has built the house, they labor in vain who build it" [Ps. 126.1]. We have the power, passed on by those to whom especially you granted it, of binding and absolving [Mt. 18.18], but just as we ought not to bind anyone unjustly, so we cannot rightly absolve anyone unless worthy satisfaction has been made beforehand. You are the knower of the hidden, you are the examiner of our hearts and loins [cf. Dan. 13.42; Ps. 7.10]. The man that we properly ought not to absolve, you can turn into one worthy of absolution.

Do so therefore, Lord, we beseech thee, do so for thy name's sake [cf. Ps. 108.21]. Inspire his mind so that he may seek you with his whole heart, in sincerity, not hypocrisy. Teach him, according to the prophet [Jer. 14.17], to wash away past sins with tears of penitence, cleanse him from present ones with your holy blessing. Mercifully cultivate his heart so that he may remove the evil of his thoughts from the eyes of your majesty; let him cease acting perversely and learn to do good. Let him search for justice, let him succor the oppressed. Let him take up the causes of orphans, let him defend widows and the fatherless, let him break bread for the hungry (but his own, not another's—that is, let him not wickedly take away from one person something to give to another *as if* in piety). In your name let him bring the homeless and the poor into his house.

When he sees the naked, let him cover him and not despise his own flesh [Is. 1.15]—that is, any blood relative or godparent or godchild. Let him loose the bundles that weigh him down [Is. 58.6]; that is, let him lay aside for your name's sake the burdens of the things which he either desires or retains contrary to the justice of your commandments. With you, O Lord, rewarding him, let him undergo no loss of the present world thereby, nay, let him rather be filled with the bounty of your gifts, O Christ. Let him set free those who are constrained, that is, are oppressed by him, and let him break the yoke unjustly put upon others [Is. 58.6]. Let him feed the hungry, give drink to the thirsty, visit the sick and those in prison, console the grieving [Mt. 25.34]. Let him be slow to punish, quick to pardon; let him prefer to take command of vices rather than of soldiers, to please God rather than men, and to do everything not for ambition of vainglory, but for love of eternal blessing. Let him rescue the weak and let him free the needy from the hand of the oppressor. Let him oppress no one unjustly; let him try to free the oppressed with all his might. Let him anxiously reflect upon how non-existent is temporal glory which eternal torments follow; how moderate is temporal affliction which eternal blessings follow.

We beseech you, Lord, holy Redeemer, generous Lover of mankind, for love of your holy name, in that true faith which works through love [Gal. 5.6], let him act so devoutly that with your help he may wipe away past sins, so that he may merit by your largesse to be loosed from the toils, past and present, of his sins, and with your protection be freed from future ones. Thus may he under your governance be able to run in the stadium of the present life so that he may more felicitously come to the prize of eternal reward [1 Cor. 9.24], and may be able to hold on to it for ever, we beseech you, who are the Way, the Truth, and the Life [Jn. 14.6], the Savior of the world, who with the Father, etc.

Appendix

Notes

Indices

Appendix

Meðieval Sources for Rather's Life

(Collected by Guiseppe Monticelli, *Raterio vescovo di Verona (890–974)* [Milan: Bocca, 1938].)

1. Folcuin, abbot of Lobbes (contemporary with Rather): *Gesta Abbatum Laubiensium*, MGH, SS, 4.[1]

c. 19.

The study of literature flourished with us at this time; the most renowned scholars in this were Scaminus, Theoduin, and Rather, the most perceptive of these; the latter, Rather, favoured Hilduin's cause and stuck to him inseparably. For when Hilduin was cheated of the bishopric of Liège, he was given the see of Verona with feudal revenue by King Hugo of Italy, with whom he had taken refuge, with the king's promise that when an opportunity for promoting Hilduin higher occurred, Rather would be given to the Veronese as bishop. How this came about and what troubles Rather suffered in that episcopacy the reader will be able to know better from his own writings, in the letter which he wrote to the highest pontiff and universal pope complaining of them thus: "In sum, etc."[2]

c. 20.

In the exile in which he said he had been placed on leaving the bishopric, he published a book which he called *Agonistic*, to which he also attached this title: "Meditations of the heart of a man called Rather, bishop of Verona, but a monk of Lobbes, arranged in six books, which he has decided to call *Praeloquia*," or "Book of *Prefaces* [to a work] which is called *Agonistic*." He sent this book to the most learned men he knew to read and approve, namely, Archbishops Sobbo and Wido and Bishops Godescalc and Aurelius, and also to Bruno and Rotbert, archbishops in Gaul, men of the highest rank and the most learned in the study of philosophy, and finally to Flodoard of Reims, sending a letter to each one (there are copies in our church's library).³ He also found a book of the life of St. Ursmar when he was in exile at Como and, since it was full of solecisms, corrected it and passed it on to us. Later, when he was staying in that part of Burgundy known as Provence, he was invited to teach literature to a wealthy man's son, Rocstagn by name, and wrote for him a book on the *ars grammatica* which he called in the local way of speaking *Sparadorsum*, because a boy who assimilated it in school could "save his back" from beatings.⁴ As a result he was given the bishopric there; leaving it he returned to Lobbes. Richarius was still living then; he was received favorably by him and allowed to live at Lobbes; not much later Richarius died.

c. 21.

Under Farabert, as previously under Richarius, everything was up for sale, to such an extent that the place was called by parasites "a valley of silver" . . . and a person was called more "holy" the more extravagant he was in giving, and "most beneficial" in proportion as he was greediest.⁵

c. 22.

Otto was at that time the most powerful king in the south, and then subdued Italy and became emperor. His brother Bruno, whose renown in Christ's Church was going to be singularly unmatched, shone like a precious stone in the diverse discussions of the philosophers. Rather was summoned and was considered the first among the philosophers of the palace. What more? He did not stop trying to make that marvellous royal talent most perceptive and accomplished in all fields of learning. . . .

c. 23.

It happened at that time that the see of Liège was vacant, after the decease of Farabert; Bruno with great energy had Rather installed as bishop there as a reward for his earlier teaching . . . [continued in Ruotger's narrative below, c. 38].

All hope of his restitution was removed. For while he was making a splendid, festive celebration of the Lord's Nativity with us [at Lobbes], a grave conspiracy was formed against him in Liège . . . [continued in Ruotger below].

c. 24.

Rather spent almost two years in this destitution, lacking the support of any knight;⁶ then he returned to Italy. To complete the story of this business (so as not to cause trouble to researchers of foreign matters): the aforesaid Bruno arranged with his brother the emperor [Otto] that the ancient see of the Church of Verona, twice taken away from him, should now be restored to him. During this same time he wrote a book which he called *Phrenesis*, because, like a "frenetic," he inveighed against Baldric very harshly and excessively. He also wrote another work which he called *Perpendiculum* [no. 28] and another which he called *Syrma* [no. 14], in which he inveighs against the same Baldric, his usurper, as he himself calls him.[7] There is also a book of his against the Anthropomorphites [no. 29] who depict God, that is the invisible Deity itself, with limbs and features; his *Synodica* also [no. 43] to the priests of his diocese and the *Conjectura* of his life [no. 41]; also his *Itinerarium* [no. 47] when he went to Rome and several sermons: On the Pasch [no. 25], On the Lord's Feast [no. 31], On the Lord's Ascension [no. 26], On the Day of Pentecost [no. 27], On the Feast of the Blessed Mary [no. 45], and many others . . . [he continues with the narrative of the Hungarian invasion].

c. 26.

To return to our theme from this digression: Baldric was bishop of the Church of Liège; he held his uncle Raginer in singular respect because he had given him the most help in obtaining the bishopric. . . .

c. 27.

Meanwhile, on the decease of Baldric, lord Everaclus, a dean from Bonne, a man well lettered in the noble arts, was made bishop at Bruno's behest. . . .

c. 28.

Rather was still at Verona. Disgusted by the insolence of the citizens and at the same time suspecting their innate treachery, he was contemplating a return [to Lobbes], thinking that it is often a good thing to live in a foreign country but a bad thing to die there. So he sent to the abbot a book which he entitled "Conflict of the Two" [not extant] on the grounds that in it, wavering in anxious uncertainty, he debated whether he should return or not, and at the same time he asked that he be sent horses and an entourage so as to speed him on his way. It was done; they were sent; he arrived, carrying with him gold and silver (I won't say "weights" but, using his own words, "masses and heaps"). Using this he bought from King Lothar the abbey of St. Amand. He held it for barely one night and—he was an extraordinarily fickle man—abandoned it, returning to Alna, which he had received on the generosity of the lord bishop. In like manner he also purchased the monastery which they call High Mount [Haumont] for a big price; there he gathered together whatever fine stuff he had in ecclesiastical vestments or adornments and whatever he had himself previously given to our church but had later taken back, making a gift of it. Leaving here also he returned to Alna once more. . . . The abbot had also given him, with the consent of the brothers, the villa Strata and Gosiniacae and the little abbey of St. Ursmar and another which they call the Waslar monastery. But always hating our place [or my position?] he kept making plots against the abbot [Folcuin], with some people spurring him on to this. In brief: things came to such a pass that, under pressure from a dangerous conspiracy, the abbot yielded his place, knowing that this also was what Bishop Everaclus wanted. About him there is nothing else for me to say. Rather, to make manifest the reasons for his previous hostility—ignoring that spiritual relationship which he had from Folcuin's baptism (for he had taken him up from the baptismal font)—invaded the place and, fearing both the abbot's animosity and his kin, who were substantial, fortified the cloister like a castle, using the money he had left (as he said) to buy the help of certain chiefs. In the same cause he deliberately gave up the church of St. Dionysius, which he had bought from Count Robert for a price of twenty librae. And he did not give a thought to what or how much he was giving for that purpose, nor to whom he was giving. What more? That year continued until Bishop Everaclus died and Notger succeeded in his place . . . who, not wanting his first actions to be thought frivolous or hasty, summoned abbots Werinfred from Stablaus and Heribert from Andagin with some brothers and first investigated the sources of the conspiracy, and, finding them, balanced them in the scale and analyzed them, and finally pronounced judgment. Seeing that the whole matter was frivolous, he reconciled the brothers to the abbot and restored him. Rather returned to Alna, where both (that is, himself and the abbot) were reconciled, and he lived out the rest of his life. He died later at Namur, when he happened to be staying there for a while with a friend. His body was brought to Lobbes and he was buried with honor, with the solemn rites due to a bishop, in the Church of St. Ursmar in the northern part.

2. Ruotger, cleric of Cologne, *Life of Bruno*, MGH, SS, 4, pp. 252–75.

c. 38.

Rather, the ordained bishop of Verona, a city in Italy, after being expelled from the honor of his own see on some slight suspicion (as is the way with that nation), was incardinated in accordance with canon law into the vacant see of Liège, after great industry on [Bruno's] part. Because of his great learning and copious eloquence, in which he was seen to flourish among the foremost in wisdom, it was thought that this was going to be of great benefit not only to the church of which he was bishop, but also to many others round about. At the same time, because in those parts, through zealotry and quarrelling— the frequent source of fickleness and depravity—certain people, even priests of the Lord, putting their trust for the most part in worldly power more than is right (even to say this is wrong), were leading the ignorant people astray, the often-mentioned—and often to be mentioned—Lord Bruno, who was now anticipating governing the whole kingdom, thought—as was true—that Rather, previously outcast and neglected, would be brought by this great favor to such loyal and true devotion that he could be seduced by no one. Bruno believed that he could thus finally block the mouths of those speaking enmity against him if no opportunity for scandal could be found in their bishop. But the hostile side prevailed to his destruction; whatever was done for their salvation they thought was destructive to themselves. What more? They went astray, they savaged him, and they did not cease until they had satisfied their cruelty and wickedness with his expulsion. All hope of his restoration was taken away; for a grave conspiracy was formed, which did not seem able to be quelled unless he should be entirely removed and Baldric (who belonged to a powerful family of that land) be promoted to that position. Into this bilgewater flowed many stormy washes from all sides; the ship of the Church rolled with struggling oars; the helmsman himself could not manage the onset of storm and squall. So he yielded; he yielded, not to be overcome by evil but to overcome evil in good; he yielded to the will of his enemies, so that he might butcher them with his sword. They were bound to him of their own accord by a sworn oath, that if they got to receive the bishop they were asking for [Baldric], they would henceforth defend the Church's authority and the king's right with invincible obduracy. So that nothing in this business be left unfinished which might cause trouble to researchers of other people's affairs: Bruno arranged with his brother the emperor that the ancient see of the Church of Verona be returned to Bishop Rather, now twice deprived.

3. A second anonymous *Life of Bruno*, twelfth century, MGM, SS, 4, pp. 275–79.

c. 14.

Leading the Church of Verona in Italy was a very energetic man named Rather, a monk in habit, an outstanding devotee of all religion, an enlightened interpreter of divine Scripture. He was elected [bishop of Liège] according to the canons in the palace of Aix at the beginning of the fast of the month of September, was consecrated the following Sunday by two archbishops, namely, St. Bruno of Cologne of worthy memory and Rotbert of Trier, and also five bishops, and with the consent of the clergy and people was enthroned in the aforesaid church. Having thus attained the bishop's seat, he attended to the affairs of the see and ecclesiastical rights strictly and to the letter of the law, scorning the ideas of those who hitherto in these matters had sought not what belongs to Christ but their own advantage. Though very upright in other respects, characters being so diverse, he was a man of rather violent temperament, and, in his eagerness for justice and fairness, a little too severe in his answers. But because, as someone says, "truth begets hatred," by this kind of zeal he aroused against himself the hatred not only of the clergy but even of citizens. Some of these, family connections of Bishops Robert of Trier and Baldric of Liège,[8] complaining of the loss of their revenues through the bishop's strong action, stirred those bishops to enmity and hatred of their own master, claiming that he was a madman [*freneti-cus*] and unworthy of the honor and name of bishop. Bishop Rather, quite touched by these taunts, did not take refuge in outside support, but turned to the armoire of books and began to write invective tracts against Bishops Baldric and Robert. Hence it came about that the rivalry and anger flared up and he was driven from his seat with considerable abuse. Expelled, he betook himself to glorious King Otto for support.[9] That king, with his instinct for piety, tried to help him but his enemies strongly opposed, and it seemed best to Rather to take refuge in the kindness of saintly Archbishop Bruno, his ordainer. Coming to him, he was kindly received and kept honorably in that one's usual charitable way; not much later he was fittingly restored to his see [Verona]. For in front of so great a man the conspiracy of all his enemies evaporated, and the weight of his adversaries' charges was put to silence before Bruno's firm testimony in his defense. For this man of all authority reminded them of the pomp of Rather's canonic election and ecclesiastical consecration; such proper ceremony ought not to be invalidated by some kind of accusation made on the testimony of lay people; in fact, all the agents of that faction could well expect the displeasure of papal censure. So the anger of Rather's opponents was softened by the medicine of Bruno's mellifluous eloquence, and, God's mercy ordaining it, he caused all to be reconciled in unbreakable harmony. And Rather was restored to his seat with all ceremony and honor by the very people who had previously expelled him with unseemly abuse, and became more reformed for the rest of his days.

c. 15. = Rather's letter to Bruno, no. 17.

4. Liutprand, *Antapodosis* book 3, in: J. Becker, *Die Werke Liutprands von Cremona* (Hanover, 1915).

c. 42.

At that time, Hilduin, bishop of the Church of Liège, expelled from his own see, came to Italy to King Hugo, to whom he was related. He was honorably received by him and granted the bishopric of Verona with use of revenue. It happened that after a while Archbishop Lampert died, and in his place Hilduin was ordained bishop of Milan. A monk named Rather had come with Hilduin; because of his religion and his knowledge of the seven liberal arts he was made bishop of Verona, where also Milo, whom I mentioned above, was the count.

c. 48.

Arnold, duke of Bavaria and Carinzia,. . . crossing from that region into Tridentina, the first march of Italy, came as far as Verona. There he was willingly received by Count Milo and Bishop Rather, since they had invited him. When King Hugo heard of this, he gathered an army and came to meet him.

c. 49.

When he had come there and was manoeuvering his horseback patrols, popularly called *caballicatae*, round about, a considerable force of Bavarians came out of the fortress called Gausening and began to fight. The Bavarians were routed, and hardly any escaped, even to tell the news to the rest. As a result, Duke Arnold was in a great quandary.

c. 50.

So it came about that he planned to capture Count Milo and, leaving Italy, take him back to Bavaria with him, so as to return with him once more when he had reinforced his army. This did not escape Milo.

c. 51.

Torn by diverse considerations, Milo was utterly at a loss what to do. . . . He was afraid to approach King Hugo, as he had certainly been entitled to, but he thought that being taken to Bavaria with Arnold meant not only death but hellfire. . . . And so in this dilemma, since he knew that King Hugo was quickly inclined to mercy, he decided to escape from Arnold and go to him. Arnold then retreated into Bavaria as quickly as he could. But first attacking the fortress which was in that city, he took Milo's brother and the knights who tried to defend the fortress to Bavaria with him.

c. 52.

When Arnold left, the city was soon returned to King Hugo and Rather, its bishop, was arrested by him and sent to exile in Pavia. There, with great elegance and refinement, he began to write a book about the miseries of his exile. Anyone who reads it will find things expressed there under this pretext which will both please and benefit the intellect of the reader.

5. Sigibert of Gembloux (post 1030–1112), *Chronica*, MGH, 6, pp. 300–374.

an. 928. Rather, a monk of Lobbes, a man of great honesty but renowned for his knowledge of the liberal arts, set out for Italy with Hilduin, who had once held the bishopric of Liège in Lotharingia, to King Hugo; when Hilduin was ordained bishop of Milan, he was appointed by Hugo bishop of Verona.

an. 932. Arnold, duke of Bavaria, coming into Italy against King Hugo was received by the Veronese and, clashing with Hugo, was defeated. Bishop Rather was expelled from his see by King Hugo because he had supported the Bavarians and was exiled to Pavia, where he wrote a book about his troubles with great elegance. He wrote also many other things of great benefit to a reader. . . . The heresy of the Anthropomorphites (that is, those who claim that God has a corporeal form) was strong in Italy; against it, Bishop Rather of Verona campaigned in both words and writings.

an. 954. After being twice expelled from the bishopric of Verona, Rather was ordained bishop of Liège after Farabert by Archbishop Bruno. . . . When he was expelled from the bishopric of Liège, Baldric took his place as bishop with the support of his uncle Raginer, count of Hennegau.

an. 974. Rather died at Lobbes. This line of verse[10] is about him:

Rather bishop of Verona but thrice an exile.

6. Anselm, canon of Liège under Wazon (1041–1048), *Gesta Episcoporum Leodiensium*, MGH, SS, 7, pp. 189–234.

After him [Farabert], Rather, a native of this country, who had been first driven from the bishopric of Verona, was installed as the forty-third bishop of Liège. But he did not hold this honor to the end of his life. For when he attacked the ways of men, both in his words and in his writings, more bitingly than he should have, the insolence of the powerful would not stand it, and he was driven from our see; and, some fields of the bishop's property being granted to him for livelihood, he gave his place to Baldric, the forty-fourth. Certain works of this Rather, composed with wit and elegance, are held in our library; even today he is accustomed to prickle the conscience of the listener with his acerbity.

7. Aegidius Aureavallensis (twelfth century), *Gesta Episcoporum Leodiensium*, MGH, SS, 25, pp. 14–129.

After him [Farabert] was Rather, a native of our country, the forty-third bishop of Verona and first expelled from the bishopric of Verona. When he attacked the ways of men too bitingly in both his words and writings and deferred to no one either high or low, he was driven from the see, certain revenues of the bishopric being granted him. . . . He ruled the Church of Liège for almost three years, under Pope Benedict, who is also called Agapet.

8. Catalogue of the abbey of St. Amand, MGM, SS, 13, p. 387.

For Rather, twice driven from the bishopric of Verona, was ordained bishop of Liège by St. Bruno of Cologne, on the death of Genulph. . . . He held the abbey of our Elno scarcely one night and was ejected by the monks on the morrow.

9. Annals of Lobbes, MGH, SS, 13, p. 234.

an. 920. Stephen, bishop of Liège, died, and dissension arose between Hilduin and Richarius about the bishopric; and because Hilduin held it only with the support of Duke Gislebert (who had broken from his oath of loyalty to his lord Charles), but Richarius was supported by Charles, Hilduin was ejected by the pope's authority.

an. 953. Farabert, bishop of Liège, died; Rather succeded him.

an. 955. Rather being driven out, Baldric usurped the bishopric of Liège.

10. Annals of Lobbes, MGH, SS, 4, pp. 16–17.

an. 953. Farabert the bishop died and Rather succeded.

an. 955. Bishop Rather was driven out, Baldric took over.

an. 974. Bishop Rather died.

Notes to Introduction

1. E. Auerbach, *Literary Language and its Public in Late Latin Antiquity and in the Middle Ages*, trans. Ralph Manheim (New York and London, 1954), 151–52.

2. For his life the Ballerini's *vita* in Migne, *PL* 136, written in 1765, though still fundamental, should be supplemented by Vogel, Kurth (1905), Monticelli, Weigle (1937–38 and 1941–42), Cavallari (1967), and Lumaghi (for all of whom see bibliography).

3. If my interpretation of no. 41 c. 13, is correct, he would have been born in 889. This date accords well with other references in his writings.

4. Rene Poupardin, *Cambridge Medieval History* (MacMillan, 1922), 3:62.

5. Quoted by Christopher Dawson, *Religion and the Rise of Western Culture* (Sheed and Ward, 1950; Image edition, 1958), 87.

6. J. D. Mansi, *Sacrorum Conciliorum Nova et Amplissima Collectio* (Florence, 1759–98), vol. 18, quoted by Christopher Dawson, 120–21.

7. Rosamond McKitterick, *The Frankish Kingdoms under the Carolingians, 751–987* (Harlow, 1983), 307.

8. Weigle reconstructs the dates for his first tenure, his imprisonment, and his exile at Como in *Briefe*, 37.

9. For an interpretation of the events see F. Weigle, in *Deutsches Archiv* 5 (1941–42): 347–86.

10. For his lack of books see *Praeloquia* 6.26. Against this, Fr. Dolbeau ("Ratherina II") has established beyond doubt that Rather in Pavia had access to, and made extensive use of, Trier Stadtbibl. 149/1195, a ninth-century collection of works of the Fathers, including: Augustine's *Soliloquies, De quantitate animae, De immortalitate animae, De anima et eius origine, De nuptiis et concupiscentia,* and *Epistula* 190, Cassiodorus' *De anima,* and Gregory's *Dialogorum liber quartus.*

11. *Decretales Pseudo-Isidorianae et capitula Angilramni,* ed. Paul Hinschius (1863). Also in Migne, *PL* 130. See "False Decretals" in *The New Catholic Encyclopaedia* (Washington, 1967), 5:820.

12. See no. 10.

13. Otto's part in Rather's restoration is proved by no. 57 c. 3, no. 47 c. 4, no. 53 c. 7, no. 37e, no. 41 c. 1.

14. Nos. 52 and 57.

15. See F. Weigle, "Ratherius von Verona im Kampf um das Kirchengut 961–968," *Quellen und Forschungen aus italienischen Archiven und Bibliotheken* 28 (1937–38): 1–35; and L. Lumaghi,

"Rather of Verona: Pre-Gregorian Reformer" (Ph.D. diss., University of Colorado, 1975).
16. No. 52, c. 7–8, no. 65, c. 4, no. 49.
17. Edited in Migne, *PL* 599–602, MGH, Diplom. Ott. I, 474.
18. See G. Misch, *Geschichte der Autobiographie* (Frankfurt, 1955), 2:527–49.
19. G. Billanovich, "Dal Livio di Raterio (Laur. 63, 19) al Livio del Petrarca (B.M., Harl. 2493)," *Italia medioevale e umanistica* 2 (1959): 103–78.
20. One manuscript of Martianus Capella, Leiden Voss. Lat F.48, was extensively glossed by Rather in his own hand; these glosses have been edited by Claudio Leonardi in the *Corpus Christianorum* edition of Rather's major works (*Continuatio Mediaevalis* 46A). Rather's glosses in another manuscript, Trier Stadtbibl. 149/1195, have been edited by Fr. Dolbeau in "Ratheriana III."
21. See Max Manitius, *Geschichte der lateinischen Literatur des Mittelalters* (Munich, 1923), 2:49–50; Benny Reece, "Classical Quotations in the Works of Ratherius," *Classical Folia* 22 (1968): 198–213; Erich Auerbach, *Literary Language and its Public in Late Latin Antiquity and in the Middle Ages*, 141. Fr. Dolbeau has pointed out ("Ratheriana III," 153) that certain allusions to Cicero (*Cato maior, De inventione*), Seneca, Juvenal, and Publilius Syrus were rather borrowings from passages in Augustine, Cassiodorus, Ambrose, Boethius, and Sedulius, where these classical sources were quoted.
22. See B. L. Ullman in *Studi in onore di Luigi Castiglioni* (Florence, 1960), 1032–33, and in *Studies in the Italian Renaissance* (Rome, 1955), 81–115, 195–200.
23. Peter L. D. Reid, *Tenth Century Latinity: Rather of Verona* (Malibu, 1981), 38–42.
24. Cf. Augustine *De Doctrina Christiana* 2.60. This approach is also discussed by E. R. Curtius in *European Literature and the Latin Middle Ages* (New York, 1953), 40, and more recently by Z. P. Thundy, "Sources of *Spoliatio Aegyptiorum*," *Annuale Mediaevale* 21 (1981): 77–90.
25. E.g., the sermon *De octavis Paschae* (no. 57), where even in the first paragraph he alludes to the actions of Count Nanno against him.
26. E.g., the *Sermon on Mary and Martha* which starts with a traditional or conventional discussion of Mary and Martha as the types of the active/contemplative life, but by c. 4 moves into his own failure to meditate on God's law night and day, since he now is reading Plautus.
27. See Lumaghi's dissertation, cited above, note 15.
28. He frequently refers to his own work as *garritus, garrulitas, garritio,* or *loquacitas* ("garrulity," "chattering," "loquacity"), a downgrading of the eloquence for which he was renowned. This self-depreciation comes from the recognition that his reputation for eloquence is based on his knowledge of the *classical* authors; but as a monk and as a bishop his duty is to meditate on *God's law* day and night.
29. Cf. *Translatio S. Metronis* c. 1 (no. 23): "he who takes on knowledge takes on labor." The preface to *Phrenesis* also makes this point.
30. See Reid, c. 2, p. 28 ff.
31. M. Winterbottom, "Aldhelm's Prose Style and its Origins," *Anglo-Saxon England* 6 (1977): 39–76 and M. Lapidge, "The Hermeneutic Style in Tenth Century Anglo-Latin Literature," *Anglo-Saxon England* 4 (1975): 67–111. Winterbottom traces the origins of this style back through Martianus Capella and St. Augustine's *sermo sophisticus* to Apuleius. What Lapidge and M. Herren say in summary about Aldhelm's style (*Aldhelm: The Prose Works*, trans. Michael Lapidge and Michael Herren [Cambridge, 1979], 4) could equally be said of Rather: "Aldhelm's Latin is extremely difficult, and sometimes impenetrable. His sentences are tediously long and complicated; his vocabulary is often bizarre and arcane, sometimes inscrutable. In-

deed, Aldhelm's love of verbiage for its own sake—he calls it 'verbose garrulity or garrulous verbosity'—must often exasperate the well-intentioned reader who, having penetrated the lexical and syntactical obscurities of a two-page long sentence, finds that he is left with a trivial apophthegm of the merest banality."

32. Auerbach, 139.

Notes to Praeloquia, Book 1

1. *Agonistic*: Rather calls it *Liber Agonisticus* (CC. p.5, l.1); Folcuin calls it *Agonisticon*. I think he means something like "Training Book for Christ's Athlete." For each book of the *Praeloquia* except book 6, Rather lists a table of contents in Roman numerals. I have supplied these Roman numerals in the text, while observing the traditional chapter numbers in Arabic numerals.

2. Rather is in prison at Pavia.

3. In the third and fourth books he tells of his own sufferings. Why then Origen? The historical Origen suffered martyrdom for his faith, as Eusebius, *The Ecclesiatical History*, 6.39.5, tells. Rather seems to be pointing out the similarity of their positions.

4. The "events" must be personal details relating to his fall and imprisonment scattered throughout the six books. He would prefer the reader to consider the arguments and moral lessons rather than the autobiography.

5. [Lk. 6.30.] He takes *te* as object of *tribue* ("give yourself"), not as object of *petenti* ("give to everyone *who asks of you*"). Cf. also Sermo II de Quad. c. 15.

6. Cf. also Exod. 20.13–17.

7. He is attacking the practice whereby lay knights received the Church's revenues as benefices, an example of which can be seen in Metr. c. 3.

8. Cf. Ps.-Maximus Taurensis *Homiliae* 44.

9. Cf. Lucan *Pharsalia* 9.898–908; Pliny *Nat. Hist.* 7.2.2.

10. Augustine wrote *incrementorum*, "growths."

11. The manuscript has: *quas dts* (*dtr?*) *genas*. Since this must (1) be a complete clause, and (2) refer in some way to witches, I suggest *quas dicunt saganas*, an echo of Horace's witch in *Satires* 1.8.25,48 and *Epodes* 5.25.

12. Augustine *Enarrationes in psalmos* 91.7.

13. Boethius *Consol. of Philosophy* 1.4.39 and 1.6.21.

14. *Cupedinarius*, a word glossed from Terence meaning "seller of fine foods," is the manuscript reading. The Ballerini emend to *cupidenarius*, "lover of *denarii* or cash," a word not otherwise attested, but likely in view of his emphasis on *cupiditas*.

15. The word Rather uses, *locotheta*, or more commonly *logotheta*, was a technical office of the Byzantine chancelery. The Langobard office was *locopositus*, defined by Niermeyer as "a duke or count's subordinate." *Comes palatii*: Count Palatine.

16. Cf. Ambrose *In psalmum* 118.20.36.

17. Source not identified; the thought comes from Isidore *Sententiae* 3.55.3.

18. Leo *Tractatus* 43.

19. A feudal lord, seigneur; Ital. *padrone*.

20. Jerome *Comm. in Malach.* 3.5.

21. Gregory *Pastoral Rule* 1.6.

22. Augustine *De Bono Coniugali* 1.1.1.

23. Boethius *Consol. of Philosophy* 3.6.7–10.
24. Benedict *Rule* 2.
25. Boethius *Consol. of Philosophy* 3.6.7–10.
26. A state officer subordinate to a duke (Niermeyer).
27. Cf. Juvenal *Satires* 3.76.
28. Juvenal *Satires* 7.201.
29. Cf. Augustine *De Quantitate Animae* 19.33.
30. Ps.-Cicero *Speech against Sallust* 2.4–5.
31. Boethius *Consol. of Philosophy* 3.6.26–27.
32. Persius *Satires* 1.7.
33. Juvenal *Satires* 3.131–32.
34. I.e., Hilduin, who, stripped of his see of Liège, had gone south to join his relative King Hugo of Italy, hoping to be given a bishopric there. The whole of this long paragraph seems deliberately obscure.
35. I.e., Rather, who could have quietly stayed secure in his monastery of Lobbes. Folcuin, *Gest. abb. Lob.* c. 19 says that "Rather in support of Hilduin's faction stuck to him inseparably."
36. As a result of the affair with Arnold of Bavaria, Hilduin's stature as archbishop of Milan increased (we know not how), while Rather lost his bishopric and was imprisoned.
37. I.e., the bishopric of Verona which he had caused to be conferred on Rather.
38. I.e., his secure monastic life.
39. One of the pieces of evidence relating to Rather's noble birth.
40. References to the wrong done him can be found in *Praeloquia* 2.24, 3.25–28, 4.5–7, 5.12, and 5.27, but no full volume is devoted to it.
41. Not Seneca but Publilius Syrus *Sententiae* B 5.
42. Publilius Syrus *Sententiae* M 1.
43. *Prov.* 96 (Friedrich, p. 279).
44. Cf. Publil. Syrus *Sententiae* 66.
45. Cf. Gregory *Homiliae in evangelia* 2.27.4.
46. Cicero *De amicitia* 13.44.
47. Gregory *Registrum epistularum* 1.34.
48. Benedict *Rule* 64.
49. *Prov.* 77 (Friedrich, p. 278); i.e., he would be cruel to everyone if he had the power.
50. Source not identified.
51. Isidore *Etymologiae* 3.47.1–3.
52. 1 Peter 5.3 *non dominantes in clero*, lit. "not domineering over the clergy."
53. Cf. Ambrose *In Psalm* 118.16.45.
54. Gregory *Moralia* 5.45.78.
55. Juvenal *Satires* 13.20–22. Juvenal wrote *ducimus*, "we think," not *dicimus* "we say."
56. Augustine *Epistulae* 166.17.
57. Cf. Augustine *Soliloquies* 1.22–24 and 1.13.23.
58. Gregory *Moralia* 23.15.28.
59. Persius *Satires* 1.26–27. The quote attributed to Augustine is actually Ambrose *In psalmum* 118.4.18.
60. Publilius Syrus *Sent.* N 2.
61. Benedict *Rule* 48.
62. Persius *Satires* 1.28.

63. Persius *Satires* 1.1.

64. Isidore *Etymologiae* 3.48.3.

65. *Myrmicoleon*; cf. Gregory, *Moralia* 5.40, who says that *m.* is an ant to other animals and birds but a lion to ants.

66. Isidore *Sententiae* 3.59.14.

67. *Proverbium* 87 (ed. E. Wölfflin).

68. Augustine *Enarrationes in psalmos* 103.16.

69. Isidore *Sententiae* 3.59.12 and 3.60.4.

70. This sentence is a combination of Bede *Homiliae* 3.66 and Jerome *Epistulae* 79.3 (Dolbeau).

71. Not Jerome but Publilius Syrus *Sententiae* T 3.

72. John Chrysostom *Homiliae* 17.

73. Jerome *Epistulae* 79.1.

74. Isidore *Sententiae* 3.59.13.

75. Augustine *Tractatus in Ioh.* 44.3.

76. Chrysostom *Homiliae* 17.

Notes to Praeloquia, Book 2

1. Following the manuscript reading, [*libellum*] *modicum pernullus, multiloquum maestiloquus*. The Ballerini read: *modicum per nullius multiloquium moestiloquus*, "dejected from lack of talk with anybody." This certainly makes better sense in English but the former smacks more of Rather's style.

2. Rather is about 45. The "wolf" is the person who took over Rather's see when he was imprisoned, i.e., Manasses.

3. Caesarius Arelatensis *Sermo* 43.

4. Augustine *De nuptiis et concupiscentiis* 1.13.15.

5. I.e., the sin of desiring [a bride's] wealth is pardoned because of the marriage.

6. Ps.-Cyprian *De xii abusivis saeculi* 5.

7. Ps.-Jerome (= Paschasius Radbert) *Epistula* 9.

8. Cf. Isidore *Sententiae* 2.39.2. The passages attributed to Prosper are from Julianus Pomerius *De vita contemplativa* 3.6.

9. Isidore *Sententiae* 2.39.

10. *Nutricius*, nourisher.

11. *Facticius*.

12. Augustine *Sermo* 9.7.

13. Gregory *Moralia in Job* 6.34.53.

14. Ambrose *Expositio in Lucam* 2.22.

15. Augustine *Enarrationes in psalmos* 99.13.

16. Cf. Persius *Satires* 3.56–57. This is a favorite classical allusion to the moral choices facing adolescence.

17. Not Augustine, but Ambrose *In Psalmum* 118.16.45; continued also in the next paragraph.

18. *Versu*, furrow or verse.

19. Luke 7.36 ff. was the Gospel reading for the Friday of the Ember Days of September (which Rather calls the seventh month); in cc. 29–30 below, which he wrote the following day,

he refers to the reading for the next day, Luke 13.6 ff. The *eighth month* from the time of his calamity establishes February as the month of his arrest and imprisonment. This is confirmed by Prael. 5.12 below, which indicates February 3 (935). The chapter is based on Gregory *Homiliae in evangelia* 2.33.1-2.

20. Augustine *De anima et eius origine* 3.14.20. Much of cc. 27-28 is drawn from Ambrose *In psalmum* 118.2.

21. Ambrose *De Helia et ieiunio* 9.32.

22. Cf. Gregory *Moralia in Job* 9.6.6.

23. Augustine *Enarrationes in psalmos* 103.3.15.

24. Cf. Augustine *Enchiridion* 65.

25. Gregory *Homiliae in evangelia* 2.31.5-6.

26. The "meadow of flowers and greenery" is Gregory's work.

27. Persius *Satires* 5.58-59.

28. Cf. Gregory *Homiliae in evangelia* 1.13.5.

Notes to Praeloquia, Book 3

1. He is saying, metaphorically, that his subject — the duties of kings and men of rank — is a dangerous one to approach truthfully and honestly; kings prefer flattering falsehoods to candid criticisms.

2. The skipper, Rather, is in prison.

3. Of king and of God; there is a complex play on words here (*incursus, cursus, excursus*). The elaborate nautical conceit is continued at the beginnings of books 5 and 6.

4. Cf. Terence *Andria* 69.

5. Isai. 30.10. By this verse, Rather means us to understand v. 9, "a rebellious people, lying sons, sons who will not hear the Lord's instructions," i.e., flatterers.

6. "The person of the citharist" is taken to be King Hugo.

7. He stresses this point because he feels that Hugo did not consider his own intentions in joining the conspiracy; Rather does not anywhere deny his complicity, but he claims that his motive was a just one.

8. Not Seneca. Cf. Friedrich, *Proverbia latina* no. 116.

9. Gregory *Moralia* 2.38.62.

10. Cf. Augustine *De quantitate animae* 17.30 and 22.38, 40.

11. Cf. Isidore *Etymologiae* 8.15.2.

12. Cf. Isidore ibid. 10.124.

13. Cf. Publilius Syrus *Sententiae* M 31.

14. Cf. Seneca *Epistulae morales* 37.4.

15. Rufinus *Historia eccles.* 10.2.

16. Cf. Cicero *De Senectute* 16.56.

17. Rather's point needs some explanation here. He is arguing that a king has no right to punish a delinquent cleric. True, a cleric ought to be scourged — because scourging will purge him of his sins and benefit him to eternal life — but the king should not be the instrument of that scourging, because rods get broken.

18. I.e., mortal flesh, a mere man, just as he uses "worm" above, c. 11.

19. Cf. Augustine *Enarrationes in Psalmos* 139.2.

20. "This true sacrifice is abused" because Rather has been removed from his office and is prevented from daily celebrating the Mass.

21. I.e., King Hugo, who punished Rather with imprisonment.

22. Rather answers the king's (hypothetical) argument that there are precedents for imprisoning a bishop.

23. Cf. Jerome *Commentarius in Matthaeum* 23.35–36.

24. This question is put into the king's mouth since Hugo's complaint is that Bishop Rather did rebel against his command when he received Arnold, duke of Bavaria, into Verona.

25. I.e., your spiritual father, the bishop.

26. I.e., attack members of the Church, your mother.

27. By "I made" Rather understands both "I appointed" and "I created." He then shows that it is ridiculous for any man to say "I created" because only God can create.

28. Rather now seems to identify two lots of enemies: those clergy who were in the original plot and made him bear the responsibility for it, and now some members of his household who flatter him to his face but are working against him behind his back. In a "Thyestean banquet" a father eats his sons, i.e., he as bishop caused the ruin of some of his lower clergy. In *Confessional Dialogue* c. 2 he refers to the executions, blindings, and mutilations which occurred as a result of his crime.

29. As we see from c. 28 below, his name was Ursus (or possibly Urso) and he was son-in-law of the arch-deacon. For translation and comment on the beginning of this letter, see Erich Auerbach, *Literary Language and its Public in Late Latin Antiquity and in the Middle Ages* (New York, 1965), 135–39. This letter is the first in Weigle's collection of Rather's letters.

30. Ursus seems to have referred to Rather as "a stinking corpse." The allusions to death and corpses can better be understood if we realize that Rather identifies death with sin. The "stinking tombs of corpses" are sinners who infect others with their example.

31. The allusion has not been identified.

32. In no. 29, *Sermo de Quadragesima 2* c. 24 he defines *fetus* ("stench") as "infecting one's neighbors with despair of recovery" (i.e., despair of salvation).

33. I.e., among the damned.

34. I.e., damnation.

35. I.e., "I do not want to be held responsible for causing you to sin."

36. Cf. John 11.39–44. The whole following passage is an extended conceit. The stench of death is the stench of sin; the sisters weeping over Lazarus are Mary and Martha.

37. A puzzling passage: the Ballerini think that he is referring to the fatal letter which Ursus wrote for the archdeacon (see below c. 28) and Rather was induced to accept responsibility for; it resulted in the fall of the spiritual father, Rather. If so, it is a very oblique reference. Alternatively, the "talk on parricide" (*sermo de parricidio*) could be a sermon or reading (of one of the Fathers?), dictated to Ursus by Rather, on attacking one's spiritual father.

38. Sisters: in John 11.39–44 Lazarus' sisters were Mary and Martha. Rather means here that he also has people praying for him, just as Mary and Martha prayed for Lazarus.

39. Alluding to Levit. 20.9 *morte moriatur*, "die in death," i.e., "death" = mortality, and "death" = damnation.

40. That is, reviling of the bishop ("husband") becomes reviling of the Church ("wife") because husband and wife share sufferings.

41. "Regeneration": spiritual fatherhood (to which "Do not touch my annointed" would apply); "generation": physical fatherhood (to which "Honor thy father and mother" would apply).

42. Alexander I *Epistulae* 7 (Hinschius, p. 98).

43. Cf. Gen. 9.25; Noah's son Cham had exposed his father's nakedness and was cursed; likewise Ursus exposing his spiritual father's shame (i.e., Rather's sin) will be cursed.

44. Cf. Ps.-Fabianus *Epistulae* 21 (Hinschius, p. 165).

45. Cf. Eusebius *Historia ecclesiastica* 6.9.

46. The leader in the rebellion against King Hugo.

47. This paragraph, our only source for the details of Rather's fall, is exceedingly obscure. For an interpretation see F. Weigle, "Zur Geschichte des Bischofs Rather von Verona," *Deutsches Archiv* 5 (1941–42): 347–86.

48. Cf. Rufinus *Historia ecclesiastica* 10.16–18.

49. The Bavarians?

50. Cf. Cassiodorus *Historia ecclesiastica tripartita* 8.1.

51. His attack on his spiritual father, the bishop.

52. "Because of it," *eius beneficio*: Weigle, Epist. 19, n. 1, takes *eius* to be God, i.e., "By God's grace." I take *eius* to refer to *infortunio*.

53. Presumably his fellow-bishops who, dumb like idols, make no protest at his treatment by the civil authority.

54. "Made" (appointed) bishop by men rather than God.

55. Because, unlike Tiberius, the emperors are now Christian and therefore subject to the Church.

56. I.e., Rather, a brother priest.

Notes to Praeloquía, Book 4

1. In *Praeloquium* 3 c. 29 above he likens those bishops who acquiesce in the king's harsh treatment of a fellow-bishop to "idols."

2. In book 3 c. 22 above.

3. Benedict *Rule* 7.

4. I.e., Rather's. Lit.: "When we already use him as censor"; this could be taken as *sui censor*, "censor of himself" (see c. 6), i.e., that he has already admitted guilt, or, more likely in view of the explanatory *nam*-clause that follows, "when his own nature proclaims him guilty." "What need of a judge/trial when his guilt is so apparent? For his reputation. . . ."

5. Publilius Syrus *Sententiae* A 32.

6. C. 5 above.

7. I.e., "What if his sons (spiritual sons, the clergy and monks of his household) are also involved in the crime?" The king's argument is: "If the clergy are also involved, then the bishop, their father, must be guilty also." The reply to this is: But some outsider might have crept in and corrupted them. Or, he goes on, the bishop could have joined them to win souls, just as one might join drinkers in a tavern. The important thing is to find out the motive, not to condemn unheard because the crowd cries "guilty."

8. *Canones apostolorum* 42.

9. Gregory *Moralia* 10.6.9. For Mauritius see John the Deacon *Life of St. Gregory* 1.40. The reference to Augustine is *Letter* 228.

10. In cc. 8–9 Rather justifies his association with those clergy in the conspiracy: first, only God can know his real motivation; second, the scriptural citations seem to establish that he ought to be on the side of God (i.e., the clergy) against the world (i.e., the king's

authority); third, being in the company of the wicked is no sin (or Lot in Sodom and Noah in the Ark would be at fault); fourth, it was his pastoral duty not to abandon the sons of the Church particularly if they were sick (i.e., criminal).

11. Cf. Isidore *Sententiae* 3.7.14, Matth. 5.23, a text of *reconciliation* to one's brother. The king, as it were, says: "You are still disaffected towards me."

12. The logic of the argument seems to be: good shepherds/bishops stand by their flock, bad ones abandon them. You (he now seems to be addressing a fellow-bishop who abandoned him, an "idol" from above) have defended the king's action in imprisoning me. In doing so, you are being worldly wise, not truly monastic. It is tempting to see all this as addressed to Hilduin, a worldly-wise monk who admired pagan literature and who seems to have abandoned Rather and sided with Hugo. The rest of the chapter largely consists of biblical texts countering the classical wisdom/rhetoric/literature so admired by prelates (including Hilduin).

13. Rather is particularly fond of this text as justification for Christian use of classical, pagan texts.

14. Cf. Sallust *Jugurtha* 113.

15. Sallust *Jugurtha* 5.4.

16. He refers to Lucan merely by the first words of the *Pharsalia*, *Bella per Emathios*.

17. Statius *Thebais* 1.417.

18. Cf. 2 Sam. 8.13, the Valley of Salt where David slew 18,000 Edomites.

19. The text of this sentence is doubtful; since the verb of the *quae*-clause has dropped out, it is not clear whether the subject of the main clause, *illa*, refers to *lepra*, "leprosy," or *Ecclesia* eight lines above.

20. Cf. Rev. 20.4; he refers to the hymn sung on the Feast of All Saints, *Quicumque in alta siderum Regnatis aula principes. . . .*

21. A reference to Rather's own treatment in prison at Pavia.

22. Publilius Syrus *Sententiae* B 21.

23. Publilius Syrus *Sententiae* I 22.

24. Publilius Syrus *Sententiae* I 25.

25. Cicero *Pro Marcello* 3.8.

26. Cf. *Proverbia Latina* 85 (Friedrich, p. 278).

27. Cf. Juvenal *Satires* 10.1–8.

28. Boethius *Consolation of Philosophy* 4.4.

29. Rather seems to be accusing Hugo of aiming to despoil the Church of Verona of some of its benefices and hence removing Rather, its bishop, who acts as its watchdog.

30. Cf. no. 10, the letter to the Pope.

31. Rather; cf. no. 10, *non consensi.*

32. Cf. Isidore *Sententiae* 3.48.7.

33. I.e., of children who have not been baptized at Easter because there has been no bishop at Verona (cf. *Praeloquia* 5.28 below).

34. *Nescioquo abscondente*; i.e., the king by imprisoning Rather has denied baptism to children and so has hidden them from the Lord who seeks them.

35. The father of the generation of the blessed is God, that of the generation of the wicked is the devil.

36. *Proverbia Latina* 18 (Friedrich, p. 275).

37. I.e., the East Frankish kingdom (Henry I "the Fowler"), the West Frankish kingdom

(Ralph), the kingdom of Burgundy (Rudolf II), and the kingdom of Provence (where Louis the Blind had died in 928).

38. Cf. Matth. 5.37, a text on swearing oaths.

39. *Proverbia Latina* 66 (Friedrich, p. 277).

40. Rather hints that another bishop (Hilduin?) has stifled into silence any other bishop who might have stood by him.

41. Cf. Gregory *Moralia* 9.16.25, where Greek *basileus* is interpreted as *basis laon* or *basis populi*, "foundation of the people."

42. Boethius *Consolation of Philosophy* 4.4; *Proverbia Latina* 92 (Friedrich, p. 278).

43. Cf. Jerome *Tractatus in Psalmos* 83.2.

44. Cf. Publilius Syrus *Sententiae* L 6.

45. Cf. Augustine *Sermo* 113.2.

46. Boethius *Consolation of Philosophy* 2.5.18.

47. Cf. Gregory *Pastoral Rule* 2.8.

48. Augustine *Sermo* 9.17–19.21.

49. Cf. Cassiodorus *Historia ecclesiastica tripartita* 9.30.

50. Because Rather himself has fallen from wealth and honor into a most abject state. He quotes Ambrose *In psalmum* 118.17.4.

51. Cf. Jer. 39.6; this difficult passage, combining several biblical texts, presupposes knowledge of Gregory's interpretation of the Jeremiah text (*Moralia* 7.28.37).

52. Augustine *De anima et eius origine* 4.6.7.

53. Avianus *Fabulae* 5.1.

54. Cf. Augustine *De quantitate animae* 33.73, and *De Genesi ad litteram* 8.24.

55. Augustine *Epistulae* 166.5.

56. Cassiodorus *De anima* 17.

57. Ambrose *In psalmum* 118.14.30.

58. Cato *Dicta*, Monost. 7.

59. *Proverbia Latina* 132 (Friedrich, p. 281).

60. Bede *In prov.* 2.16.10 and 2.21.1.

61. Isidore *Sententiae* 3.51.2.

62. *Proverbium* 87 (ed. E. Wölfflin).

63. Isidore *Sententiae* 3.51.4.

64. Cf. Gregory *Epistulae* 1.34.

65. Cf. Gregory *Homiliae in evangelia* 2.27.4.

66. Hegesippus *Historiae* 1.40.4.

67. Juvenal *Satires* 8.87–89.

Notes to Praeloquia, Book 5

1. Cf. the beginning of book 3 where he used the same phrase, *tricipiti voluminum lintre*. The three heads are the king, the clergy, and the laity.

2. That is, the bishop will have to answer for the actions of his whole flock.

3. Vergil *Aeneid* 7.141.

4. Vergil *Aeneid* 7.612.

5. Persius *Satires* 3.49.

6. Persius *Satires* 3.49.

7. Persius *Satires* 5.148.

8. *Milvus*; "stork" in standard translations of the Old Testament.

9. Ps.-Alexander *Epistulae* 14 (Hinschius, p. 102–3).

10. I take it that he means that it is not so much the material costs that make luxury objectionable as the morality of its lifestyle.

11. Gregory *Homiliae in evangelia* 1.12.1.

12. He borrows a phrase from Martianus Capella *De nuptiis Mercurii et Philologiae* 1.16.

13. Falerii, in Etruria, was famous in classical times for its sweet pasturage (cf. Ovid *Amores* 3.13.14).

14. Vergil *Aeneid* 7.277–78.

15. Vergil *Aeneid* 6.642–43.

16. Vergil *Aeneid* 7.163–65.

17. Not Augustine but Ambrose *In Psalmum* 118.20.22.

18. I.e., February 3.

19. Cf. *Praeloquia* 3.28.

20. *Praeloquia* 3.1. The letter to Wido that follows is no. 2.

21. Cf. Augustine *Tractatus in Ioh.* 87.2.

22. I.e., the powers of the world, civil authorities.

23. *Proverbia Latina* 125 (Friedrich, p. 280). The Augustine citation comes from *Enarrationes in psalmos* 96.17. The other comes from Venantius Fortunatus *Carmina* 9.2.40.

24. Cassiodorus *De Anima* 4.

25. Sallust *Jugurtha* 10.6.

26. Juvenal *Satires* 3.30.

27. Ambrose *In psalmum* 118.21.24.

28. Juvenal *Satires* 13.2–3.

29. Leo *Tractatus* 85.

30. Ambrose *In psalmum* 118.16.45.

31. Bede *Homiliae* 3.15.

32. The text is in doubt here; the manuscript has *omnium sacratico* with an alternative *socratico* added in the margin. I follow the Ballerini's emendation of *omnium memor execrato*, though it is tempting to try to retain *socratico*.

33. Gregory *Epistulae* 10.63; *Moralia* 9.45.68.

34. As so often (cf. *Praeloquia* 6, c. 26), Rather turns his general admonition onto his own personal situation; "you" here is Rather himself.

35. Rufinus *Historia eccles.* 2.5.5.

36. Cf. no. 44, line 31: *clericus ideo vocetur quod de sorte sit Domini*.

37. E.g., St. Paul; cf. 1 Tim. 1.13, where Paul admits his persecution of Christ but received mercy because he had acted ignorantly.

38. Because Rather had left the sheepfold of the monastery to come south with Hilduin and became a prey for wolves/enemies.

39. Ambrose *De bono mortis* 8.35.

40. In the surviving manuscript, the passage starting here and ending with the penultimate sentence of book 5 is written on another folio by a different scribe and pointed to here. It is evidently written later, as the Ballerini surmise, from the reference to Rather's presence in Laon on Christmas Day "this year." Rather became abbot of Alna in 960.

41. Benedict *Rule* 33.

42. Rather seems to have returned to Lobbes in 944, so this probably refers to Christmas

of that year. We may infer from his reference to St. Amand and its governance, particularly from the words "Ought you then to be made an abbot . . .," that he was considering being made abbot of the monastery. Many years later, after he left Verona in 968, he is said by Folcuin to have bought the abbey of St. Amand from King Lothair, but to have left it after staying only one night. It is possible that this whole passage was added to the text after 968, though that is unlikely: he would not have had such qualms at that time, since he had already, in the 950s, been abbot of both Lobbes and Alna.

    43. Jerome *Commentarius in Matthaeum* 4.23.35.

    44. In prison, Rather's hair has grown to a length unsuitable for a monk.

Notes to Praeloquia, Book 6

    1. Gregory *Pastoral Rule* 3.34.

    2. Leo *Tractatus* 18.

    3. Leo *Tractatus* 59.

    4. Augustine *De immortalitate animae* 7.12.

    5. Cf. Gregory *Moralia* 2.9.15.

    6. Cf. Ambrose *In psalmum* 118.1.15.

    7. Cf. Jerome *Epistulae* 132.1 and Augustine *Sermo* 9.7 and (below) 9.13.

    8. Gregory *Dialogi* 4.60.

    9. *Proverbia Latina* 133 (Friedrich, p. 281).

    10. The words of Archytas of Tarentum reported in Cicero *Tusculans* 4.36.78 were probably known to Rather through Jerome *Epistula* 79, cited in *Praeloquia* 1.38 and 43 (Dolbeau).

    11. Gregory *Homiliae in evangelia* 15.2.

    12. Augustine *Enarrationes in psalmos* 99.16.

    13. Augustine *Enarrationes in psalmos* 106.10.

    14. Augustine *Sermo* 117.1.

    15. *Stultus*: in this paragraph mostly means "ignorant," sometimes "foolish."

    16. Augustine *De anima et eius origine* 3.1, *De quantitate animae* 23.41, and *Enarrationes in psalmos* 103.4.2. "The same" in the next paragraph is Ambrose *In psalmum* 118.2.25.

    17. Clemens *Epist.* 3.64.

    18. Augustine *De quantitate animae* 1.19.33.

    19. Cf. Gregory *Vita S. Benedicti* praefatio.

    20. Augustine *Enarrationes in psalmos* 42.8.

    21. Ibid. 91.5.

    22. Ambrose *In psalmum* 118.12.9.

    23. Gregory *Homiliae in evangelia* 2.39.3.

    24. Augustine *Enarrationes in psalmos* 93.6.

    25. Gregory *Moralia* 11.9.13.

    26. Cf. Boethius *Consol. of Philosophy* 3.9.99–102 (Plato *Timaeus* 27C).

    27. Cf. Gregory *Moralia* 1.25.34.

    28. *Agonisticum.*

    29. *Interitus* (manuscript): I take to be an error for *interritus*, but it could be a noun, i.e., "struggle to the death."

    30. Isidore *Etymologiae* 12.4.6–7.

    31. Cf. Gregory *Moralia* 7.28.36; cf. Physiologus, *Versio Y*, no. 15, *De Syrena et Onocen-*

tauro, where the onocentaur has the figure of a man above the waist but that of an ass below.

32. Cf. Gregory *Moralia* 8.42.66.

33. Ambrose *In psalmum* 118.8.35.

34. Two further points because he has already been discussing superfluous words. The source is Bede *Homiliae* 2.6.

35. Cf. the preface to *Praeloquia* 1, where he refers to a reader who might be a recluse, shut in either by his own choice or by another's command.

36. He uses *ancient* to denote the Scriptures, *modern* to denote the Fathers.

37. Basil and Gregory Nazianzenus (Rufinus *Historia eccles.* 11.9).

38. Gregory *Homiliae in evangelia* 1.12.1.

39. *Priorum librorum*.

40. Persius *Satires* 1.2.

41. I.e., the six books of *Praeloquia*.

42. Not included in the manuscript.

Notes to 2-10

1. Perhaps Alcherius of Grenoble (Weigle).

2. Rather is still in exile in Como.

3. Persius *Satires* 4.23.

4. Terence *Andria* 185.

5. Without address; the manuscript entitles the letter: *Item exemplar Ratherii Veronensis ad Petrum Veneticum*. The text consists of two lengthy extracts from the letter.

6. Cf. Benedict *Rule* 1.

7. Vagrant or itinerant monks, cf. Benedict *Rule* 1.

8. Cf. Benedict *Rule* 7.

9. *Reclausum*, "recluse."

10. Jerome *Epistulae* 118.5.

11. Another excerpt begins here under the title *Item ex eadem epistola*.

12. Cf. Benedict *Rule* 1.

13. Cf. Isidore *Sententiae* 4.4.3.

14. This work in its original form, along with Anzo's Preface, can be found in MG.SS Rer. Merov. vol. 6, pp. 445–61. Rather's corrected version can be found there and in Migne, PL 136.345 ff.

15. Cf. Augustine *Contra Faustum* 21.10 and passim.

16. Cf. Augustine *De trinitate* 8.3.4.

17. Nevertheless, his style is full of classical erudition; cf. also *Phrenesis* below, also addressed to Rotbert.

18. I.e., since leaving the monastery of Lobbes in 926.

19. I.e., after he came south with Hilduin in 926 but before he was promoted to bishop of Verona. The questions are not known but they must have concerned pagan (i.e., classical) literature; after becoming bishop he felt that his study should be given to Scripture and the Fathers.

20. Twenty-two years later, in the sermon *De Maria et Martha* c. 4, he rebukes himself for reading Catullus and Plautus when he should be meditating on God's law day and night.

21. Juvenal *Satires* 10.174.

22. Persius *Satires* prolog. 1.2.

23. "Foreigner" (*alienigenam*), i.e., the pagan classics. Rather is saying that one can use the pagan classics, after removing "superfluities," to decorate the Lord's Temple; that is, that one can borrow from pagan rhetoric to serve Christian teaching.

24. Exod. 3.22; a similar use of this text can be found in *De translatione S. Metronis* c. 2.

25. I.e., use my talent, my knowledge of classical rhetoric and poetry, in the service of Christ.

26. I.e., the *Praeloquia*.

27. François Dolbeau, "Un sermon inédit de Rathier pour la fête de Saint Donatien," *Analecta Bollandiana* 98 (1980): 335–62. These notes owe much to this article.

28. Jerome *Epistulae* 60.1.

29. Cf. also *Praeloquia* 2, c. 29.

30. *Viridis et amenus*, green and pleasant.

31. Cf. Ambrose *Epistulae* 31; man's head is septiform because it has seven openings on the outside world: two eyes, two ears, two nostrils, and a mouth.

32. Cf. Augustine *Sermones* 51.34: three in the soul reflecting the Trinity, four in the body.

33. Cf. Gen. 4.24, where Lamech, the seventh generation, says: "Cain is avenged sevenfold."

34. The seventy-seventh generation was that of Christ.

35. I.e., Enoch; cf. Gen. 5.24, Jud. 14, Hebr. 11.5.

36. The Holy Spirit which is septiform (Isai. 11.1–3) descended on Christ in the form of a dove (Matth. 3.16); hence the dove in Genesis can be called septiform, apart from the fact that it was sent out after seven days.

37. A conflation of Exod. 25.31–38 and Rev. 1.12.

38. For Bathsheba meaning "seventh well," cf. Augustine *Contra Faustum* 22.87.

39. The proud king is Nebuchadnezar.

40. He refers to the seven Epistles of James, Peter (2), John (3) and Jude, and the fourteen Pauline Epistles.

41. Athanasian Creed, 3.

42. Reading *dissociaverint vitia* (H. Silvestre's suggestion), rather than *dissociaverit vita* (manuscript).

43. Deriving Donatianus from the root *donum*, *donare*, "gift," "give."

44. *Eumorfam indolem*; this is the only use of this Greek word in Latin cited in Blaise's *Lexicon Latinitatis Medii Aevi* (1975).

45. See *Phrenesis* cc. 20–21 for verses of his, both hexameters (seventy lines) and elegiac couplets (fifty-two lines), which have survived.

46. The manuscript has *Iohanni*. Weigle shows that this is an interpolation, by establishing that the pope must have been Agapet II.

47. Ps.-Alexander c. 14 (Hinschius, p. 102).

48. A rhetorical conceit rather than a statement that he has visited either Greece or Spain.

49. *Gyrovagum*; cf. Benedict *Rule* 1.

50. Notger, bishop of Verona, died August 10, 928.

51. Bishop of Liège 920–922. Rather had supported him against Richarius in the dispute for the see of Liège that arose after the death of Bishop Stephan (d. 920). In 926, after Hilduin had yielded his claim, Hugo, count of Arles, entered Italy and summoned Hilduin, his cousin, making him bishop of Verona when Notger died (928).

52. In June, 931.

53. Weigle identifies him with Hugo's son Gotfried, later abbot of Nonantola. Aquitanus (or "an Aquitanian") cannot be identified.

54. For the details of these actions, most of which we draw from the *Praeloquia*, see the introduction.

55. Cf. *Praeloquia* 5, c. 13.

56. Augustine *Sermones* 46.12.27.

57. I.e., the two and a half years while he was bishop and subject to Hugo's harassment.

58. In 945, following Berengar's return (Weigle).

59. Manasses, archbishop of Arles, had become bishop of Verona after Rather's expulsion, then became archbishop of Milan also. Rather is of course being ironic in his praise.

60. Cf. Josephus *Jewish Antiquities* 17.1.

61. Cicero *In Catilinam* 1.1.2.

62. He speaks of Manasses' former position; he had been archbishop of Milan since 948.

63. Cf. Prov. 22.28; Siricius *Decreta* 17.1 (Hinschius, p. 524).

64. Ps.-Calixtus c. 13 (Hinschius, p. 139).

65. Source not identified.

66. Son of King Hugo and married to Adelaide, the future wife of Otto I.

67. That is, abandon his see. Elsewhere he tells of his desire to quit his turbulent life as bishop and retreat to his cloister, but cannot do so for fear of John 10.12-13.

68. Liudolf (930–957) came to Italy in 951, soon followed by his father Otto, to drive Berengar from his kingdom.

69. Liutprand *Antapadosis* 4, c. 6, says the same thing.

70. Bonifatius *Decreta* 3; cf. Ps.-Julius c. 11 (Hinschius, p. 467).

71. Gregory *Moralia* 22.21.52.

72. Cf. *Concilium Carthaginiense* c. 87; Ps.-Felix c. 10 (Hinschius, p. 201).

73. Cf. Paulinus *Vita Ambrosii* 5.8.21, 25; Count Milo of Verona and Archbishop Manasses of Milan are meant.

74. Cf. *Concilium Chalcedonense* c. 6.

Notes to 11-15

1. Cf. no. 11 above.

2. Ps.-Julius c. 11 (Hinschius, p. 465).

3. *Concilium Carthaginiense* c. 87.

4. Ps.-Callixtus c. 8 (Hinschius, p. 138).

5. Ps.-Alexander c. 14 (Hinschius, p. 102).

6. Not Gregory, but cf. Augustine *Enarratio in psalmos* 40, c. 2.

7. Not Augustine, but Ambrose *In Psalmum 118* 17.4.

8. Jerome *Liber contra Vigilantium* c. 14.

9. It is not known to what country (*ista patria*) he refers. Weigle notes the use of *ista patria* also in no. 53 (fifteen years later), referring to North Italy.

10. I.e., the Church and congregation of Liège.

11. I.e., Baldric the younger, who had usurped the see.

12. Perhaps he means those of the clergy of the diocese who were loyal to him.

13. Baldric, by "marrying" a church already "married" to another bishop, had committed an "adultery."

14. Rather was native to the Liège area.

15. The Synodica Tridentina (*sess. 23 de deform.* c. 1) laid down that bishops' absence from their churches must not exceed two, or at most, three months.

16. I.e., that I not first repudiate the Church of Liège so that it can justly expel me.

17. The oath-breakers are presumably those who had changed their loyalties from Rather to the usurper.

18. The "False Decretals," which Rather takes as genuine throughout, allowed that a bishop who had been removed from one bishopric could obtain a bishopric in a vacant church elsewhere.

19. Cf. Os. 6.6 and Matth. 12.7; Christ uses the text from Hosea to refute the Pharisees, who had criticized the disciples who in their hunger were eating ears of grain in the fields, saying that it was not lawful to do this on the sabbath. Christ meant that under necessity some things were allowed which were not allowed otherwise; "For I am lord of the sabbath." Rather therefore is saying that his holding of the bishopric of Liège, perhaps technically questionable, was nevertheless allowable owing to *necessitas*, as per Antherus' decree.

20. He implies that it was Otto's authority which won him his promotion to Liège.

21. He implies that any who attack his own elevation are in fact asserting that Bruno, who had sworn to obey the canons, had openly denied the canons.

22. Rodbert, archbishop of Trier, and his nephew Bruno, archbishop of Cologne. Rodbert had been ordained archbishop in 928 on the same day of the year (25 September—according to the Ballerini) that he ordained Bruno.

23. Bruno was not only archbishop of Cologne but also duke of all Lotharingia and as such responsible for harmony in the area under his supervision. He must in fact have yielded to the anti-Ratherian faction for Rather to be expelled. What Rather is saying here is that he will not accuse him of having yielded—that his yielding to their demands would be putting inferior men before God, of negating his own lawful actions and of confirming wrongdoing.

24. The seven are named in *Phrenesis* c. 1; the primates are Bruno and Rodbert.

25. Rather had been ordained in the church in Cologne, then accompanied to Liège by the *legati* who had been appointed in Cologne and whose responsibility it was to turn Liège over to him. The metropolitan bishop was Bruno, Cologne being the metropolitan church of Liège.

26. Rather feels that if he quietly accepts the pressures of his opponents to oust him, he will thereby be doing a disservice to other bishops in similar circumstances in the past or in the future. To create such a precedent would be damnable.

27. I.e., of Gaul.

28. Cf. Ps.-Antherus c. 2 (Hinschius, p. 152), Gregory *Registrum* 1.77 and *Epistulae* 1.79, 2.37, 3.13, and Cassiodorus *Historia ecclesiastica tripartita* 12.8, where the names of bishops transferred to other seats appear in the same order.

29. That is, he would rather have force used against him than retire of his own accord, since the latter would be abandonment of his office and therefore criminal.

30. I.e., Baldric the younger.

31. Egypt as the type of wickedness is a frequent conceit in Rather's works.

32. We understand from this that he had previously used the first sixteen clauses to answer those urging him to retire from Verona in 948.

33. The reference to Otto's *imperial* power (and the fact that this work appears in the Laon manuscript, which contains only works from his third period in Verona) shows us

that Rather also used this document later in Verona, when being pressed to retire from that see by the usurper Milo (see no. 41, *Qualitatis coniectura* c. 16). Otto did not become emperor (Caesar) till February 2, 962.

34. A consul Olybrius was the addressee of one of Claudian's poems (*Epistula ad Olybrium*). More likely is the prefect Olybrius in the legend of St. Margaret, AA. SS. Jul. 5, 35A (Weigle).

35. Or "changing his opinion" (*perverso iudicio*).

36. Terence *Phormio* 950.

37. Cf. Ps.-Zeppherinus c. 4 (Hinschius, p. 131).

38. Cf. Gregory *Regula pastoralis* 1.77.

39. Terence *Andria* 907.

40. Compare the account of Ruotger, c. 38, in the Appendix.

41. *Dirae* 98–99 (Appendix Vergiliana).

42. Cf. Phaedrus *Fabulae* 1.2.

43. Referring to the Lotharingian wars of 954.

Notes to 16

1. Spelled *Frenesis* in other autograph manuscripts of Rather.

2. Cf. the letter to him, no. 5.

3. See c. 6 below for the twelve books (originally twenty) for which our *Phrenesis* acts as a preface.

4. I.e., after the death of Farabert, bishop of Liège, in August 953.

5. Conrad the Red, the former duke of Lotharingia.

6. Archbishop William of Mainz, son of Otto I.

7. Cf. Horace *Epistles* 2.2.53.

8. Cf. Horace *Satires* 1.4.35.

9. The text is doubtful.

10. Similar self-criticism is found in no. 41.

11. Cf. Boethius *Consolation of Philosophy* 1.1.9.

12. This summing-up is deliberately vague, I think—and the Latin is exceedingly difficult. He realizes that he has been overly hard on himself, perhaps even giving his enemies some handle against him, and he wants to sum himself up in a more favorable light; yet out of a false sense of modesty he shrinks from overt bragging. He seems to be saying: He is not as bad as all that and anyone who says he is runs the risk of being accused of envy.

13. *Exemplo si non aliquis nocuisset innoxius*; his meaning is obscure.

14. Rodbert died of the plague on May 9, 956.

15. Cf. Augustine *De doctrina christiana* 2.6.7. There are difficulties in the text and syntax here, and I am not sure that this translation is correct; but this seems to be the sense of the passage. We find in the opening chapters of *Translatio S. Metronis* the same kind of justification for using pagan *sententiae* in Christian works.

16. Horace *Epistles* 1.19.19.

17. Cf. Boethius *Consolation of Philosophy* 1.3.7.

18. Vol. 1: *Phrenesis*.

19. Vol. 2: *Professio Fidei* (*Praeloquia* 3, cc. 31–32), attached to the end of *Phrenesis*, plus no. 6 above plus no. 7 above.

20. Vol. 3: lost (though perhaps no. 8 above was included).

21. Vol. 4: lost.

22. Vol. 5: lost.

23. All lost, unless no. 11 is a fragment of one.

24. Vol. 9: lost.

25. Vol. 10: lost; the congregation is that of Liège, led astray by the expulsion of their rightful bishop.

26. Vol. 11: the *Conclusio Deliberativa*, no. 10 above.

27. Vol. 12: lost.

28. Rather is referring to: Martianus Capella *De nuptiis Philologiae et Mercurii*; Fabius Fulgentius Afer *Mythologiae*; Boethius *De Consolatione Philosophiae* (Weigle).

29. The text here as recorded by Dolbeau, *Ratheriana I*, needs emendation. The eighteenth century copyist of Verona, *Bibl. Civica, Busta, 809, fasc. isole*, p. 1–16, wrote: *osorum ut latratibus rappalam contraponamus obstaminis huius iuvenalis acronitatimante scripsisset satyrographis omnibus preferendum flaccum horatium.* I suggest, and translate: [*apud seculi vero scriptores Tullium, Senecam, Plinium ipsum quoque epistolares metro condidisse et appellasse libros, et,*] *osorum ut latratibus rabidam contraponamus obstantibus his iuvenalis animositatem, scripsisse et satyrographis omnibus praeferendum flaccum horatium.*

30. Cf. Suetonius *Nero* 7.

31. Not known; Weigle suggests A. Leodicensis Diaconus.

32. Cf. Augustine *Sermo* 71.7.11.

33. Cf. Boethius *Opuscula sacra* 3.

34. Horace *Epistles* 2.1.13–14.

35. Cf. Terence *Andria* 941; a proverbial expression.

36. Rather refers to himself in the third person as well as the first throughout this.

37. Rodbert called it "Madness" or "Ravings" but Rather later hints that what may appear "madness" to some is really rhetorical and literary talent.

38. From Liège to Mainz.

39. *Quorum tangat ceterum specialius actum*, an exceedingly obscure clause which I do not understand. I construe: [*ei*] *tribuunt. . .quorum specialius actum* ["whose particular action"] *tangat* ["is to touch, attack," subjunctive of purpose] *ceterum*.

40. Vergil *Eclogues* 4.63.

41. Terence *Andria* prol. 20–21.

42. Some of the precedents he chooses are listed in no. 14, *Conclusio deliberativa*, above.

43. Rodbert's announcement of Rather's elevation in Cologne Cathedral is referred to in c. 1 above.

44. Gnatho was the flatterer and parasite in Terence's *Eunuchus*.

45. Rather seems to be claiming here that if he has done Rodbert any wrong which Rodbert now holds against him, it was out of negligence rather than treachery. He confesses that he has been ill-disposed to Rodbert but hopes that this confession will bring about a reconciliation, whereby Rather may once again look to him as a patron. He offers henceforth his gratuitous service (hoping of course for support as *quid pro quo*) but only where it will not interfere with God's service.

46. Some of these precedents (of bishops without a seat being appointed to churches without a bishop) taken from the false decretals (of Antherus, Alexander, and Calixtus) are included in the body of the text; but others, including names of individuals such as we find in the *Conclusio deliberativa* were probably appended in a separate document.

47. Alexander *Epistulae* 1.14 (Hinschius, pp. 102–3).

48. His request here is that Rodbert should circulate his arguments among the other six bishops (named in c. 1); those who then failed to help him, he implies, would be "judged not priests but schismatics," from Alexander's decretal.

49. Alexander *Epistulae* 1.14 (Hinschius, p. 106).

50. Cf. Telesphorus *Epistulae* 4 (Hinschius, p. 112).

51. This obscure passage, alluding to four biblical texts and Gregory's interpretation of one of them (cf. also *Praeloquia* 4, c. 28), is a conceit to say: "obvious to anyone except him who is so blinded by worldly concerns that he cannot see the eternal verities."

52. Gregory *Moralia* 7.28.37.

53. He now addresses *Phrenesis* (i.e., himself) as a personification, but he continues to refer to himself in the third person ("he who had been enthroned . . ."). But his address to *Phrenesis* gradually turns into a dialogue between Rather and an imaginary objector.

54. I.e., the introduction of Zedekiah.

55. Not only the Zedekiah of Jer. 39.6, but all those today who are too blinded by worldly interests.

56. Cf. Terence *Heauton* 222; Horace *Epistles* 2.1, 199–200.

57. Because failure to help such a bishop (according to Alexander's decretal quoted above) was schismatic.

58. I.e., Rodbert in his praise from the pulpit of Cologne Cathedral. Rather in his *Dialogus confessionalis* admits to greed for praise.

59. Ambrose *In psalmum* 118.9.15.

60. I.e., the people of Liège because they had no bishop.

61. There are some problems with the text in this chapter and I am not sure I have interpreted it correctly. Rather seems to be saying that their similar intellectual and rhetorical natures made rivalry/envy inevitable, and from this arose hatred.

62. Jerome *Epistulae* 52.8.

63. Cf. Matth. 23.27; Gregory *Moralia* 18.7.13.

64. Horace *Epistles* 1.16.45.

65. Ambrose *In Psalmum* 118.20.

66. Isidore *Synonyma* 2.85. Cf. Cicero *De oratore* 2.43.183.

67. C. 15 provides scriptural justification for Rather's arguments in c. 14. (1) Rather had publicly excommunicated some one who scorned penitence. He justifies this excommunication by saying that God will visit men's sins with blows but will not withhold mercy (i.e., from the penitent). (2) Rodbert had called the excommunication invalid, because Rather was no longer bishop; Rather's defense is that it is merely human politics that he is no longer bishop; in God's eyes he is bishop (and therefore the excommunication is valid) and divine authority far surpasses human. (3) We are told to worship God corrected by blows, i.e., under discipline and punishment, and excommunication is such a punishment—though the punisher can be hurt as much as the punished (this latter point is irrelevant but Rather frequently adds it to any discussion of scourging). (4) The office (of bishop) is more important than the person holding the office (that is, Rather's own quality is immaterial), as the altars of the sons of Levi show. (5) Rodbert had said that Rather was not bishop because he had been expelled; in c. 14 Rather had countered this with the observations of Augustine and Isidore that guilt depends not on punishment and accusation but on the facts of the case.

68. Augustine *City of God* preface to book 1.

69. Reading *provisa* with Boethius. Dolbeau records that the apograph of the Lobbes

manuscript available to the Ballerini read *praevisa*; the Ballerini printed *premia*, followed by CC.

70. Boethius *Consolation of Philosophy* 1.4.

71. Boethius *Consolation of Philosophy* 1.4.155–163.

72. This chapter, difficult in its Latinity, its confusion of persons, and its problems of text, seems to suggest the following sequence of events: After Rather's forcible removal, Rodbert (as metropolitan bishop) put on Rather's chasuble to celebrate Mass at the Feast of the Lord's Supper. As he was about to place the offerings of the women on the altar, someone, prompted by Rather, called out the text from Matth. 5.23–24, "If you offer your gift at the altar and there remember that your brother has something against you, leave there your gift before the altar and go first to be reconciled to your brother"—challenging him, in other words, to be reconciled to Rather. Rodbert evidently ignored the challenge, thereby incurring God's displeasure, Rather maintains. For this, Rather "dared to excommunicate the archbishop," but it is not likely that he did so literally; he merely uses those words to show Rodbert how heinous is his sin before God. In later chapters, Rather, who is appealing for help, says that Rodbert would effect the reconciliation, demanded by God before the offering could be made, if he gave him that help.

73. The text here is obscure and the interpretation of it hazardous. I construe: *ad cumulum, quasi affectatus* [deponent participle] *multa genera vesaniae per curricula annorum, sepe garriens, ut mos insanientis est, favor vestrae dicacitatis ita desiperet ut.* . . . If this is the correct text and the proper construction of it (*vobis* still being unexplained), Rather would seem to turn the accusation of *phrenesis* against Rodbert. He begins to moderate the meaning of *phrenesis*, understanding it not as lunacy but as a kind of literary garrulity, of witty eloquence and conceit, that raises the possessor of it above the ranks of the pedestrian (such as he seems to regard Baldric).

74. Rodbert had, for instance, supported Rather's elevation to Liège.

75. Rather is at Mainz.

76. Gregory *Dialogi* 4.60.

77. As so often, Rather ties in an Old Testament sentence to a gospel incident. The whip is the symbol of God's punishment; it cannot easily be broken, nor can God's punishment be evaded.

78. Reading with Dolbeau *cuiuscunquemodi remedio resolidare*.

79. Antherus *Epistulae* 4 (Hinschius, p. 153).

80. Terence *Heauton* 483.

81. Cf. above c. 7.

82. Cf. c. 2, where he says that the slur *phreneticus* has rekindled his ardor for writing.

83. Rather now addresses himself, having heard of Rodbert's death.

84. Persius *Satires* 1.2.

85. Juvenal *Satires* 7.30–31.

86. Horace *Epistles* 2.2.58.

87. The Ballerini brothers comment that the following verses appear to have been written very inaccurately so as to seem the ravings of a lunatic. "The meaning is very obscure and difficult, so that in the end scarcely anything can be elicited." The Latin *is* obscure, but by changing the punctuation of the Ballerini edition, one can at least construe the Latin. Its themes are familiar from Rather's other writings: lack of unity and harmony among Church leaders, confusion of temporal and eternal values, the increasing disrespect for the Church and its institutions, his own leadership in fighting for clerical rights against overbearing civil authority in a struggle which he equates with that between God and the devil. The versifica-

tion is crude and uninspired, more like prose (and Ratherian prose at that!) in a metrical form. When Rather said in no. 5 above, "Believe me, I am no poet," he was for once not being falsely modest.

88. Cf. Horace *Epistles* 1.1.100.

89. Cf. Horace *Odes* 1.37.14.

90. Lucan *Pharsalia* 1.12.

91. Cf. Telesphorus *Epistulae* 4 (Hinschius, p. 112).

92. In this set of elegiacs he prays for Rodbert, whose death has just been reported to him. He prays that Rodbert will not go to hell—a singularly pagan hell owing much to the *Aeneid* (which Rodbert as a good classical scholar would have appreciated)—but will hear Christ summon him among the elect.

93. Cf. Juvenal *Satires* 3.265–67 (reading *trientis*, Dolbeau's suggestion).

94. Cf. Vergil *Aeneid* 6.134–35, 265, 280, and 295.

95. Cf. Vergil *Aeneid* 9.503.

96. Horace *Ars Poetica* 390.

Notes to 17-20

1. This paraphrase of a letter of Rather's to Bruno, archbishop of Cologne and brother of Otto I, comes from an anonymous *Life of Bruno*. It refers to his appointment by Bruno to abbot of Alna in September 955.

2. A Lotharingian cleric, otherwise unknown.

3. A cleric of high rank otherwise unknown.

4. Cf. Prov. 6.16–17. The last of the seven vices listed there is *slander* (*et eum qui seminat inter fratres discordias*).

5. Cf. Chrysostom *Homiliae in epistulam ad Hebraeos* 17, c. 4.

6. Cf. Benedict *Rule* 36.

7. *Canon Missae*; cf. Lk. 22.19–20; Mt. 26.26.

8. Cf. Gregory *Moralia* 6.15.19.

9. Cf. *Qualitatis coniectura cuiusdam* c. 8. That our text consists of excerpts is clear from the recurrence of *Item*, e.g., in c. 23 and c. 33.

10. Migne PL 136.142, Epitaph, line 3.

11. The Ballerini (PL 136.393–94) cite Rotger *Vita S. Brunonis* 34, Folcuin *Gesta abbatum Lobiensium* c. 23.

12. He does the same in no. 16 *Phrenesis* and no. 41 *Qualitatis coniectura cuiusdam*.

13. PL 136.397 n. 525.

14. PL 136.306 n. 523.

15. See F. Dolbeau, "Ratheriana I: Nouvelles recherches sur les manuscrits et l'oeuvre de Rathier," *Sacris Erudiri* 27 (1984): 419–21.

16. The "perjury" must be this confession. He now points out that the inciter to perjury (i.e., the confessor or reader or addressee) is as guilty as the perjuror (i.e., himself).

17. The Ballerini brothers, who found this passage *perdifficilis et mendosa*, construe and punctuate it differently.

18. He is referring to the events of the year 934. King Hugo had been responsible for his promotion to bishop of Verona, but when the nobility of Verona, unhappy with Hugo's discipline, supported Arnold of Bavaria and even received him in Verona, Rather seems to

have welcomed him (so Liutprand *Antapodosis* 3.48). He seems here to blame himself for the troubles that followed that rebellion. For this confusing period see the Introduction; also L. Lumaghi, "Rather of Verona: Pre-Gregorian Reformer" (Ph.D. diss., University of Colorado, 1975), 22–23. As a result of his participation, he was imprisoned in Pavia and then wandered in exile (hence "Norica, Italy, Germany . . .") for a while.

19. His "marriages" to the churches of Verona and Liège, "broken" because he was expelled from both. The image is continued in "You took husbands from two women" below.

20. Duke of Lotharingia (died 955); though married to Otto's daughter Liudgard, he had worked against Otto's interests in Lotharingia (see also *Phrenesis* c. 1). It was because of the threat that the powerful counts Regener and Rudolf/Ruodvolt might join him in opposition to Otto that Bruno yielded in his support of Rather in Liège (see *Phrenesis* c. 1). Rather can accuse himself of "taking his lot with adulterers," because, by leaving Liège, he acquiesced in its "adultery," i.e., Liège's adulterous liaison with a new bishop [Baldric], not the rightful bishop [Rather].

The last sentence in c. 3 is puzzling: the Ballerini simply noted, "Let him interpret it who can" (*interpretetur qui potest*). "This summary" must refer to cc. 4–9, which is not a specific confession individual to him but a general confession covering most of the sins that one might possibly have to confess. "Though put together by someone else" (*collectione licet alterius*) then refers to the fact that the summary is someone else's collection of sins for a general confession. However, some items do seem specific to Rather, e.g., c. 5 "In addition . . ." (*adiciendum quoque . . .*).

21. Dolbeau, "Ratheriana I," 410, refers the reader to *Confessio Penitentis* (ed. M. Andrieu, "Les *ordines Romani* du haut moyen âge," vol. 5 [Louvain, 1961], 112).

22. Cf. Acts 7.58; cf. Augustine *Sermo* 279.1.

23. Isidore *Sententiae* 3.7.14.

24. In the Church of Sts. Peter and Paul, the church of the monastery of Lobbes.

25. We know nothing of these incidents, nor whether they are factual or allegorical.

26. In the next few lines there are several lacunae in the text, making interpretation difficult.

27. Prov. 28.13; i.e., "Whoever has confessed . . . will obtain mercy."

28. There is frequent allusion in what follows to Paschasius Radbert's *Liber de Corpore et Sanguine Domini*, a work which in the Lobbes manuscript was added to the end of this confession.

29. The next 94 lines are also found in a Brussels manuscript, Koninklijke 5576–5604.

30. The Ballerini read *scriptorum* ("of writers"), which seems to me unlikely. I have emended to *sacerdotum*. The invocation of the Holy Spirit is *verax* if the *priest* who invokes it is sinless.

31. Cf. Gregory *Moralia* 1.36.53.

32. Jerome *Epistulae* 130.9.

33. The text we have is an *excerptum* of the *Dialogus Confessionalis*.

34. "Let him who is without sin among you be the first to throw a stone at her."

35. Cf. Gregory *Regula pastoralis* 9.81; 9.125.

36. An allusion to the resuscitation after four days of Lazarus, brother of Martha and Mary (Jn. 11). Lazarus's death and resuscitation are explored as a type for the sinner and forgiveness. Mary and Martha are seen as the types of pious action and pious meditation, hence the "two orders in the Church" (below).

37. Cf. the sermon *De Maria et Martha* cc. 1, 2.

38. *Familiaritatis*: referring to the "family" of monks but alluding to Mary and Martha's interceding for their brother Lazarus.

39. Referring to his leaving the see of Liège.
40. Horace *Epistles* 1.16.52.
41. Septuagenarian: this puts Rather's birthdate at 890 or earlier.
42. He seems now to be addressing an elderly monk in his monastery (Alna).
43. "You all" here seems to refer to the monks.
44. As abbot.
45. *Rodis*, a use common in the classical satirists (e.g., Horace *Satires* 1.6.46).
46. Cf. Benedict *Rule* 33.
47. Benedict *Rule* 57.
48. The elderly monk above who had embezzled the communal funds.
49. *spoliavi*; see below c. 24 for another reference to this "theft" from the monastery, referring to himself as twenty-two pounds in *debt*. It would seem that the other monk, named Oderadus in c. 34 below, had borrowed eighty pounds from the monastery in order to buy the position of abbot at another monastery.
50. Benedict *Rule* 36.
51. Horace *Epistles* 1.19.19.
52. Cf. Benedict *Rule* 2.
53. Cf. Terence *Phormio* 1012–13.
54. The reference is to the troubles that followed the rebellion against Hugo in 934. Rather, as one of the principals in the rebellion, assumes responsibility for the troubles; see *Praeloquia* 5, c. 27.
55. The sending of the letter to Hugo.
56. That is, Rather's own debt (see c. 23) and the monk's embezzlement of eighty pounds.
57. The seemingly religious abbot of c. 23 above.
58. Jerome *Epistulae* 84.7.
59. Benedict *Rule* 4.20.
60. Cf. Jerome *Commentarius in epistulam ad Ephesios* 2.4.27.
61. Gregory *Moralia* 1.36.55.
62. Cf. Statius *Thebaid* 5.743.
63. *In arduo constitutus*, i.e., in the pulpit.
64. Levit. 21.18; for the following interpretation cf. Gregory *Regula pastoralis* 1.11.
65. Cf. c. 21 above.
66. Rather frequently wonders whether his writings are the product of pride.
67. Cf. Persius *Satires* 6.11.
68. Cf. Gregory *Moralia* 23.11.18.
69. Benedict *Rule* 31.
70. A difficult rhetorical passage detailing the joys of honor and some of the rewards of ambition achieved; but Rather counters it with the reflection that all honor carries with it responsibilities and anxieties. He himself has paid a price (simoniacal) to become abbot; but an abbot carries a heavy burden of responsibility.
71. *Exercitus*; he seems to be recalling the splendor of his departure from Liège. In *Praeloquia* c. 5 he criticizes prelates in general for such worldly pomp.
72. Cf. no. 41, *Qualitatis coniectura cuiusdam* c. 3, for his habit of lamenting aloud in private.
73. Benedict *Rule* 31.
74. Benedict *Rule* 3.
75. Ibid.
76. Cf. Ovid *Ex Ponto epistulae* 2.2.2.

77. Gregory *Registrum epistularum* 9.219.
78. Ps.-Sallust *In M. Tullii Ciceronis de oratore* 7.
79. Cf. Gregory *Dialogi* 4.38.
80. Cf. c. 35 above.
81. In *Qualitatis coniectura* c. 5 he notes a similar inconsistency of behavior in himself.
82. Bishop or abbot.
83. Cf. *Concilium Gangrense* 8.
84. Rather frequently chides himself for his pride in his literary reputation.
85. The Ballerini point out that since it is unlikely that any physical edifice was torn down by Otto's command, Rather must be speaking allegorically, i.e., not of a church but of *the* Church of Liège, "torn down" by the expulsion of its bishop, who had "enlarged" it by the imposition of discipline. But elsewhere (e.g., no. 41, c. 2) he does talk of his passion for constructing physical buildings.
86. *Vitae Patrum* 5.29.
87. Cf. Jerome *Epistulae* 84.7; "mole" — i.e., blind; "she-goat" — i.e., sharp-sighted.
88. Horace *Epistles* 2.1.117.
89. Cf. 1 Mach. 6.43–46; Eleazar killed an elephant in battle, which fell on him and, in turn, killed him.
90. Benedict *Rule* 2.
91. Rather equates the Canaanite woman of Mt. 15.22 with Gen. 9.25, "Cursed be Canaan"; that is, he finds it significant that the woman of Mt. 15.22 was a *Canaanite*.
92. Mt. 5.22: "whoever says *racha* to his brother shall be liable to the council and whoever says *fatue* shall be liable to hell-fire." *Fello*: knave (only attested once before Rather); *puta*: strumpet.
93. Possibly Odo, king of the West Franks from 888 to 898, approximately the period that Rather would have been offered as an oblate. Since Odo died without issue it is easy to understand how he would not be remembered seventy years later. For Odo see Rosamond McKitterick, *The Frankish Kingdoms under the Carolingians, 751–987* (Harlow, 1983), 266–72.
94. Gregory *Moralia* pref. 12.
95. Cf. c. 21 above.
96. Cf. Horace *Epistles* 1.16.52.
97. In *De Officiis* book 3 passim. Cf. Gregory *Pastoral Rule* 3.13.
98. Cf. Augustine *Sermones* 82.14; the raven says "*Cras, cras.*"
99. Dolbeau, "Ratheriana I," 418.
100. Cf. Augustine *Confessions* 1.6.7.

Notes to 21-27

1. Rather at this time was abbot of the little monastery of Alna.
2. I.e., if he fails to win restitution, that shame would be added to his current one, his lowly position.
3. Judicial assemblies (*malli*).
4. This implies that the pallium belongs to the Church of St. Peter, presumably at Alna.
5. *Solidus* (sc. *aureus*): a gold coin.
6. *Translatio S. Metronis* is discussed, together with a translation of the first five chapters, in my *Tenth Century Latinity: Rather of Verona*, 7–27.

7. Cf. Orosius *Historia* 7.42.

8. A circumlocution for the Old Testament.

9. "Fraud": i.e., borrowing with no intention of repaying.

10. Cf. Augustine *Tractatus in evangelium Ioannis* 24.5.

11. Millstones commonly signify the two Testaments; the Old is "inactive" (*otiosus*) compared to the New, which it prefigures.

12. I.e., the pagan classics; Rather frequently uses this example to justify secular rhetoric.

13. *Carmen de S. Cassiano* lines 77–79.

14. Cf. Juvenal *Satires* 10.174.

15. Otto I entered Italy in 961 and was confirmed emperor in February, 962. The tenses of the Latin (*intraverat . . . triumphaturus*) indicate that the removal took place between Otto's entering Italy and his coronation, i.e., January 27, 962.

16. I.e., Rather himself (he frequently notes his own unworthiness).

17. *Carmen de S. Cassiano* line 80.

18. Rather here hints at enemies in the community already undermining him.

19. That is, Rather could find no written life of St. Metro but had to rely on the oral tradition.

20. Cf. Augustine *Sermo* 247.7.

21. Gregory *Homiliae in evangelia* 37.1.

22. Vergil *Eclogues* 5.70.

23. *Stipularis illa ritus Saxonici camera*: the Ballerini interpret *camera* ("vault") as "hat." The word is not attested elsewhere in this sense.

24. Horace *Epistles* 1.16.52.

25. Cf. Zeno, *Sermo* 1.54.41.

26. Quotation not identified; also used in no. 19, *Confessional Dialogue* c. 33.

27. The boxer in Vergil *Aeneid* 5.387 ff.

28. A dialect word meaning "bag" or "balloon," hence "stupid" (Fr. *fou*).

29. Cf. Cassiodorus *Historia eccles. trip.* 8.

30. Cassiodorus *De anima* 17.

31. Cf. Persius *Satires* 5.185.

32. Cf. Tertullian *De praescriptione haereticorum* 36.

33. *Antiphona in fest. S. Vincentii.*

34. Quotation not identified.

35. Gregory *Homiliae in evangelia* 2.30.2.

36. For the interpretation that follows, cf. Gregory *Moralia* 33.3.

37. Cf. Pliny *Natural History* 20.26: he identifies four kinds of *lactuca*; one (*caprina*, "goat-lettuce") he recommends as a mouthwash; another (*heiracion*, "hawkweed") is used by hawks to dispel poor vision.

38. *Potentissime* is in fact a vocative ("Almighty one"), but Rather's gloss *id est fortiter* shows that he takes it as a superlative adverb.

39. See above in the Sermon on Lent, no. 24.

40. See above in the Sermon on the Pasch, no. 25.

41. Taphnitic: an adjective formed from Tanais, a city in Lower Egypt (Is. 19.11, 30; Ps. 77.12, 43). See also no. 23, *Translatio S. Metronis* c. 5.

42. Perhaps alluding to Daedalus. The words have been taken by some to be an allusion to Catullus *Carmen* 58b, 2–3, but such an interpretation requires *poeticus noster* to be understood as *poeta noster*, which makes little sense in the context. In any case, two years later

Rather notes that he has not read Catullus (no. 45, *Sermon on Mary and Martha* c. 4). The Brussells manuscript adds: "if it is right to give any credence to this, inasmuch as it is a fictional story which should not be accepted with trust."

43. Gregory *Homiliae in evangelia* 30.1.

Notes to 28

1. The Laon manuscript includes a marginal notation which seems typical of Rather: *Volumen perpendiculorum Ratherii Veronensis vel visus cuiusdam appensi cum aliis multis in ligno latronis*; "Volume of thoughts of Rather of Verona, or the perception of a certain one hung with many others on the robber's cross." Later, in no. 52, he refers to this work simply as "the letter addressed to Bishop Hubert."

2. Sallust *Jugurtha* 3.3.

3. I.e., the rebellion of the Veronese clergy during his second episcopacy, 946–948; cf. the letter to the pope, no. 10.

4. Referring to his expulsion from Verona by King Lothar in 948 (see no. 10).

5. Paragraphs 2–5 form a self-standing section, as is apparent from their insertion also in no. 52. He calls them *neniae*, "trifles," "nonsenses," ironically, a word the scorners of the canons might use.

6. The Ballerini point out that Rather notes only the *possibility*, not the *actuality*, of their swearing loyalty to another bishop.

7. I.e., the lower orders of the clergy, who are the victims of the higher orders' greed.

8. The senior clergy seem to have claimed: "This is the way it has always been done in Verona." Rather argues that canon law puts control of the resources of the cathedral in the hands of the bishop.

9. Jerome *In Ezech.* 3.9; *In Hieremiam* 4.35.

10. Gregory *Moralia* 4.27.52.

11. Not Rather as the Ballerini maintain but the ideal bishop of "Feed my sheep" above (c. 3).

12. Cf. Justin's epitome of Pompeius Trogus's *Historiae Philippicae* 1.3.3.

13. Cf. *Martyrium S. Sexti* c. 3, c. 8.

14. Ps.-Evaristus c. 4 (Hinschius, p. 90).

15. Cf. Horace *Ars Poetica* 94; Chremes is an avaricious old man in the *Andria*, *Phormio*, and *Heautontimorumenus* of Terence.

16. *Solibus*, "suns": it is not clear whether Rather uses it temporally (i.e., "times") or geographically (i.e., Italy). Later, he singles out Italians for their abuse of the canons.

17. He means Pope John XII.

18. Cf. Boethius *Consolation of Philosophy* 2.7.12.

19. *Concilium Nicaenum* c. 3.

20. Cf. Possidius *Vita S. Augustini* c. 26.

21. I.e., "Scripture, canons, etc. have no more validity than anything else written on sheepskin."

22. August 962–December 963.

23. Not known, but possibly Bishop Baldric is meant (Vogel, 1.278, Monticelli, p. 211, Weigle *Briefe*, p. 82).

24. *Concilium Sardicense* c. 1.

25. From Verona in 948 and 951.
26. See no. 16, *Phrenesis* c. 1.
27. Vergil *Eclogues* 6.15.
28. *Concilium Sardicense* c. 15.
29. *Concilium Toletanum* 4.45.
30. *Concilium Neocaesariense* 1.
31. Cf. *Concilium Nicaenum* c. 9.
32. *Concilium Neocaesariense* c. 1.
33. Ibid.
34. *Concilium Toletanum* 4.45.
35. *Canones Apostolorum* 17.
36. Rather here has Pope John XII in mind. Milo, supporting the canons in their feud with Rather, has challenged Rather's legitimacy as bishop of Verona. In the next three pages Rather shows why he can hope for no support from the pope: John XII is so reprobate that he would side only with the reprobate.
37. *Ordo Romanus* 8.6.
38. Cf. Augustine *City of God* 4.4.
39. Gregory *Pastoral Rule* 3.23.
40. *Canones apostolorum* 31. Rather's reason for having no confidence of receiving help is this: John has climbed into the sheepfold not by the door, that is, he has become pope illegally; therefore, he will not condemn the action of Milo, who is also trying to climb into the sheepfold, i.e., the church of Verona, not by the door.
41. From this we gather that Bishop Hubert had a chance of becoming pope.
42. I.e., if Rather accuses Milo before the pope of invading his church (that of Verona), he will not get justice because the pope could not rebuke Milo without fear of hearing "Let him who is without sin. . . ."
43. Weigle notes here the synod of November, 963 against John XII.
44. Horace *Satires* 2.3.326.
45. Cf. Isidore *Etym.* 7.12.17.
46. A passage is assumed to have dropped out here (see Ballerini, p. 355 n. 55).
47. Cf. Regino *De synodalibus causis* 2.55.
48. *Canones Apostolorum* 28.
49. He refers to the *privilegium* given to Milo, the usurper of his seat at Verona; or possibly that given to Baldric, who took over when he was expelled from Liège.
50. Gregory *Regula pastoralis* 1.11.
51. Zeno *Tractatus* 2.14.4.
52. Reading *verendum* (Laon manuscript). Weigle has *verendam*.
53. Chrysostom *De proditione Judae* 1.6.
54. Augustine *Tractatus in evangelium Ioannis* 61.6; 62.1.
55. Zeno *Tractatus* 2.14.4.
56. Jerome *Epistulae* 60.1.
57. Cf. *Concilium Nicaenum* 9.
58. Gregory *Registrum epistularum* 9.218.
59. By "sect" Rather means simoniacs.
60. Cf. Vergil *Aeneid* 8.727.
61. Gregory *Expositio in librum I regum* 2.17.
62. Isidore *Etymologiae* 7.12.11. *Episcopus*: lit. "over-seer."

63. From the Athanasian creed.
64. Cf. Jerome *Epistulae* 84.7, a favorite allusion of Rather's.
65. Cf. Gregory *Moralia* 9.6.
66. *Pigmenta*: spicy foods and drinks. The Ballerini cite a contemporary of Rather deploring this practice in Italy.
67. Martianus Capella *De nuptiis Philologiae et Mercurii* 1.7.
68. Cf. Gregory *Moralia* 1.3.
69. Cf. Isidore *Etymologiae* 3.7.14.
70. Cf. Gregory *Homiliae in evangelia* 2.37.1.
71. Cf. Horace *Satires* 1.10.34. The rest of the sentence comes from Gregory *Moralia* 8.41.65.
72. This Hubert is unknown.

Notes to 29

1. One manuscript, Brux. 5463–67, entitles this work *Chronographia*, a title also mentioned in nos. 41, 47, and 60.
2. Gregory *Homiliae in evangelia* 2.34.16; *Moralia* 5.11.17.
3. *Concilium Laodicense* 153; *Concilium Gangrense* 127.
4. Gregory *Homiliae in evangelia* 1.16.5.
5. Jerome *Epistulae* 54.10.
6. Cf. Cassianus *Conlationes* 5.11.
7. Isidore *Sententiae* 2.44.10–11.
8. Gregory *Dialogi* 3.15.16.
9. Augustine *Sermones* 113.2.
10. Jerome *Epistulae* 120.1; *Tractatus in psalmos* 83.2.
11. Isidore *Synonyma* 2.96.
12. Ambrose *De Joseph* 5.25.
13. Lk. 6.30: *omni petenti te tribue*. Rather takes *te* with *tribue* ("give yourself") instead of with *petenti* ("anyone asking you").
14. *Symbolum Athanasium* 1.
15. Cf. Zeno *Tractatus* 1.3.5; cf. *Praeloquia* 4.13.
16. Benedict *Rule* 2.
17. This sentence occurs also in *Qualitatis coniectura* c. 6.
18. Much of this chapter echoes Gregory *Moralia* 4.27.52.
19. Cf. Augustine *Sermones* 117.3.
20. Augustine *De Mendacio* 14.
21. Cf. Gregory *Moralia* 1.36.54.
22. Fulgentius *Sermo* 8.4.
23. For this polemic on the anthropomorphites (cf. Augustine *De haeresibus* 50), Rather begins by quoting their viewpoint ("they say") but soon puts their argument into the mouth of a single addressee ("you say"). Thus the sermon becomes a kind of dialogue in the manner of the satirists. The exchange gets its momentum, as often in Rather, from the addressee raising a scriptural citation as an objection, which the speaker then disposes of either with another citation or by a metaphorical interpretation of it.
24. Cf. Gregory *Moralia* 27.5.8.
25. Augustine *Sermo* 130.2.

26. Cf. Zeno *Tractatus* 2.3.63.

27. Zeno *Tractatus* 2.14.4.

Notes to 30-36

1. The text for the last three lines is in doubt.

2. Rather assumes in the listener knowledge of the rest of this psalm, particularly v. 3: *exacuerunt ut gladium linguas suas*, "they [i.e., slanderers] have sharpened their tongues like a sword." V. 8 is then taken to mean that they will be struck down by God.

3. Cf. no. 16 *Phrenesis*, c. 15 and no. 41, c. 15; Rather alludes to Is. 47.6–11, where God says that he has handed the Israelites over to the Babylonians to be their punishers; in dealing out punishment the rod [Babylonians] gets broken.

4. Cf. Augustine *Enarrationes in psalmos* 117.27; Gregory *Moralia* 9.43.

5. Or "mistake"—*de proprio lapsu*.

6. This establishes the date: Pentecost.

7. No. 41 *Qualitatis coniectura*, c. 7, confirms that it was Rather who committed this sin, whatever it was.

8. Weigle's dating. Two details, however, suggest a dating of late 962: he says that Bucco has been secretly working against him "for a full year," and he says that his arm, which was broken "on that day of pain" (presumably the day of his return in early winter, 961), "still has not mended," an unlikely statement for late 964.

9. Caesar: Otto I. He refers to his return to Verona in 961, when he was not received by the clergy of Verona with the love due to a father.

10. He refers to his expulsion from Verona in 948.

11. Garda, a fortified castle on the shores of Lake Garda in the diocese of Verona, fell at Christmas, 963. See also no. 28, *On Contempt of the Canons*, c. 8.

12. In Apoc. 2.6, the Nicolaitans are referred to as hated by God; not much is known about them. They seem to have approved of adultery, which Rather understands here as the bigamous marriage of a bishop with a second church.

13. The diploma of King Hugo for Bishop Notker of Verona, dated August 7, 926 (Weigle, *Urkunden und Akten*, 19).

14. This incident is also referred to in no. 41, c. 11.

15. The text is questionable here and the result of the incident unclear. It would seem, however, that the fined cleric could not get his fine from the bishop, so he went to Rather's enemies, the higher clergy, and they helped him pay his fine by taking a *pallium* from the Church—with the bishop's knowledge; see Weigle, *Urkunden und Akten*, 7–8.

16. Cf. Cicero *Pro Milone* 4.10.

17. I.e., Gal. 6.3: "If anyone thinks he is something when he is nothing, he deceives himself."

Notes to 37-40

1. Cf. Jerome *Epistulae* 69.2.

2. Lanzo's son (Weigle).

3. A Veronese vassal of the bishop (Weigle).

4. Count of Verona 964–967.

5. Probably, but not certainly, Bishop Odelric of Bergamo (Weigle).

6. The *Mittellateinisches Wörterbuch* cites this passage under "castaneus II de textilibus, A pannus," understanding the word to mean chestnut-brown (of textiles). However, under *cantherus*, "a gelding," an alternate spelling *castanus* is noted. Since Rather probably did not send a *chestnut cloth* with a pallium (denying sense to the relative clause describing pallium), but could very easily have sent a *chestnut horse* with a piece of cloth to cover it, I have translated accordingly.

7. In no. 64, he also sent Count Nanno a Venetian cloak.

8. Juvenal *Satires* 1.161; Persius *Satires* 1.119.

9. He seems to be saying: others speak only flatteries, they do not dare to criticize; he has to speak candidly, even if it brings him ill will. The text is fragmentary and typically obscure.

10. I.e., he will speak out, and he hopes that the object of his candid remarks [Odelric] will not take it amiss.

11. Gauslin must have asked: "I am told by Scripture to live peaceably with all men; how can I keep this commandment without breaking my oath of loyalty to the emperor if he commands me to fight? Particularly since Rom. 13.2 demands obedience to *potestas*, authority." Rather's answer is a compromise: keep your oath to the emperor and attack them, but in goodwill.

12. Weigle points out that this provides decisive evidence for Otto's role in Rather's restoration.

13. The properties are referred to in *Qualitatis coniectura* c. 13. His predecessors in the previous thirty years would be Manasses and Milo.

14. The monastery of Lobbes.

15. Leo VIII has died and John XIII has not yet been elected.

16. "Invasion": by Manasses (948) and Milo (950).

17. Judith, duchess of Bavaria, had shown particular support for Rather. Verona was a march of Bavaria.

18. Cf. Terence *Brothers* 870: "I have worn out my life and my years in seeking [*supply* and getting it]" (Weigle).

19. That is, Rather cannot leave Verona in flight or he will be like the hireling who flees in the face of the wolf.

20. Rather interprets this figuratively: his "wife" is the Church of Verona.

21. Cf. Apoc. 2.6. The Nicolaitans approved of adultery (which to Rather means the bigamous marriage of a bishop with a second church).

22. I.e., Rather's re-instatement.

23. I.e., the Lombard bishops supporting Milo (?).

24. "Father": the bishop (Rather himself); "sons": the clergy of Verona.

25. Anathemas: notices of excommunication.

26. Ps.-Alexander c. 14 (Hinschius, p. 102).

27. Jerome *Commentarius in Matthaeum* 4.23.

Notes to 41

1. For example, in *Praeloquia* 5, cc. 6–12.

2. I.e., he dare not have people of class as his aides because he is likely to abuse them in unseemly fashion.

3. He is referring to the events of 965; see the introduction and no. 40, the letter to Milo.

4. I.e., if a cleric marries, he breaks his vows of celibacy and has no true marriage.

5. The higher clergy who were attacking him claimed that "custom" (or current practice) allowed them a larger share of church revenues than canon law did.

6. Gregory *Homiliae in evangelia* 2.37.1.

7. One manuscript of no. 29, *Sermo II de Quadragesima*, gives that work this name as an alternative title, but it does not fit this description. In fact, he uses this name to refer to all his writings in general, rather than to one particular work, as its use in nos. 47 and 60 indicates.

8. Referring to his Belgian origin.

9. Cf. Persius *Satires* 1.115.

10. "A young nobleman" is what he means (though the *Mittellateinisches Wörterbuch* [Munich, 1967–] takes the word to be "agent" or "bailiff" *sensu despicabili*), and it is likely that he was of noble birth (cf. *Confessional Dialogue* c. 11); but his delight in building invited the sneer that he was "a carpenter's son."

11. Sallust *Catilina* 1–5.

12. Cf. Horace *Satires* 1.3.82: *Labeone insanior inter sanos dicatur* ("Among the sane he would be called madder than Labeo"). This Labeo cannot be identified.

13. Presumably referring to his *Confessional Dialogue*, of which we have only *excerpta*.

14. Rather frequently refers to his own eloquence in unflattering terms; cf. for example, *Phrenesis* passim, and the title of no. 29, *inefficax . . . garritus*.

15. It is interesting to compare this picture of his own behavior with his criticism of worldly bishops in *Praeloq.* 5, cc. 6–12. His enemies ask how he can *be* a bishop if his behavior is so untypical of bishops in general.

16. Judith of Bavaria; or perhaps *dux* is to be taken as *duke*, i.e., her son Henry; but c. 14 suggests that the duchess is meant.

17. Rather alludes elsewhere to losses of the Church of Verona's properties; some of these losses will be made good in Otto's *Privilegium* to Rather (no. 48).

18. In *Confessional Dialogue* c. 6 he confesses the same fault.

19. See Levit. 3.9. He means that he does not carry good works through to a conclusion.

20. Rather is about 76.

21. I.e., the previous year, 965. See the introduction.

22. Cf. no. 29, *Sermo II de Quadragesima* c. 23.

23. See no. 32, *De proprio lapsu* c. 4; no. 46, *De otioso sermone* c. 5 also seems to recall this.

24. Sikerus, anticipating that Rather would be replaced, seems to have wanted to ensure his continued possession of land which he had received from Rather as a gift, by having it on record that he had bought it (though the money paid seems rather to have been payment of a fine).

25. I.e., he would give him nothing at all.

26. The story of this doctor is not known, but presumably the breastplate did not go to his intended heir.

27. That is, he would always lie if he thought that he would not be required to swear an oath as to his truthfulness.

28. Lamentations 4.20. Rather interprets the text as "We Jews will live under you Christians."

29. See no. 33 for another reference to this incident.

30. Cf. Terence *Phormio* 375. The same phrase occurs in no. 44, *De Nuptu Illicito* c. 3, though the name Erimbertus is withheld. Weigle, *Urkunden und Akten*, 8, notes that Erimbertus' signature appears on Milo's will, dated 955 (see also F. Ughelli, *Italia sacra* [Venice, 1717], 5:740).

31. He is saying: "Why do kings not see that Christ's relationship with the Jews is the same as that between themselves and their disloyal subjects?"

32. The last chapter was a digression in Rather's own persona, as it were, giving Rather's own anti-Semitic views.

33. According to Isidore, the sixth—and last—age is *senectus*, old age.

34. Augustine *Enarrationes in psalmos* 26.14.

35. Rather evidently did petition Otto about this when Otto visited Verona in November, 967; see the *Privilegium*, no. 48.

36. *Isto triennio morituro*: if Rather takes 80 as the term of his life (cf. Ps. 89.10) this would mean that he is now 77, placing his birthdate in 889. This accords with other references to his age.

37. Forty years earlier, in 926, Hilduin came south to Italy, bringing Rather with him.

38. Gregory *Homiliae in evangelia* 2.37.1.

39. State officers; see *Praeloquia* 1.23.

40. I.e., Manasses, who, though archbishop of Arles, had replaced him in 934, and Milo, the nephew of the count of Verona, who had replaced him in 948.

41. Technical terms for property deeds. Rather shows that local barons have taken for themselves, by one questionable means or another, properties which Otto's predecessors had conferred on the Church of Verona. Niermeyer defines the terms as follows: *commutatio*: exchange contract; *libellarium*: long-term lease; *precaria*: precarial deed.

42. Otto's *Privilegium*, no. 48, next year did in fact rescind those fraudulent deeds and did restore the properties in question to the Church of Verona.

43. Cf. no. 37, his letter to Otto.

44. Destroyed by Hungarian invasion.

45. Otto did give him resources for this, since later (no. 53) Rather defends himself against a critic who accuses him of spending money given him by Otto for feeding the poor on building and restoring churches.

46. The Ballerini note that this hill was the walled enclosure across the River Athesis where the Church of St. Peter stands (PL.136.541, n. 896).

47. Cf. the phrasing in Otto's *Privilegium*, no. 48.

48. By Milo, cf. no. 47, *Itinerarium* c. 4.

49. By the help of Duchess Judith; see no. 47.

50. *Palatium*

51. I.e., the bishop's palace, where he had been arrested earlier.

52. *Curtis Alta*: a public building not far from the cathedral more secure than the bishop's palace; the Ballerini note that it is still called *de Curte Alta* (PL.136.542, n. 903).

53. The bishop's palace.

54. A fortress in the diocese of Verona.

55. Ovid *Ars amatoria* 3.49; cf. no. 64, the letter to Nanno (who had succeeded Bucco as count), c. 3. He means: "when Nanno took over as count of Verona from Bucco."

56. Manuscript: *promisit* and *distulit*, but the sense demands that Rather promised help to the deacon.

57. That is, "when I have completed the repair of St. Peter's, I will return to the episcopal palace."

58. These words seem to be addressed to Milo, the bishop whom Rather replaced, who seems to have expected that Rather would not last long, so that he could return to his former office; he has been the inspiration of the clergy's rebellion against Rather. In c. 15, Rather more or less accuses him of trying to murder him.

59. An echo of an old proverb, *Qui fuit in furno, pares suos inibi querit*. See no. 65 below, the letter to Ambrose.

60. I.e., the restoration of St. Peter's; another reason becomes clear from no. 57 and no. 65, where he says that the Bavarians and the clerics living nearby are wrecking it.

61. Jerome *Epistulae* 125.7.

62. Rather likens himself to the Lord's children who are scourged (in his case by his political troubles) but loved by the Lord; and he likens his enemies to those who prosper but are damned. The Lord's children (Rather) were handed over to Babylon (the symbol of wicked material prosperity) but Babylon (i.e., Rather's enemies) showed no mercy, so sudden ruin will come upon it (i.e., these enemies).

63. The critic who points out another's faults so that they can be corrected and the sinner saved, risks being abused according to the Lord's words; to point out another's faults is therefore a "sacrifice" or worthy risk.

64. This is an appeal to the emperor to investigate what has been going on in Verona (cf. also no. 63, the letter to the empress Adelaide) and not to rely on the false information of informers. Hatred of informers is a frequent theme in Rather's works. The quote from Gregory is from *Dialogi* 1.4.19.

65. Hegesippus *Historiae* 1.40.4 and Horace *Epistles* 1.18.69.

66. Rather is particularly sensitive to the fact that his enemies are working against him behind his back at Otto's court. Here, as in the letters to Adelaide and Ambrose, he urges the emperor to learn the true facts and not listen to false information against him.

67. Hubert, bishop of Parma, was the one to whom his work *On Contempt of the Canons* (no. 28) was addressed. We do not know of further correspondence between the two.

68. *Accepto animarum pretio*: what precisely *pretium animarum* means is not clear; it might be something like "weregeld," i.e., the price of many souls or lives (as we might say "a king's ransom").

69. *Nostram ducem*: Judith of Bavaria.

70. I.e., with being disloyal or disobedient to the emperor and so breaking his oath to the emperor.

Notes to 42-46

1. Augustine *Sermones* 46.27.

2. Benedict *Rule* 33.

3. Cf. Levit. 16.6–28 for the following lines.

4. "Especial" because Zeno was Veronese.

5. Cf. Zeno *Tractatus* 2.14.4.

6. Rather inserts here the well-known *Admonitio Synodalis*.

7. I.e., a twenty-day fast instead of one of forty days.

8. Cf. Benedict *Rule* 48.

9. I.e., John was a cleric.

10. *Qualitatis coniectura* c. 11.

11. Cf. below no. 47.

12. Gregory *Moralia* 15.51.57.

13. I.e, the aunt of the girl married to John's son. The girl's father is dead and has been buried, not in a public cemetery open to the rain, but in some shrine or private sepulchre.

14. Augustine *Enarrationes in psalmos* 103.2.4.

15. Gregory *Regula pastoralis* 2.8.

16. Gregory *Homiliae in evangelia* 1.12.1.

17. Cf. Cassianus *Conlationes* 21.34.4.

18. Cf. Benedict *Rule* 48.

19. Cf. Cicero *Disputationes Tusculanae* 5.21.62 (the story of the tyrant Dionysius and Damocles).

20. One of the few references to Catullus in the Middle Ages. See the introduction for discussion of Catullan manuscripts in Verona.

21. Juvenal *Satires* 6.179.

22. Gregory *Homiliae in evangelia* 2.39.8–9.

23. Gregory ibid.

24. Prosper *Epigrammata ex sententiis Augustini* 75.

25. In fact we find this cited seven times: no. 19, *Confessional Dialogue* c. 26, no. 27, *Sermo 1 de Pentecoste* c. 7, no. 28, *On Contempt of the Canons* part 2, no. 29, *Sermo 2 de quadragesima* c. 23, no. 32, *De proprio lapsu* c. 3, no. 44, *De nuptu illicito* c. 6, and no. 47, *Itinerarium* c. 10. The "four times" he cites must be nos. 27, 29, 32, and 44.

26. Prosper *Epigrammata* 5.5–6.

27. "Someone" is himself, cf. no. 41, *Qualitatis coniectura* c. 7, no. 32, *De proprio lapsu* c. 3.

28. In this last chapter his conscience—or a confessor, as it were—addresses him. "You" is then Rather himself. Cf. *Dialogus confessionalis* for similar style.

29. Augustine *Tractatus in evangelium Ioannis* 22.5.

30. Augustine *Tractatus in evangelium Ioannis* 22.5.

Notes to 47

1. Gregory *Moralia* 33.12.24.

2. *Canones apostolorum* 6.

3. *Concilium Nicaenum* c. 3.

4. Cf. *Concilium Antiochenum* c. 2.

5. Augustine *Epistulae* 250.

6. Cf. Gregory *Registrum epistularum* 3.26.

7. Cf. Jerome *Interpretatio Hebraicorum nominum* 69.16: *Iohannes . . . Domini gratia,* "John . . . grace of the Lord."

8. Juvenal *Satires* 1.160.

9. I.e., the bishops of both Italy and Germany.

10. Cassiodorus *Expositio in psalmos* 139.1; cf. Mt. 13.39.

11. I.e., in 934, 948, and 965 (in the attack on him described in *Qualitatis coniectura* c. 2—Weigle); the Ballerini, however, take the third to be his failure to regain the see of Verona in 951.

12. For these events cf. no. 41, *Qualitatis coniectura* c. 16.

13. Judith, widow of Henry, duke of Bavaria, and mother of Henry the Wrangler, was Otto's sister-in-law. Since Verona was a march of the duchy of Bavaria, Rather naturally looked to her for political support and received it. See also references to her in no. 41, chapters 4 and 9.

14. In Lent, 966. See his Address in Synod above.

15. Cf. *Canones apostolorum* 38.

16. Cf. *Concilium Rothomagense* c. 16.

17. *Concilium Nicaenum* c. 3.

18. *Concilium Neocaesariense* c. 1.

19. *Canones apostolorum* c. 17.

20. No 14 above.

21. See no. 41, *Qualitatis coniectura* c. 2 above, and no. 60, *Sermo 2 de Pentecoste* c. 3 below.

22. *Concilium Sardicense* c. 1.

23. Cf. *Decretum Gratiani* (ed. E. Friedberg, 1879) 11, c. 1.

24. Cf. *Concilium Nicaenum* c. 9.

25. Athanasian creed.

26. *Concilium Toletanum* 4, c. 45.

27. *Canones apostolorum* 42.

28. Cf. *Concilium Constantinopolitanum* 2.3.

29. Cf. *Concilium Constantinopolitanum* 4.29.

30. Cf. *Concilium Romanum* [769] act. 3.

31. "I": the tiller of the vineyard, i.e., the priest in charge of souls.

32. Cf. Innocent *Letter to Rufus and Eusebius* 5.

33. I.e. Irishmen. The source of the story has not been identified.

34. The following paragraph implies that the expeller, through penitence, achieved sanctity. Hence I would suggest that the end of the story is missing.

35. Gregory *Homiliae in evangelia* 1.10.6; cf. Joel 1.17.

36. Cf. Gregory *Moralia* 12.4.5. Rather understands himself as "the wood of the vine," which is to be thrown on the fire.

37. Source not identified.

Notes to 48-52

1. The Ballerini note the ancient origin of the *ripaticum*—fees due on land with river frontage—still paid to the Church of Verona in their day.

2. Cf. *Praeloquia* 1.23.

3. All technical terms for property tenants: *mansarii* or *massarii* were tenants of a *massaritia*, a larger property. Rather's *Judicatum* (no. 49) refers to three *plecticii* on a *casale*, which must be a smaller property. *Incensiti* must be those bound by a *census*, i.e., tenancy dues on manorial holdings (Niermeyer, s.v. *census* 5b), not "tributary owing incense," the translation

Niermeyer gives citing this passage (s.v. *incensitus*). *Castellani* are those living on a *castellum* (castle-property).

4. Cf. no. 41, c. 14.

5. Cf. *Praeloquia* 4.12. This "protection" guarantees the safety not only of his person but also of his rights.

6. The Ballerini note this marginal gloss, perhaps written or dictated by Rather: "The rebel clerics are properly those who refuse to obey him and seek the patronage of certain people without his permission. If anyone adamantly challenges this true statement or in malice mutilates it or perhaps erases any of it, let him be deleted from the book of the living and not written down with the righteous."

7. See no. 41, c. 13.

8. Balsemate was a parish of the diocese of Verona. Saxo, in his annals under the year 967, records that Otto celebrated the feast of All Saints, November 1, in Verona, then proceeded to Mantua.

9. Cf. no. 52, chapters 7 and 8, below.

10. *Forica* was a privy in classical times and that is how the Ballerini take the word here. I take *foricis* as equivalent to *forensibus*, i.e., "men of the forum" or "lay people." "Taverns" is a compromise.

11. I.e., only the bishop. Rather is determined that the senior canons who are his particular enemies should not be able to remove his protégés.

12. Prosper *Epigrammata ex sententiis Augustini* 1.

13. Cf. *Concilium Chalcedonense* c. 2.

14. Cf. *Concilium Gangrense* c. 8.

15. The citations in the first four paragraphs are taken from Isai. 30.9–18.

16. Gregory *Moralia* 31.24.43.

17. Cf. the Itala version of Rom. 2.4 (*Patientia Dei te expectat ad salutem*) which he uses elsewhere.

18. Cf. no. 47 above. He seems to include the events of 951 as the fourth (Weigle).

19. The Ballerini note that by this he seems to be banning them from serving in the cathedral.

20. In 934, 948, and 965; see above nos. 47 and 51, p. 490, where he refers to *four* expulsions.

21. Cf. Sallust *Catilina* 20.4.

22. Cf. Cicero *De amicitia* 20.61.74.

23. I.e., homosexuality; cf. Rom. 1.27.

24. Cf. Isidore *Etymologiae* 7.12.1.

25. "You" is not Ambrose, of course, but an imaginary opponent.

26. Cf. Terence *Andria* 505.

27. Not found in St. Columban's works. Weigle suggests that he means a book belonging to the monastery of Bobbio.

28. Weigle suggests that Ambrose may have well have cautioned Rather to avoid a scandal in the Church.

29. Cf. Gregory *Homiliae in Ezechielem* 1.7.5.

30. In Verona in October 967.

31. Cf. no. 28 above.

32. Gregory *Homiliae in Ezechielem* 2.5.14.

33. Augustine *Tractatus in Ioh.* 87.2.

34. At the Imperial Synod held in Ravenna in Apr. 967.

35. He refers to the knight's benefices (*beneficia militaria*) given to ten cathedral clerics (see above no. 47).

36. *Massaritia*: tenancies; see no. 48 above.

37. This indicates Rather's celebrity.

38. Weigle suggests that this missive must be *Qualitatis Coniectura* (no. 41) of early 966; if that is unacceptable in view of *nuperrime*, "very recently," it must be some other work which has not survived.

39. I.e., Count Nanno and other magnates in Verona; cf. no. 57, c. 1.

40. I.e., by his *Judicatum*, no. 49 above.

Notes to 53

1. Rather's own knowledge of Martianus Capella is demonstrated by his autograph glosses on the Leiden manuscript (Voss. lat. F.48), which have been collected and edited by Claudio Leonardi in Corpus Christianorum 46A.

2. Cf. Juvenal *Satires* 6.181.

3. The emperor's visit to Verona was in November, 967.

4. Burnt by invading Hungarians.

5. Augustine *Sermones* 46.27.

6. Gregory *Moralia* 35.14.29.

7. Indicating that the unknown critic is not Veronese. The maxim that follows comes from Isidore *Synonyma* 2.96.

8. Cf. Gregory, *Moralia* 22.14.27–28.

9. Cf. Persius *Satires* 1.115.

10. Cf. no. 57.

11. Cf. Juvenal *Satires* 3.30.

12. Cf. Gelasius I *Epistulae* 14, c. 27.

13. *Concilium Antiochenum* c. 25.

14. *Concilium Romanum* c. 23; *Canones Apostolorum* 41.

15. Cf. Gen. 9.22–25; Rather as bishop is "father" to his clergy.

16. The manuscript reading here is uncertain.

17. I.e., in the style of Martianus Capella, cf. above c. 1.

18. I.e., one of the higher clergy of Verona, his enemies.

19. Sallust *Jugurtha* c. 8. That the higher clergy have sent a representative to Otto's court to register their complaints against Rather is clear from no. 51, the "Address to his Rebellious Clergy," and no. 53; it seems probable from this passage that the same canon had continued on to the Curia in Rome.

20. Donatus *Ars Grammatica* 4.373 (Keil).

21. I.e., when he was restored to the bishopric of Verona in 961.

22. Isidore *Etymologiae* 7.12.11.

23. Cf. Vergil *Aeneid* 5.472–81.

24. Unknown. Candidates that have been suggested: Antony, bishop of Brescia, 952–969 (Ballerini); Bishop Atto of Vercelli (Vogel). The "weakling" is Rather himself (now about 78).

25. This lengthy sentence is confusing. Weigle seems to accept the manuscript text without question; but surely *ipse miserrimus cogitans* needs explanation? The indefinite *quis* ("one") of line 21 seems to become a more definite person in Rather's mind, as he heaps up his accu-

sations. Since it would be inappropriate (though not uncharacteristic) to accuse himself in this letter, the object of his accusations would seem to be the addressee.

Notes to 54-66

1. Jerome *Apologia contra Rufinum* 1.1.

2. On Easter Sunday, see no. 54 above.

3. Count Nanno (whose name is declined with the same inflections as *Pharao*) and, presumably, the vice-count. He used the same text (Exod. 18.10) of Count Bucco (cf. no. 64, the letter to Nanno), but, as he points out there, Bucco had given Rather some support before he departed. Nanno had been count of Verona since May 967.

4. In no. 41, c. 14, he tells us why he has left the episcopal palace for greater security. In his absence the palace has been looted by Bavarians and neighboring clerics, and his enemies appear to have used this wanton destruction as a further pretext for attacking him before the count.

5. I.e., Otto's officers passing through Verona. Rather is not residing in the episcopal palace and is unable to stop either Otto's officers or local noblemen from despoiling it; see also no. 65, the letter to Ambrose below.

6 Sedulius *Carmen Paschale* 3.76–77.

7. Cf. Phaedrus *Fabulae* 1.2.

8. Cf. L. Hervieux, *Les Fabulistes Latins*, 2:132: *Mus et Rana*.

9. He seems to be referring to Otto's presence in Verona in November 967 (see no. 48) and the synod at Ravenna in April 967 (see no. 65).

10. *Missale Gregorianum: Die Dominica post Albas*.

11. In no. 54, Sermon 2 on the Pasch above.

12. "If a priest confess that before ordination he sinned carnally, he should not consecrate the offerings. . . ."

13. Particularly in his sermons around Easter, nos. 54, 57, and 58 above.

14. Cf. his Sermon 2 on the Pasch, c. 2, above.

15. Rather means himself.

16. For a figurative interpretation see no. 26, c. 3.

17. Cf. Augustine *Confessions* 1.6.7.

18. Gregory *Homiliae in evangelia* 2.30.2.

19. Publilius Syrus *Sententiae* A 6.

20. Count of Verona since May 967.

21. Cf. Juvenal *Satires* 6.179–83.

22. By this he asks her to excuse his blunt criticism (that Otto and Adelaide had made no effort to hear his side of the story).

23. He refers, perhaps, to some criticism he had made privately of Nanno which was later reported to Nanno.

24. Cf. no. 63, the letter to Adelaide above.

25. We may infer from this that Rather's *impudentia* had been reported to Nanno by someone to whom Rather had given a Venetian cloak as a gift.

26. Source not identified.

27. Referring to his attempt to hold a diocesan synod in May 967.

28. I.e., the decree of the Council of Ravenna in May 967, which was held at the emperor's command and attended by Pope John XIII.

29. Cf. Isidore *Etymologiae* 3.48.7.

30. Ovid *Ars Amatoria* 3.49. He refers to no. 41, *Qualitatis coniectura* c. 14 above.

31. The Ballerini read *Buccone*, i.e., "a better man than Bucco." Weigle does not note this.

32. I.e., "May he who freed Israel out of the hand of Pharaoh . . ." etc.

33. The Council of Ravenna reaffirmed the traditional canons concerning clerical celibacy.

34. I.e., restoration of the Church of Sta. Maria.

35. *Fellonem, bausiatorem, periurum.*

36. Cf. above no. 57, *De octavis Paschae* c. 1. The Bavarians are Otto's officers passing through Verona.

37. Count Bucco left Verona in May 967. The "plot" refers to the revolt of 965, in reaction to Rather's rejection of the clerics who had been ordained by the usurper Milo.

38. Rather puts the blame for the damage to the palace on Count Nanno. The "outsiders" are Otto's officers mentioned above.

39. In the revolt of 965; see above.

40. *Ex vestratibus* indicates that Nanno was a Bavarian also.

41. I.e., those detailed in c. 2 above.

42. Terence *Andria* 105.

43. Cf. Jerome *Dialogus adversus Pelagianos* 3.7; cf. also *Praeloquia* 4.22.

44. Augustine *Soliloquies* 1.6.

Notes to Sources for Rather's Life

1. François Dolbeau, "Ratheriana I," *Sacris Erudiri* 27 (1984): 373–431, using a seventeenth-century witness (Paris, B.N., *lat.* 17188, f. 281), records an earlier version of c. 28, which omits the six lines referring to Hainault but adds the interesting fact that Rather had taken part in Folcuin's baptism.

2. I.e., no. 10.

3. See nos. 2, 5, 6.

4. Not extant. The word seems to be a coinage based on the German root *sparen*, "spare," and Latin *dorsum*, "back."

5. Cf. *Praeloquia* 5.7.

6. The text here has been questioned. Rather left Liège in 955 and was not restored to Verona until 961. Since he was in Liège for almost two years (953–955), the Ballerini suggest that *institutione* should be read instead of *destitutione*; i.e., "he spent almost two years in his episcopacy of Liège, but lacking the support of any knight (or magnate of Liège, *deficiente militari copia*), returned to Italy."

7. *Perpendiculum* (called *Volumen perpendiculorum* in the Laon manuscript) is no. 28, the letter to Hubert of Parma, otherwise known as *De contemptu canonum. Syrma (Climax Syrmatis* in the manuscript) is no. 14, the *Conclusio Deliberativa. Phrenesis* deals with Baldric of Utrecht, not the same Baldric as that in *Conclusio Deliberativa* (Baldric of Liège).

8. Not Baldric of Liège but rather his uncle, Baldric of Utrecht.

9. Cf. *Phrenesis* c. 1, where Rather says that it was after his expulsion from *Verona* that he went to Otto and thence to Bruno.

10. *Veronae praesul, sed ter Ratherius exul.* The rest of this epitaph is to be found in Valenciennes 843 (CC XLVIA, p. viii): "previously a monk *(cucullatus)*, then afterwards, Lobbes, yours. Noble, urbane, honest for the time, he asked that this be inscribed on his tomb: 'Trample, feet of men, this useless salt *(sal infatuatum* [Mk. 9.49, Lk 14.34; cf. no. 47, c. 13]); may the propitious reader help him with prayers.' "

Index
to Scriptural Citations

Index to Classical
and Patristic Citations

General Index

Thieves 404, 476
Throne, of apostles 132
—twelve 134
Thuringia 3
Thyestean banquet 113
Tiberius 112, 555
Tobias 350, 505, 516
Tombazosana 485
Tongue 201–2
Trinity 222, 350, 394, 397, 448, 450, 482, 517
Truth 22
Tythe 26, 356

Ulysses 33
Ungodly 387
Unleaven 315, 340
Ursmarus, Veronese property holder 223
Ursus/Urso, letter to 15, 114 ff., 554
Usury 35
Uzzah 101

Vainglory 3, 80, 169, 371, 382, 402, 429
Valley 129
—of Salt 129
Vanity 301
Varro 42
Venetian cloak 417, 577
Venetic denarii 433
Vengeance, of God 25
Vergil 13, 247, 504
Verona, second only to Athens for writers 324
—buildings in 438–39, 579
Verona, Church of, canons of 489–91
—property of 433–34, 438, 482–83, 579
—churches destroyed 438
—poverty of clergy 484–85, 495
—pride in singing 489
—revenues of 356, 438, 443–44, 495
—revenues in four parts 501–2
—revenues unfairly divided 493–94
—revenues redistributed 484–86, 489
Versus, furrow 79
Vicentia, neighboring Verona 391
Vice 521
Vices 329, 389, 404
—to be chastised by self 404
—appear as virtues 96
—cruelty 96
—flattery 94–96
—hardened in 399
—impatience 96

—vainglory 80, 169, 371, 402, 429
—sensuality 64
—slander, the seventh 263, 568
—sloth 96, 433
Vigesima 380, 451, 581
Vigils 177, 191, 208, 312, 391
Vikings 3
Vincentius the Levite 333
Vineyard, interpreted as the Church 86, 478, 582
Vir, etymology of 64
Virago 64
Virgin 492
—duties of 77
Virtue 521
Virtues, humility 80
—obedience 64
—of a king 95, 97
—prudence 97
Vows 280, 317

Walbert's castle, Pavia 227
Warner, brother of Conrad the Red 272
Waslar, monastery 541
Waters, of Israel 130
—of Siloe 129
Wealth, damages soul 34
Werinfred, abbot of Stablaus 542
West Franks 3
Whip 258, 567
—of Ps. 37.8 425
Wicfrid, bishop of Cologne 235
Wido, archbishop 558
—letter to 6, 166, 209, 539
Widow 535
—duties of 77
Wife, duties of 65, 72–74
—image for Church 272, 424, 577
—sex with 24, 62
Wiffa, token of royal protection 131
William/Willihelm, archbishop of Mainz 7,
   244, 245, 266
Wine of sacrament 264, 397–98, 400–401
Witch 32, 550
Wisdom 21
—order for acquiring 50
—defined 97
Wise, duties of the wise 194
Witness, duties of 38
Witches 32
—inspired by Devil 33
Wolf, image for Devil 475

The Complete Works of Rather of Verona is a translation of the writings of one of the most interesting and controversial figures of the tenth century — Rather of Verona (ca. 890–974), learned monk of Lobbes and bishop, thrice of Verona and once of Liège. A Belgian from the north, he attacked the corrupt practices and lax discipline of the Italian clergy and was three times expelled from his see of Verona.

Rather's works, here translated into a modern language for the first time, provide a fascinating glimpse into ecclesiastical and intellectual life in the period before the Gregorian reforms. Much of his work is polemical self-justification — and consequently autobiographical — at a time when there were few models for autobiography. His literary output includes the *Praeloquia*, written in prison in Pavia, thirty-three letters to significant lay and church figures, including Otto I and his chancellor, three long works that contain much self-analysis, a dozen sermons, and some twenty shorter works.

This book translates Rather's entire corpus, as edited by F. Weigle in *Die Briefe des Bischofs Rather von Verona* (1949) and by Peter L. D. Reid in two Corpus Christianorum volumes, as well as the *testimonia* collected by G. Monticelli (1938). It will be of particular interest to medieval historians, church historians, students of patristics and of the classical tradition, and medieval Latinists.

Peter L. D. Reid is Associate Professor of Classics at Tufts University. He is the author of *Tenth Century Latinity: Rather of Verona* (Malibu, 1981) and the editor of the complete works of Rather of Verona, published in the Corpus Christianorum series, *Ratherii Veronensis Opera Minora* (Turnhout, 1976) and *Ratherii Veronensis Opera Maiora* (Turnhout, 1984).

mRts

medieval & Renaissance texts & studies
is the publishing program of the
Center for Medieval and Early Renaissance Studies
at the State University of New York at Binghamton.

mRts emphasizes books that are needed —
texts, translations, and major research tools.

mRts aims to publish the highest quality scholarship
in attractive and durable format at modest cost.